# TOTAL ONSLAUGHT

**Recent military history by Paul Moorcraft**

*African Nemesis: War and Revolution in Southern Africa; 1945–2010*
*Axis of Evil: The War on Terror* (with Gwyn Winfield and John Chisholm)
*Guns and Poses: Travels with an Occasional War Correspondent*
*Inside the Danger Zones: Travels to Arresting Places*
*The Rhodesian War: A Military History* (with Peter McLaughlin)
*Mugabe's War Machine*
*Shooting the Messenger: The Politics of War Reporting* (with Philip M. Taylor)
*Total Destruction of the Tamil Tigers: the Rare Victory in Sri Lanka's Long War*
*Omar al-Bashir and Africa's Longest War*
*The Jihadist Threat: The Re-conquest of the West?*
*Dying for the Truth: The Concise History of Frontline War Reporting*
*Superpowers, Rogue States and Terrorism: Countering the Security Threats to the West*
*Deadlines on the Front Line: Travels with an Old War Horse*

**On mathematics**

*It just doesn't add up: Explaining Dyscalculia and Overcoming Number Problems for Children and Adults*

**Recent fiction**

*Anchoress of Shere*
*Regression*

# TOTAL ONSLAUGHT

*War and Revolution in Southern Africa since 1945*

PAUL MOORCRAFT

Pen & Sword
**MILITARY**
AN IMPRINT OF PEN & SWORD BOOKS LTD.
YORKSHIRE – PHILADELPHIA

First published in Great Britain in 2018 by
PEN & SWORD MILITARY
an imprint of
Pen & Sword Books Ltd
Yorkshire – Philadelphia



ISBN 978 1 52670 488 7



A CIP catalogue record for this book is available from the British Library.



Typeset in 10/12.5 & Times New Roman
by Aura Technology and Software Services, India

Printed and bound in England by TJ International Ltd, Padstow, Cornwall.

Pen & Sword Books Limited incorporates the imprints of Atlas, Archaeology, Aviation, Discovery, Family History, Fiction, History, Maritime, Military, Military Classics, Politics, Select, Transport, True Crime, Air World, Frontline Publishing, Leo Cooper, Remember When, Seaforth Publishing, The Praetorian Press, Wharncliffe Local History, Wharncliffe Transport, Wharncliffe True Crime and White Owl.

For a complete list of Pen & Sword titles please contact

PEN & SWORD BOOKS LIMITED
47 Church Street, Barnsley, South Yorkshire, S70 2AS, England
E-mail: enquiries@pen-and-sword.co.uk
Website: www.pen-and-sword.co.uk

Or

PEN AND SWORD BOOKS
1950 Lawrence Rd, Havertown, PA 19083, USA
E-mail: Uspen-and-sword@casematepublishers.com
Website: www.penandswordbooks.com

# Contents

# About the Author

**Professor Paul Moorcraft** has written numerous non-fiction books on military history, politics, international relations and mathematics, as well as being an award-winning novelist. In southern Africa he taught fulltime (consecutively) at the universities of Rhodesia/Zimbabwe, Natal, Cape Town and the Witwatersrand. He also worked as a freelance foreign correspondent for most of the major international TV networks as well as being a fulltime stringer for *Time* magazine. He was editor in chief of the region's largest publishing house, and a controversial political columnist for the weekly *Sunday Express*, Johannesburg, and for the *Star*, Africa's biggest English-language daily newspaper. Besides that, he produced dozens of award-winning TV documentaries on the politics of the sub-continent.

More particularly, he spent five years covering the transition from Rhodesia to Zimbabwe, producing the well-known *A Short Thousand Years: the End of Rhodesia's Rebellion* (1979); in the same year he was elected by his local and foreign colleagues to be the vice-chair of the Press (Quill) Club and to aid the hundreds of correspondents coming to Rhodesia to cover the two elections that led to the country's independence in 1980. It was probably this media position that kept the author out of a threatened prison cell because the government wanted the elections to succeed. In addition, he later served as a uniformed reserve officer in the British South Africa Police/Zimbabwe Republic Police.

Paul Moorcraft later worked with the South African Police to co-author *Stander: Bank Robber* (1984) which was made into a major feature film in 2003. In the US and UK one of his best-known books on Africa is probably *African Nemesis* (1990). In 2008 Dr Moorcraft updated his 1982 book *Chimurenga* (written with Peter McLaughlin) to produce *The Rhodesian War: A Military History.* This went into a series of editions in the UK, South Africa and the USA and became one of Pen and Sword's most successful books. *Mugabe's War Machine* (2011) was a complement to the earlier book on the Rhodesian war. After Mugabe's ejection in a military coup, the author was vindicated. He was the only one to predict such military intervention six years before it happened. Paul Moorcraft also included chapters on his African experiences in a series of four memoirs and various books on war reporting such as *Inside the Danger Zones: Travels to Arresting Places* (2010) and *Dying for the Truth: The Concise History of Frontline War*

*Reporting* (2016). Although his main continental focus was on southern Africa, Dr Moorcraft has worked extensively throughout the continent, for example, in Sudan, especially Darfur and South Sudan. *Omar al-Bashir and Africa's Longest War* was published in 2015.

He wrote the first comprehensive inside history of the conflict in Sri Lanka, *Total Destruction of the Tamil Tigers: The Rare Victory in Sri Lanka's Long War* (2012). The author is unusual in having had direct front-line combat experience of working with jihadists, starting with the Afghan *Mujahedin* in 1984. *The Jihadist Threat: The Re-conquest of the West?* (2015) was shortlisted for the British Army Military Book of the Year (2016). His most recent books are *Superpowers, Rogue States and Terrorism: Countering the Security Threats to the West* (2017) and *Deadlines on the Frontline* (2018), both by Pen and Sword.

Besides the southern African universities, Dr Moorcraft taught fulltime at six other major international universities in the USA, UK, and Australasia as well as being a visiting professor at other universities and military colleges. He also served extensively in the UK Ministry of Defence in theatre in the Balkans and the Middle East, as well as in Whitehall. For five years he was a senior instructor at the Royal Military Academy, Sandhurst, and later at the Joint Services Command and Staff College, which became part of the UK Defence Academy. In 2004 he was the founding Director of the Centre for Foreign Policy Analysis, London, a think tank dedicated to conflict resolution. In this role he was, for example, the Head of Mission for fifty British observers in the 2010 election in Sudan. He lives in a riverside cottage in the Surrey Hills, near Guildford, England.

# List of Maps

# Acknowledgements

In my books on wars, most people tried to hinder or occasionally shoot me rather than assist me. Yet I could not have spent so many enjoyable years on the sub-continent unless generous locals gave me a regular helping hand.

Jack Spence inspired me as an undergraduate to study southern Africa over fifty years ago and we are still friends. Jenny Shaw, also a student taught by Jack, published two of my early books when she was at Brassey's. Peter McLaughlin was a friend in Rhodesia (and in the same regiment), not least when we wrote *Chimurenga* together. Ariston Chambati of ZAPU was a reliable and regular guide on African politics. Ken Flower and his two charming daughters were always kind to me, as were the Whaley family in what was then Rhodesia. Fred van der Merwe, thank you for believing in me enough to publish my first four books on Africa.

Sandy Johnston was a genial drinking buddy when I taught at Durban University. Deon Fourie in Pretoria was a patient supervisor of my doctorate. Tim Lambon saved my bacon a few times, not least on my first trip to RENAMO territory. Marie Bruyns was a fabulously elegant companion in many of my earlier filmmaking forays, not least in Soweto and the Cape Flats. Denis Beckett was a patient (and usually non-paying) editor when I wrote for *Frontline.* Ken Owen was an indulgent newspaper editor when I wrote a column for his *Sunday Express*. Harvey Tyson also put up with me as a controversial political columnist for the *Star*. Sanette Roos of Stellenbosch University was equally indulgent about my study of Afrikaans and Cape wines. And there were other female domestic companions who put up with me (notably, and consecutively, Veronica, Jenny and Glenda), especially my regular disappearing acts into the bush when we had dinner parties planned.

After 1997 when I returned on a number of occasions to government service, I would like to thank officials in the MoD and FCO, who I think turned a blind eye (or simply failed to notice) their funding of my various trips to southern Africa that came under the rubric of 'defence diplomacy', shared by both departments. I just noticed the gaps. Some of these later adventures are covered in a companion memoir published by Pen and Sword, *Deadlines on the Front Line* (2018).

Richard Doherty deployed his usual editing skills to knock this lengthy tome into shape. Matt Jones worked his production magic at Pen and Sword. And my commissioning editor, Henry Wilson, let me get away with a longer book than was contracted. Thank you all. All the mistakes and potential contraventions of the Official Secrets Act are my own fault, Your Honour.

# Abbreviations

**ANC:** African National Congress
**APLA:** Azanian People's Liberation Army
**AWB:** *Afrikaner Weerstandsbeweging* (Afrikaner Resistance Movement)
**BDF:** Botswana Defence Force
**BMATT:** British Military Advisory and Training Team
**BOSS:** Bureau of State Security (South African intelligence agency that operated at home and abroad)
**BSAP:** British South Africa Police (Official title of Rhodesian police)
**CCB:** Civil Cooperation Bureau
**CF:** Citizen Force
**CIO:** Central Intelligence Organization (Rhodesia)
**CODESA:** Convention for a Democratic South Africa
**ComOps:** Combined Operations HQ (Rhodesia)
**COSATU:** Congress of South African Trade Unions
**DGS:** *Direcção-Geral de Segurança*, Portuguese security police
**DONS:** Department of National Security (South Africa)
**DTA:** Democratic Turnhalle Alliance (Namibia)
**EPG:** Eminent Persons Group (from the Commonwealth)
**FALA:** *Forças Armadas de Libertação de Angola* (the military wing of UNITA)
**FAPLA:** *Forças Armadas Populares de Libertação de Angola* (the military wing of the MPLA)
**FNLA:** *Frente Nacional de Libertação de Angola* (a group led by Holden Roberto)
**FPLM:** *Forças Armadas Populares de Libertação de Moçambique* (the military wing of FRELIMO)
**IFP:** Inkatha Freedom Party
**JMC:** Joint Management Centre
**JOC:** Joint Operations Command (Rhodesia)
**LLA:** Lesotho Liberation Army
**MK:** *Umkhonto we Sizwe* (Military wing of the ANC)
**MNR:** See RENAMO

| | |
|---|---|
| **MPLA:** | *Movimento Popular de Libertação de Angola* |
| **NIS:** | National Intelligence Service |
| **NP:** | National Party |
| **NSMS:** | National Security Management System. |
| **NUM:** | National Union of Mineworkers |
| **OAU:** | Organization of African Unity |
| **PAC:** | Pan-Africanist Congress |
| **PF:** | Patriotic Front |
| **PFP:** | Progressive Federal Party |
| **PIDE:** | *Policia Internacional de Defesa do Estado* |
| **PLAN:** | People's Liberation Army of Namibia |
| **RAR:** | Rhodesian African Rifles |
| **RBC:** | Rhodesian Broadcasting Corporation |
| **RENAMO:** | *Resistência Nacional Moçambicana* |
| **RLI:** | Rhodesian Light Infantry |
| **RF:** | Rhodesian Front |
| **SAAF:** | South African Air Force |
| **SABC:** | South African Broadcasting Corporation |
| **SACP:** | The South African Communist Party |
| **SADF:** | South African Defence Force |
| **SANDF:** | South African National Defence Force (after 1994) |
| **SAP:** | South African Police |
| **SAS:** | Special Air Service |
| **SB:** | Special Branch |
| **SSC:** | State Security Council |
| **TTL:** | Tribal Trust Land |
| **UANC:** | United African National Council |
| **UDI:** | Unilateral Declaration of Independence |
| **UNITA:** | National Union for the Total Liberation of Angola |
| **ZANLA:** | Zimbabwe African National Liberation Army |
| **ZANU:** | Zimbabwe African National Union |
| **ZANU (PF):** | Zimbabwe African National Union (Patriotic Front) |
| **ZAPU:** | Zimbabwe African People's Union |
| **ZIPA:** | Zimbabwe People's Army |
| **ZIPRA:** | Zimbabwe People's Revolutionary Army |
| **ZNA:** | Zimbabwe National Army |

# Glossary

***aldeamentos*:** Strategic hamlets, introduced by the Portuguese to separate the black population from the guerrillas.

**Apartheid:** Literally 'separateness', official policy of racial segregation practised in South Africa (1948-1994).

***Assimilado*:** A black in the Portuguese colonial territories who had satisfied very stringent educational and cultural requirements.

**Auxiliary:** Ex-guerrilla who was affiliated to the Rhodesian security forces.

**Azania:** The name adopted for South Africa by the Pan-Africanist Congress.

**bantustan:** A homeland for different 'tribal' nations of South Africa, the cornerstone of old-style apartheid.

***Bittereinder*:** Afrikaners who did not want to sign the peace agreement that ended the Boer War in 1902.Also applied to later last-ditchers.

**Boer:** Literally a 'farmer' but came to be applied to all Afrikaners; often derogatory.

***Broederbond*:** A secret society to promote Afrikaner interests.

***Chimurenga*:** From the chiShona word meaning 'resistance'; applied first to the war against the Rhodesian settlers in the 1890s, then to the war in the 1970s.

**contact:** Military engagement.

**Contact Group:** Five Western states – USA, UK, France, West Germany and Canada – that negotiated with Pretoria about Namibian independence.

**fire force:** Highly mobile Rhodesian heliborne troops.

**House of Assembly:** White chamber in South Africa's tricameral parliament.

**House of Delegates:** Indian chamber of tricameral parliament.

**House of Representatives:** Coloured chamber of parliament.

**impis:** Zulu regiments.

**Inkatha (yeNkululeko ye Sizwe):** Zulu cultural/political party led by Chief Gatsha Buthlezi.

***Koevoet* (crowbar):** Paramilitary police counterinsurgency unit in Namibia.

***kragdadig*:** Afrikaans for hard-line.

**laager:** literally a defensive circle of ox-wagons. Later applied to the defensive mentality of Afrikaners.

***Liqoqo*:** Royal council in Swaziland.

***mestiço*:** A person of mixed white and black ancestry.

***mujiba*:** A young boy or girl who acts as a scout and helper to guerrillas. Term usually applied to the Rhodesian war.

**necklacing:** the practice of killing alleged collaborators with a tyre, filled with petrol, which was then placed around the victim's neck and set alight.

**pass laws:** Former South African laws that prevented black people from living and working in certain areas. Repealed in 1986.

***platteland*:** Afrikaans term for the rural areas.

***Poqo*:** A Xhosa word that means 'alone' or 'pure'. The military wing of the PAC especially in the 1960s.

***povo*:** Portuguese word for the common people or the masses, used extensively in the Mozambique and Rhodesian wars.

**protected villages:** Guarded settlements in Rhodesia to prevent the peasantry from supporting the guerrillas.

***sjambok*****:** A whip.

**townships:** Areas of settlement for non-white groups, usually situated near 'white' urban areas or towns to serve as a convenient workforce. Townships were sometimes also referred to as 'locations'.

***tsotsi*****:** Young criminal.

***uitlander*****:** Literally an outsider. An Afrikaans word for a foreigner.

***Umkhonto we Sizwe*****:** The military wing of the ANC. Also called MK for short.

***verkrampte*** (adj. ***verkramp***): An Afrikaans term for an ultra-conservative or 'narrow' person.

***verligte*** (adj. ***verlig***): Liberal or 'enlightened' person.

***Voortrekker*****:** An Afrikaner/Boer pioneer who *trekked* (travelled) north with the Great Trek.

***witdoeke*****:** Literally, 'white cloths/head scarves', worn by conservative vigilantes in the Cape to distinguish themselves from the comrades. Then applied to conservative groups as a whole.

# Timeline

| | |
|---|---|
| 1652: | Jan van Riebeeck lands at the Cape. |
| 1806: | Britain re-occupies the Cape. |
| 1814-40: | *Mfecane* (literally the 'crushing'); aggressive Zulu expansion causes widespread dislocation of other tribes. |
| 1836: | The Great Trek begins. |
| 1838: | Battle of Blood River. |
| 1867: | Diamond mines opened in Griqualand West. |
| 1880-81: | First Anglo-Boer war. |
| 1884: | Germany annexes South West Africa. |
| 1890: | Pioneer column reaches Salisbury, Rhodesia. |
| 1895: | Jameson Raid. |
| 1899-1902: | Second Anglo-Boer war. |
| 1910: | Union of South Africa formed. |
| 1914-18: | First World War. South African forces conquer South West Africa. |
| 1939-45: | Second World War. |
| 1948: | National Party comes to power, establishes apartheid. |
| 1960: | Belgian Congo becomes independent; Sharpeville massacre; banning of the ANC and PAC. First state of emergency. |
| 1961: | South Africa becomes a republic, leaves the Commonwealth. Uprising in northern Angola. Beginning of armed struggle in South Africa. |
| 1964: | Rivonia trial. Guerrilla war begins in Mozambique. |
| 1965: | Rhodesia declares UDI. |
| 1966: | SWAPO begins insurgency. |
| 1974: | Coup in Lisbon. |
| 1975: | Mozambique and Angola gain independence. |
| 1976: | Soweto uprising. |
| 1977: | Murder of Steve Biko. |
| 1980: | Independence of Zimbabwe. |
| 1983: | UDF formed to oppose the tricameral parliament. |
| 1984: | Nkomati agreement. |
| 1984-86: | 'Unrest' throughout South Africa. |

| | |
|---|---|
| 1985: | Second state of emergency declared. |
| 1986: | Third state of emergency. |
| 1988: | Agreements on Angola and Namibia. |
| 1989: | UN-monitored elections in Namibia. F.W. de Klerk wins South African election. |
| 1990: | Release of Nelson Mandela; unbanning of ANC, PAC and SACP. |
| 1992: | Settlement of Mozambican civil war. |
| 1994: | Mandela becomes first black president of South Africa. |
| 1998: | South African and Botswanan troops intervene in Lesotho. |
| 1998-2003: | 'First World War' in the Congo. |
| 2002: | Jonas Savimbi killed in Angola. |
| 2013: | December, death of Nelson Mandela. |
| 2017: | Robert Mugabe deposed in a coup. |
| 2018: | Cyril Ramaphosa replaced Jacob Zuma as South African president. |

*Introduction*

# The lure of Africa

My interest in Africa was partly kicked off by an inspirational teacher, Jack Spence, when I was an undergraduate at Swansea University in 1967. So that now makes my addiction to African politics over fifty years old. Professor Jack Spence was a liberal South African who left his homeland because of its apartheid policies. I took a slightly different perspective, partly because my Welsh nationalist hero, David Lloyd George, had been sympathetic to the Boers (Afrikaans-speaking white South Africans) during their rebellion against the British Empire. When I first visited South Africa few years later I was more inclined to try to understand their language and culture rather than indulge in easy knee-jerk moralizing. I used to joke (in Afrikaans) to Afrikaners, 'The Welsh and the Afrikaners are both the same: too near the English and too far from God.'[1]

Part of my joint honours degree in modern history and politics was about Africa, though that continent did not impinge much on my post-graduate studies at Lancaster and Cardiff Universities. I studied later at universities in the Middle East and Africa, securing, for example, a D. Litt et Phil. at the University of South Africa in Pretoria. My supervisor there, Deon Fourie, was a professor who had also been a senior officer in the South African Defence Force. He was probably the only academic who had the right background to co-ordinate my doctoral thesis on the intelligence failures of the Rhodesian republic.

I was always attracted to societies under siege. My first trip to Israel had been in 1970 when I lived on various border *kibbutzim*; I returned there in 1975 for a scholarship before my first long and continuous African odyssey (1976-87). Despite my deep roots in Wales perhaps I became addicted to exile, to always being a foreigner, a lone stranger in an unfamiliar setting. Maybe I found wandering more stimulating than belonging. I wanted to prove that I could stay away longer and longer but the people I wanted to impress with my rugged independence seemed to carry on perfectly well without me, or sometimes didn't even notice my absence; so I kept travelling, almost by default. The first of my long journeys without maps was to Kenya and then white-ruled southern Africa.

I started with all the keyboard courage of an academic. True, I had improved some practical skills, such as riding and shooting, during my two years at the Royal Military Academy, Sandhurst; I found it rather like Hogwarts but with more guns. I was too much of a rebel to fit in. It was ironic that I was later happy to be commissioned into a foreign regiment, when I was a bit more mature perhaps. I was called a rebel in the Sandhurst officers' mess. Perhaps it was inevitable that I should travel to a colony in rebellion against the Crown — Rhodesia.

'Rhodesia is a well-armed suburb masquerading as a country.' The first (probably unoriginal) sentence I ever wrote about the place just about summed up my early political views on Rhodesia. I was intellectually curious about the rebellion. How could whites, outnumbered 25:1 by blacks and ostracized by the world, hang on to power for so long? How could they argue with both history and arithmetic? Because of the political furore, Rhodesia and, more especially, South Africa had almost ceased to be geographical entities. To the outside world they were more a *condition*, a disease. South Africa was no longer a country but a map of the mind in which anyone could find his or her own place. As a schoolboy I had been seduced by the African tales of writers such as Henry Rider Haggard. As a university student I had been touched by the continent's apparent mysticism as well as robust complexity. And at Sandhurst I learned a few things about the military realities.

From the mid-1970s I was to travel continually for more than a decade on foot, on horseback, on motorbikes, stripped-down Land Rovers, in armoured vehicles and helicopters throughout southern Africa. I crashed in both an old South African Dakota aircraft and a Rhodesian Alouette helicopter, while I spent hairy times with the rebels in Angola and Mozambique. In Rhodesia (now Zimbabwe) and South West Africa (Namibia) I travelled frequently, and more safely, with government security forces. Often in the chaos of the riots in South African cities in the 1980s I was on my own, or with a civilian film crew. I journeyed regularly in the smaller countries of Lesotho and Swaziland, and the bigger ones such as Botswana and Zambia. And yet my first love in Africa was always the fauna and the flora – if not the governments – of Rhodesia, renamed Zimbabwe.

South of the famous Victoria Falls the Rhodesians had set up a game reserve, as big as Northern Ireland. It was called Wankie; I will use the names of places as they were called at the time of my visits — it is now called Hwange. When the rains came in late October or November the *sandveld* was verdant with grass and foliage; the gemsbok, hartebeest, wildebeest and giraffe of the dry savannah rubbed shoulders with waterbuck, reedbuck, buffalo, elephant and zebra. To the south-east lay Bulawayo, the charmingly colonial capital of Matabeleland, with streets designed to be wide enough to turn around a wagon with a team of twelve oxen. To the far south-east lay Beitbridge and the Limpopo border with South Africa. On the long drives through Matabeleland the granite castle *kopjes* standing proud against the setting sun, the smooth trunks of the upside-down giant baobabs with their coppery sheen, the *mukwa* (bloodwood) trees with their round bristling pods hanging like medals, and colourfully dressed African women trudging along dusty tracks with massive bundles on their heads — they all convinced me that if I left Africa it would break my heart. Then I would come across a newspaper and the idiocies of the politicians (black and white) would almost convince me to bribe my way onto the first flight out. To me, Africa is about strong passions that match the strong colours, the sensual smell of the first rains on the dry earth, the violence of the storms that match the violence of the politics; the spontaneity of its peoples … the sheer lack of conformity with nearly everything manmade. By comparison, I thought, Europe bred indifference and greyness.

I spent some of my time in the bush or on isolated farms (occasionally under guerrilla attack) but my permanent address was usually a safe berth in the national capital, Salisbury. I learned some of the main local language, chiShona, and the protocols of the Rhodesian art of war by propping up the bar in the Quill Club, the press bar. Slowly, I started to understand the white Rhodesians' love affair with the land – the rolling hills of Inyanga, the mysterious balancing rocks, the crystal-clear

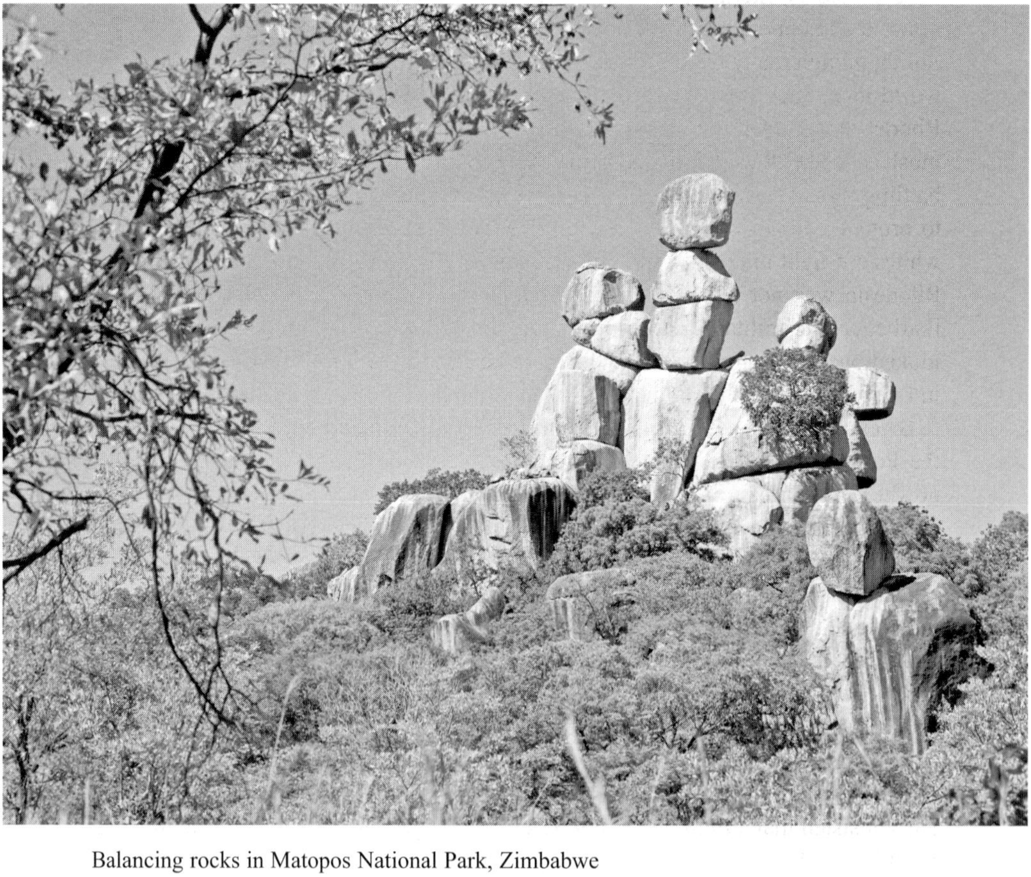

Balancing rocks in Matopos National Park, Zimbabwe

champagne quality of the air, the invigorating climate, the sense of space, the perfume of jasmine in the suburban gardens – but not with its native peoples. White Rhodesians paid more attention to their roses, their Currie Cup cricket, horses, dogs and the level of algae in their pools than to the black people whose land they shared in unequal proportions. Rhodesia may have appeared boundless to the white man because his five per cent of the population owned 50 per cent of the land and *all* the political power. It could not last – the white regime was, I believed, doomed. I hesitate to use the word 'damned' as well because I made so many good, and lasting, friends, both black and white. When some of them were killed in the war, the mourning disregarded race. Later I served (fairly briefly) in the security forces, as a reservist, and those forces were 77 per cent black. If I may use the vernacular, I learned that generally Africa was full of great people but shit governments. Appalling governance has emasculated the continent.

The censorship of news and tiny foreign holiday and emigration allowances, necessitated by international sanctions, made many of the 250, 000 whites captives rather than supporters of the Rhodesian Front regime, led by Prime Minister Ian Smith, though many were also true believers. The negative portrayal of the outside world intensified the cancer of isolation in what was already a parochial society. Rhodesians seemed to understand little of the modern world and heartily disliked most of what they did understand. Many whites believed they were sincerely battling against communism to preserve a civilized Christian order, not merely to protect a three-servants, two-cars, one-swimming-pool lifestyle. Although the whites did fight long and hard, and despite the ubiquitous weaponry and uniforms, Rhodesia was not a militaristic society. They much preferred beers and *braais* [barbeques] to military parades. Later, as black rule became imminent, the whites looked back in sorrow and resignation rather than anger, and with a bruised pride in having survived for so long against the odds.

Black rule was inevitable in all the white redoubts in southern Africa – Rhodesia, the Portuguese colonies and South Africa itself. The liberation mantra was that nowhere in Africa could be properly free until the *whole* continent was purged of white rule. The Portuguese colonies were given independence in 1974-75 but the anti-colonial struggles were replaced by long civil wars in Mozambique and, especially, Angola. The Rhodesian whites declared their illegal declaration of independence in November 1965 and did not return to formal British rule until December 1980. Nelson Mandela became president of South Africa in May1994. This book covers the prolonged series of wars that ran from the 1960s to the formal end of apartheid. I also consider briefly the earlier conflicts that helped to engender these wars, and the turmoil that ensued after 1994. The core of the struggles, however, was centred on the Afrikaner resistance to black rule. The ruling National Party insisted that a *total onslaught* was being waged against the white-dominated republic. And it would be met by a 'total strategy'.

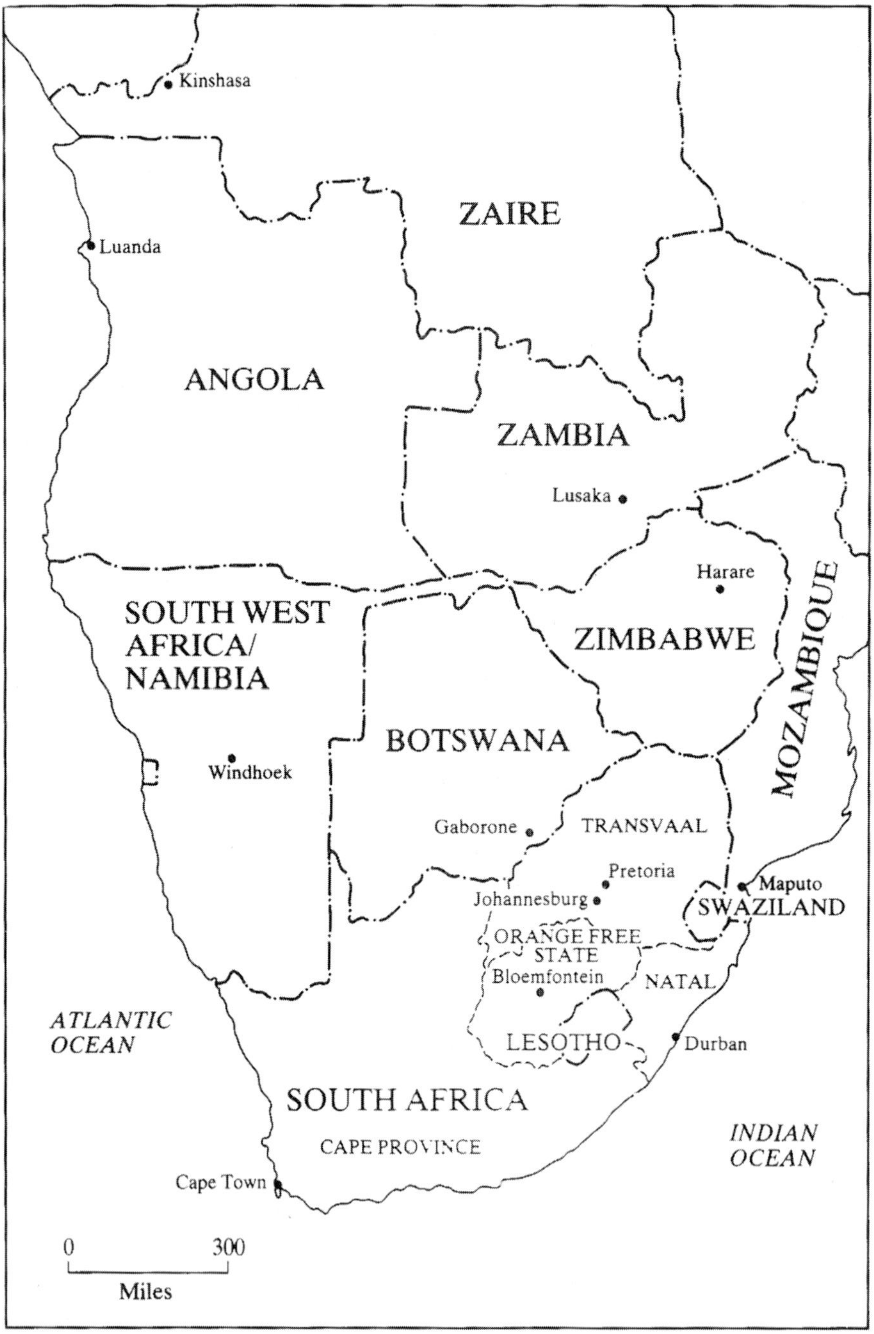


Southern Africa

Writing in 2018 black rule was unarguably as inevitable as gravity. I also thought so when I first travelled in the region but most whites certainly did not. Even after the Portuguese gave up the game in 1974 after a revolution in the metropole, Lisbon, it was assumed that the Rhodesians, comprised of tougher Anglo-Saxon stock, would not follow the path of the 'Porks' who were seen as rather feckless and certainly less martial by the Rhodesians and white South Africans. And above all, as long as the Afrikaner government in Pretoria remained steadfast, then white Rhodesia would survive – for a thousand years, as Ian Smith was (mis)quoted as saying.

South Africa was not a cause of delayed decolonization as in Portuguese Africa and Rhodesia – the Afrikaner *volk* was an indigenous people who had first settled in the seventeenth century. Only in Algeria had so many poor whites sheltered under the umbrella of a discriminatory regime. Most of the Rhodesians – about 20 per cent were Afrikaners – had migrated fairly recently from Britain, especially after the Second World War. They were expatriates as much as patriots. Many would have voted Labour or even Liberal 'at home'. Crossing the Equator did not suddenly turn them into racists. Many had seen with their own eyes traumatized refugees who had fled the carnage in the Congo and Mozambique. And once-prosperous Zambia, formerly Rhodesia's partner in the Central African Federation, had turned into an economic basket-case after independence. Living conditions in Rhodesia for both whites and blacks were very favourable compared with most of Africa's ramshackle states. Unlike the Berlin Wall, Rhodesia and South Africa initially built fences to stop Africans trying to get *into* their states to look for jobs and security. Whites had good reason to fear for 'standards'. It had to be admitted that Rhodesia was an extremely well-administered state, and not just for whites.

The whites, however, like their black successors, were history's slow learners: they repeated all the same mistakes that impoverished the whole continent. The transition from Rhodesia to Zimbabwe was inevitable and it could perhaps have been accomplished by clever diplomacy and not brutal war, and thus saved tens of thousands of lives. Rhodesia had been run by an *efficient* racist white elite that was replaced in Zimbabwe by an *inefficient* black racist elite. Zimbabwe became almost the poorest state in the world. Then South Africa under the African National Congress was rapidly Zimbabweanized.

If black rule now seems unarguable why did so many Portuguese, Rhodesians and South Africans pour out so much blood and treasure to avoid it? Obviously context is all. People thought differently a generation or two ago. And it is important to remember that the African wars were contemporaneous with, if not necessarily integral to, the Cold War. It is likely that wars of liberation would have developed even if the Chinese and Russians had not shepherded their respective protégés. Many whites passionately believed they were fighting for Western Christian democracy against the godless evils of foreign communism. Eventually tens of thousands of Cuban soldiers, along with Russian and East German advisers, fought big tank battles not seen in Africa since Rommel; they provided some tangible substance to the white phobias of communist aggression. At times the Americans shored up the white resistance – for example in Angola.

South Africa became the *cause célèbre* among the chattering classes in Europe and the USA. Apartheid had created a cargo cult on a gigantic scale for many whites. The Republic had become an economic giant but a moral pygmy. It was the richest state on the continent – and, despite many press restrictions, it had arguably the freest media. It was also the continent's military superpower, armed with nuclear weapons. It was a sociologist's paradise but a statesman's hell. It was often assumed that perhaps apartheid was not amenable to political resolution – as in Rhodesia, the whites would have to be fought to a standstill. It was as if the sorcerer would never re-appear to sort out the mayhem of his apprentice. Against all the odds, though, the two dominant lawyer-politicians – Nelson Mandela and F.W. de Klerk – managed to reach a deal. Against all the odds too, the US quietly ensured that the nuclear weapons were spirited away. Nobody in Washington wanted the ANC and its communist allies to take over the nukes.

Peace of sorts came to the new 'rainbow nation' that crystallized under the leadership of the secular saint, President Nelson Mandela. The fighting in Namibia had ended, and the apparently endless war in Angola also stopped with the assassination of Jonas Savimbi, white South Africa's long-term ally. In Mozambique, too, the civil war wound down, with help from South Africa and Zimbabwe, plus some European intercession. On the perimeters of southern Africa's war zones, bloodshed accelerated, however. Rwanda endured a more rapid genocide than even the Germans had inflicted in the Holocaust. In the Congo, all the neighbouring states were sucked into what was dubbed 'Africa's World War'.

The ruling liberation parties – with South Africa's ANC and Robert Mugabe's ruling kleptocracy as the core – formed a trade union of old comrades and cronies in the south. Despite the economic implosion in Zimbabwe and the epic corruption in South Africa, no rival parties were permitted to threaten the dominance of this liberation trade union. In military terms, the region was largely left to its own devices by the great powers once the Cold War had spluttered out, especially as the dangers of Marxism were later replaced by jihadism. A second version of the Cold War phoenixed under President Vladimir Putin, but the key members of the North Atlantic Treaty Organization had exhausted themselves in Iraq and Afghanistan and were humbled by the chaotic outcome of intervention in Libya. The growth of jihadism in the ungoverned spaces from A-Z – Algeria to Zanzibar – prompted some Western intervention in North Africa, even after the debacle in Libya. The European Union states were desperate to curb not just jihadist strikes against the soft underbelly of Europe but also the mass migration, not least from Africa, which was swamping the EU.

The wars and revolutions in southern Africa were inspired by a different drumbeat in the decades that followed the Second World War. It was a time of decolonization and mutual assured destruction between the nuclear superpowers. Much of that has changed. Some things never change however – questions of democracy, human rights and media freedoms are more enduring.

Some of the military lessons are equally enduring, too. This book is not a moral tract; it is about the exercise of military power in the sub-continent. I have tried hard not take sides, although I have focused more on white power, especially in the epicentre of resistance to the perceived total onslaught – Pretoria. Throughout the fifteen years of their rebellion the Rhodesian forces generally fought well, especially given the overwhelming odds stacked against them. The South Africans fought with some élan against the massed Angolan-Cuban armoured forces, backed by Soviet airpower. The Rhodesian war and South African counter-insurgency (COIN) in Namibia and Angola will be studied by professional soldiers for generations. The tactical and operational achievements of the Rhodesians, especially their use of their 'Fire Force', were very impressive. Where the Rhodesian military leaders failed was in their inability to persuade or cajole the political architects of the unilateral declaration of independence to provide a matching *strategic* vision. In both South Africa and Rhodesia the military-intelligence nexus came close to dominating the state and in Rhodesia a coup was just about avoided. In the end the British at the Lancaster House talks in London saved the white Rhodesians from themselves and from total defeat. It was different in Pretoria where the new president, F.W. de Klerk, sidestepped the national security state that his predecessor, P.W. Botha, had erected. In 1980 in Zimbabwe and in the early 1990s in South Africa black and white politicians were largely responsible for ensuring that it was dealmaking not tanks that ended the long wars. Nuremberg trials and lynch mobs hanging opponents upside-down, Mussolini-style, were avoided. Both countries teetered on the brink of major post-bellum civil wars, however. More recently, the much more powerful armies in NATO also could not construct and implement a desired end state for their failed wars in the Islamic world. A study of the epic Portuguese, Rhodesian and South African strategic failures, as well as operational successes, still provides contemporary lessons to all who decide to use force to resolve fundamental political challenges.

# PART I

# PAX PRETORIA

## *Chapter 1*

# Pax Britannica

The modern military story began as a struggle between white settlers and the indigenous African tribes, and then developed in the nineteenth century as a Boer/Afrikaner conflict with British imperialism. In the twentieth century both British and Afrikaner historians turned history into myth to suit their own ends. Afrikaner writers often re-created their own past to fit their contemporary racist ideology: a mixture of nationalism and Calvinism. In dominating the blacks, Afrikaner nationalists liked to believe they were fulfilling God's will. On the other hand, the Kiplingesque notions of British imperial 'race patriotism' had something in common with the Soviet communism of half a century later: 'an innocent optimism, a facile disregard for unwelcome truths, an instinct to simplify and categorize, and a dreadful taste in propaganda'.[1]

War, nationalism and a sense of manifest destiny made Afrikaners paranoiacally independent. The enmity of British imperialism and, after 1948, world opinion merely reinforced the Afrikaner tribe's determination to stand alone, if necessary. Afrikaner society developed largely in isolation from the mainstream of Western thought. It rejected or corrupted three of the four most dynamic twentieth-century impulses: liberalism, democracy and socialism. The fourth, nationalism, emerged as a crude form of national socialism founded on white tribal exclusivity.

Boer, Britons and blacks fought each other in a farrago of alliances until the twentieth century when South Africa's whites tended to coalesce in joint opposition to the black demands for equal rights. Despite public nods to the (sometimes) more liberal sentiments in the imperial capital, London, the colonial and the local English-speaking authorities laid the foundations of racial discrimination in the region.

Permanent white settlement had begun in 1652 when Jan van Riebeeck had established a victualling station for the Dutch East India Company near the African continent's southernmost point, the Cape of Good Hope. Afrikaners used to compare 1652 with the early Pilgrim Fathers. Unlike the first American settlers, however, the Dutch motivation was entirely commercial. The Cape's victualling station provided fresh produce for the merchantmen on the long hazardous sea route to the riches of the east. The company's settlement expanded and intermittent wars against the indigenous Khoikhoi and San (Bushmen) set the pattern for the next 300 years as more and more frontier wars were fought against black tribesmen. The nature of the company's tiny colony changed as new immigrants arrived: French, Germans and, after 1820, British settlers. In 1795 the British had taken over temporary control from the Dutch but it was only at the end of the Napoleonic wars in 1815 that the British, for the price of £6 million, took formal possession of the Cape. The Cape station was a major outpost on the way to the proverbial jewel of empire, India. The English were often insensitive overlords who regarded the Dutch, or Boers and Afrikaners, as they came to be known later, as obstinate and inferior. Afrikaners, excluded from jury service because of their language (Dutch which evolved into Afrikaans), were incensed by all sorts of English laws, not least those which encouraged black servants to give evidence against their masters in courts. In sum, Boers resented paying taxes for the privilege of being browbeaten by an English master race. Then the British abolished slavery, without fair compensation in Boer opinion.

Abolition prompted a seminal event in Afrikaner history: the Great Trek. In the mid-1830s thousands of Boers fled British control. Without navigable rivers, they deployed their heavy ox-wagons to seek refuge and independence deep in the African interior. According to one of the most respected of South African historians,

> The Trek was, at bottom, inspired by a desire to escape from the distant authorities which seemed to be both wrongly motivated and at the same time more effective than any other that the frontiersmen had previously known …. [the expansion north and later eastwards] was, in its essentials, a story of black-white confrontation in which the white man with his superior weapons and notions of individual ownership, his theodolite and his title deed, generally gained at the expense of the black. Black chieftains seldom became involved in inter-white quarrels, whereas the advancing whites were often able to exploit the divisions in black societies which developed all too frequently as a direct result of the initial loss of land.[2]

Some of the white pioneers, or *Voortrekkers* (literally 'forward movers'), travelled north-eastwards into Natal to set up an independent republic. There, a small band of trekkers, led by Piet Retief, was treacherously slaughtered by Dingane, the Zulu king. Dingane ordered his impis to wipe out the remaining Boer laagers. The loose and fractious organization of the Boer commandos aided the Zulu onslaught. The *Voortrekker* presence in Natal might have been completely eliminated but for Andries Pretorius (the eponym of Pretoria), who organised a commando of 500 Boers (and some Englishmen from Port Natal) into a disciplined fighting force. On 15 December 1838 the trekkers laagered in a strong defensive position on the banks of the Ncome river. The next day the Zulu army, over 10,000 strong, wasted itself in heroic but futile assaults on the well-defended laager. Cannon and musket

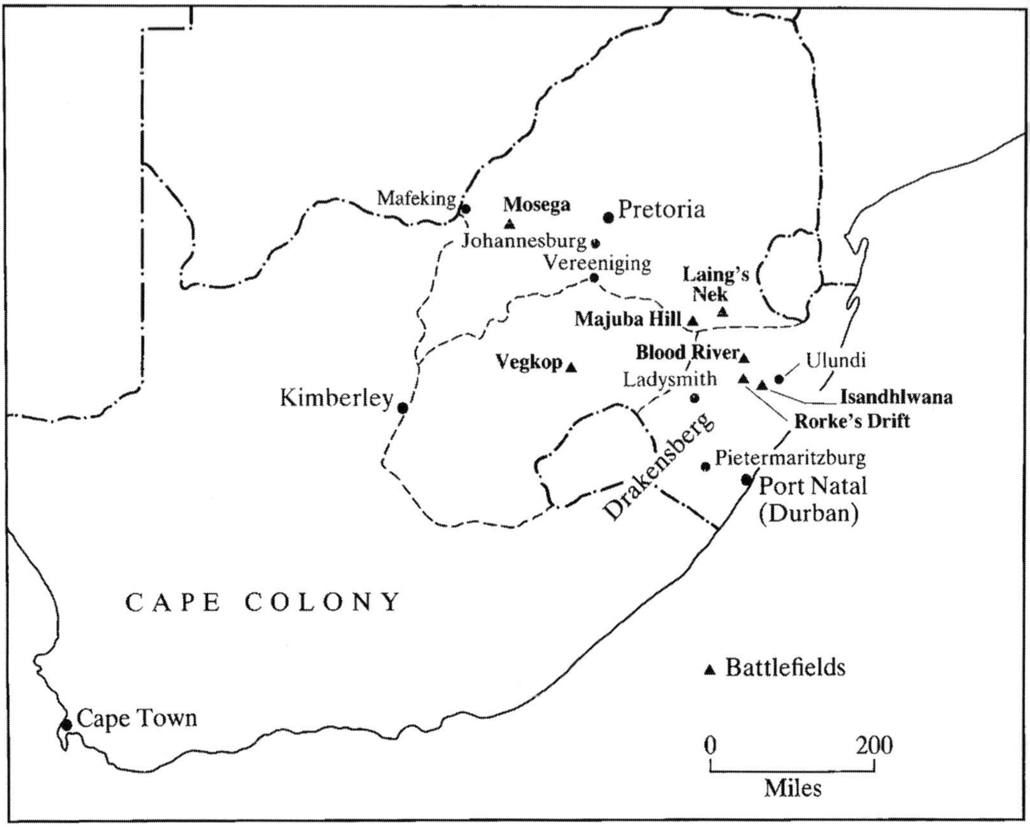


Major battlefields and sieges

fire ravaged the Zulu ranks which broke and ran when mounted Boers charged from the laager to complete the rout of the demoralized surviving impis. To quote from *The Oxford History of South Africa*, the Battle of Blood River, as it became known, was 'a classic example of the devastating superiority of controlled force, by resolute men from a defensive position, over Africans armed with assegais and spears, however numerous and brave'.

Blood River, as much as the Great Trek, became enshrined in Afrikaner mythology. Before the battle, the Boers had sworn a covenant with God that if they were victorious they would honour that day for ever as a thanksgiving. So 16 December became 'the day of the vow'. From this a whole series of racial myths emerged: that Blood River saved the Great Trek; that it marked the birth of the Afrikaner nation; and that the battle was a symbol of white Christianity's triumph over black heathens. Blood River was run in tandem with the fundamental Afrikaner myth: that there were no blacks in South Africa when van Riebeeck arrived (except for a few Bushmen). Blacks were said to have moved south as the whites moved north, ignoring the evidence of hundreds of years of black settlement in the Cape. In short, argued Afrikaner nationalists, God had sided with them at Blood River, proof that He had called upon the Afrikaner *volk* to keep South Africa white.

The trekkers had temporarily contained Zulu power but the might of the British imperium was to prove too great for them. By 1842 the majority of the Boers had been ejected from Natal by British forces. Most of them had retraced their steps over the Drakensberg mountains to rejoin their Afrikaner brethren living in the Transvaal with their republicanism and Jehovah. Their God did not help them much against the expanding British, however. The Empire annexed the Transvaal in 1848 but relaxed its grip in 1854, only to take back control from 1871 to 1881. In 1854 the British had reluctantly recognized the independence of the two fledgling Afrikaner republics in the Transvaal and the Orange Free State. Then they achieved (temporary) independence but little peace. The poorly-governed republics squabbled among themselves and they even went to the brink of war in 1857. Meanwhile, the intermittent conflicts with the neighbouring black tribes continued to fester. Then, in 1867, diamonds were discovered near the confluence of the Vaal and Orange rivers where the diamond town of Kimberley was destined to rise. Fortune hunters from the four corners of the globe, but mainly from Britain, surged into the area and threatened to overwhelm the small, conservative Afrikaner communities.

The Transvaal republic, which claimed the diamond fields, ironically found itself in dire economic straits not least after a military campaign against the Pedi

Battle of Blood River

tribe in the eastern Transvaal had fared badly. This was the chance the British had been waiting for. Lord Carnarvon, the British colonial secretary, had long cherished the unification of the Afrikaner states with the Natal and Cape colonies to forge a British-dominated federation. Lord Carnarvon's nickname at Eton was 'twitters' because of his nervous tics and twitchy behaviour, yet his immense family wealth helped him to develop a relatively successful political career (though his son's historical legacy is greater because he funded and witnessed the excavation of Tutankhamen's tomb). Carnarvon père was obsessed with emulating the remarkable confederation in Canada in 1867. South Africa was entirely different, not least in that it comprised a number of white and black states and nations which were hostile to one another.

In 1877 Britain annexed the Transvaal republic under the pretext that it was unable to govern itself or contain the Zulu threat from the south-east. The Boers offered only token resistance. The bigger obstacle confronting the British plan for federation was the still-menacing Zulu army led by Cetshwayo. Blood River had demonstrated that the Zulu military machine, though highly effective against African opposition, was too inflexibly offensive. Yet the British, who were soon to clash with the Zulus, were themselves weakened by outmoded tactics. Cetshwayo became the Zulu king in 1873. He was a nephew of the mighty King Shaka and of massive stature – many accounts put him at over 6 feet by six to eight inches – and ruthless: he was believed to have killed many of his own family, including his own mother. Yet he was reluctant to provoke the technology of the British army. He tried hard to appease the imperial power and to avoid entanglements in the Anglo-Boer disputes. The presence and size of the Zulu impis, however, were anathema to the British federalists especially Sir Bartle Frere, the new governor of the Cape. Frere issued the Zulu king an impossible ultimatum that would have meant dismantling the whole structure of his kingdom. When Cetshwayo unsurprisingly refused, the British governor launched an invasion.

The Zulu war of 1879 composed a pattern that became almost compulsory for the later military campaigns of the Victorian empire: the opening tragedy, the heroic redemption and the final crushing victory. The tragedy was Isandhlwana. Six companies of the 2nd Warwickshire Regiment were entirely wiped out. In all, 858 Britons and 470 men from native levies were killed. It was the worst British military disaster since the Afghan retreat of 1842. The general in command, Lord Chelmsford, had served well in the field beforehand – in the Crimea, India and Abyssinia. He had also crushed the neighbouring Xhosa tribes easily and so he had underestimated his Zulu foe. The heroic redemption came at Rorke's Drift where 110 Britons gallantly warded off waves of charges by 4,000 Zulu warriors. Six months later, Lord Chelmsford, determined to redeem his reputation after the shame of Isandhlwana, rejoiced in a crushing victory at the Zulu capital of Ulundi. The imperial forces formed up in the classic formation, the hollow square,

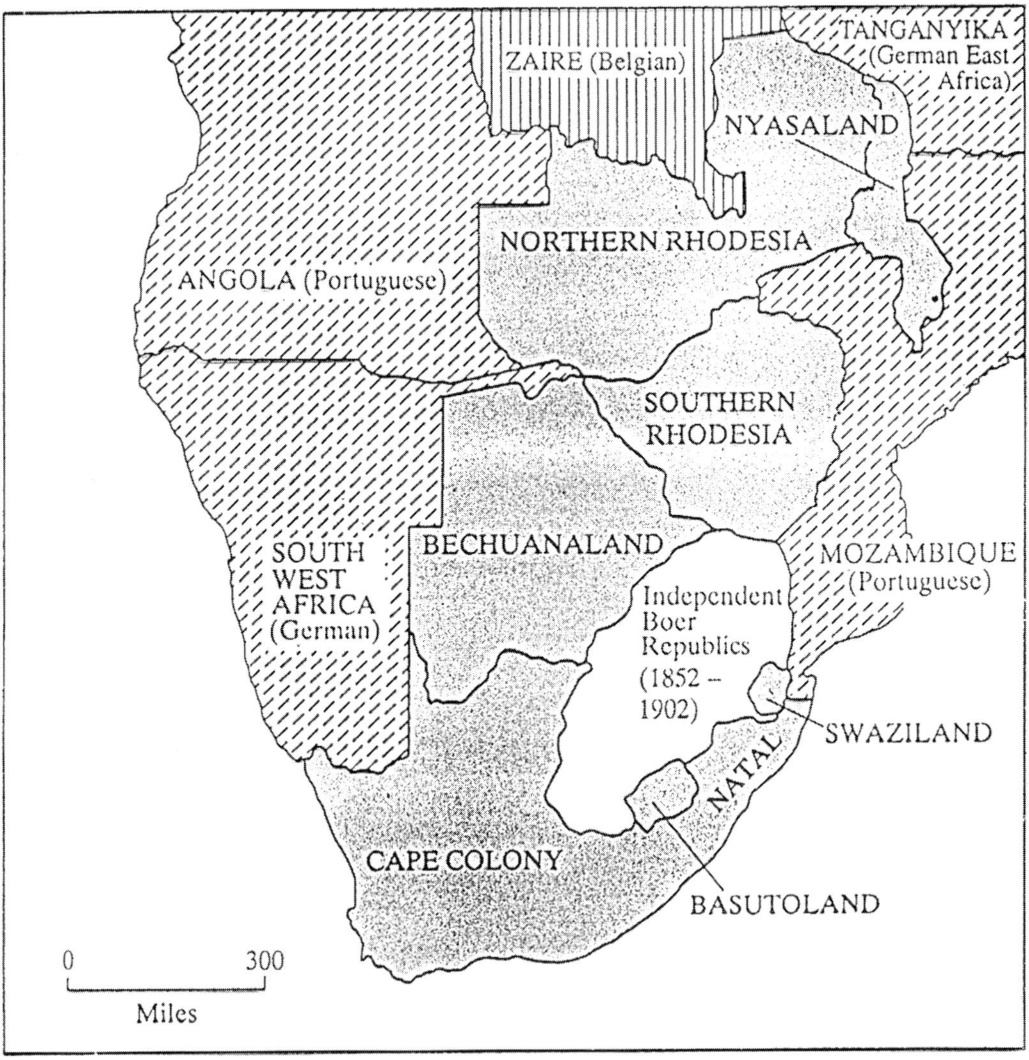


Colonialism in Southern Africa

four deep with fixed bayonets, with field guns and Gatlings, at each corner. There was no digging in, no Boer laager. 'They'll only be satisfied,' said Chelmsford, thinking of his critics in London, 'if we beat them fairly in the open.' The Zulus flung themselves in suicidal waves against the walls of disciplined fire. Hardly a single warrior got within thirty yards of the redcoat square. When the impis faltered, Chelmsford unleashed the cavalry, the 17th Lancers. The British suffered a handful of fatalities. Chelmsford was supposed to have been replaced and had moved on Ulundi instead of waiting for his successor. The final victory partly redeemed his reputation but he never led in the field again. Zulu power was broken, however. Zululand was divided up and later incorporated into the Natal colony.

Isandhlwana had revealed British vulnerability, not least to the Boers who took heart from the pricking of the myth of the British Lion's invincibility. And they had a powerful new leader, Paul Kruger, 'a coarse man, a man of spittoons and pipe smoke, home-spun philosophies on the stoep, religious bigotry; but so absolute that he moved among his people like a prophet'. This was the view of a later British imperial historian.[3]

At Christmas 1880 Kruger led the Transvaal Boers in their first war of independence, perhaps the first modern national liberation struggle against foreign colonialists in southern Africa. No retributive British victory rescued imperial prestige this time: the three-month war was ignominy from start to finish. The British army, facing its first 'European' foe since the Crimea, was disastrously defeated at the Battle of Majuba in February 1881. Overwhelmed by 'arrogance and the sun', as the South African poet Roy Macnab put it, and the revolutionary guerrilla tactics of individual rifle fire, 280 Britons were killed for the loss of one Boer. The Transvaal became independent once more, although the South African Republic (as it became known) was still bound by a vague British 'suzerainty'. It was one of the rare occasions in the Victorian empire when the British negotiated a settlement from the loser's side of the table. It was not the end of the Boer struggle but rather the beginning. And it was an indication that a unified South Africa would emerge only by force: British, Boer or, later, black.

In 1886 gold was discovered in the Transvaal, on the Witwatersrand. This area was to become the biggest single producer of gold in the world. The imperialists had seized the diamonds; gold would be next. Initially, the gold rush brought prosperity to the South African Republic but it also enticed an influx of gold-hungry *uitlanders* (outsiders) who threatened to destroy the traditional fabric of the young republic. *Uitlander* grievances, both real and imagined, grew rapidly. Britain's *fin de siècle* imperialists, British High Commissioner Sir Alfred Milner and the visionary freebooter Cecil Rhodes, could not resist exploiting *uitlander* demands for franchise rights in the Transvaal. Paul Kruger, however, had no illusions about British intentions: 'It is not the vote but my country you want.'

With the connivance of senior members of the British government, Rhodes plotted an *uitlander* rebellion against Kruger but the premature Jameson raid in 1895 undermined his plans. The Jameson debacle fired up Afrikaner nationalism from Cape Town to the Limpopo: in the following year an alliance was made between the Transvaal Republic and the Orange Free State. The Jameson raid (organized from the fledgling British colony of Rhodesia) had given the Boer republics a genuine reason to re-arm, yet this escalation also encouraged those in

British imperial circles who asserted that Kruger was trying not only to preserve his republic. He was alleged to be constructing a 'dominion of Afrikanerdom' throughout southern Africa. The raid, led by a confidant of Cecil Rhodes, Dr Leander James Starr Jameson, provoked the resignation of Rhodes as Cape premier; it also denuded Rhodesia of troops and led to an uprising by the indigenous tribes. Worse, the raid prompted a congratulatory telegram to Kruger from the German Kaiser. This helped to poison Anglo-German relations. In southern Africa the hostilities between Briton and Boer reached a climax in 1899. The Boers were faced with a stark choice: to reform themselves out of existence or to fight. Kruger was not 'bluffing up to the cannon's mouth' – he chose war over surrender.

### *The first twentieth-century war*

The Anglo-Boer war (or the 'Second War of Independence' as the Afrikaners judged it) began on 11 October 1899. This conflict proved to be arguably the British Empire's Vietnam in moral terms, though the British eventually won in Africa while the Americans eventually lost in Asia. The imperium was potentially doomed the moment the Boers showed how a professional British army could be outwitted by a relatively small number of determined guerrillas. Britain was ill-prepared for this clash of wills: imperial troops marched into the first twentieth-century war ready to fight with nineteenth-century tactics. The mounted, highly mobile Boers, with their magazine-loading Mausers and their devastating 'Long Tom' artillery, soon drove the imperial forces into siege positions at Ladysmith, Kimberley and Mafeking. Mafeking, in particular, became world famous as the town that resisted the Boers for seven long months. The commander of British forces there was Robert Baden-Powell. He later founded the Boy Scouts but behaved abysmally towards the town's blacks whom he reduced to starvation by keeping the garrison's whites comfortably fed. (That at least was the judgement in Thomas Pakenham's well-known book, *The Boer War*, though more recent historians, notably Tim Jeal, have refuted the allegation.)

The war became one of attrition. Eventually, the Empire fielded over 450,000 men; the Boers could never muster more than 35,000. It was, therefore, inevitable that the British would win the conventional aspects of the war. Lord Kitchener, the hero of Omdurman, smashed into the Boer republics and captured the main towns. In reply, the Boers resorted to guerrilla tactics. The Boer commandos were more than a match for Britain's unwieldy war machine, which was entirely off-balanced by this sort of mobile irregular warfare. The Boers sabotaged railway lines, the main means of supply, and learned how to transform retreat into assault by suddenly turning on their exhausted pursuers.

The Boer war is sometimes called the last of the gentleman's wars. Yet some British commanders, frustrated by their opponents' irregular style of combat, reacted with brutality. Kitchener intensified his scorched-earth policy by burning

Boer War Commandos: Three Generations

down farms and herding women and children into refugee camps. They were called 'concentration' camps after the *reconcentrado* camps used by Spain in her Cuban colony. Disease killed thousands of Afrikaner non-combatants in the squalid camps, especially undernourished children. Emily Hobhouse, a pacifist and early feminist, campaigned in South Africa and England and carried her cause to the general public, especially the terrible fate of Boer children. (She later became a heroine in South Africa, and one of the three Daphné-class submarines was named after her, although it was soon changed to the SAS *Assegai* under African National Congress rule.) Hobhouse's energetic crusade fuelled the anti-war movement led by David Lloyd George, the British Liberal leader. International criticism finally stung the London government into allowing the Boers to negotiate a peace settlement. Britain had won a savage war and introduced a moderate peace, which was negotiated at Vereeniging in May 1902 – despite the passionate opposition of Afrikaner *bittereinders* who wanted to fight on. And so the young republics were dragged back under the British flag.

In money and lives, no British war since 1815 had been so prodigal. Lord Milner, the High Commissioner, had been a dedicated warmonger and a passionate believer in the imperial mission. His 'little Armageddon' had cost the lives of over 22,000 imperial troops and 7,000 Boer combatants. As many as 28,000 Boers died in the camps, of whom about 22,000 were under 16. Many blacks suffered too: over 14,000 died in separate camps for African prisoners. The Afrikaners might have forgiven Britain's heavyhanded treatment in the Cape, their expulsion from Natal, the shifty seizure of the Kimberley diamond mines, even the notorious Jameson raid but the bodies of concentration camp victims were to be dragons' teeth, sowing a fierce and bitter xenophobia among Afrikaners. And what was the barbarous and unnecessary war intended to achieve? 'It's all for the gold mines,' says a British Tommy in Pakenham's sweeping classic, *The Boer War*. Maybe Tommy was right. The British parliament rewarded Kitchener with a £50,000 victory purse, which he immediately cabled his brokers to invest in South African mining stocks.

According to Pakenham, the arrogant imperial generals failed to heed the military lessons of the tragedy:

> The central tactical lesson of the Boer War eluded them. The reason for those humiliating reverses was not the marksmanship of the Boers, nor their better guns or rifles, nor the stupidity of the British generals – all myths which British people found it convenient to believe. It was the smokeless, long-range, high-velocity, small-bore magazine bullet from rifle or machine gun – plus the trench – had decisively tilted the balance against attack and in favour of defence.[4]

They would soon re-learn the lesson the hard way in Flanders.

### *The Union's wars*

Despite the acrid bitterness of the Boer war, the four white-ruled colonies reconciled themselves to unity: in 1910 the Union of South Africa was forged. This was not quite the federation that Milner and his ilk had imagined, however. Milner had wanted a mass influx of British immigrants but the Afrikaner birth rate, political determination and immigration controls on *uitlanders* created an Afrikaner majority among the whites. The 1910 Union enshrined the principle of white domination. The London government traded its halfhearted protections of 'native' interests for the sake of Anglo-Boer reconciliation, greed for gold and imperial strategy – not least defence. In 1912 the Union Defence Force (UDF) was established, merging both the traditions of the Boer commando and the British regiment. An imperial garrison tarried until 1921, although British influence remained paramount in the local armed forces until 1948. Yet the bitterness of the Boer war never died. As the South African writer William Plomer noted: 'Out of that bungled unwise war/an alp of unforgiveness grew.'

Many Afrikaners, including members of the UDF, were reluctant to fight on behalf of the Empire that had just defeated them. The litmus test was German

South West Africa. Many Boers regarded Germany as a friendly power, especially after its support during the 1899-1902 war. The crunch came in 1914 when the British king declared war on Germany on behalf of the Empire. The South African prime minister, Louis Botha — a former Boer general — promised to invade German South West Africa. Botha sent a telegram to one of his Boer war comrades to take up arms and drew the reply: ‘Certainly but on which side do we fight?’ Some senior Boer commanders rose in revolt and summoned veterans from their old commandos. After 150 rebels and 132 members of the UDF had been killed, the revolt was contained by UDF loyalists. The Afrikaner rebellion was over but more martyrs had been added to the nationalist pantheon. Despite the internal frictions, UDF troops conquered the German colony: the German forces surrendered in July 1915.

The South African forces were then sent to German East Africa where they fought a protracted war against the wily German commander, General Paul von Lettow-Vorbeck. The Prussian aristocrat transformed himself into one of the greatest guerrilla leaders in history. He eventually formed an army of 3,000 Germans and 11,000 black Askari troops, who responded well to his charismatic leadership, use of Swahili and promotion of black officers. The German general realized that East Africa was a sideshow but he determined to tie down as many Entente troops as possible and to keep them from the Western Front. Eventually he faced a combined army of 300,000 British, South African, Rhodesian, Belgian and Portuguese troops. He was the only German commander to take imperial territory when he moved into British East Africa and later into Portuguese Mozambique. The German colony he defended was ravaged by war and starvation because of the naval blockade, yet General von Lettow-Vorbeck remained undefeated at the time of the armistice. The German became a close friend of General Jan Smuts, the South African leader, and later an avowed opponent of Adolf Hitler. Yet, unwittingly, von Lettow-Vorbeck’s military determination augmented the Hitlerian myth of the undefeated German army’s stab in the back. Hitler offered him the ambassadorship in London, where he was still regarded with grudging respect. He declined with ‘frigid hauteur’. After his death in 1964 at the age of 94, his nephew was asked whether it was true that the so-called ‘Lion of Africa’ had personally told Hitler to fuck himself. The nephew replied, ‘I don’t think he put it that politely.’ After the Second World War, his reputation as a ‘good’ German gave some respectability to the fledgling Bundeswehr, which named a number of barracks after him.

The Union’s campaigns in Africa had led to the genesis of the South African Air Force, the second oldest in the world. South Africans had also first used armoured cars in combat, while deploying one of the last major cavalry operations, with camels and horses. South African troops also fought in the Middle East and Flanders during the Great War. For South Africa, the most famous battle took place at Delville Wood, where in a few long days the UDF suffered 2,815 casualties.

Transvaal Scottish preparing to leave Johannesburg for the front in the First World War

To the Entente side the South Africans contributed 190,000 white and 60,000 'non-white' soldiers, as well as 25,000 non-white auxiliaries. At home, the blacks who had volunteered – encouraged in some cases by the African National Congress (then the South African Native National Congress) – received scant reward or political concessions for their service to the country.

The Maritz rebellion of 1914 and the refusal of the Botha government to provide forces directly under the command of the Union Defence Force to fight for the British Empire in the Middle East and Europe vividly displayed the internal splits in South Africa. The South Africans who fought at Delville Wood were part of the South African Overseas Expeditionary Force (SAOEF) which came directly under British War Office command, a deliberate fudge on the part of both Botha and the British government to avoid infringing the ban imposed by the Pretoria government in 1914 on sending men to fight beyond Southern Africa.

In the inter-war period the UDF saw action on the domestic front against black protesters in 1922 when it suppressed the Bondelswart rebellion in South West Africa; the army also crushed a white mineworkers' revolt on the Rand in the same year. Meanwhile the imperial government had helped to build up a local air force with the gift of a hundred aircraft. Despite various attempts to develop a South

African navy in this period, however, the Royal Navy dominated the important Cape route from its base in Simonstown (leased from 1921 until 1975).

Within less than a generation after the war to end all wars, the call to arms sounded again. And, like the Allies, South Africa was almost completely unprepared. The cabinet and the parliament split along the old (white) tribal fault lines on whether to stay neutral or fight but a decision to join the Allies was taken in parliament by eighty votes to sixty-seven.The prime minister, J.B.M. Hertzog, who was in favour of neutrality, resigned and General Jan Smuts took over the premiership for the second time. The more conservative nationalists veered even more to the right in open sympathy with Adolf Hitler; some of them, including the future prime minister, B.J. Vorster, were interned. Conscription was not introduced, partly because of Afrikaner resistance. A massive recruiting drive did take place, however. Over 200,000 uniformed South Africans joined up, of whom about 9,000 were killed. Blacks volunteered in their tens of thousands. Despite the official policy that they should remain non-combatants – the deepseated fears of an African uprising was part of the DNA of most whites in colonial Africa – many took an active part in the fighting, especially in North Africa. Black leaders were more guarded in their support this time: they were sceptical about the chances of the Atlantic Charter's freedoms being extended to southern Africa. During the 1942 scare that the Japanese might invade, Smuts talked about training and arming a large non-European army; the plan was quietly dropped as the Axis threat waned. South Africans of all races fought with gallantry and distinction, excelling notably

*Above left*: Emily Hobhouse, champion of Boer rights

*Above right*: General von Lettow-Vorbeck, undefeated in 1918

as pilots in the North African and European theatres. One of their most famous operations was during the 1944 Warsaw uprising, when South Africans flew Liberators to drop supplies to the Polish underground army besieged in the capital by Nazi forces. Of the forty-one planes flown by South African squadrons, eleven were shot down in the vain attempt to relieve the garrison.

In the Second World War those members of the UDF who wished to fight outside Southern Africa wore a circular red patch on their shoulder straps to indicate their willingness to fight alongside other British Commonwealth forces. South African servicemen wearing these badges often ended up in punch-ups with Afrikaners who generally supported Nazi Germany on the principle of my enemy's enemy is my friend, including B.J. Voster and his *Ossewabrandwag* neo-Nazi friends.[5] NCOs and commissioned officers in the UDF carried on wearing these patches until 1948 when the Nationalist Party victory made such outward signs of loyalty to the British Commonwealth harmful to their career prospects. As a consequence many resigned their commissions.

After the Second World War, South Africa once more rallied to the Allied side, this time during the onset of the Cold War. South African pilots once more distinguished themselves, during the Berlin Blockade (1948-49) and the see-saw war in Korea (1950-53). In the immediate postwar period, Jan Smuts strode the Western stage as a world statesman. From 1917 to 1919, he had been one of the members of the British Imperial War Cabinet and he was instrumental in the founding of what became the Royal Air Force. The Boer War rebel warrior (and Cambridge scholar) even became a field marshal in the British Army in 1941, and served again in the cabinet alongside his friend, Winston Churchill. He was the only man to sign both of the peace treaties ending the First and Second World Wars and played an important role in the creation of both the League of Nations and its successor, the United Nations. At one stage it was even suggested that Smuts could have succeeded Churchill if the prime minister had been struck down by a stray bomb or an alcohol-induced heart attack. This remarkable Afrikaner was a visionary to be sure, but his loftier ideals were also infused with cynical attempts to extend white *Lebensraum* in Africa, especially in the League's mandated territory in South West Africa. He had also hoped to swop former German East Africa in exchange for South Africa absorbing Portuguese Mozambique south of the Zambezi river. In addition, he intended to include Southern Rhodesia, and even the British protectorates (modern-day Botswana, Lesotho and Swaziland) could fall into the Union's embrace. Then Pretoria would have controlled territory three times its size before the Second World War.

As a leading world statesman Smuts attended the opening conference of the United Nations in San Francisco in April 1945. It was Smuts who helped draft the original declaration of aims in the preamble of the UN Charter, with its soaring words sanctifying human rights. Ironically, Smuts had created a massive rod for his own country's back and it would help to drive South Africa from the community of nations. At home Smuts had little vision: his race policy was a muddled paternalism subordinated to the unshakeable principle that white interests must always come first. Even if Smuts, distracted as he was by international affairs, had tried to practise at home what he preached abroad, he would not have been able to carry his fellow Afrikaner leaders, who were obsessed with domestic racial issues.

Soon the erstwhile Nazi sympathizers in the National Party would rise to power. In futile counterpoint, some of the returning soldiers who had fought in the name of democracy and human equality adopted more liberal attitudes; these were to surface in ex-servicemen's organizations such as the Springbok Legion and the Torch Commando. The Torch Commando was led by the RAF fighter ace, 'Sailor' Malan, and he attracted tens of thousands of followers, much to the annoyance of the National Party leaders, who did everything to stop civil servants associating with the liberal ex-servicemen and ex-servicewomen. Racial policy hardened in the immediate postwar years. In the UN General Assembly, in December 1946, Vijaya Pandit, the Indian representative, excoriated South Africa's racial discrimination. At the same time, Dr A.B. Xuma, the ANC leader, was busy lobbying UN delegates. Soon South Africa, the West's 'honoured ally', was to be branded a 'polecat among nations'. Britain, it is true, held the line in the UN Security Council. Yet the trumpets were sounding the imperial retreat for Pax Britannica, especially in Africa. Elsewhere on the continent the other colonial empires began their long recessionals in haste, or slowly and in anger. From these winds of war and change a new great power was to emerge in southern Africa. It was to be a harsh imperium based upon the naked assertion of white power: Pax Pretoria.

*Chapter 2*

# Winds of Change and War

In 1945 South Africa was a small military power, still nestling in the protective bosom of the British Empire. The imperial power was exhausted, however. At the UN, Jan Smuts epitomized South Africa's respectability. Yet after 1948 the paragon was destined to become a pariah. The South African government, once in the vanguard of the lobby that advocated economic sanctions by the League of Nations as the best guarantee of collective security – even to the extent of urging an oil embargo on Italy in 1935 – would soon find itself facing an unprecedented range of UN sanctions.

The UN began its long vendetta with criticisms of Pretoria's treatment of its Indian community, then the illegal control of South West Africa and later the South African Defence Force's attacks on neighbouring states. Above all, the main cause of the obloquy was the government's policy of apartheid – racial separation. Many of the tirades were based upon sanctimonious ignorance, ceremonial angst and downright double standards. Other obnoxious regimes were more repressive or the behaviour of their police no less outrageous but no other state had based its oppression so 'legally' and so overtly on race. Pretoria was condemned because its policy was both impolitic and immoral. To quote American writer William Faulkner: 'To live anywhere in the world today and be against equality because of race or colour is like living in Alaska and being against snow.'

Many volumes have been written on the political manifestations of apartheid. This book is concerned primarily with a military – not moral – analysis, in so far as such a distinction is possible. The system of racial discrimination and domination was founded upon an ornate (if spurious) system of laws. Afrikaners set themselves a Herculean task: 'a womb-to-tomb surveillance plan for the subjugated population'.[1] Perhaps only Hitler and Stalin had attempted social engineering on such an audacious scale. Their regimes had the manpower, though. History of course is more than a numbers game – ask the Israelis – but demography counted, especially in Africa.

The period of high apartheid (especially in the 1960s and 1970s) was an attempt to command the waves to stop. Over 30 million were classified, usually for life. Eight million citizens were denationalized in the so-called independent homelands programme. At least 3.5 million were ethnically cleansed – except for a tiny fraction of whites, all were coloured, blacks or Asians. (Perforce I have to use the contemporary classifications to define the conditions and categories of the time.) These 'non-white' millions were physically removed or 'relocated', as Afrikaner bureaucrats termed it, often to the impoverished 13 per cent of the country, designated as Bantustans (allocated to the 75 per cent majority of the population). African politics – across the continent – has usually been based on land: shoehorning so many land-hungry people, often rooted in ancestral terrain, into such small rural and urban ghettoes and gulags was bound to inspire revolutionary anger. The UN talked of 'crimes against humanity': apartheid, the slave trade and the Holocaust became near-synonyms of human evil.

And yet Afrikaners were not uniquely evil people. The architects of apartheid saw it as a rational, even idealistic, segregationist alternative to an unacceptably integrated future. The homelands, to the racialist philosophers who designed apartheid, were deemed to be black counterparts of Afrikaner nationalism. Blacks were not thought fit to vote in white South Africa but they could vote in their Bantustans to re-affirm, in the sham parliaments, the tribal oligarchs groomed by Pretoria. If the Afrikaner leaders had been inclined to take their grand vision to its logical conclusion and share the land *proportionately*, the many foreign critics might just have been prepared to accept partition – as in Ireland, the Raj, Palestine, Korea, or Germany – as a stalemated temporary resolution of endemic tensions. Pretoria did not proceed to finesse a logical extension of apartheid, a white homeland, and ended up using overwhelming military force to retain its unequal patrimony.[2]

Afrikaners were to pay a huge price for their misplaced idealism and selfish cruelty. On the fortieth anniversary of coming to power – in 1988 – the National Party held a big celebration, despite the massed opprobrium of the world community, even from erstwhile allies such as the Americans and the British. But

A typical petty apartheid sign

the opposition white Progressive Federal Party asked 'What is there to celebrate?' and launched a campaign to advertise '40 years in the wilderness'.

The small liberal opposition pointed out that in 1948 the National Party ended a white immigration scheme that brought in 51,000 per year. Now white skilled people were *emigrating* in droves. In 1948 South Africa had won medals at the Olympic Games, whereas in 1988 Zola Budd – running for Britain – was pilloried because she had once been a South African citizen. In 1948 the country managed with twelve cabinet ministers and 153 MPs. In 1988 Pretoria was augmenting the 144 cabinet ministers and 1,369 MPs in the various tri-cameral (for Indians, whites and coloureds) and homeland parliaments (for blacks). In 1948 Pretoria had lent war-weary Britain £80 million. In 1988 it was estimated that in the previous three years R18 billion in private capital had been lost to South Africa because of disinvestment. Official foreign government and UN sanctions had increased that tally by many more billions. Within four months of taking office in 1948 the minister of defence disarmed the South African Cape Corps and the Native Military Corps, both of which had distinguished themselves in the Second World War. They were told not to wear their military uniforms. Non-white soldiers were later recruited in small numbers into the regular army's order of battle and saw service in South West Africa. Nevertheless, by 1988 some of the black veterans had not received their military pensions from service in the Second World War. At the same time in the training camps outside South Africa, the African National Congress was welcoming tens of thousands of young blacks, Asians and coloureds who were all too eager to put on battledress to fight apartheid.

The white liberal opposition had been reduced to a feuding rump in parliament by 1988. Many traditional English-speaking supporters of the opposition had crossed over to the National Party which promised security, while the far-right Conservative Party became the official opposition in 1987. The government did promise, and even promote, some reform, but it was too late and too little for most critics inside and outside the beleaguered country. Although reforms had been granted the Afrikaner rulers still relied largely on their strength of arms. The small Union Defence Force had been transformed into the South African Defence Force (SADF) – the mightiest military machine on the continent, with a vast arms industry and a secret arsenal of nuclear weapons, courtesy of some help from Jerusalem. But it was a military giant with the proverbial feet of clay. Incessant wars on the borders and intermittent domestic insurrections had caused South Africa to suffer imperial overstretch. Like all profligate empires, Pax Pretoria was beginning to collapse under its own weight. Empires tend to show signs of crumbling at the edges even though the rot usually starts at home, in the centre. 'Far-called our navies melt away,' wrote Rudyard Kipling as Britain entered its Edwardian twilight. By 1988 the South African navy had ceased to exist as far as a blue-water strategy, capable of a conventional defence of the Cape sea route was concerned. And that was not the only vulnerability in the ramparts of the Afrikaner laager.

The architects of Total Strategy: P.W. Botha and General Magnus Malan

International pressures on South Africa were based on a number of assumptions. The most obvious was that neither the black-ruled neighbouring states, as they became independent, nor the internal black majority were strong enough to overwhelm the well-armed white minority on their own. Short of joint military intervention by the great powers, isolation and sanctions, it was argued, would nudge history along and persuade the dominant white oligarchies that timely political negotiation, rather than eventual, and inevitable, military surrender or defeat, was in their own interests. The economic, political, military and, crucially, the psychological dimensions became enmeshed in a complex international matrix; South Africa became a political football for many campaigners to kick towards their own, often vastly different, goals. By the end of the 1980s, and before covert settlement talks, Pretoria was totalitarian, paranoid, motivated in part by ideology, reliant on its army, police, its reserves of gold and scarce minerals, its helot workforce, and deluded by its own propaganda and real and imagined external hostility into believing in a cosmic cleavage: preserving an advanced civilization against the enveloping foreign threat. Pretoria's Manichean vision, aptly summarized as 'a total onslaught [which] equates the "red peril" with the "black peril", and defence of apartheid with defence of Western Christian values' lacked real substance.[3] The white supremacists were fast using up their future.

### *The gathering storm*

In 1945 the African National Congress was an insignificant organization and the NKVD (later KGB) had far more important things on its mind than Pretoria's racial eccentricities. The Russians did make a play for a piece of Africa when Foreign Minister Molotov demanded not only a Soviet mandate over ex-Italian Libya but also Russian control over the ex-Italian Eritrean port of Massawa (which it later accomplished, for a time, by its support of the radical Dergue regime in Ethiopia in the 1970s). Elsewhere, colonial Africa and Asia afforded Moscow many opportunities. The USSR was in the business of franchising revolutions, so Moscow rushed to sponsor 'wars of national liberation'. In the beginning the Soviet Union sought influence rather than real estate. Moscow had many advantages: it was not tainted with the original sin of imperialism; its superpower status, ideology and industrialization offered a model to African socialists; and it did not have to contend with squeamish public opinion at home. Plus it could provide a constant supply of cheap, reliable and simple-to-operate small arms. In later years a new generation of African leaders found Russians to be tactless colonizers. They were ruthless, arrogant and, after all, white. The Chinese were not and could be used as a radical alternative, though in the early years of decolonization the Chinese had little money to spare; that was to change in the twenty-first century when Beijing could afford to buy up much of Africa's mineral resources.

In the first flush of decolonization the Russians were the main military backers for African revolutionaries. Moscow's great ally in the scramble to decolonize was Washington. The USA did as much as the USSR to undermine Britain's often halfhearted (and France's fullthroated) efforts to hang on to imperial possessions. Equally important was the European left's hostility to empire. The new African nations were expected to choose sides in the Cold War. The older imperial powers, perhaps more cynical about the nuances of African politics, generally eschewed such simplistic notions. They tended to see African events in terms of the North/South divide, sometimes black versus white, but not usually only East versus West. In South Africa's case Britain combined sanctimonious moral disapproval with the almost uninhibited pursuit of economic self-interest. France, typically, buttered its bread on both sides: it managed in the 1960s to build up its military and economic ties with francophone Africa while playing a major role in the modernization of the South African Defence Force.

Despite the major disagreements over colonial policy, with America, and each other, the British and the French tended to close ranks during major Cold War confrontations, not least in the UN Security Council. Initially the Western powers protected South Africa from the increasingly hostile array of third-world states. Pretoria was also shielded by its membership of the Commonwealth (until 1961). Pretoria was unhappy with Britain's invasion of the Suez Canal Zone in 1956, however, because it provided the ideal opportunity for the USSR to lure Africa ever more into the Cold War arena. Egypt's leader, Abdel Nasser, turned to Moscow after his humiliation at the hands of the Anglo-French and Israeli forces. Then Russia backed Kwame Nkrumah's Ghana and in 1958 Sékou Touré's Guinea.

Katanga province of the Congo

Soviet advance was impeded by the relatively graceful French and British retreat from Africa, which became more an issue of timetables than principles. The important exceptions were Algeria and Rhodesia. The mayhem, however, induced by Belgium's precipitous exit from the Congo did allow for Soviet meddling, although Moscow lacked the military throw-power, then, to intervene decisively.

The Congo will not be analyzed in detail – here or later – because it is not usually considered part of the southern African region. Nevertheless, the continuous bloodbath that was Congo's style of politicking regularly infected the pattern of politics farther south. The mass rape of whites, especially nuns, became a staple of tabloid reporting in European papers in the first years of Congo's independence after 1960. *Newsweek*'s Edward 'Teddy' Behr's infamous title of his memoir of the period – *Anybody Here Been Raped And Speaks English?* (supposedly the gauche indiscretion of a BBC man) – cynically characterized the media approach.[4] Many of the dramatic stories were true. Train loads or car convoys of Europeans – 'beaten men, crying children and women bleeding down their thighs' – were regularly recorded. Many white refugees escaped into Northern Rhodesia; the blood-spattered reports spread like a bush fire and hardened the politics of a generation of whites in Southern Africa to the future possible excesses of black rule. The explosion of racist rage among the Congo's supposedly disciplined black policemen and soldiers caused particular concern:

> Frustrations over money, rank and years of bigotry burst onto the streets. Drunk or drugged soldiers ordered whites to kiss their feet. Those who did were kicked in the head; those who refused were beaten to the pavement with rifle butts.[5]

Even a senior UN diplomat such as Brian Urquhart was seized by mutinous gendarmes and beaten for two hours. 'Better beaten than eaten,' he said with a black humour in the pre-PC era, when he was finally released. He was referring to the real incidents and false rumours of widespread cannibalism. It was a stirring saga – frenzied white exodus and European businesses trying to secure the secession of Katanga for its mining wealth. The influx of white mercenaries to defend Katanga and the intervention of UN forces, and then the mysterious death of the UN secretary general (Dag Hammarskjold) in a plane crash: this was mayhem in the original heart of darkness. It was made worse by the intrigues of the great powers. Belgium, the colonial power, France and the US were the most active militarily but Russia and Britain were involved too, not least in the spying game. Britain's Daphne Park was a famous SIS (MI6) fixer. 'Very high on intelligence, if low on glamour', she was then a 39-year-old consul in Léopoldville at the time of Congo's independence. Intelligence lore has it that she had attempted to grab Nazi scientists in postwar Berlin but her inadequate German confused a missile scientist with an expert on bumble bees. She improved later while working in Moscow and in the Congo she is still associated with the assassination of Patrice Lumumba, the first democratically elected leader of the Congo who was considered too pro-Soviet by the UK and American agencies.

The Congo – in its various names – was later to become the site of Africa's so-called first world war in the 1990s and at the time of writing is still awash with the blood of civil conflicts. In the 1960s the Congo independence debacle radicalized the new balance of forces in the UN General Assembly, where the Afro-Asian blocs had risen from fifteen out of fifty members in 1956 to seventy-three out of 125 in 1965. The rowdy newcomers increasingly sided with Moscow and Beijing, especially in the ritual denunciation of Pretoria. The Sharpeville massacre by South African police in March 1960 – although it was not like the calculated slaughter of Indians by British forces at Amritsar in 1919 during the Raj – raised the tempo of UN members' righteous indignation. It was in the same year that Harold Macmillan, the British premier, delivered his famous 'wind of change' speech in Cape Town. That was the last visit of a British prime minister to the pariah state. Despite Macmillan's (gentle) warning, London refused to accede to the UN's calls for economic boycotts. In 1961 South Africa felt compelled to leave the Commonwealth and in the same year it became a republic. In 1963 the UN slapped a ban on the sales of arms to South Africa. The ban was not (then) mandatory. In the same year the Organization of African Unity (OAU) was set up, even though it was the ultimate misnomer. Despite the incessant and incestuous backbiting, it was an important forum for the verbal assaults on apartheid – the one thing all the members could (nearly) always agree upon. In the following year South Africa was pushed out of active participation in the General Assembly, which continued to hammer away at the new republic's continuing occupation of South West Africa.

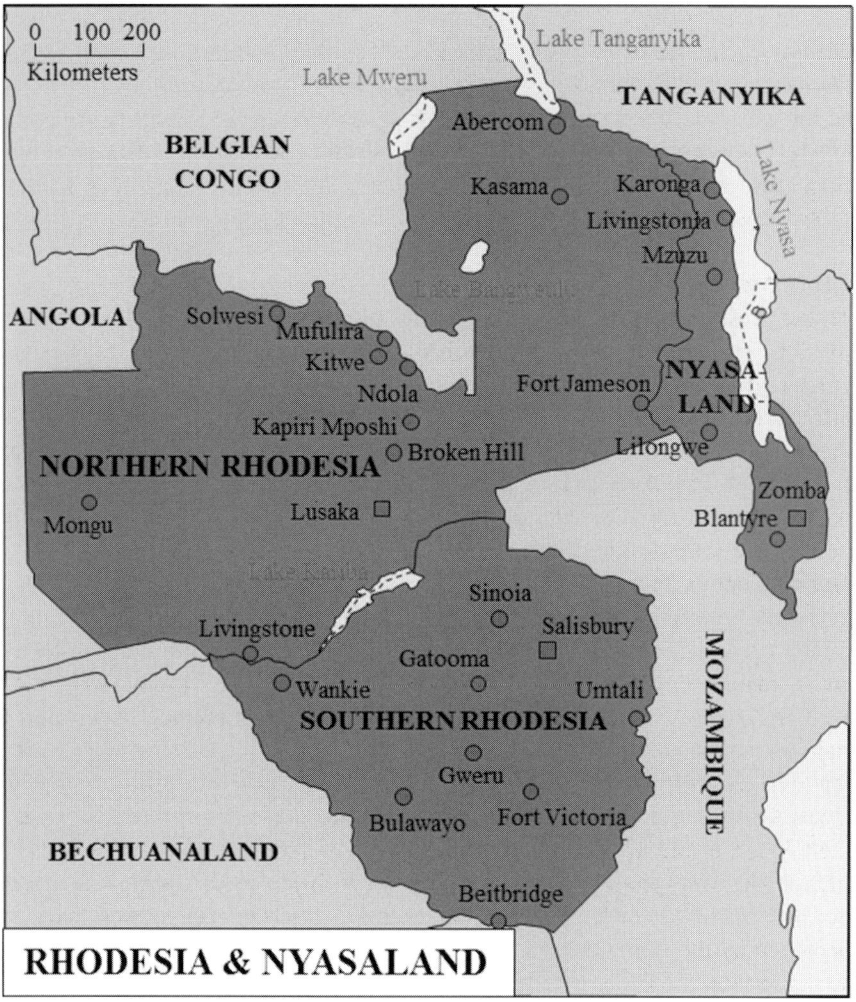


Flawed Federation of the Rhodesias and Nyasaland

Rhodesia's illegal declaration of independence in November 1965 sharpened the UN's focus on southern Africa. Pretoria blamed the collapse of the two British-sponsored federations in east and central Africa on the evils of African nationalism and communist intrigue but the ambiguity of British colonial policy was the most likely culprit. In both regions London had vacillated between the themes of responsible government for whites and trusteeship for blacks. As a result the Kenyans were denied what the Rhodesian whites got in the 1920s. Despite the influence of the Kenyan settlers' lobby and because of the Mau-Mau emergency (from 1952-1960), it became impossible to grant self-government to Kenya's

60,000 white settlers. In the end Pretoria had to face not two white-dominated federations but five black republics, all hostile except for docile Malawi (originally Nyasaland). It also had to succour a rebellion in Rhodesia. South Africa was castigated at the UN for its economic and military aid to the 'bunch of cowboys' in Rhodesia's capital, Salisbury. The former British protectorates (Bechuanaland/Botswana, Basutoland/Lesotho and Swaziland) had escaped Pretoria's official control but not its economic orbit.

### *Tar Babies*

To the Western powers, trade with South Africa seemed more important than pious UN resolutions, especially when white power appeared firmly entrenched in the region. This was the conclusion drawn in 1969 by President Richard Nixon and his security adviser, Henry Kissinger. The German-accented professor backed the key decisions that originated from National Security Study Memorandum (NSSM) 39. This document tried to sidestep America having to choose between white and black Africa, and the compromises had to satisfy the increasingly vociferous domestic black-American constituency. The essence of NSSM 39 (actually option two of the study) was that black states should not needlessly be upset – although the ANC called the study an 'infamous document' – but trade with South Africa would continue. The white-ruled republic was virulently anti-communist, wasn't it? And, unlike South Vietnam (then a strategic priority for Washington), it could fight its own battles, provided it secured some foreign military equipment. This fitted precisely with the so-called Nixon Doctrine that was then in vogue. The doctrine encouraged pro-Western states to defend themselves with American help but not with American troops. South Africa was, therefore, a useful ally, and so was Portugal. The Portuguese Azores islands in the mid-Atlantic proved vital in the urgent air shipment of US arms to Israel during the 1973 Yom Kippur War, for example. NATO weapons were happily deployed by the Portuguese in their African wars. And South Africa's efficient secret service, the Bureau for State Security (BOSS), enjoyed close ties with the CIA. Pretoria was not only a major trading partner but amenable in other ways such as helping the National Aeronautics and Space Administration set up a tracking station in South Africa.

And Rhodesia? Why treat it like a leper? Rhodesian sanctions were not working so why should a passionately pro-capitalist administration such as Nixon's penalize American businessmen in the name of a policy that had failed? This applied especially to the strategic metal chrome. After all, the Russians were surreptitiously buying the supposedly sanctioned ore and then re-selling to the Americans at a sweet profit. Why should Washington buy this more expensive 'Russian' chrome when they could get a better bargain from pro-Western Rhodesia, and at a good discount? In 1971, with the passage in Congress of the Byrd Amendment, the USA traded openly in chrome with Salisbury.

A section of NSSM 39 read:

> The whites are here to stay, and the only way that constructive change can come is through them. There is no hope for the blacks to gain the political rights they seek through violence … which will only lead to chaos and increased opportunities for the communists …. We can, through selective relaxation of our stance toward the white regimes, encourage some modification of their current racial and colonial policies …. Our tangible interests form a basis for our contacts in the region, and these can be maintained at an acceptable political cost.

The US National Security Council seemed to have discussed this new policy in a fog of ignorance. Vice President Spiro 'Ted' Agnew praised the South Africans for having achieved independence with a declaration modelled on America's until Nixon gently suggested, 'Ted, I think you mean Rhodesia, don't you?' These conservative views dismayed State Department officials who quoted the Uncle Remus story: Brer Fox made a Tar Baby to catch Brer Rabbit; each time Brer Rabbit hit the Tar Baby he became more stuck to it. So they dubbed it the 'Tar Baby Option'. The name, and the policy, stuck.

After this green light, American support for the whites became much more overt. In 1971, for example, the US Export-Import Bank changed its policy to allow longterm loans to Pretoria. IBM and ITT supplied computers and other electronic equipment

The Simonstown naval base was long a symbol of the British-South African military relationship

to the SADF. Between 1967 and 1972 the USA sold 1,376 aircraft of various types to the ex-pariah, including ten C-130 troop carriers. In 1972 NATO secretly requested the supreme allied commander in the Atlantic to devise plans to protect the Cape sea route – in close collaboration with the SADF. From 1972 NATO provided sophisticated electronic equipment for Project Advocate, a huge surveillance and communications base near Simonstown. In March 1974 the French and South African navies held joint exercises.[6] Even when Britain announced the withdrawal from its long-cherished base in Simonstown in October 1974, NATO officials hinted to Pretoria that contingency plans for the allied defence of the Cape would not be affected. Pretoria desperately wanted *formal* membership of NATO or some South Atlantic equivalent. That would have been political dynamite for the West. But the secret accords, from Pretoria's perspective, were a lot better than nothing.

The British exit from the large naval base in Simonstown, first used by the Royal Navy in the 1790s, signified the end of formal South African-British military ties. It caused some unease in naval circles in the UK but real bitterness in Pretoria. According to a later detailed conversation I had with Vice Admiral James 'Flam' Johnson, the chief of the South African Navy, just after the naval knot was cut, P.W. Botha (the defence minister) summoned his SADF commanders to their weekly meeting. The hardline Botha turned to the anglophile admiral and said, very emphatically, in English, 'What of your old English friends now?' Johnson had no reply.

Despite the stickiness of the Tar Baby option, the tide of events was moving against white supremacy in southern Africa. In 1972, for example, the pro-French and pro-South African regime in the Malagasy Republic was overthrown by a military coup whose leaders then veered towards Moscow. Above all, the anti-fascist coup in Lisbon in 1974 proved Kissinger and the Tar Baby option completely wrong. Russia had kept a relatively low profile in Africa after the Congo crisis, a tendency perhaps reinforced by the relative humiliation of the climbdown during the Cuban missile crisis of 1962. While the Portuguese army retreated rapidly from Mozambique, Angola and Guinea-Bissau, the ancient monarchy in Ethiopia was usurped by the savage Dergue, which became dependent on Soviet arms and Cuban troops. Russia was ousted from Somalia in 1977 but there were much bigger pickings in nextdoor Ethiopia, Somalia's enemy. After the largest airlift in African history and the biggest African battles since the desert war of the 1940s, Russian generals and their Cuban allies broke the back of the Somali army they had created a few years before. Then the USSR helped the Ethiopian army to stamp on, but not out, Cuba's erstwhile allies among the rebels fighting for Eritrean independence. The Soviets proved themselves inconsistent allies and yet supreme opportunists. Traumatized by the defeat in Vietnam, Washington's diplomats stood and gawked while Moscow chalked up crushing victories in Angola and Ethiopia. African states could not but be impressed by Moscow's mailed fist.

*Before* 1974 the occasional African revolution had fallen into Moscow's lap. *After* 1974, especially in southern Africa, the Kremlin perceived a consistently advantageous revolutionary pattern. The Russians placed

> a special faith in the men and regimes coming to power in Ethiopia, Mozambique and Angola. These were revolutions, as the Soviets judged them, made of stiffer stuff, in part because they were won in armed struggle, led by men who bore arms rather than pamphlets, and in part because they faced real and powerful external threats that would keep them from growing soft. For five years, from 1974 to 1979, Soviet excitement mounted.[7]

The apartheid regime was badly shaken by these developments. Angola and Mozambique had become ideological enemies and military threats almost overnight after the Lisbon coup. The SADF pulled back from full involvement in the Angola civil war in early 1976. In 1974-75 it had been urged to get stuck in by Washington and then America stabbed South Africa in the back, according to Pretoria. Britain had exited the Simonstown agreement and France reneged on its arms deals with South Africa. Kissinger's hectic 'shuttle diplomacy' had not ended the war in Rhodesia; in fact it had escalated after the abortive Geneva conference of late 1976. Moreover, the dramatic revolt in the black Johannesburg township of Soweto had coincided with Kissinger's attempt at peace brokerage in the region. South Africa's image of toughminded stability had been eroded. Nor had progress been made on the border war in South West Africa/Namibia.

By the end of 1976 Kissinger was out of a job as secretary of state and South Africa had secured few tangible gains from the Nixon doctrine. True, some important military equipment had been procured. Yet, according to R.W. Johnson (in his *How Long Will South Africa Survive?,* a highly influential book at the time), Kissinger's diplomacy had involved the manipulation (downwards) of the gold price, the mainstay of the South African economy, particularly during the big squeeze on the stubborn Rhodesian premier, Ian Smith, in mid-1976. Earlier, Nixon, forced ultimately by the deficit financing of the Vietnam War, had allowed the gold price to float above the traditional $35 an ounce. The upwards movement ($220 an ounce when Nixon resigned) had helped South Africa during the international recession induced by the 1973 massive OPEC oil-price hikes and the supply problems caused by the Arab oil embargo against Pretoria. By 1974, however, the US had several reasons to depress the gold price: such as reducing the value of Russian gold sales, hostility to French fiscal policy and re-asserting the primacy of the dollar. So Kissinger's

Henry Kissinger in 1976

alleged gold-price conspiracy against South Africa may not have been paramount. Nonetheless, IMF gold auctions had helped to push the price down to around $100 by July 1976. So South Africa's vast gold reserves were not an invulnerable hedge against international recession or economic pressure. The fall of the Shah of Iran in 1979 pinched another vulnerable pressure point: oil supplies.

A far greater step-change, however, was the arrival of a born-again peanut farmer and Democrat contender, Jimmy Carter. In 1977 President Carter entered the White House hellbent on taking a much tougher line on Rhodesia and apartheid. He appointed a vociferous black rights activist, Andrew Young, to be the first African-American to hold the position of US Ambassador to the UN. Young, a pastor, rode shotgun on the new American policy on Africa with a fullthroated religious fervour. He went as far as calling the Cubans a 'stabilizing force' in Africa. This was too much for pro-Western African leaders such as Zaire's General Mobutu. The Afrikaner government regarded Carter as held in thrall to the black voters in America. Pik Botha, the always blunt politician who later became foreign minister, expressed the angry mood of his government when he said, 'Must I pay the price of Mr Young's hatred of white America?'

Carter had other counsellors. His national security advisor, Zbigniew Brzezinski, was as hostile as Kissinger to Soviet penetration of Africa. On occasions, particularly after the 1978 invasion of Zaire's mineral-rich Shaba province via Angola and the bestial slaughter of whites in Kolwezi, Carter turned on the Russians. If they could use proxy forces in Africa – the Cubans – then America could deploy proxies too. The USA assisted the rapid deployment of the French Foreign Legion and Belgian paratroopers. The Legionnaires went in fast and hard and restored order, saving thousands of lives, both Zairians and white ex-pats. The French Legionnaires had become the West's Cubans. Paris was determined to counter Soviet encroachment especially in francophone Africa.

Yet Carter continued to confuse friend and foe alike. At the beginning of his presidency he scoffed at the Soviet menace: Americans, he advised, should throw away their 'inordinate fear' of communism. In this he was Andy Young's alter ego. But later, as Soviet adventurism increased, notably after the invasion of Afghanistan, Carter chose to echo Brzezinski. The president appeared to be not the conductor of American foreign policy but rather the arbiter at best or, at worst, merely the inconsistent mouthpiece of the traditional warring interests within the CIA, State Department, White House and Congress. To many Americans Carter looked as though he could not control unruly members of his own family let alone contain a rampant rival superpower. No wonder the Russians thought 1974 to 1979 were wonderful years in Africa.

They were lean years for Pretoria. In 1977, at a meeting in Vienna, US Vice President Walter Mondale told John Vorster, the South African prime minister, that his country should have one man, one vote – the ultimate insult to Pretoria. And Young had described the Afrikaner government as 'illegitimate'. By the end of the Carter administration the harsh rhetoric had been muted. The Democrats' crusading idealism had lost its drive after the Afrikaner republic had re-stabilized after the 1976 Soweto insurrection, just as President John Kennedy's passion for Africa faded once the furore of the 1960 Sharpeville emergency had died down. In essence, until 1984, American foreign policy concentrated on the East-West dimension of conflict in southern Africa. Nearly all American leaders applied the Tar Baby option in practice: as long as US investment in South Africa was large and profitable and as long as white supremacy looked secure, then US foreign policy would not rock the boat by putting African liberation before, firstly, the containment of Soviet penetration, secondly, the protection of trade, especially in strategic minerals, and thirdly, and least important, the defence of the Cape sea route. There was a gut feeling in official Washington that it was better to stick with familiar allies, whatever their nature, as long as they were anti-communist. And, frankly, was Pretoria any worse than, say, the dictatorships in Haiti, Chile or the Philippines?

Pretoria survived Carter's foreign policy. The outcry over the callous police murder of black consciousness leader Steve Biko in September 1977 had precipitated worldwide condemnation and a mandatory UN arms embargo. A domestic political and financial scandal, dubbed 'Muldergate', that revealed gross corruption in the citadel of Afrikaner power, toppled Vorster and led to P.W. Botha

Ronald Reagan swore to end the 'evil empire'

becoming prime minister. The former defence minister marched his generals into the central decisionmaking process via the reconstituted State Security Council that came to run the country behind a parliamentary façade. P.W. Botha's containment policy rested upon a total strategy to defeat the black/communist threat. By the late 1970s a central pillar was to be a pliant black bishop, Abel Muzorewa, as leader of 'Zimbabwe-Rhodesia'. A moderate Zimbabwe was supposed to join P.W. Botha's pet scheme: a 'constellation' of southern African states. Robert Mugabe's tumultuous victory in the 1980 Zimbabwe election, however, was a death blow to the constellation. It was also a major setback for Moscow, which had assiduously courted Mugabe's main rival, Joshua Nkomo. Owing a debt of loyalty to the Chinese, who had armed and trained his guerrilla forces, Mugabe now led a state with a relatively modern industrial base and a large, battletested army. Zimbabwe emerged the most militant, and articulate, front-line enemy of apartheid.

The early 1980s introduced a decade of major destabilization of the front-line state by the SADF. Wars consumed Angola and Mozambique, where South Africa nourished insurgent armies fighting the Soviet-sponsored Marxist governments. This was a novelty. It was now America's turn to sponsor liberation struggles around the world, all aiming to overturn the status quo powers armed by the Russians. The tables, it seemed, were being turned.

### *Destructive engagement?*

One of the architects of this turnabout was President Ronald Reagan who replaced Carter's zig-zags with a big-budget war on Russia's 'evil empire'. The new 'Reagan doctrine' bolstered support for anti-Marxist guerrillas, most notably in Angola. Reagan's election and the 1979 Conservative Party victory in Britain came as sweet music to the ears of the hard men in Pretoria. The heat was off apartheid — for a while.

Washington's re-jigged approach to southern Africa was dubbed 'constructive engagement', a stickier version of the old Tar Baby. Its prime exponent was Assistant Secretary of State Chester Arthur Crocker. In his Pulitzer-winning book on South Africa, *Move Your Shadow*, the American writer Joseph Lelyveld described Crocker thus: 'with a precisely trimmed moustache and a banker's caution with words, he was guarded, remote, resolutely non-telegenic'. To its many liberal critics the new policy Crocker was trying to sell was a curious concept: only the minority regime would end minority rule, provided not too much pressure was applied. To the right in the USA, Crocker was a dangerous liberal even though the anti-apartheid lobby had termed him Pretoria's ally. He was neither. Nonetheless, the ban on non-military exports for use by the SADF and the South African Police was lifted. US loans, powerful computers and nuclear-related technology started to flow into the pariah republic. Despite the escalating economic and military campaigns against the front-line states of Mozambique,

Angola and now Zimbabwe – in short, destabilization — the SADF was a 'lobby of modernizing patriots', to use Crocker's words, that would assist P.W. Botha's reform programme.[8] But could apartheid be reformed or was its root-and-branch abolition the only way to end the main cause of conflict in southern Africa? The success of constructive engagement was predicated upon real political change in South Africa. Domestic reforms indeed there were – although most critics said they were merely cosmetic – but the wars in Angola and Mozambique and the insurrection at home intensified. And a settlement in South West Africa/Namibia, the immediate goal of US policy in the region, looked like a distant mirage. So Pretoria had to supply some political ammunition to its right-wing allies in London and Washington: hence the constant stream of promises of change. As veteran South African observer Stanley Uys noted: 'Diplomats are always looking for glimmers of hope. They have to find a reason for doing nothing. Pretoria has a special department to supply glimmers.'

To the army of Western opponents, constructive engagement was appeasement. Sticks were needed, not carrots dangled as rewards for mere glimmers. As prominent American critic William Minter noted, 'Washington bolstered Pretoria's capacity to delay at home and intervene abroad, emboldening the hawks and postponing the day of reckoning.'[9] As with Nixon's administration, however, Reagan intuitively rejected further sanctions. He argued that South Africa combined large mineral resources, skilled technology, stable capitalist economics and good transportation, all of which were sorely needed in southern Africa. Blacks in South Africa and the neighbouring states would suffer if mandatory sanctions were imposed. So the argument ran. As with the military rationale for the Cape route, however, the more Pretoria over-traded on its strategic allures, the more her trading partners in Africa and the West resolved to find alternatives. In short the more leverage was attempted, the more likely the lever was to bend. That principle worked both ways. If South Africa overplayed its hand over the strategic importance of the Cape and scarce minerals (especially chrome, manganese, platinum and vanadium), her enemies did the same with the potential efficacy of embargoes on oil and arms. South Africa was inevitably going to search for alternative supplies and build up her domestic infrastructure to produce a successful indigenous arms industry and oil-from-coal technology.

By mid-1984 South Africa looked as if it had weathered the worst of the storms because of its economic and military strengths as well as the blessings of the Reagan doctrine. Pretoria had forced Mozambique to sign the humiliating Nkomati non-aggression pact and Washington had started to pour in arms to Jonas Savimbi, South Africa's ally in Angola. At home, P.W. Botha had introduced his big glimmer: a tri-cameral parliament with separate chambers, of course, for Indians, coloureds and whites. One vital ingredient was missing, however, in Pretoria's containment diplomacy: the acquiescence of the country's majority. The blacks had been totally left out of the new tri-cameral 'dispensation'. This startling omission was a major cause of the massive insurrection that spread throughout South Africa in late 1984 and continued to suppurate until 1986.

Winnie Mandela, the wife of the jailed ANC leader Nelson Mandela, summed it up precisely: 'Constructive engagement,' she said, meant telling blacks to call off the struggle because 'the bosses are working it out'. The struggle was very much on again, both locally and internationally. As during the Vietnam War, dramatic TV footage of the revolution in South Africa brought the apartheid drama nightly into American homes, and into Congress. Daily anti-apartheid demonstrations and, more seriously, the resulting business disinvestment became popular American moral fads. The anti-apartheid holy-rollers strongarmed Congress into passing a series of fresh sanctions that Reagan could not prevent. Even Margaret Thatcher, a heroic figure in Pretoria, was forced to concede to Commonwealth pressures to allow further 'tiny' sanctions. As stubborn as any Boer, Thatcher more than Crocker held the line against comprehensive sanctions.

Nevertheless, the Great Crocodile (one of P.W. Botha's more polite nicknames) was in deep trouble. The local business community bayed for his resignation, as private US disinvestment, not UN sanctions, rocked the South African economy. A national state of emergency continued to discourage foreign bankers, even after the two years of black 'unrest' petered out in late 1986 because of draconian laws and severe repression by the security forces. The ANC tried to capitalize on a revolt it did not control. More effectively it capitalized too on the international pressures on Pretoria, even after the blanket censorship banished the TV cameras from the unrest areas. The ANC gradually made itself respectable in the West as British and American officials started talking publicly with the 'terrorists'. The diplomats were hedging their bets, although not necessarily changing sides. Yet it all helped to augment the ANC's credibility. That, as much as changing the hard hearts of Afrikanerdom, was perhaps the fundamental aim of sanctions. Above all, political pressures and superhyped pop concerts boosted the worldwide demand for the release from jail of the ANC's imprisoned hero, Nelson Mandela.

### *Gorbachev's 'new thinking'*

Paradoxically, the Russians also started to talk openly with Pretoria. Clandestinely, South Africa and the USSR had long operated a cosy arrangement to sell their gold and diamonds, once a near monopoly they jointly manipulated. Then came Mikhail Gorbachev. His *perestroika* and *glasnost* inspired a 'new thinking' in foreign policy and a greater fluidity in international relations. And yet Soviet reforms threatened the cornerstones of South African as much as NATO security systems. As George Arbatov, the Kremlin's best-known America-watcher, suggestively observed: 'We are going to do something terrible to you – we are going to deprive you of an enemy.' Russia not only withdrew her army from Afghanistan (in early 1989) but also agreed to start pulling out Cuban troops from Angola, and hence hasten the process of Namibian independence. And Soviet experts began to muse publicly that evolutionary change, not violent revolution, was likely in South Africa. Had pragmatism replaced ideology?

Criticism of apartheid in the West emanated initially from small exiled groups and the left wing. The early calls for sanctions had come from countries with nothing to lose and, sometimes, with something to gain. But by the late 1980s the old assumptions had withered, for a number of reasons. The 1984-86 uprising had concentrated world attention on Pretoria's misdeeds. The relative importance of the South African gold-based economy had declined. Trade with the European Community and the US had been reduced, although for the UK South Africa was still an important trading partner. The pressures to disinvest, the 'hassle' factor, made many multinationals decide that South African profits were not worth the political, economic and moral costs. Moreover, the Cape route had always been an overblown strategic argument. Few military analysts expected the Soviets, particularly in the Gorbachev era, to resort to Second World War naval stratagems to blockade supply lines. And, it was commonly argued at the time, a stable black regime in Pretoria could be a more reliable supplier of strategic minerals than one run by Afrikaner *bittereinders* prepared to pull down the economic pillars on their own heads. In short, Western interests were being pushed towards the advantages of a peaceful transition to black rule.

Nobel Laureate Archbishop Desmond Tutu's emotive appeals to end apartheid and the dismally hamfisted behaviour of the South African government towards the Commonwealth peace mission of 1986, as well as the famously bungled Rubicon reform speech by President Botha, all conjured up an image of an irredeemably ruthless and savagely inept regime. The old selling points – that blacks would suffer most from economic embargoes, that Pretoria should not be singled out for its human rights abuses and it stood as a bastion of anti-communism – all looked desperately thin. And the sporting bans appeared to have had an ameliorative impact on the many sports-mad whites in South Africa. Nevertheless, by the end of the 1980s, compulsory comprehensive sanctions had not been adopted by South Africa's main Western trading partners.

The Afrikaner power structure had paid an enormous price for its stubborn, if often understandable, reluctance to bend its knee to international demands. In 1989 the regime looked stable. The men on horseback, the soldier-politicians in the State Security Council, had called many of the shots in the 1980s. Military power had been the bedrock of the minority regime. Despite the continuous drumbeat of world condemnation, how did South Africa become the single most powerful military machine on the African continent?

*Chapter 3*

# The Rise of Africa's Superpower

The core strategy of the ruling National Party in Pretoria had always been the preservation of white rule by any means. The military nightmare was the possible combination of a massive internal insurrection with an external invasion. The latter seemed unlikely and all the domestic revolts were crushed with utmost vigour. Both threats, however, were twinned in Pretoria's ideological perspective: internal unrest was viewed as the instrument of the international communist conspiracy. One of the first major measures of the apartheid regime was the passage of the Suppression of Communism Act in 1950; this outlawed the tiny pro-Moscow South African Communist Party. In 1960 the ANC and the Pan-Africanist Congress were also banned. Although internal security was the prime concern, Pretoria felt that this was best achieved by grandstanding as the Western world's chief ally in the Cold War, especially in Africa.

South Africa was in fact a minor element in the East-West confrontation; nevertheless Pretoria developed what Kenneth Grundy called the equivalent of the Ptolemaic theory of the universe: just as the planets, sun and stars were once thought to revolve around the earth so South Africa imagined itself to be epicentre of the 'free world's' war on communism.[1] Though apartheid came to provide the most convenient pretext for Soviet penetration of Africa, Pretoria's sense of its own importance was grotesquely exaggerated. The regime wanted to be the centre of attention for the right reasons: as a pro-capitalist bastion in order to lock the NATO powers into the defence of white supremacy.

Such diplomatic arabesques prompted a supreme irony. Afrikaner nationalists had been committed to jettisoning defence ties with its former imperial overlord. In the early days, Anglophile English-speaking officers were hounded out of the armed forces. Yet at the same time Pretoria was trying to entice Britain into a joint security pact. Initially, Pretoria suggested an African Defence Organization, a wannabe southwards extension of NATO to include South Africa and the colonial powers such as France. The then British Labour government, despite its commitment to decolonization, was not averse to the military (and gold and uranium) connections. Pretoria accepted a provisional invitation to join the ill-fated British-sponsored Middle East Defence Organization. But MEDO proved abortive partly because of possible South African participation. The only concrete achievement of Pretoria's strategic soliciting was the 1955 Simonstown agreement with Britain. This agreement, *not* a formal defence pact, specifically excluded any British commitment to internal security. In the spirit of Pretoria's apparent willingness to help the UK in the Middle East, South Africa purchased sixty-eight British Centurion tanks and various aircraft between 1955 and 1959. Also, thirty-six Sabre jets were obtained from Canada. So Pretoria had secured some hardware and joint naval exercises with the Royal Navy but the goal of a military alliance slipped further away. Although both Labour and Tory administrations allowed British arms to reach South Africa, a formal pact was politically impossible because of apartheid.

Thus emerged Pretoria's peculiar love-hate relationship with the West in general and Britain in particular. South Africa frequently talked of standing alone, flirted with armed neutrality and even suggested overtures to Red China but in the end its threats of unfaithfulness could never be consummated because Pretoria needed the West for arms and for psychological reassurance. Moreover, Moscow's identification of South Africa as part of the imperialist camp reinforced Pretoria's self image. At this stage the West had it both ways. In the event of the Cold War turning hot, South Africa would have had little alternative but to place its military facilities at the disposal of its old allies. This situation guaranteed Pretoria's availability without the political costs demanded by a formal alliance.

The ambivalence to the West persisted. It was probably best expressed in John Vorster's famous statement of August 1977 when he said that the result of American pressure on southern Africa 'would be exactly the same as if it were subverted by the Marxists'. Vorster added: 'In the one case it will come about as a result of brute force. In the other case, it will be strangulation by finesse.' And yet however much the South African government disliked Washington's policies, Pretoria still acknowledged that the US 'remains the leader of the West and ... only America stands between the continued freedom of mankind and slavery' in the words of Foreign Minister Pik Botha in the South African House of Assembly in May 1980.[2]

In 1960 South Africa was puny in military terms. The state had a small obsolete military structure and no formal defence pact. Although disconcerted by the rapid pace of decolonization, Pretoria did not feel threatened externally. Rather, the Sharpeville massacre on 21 March 1960, when the police killed sixty-nine blacks protesting against the pass laws, and the ensuing state of emergency, generated a renewed concern with internal security. If the 1950s had been characterized by the search for military alliances, the first half of the 1960s was a period of military introversion and planned reform. The decision was made to build up a large modern defence force, committed initially to internal security. The army was rapidly enlarged. The permanent force (PF), the regular command-and-training nucleus for the expansion of the reserve citizen force (CF), was increased from 9,000 in 1960 to 15,000 in 1964. Almost 20,000 national servicemen were in training in 1964, a tenfold increase over the number trained in 1960. Compulsory military service for whites, the sole example of apartheid discriminating *against* whites, replaced the selective ballot system in 1967. By 1969 South Africa had 200,000 armed and trained men.[3] This new force needed better equipment. Under the terms of the Simonstown agreement, Britain supplied a small fleet of secondhand frigates and fifteen Buccaneer aircraft.[4] After 1964 London imposed an arms embargo and the ever-cynical French stepped in quickly to replace British sales. The old Fashoda complex was back with a vengeance. Pretoria now had the chance to develop both its conventional and counter-insurgency capabilities. The army got the lion's share of the burgeoning defence budget. French armoured cars boosted the army's strength and the air force also received prized new Mirage jets, helicopters and missile systems. Three Daphné-class submarines were delivered to the navy in 1971-72. Much of this new hardware was assembled from kits or built in South Africa from largely imported components, mainly on the basis of licences from French, Italian and Belgian companies. Small arms were purchased from or via Portugal, Spain, Greece and East European states. The domestic production of tear gas, napalm and ammunition was begun with the assistance of mainly British-based companies. America continued to be a major supplier. In the fiscal years 1981 to 1984, for example, the State Department authorized commercial sales of more than $28.3 million-worth of military-related equipment to Pretoria. In addition, aircraft worth $556 million – technically for civilian use but in many cases suitable for military adaption – were sold during 1980-82.

Pretoria flexed its new muscles not only at home but also in covert involvement in the wars in Rhodesia, Mozambique and Angola. Stung by criticisms about these adventures, and especially its illegal retention of Namibia, Pretoria continued to manifest its strange dualism towards the West. Pretoria kept on stressing that its arms build-up was a commitment to Western goals and its readiness to join an expanded NATO. Yet the reality of standing alone began to sink in, especially as the Western 'allies' became increasingly reluctant to provide arms, above the counter, for the pariah. Hence Pretoria displayed a growing interest in scouting around for new friends – in Latin America, Israel and Taiwan. The precariousness of South Africa's position was dramatized by the invasion of Angola in 1975-76, when the US backed off from its initial support. This epitomized to Pretoria both the communist threat and Western unreliability. The UN arms embargo of 1977 and the domestic insurrection of 1976 all helped to convince the Afrikaner leadership, if they needed any convincing, that South Africa was now facing a total communist onslaught. And the answer was a 'total strategy'.

## *Total Strategy*

The concept of a total national strategy was developed in a number of defence white papers in the 1970s. In essence, it articulated the philosophy of a world communist conspiracy aimed at South Africa. Thus the fundamental problem was perceived as not the manifold injustices to blacks but Kremlin intrigue. And the purported solution was a total economic, political, psychological and military mobilization of the state's resources to defeat this onslaught. As with the Bolshevik concept of capitalist encirclement in the 1920s, there was just enough truth to the notion to lend it some credibility. Tens of thousands of Cuban soldiers in Angola was one (large) concrete piece of evidence. That bit of truth was ruthlessly manipulated by the government's increasing domination of the media. As in Rhodesia, the perceived illegality of the international conspiracy implied that black nationalist guerrillas and their political leaders were not freedom fighters but criminal stooges of foreign powers.

Although the mailed fist was the primary response to threats, political reform was also included: the axiomatic mixture was supposed to be 80 per cent political and 20 per cent military. Yet because of the threat-oriented politics of white survival, the characteristic emphasis on military and police repression swamped the belated political initiatives. Reform for blacks, essentially the formation of a co-opted black middle class, in itself a highly dubious strategy, always came a very poor second.

The intellectual substance of the total strategy was essentially the writings of Frenchman General André Beaufre and the American Colonel John J. 'Jack' McCuen – but writ large and awkwardly updated and misapplied to South African conditions.[5] In the mid-1980s the South African analyst Philip Frankel summarized the local approach:

> Total strategy selectively interprets the world in the narrow, dialetic and melodramatic terms with which white South Africa is so familiar, confusing communism, nationalism, dissidence, subversion, racism and imperialism in an impenetrable mélange from which only the security of the white state merges as constant and paramount .... Total strategy at its present level of development is not an exception to the general rule that most proto-ideologies developed by soldiers are primitive, transparently self-rationalizing and largely devoid of any practical positive content. Total strategy is important in generating and justifying siege psychologies and structures through which the Defence Force can accumulate social power.[6]

The implementation of total strategy did indeed mark the growing influence, although not necessarily the complete dominance of the military in South African society. The concept was assiduously fostered by Defence Minister P.W. Botha and by his successor, General Magnus Malan. Botha revived the State Security Council (SSC), originally established in 1972, and made it the central organ of his counter-revolution. Run like a politburo, it became more important than the cabinet. Perhaps 70 per cent of its members and staff were drawn from the security forces. Throughout the country the SSC constructed a shadow, parallel administration called the National Security Management System. The restructuring of the Afrikaner security network did not solve the intractable domestic political grievances; indeed, they became worse. But the SSC did help to co-ordinate the growth and deployment of the rapidly expanding war machine. Military strategy became almost an end in itself. The 20 per cent solution became god and the 80 per cent political input almost disappeared amid the gun smoke. Clausewitz had been turned on his head.

### *Apartheid weapons*

Pretoria spent a lot of money quickly on the SADF. In 1960 the defence budget was R44 million; the 1988-89 budget was R8.09 billion. The police, a paramilitary formation, saw its budgetary vote expand from R129 million to R1.8 billion in the same period. True, the economy was growing rapidly and could absorb some of the strain before the sanctions and the disinvestment of the 1980s. Inflation played a part as well. But even allowing for inflation, the astounding growth in defence expenditure was a heavy burden on the state. And the official figures excluded Namibian defence costs as well as the large secret intelligence funds. Of course, many totalitarian states officially have undersold their defence spending. UN estimates put the figures at 35 per cent higher than the official SADF figures at the time. At the height of the apartheid war campaign, perhaps as much as 20-25 per cent of the total national budget – at least R20 million a day – was being spent on defence.

Much of the expenditure was used to buy or develop weapons systems, co-ordinated by the Armaments Corporation of South Africa (Armscor).[7] Armscor was a paradox: a state corporation run almost exclusively by private enterprise. Once, private enterprise, dominated largely by English-speaking capitalists, had been portrayed as part of the onslaught but under P.W. Botha it became a component of the counter-revolutionary machinery – though it would be simplistic to describe this synergy as a sinister military-industrial complex because many of the senior entrepreneurs nursed serious misgivings about government strategies.[8] Indeed, some of these same entrepreneurs provided funds to the white liberal opposition to apartheid. Some senior industrialists publicly criticized the government about the distortions caused to the economy by excessive defence spending, especially the insistence on costly import substitution for political non-economic reasons. Nonetheless, there were big profits to be made.

Mirage III EZ

Minister-class strike craft

South African Air Force Super Frelon

Pretoria obtained its arms in a variety of ways. In the 1960s and 1970s South Africa largely shopped on the open market for goods from NATO countries. Between 1960 and 1983 the French were the biggest suppliers. The most important weapons purchased were Panhard armoured cars, Alouette, Frelon and Puma helicopters, Mirage fighters, the three submarines and the Franco-South African development of the Cactus (Crotale) surface-to-air missile system. As historian R.W. Johnson drily observed: 'For such a haul as this Pretoria may well have been willing to pay in blood. As it was, she paid in gold, which, as was well known, Gaullists preferred.' The deals continued for a while even after the socialists replaced the right-wing Gaullists. The British firms Marconi and EMI established electronic component subsidiaries in South Africa that produced military equipment. Such subsidiaries were sometimes used to circumvent the arms embargo. British Leyland (SA) produced vehicles for the SADF and ICI South Africa, wholly owned then by its parent company in the UK, helped to set up an explosives factory. Many NATO countries ignored or sidestepped UN restrictions, as did Israel and Taiwan more openly. The SADF's acquisitions from the Jewish state were especially significant: for example, the Reshef- and Aliyah-class fast-attack boats and their accompanying missile systems, RPV pilotless reconnaissance drones and assistance with the upgrades for the ageing Mirages (from experience gained with the Israeli Kfir aircraft and aborted Lavi projects). Before covert Israeli co-operation, the South African Atlas Aircraft Corporation had built a range of aircraft under licence, first the Impala from Italy's Aermacchi MB-326 and then the Mirage F1AZ.

Increasingly Armscor and its subsidiaries were forced to resort to subterfuge: military deals through third parties via front companies or purchase of equipment with nominally 'civilian' use. Perhaps the most spectacular and best-documented breach of the arms embargo was the acquisition of the US/Canadian-designed 155mm howitzer that was used to such effect in the fighting in Angola in the late 1980s. In various configurations, it also became a money-spinner for Armscor when it moved into the export market. The arms market has always been renowned for its utter cynicism. One British arms merchant symbolized this truism when he said:

> We were able to sell them [the South Africans] some helicopters because they were half-French. And they're of course the deadliest machines against natives. When the South Africans came through with an order for patrol boats we told them to redraft the order to make it look as if they were for civilian use – 'Surely you must have some *black* fishing boats that need protection.'[9]

By and large, Armscor officials and South African intelligence agents seemed to have operated with great ingenuity and many bribes, some of which went into Switzerland, not weaponry for the Afrikaner fatherland. Another arms dealer noted: 'They're just like other Africans: they all want to get their money out.' During the late 1970s there had been a degree of corruption and embezzlement associated with the disgraced Information Department, the 'Muldergate' scandal, but P.W. Botha cleaned up much of the mess when he streamlined defence procurement after 1978. On the whole, Armscor was a remarkable success story for the besieged South Africa. Its adaption, inventiveness and sheer chicanery resulted in excellent weapons such as the G-6 self-propelled 155mm cannon and the 127mm Valkiri multiple-rocket launcher. Many Warsaw Pact and NATO weapons were not well suited to the terrain, structure or skills of smaller armies in developing countries. More important, the SADF had successfully tested and proved Armscor products in combat. Thus, not only in some areas did the arms embargo backfire, but Armscor moved into the top league of arms exporters, selling its wares under the slogan 'Born in necessity and tested under fire'. African countries such as Morocco bought the impressive Ratel range of infantry combat vehicles, while Sri Lanka purchased a series of mine-resistant armoured troop carriers. Iraq bought the 155mm guns. And South Africa was accused of selling Argentina its very advanced frequency-hopping radios, some of which were reported to have been captured by the British during the Falkands war of 1982.

Armscor became the largest single-exporter of manufactured goods in South Africa with sales to twenty-three countries at $2 billion per year in the last period of apartheid. It claimed to be ranked fifth in the world league of defence contractors. It had ten wholly owned subsidiaries with 23,000 employees and 975 private sector sub-contractors supporting a total of 90,000 employees. Efficiency was usually achieved because of its unusual status as the sole procurement authority for the SADF and as the systems management organization for all projects. By the end of the 1980s it was producing more than 4,000 items, including forty types of ammunition. This was blowback with a vengeance – a classic example of the laws of unintended consequences from UN intentions.

Pretoria liked to boast that it was 95 per cent self-sufficient in weaponry. But was that the whole truth? That boast, partly intended to boost white morale, tried to demonstrate that further economic and defence sanctions would not work and, crucially, it was a bluff to disguise the foreign expertise and components that were still deeply involved with the so-called 'homemade' weaponry. In fact, despite the undeniable skills in adaption to local conditions and the tenacity in circumventing sanctions, the South African arsenal was highly derivative and still vulnerable to a strictly enforced arms embargo, especially from fellow members of the 'league of the desperate', Israel and Taiwan. By the late 1980s, as the war in Angola escalated, South Africa had an urgent shopping list. The South African Air Force, for example, was alarmed by the competition from the MiG-23s and the SU-22s and the integrated Soviet defence systems of radar, anti-aircraft artillery and surface-to-air missiles. The navy desperately needed large surface ships such as modern frigates as well as new submarines. The SADF had no replacements for long-range maritime reconnaissance aircraft when the aged Shackletons were finally phased out in the early 1980s. The Air Force had thirty Dakotas, probably the largest surviving fleet in the world. Some of these venerable old warriors, dubbed 'Dackletons', had been used as crude substitutes for the Shackletons. Apparently without irony, officers in 35 Squadron, flying the Daks, talked proudly of 'modernizing' from a thirty-year-old aircraft to one ten years older.

Nevertheless, the very professional air force was in better shape than the navy. It had adapted some of the twenty-year-old Mirage IIIs, with Israeli help, to produce the Cheetah aircraft. The South Africans also developed the Puma XTPI (based on its French namesake) and the Alpha XHI (based on the Alouette III). The Alpha was not entirely successful as it proved unstable. Even the more successful Puma adaption paled alongside the Hind gunships it was supposed to contend with. In short, the SADF and Armscor had done well, despite or because of the embargoes, but could not compete, nor be expected to, with up-to-date weapons systems provided to the front-line states by the USSR. The SADF was rumoured to be developing a cruise missile, courtesy of Israeli designers, and some advanced avionics and electronic countermeasures. But the SADF desperately needed more and better combat and transport helicopters. It had other vulnerabilities too. The Olifant Mk1A, the army's main battle tank, was based on the British Centurions purchased from the UK in the late 1950s and additional ones procured, in various states of repair, from Jordan and India in the 1970s. It was not up to NATO standards, but it had proved useful against the older generation of Soviet tanks operating in Angola. Besides, South African army's tactics were built around highly mobile, *wheeled* not tracked, armoured vehicles.

Despite all the bravura of apartheid apologists, the SADF faced serious hardware deficiencies in the twilight of white rule. More military pressures in Angola and tougher Western sanctions were bound to make things worse. Originally, Pretoria's hunt for Western arms was a means to secure a political certificate of respectability, to 'get pregnant' by the Western powers, as one Pentagon official tartly observed. Pretoria desperately needed state of the art military hardware, or a political settlement, if the whites were to survive. Or could doomsday weapons deter the total onslaught?

## *Nuclear weapons*

South Africa's nuclear programme began in the closing days of the Second World War. Then, at the request of the USA and Britain, a secret study of the country's uranium resources was commissioned. The US supplied Pretoria with its first nuclear reactor, Safari I, which became operational at Pelindaba in 1965. Thereafter, Britain, France and West Germany (the last prohibited from developing nuclear weapons on its *own* territory) aided the construction of Pretoria's nuclear capacity. Israel helped to turn the civilian capability into a nuclear military option. In 1979 the CIA made an assessment that a joint Israeli-South African nuclear test had been conducted in the South Atlantic on 22 September. Jerusalem and Pretoria had apparently thought that their small 'clean' test would not be spotted but a US satellite picked up the flash. Two underground test sites were readied in the Kalahari but US arm-twisting stopped the tests. Pretoria, meanwhile, refused to sign the Non-Proliferation Treaty. By the late 80s South Africa had built six atomic bombs with one under construction via a secret Armscor project called Hamerkop. Israel was the main partner, although intelligence reports indicated that Pakistan had possibly been bribed sufficiently to give some technical help.

Initially Pretoria considered an air drop from one of its ageing bombers, then concentrated on missile delivery. The secret missiles looked uncannily like the short-range Israeli Jericho and the Shavit with a longer range of 2,000 miles. The big fission bombs would have to be miniaturized to fit on a missile warhead, though the bonus could be a 'tactical' nuclear weapon. Pretoria's Dr Strangeloves wondered whether they could be used to deter a feared Cuban-Soviet invasion of Namibia from their Angolan strongholds. Pretoria had the will, the cash and the perception of threat to go nuclear. With Israeli help it then managed to join the nuclear club by acquiring the weapons and delivery systems. Except for the doomsday scenario of a large communist invasion, who could be targeted by the nuclear weapons systems, however? Certainly, by emulating Israel's 'bomb in a basement' strategy, Pretoria could boost its deterrent posture. Some Afrikaner leaders could not help themselves by boastfully hinting at their secret arsenal from time to time.

Pretoria also produced other weapons of mass destruction, not least chemical weapons, despite international conventions. Pretoria also helped the Rhodesians in a secret bio-weapons programme, and used their new arsenal on Zimbabwean insurgents.[10] In 1968 South Africa announced that it had begun domestic manufacture of napalm and defoliants were used on the Angolan border to establish free-fire zones.

The whole elaborate nuclear weapons project was wound down at the end of 1989, partly because of large-scale political developments in the region. Ironically, more secrecy was deployed than before when the Americans, British and the International Atomic Energy Authority stepped in to remove the weapons they did not want to fall into the hand of the communist-leaning ANC. All the data and research papers were destroyed as well as part of Operation MASADA. South Africa signed the NPT agreement in 1991 after the nukes had been spirited away. It was a very rare example of unilateral nuclear disarmament – partly because neither the CIA nor the Afrikaner leadership could bear black radicals getting their hands on the ultimate weapon. Mandela used to hand out to VIPs small ploughs made from the non-nuclear metal parts of the former apartheid A-bombs.

### *The SADF structure*

The style of the SADF was inherited from elements of the British regimental traditions superimposed on the heritage of the Boer commandos of the nineteenth century. 'Commando' had a specific connotation in southern Africa. It did not denote specialized professional forces but rather the concept of the Afrikaner farmer-soldier who volunteered to fight with his horse and rifle at his own expense. The SADF's largest service, the army, was essentially a militia force that relied on the core permanent force (PF) members to train and lead the national service personnel who provided the bulk of the standing army and the citizen force (CF) of part-time soldiers to provide the reserves. The navy, the air force and medical services, the three other wings of the SADF, relied more heavily on fulltime personnel as they were more technology intensive. And, in practice, the special forces were also considered almost an independent fifth wing of the SADF. (For a detailed breakdown of the SADF structure, see the Appendix.)

The SADF liked to think that it was similar to Switzerland's citizen army, although this was difficult to reconcile with the fact that it was fighting largely a civil war where 75 per cent of the population were not full citizens. Only whites were conscripted though blacks, Indians and coloureds could, and did, volunteer – though probably mainly for economic, not patriotic, motives.

Counter-insurgency (or counter-terrorism) was to be met first by the police and local commandos. This was the first line of 'area defence'. If the threat became serious, the standing army – the PF plus national servicemen and elements of the CF reservists – would form a reaction force for a conventional response. This was the pattern for major operations in Angola. The standing armed forces were estimated at 103,500 in 1989, according to the International Institute for Strategic Studies. The SADF could get further back-up from an array of allied forces, of varying quality and commitment. These included the various police forces, homeland armies and, until 1989, the South West African Territory Force. The full mobilization figure was usually estimated at around 425,000 although in an extreme emergency such as a full-scale invasion, it was considered possible to mobilize as many as 800,000 trained men and women using all reserves and auxiliaries. That was a far higher figure than the total of all the mobilized forces of the front-line states plus the ANC fighters and the late 1980s tally of Eastern bloc troops and advisers in the region.

The conventional forces were shaped very much like their Western counterparts in NATO. Their uniforms and equipment would seem familiar, if sometimes a little quaint, to any NATO officer. Our hypothetical NATO observer would recognize some of the tactics learnt from the Rhodesian army, and the flamboyant style, copied somewhat selfconsciously from the Israelis. The SADF, however, although not as formal as British regiments, was decidedly more hidebound than the Israelis.

South African Ratels carried ten men and were armed with a 20mm cannon

Ex-Rhodesians who joined the SADF found the formality rather tedious. A 'prayer meeting' in Rhodesian army slang meant a drinks party; in the SADF, which tended to take God and country rather more seriously, the regular prayer meetings could mean just that. Despite its multi-racial and officially bilingual composition, the SADF was Afrikaner-dominated. Official rules to the contrary, Afrikaans was the prevailing language and culture. Technically the languages, English and Afrikaans, were supposed to alternate on a daily basis. That didn't happen, especially on the front line. It was a no-nonsense force – there was no talk of hairnets for long hair as in some of more liberal NATO military establishments. Unlike the US army in Vietnam, drugs were not a major problem. And the 'fragging' of unpopular officers was unheard of. Conscription also brought in a large proportion of bright young graduates who were often '*verlig*' – liberal/open-minded – to use the Afrikaans phrase of the time. Many of the young officers I met in Namibia and Angola in the 1980s impressed me with their political insights – by asking, for example, why were they fighting so hard on the Angolan border when the young lions of the ANC were running amok in the South African townships? And provided you were prepared to drink beer and listen in Afrikaans, even the more conservative and less-educated troops would discuss acute political issues. The white soldiers were not robots, by any measure. Nonetheless, many of the young conscripts disliked their time on the border war and counted the days until they could get out. The permanent force and the older 'campers' (reservists) were usually more committed than the conscripts doing their national service. And, as in any army, it depended on whether you were talking to elite well-motivated troops with dedicated officers; the closer to the front line, the higher the morale. The problem was that 'down south' in South Africa no front line existed – the battle lines ran through town and country, dissecting families, classes and hearts, and yet nearly always cleaving to racial boundaries.

*Assessment*

Despite its frantic search for allies, the South African government ended up on its own, with an atomic bomb in the basement that seemed to deter no one. Even its fellow pariah, Israel, had distanced itself and started applying sanctions. The rusty old arguments, the defence of the Cape sea route and the resource-war thesis, had lost their power to persuade. While still wedded throughout the 1980s to the total strategy, Pretoria started to play down the total onslaught theme. Its alarmist nature was becoming counter-productive not least in boosting the ANC on the left and, on the right, the main opposition Conservative Party, which lambasted P.W. Botha for being *soft* on the communist threat. Yet after decades of official propaganda, the idea of the red menace had become deeply embedded in the Afrikaner collective psyche, not least among members of the security forces, especially in the police. This was especially sensitive politically as the Botha regime's reform programme tried to backtrack on some elements of traditional apartheid doctrine. The white right-wing organizations grew as they replayed precisely the former National Party songs to a burgeoning army of voters who were led to believe that Botha and his new English-speaking 'liberal' allies were betraying the *volk*. The reform elements of the total strategy depended fundamentally upon sanitizing primitive apartheid so as to create a black labour aristocracy in the urban areas. In addition, a co-opted black middle class and the near-feudal ruling elites in the homelands were supposed to drive a wedge between the ANC and its potential supporters. It didn't work.

As all good counter-insurgency texts preached, President Botha did centralize his counter-revolutionary strategy in his imperial presidency through the State Security Council. This might have been more effective if this centralized machinery had offered an alternative vision of society. Short-term military tactics had become long-term strategy and the possibility of genuine political resolution with the ANC seemed to recede. Like the white minority in Rhodesia, Pretoria could offer no persuasive alternative to its hostage black majority. As Alexis de Tocqueville had long ago warned, reform is always the most dangerous period for a repressive government. For the restless black masses the reforms of the 1980s had come too late. The repeal of the hated pass laws would have been welcomed in the 1960s. By the 1980s political power was all that mattered.

Even if a convincing political programme had been fashioned as part of the total strategy, it would have demanded a high degree of resolve and unity among the Afrikaner *Herrenvolk.* During most of their war white Rhodesians exhibited this in the crucial areas of effective counter-insurgency: competent security forces, an efficient and honest civil service and high morale among the majority of the ruling group. P.W. Botha, however, split Afrikaner ranks. His civil service remained an ultra-conservative, often bungling, leviathan that frequently obstructed reform measures. Only the SADF remained as a trusted and competent tool of Botha's imperium.

Yet even the SADF was riddled with paradoxes. The armed bureaucrats in the State Security Council tended to be moderate at home but militant abroad, domestic reformers (up to a point) but hawkish destabilizers in the neighbouring states. Despite the SADF's attempts to forge a multi-racial army, for practical and propaganda reasons, and to the fury of the Conservative Party, Pretoria still continued to build up tribal forces in both the 'independent' and non-independent homelands. Although it emphasized the combat efficiency of its black soldiers, promotion opportunities for black (and sometimes English-speaking white South Africans and ex-Rhodesians), were impeded by the Afrikaner caste system. And for all the spirited forays to finagle modern weaponry, the key component of military counter-insurgency – good intelligence – began to dry up as the angry 'comrades' mercilessly rounded upon blacks accused of being 'sell-outs', collaborating with the regime. Even the much-vaunted security police informer network began to break down in the mid-1980s. The SADF was supposed to hold the proverbial ring to allow time for the politicians to settle the 'political problem'. Far-reaching reform, it was then said, would have to wait until the unrest was crushed. But the state of emergency was declared in 1985, and the wars on the borders festered. The jackboot became the symbol of both short-term and long-term 'solutions'.

Despite its pariah status, South Africa had constructed a powerful defence apparatus by the late 1980s. It would be naïve, and inaccurate, to paint a demonic picture of a rampant military junta, slavering behind a civilian façade and gobbling up the country's wealth while stamping out all protests. There was no doubt about the ruthlessness of the Afrikaner regime but the image of an SS state portrayed by many anti-apartheid organizations did a disservice to accurate history. The interplay between the military and civilian elites was very subtle and complex as the conduct of destabilization in the neighbouring states demonstrated, for example. Military influence was very important but not always decisive. The concept of a 'creeping coup' was a little simplistic. Even with hidden costs, expenditure on the armed forces had been fairly modest compared with states such as Israel and Taiwan. According to IISS figures, the percentage of the GDP spent on the military actually declined from 4 per cent (1984) to 3.8 per cent (1986). The comparative figure in Israel, where civilian control of the military was not generally in question, were 22.4 per cent of GDP to 18.9 per cent in the same period. Despite a growth in police numbers in the 1980s, by Western standards South Africa was *under-policed* in terms of police-officer-to-population ratios. It is true that the apartheid society, especially the separate black group areas, physically designed to be contained easily by security forces, provided extra control measures which did not exist in democratic countries. Nor can figures alone represent the phobias and militarization of an increasingly gun-happy white population upon whom the financial and conscription burdens weighed so heavily.

Before analyzing the details of the domestic insurgency, the civilian-military nexus will be examined in how Pretoria operated in its neighbouring states. First, South Africa worked hard to uphold white colonial rule. Then Pretoria employed its economic power as both a club and a magnet to maintain its regional dominance once its neighbours had broken free of white supremacy. Throughout southern Africa Pretoria sought to buy hegemony with gold and cheap black labour. Whenever that failed, the *swaardmag* (sword-power) of the SADF could be thrust deep into the fragile polities. But for how long? In 1989 the question was: could the SADF hold the ring for an eventual political settlement in South Africa or was it rather the pin in the grenade for all-out war in the region?

# PART II

# THE COLONIAL WARS

*Chapter 4*

# Angola (1961-1976)

*Buffer states*

The survival of the white 'buffer' colonies in Angola, Rhodesia and Mozambique was a vital element of Pretoria's defence strategy throughout the 1960s and early 1970s. Secretly in Portuguese territories and more overtly in Rhodesia, South African security forces provided men, equipment and intelligence to their increasingly beleaguered white allies. Lisbon might have insisted that her African possessions were 'overseas provinces' of metropolitan Portugal, not colonies, and Ian Smith's UDI might have converted the erstwhile self-governing colony of southern Rhodesia into a rebel republic; nonetheless, the guerrilla struggles waged against the Portuguese and white Rhodesians fitted into the mould of African anti-colonial wars.

The civil war in South Africa, not a colony but a recognized – if reviled – sovereign state, was to assume a different pattern. Nevertheless, the political and military experiences in these colonial wars were destined to shape the future conflict in the heartland of white supremacy. In four of her neighbours, Pretoria was forced to swallow the victory of its most radical Marxist opponents; so much for the fruits of years of 'destructive engagement'.

The long Angolan war was to prove the most costly in terms of SADF lives lost and the commitment of military hardware. The saga entailed, initially, the defeat of Pretoria's Portuguese allies in the colonial war (1961-75) then the debacle of the South African invasion (1975-76), the rapid decline of Pretoria's guerrilla protégé, Jonas Savimbi (1976-80) and the expensive and dangerous series of conventional battles to protect his military resurrection (1985-89). In Mozambique, Pretoria backed Portugal to win, then – reluctantly – strained to reach a *modus vivendi* with new black Marxist rulers. After 1980, however, Pretoria stoked the fires of civil war by supporting the *Resistência Nacional Moçambicana* (RENAMO) against the Maputo government. Next door, Rhodesia demanded fifteen years of political attention and military largesse from Pretoria, although South Africa's support sometimes wavered.

From the perspective of black South Africans, African nationalism had triumphed over white firepower in Lusophone Africa, Rhodesia and, finally, Namibia in early 1990. The ANC's armed wing, *Umkhonto we Sizwe* (MK), had adapted its tactics and organization, because of lessons learned from these four examples of failed counter-insurgency. The direction of travel was fatally obvious for the remaining relic of white domination. Yet right to the end Pretoria argued that each of these neighbouring conflicts was *sui generis*. They set no precedent. Like its opponents, the SADF had also learned from these wars. The highly successful counter-insurgency campaign in Namibia was an example of how to contain guerrillas by *military* means, although Pretoria had lost the *political* war there. Its most radical opponent, Sam Nujoma, won the election after independence in March 1990.

As long as white rule had looked firm in the buffer states, Pretoria had been prepared to bolster their war efforts. Once the tide of war had begun to turn the South African government launched into a frantic search for the ever-elusive black 'moderate' alternatives (Savimbi in Angola or Bishop Muzorewa in Zimbabwe were two such examples). Failing that, Pretoria's policy degenerated into debilitating its enemies by economic and military means. This destabilization assumed its most dramatic manifestation in the creation of surrogate guerrilla movements in Angola, Mozambique, Zimbabwe and, on a small scale, in Lesotho. When necessary, these proxies could count on continuous armed intervention by the SADF (Angola) or intermittent raids (Mozambique).

Thus South African grand strategy was initially to keep the white-ruled neighbours strong; then Pretoria tried to keep the black-governed neighbours as militarily weak and economically dependent as possible. The colonial *cordon sanitaire* became a twilight zone of post-independence instability. Underpinning this racist contrast was a complex web of political intrigue and military force. How Pretoria reacted to the destruction of its colonial buffers is considered in the following survey of military events in four key territories: Angola, Mozambique, Rhodesia and South West Africa/Namibia.

### *Portuguese withdrawal*

After 400 years the Portuguese were in no mood to sail with the new winds of change, not least because during the 1960s, despite the onset of insurgency, Angola enjoyed an economic boom. The exploitation of new oilfields, the expansion of diamond mining and rich revenues from coffee boosted the confidence of the more than 300,000 white settlers. This bonanza was not shared equally with black Angolans. Portugal claimed, often with apparent sincerity, that racial discrimination did not exist in her African domains but the privileged *mestiços* (mixed-race) and *assimilados* (assimilated or 'civilized' Africans) constituted a miniscule portion of society.[1] The Mozambican nationalist leader, Eduardo Mondlane, described the assimilated status as 'at best simply bourgeois social clubs, often called up to shout their part in the militarized chorus of allegiance to Salazar'. Mondlane was referring to the Portuguese dictator, António de Salazar, who ruled from 1932 to 1968.

The 'uncivilized' remainder of blacks suffered under a harsh regime of racial injustice, sometimes not far removed from the days when Angola was a penal colony. True, poor whites were plentiful too, but they were often recent immigrants. And a few examples of rapid black mobility had been allowed,

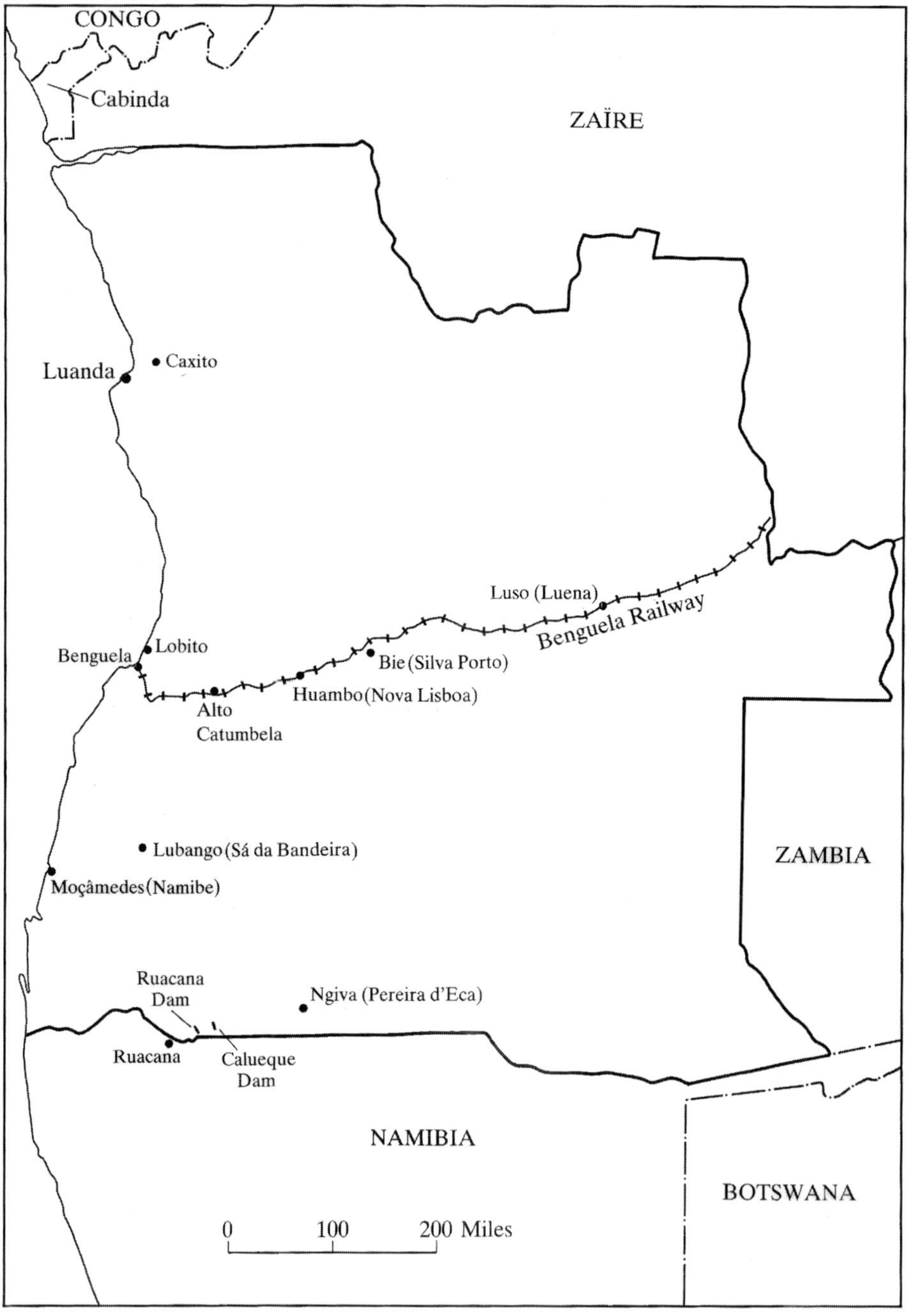


Angola

The war against the Portuguese

for instance, a black Angolan general. The whites elsewhere in southern Africa, especially the Anglo-Saxons, tended to look down on the 'Porks', the Portuguese, and make comments that racial integration in Angola reflected the downward mobility of the Portuguese rather than upward mobility of blacks. Nevertheless, the overall pattern was one of white privilege and black oppression. Harsh labour laws and poor schooling were two of the most resented aspects of alien rule. Lack of schools militated against blacks achieving educational qualifications required to attain *assimilado* status. By 1961 only one per cent of blacks had been 'assimilated'. Any signs of black (or white) disaffection were rooted out rapidly by the secret police, *Polícia Internacional e de Defesa do Estado* (PIDE, later known as the DGS). PIDE was no exception to the maxim that the secret police are usually the most (sometimes only) efficient arm of the totalitarian state. Despite the gradual liberalization in the metropole, the semi-fascist Salazarist regime in Lisbon – for historic and economic reasons – refused to loosen the grip on the African colonies. As Marcello Caetano, Salazar's successor, put it, 'Without Africa we would be a small nation, with Africa we are a big power.' Fledgling black nationalist movements did surface in the early 1960s in Angola, Mozambique and Guinea-Bissau, mostly led by *mestiços* and *assimilados*, the very embryonic 'moderate', middle-class allies that the authorities hoped to buy off with privileges.

In 1961 most of these nationalists had been driven underground or into exile in neighbouring states and Portugal. Thus, in March 1961, when the night of the long knives came – often quite literally – to settlers of northern Angola, the Portuguese security forces were caught entirely offguard. Marauding bands of Africans armed with machetes and old muskets attacked isolated white settlements and plantations in the Uige region. Gradually, the violence spread until by June it affected much of north-western Angola. Only 3,000 Portuguese troops were stationed in the whole of Angola and none were deployed in the north. By August the Portuguese had 17,000 troops in the field, aided by white vigilantes who exacted merciless reprisals for the earlier savagery. The uprising lasted six months, and perhaps 50,000 blacks and 700 whites were killed. The whites resumed their hold on Angola, but the foundations of empire had been shaken.

The 1961 uprising had been organized – 'organized' is a loose term for the often random racial slaughter – in part by an Angolan exile group based in the recently independent Belgian Congo. The group was led by Holden Roberto, a somewhat effete chairbound warrior, who managed to get paid by the CIA from 1962, and then finagled a little support from Israel, and then much more from China and Zaire. He was a descendant of the monarch of the Kongo kingdom and did not let his associates forget it. Many colleagues were later to desert him because of his tribalism and lack of pan-Angolan instincts. He led an alphabet soup of groups but they eventually became known as the FNLA (*Frente Nacional de Libertação de Angola*). Exploiting the land grievances of the Bakongo people, who straddled both sides of the ill-defined Congo-Angola border, Roberto hoped that violence would prompt the Portuguese to depart as rapidly as the Belgians had scuttled from the Congo. The Portuguese, however, chose to fight … and to reform their archaic empire. After years of 'colonialism by neglect' the authorities abolished compulsory labour and launched a widespread programme of social, educational and economic development. There was no change in the political status quo, however. Lisbon re-affirmed that the African 'provinces' were inalienable parts of Portugal. The insurgents fought on, not only in Angola but elsewhere. In January 1963 the guerrilla war in Guinea-Bissau began. In Mozambique FRELIMO *(Frente de Libertação de Moçambique*) commenced its war of independence in September 1964.

By 1970 Portugal was fielding 150,000 troops in Africa, with 60,000 stationed in Angola. For the poorest country in Western Europe, it was no mean feat to contain the guerrillas in remote areas, far from the main towns and major faming areas where the vast majority of the settlers were concentrated. But it was the divisions among the nationalists as much as Portuguese organization (or often lack of it) that determined the course of these colonial wars. The colonialists frequently manipulated traditional inter-tribal animosities to divide and rule. Suppression, exile, infiltration and assassinations frequently, but not always, perpetrated by the secret police – who inevitably put the blame on rival nationalist factions – all took their toll. As the distinguished historian of the Angolan revolution, John Marcum, suggested, 'clandestinity left its mark too. Decimated by infiltrators and corroded by insecurities and tensions of underground politics, Angola's nationalists became obsessively distrustful of everyone, including each other.' The major nationalist parties spent as much time fighting each other as trying to defeat their mutual Portuguese foes. Sometimes, guerrillas would co-operate with the colonial army to inflict local reversals on rival factions.

Holden Roberto rarely ventured into the field in Angola, preferring instead to enjoy the nightlife in Leopoldville and the style of his brother-in-law, General Mobutu Sese Seko, perhaps the most corrupt leader to emerge in Africa. Roberto's FNLA was run as a personal fiefdom riddled with poor morale, venality and splits. The FNLA's half-hearted armed forays petered out by the mid-1960s. The MPLA (*Movimento Popular de Libertação de Angola – Partido do Trabalho*) was founded in 1956 and it had a more secure intellectual basis. Its elite mostly comprised *mestiços* and some whites with links to the banned Angolan communist party, which was in turn connected to the Portuguese communists. The MPLA attracted a mainly middle-class following among civil servants and students in the capital Luanda and in the Kimbundu region. Later the MPLA was to recruit heavily, but not exclusively, from the 1,400,000-strong Mbundu tribe. The MPLA's leader, Agostinho Neto, a doctor with a penchant for poetry, had been driven into exile. His movement, also riven by factionalism, was forced to shift its offices from Paris to Conakry, to Leopoldville then to Brazzaville and even, briefly, Lusaka. After meeting Neto in 1965 that most romanticized of revolutionaries, Che Guevera, provided a small corps of Cuban military instructors. The USSR also donated some money and training. Moscow later (in 1973) despaired of the military performance of the armed wing of the MPLA, only to recharge its support to counter Chinese intervention in Angola. The third leading protagonist was Dr Jonas Savimbi, a soldier imbued with ever-changing ideologies but a charismatic leader and talented guerrilla tactician until power drove him mad decades later. He broke from the FNLA in 1964 and two years later he formed UNITA (*União Nacional para a Independência Total de Angola*). This movement drew its main strength from the Ovimbundu people, about two million in number, and Angola's biggest tribe. Unlike Roberto and Neto, Savimbi spent most of his time leading his troops in the field. Scorning – initially – the public relations of the politics of exile, he secured little foreign support. His guerrillas were few in number and poorly trained and equipped. Except for a brief period of Zambian assistance, he could not rely on a regular sanctuary.

All three major parties tried to capitalize on their relationships with fickle foreign patrons in order to counteract their frequently dismal military performance against the Portuguese army. Roberto and Savimbi, sometimes in concert, often in conflict, received aid from the USA, France and Britain but also from the People's Republic of China, Romania, North Korea and, later, and most significantly, from South Africa. Some observers saw this alliance as 'pro-Western' while others strained to call it 'pro-Chinese'. The MPLA, on the other hand, ranged equally widely across the political spectrum: the USSR, Cuba, Sweden, Denmark and Nigeria. It also recruited to its side former Katangese mercenaries loyal to Moise Tshombe. To many this was the 'pro-Soviet' side while others preferred the term 'non-aligned'. Thus a pattern emerged that persisted during the post-independence civil war where the favoured party was portrayed as enjoying broad ethnic and national domestic support and the rival side was characterized as mere surrogates of foreign imperialism (especially Russian or South African). In fact, none of the three movements could be legitimately or intelligently defined by the ideology or interests of their patrons. Instead each was an expression of internal Angolan differences based upon a melange of historical, ethno-linguistic, regional and personal factors. Foreign meddling, however, played a crucial role in the war's outcome.

Theoretically, the FNLA was the strongest military force. In 1971 Roberto claimed to control up to 8,000 guerrillas although fewer than 1,000 were usually active inside Angola. During the final years of the colonial war the FNLA plunged into a military decline. In 1970 UNITA – operating in the south – was estimated by Portuguese intelligence to have no more than 300 insurgents, whereas the MPLA at the same time had approximately 1,500 fighting men in-country, with two to three times that number stationed outside. (Nationalist figures were usually wildly inaccurate; Portuguese estimates were generally much nearer the mark.) A series of Portuguese offensives between 1968 and 1973 as well as the withdrawal of

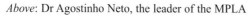

*Above*: Dr Agostinho Neto, the leader of the MPLA

*Right*: Dr Jonas Savimbi (left)

Zambian backing, plus the split of the MPLA into three warring factions, resulted in major military reversals for the MPLA by 1973.

As in many African insurgencies, the guerrillas were frequently their own worst enemies. Many of their initial advantages were squandered. The terrain was frequently suitable for insurgency. The FNLA, for example, operated along a 1,300-mile frontier of swamp, mountains and jungle, while the MPLA forces in eastern Moxico region could range over a vast plateau of savannah and forest covering 150,000 square miles. But the great distances also hampered the guerrillas who could never match the logistics of their conventional opponents. The weather also worked both ways. In the south the style of campaigns depended upon the season. The dry season (usually April to September) facilitated conventional vehicle-borne troop movements, with clear skies for air support. In the rainy season Angola's dirt roads turned into quagmires. The extra foliage provided more cover for the insurgents, water was then plentiful and low cloud deterred aerial interdiction.

The long frontiers were porous, so the key neighbouring sanctuary states, the Congo Republic, Zaire and Zambia, provided convenient infiltration routes from external bases. The first 300 MPLA cadres were trained in Algeria; later MPLA units received instruction in Bulgaria, Czechoslovakia and the Soviet Union. In addition, some of these states, as well as the Organization of African Unity, offered important diplomatic assistance in the propaganda war. Internally, the guerrillas' political warfare was less effective. All the insurgent groups in the three main Portuguese African territories attempted to set up 'liberated' zones to politicize the inhabitants. The most successful was the *Partido Africano da Independência da Guiné e Cabo Verde* (PAIGC) in Guinea-Bissau, which formally established a government in its extensive liberated areas in 1973. The least effective was the FNLA that concentrated almost exclusively on military action. This was one of the reasons for the breakaway of UNITA, which set a high priority on political education. Internecine feuds within and between the Angolan movements, often deliberately exacerbated by their external mentors, resulted in a failure to evolve an overall military strategy, let alone a concerted political programme.

Most of the guerrilla activities consisted of short-range incursions by relatively small groups, which, after operations returned to their sanctuaries – if they had survived. Both sides, however, tended to avoid direct confrontation. Indeed the Angolan war has been characterized as 'mines versus helicopters', with relatively few 'contacts' on the ground. In 1970, for example, mines accounted for perhaps as many as 50 per cent of Portuguese casualties. Guerrilla weaponry was essentially basic. Typically, they carried the temperamental Simonov automatic rifles and the ubiquitous and hardy AK-47s; Russian 82mm mortars, 75mm cannon and the various types of 'bazookas' were also deployed. In the final stages of the war the weaponry became more sophisticated. In 1973, for example, the PAIGC was successfully operating ground-to-air missiles.

Caught offguard in 1961, the Portuguese security forces were slow to consolidate their position after the vengeful savagery of their initial reprisals. Until troop levels were built up, their strategy was defensive and hesitant. By 1967, however, some 75 per cent of the metropolitan army was overseas. By 1970, with 150,000 troops stationed in Africa, this deployment in proportion to the Portuguese population as a whole was five times greater than that of America's in Vietnam in the same year. Nevertheless, the Portuguese struggled to quarantine insurgency in the remote areas. For political reasons the Portuguese were reluctant to engage in full-scale cross-border raids to wipe out insurgency bases in their sanctuaries. Portugal was already under attack in both NATO and UN circles for its African operations. Many border infringements did take place, however, and Portugal also manipulated Zambian dependence on the Benguela rail-link, which traversed central Angola to the sea. The Portuguese army did try to cut the supply routes from sanctuaries and to destroy the internal bases with a regular series of co-ordinated sweeps. Airpower, using napalm and defoliants, was combined with swamping targets with ground patrols. Vital to these tactics were the newly introduced helicopters. By 1971 sixty Alouette choppers had been deployed. Delving into their NATO arsenal, the Fiat G91s, American F-84 Thunderjets and Lockheed P-2Vs were used for offensive air support, although the F-86 Sabre was withdrawn from African service in 1967 at Washington's insistence. The guerrillas had little to deter Portuguese airpower. Thus, Lisbon could claim that Operation ATTILA in 1971, for example, had eliminated half the insurgents operating in eastern Angola.

The Portuguese used NATO weaponry including US-supplied Sabre fighters

With the exception of elite units, Portuguese forces tended to lack an offensive spirit. They relied upon their (outdated) technological superiority over their opponents. The Rhodesian army, which frequently co-operated with the Portuguese in Mozambique, adopted a much more aggressive hands-on approach by a continuous and forceful use of small foot patrols to engage the enemy regularly in the bush. Rhodesian 'troopies' frequently derided their colonial allies for taking siestas in the afternoon while on operations and for their use of the *pica* (a sharpened stick) to probe for mines ahead of patrols. Some of these primitive methods were very effective. The Portuguese would suspend empty beer bottles on wires around their outposts as early warning devices. They were often just as effective as modern American sensors that were anyway not available to the Portuguese. And, like the Rhodesians in the 1970s and South Africans in Namibia in the 1980s, the Portuguese deployed cavalry quite successfully. Supplied by air, horses could patrol vast areas. In the flat terrain of southern Angola, a mounted soldier had the advantage of silent mobility and elevated observation. Although troops normally dismounted to engage the enemy, many guerrillas displayed an extra wariness of horse soldiers. Besides this psychological factor, the horse itself was also an (unfortunate) shock absorber in mine warfare.

In contrast to the often reluctant conscript troops, elite formations of volunteers, often with a large component of black soldiers, such as the *Grupos Espeçiais*, the airborne *Grupos Espeçiais* de *Paraquedist* and the *Commandos Africanos* achieved very high kill rates. Perhaps as many as 40 per cent of Portuguese forces in Angola were comprised of black Angolans, often recruited from tribal groups hostile to local rival clans that favoured the nationalists. (At the end of the Rhodesian war, blacks constituted 77 per cent of the security forces.) Also many captured guerrillas and deserters, given 'offers they could not refuse', were turned and used to penetrate their former bases.

A major element of Portuguese strategy was the concentration of population in strategic hamlets or defended villages. Approximately one million blacks were resettled in these villages or *aldeamentos*. Allied to this was a prodigious roadbuilding programme: 5,000 miles of roads were constructed by 1974, partly to avoid mines but also to provide the infrastructure for the 'social promotion' policy. As one official said, 'Revolt starts where the road ends.' Clinics, cattle dips and schools were rapidly developed in the rural areas. Improvements were certainly made but the 'hearts and minds' campaign could not alter the political alienation felt by the majority of blacks. Resettlement was largely a failure (as it was in South Vietnam and Rhodesia). It appeared as just another phase in the cycle of destruction of traditional life, 'a chronicle which began with slavery, continued through the pacification wars and contract labour period, and finally ended with forced resettlement programmes during the war'.[2] A minority of traditional tribal chiefs, with reasons to fear guerrilla intimidation, may have welcomed the protection afforded by resettlement but many Africans translated resettlement as land-grabbing by the white farmers. Even when a military rationale dominated, rather than selfish land expropriation, guerrillas often infiltrated the system and the various types of protected villages as sources of food, and information.

The Portuguese army was not defeated in Africa. By 1974 even the most successful insurgency, in Guinea-Bissau, had resulted in a no-score draw. The verdict on the Angolan war may perhaps have been a 'low-intensity stalemate'. And in Mozambique the Portuguese could possibly have defeated the insurgency – Kenya might have been a parallel – if the war had continued. One British military historian concluded:

> In many respects it was a considerable achievement for the army of arguably the poorest and least developed country in Western Europe to fight three wars simultaneously for such a prolonged period without suffering military defeat.[3]

The strains induced by the African wars played a part in destroying the civil-military balance in the metropole. The coup of April 1974 ended almost overnight the historic 'mission' in Africa and turned the armed forces into a debating society. Troops in the field refused to fight. The costs had already been enormous: the proportion of the national budget spent on defence had risen from approximately 25 per cent in 1960 to a peak of 48 per cent in 1968. Only in Angola was indigenous production sufficient to fund a large proportion (50 per cent) of the local war effort. Revenue from the oilfields, the diamond and iron ore mines and the coffee and cotton plantations were drained away to fund the counter-insurgency campaigns. Lisbon admitted to a total of 3,265 men killed in action in Africa, though independent observers suggested that the real figure was four times that number. Guerrilla casualties were very much higher still.

An artistic interpretation of General António de Spinola

The Portuguese armed forces were the exception to the European pattern: they alone revolted against fighting the 'war of the flea' in the colonies. Officers will risk their lives, it is said, but rarely their careers. General António de Spinola, the army's deputy chief of staff, was an exception. In his book *Portugal and the Future*, published in February 1974, he stated clearly that the African wars as a whole could never be won militarily. This monocled warrior, a public hero after his campaigns in Guinea-Bissau, tried to emulate Charles de Gaulle during the Algerian crisis. Yet de Spinola did not want to grant total independence to the African possessions; he hoped to create a 'Lusitanian' federation of self-governing states. Although his views on the futility of the wars were shared by the majority of the officer corps, he was sacked. Re-installed as head of the military junta after the coup he was outmanoeuvred by officers with more radical opinions.[4] The endgame for the Portuguese forces was their supervision of the transfer to full independence of the African territories. One series of wars was ending but a much more bloody saga was about to begin.

The military revolution in Lisbon in 1974 ended colonial rule in the Portuguese territories

## *The transition from colonial war to civil war*

At the time of the Lisbon coup, Holden Roberto's FNLA looked the strongest, partly because the Zairean army had quashed a mutiny against his erratic leadership. Then in June 1974 an advanced party of Chinese instructors arrived at Kinkuzu, the FNLA's main military base inside Angola; soon lots of Chinese arms also arrived. As the Portuguese troops disengaged, the FNLA moved in to set up a liberated zone in north-eastern Angola. Part of the reason for the FNLA's apparent strength was because of the weakness of the rival nationalists. The MPLA was utterly divided. One faction was led by Daniel Chipenda who happened to be good at both kicking football (as a professional player) *and* kicking arse as a guerrilla commander. His main rival, Agostinho Neto, called him a drunken diamond smuggler and bank robber. Fearing the Chinese would steal a march, the Russians resumed their backing for Neto. He now made some headway in mobilizing political support in Luanda and the surrounding Kimbundu area. Portuguese officials in the capital started to favour him and the overall military commander in Angola, Admiral Rosa Coutinho, sent there after the coup, was an energetic supporter of Neto. Nevertheless, MPLA activism was limited to central Angola. The Bakongo in the north and the Ovimbundu in the south were reluctant to commit themselves to Neto's pro-Soviet party.

In the south, Savimbi had secured much popular support for his (ineffectual) campaign against the Portuguese, plus he received some Chinese backing. Religion also counted: Savimbi's father had been a part-time Congregationalist preacher (as well as being a fulltime stationmaster). The Ovimbundu elite were largely Congregationalist-educated, many of the Bakongo leaders tended to be Baptist mission-educated, while the MPLA leadership was influenced by Methodist-trained Mbundu intellectuals. Savimbi's clandestine relations with Portuguese intelligence resulted in a rapid ceasefire with the colonial army. He also made overtures to remaining members of the white business community by offering himself as the moderate option for Angolan leadership (while promising radical Africanization when addressing black supporters).

The OAU tried to resolve the chaos with the Alvor Agreement. The three main movements would form a coalition government with the Portuguese and take part in national elections for a constituent assembly to achieve independence in November 1975. Portugal would retain a 24,000-strong army and the three main nationalist armies would contribute 8,000 each as well. The FNLA had the numbers but the other two had to recruit and train feverishly. In early 1975 the transition government met in Luanda and tried to integrate the guerrilla armies (both the three bigger ones and the smaller ones such as those fighting in the oil-rich Cabinda enclave). No political consensus existed and the reduced Portuguese army could not keep order, even in the capital where the FNLA and MPLA were soon at each others' throats. The Russians tried to bolster its proxy, the MPLA. When the FNLA massacred more than sixty MPLA supporters in March in the strategic coastal town of Caxito, Neto duly proclaimed this incident as the formal start of a civil war. Within six months around 300,000 whites had panicked and quit the country, the largest exodus of whites from the continent since the Algerian crisis. In June the Portuguese army stormed the FNLA and MPLA strongholds in Luanda to try to maintain some semblance of order. In the same month 230 Cuban instructors arrived to set up four military training bases for the MPLA. Freshly equipped with Soviet arms, and allied with now notoriously bloodthirsty Katangese mercenaries, the MPLA drove the FNLA and UNITA out of the capital in July 1975.

Neto's seizure of the capital, with some Portuguese connivance, spelt the end of the utterly fragile transitional government. Some elements of the Portuguese security forces, especially in Luanda, helped the MPLA. Elsewhere they huddled in their barracks, sometimes making forays to protect terrified Portuguese refugees, and occasionally to assist the MPLA's rivals in more isolated parts of the country. Portugal's military role had come to an end –after four centuries in Africa. The big powers were now entering the fray. With Luanda in the bag, the MPLA concentrated on capturing the provincial capitals so that it could exert maximum diplomatic pressure at the OAU when Angola attained formal independence in November. By the end of August the MPLA held eleven of the fifteen provincial capitals, although much of the countryside surrounding these towns was beyond their grasp. Crucially, the MPLA dominated Cabinda, despite French and Zairian support for FLEC (the Front for the Liberation of the Enclave of Cabinda). In September alone the American Gulf Oil Company paid $116 million in royalties to the MPLA administration. The diamond mines in Luanda province were also controlled by the MPLA. Their hold on the key ports of Luanda, Lobito and Moçamedes permitted the re-supply of Cuban and Eastern bloc weaponry and also stopped arms reaching the FNLA and UNITA areas farther inland.

On the eve of Angolan independence, Russia and America stepped up their involvement. Like China, each superpower had previously hedged with side bets on a number of early starters. East-West rivalry and superpower prestige demanded that the favoured horse had to win. But the armed intervention of an outsider, South Africa, was greatly to complicate the prestige stakes. Understanding Angola's travails has always been a complex business that requires longterm, close-up study. As the historian Christine Messiant has observed, 'Here in Angola, even the past is unpredictable.'

## *The South African invasion*

Once Pretoria intervened in a big way, the Angolan stage was set for high drama. Some depicted the South African invasion of Angola in 1975-76 as a morality play decrying the unholy alliance of apartheid, Western imperialism, CIA recklessness and Chinese revisionism. Alternatively, Russian opportunism and Cuban aggression were denounced. The initial intervention was seen as the biggest defeat for Afrikaner power since the Boer War but not by South Africans because they were kept completely in the dark about what their army was doing next door.

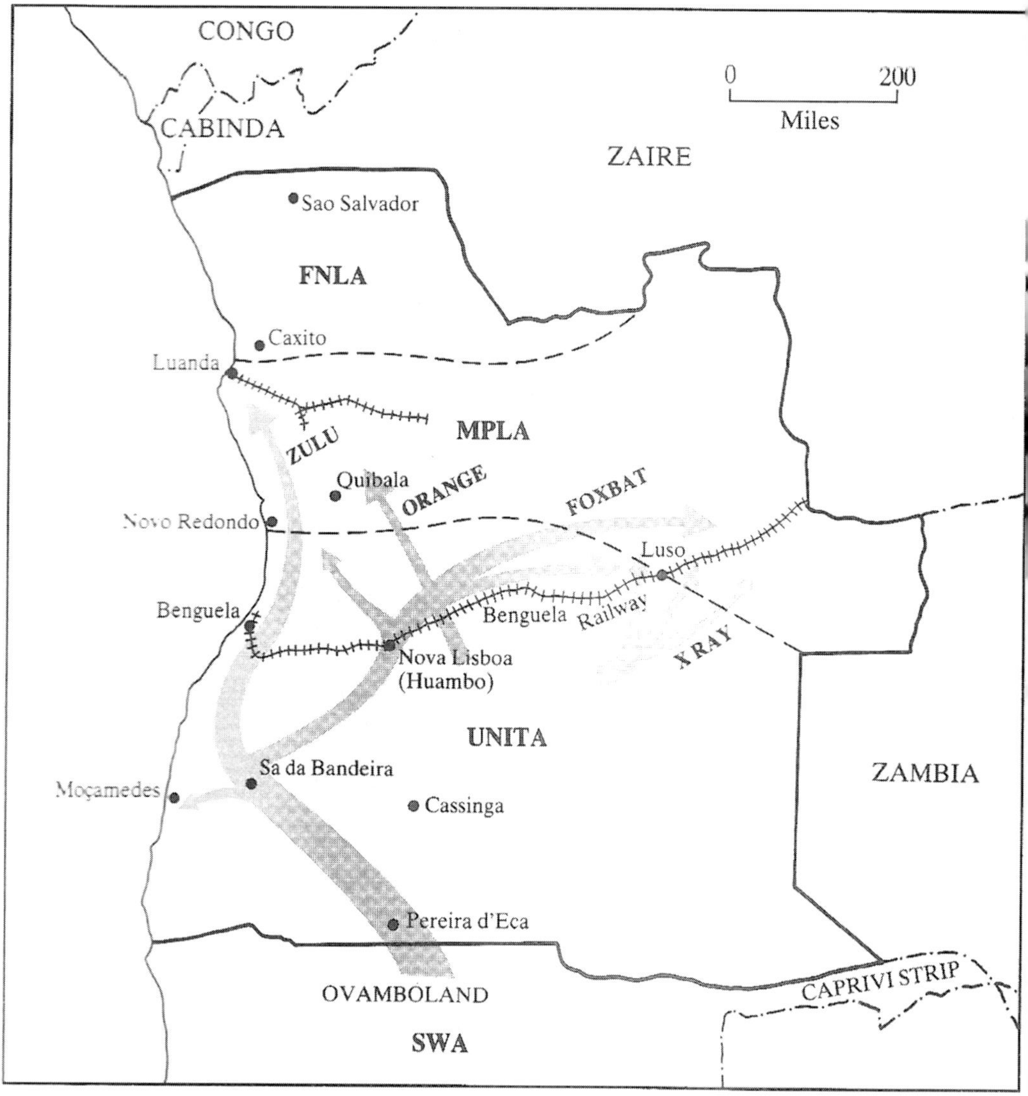


The South African invasion of Angola

During the anti-colonial wars in Angola, Pretoria had acted very cautiously. The SADF covertly supplied intelligence, and then later some arms, helicopters and pilots to the Portuguese. Lisbon was always very touchy about admitting South African aid in Angola or Rhodesian backing in Mozambique, partly because Portugal always wanted to maintain the fiction that its oversees territories were under a firm metropolitan grip. Nor did Lisbon want to further hobble itself in world forums by being seen to march under the same banners as apartheid and UDI. Black nationalists naturally overplayed the triple white coalition and exaggerated South African military intervention. South Africa did set up joint command posts at strategic centres, for example at Cuito Cuanvale, the scene of fierce battles in the late 1980s. Pretoria received no direct return on its investment. The purpose, as ever, was to preserve the Angolan link in the white shield.

Mozambique was also a vital segment of this racial bulwark. There South Africa was sufficiently self-confident to leave FRELIMO – initially – to its own devices. The important Cabora (Cahora) Bassa dam was left undefended by the SADF. The dam was the biggest hydroelectric scheme in southern Africa and much of the electricity was scheduled to go to South Africa after it was completed in 1974. Pretoria also scorned the hardline white Mozambicans who wanted to set up their own UDI republic in southern Mozambique adjacent to South African territory. So why didn't Pretoria stand back in Angola as it did in Mozambique? FRELIMO, after all, was almost ideologically indistinguishable from the MPLA.

In Mozambique one nationalist party inherited the mantle of power and the country's weak economic infrastructure was largely at the mercy of South Africa's capitalism. No single party had inherited the keys to the kingdom in Angola, potentially a very rich country. With few economic ties with the financial powerhouse in Johannesburg, and thus lacking an economic stranglehold, the military option became more enticing. Above all, the SADF was extremely anxious to prevent eastern bloc troops from lining up on the 1,200-mile Namibian/Angola border, where for ten years the South African army had been skirmishing with insurgents loyal to SWAPO (the South West Africa People's Organization). An MPLA victory would inevitably boost the moral and striking power of its SWAPO ally. Moreover, Angola's excellent ports could also be a strategic bonus for the Russians who might also manipulate the Benguela rail link with Zambia and Zaire, countries which were targets of Pretoria's détente policy.

Pretoria did not have a master plan for invasion, nor did Washington. In retrospect, the FNLA drive from the north and the SADF-led strikes from the south did take on the appearance of deliberate pincer movement against the MPLA. Instead, constant improvization marked the 'pro-Western' war effort. South Africa's full-blown participation was a result of almost inadvertent steps up the ladder of escalation in mid-1975. In August the SADF had moved into south-western Angola, ostensibly to protect the large hydro-electric projects at Calueque and Ruacana. 'Ostensibly' because some analysts suggested that this move was an excuse to draw off MPLA troops from the north, and thus weaken the capital for a swift sweep south by the FNLA. This theory holds that as the SADF did not send in troops to guard the much more important – and expensive – dam projects in Mozambique, Pretoria was participating in a carefully calibrated gesture that might have caught the MPLA completely off balance. The Angolan dam projects, funded by South African and Portuguese finance, were vital to agricultural development on both sides of the southern border. Workers on the unfinished schemes had complained of harassment by MPLA soldiers. The South African army also moved into Angola for humanitarian reasons: to set up and guard refugee camps in southern towns; later many thousands of white Portuguese and black Angolans were allowed to travel on to South West Africa.

Economic factors (the dams) and humanitarian concerns were less important than the military rationale. The SADF's limited deployment along the southern Angolan border was an attempt to create a *localized* buffer against Cuban/MPLA/SWAPO encroachment into Namibia. But the fluidity throughout Angola prompted Pretoria's military planners to consider wider possibilities. Perhaps South Africa could influence the *national* outcome of the civil war?

In August 1975 South Africa had officially withdrawn its 2,000-strong police contingent from Rhodesia (albeit leaving equipment, pilots and advisers behind – unofficially). After pulling out 2,000 men from one war which Pretoria thought was probably lost, why should it commit the same number of men to a much bloodier conflict where South Africa had far fewer traditional ties? That was a dominant question among the doves in the South African department of foreign affairs. Even the military commanders who were advocating intervention were secretly voicing some concern about the risks of sending their troops thousands of miles from their own borders into a largely unfamiliar territory against possibly superior Russian weapons. Actual defeat at the hands of communist-sponsored black troops, perhaps because of vastly superior numbers and modern weapons, and with the UN cheering from the sidelines, was a persistent hidden fear that underlay a racist arrogance that publicly dismissed the possibilities of a major reversal in the field. Only one scenario could induce South Africa to take such a risk: an anti-communist alliance with the West, particularly America.

Angola had been largely ignored by the US State Department. As the battles shifted in the MPLA's favour, the competitive juices were aroused, not least in the CIA, so diplomatic priorities were re-jigged. Henry Kissinger had previously tried to ride two horses in Portuguese Africa: officially he supported his NATO ally, while allowing the CIA to sponsor in a small way some of the likely contenders among the guerrillas. The pro-Western FNLA had been given extra funds to boost its position in the provisional government, though Jonas Savimbi's initial requests were turned down. Washington's humiliation in South Vietnam in the summer of 1975, coming so soon after the Watergate scandal, encouraged Kissinger to re-assert US prestige elsewhere. Soviet intercession in Angola was tilting the global balance, he believed. If the West allowed this to happen then friendly Zambia and Zaire, a client state of Washington, could fall into the communist net. Malawi and Kenya could be next. As Kissinger later declared to the Senate Africa Sub-Committee in January 1976:

> Angola represents the first time since the aftermath of World War Two that the Soviets have moved militarily at long distance to impose a regime of their own choice. It is the first time that the US has failed to respond to Soviet military moves outside their immediate orbit.

Kissinger was particularly worried about Zaire, which had allowed its regular troops to fight alongside the FNLA since February 1975. After the recent traumas in South East Asia, Kissinger's own experts on Africa in the State Department were hostile to any American intervention in the Angolan conflict. Kissinger ignored them. With the CIA, he organized a covert operation, partly to avoid a clash with a highly sceptical Congress, and partly to reduce the risks of an open breach with the Soviet Union. On both counts 'deniability' would be possible. As Kissinger later admitted, it kept American 'visibility' to a minimum. The '40 Committee' (a four-person sub-committee of the National Security Council) initiated a $30 million programme to provide arms and cash to the FNLA and UNITA. Much more was to follow and Zaire was the main conduit for this subvention. Encouraged by his patron, General Mobutu sent armoured car units into Angola, then Zairian paratroopers joined the expeditionary force.

Although it would be naïve to interpret great power diplomacy in Angola purely in terms of knee-jerk rivalry, that such instincts were involved is indicated by CIA Director William Colby's testimony before the House Select Committee on Intelligence on 12 December 1975. Congressman Les Aspin asked Colby why certain countries backed different Angolan parties:

> Aspin: And why are the Chinese backing the moderate group?
> Colby: Because the Soviets are backing the MPLA is the simplest answer.
> Aspin: It sounds like that is why we are doing it.
> Colby: It is.

A great deal of historical debate about Angola is based on who started the build up of foreign weapons and troops. Most Western sources blame the Russians and Cubans. After all, Cuban advisers had been involved since 1965 and, by 1976, 20,000 Cubans troops were operational. How much persuasion did Washington exert on Pretoria to go in big? And was the extensive Cuban intervention the cause or effect of the South African invasion? Many fingers were jabbed into the pie. Besides the great powers, Cuba, Romania, Zaire, Zambia and the Congo Republic, as well as South Africa can be blamed. Western slush funds probably in the end matched the $200 million Kissinger estimated the Russians had spent. According to John Stockwell, the head of the CIA's Angolan task force, and who later repented and wrote a scathing account of American involvement, 'Each major escalation was initiated by our side, by the United States and our allies'.[5]

Russian intervention was 'end-loaded': it rapidly accelerated towards the close of 1975. Between November 1975 and March 1976, approximately twenty Soviet ships and seventy flights deposited their contents of arms and Cuban troops inside Angola. Despite the fact that Stockwell insisted he saw no formal evidence of Washington arm-twisting of Pretoria it was obvious that the US gave a series of green lights to South Africa. Later, South African recriminations, both private and in public, strongly suggested American enticement. The then South African defence minister, P.W. Botha, told parliament that Washington, after encouraging South Africa to invade, then 'recklessly left us in the lurch'.

Besides superpower pressure, many of the smaller powers had their own ambitions. Pretoria was always extremely anxious about communist penetration of South West Africa. And the Cubans cannot simply be designated as mere puppets of the Kremlin. Fidel Castro's Marxism had a tropical flavour all its own. The Cuban politburo operated with a large measure of discretion within the general framework of 'progressive' goals. Castro himself displayed a sense of personal 'mission' about revolutions in Africa, despite the high costs, both in blood and treasure, of his island's intervention in Angola.

For both Pretoria and Havana, wading into the Angolan quagmire was not the result of a sinister blueprint or even a single decision. More prosaically it was caused by a gradual escalation: first, military advisers sent in to train; then advisers getting sucked into combat; next, small specialized support units were required; and, finally, regular army infantry units, with the air force in close support, were deployed. Thus no single *casus belli* can be flagged up, nor a single villain demonized. All the actors in the tragedy became embroiled in a bloody cycle of reaction and counter-reaction. To lay the exclusive blame for the length and bitterness of the Angolan civil war on either Havana's or Pretoria's doorstep is propaganda, not history. The military style was different, however. Cuban instructors became involved – integrated – at every level of the FAPLA forces (*Forças Armadas Populares de Libertação de Angola,* the military wing of the MPLA). Not surprisingly perhaps, the SADF retained a distinct and separate identity. The Russian advisers were notorious for their aloofness towards black Angolan troops.

South Africa's determination to prevent an MPLA victory led almost inexorably to military support for the rival factions. The 'pro-Western' rival leaders met South African military and intelligence specialists in Zaire, Windhoek, and finally Pretoria. An SADF programme was set up to train FNLA and UNITA troops in the south (later a team of South African advisers was sent to the northern Angolan front). One camp in southern Angola was at Calombo, to train UNITA; another, at Mapupa, attempted to train soldiers loyal to the FNLA. Together these two camps were supposed to produce 6,000 'trained' soldiers within six weeks. South African instructors were taken aback by the poor material they were told to work with. Colonel Jan Breytenbach, one of South Africa's finest combat soldiers, was largely responsible for the shaping of the FNLA southern forces. In his memoirs he commented on the quality of his charges. 'They were without a doubt the scruffiest, most underfed, worst armed and most unwarlike troops I had ever seen in my life.' Then 43, Breytenbach had learned his style of discipline in the Royal Navy and later helped to found the Reconnaissance Commandos, becoming South Africa's foremost authority on special forces and guerrilla warfare. Despite the unpromising manpower, South African officers led these men in one of the most rapid military advances in history. It was called Operation SAVANNAH.

The SADF training programme took shape in late August. The independence date was set for 11 November 1975. Pretoria's military planners asked themselves: could the MPLA coalition be weakened enough to prevent its official recognition by the OAU on independence day? It was to be a race against the diplomatic clock. Savimbi and Roberto conjured with plans for a triumphal march into Luanda, whereas some of their South African and American advisers privately wondered whether the anti-Neto forces could survive, let alone win. In August 1975 two opposing armies lined up for the decisive contest to control Angola. On the battle 'fronts' the military mosaic was as complex as the political network of alliances. Neto and his MPLA held Luanda as well as most of the towns of central and southern Angola. Crucially, the MPLA still retained the Cabinda exclave,

Eland column advancing north into Angola, near Rundu (SADF)

formerly known as Portuguese Congo. It had 2,810 square miles of territory and a small population but its coast was adjacent to one of the largest offshore oilfields in the world. Zaire and the French backed local secessionists in an on-off war that was to last for over four decades. In late 1975, however, the oil money was going to the MPLA. The MPLA were also allied then to 4,000 experienced Katangese fighters as well as a small but growing number of Cuban troops and a burgeoning Soviet arsenal. On the other side, Roberto's FNLA and Zairian regulars occupied parts of the north and the south where Daniel Chipenda's wing was active. Roberto had as allies the Chinese, his brother-in-law Mobutu and the CIA and the latest recruit, South Africa. UNITA, tribally rooted in central and southern Angola, was supported by the CIA, Zambia and South African arms and instructors. Scattered around the country were demoralized units of Portuguese troops. Most now did their best to avoid the war, although small numbers, along with desperate white settlers, joined the anti-Marxist Portuguese Liberation Army. In contrast, a handful of white Angolans fought on the side of the MPLA. Such was the line-up for the next six months of intense and often highly mobile warfare.

The fighting was divided into two main fronts although that term can only loosely be used to describe advances which often ignored much of the countryside. What mattered most was the domination of ports, main towns, vital bridges and road and rail links. In the north, Roberto chose to disregard his small number of American and South African advisers, who told him to consolidate the areas he had already just about held. In the South the much larger contingent of South African

SADF column in Eland armoured cars near Rundu (SADF)

Armoured cars crossing on pontoon between Rundu and Calai, southern Angola (SADF)

officers enforced a much more disciplined command-and-control system on their black allies. In the north, the South Africans advised from the rear; in the south they commanded and led from the front.

South African-led UNITA forces clashed with an MPLA/Cuban unit on 5 October near Nova Lisboa (Huamba). A section of UNITA was ambushed on a bridge and retreated under heavy fire from light artillery, recoilless riflles and mortars, supported by a few ageing T-34 tanks. One of the South African Panhard AML-90s managed to knock out a T-34. Another tank was destroyed by a 106mm recoilless rifle mounted on a jeep. The South Africans next fired anti-tank missiles at the enemy position which was then abandoned.

This encounter with Cuban-manned armoured units prompted the SADF to expand its intervention by forming a number of flying columns. The first column was designated 'Zulu'. Zulu comprised one battalion, largely of Bushmen from Caprivi, plus 1,000 FNLA troops with a sprinkling of white officers and NCOs in command. Some of the FNLA men had received just three or four days' training. When they came under fire for the first time, especially from artillery, their lack of training and discipline soon became apparent. The South Africans had no choice but to train their allies in real combat conditions. Besides Panhards, transport included jeeps and a convoy of 'borrowed' Portuguese vegetable trucks. In some cases the drivers were 'volunteered' as well; at least one stayed with his vegetable truck for the duration of the drive north and back again. Zulu also had on board some 81mm mortars and several old Vickers MMGs.

For the SADF this was very deliberately a limited war. Pretoria went out of its way – after the invasion was made public – to sustain the image of penny-packet commitments, and deliberately underplayed the number of troops committed. Domestic constraints forced the military commanders to restrict the size and firepower of Operation SAVANNAH, which was a very small portion of the SADF's fully mobilized strength. South Africa later admitted to contributing up to 3,000 of its own officers and men, although some foreign experts doubled that figure. Besides limitation of manpower, other self-imposed restrictions were the non-use of tanks and fighter-bombers. The restriction on size was partly to reduce casualties. The government for long denied the very existence of the invasion and placed a blanket of censorship on the local media. Nonetheless, it would have been impossible to conceal a large number of white fatalities. Too many body bags would have proved politically contentious in the often close-knit Afrikaner communities. Later, the SADF officially acknowledged 128 dead and 100 wounded SADF personnel during the operation.

Pretoria may have had good reasons to hide its invasion – to avoid embarrassing 'friendly' black states such as Zambia, for example, and to discourage Soviet escalation. But the clumsy total censorship was a domestic disaster. Gradually the world would find out what South Africans were not supposed to know: the fact that their country was fighting an (undeclared) war in a neighbouring state. South African troops, often dressed in green Portuguese army uniforms, were told to pretend to be American mercenaries, if they met journalists. Afterwards, South African soldiers started calling their country 'the States', army slang which persisted, especially during the future operations on Angola. Some SADF personnel insisted, in the very thick Afrikaans variant of South African English, that they were in fact from the UK, hardly effective linguistic camouflage against the British journalists who recorded such incidents.

Although the South Africans managed to hide major setbacks in the north, nothing succeeded like success in the south; there, the Zulu taskforce covered just under 2,000 miles in thirty-three days after starting out on 19 October 1975. A journalist reporting from the Cuban side compared the push to a 'Sunday drive'. That was obviously an exaggeration as the South Africans dealt with a number of serious ambushes and firefights as well as skirmishes.

The Sunday drive began with the capture of Pereira D'Eca, near the Namibian border, on 19 October. Sá da Bandeira, the regional MPLA HQ, fell three days later. On 28 October one section of the Zulu column captured the port of Moçamedes, where the South Africans confronted the infamous Stalin Organs for the first time. The 122mm truck-mounted rocket-launchers had gone through many marks since the days of the Soviet dictator but the name had stuck. Against inexperienced and undisciplined troops the inaccurate artillery weapon can be very effective, partly because of the tremendous noise the rockets make. These weapons had demoralized the FNLA troops during their sally on Luanda from the north. In the south the South African officers kept a firm grip on their new subordinates. According to South African sources, at Moçamedes port the Zulu officers threatened to sink a Portuguese corvette if it did not up anchor and leave before morning. It did. This section of Zulu then raced along the coast road taking Lucira and advancing on the key communications hub of Benguela. Another element from Zulu, mainly UNITA troops, converged on Benguela from Nova Lisboa in the east. On 4 November Benguela airport was seized as well as the adjacent MPLA and Cuban bases – which happened to contain much-needed fuel supplies. The next day a three-pronged assault overran Benguela. Two days later Lobito fell. Zulu joined up with elements of another taskforce, Foxbat. Once the South Africans moved forward, they left behind UNITA or FNLA 'administrations'. Thus a few days before independence, the SADF-led thrust had taken two vital ports and command of the Benguela railway to enable vital supplies to reach UNITA and FNLA units in the central highlands.

On 11 November the Portuguese flag flew for the last time above the old hilltop fortress of São Miguel in Luanda. It was built in 1576 and had served as the main centre for the slave trade to Brazil. Until 1975 it had been the HQ of the Portuguese armed forces in Angola. Admiral Leonel Cardosa held a brief ceremony recognizing independence and handed over power to the 'Angolan people' even though not a single senior nationalist was present. The last 2,000 Portuguese troops in the capital boarded the ships that were waiting and they sailed away, leaving the 400-year-old colony swamped in violence. The MPLA set up a government in Luanda that was immediately recognized by a large number of predominantly socialist states. No state recognized the rival FNLA/UNITA republic established in Huambo. Despite the diplomatic gains, the MPLA now faced a serious military crisis; the rival troops threatened water, power and food supplies to the capital. The MPLA leadership even discussed the possibility of decamping to the Cabinda exclave.

In the south FAPLA (the MPLA's armed wing) was retreating on all fronts. The northern campaign was different. On independence day an FNLA force supported by Zairian regulars advanced across the wide, flat Quifangondo valley, twelve miles from the outskirts of Luanda. The small army was supported by twelve armoured cars and six 106mm recoilless rifles mounted on jeeps. The South African advisory team, plus four 5.5-inch artillery pieces manned by the SADF, positioned themselves on a ridge overlooking the valley. They were accompanied by a contingent of CIA officers. Holden Roberto felt his hour of destiny had arrived: Luanda was now almost in his grasp. Morale among his 1,500 troops was high. The foreign advisors were relaxed, even though Roberto had ignored their original advice to consolidate, not march on the capital.

The Cubans were waiting – even though many of them had been in Angola for only a few days. They opened up with salvos, twenty at a time of the 122mm rockets. Caught in open ground, with no cover at all, 2,000 missiles rained down on the FNLA. Roberto's dreams vanished as his men broke and ran. They fled, leaving weapons and wounded alike. The South Africans kept pounding away but their firepower was very limited compared with the Cubans' 120mms that had twice the range of the 5.5-inch guns. This was an important lesson learnt from the Cubans which the South African arms industry religiously applied in their later development of their famous G5 and G6 artillery systems.

The rout at Quifangondo knocked the FNLA and Zaire out of the war. And it was an embarrassing setback for the SADF which had to call in the navy for their first major intervention of the invasion. Ambrizete, north of Luanda, was chosen as a pick up point for the South Africans who had to make a quick getaway. The old frigates, the SAS *President Kruger* and SAS *President Steyn*, deployed inflatable boats to extract twenty-six personnel successfully from the beach on 28 November. The guns were extracted separately. General Constand Viljoen later confessed that the safety of his soldiers and (temporarily) abandoned field guns made this 'the most difficult night in my operational career'.[6] As thousands more Cubans arrived in Angola, some were assigned to mop up the FNLA limping northwards. Disciplined troops such as the Vietcong could survive heavy bombing and artillery assault by building fox-holes, tunnel networks and by orderly withdrawals and counter-attacks. But the CIA's John Stockwell commented laconically on the retreat: 'The FNLA guerrillas and Mobutu's commandos were not diggers.'

The CIA tried to stabilize the collapsing northern front by organizing the arrival of French and Portuguese mercenaries as well as supplying Roberto with funds to hire British and American soldiers of fortune. The latter included psychopaths and deadbeats with no military experience and two recently retrenched dustmen. Their positive military impact was predictably zero, although the atrocities examined at the Luanda trial of some captured mercenaries provided wonderful ammunition for MPLA propaganda.

As the CIA money dried up, the FNLA retreat turned into anarchy. Zaire's best troops, humiliated and beaten, conducted an orgy of rape, killing, looting and wanton destruction as they withdrew to their own borders. On 11 February 1976 the last FNLA stronghold, São Salvador, fell. It had been the capital and spiritual heart of the Kongo kingdom from 1390 to 1914 and yet many of the Bakongo tribesmen and women who had been ardent, long-term supporters of Roberto welcomed the MPLA and Cubans as liberators.

The SADF had ventured little in terms of assets in the north. In the south, however, the South Africans had committed at least 3,000 men along a front of hundreds of miles. Two days after independence the South Africans occupied Novo Redondo; here the Zulu Taskforce had suffered its heaviest casualties since

General Constand Viljoen: 'The most difficult night in my operational career.' (SADF)

the first days of its lightning advance. From well-placed dug-outs the Cubans unleashed a barrage of rocket fire and mortars. One of the mortar bombs exploded in the middle of the South African column. Eighteen South Africans were wounded and one was killed, the first South African fatality in the southern invasion. The Cubans were now determined to repel the SADF/FNLA/UNITA onslaught. Battlefield constraints and, more important, international politics were now starting to curb Pretoria's big push. The South African advance troops asked for more reinforcements, including a paratrooper drop behind the enemy lines. Both were refused. Zulu was told to sit tight at Novo Redondo (after withdrawing from Port Amboim).

Zulu's advance was the most dramatic but four other taskforces were engaged in Operation SAVANNAH. Foxbat had been formed in mid-October; it originally comprised South African-trained UNITA forces and a squadron of vintage Panhard armoured cars. This group, reinforced with 120 Zairian regulars, guarded the FNLA/UNITA capital at Huambo. On 25 October Foxbat had blocked the Cuban/FAPLA advance on Silva Porto; a Cuban general was killed in the fighting. When Foxbat and Zulu had joined up in mid-November, the South African forces had recaptured virtually all the territory the FNLA and UNITA had lost in the preceding months. At independence, the FNLA forces had held much of the north as well – though they were soon to have it all wrested from them. In the south the SADF commanded a front from Novo Redondo to Santa Comba to Luso in the far east.

Something had to give soon, as Havana started to ship in many more combat troops and equipment despite minor harassment by the US Navy en route. The CIA even considered making a feint against Cuba itself in order to distract Castro's new *conquistadores* from their African adventures. By January 1976 approximately 12,000 Cuban combat troops were in theatre. Besides Cuban/Russian sea transport from the Caribbean, Moscow operated a number of supply routes. For example, Soviet An-22 transports flew to Maya Maya, near Brazzaville in the Congo Republic, where equipment was forwarded to MPLA strongholds north of Luanda. Some Antonovs flew directly from the southern USSR to Luanda or Henrique de Carvalho, stopping only to refuel in Guinea, Mali or Algeria. Soviet cargo vessels delivered small arms in Point Noire in the Congo or to Guinea, which were then ferried to MPLA-held areas. In a well-executed and complex logistical operation, T-34 and T-54 tanks, armoured personnel carriers, MiG-21 fighters, anti-tank missiles, BM-21 rocket-launchers, SAM-7s and AK-47 rifles were transported over great distances to Angola. Moscow was taking its African mission very seriously.

Initially the South African army tried to contain this influx of communist weaponry and troops. Another task force, Orange, was set up on 12 December. It comprised a UNITA battalion, a South African armoured car squadron and a SADF infantry company with artillery. This column occupied the Salazar Bridge over the Cuanza river at the northernmost extremity of UNITA territory. On 15 December Orange fell upon a large group of Cubans near Quibala. The Cubans deployed MiGs and tanks, while South Africans had to rely upon old armoured cars, light reconnaissance aircraft, and Alouette helicopters. Pretoria's 'limited' war was falling apart at the seams.

While Orange was engaged at Quibala, Foxbat fought perhaps the hardest action of the campaign at the so-called 'Bridge 14', north of Santa Comba and over the Nhia River. Foxbat consisted then of three UNITA/FNLA companies, an SADF infantry company, a squadron of Elands, a company of engineers and a mortar platoon supported by eight 5.5-inch (140mm) and 25-pounder guns. A Cuban/FAPLA group, armed with several battalions of BM-21 122mm rocket-launchers, had blown up the bridge and entrenched itself in the hills beyond the river. It was the morning of 10 December, exactly a month after a similar Cuban ploy had routed Roberto's advance on Luanda. There, time and time again, the Cubans had deployed the Stalin Organs to great effect. Each rocket pallet of forty tubes was usually mounted on a rotating platform. A textbook deployment was a battalion of eighteen that could fire 720 rockets in thirty seconds. These could be fired in salvo, 'rippled' or selected individually. The vehicle, the Ural 375, had excellent cross-country capability – particularly important in Angola's rough terrain. But the Ural had to be parked obliquely to the target to avoid blast damage to the unprotected cab, although this was not always done and occasionally the cab was blown away. Despite the noise and psychological impact of the BM-21s elsewhere, they did not prove to be decisive against the SADF near Bridge 14. The troopers nicknamed the rocket launchers *Rooi Oog* – Afrikaans for Red Eye.

At Bridge 14 a company of Foxbat sappers, protected by two Elands, examined the remains of the blown bridge. After they had de-activated a number of mines, the engineers started to rebuild the bridge using local material: scrap iron and bluegum logs. The Cuban/FAPLA force did not react as the engineers constructed a footbridge to secure a bridgehead on the opposite bank. But as soon as an attempt was made to rebuild the main bridge to carry the vehicles, the Cubans opened up with the BM-21s and mortars. Shells exploded all round the engineers but the bridge was never hit. The sappers withdrew and the SADF replied with less powerful but more accurate artillery. During the night a small group of Reconnaissance Commandos went over to the other side to scout and create some mayhem. The next morning in the mists and later rain the column crossed over the new bridge, despite the heavy but ineffectual fire. Foxbat then stormed the Cuban/FAPLA positions. Pro-communist sources admitted that this battle was a disaster for the Cubans, who lost over 200 of their men, and their commander, Commandant Raul Diaz Arguelles. Over 200 FAPLA were also killed. The South Africans had lost four men. Among the equipment captured were ten 76.2mm field guns, twenty-two 120mm mortars and five BM-21s. Crucially, one of the BM-21 multiple rocket launchers was salvaged intact. It was taken back to South Arica where Armscor used it as the pattern for their own Valkiri. The SADF became absolutely determined to remedy its artillery deficiencies.

Later a film in Afrikaans was made about the battle (*Brug 14*), in which one of the heroes of the battle, Sergeant Danny Roxo, shot from the hip 'like Audie Murphy', killing twelve FAPLA/Cubans who rushed him. For this and other actions, Roxo received his country's highest gallantry award, the Honoris Crux. Other soldiers were given the award posthumously. The film only slightly glamourized the successful battle that proved that speed, surprise and aggressive offence can tip the balance in favour of numerically weaker forces with fewer heavy weapons.

In December another taskforce, X-Ray, had been formed at the specific request of Savimbi to guard the Benguela railway. X-Ray split into three roving combat groups, which conducted mopping-up operations east of Bucaco. The fifth task force was the hastily evacuated group which had been backing Roberto in the north.

Such was the highwater mark of Operation SAVANNAH. Despite the claims of higher numbers, the SADF insisted that it had not committed more than 3,000 of its own troops with back-up of a small number of armoured cars, light planes and helicopters. Few could doubt that the South Africans performed well in military terms, not least given their small numbers and light weapons. As John Stockwell concluded:

> The South African armoured columns … teamed with UNITA to make the most effective military strike force ever see in black Africa, exploding through the MPLA/Cuban ranks in a blitzkrieg which in November almost won the war.

This was an old African lesson, however; good trained black soldiery with excellent white officers and NCOs had proved the value of the Askari principle in German East Africa, Kenya and Rhodesia and elsewhere. The SADF had been outgunned and outnumbered, however. Of particular concern to Pretoria was the presence of the MiG-17s and MiG-21s. The superior firepower enabled the MPLA to go back on the offensive in the south. FAPLA also began to counter with guerrilla harassment behind the over-extended lines of their opponents. On 18 December Zulu suffered further losses around Quibala. Elsewhere, four SADF mechanics, who had accidently strayed into MPLA-controlled territory, were captured. The captives were paraded as proof of South African aggression. Pretoria was pilloried internationally. An increasing number of African states that had previously condemned Cuban and Soviet adventurism now switched to the side of the MPLA. On 19 December the US Senate voted to block all additional covert funds, thus forcing the CIA to abandon its allies in Angola. Pretoria, however, was persuaded by Washington and a number of conservative black states to continue fighting until 22 January 1976 when the OAU voted on which party to recognize as the Angolan government. The vote was an inconclusive 22-22 stalemate but the MPLA was nevertheless gaining ground rapidly. Kenneth Kaunda, who had encouraged Pretoria's gamble, also changed sides and, with a wave of his ubiquitous white handkerchief, dismissed his old allies as 'racists'. The South Africans were now left high and dry.

The SADF withdrawal duly began on 22 January 1976. On 11 February the rebel capital of Huambo fell. The FNLA had given up. UNITA went back into the bush to fight on with a few thousand guerrillas. As a face-saving device, Pretoria obtained from the MPLA government the promise not to interfere with the southern hydro-electric schemes. South African forces remained in an occupied strip along the southern border until the end of March. Cuban/FAPLA units finally arrived at the Namibian border on 1 April, a suitably ironic day to confirm the realization of the nightmare scenario the South African invasion was intended to forestall.

### *What the invasion meant*

The defeat snatched from the jaws of victory meant that the stature of American and South African foreign policies were diminished throughout the continent, and elsewhere. Kissinger had tried to win friends in Africa but his first excursion had been a dramatic failure – though that didn't stop him from trying to deal with the Rhodesian imbroglio a few months later, with equally unpromising results. One of the foundations of US failures in the region had been the Tar Baby option which discounted the longterm role of Southern African guerrilla movements. The Lisbon *putsch* caught the CIA completely offguard. The agency then fundamentally underestimated the money and weapons Moscow was prepared to commit. The American financial contribution was not just small by comparison but was also very poorly spent. As John Stockwell confessed, 'For the CIA, nothing had worked.'

His revealing account of CIA operations (*In Search of Enemies*) contained a long list of shortcomings. Much of the weaponry sent through Zaire lacked ammunition, instructors, training manuals or simply failed to work, such as the SAM-7s bought from Israel. The Swift patrol craft, he wrote, 'disintegrated in short weeks of Zaireans' pounding misuse'. Twenty-four rubber boats were simply 'lost'. Much of the CIA cash slipped into Mobutu's personal coffers. 'Most serious of all,' concluded Stockwell, 'the United States was exposed, dishonoured and discredited in the eyes of the world.'

Like Pretoria, Washington ignored Clausewitz in that they had no clear political aims for their intervention in Angola. The USA vacillated from a policy of intervention to tacit acceptance of the MPLA to possible intervention again (in late 1976) and then veered back to tacit recognition. The last three stages occurred in less than a year. Initially, Washington wanted merely to stalemate the MPLA. But US aid was too small to win, and yet too large to be kept secret. Thus a well-disclosed debacle resulted. It was argued at the time that Kissinger, and Pretoria, should have gone for broke. There was some evidence that Kissinger, in late 1976, did indeed consider completing the 'unfinished revolution' in Angola by injecting UNITA with a massive dose of American military support. Congress, however, feared a replay of Vietnam. Kissinger hovered like Banquo's host at the table of the newly-elected President Jimmy Carter. The lacklustre Carter administration, while not formally recognizing the MPLA, moved towards a compromise with Neto's regime in Luanda, partly in the hope of generating stability in Zaire and Zambia and, crucially, finessing the removal of Cuban troops, which in turn could have triggered the independence of Namibia. The Cubans remained, as did the stigma of Pretoria's blunder. If Washington had to suffer a political embarrassment, then Pretoria had to endure a traumatic political defeat.

President Jimmy Carter moved towards a compromise with the MPLA regime (Library of Congress)

The military withdrawal, after nearly reaching Luanda, rankled among some senior SADF officers. As in Israeli messes after the retreat from Egypt following the Yom Kippur war, muttering could be heard about 'victorious soldiers and defeatist politicans'.[7] But the widely accepted view (especially in South Africa) that the SADF retrocession was caused by purely political factors was not accurate. Certainly the self-imposed limitations on the invasion force were largely political but the fighting revealed a number of *military* deficiencies, not least the need for longer-range artillery and better armoured vehicles. After hinting at some of the big-ticket deficiencies just before the final withdrawal, Prime Minister John Vorster said, 'Only big powers can effect this arsenal. It is certainly beyond our limits.' After years of counter-insurgency in Namibia, without any official South African military fatalities, the toll in Angola was forty-three killed. The white electorate's distress at finally being told about such a sacrifice in lives for a war which the government originally said did not exist was compounded by the embarrassment of seeing in the media the first-ever SADF prisoners of war paraded as MPLA propaganda.

Nevertheless, political factors were paramount: Pretoria had been left in the lurch by its allies. It was a lesson that the apartheid government would not forget. As Vorster put it so succinctly, 'When it comes to the worst, South Africa stands alone.' Above all, Washington had turned its back. Far from cementing South African-American ties, the failed joint venture had soured relations, soon to be made worse by the effects of President Carter's substitution of Kissinger's cool *realpolitik* with self-righteous moralizing. At least Moscow and Beijing as well as Pretoria could understand the style and content of the latter-day Metternich. No-one, allied or hostile, could fathom Carter's patently sincere but ineffectual foreign policy. Kissinger had talked of defeating communism in black Africa; now Carter was sermonizing on majority rule in white southern Africa. Meanwhile, Paris had been at its cynical best. After nurturing closer ties with Pretoria, via proxies in Ivory Coast and Gabon, and cheering on the SADF advance in Angola, in a sudden *volte face* the French government embargoed vital arms supplies to South Africa. Pretoria's détente with black southern African states was ruptured, even with those countries that had almost begged Pretoria to move into Angola. Kaunda no longer described Russia and Cuba as a 'plundering tiger and her cubs'. Tigers, he had no doubt been informed, were not to be found on the African continent.

While foreigners were reading about the invasion in minute detail, on the domestic front the blanket censorship generated widespread disillusionment with the government, especially at the same time as the unfolding of the Muldergate scandal. That prompted ministers to fall on their swords but no heads rolled for the Angolan disaster. No minister or officer resigned. The whites were partly used to living in the 'mushroom club' and perhaps most *wanted* to believe the government line. Opinion polls soon registered support for the government's *post hoc* rationalizations for the invasion that said, in essence, that the republic had struck a mighty blow against Soviet expansionism. White quiescence was not replicated in the much more politicized black communities. Many blacks perceived the SADF's withdrawal as a military defeat of Afrikaner racism by African nationalism; some blacks depicted events as the triumph of socialism over Western imperialism. At the nub of these interpretations was the conviction that the bubble of apparent Afrikaner invincibility had been pricked. The so-called 'awe factor' – the alleged black fear of, and respect for, white repressive power – had been severely undermined. The humiliation of the SADF's exit from Angola in March forged a direct psychological continuum with the Soweto uprising in June. Soweto youngsters knew precious little Portuguese but they could readily chant *Viva MPLA* and *A Luta Continua* – The Struggle Continues.

A Western diplomat in Lusaka summed up the repercussions of the Angola fiasco:

> I sometimes think that South Africa went into this war to assure an MPLA victory. They went in with a weak force at the wrong time, and got out on the wrong foot. In between they lied and lied to a world that knew the truth.

So much obloquy and for what? Pretoria had no clear political aims for its war effort. Obviously it wanted to influence the outcome of the war at the expense of the MPLA. This was a woolly ambition, not a precise war aim. Did the South Africans anticipate the possibilities of a rapid Cuban and Soviet armed intervention? Probably not. The Americans had not expected it and presumably their intelligence on Cuban/Soviet intentions was better than Pretoria's. The CIA shared much of its Africa-related information with South Africa's Bureau of State Security. Perhaps both fed off the same misperceptions and Chinese whispers. Once the communist military bridge was operational, did the SADF believe it could defeat the pro-MPLA alliance? Or, more modestly, was Pretoria backing the FNLA and UNITA to strengthen their hands should a coalition government with the MPLA finally emerge from the bloody transition from colonialism to black rule. Or rather, was Pretoria hoping to Balkanize Angola by prompting a Katanga-style secession in, at least, southern Angola? A greater Ovamboland, covering northern Namibia and southern Angola, had always been one of Pretoria's pet schemes to divide and rule. It seems likely that Pretoria had juggled with all these scenarios and, in the end, simply hoped for the best.

Precise war aims were missing and so was able political leadership. Political direction, such it was, appeared to have been centred on Vorster and P.W. Botha. The cabinet and the State Security Council were left out in the cold. The senior military commanders and military intelligence provided the prime input, even though both the influential chief of BOSS, General Hendrik van den Bergh, and the department of foreign affairs preferred a hands-off policy, as in Mozambique. Van den Bergh, who usually had the ear of the prime minister, was personally hostile to the growing influence of military intelligence. (During his regular meetings with his Rhodesian counterpart, Ken Flower, van den Bergh enjoyed regaling him with a multitude of stories about the blunders made by SADF military intelligence. According to Flower's discussions with me, van den Bergh was particularly bitter about the Angolan escapade.) Apparently a number of US intelligence sources outside the CIA warned van den Bergh early on about the precarious nature of American commitment to the war, And the traditionally dovish department of foreign affairs stressed that South Africa could score an own goal if she broke her (purported) golden rule of not interfering in her neighbours' affairs. Direct armed intervention could boomerang, said the doves, and generate intervention against South Africa, not least further economic sanctions. P.W. Botha had the full confidence of the military commanders. The long-serving defence minister had temporarily eclipsed van den Bergh in the role of primary security advisor to the prime minister. In sum, Vorster sided with the hawks and allowed the operational discretion of his commanders to dictate grand strategy. The military dimensions of this strategy were well-executed, especially as the SADF fought with one hand tied behind its back. The military offensive had been divided into four escalating phases, with phase four being the capture of Luanda. The decision to cross from one phase to the next rested with Vorster. On the ground, however, operational imperatives, with the overzealous commanders emphasizing local requirements, encouraged a rapid shift through the first three gears, despite Vorster's prevarication. Thus the tactical tail came to wag the strategic dog, with predictable results.

The invasion of Angola altered the balance of civil-military relations in South Africa, for a decade or more. Paradoxically, P.W. Botha, destined soon for the premiership, became even more determined to forge a comprehensive politico-military framework for his 'total strategy'. This implied the dominance of clear-cut political goals. Simultaneously, the SADF embellished its newly acquired status as a major quasi-independent actor in national decisionmaking. Greater military influence *and* stronger (that is, more authoritarian) political leadership were to be the hallmarks of the dawning Botha era. The two contradictory tendencies could operate in tandem mainly because of Botha's symbiosis with his generals. But this dangerous equilibrium, the elevation of military force to the status of primary political principle, became *the* problem, not an answer to the fundamental dilemmas of white supremacy in South Africa. After the Angolan invasion, the generals said, in effect, to the politicians 'give us your backing and next time we will do much better'. Meanwhile, the SADF swiftly applied the tactical lessons of its first taste of conventional warfare since Korea. A new generation of armoured vehicles, missiles, artillery and aircraft, skilfully adapted to local conditions, but also suitable for the export market, began to roll out of Armscor factories.

South Africa forged an impressive military arsenal but its political problems accelerated exponentially. The local debits of the failed invasion were immediately obvious. The MPLA, always hostile to Pretoria, became an even more implacable foe. And Savimbi, by supping with the devil, had lost his chance of playing a moderating role in Angolan politics. States throughout the region, particularly Mozambique, grew even more suspicious of Pretoria and more susceptible to Moscow's blandishments. All this made America's role much harder, especially in Rhodesia, where the mounting conflict was to draw away much more of South Africa's defence budget. For white Rhodesians, the bloodletting in Angola recalled the Congo's slaughter of Europeans and made them even more paranoid about black rule, and thus even more determined to play upon white racist sympathies 'down south'. The MPLA victory had also boosted the morale of Zimbabwean insurgents, thus further complicating Pretoria's search for a black 'moderate' leader to replace the stubborn Ian Smith: better a Muzorewa than a Neto or a Machel.

South Africa's withdrawal in March 1976 was not an end but the beginning of a different kind of war in Angola. The MPLA became the officially recognized government (though Washington still held out against recognition). Once it had won – for the time being – its own war, the MPLA proceeded to support the poorly-organized guerrilla campaigns of not only SWAPO but also the ANC. Bases for South African insurgents were set up in central Angola, while numerous SWAPO camps were re-established in the south. Over the next decade or so the SADF attacked these insurgent bases regularly. The SADF's self-limitations of 1975-76 were whittled away as the levels of manpower and of the sophistication of weaponry rose on both sides. The South Africans often applied their considerable strength in short, sharp strikes as well as later re-occupying large swathes of southern Angola. The continued presence of the Cuban army, and the upgrading of FAPLA, armed with modern Soviet hardware, dictated a measure of caution. Pretoria always did its best to avoid any hint of a local SADF 'defeat' again. The increasing deployment of modern Soviet weaponry, particularly air-defence radar and combat aircraft, made that a real possibility by the mid-1980s. Meanwhile, the entrenchment of the Soviet and Cuban position prompted Pretoria to be all the more reluctant to withdraw from Namibia. The pattern of events in Angola strongly influenced the very distinct but inevitably related bush war in Africa's last colony.

# *Chapter 5*

# Namibia (1966 to 1976)

'The land God made in anger.' That was one lyrical designation for Namibia, or South West Africa as it was called before independence. It *is* an angry tough landscape but also beautiful; and very big, albeit with a small population of today around two million. It is the same size as France, Belgium, and what was once West Germany combined. It boasts the second lowest population density on earth (after Outer Mongolia). Yet the wild symphony of harsh desert, lunar landscapes, pastoral serenity and almost untouched wildlife formed also the reluctant requiem for the longest and perhaps one of the most under-reported of African guerrilla wars. Never had so few fought so bitterly for so long for so much territory in this, Africa's last colony. Pretoria had interceded in other colonial wars; in Namibia it had its very own colony to run, albeit illegally held, in defiance of international law and world opinion.

Namibia was, arguably, the final unresolved legacy of the German defeat in 1918. In the 1880s the German Reich had begun to colonize the territory during the 'scramble for Africa'. Almost prophetically, the first commissioner was Dr H.E. Göring, the father of the infamous Nazi leader. When the Herero tribe, and later also the Nama, rebelled against imperial rule, the German authorities issued an extermination proclamation (*Vernichtungsbefehl*). About 70 per cent of the black population in the centre and south of the colony were exterminated.[1]

Just what is it about Germans and extermination policies? The Germans made even racist white South Africans look like paragons of rectitude. In 1915 South African forces occupied the colony as part of the Entente war effort. In 1920 South Africa was mandated the territory as a 'sacred trust' by the League of Nations. To the Afrikaner leaders, 'trust' meant annexation. In 1922, during the Bondelswart uprising, the South African air force bombed the rebels into submission. Over a hundred men, women and children were killed, a tragedy, but a small number compared with the previous German genocide.

After the demise of the League, Pretoria commenced its long legal wrangle with the UN over the status of the mandate. Regardless of legal debate, South Africa began the process of integration. The territory's whites (about 14 per cent of the population) were granted representation in the South African parliament in 1949. Apartheid was entrenched. Much of the best land and all the political power was

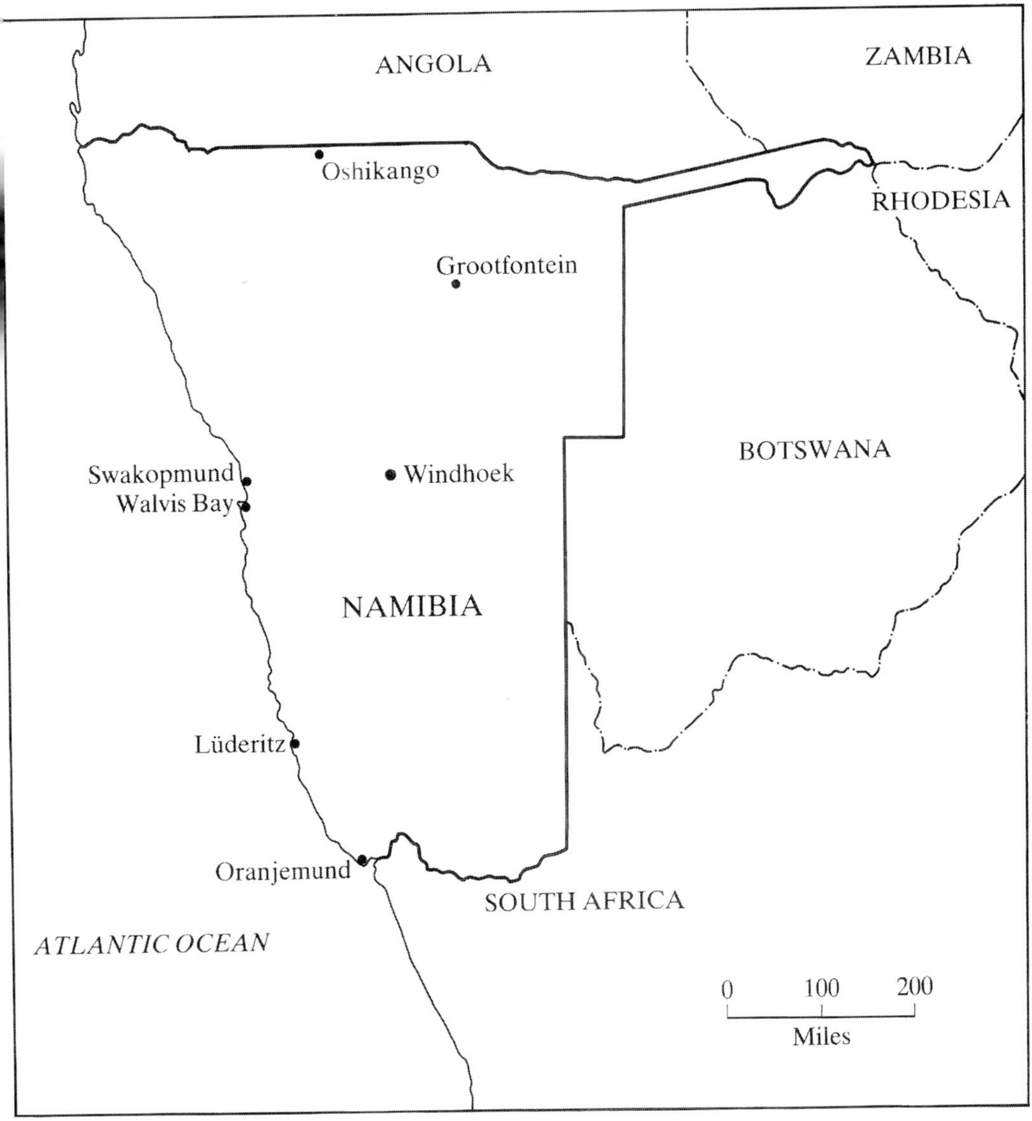


South West Africa/Namibia

reserved for whites, while the ten other ethnic groups were offered various degrees of limited autonomy. It was bantustans again, but with a Namibian face.

The UN continued to protest at South Africa's behaviour in Namibia but to little avail. In 1958 Andimba (Herman) Toivo ja Toivo, a leading black nationalist, sent a petition to the world body in a recorded message hidden in an old copy of

*Treasure Island.* He also wrote to the Pope and to Queen Elizabeth. The letter to the Queen was, however, duly returned with a note saying it should be forwarded through her representative, the governor-general of South Africa. (South Africa was still in the Commonwealth.) The small and quarrelsome group of nationalists, mainly from the dominant Ovambo tribe, decided that, should the UN fail to act, Namibia should become a British protectorate, like Basutoland (now Lesotho), Bechuanaland (Botswana) and Swaziland. There were even demands for the territory to be designated a protectorate of the USA. Clearly, the nationalists were desperate men.

In July 1966, on a technicality, the International Court of Justice delivered a non-committal legal opinion on the status of Namibia. Pretoria interpreted this as a victory and Namibia's 100,000 whites were jubilant. 'The bars in Windhoek stayed open all night,' wrote one reporter from the Namibian capital. In October, however, the UN General Assembly revoked the mandate and in July 1971 the International Court of Justice declared South Africa's presence to be illegal. And yet no amount of legal argument was going to lever Pretoria out of what had become *de facto* a fifth province of South Africa. Namibia was set to take the same route as its minder: both black and white nationalists talked past each other and left the diminishing band of 'moderates' lost in the middle of nowhere. Many of the Namibian nationalists had worked in South Africa alongside ANC activists. The same pattern emerged: petitions, passive disobedience, strikes and, finally, armed struggle. In both countries, entreaties fell on deaf ears and protest invoked repression. The Afrikaner obsession with ethnicity was rigorously applied to the administration of the new 'province'. But here the divide-and-rule tactics did prove unusually divisive for a number of reasons. Firstly, some kind of decentralization was almost inevitable in a vast and often arid land where communities, frequently dirt-poor, were widely and thinly dispersed. Decentralization did not have to be the same as ethnic segregation of course, yet Namibians were very ethnically conscious no matter how often their politicians substituted 'Herero-speaking' or 'Ovambo-speaking' as tribal euphemisms. Secondly, the ten smaller ethnic groups (ranging from the 7 per cent Herero population to the 2.8 per cent San, Bushmen, fretted about the predominance of the 50 per cent Ovambo group). The whites were themselves made up of sometimes rival groups speaking German, English or Afrikaans (as well as Portuguese). They were especially hostile to any notion of universal franchise that could swamp them with the Ovambo which many whites equated with SWAPO (the South West African People's Organization).

Pretoria's propagandists always played upon the ethnic fears of the Ovambo population power, especially after April 1960 when SWAPO, originally largely an Ovambo party, was formed. SWAPO's previous designation had been the Ovamboland People's Organization. Through persistence, and some ruthlessness, SWAPO gradually came to be identified as a major *national* symbol of independence for all Namibia's ethnic groups.

Sam Nujoma, the SWAPO leader

In 1961 Samuel Daniel Nujoma and other SWAPO leaders set up their HQ in Dar es Salaam, Africa's oasis of revolution. Nujoma was to prove a determined and longlasting guerrilla leader. Born in 1929, the first of eleven children of a poor farming family, he worked in a general store, a whaling station in Walvis Bay, and then as a cleaner for the South African Railways, while trying to improve on his poor education. He experienced the hardships of black contract labour and moved towards the trade union movement. He came to despair of political reform at home or the UN's ability – or will – to oust Pretoria, so he supported SWAPO's decision to prepare for protracted war. Training camps for the initial cadres were established in Tanzania and Zambia and, like all the other alphabet soups of African insurgents, were equipped by the Chinese and Soviets. Guerrillas began to infiltrate into Namibia during 1965 and they established bases in Ovamboland. The terrain is suitable for partisan warfare. With the exception of a small section in the north-west, along the Cunene river, the Angolan/Namibian border is a straight cartographic line. In the centre the Ovamboland/Angolan border runs straight for 280 miles. The line divides, in theory, the Angolan Ovambo from their Namibian kinsfolk. Ovamboland is exceptionally flat, covered in the west by often dense *mopani* bush and in the east by forest. In the sub-tropical climate, the rainy season, usually October to April, provides ample water and luxuriant foliage for guerrilla penetration. Anthills are abundant, all for some reason pointing north. And almost everywhere, too, there used to be *Cuca* shops: tiny general stores with very little on sale but which sported grandiose titles such as 'California Inn' or 'Country Club'. The Ovambo were said to be born capitalists and yet many of them were driven in to the arms of the Moscow-leaning SWAPO.

The Namibian war began at 7.30 am on 26 August 1966. A South African security police unit of thirty-two men, led by Major Theunis Swanepoel, attacked the Ongulumbashe SWAPO base inside Ovamboland. The guerrillas were expecting an attack and had decided to stand and fight. In the heliborne assault two insurgents were killed and nine were captured, after a brief resistance lasting two minutes. A sizeable hoard of equipment and documentation was also seized. No South Africans were injured, despite (according to South African accounts) an irregular application of irregular warfare. One SWAPO warrior, Agapepe Ipangelwa, deployed a bow and arrow tipped with poison, though the other fighters were armed with AK-47s. As with the Sinoia 'battle' in the same year, which marked the onset of the Rhodesian war, this guerrilla struggle started with a military fiasco. And as with many similar African liberation movements, constant military setbacks were nearly always transformed into great victories by glowing propaganda statements issued in faraway foreign capitals. In the case of Ongulumbashe, a SWAPO statement – claiming fifteen South Africans had been killed – concluded with a dramatic sentence: 'Rivers of blood have to be crossed but, as night follows day, victory – will be ours.' It seemed vainglorious at the time and yet it was proved completely accurate twenty-four bloody years later.

In 1966 SWAPO's prospects of military victory looked decidedly slim. Access to Ovamboland was exceptionally difficult, especially from the first SWAPO bases in Zambia. Guerrillas were forced to make their way on foot via the 250-mile-long panhandle of the Caprivi Strip. Carrying heavy equipment for weeks across sandy soil was arduous. Dangerous wild animals would sometimes make things worse. South African Police (SAP) patrols took even bigger bites from SWAPO morale, and politically hostile locals from rival tribes would often report sightings of armed strangers to chiefs in the pay of Pretoria. And, until 1974, the Portuguese patrolled parts of southern Angola – not very well, but they were still a deterrent. Initially, UNITA guerrillas helped their kinsmen in SWAPO but later turned on them because of SWAPO's alliance with their enemy, the MPLA. It all added up to a political and logistical nightmare for SWAPO.

Caprivi continued to be an international pain in the diplomatic rear. Long after Namibian independence in 1990 amid the complex tribal groupings some wanted independence for Caprivi too, and a minor civil war ensued during the latter part of the 1990s. South Africa had encouraged the micro-nationalism from 1976 partly because of its tribal divide and rule. Of course the European colonialists had stirred the pot even earlier. In 1890 the German Chancellor, Leo von Caprivi, purchased the strip (*Caprivizipfel)* from the British (as well as gaining Heligoland

Traditional Ovambo huts

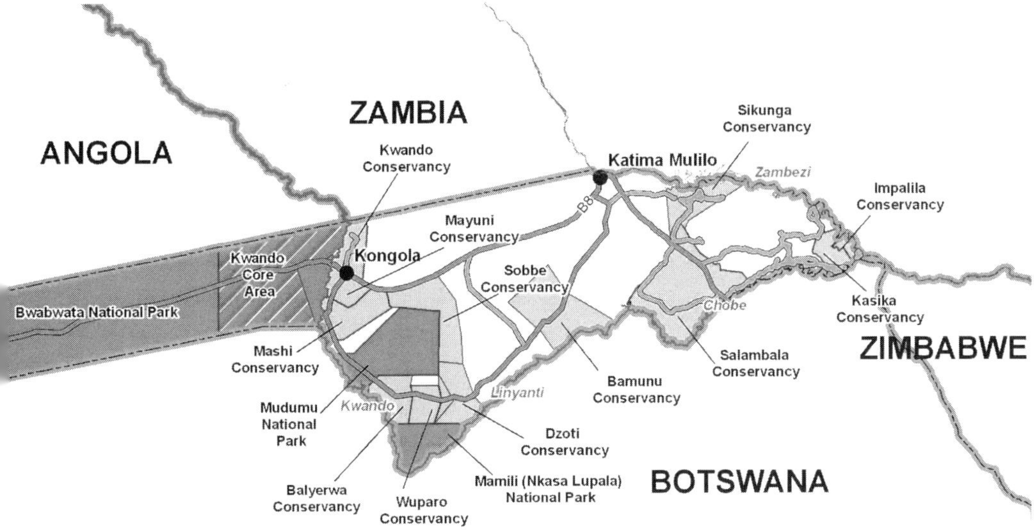


The Caprivi Strip

in the North Sea) in exchange for full British control in Zanzibar. The Germans had hoped to reach out and touch their possessions in German East Africa by navigating along the Zambezi, without recognizing fully the problems of rapids and obstacles the size of Victoria Falls. The former chancellor, Otto von Bismarck, said von Caprivi had given up 'his trousers in exchange for a button'. The Caprivi Strip, also called the Okavango Strip, became embroiled in the Angolan, Namibian, South African and Zimbabwean wars, not least when Rhodesian special forces blew up the Kazangula ferry. The strip was argued over well into the current century when Kazangula in southern Zambia formed the international boundaries with Botswana, Namibia and also Zimbabwe (for a few hundred yards, one of the world's shortest borders).

The area had tremendous beauty and splendid wildlife. When I first wandered around the region in the 1980s I regularly saw four to five hundred elephants roaming on their traditional corridor from southern Angola thorough Caprivi into Botswana and the famous game reserves such as Chobe. I was travelling with South African forces usually and sometimes with their Bushmen troops. The guerrillas had a much harder time. A SWAPO commander, Rahimisa Kahimise, summed up the difficulties of infiltrating along the Caprivi route in the late 1960s.

> We had to walk a long distance from Zambia through Angola. Some of our people died in Angola and some missions could not reach Namibia because

> they had to fight through Angola .... The battles we were involved in, most of them were in Angola with the Portuguese ... but even the South African soldiers were also involved in Angola and really we worked hard because by then we had to train the new recruits and we also had to fight to get food as we had to walk long distances and we had to try and get transport, also after a battle then you must have more ammunition .... I could say by the time we crossed into Namibia we were a bit tired but a bit more experienced.[2]

SWAPO persevered. They sabotaged government installations, killed pro-government blacks and occasionally took on the security forces deliberately. Through such 'armed propaganda' they persuaded and/or intimidated the increasingly politicized Ovambo population. SWAPO's military forces, PLAN (the People's Liberation Army of Namibia), were countered by increasingly sophisticated South African counter-insurgency techniques, supervised initially by the SAP and later by the SADF. The internal political wing of SWAPO, based in the capital, Windhoek, remained a legal party, even though it was constantly harassed by the security police. In contrast to the ANC but similar to London's distinction between Sinn Féin and the Irish Republican Army, Pretoria decided not to ban SWAPO's domestic wing. Such limited, and unusual, forbearance was partly a recognition that South Africa could not defeat Namibian nationalism by brute force alone. Hence the policy of 'co-optive dominance', enticing 'moderate' nationalists with limited power and sufficient room for their snouts in the trough. Thus Pretoria created a two-track policy: of keeping the UN politely at arm's length, while attempting to destroy SWAPO's military wing; and simultaneously encouraging 'internal' black nationalists, including SWAPO members, to accept a domestic settlement engineered by South Africa and its white allies in Namibia (and Europe). Always pretending to juggle with two entirely different balls – a UN settlement or UDI – Pretoria quietly entrenched its own power in the 1960s and 1970s. By the late 1970s Namibia had almost become a SADF fiefdom.

On the purely military level, the SADF conducted an almost textbook counter-insurgency campaign in the territory. The lessons of Malaya, Vietnam, Algeria, Rhodesia, Angola and Mozambique were skilfully synthesized and applied, often with the assistance of ex-Rhodesian officers and occasionally Israeli experts.[3] Like the Bourbons, Pretoria had learned little on the political level, at least as far as Namibia was concerned in the 1970s. Above all, Pretoria was determined to prevent a military defeat in the field. Until 1976, the SADF was entirely on top of SWAPO. Indeed, the security forces tended to regard SWAPO more as a public nuisance than a military threat.

Nevertheless, SWAPO did tie up thousands of security force members and SWAPO's political activity did tilt South Africa closer to pariah status. Like

Pretoria, SWAPO was running a dual track: fighting and talking. The volatile Sam Nujoma, the external guerrilla leader, looked around Africa and judged that time was on his side.

For its part, Pretoria was buying time to build up internal proxies and to destroy SWAPO's domestic political base. During 1966 to 1977, the security police arrested thirty-eight SWAPO leaders, including John Ya Otto, the acting secretary-general, and Ja Toivo. Before the trial, under the Terrorism Act of June 1967, both men claimed they were tortured. Ya Otto described his treatment thus:

> When electricity tears through your body, you cannot think, let alone speak. I discovered that for the [SAP] Special Branch this was the last stage of priming their detainees for co-operation – the last torture before sitting down to 'talk reason'.... Each time if felt as though a bomb of a thousand sharp needles was exploding inside me, tearing my guts apart, pushing my eyes out from their sockets, bursting my skin open in a dozen places.[4]

When the SWAPO leaders were finally put in the dock in June 1967, Ja Toivo was elected to speak for the group. Addressing the South African judge, he declared:

> We are Namibians and not South Africans. We do not now, and will not in the future, recognize your right to govern us; to make laws for us in which we had no say; to treat our country as if it were your private property and us as if you were our masters. We have always regarded South Africa as an intruder in our country.

After the trial, in which the main SWAPPO leaders were sentenced to long terms of imprisonment, PLAN stepped up its armed propaganda on the border. Recruitment was increased as was infiltration through the Caprivi. The initial, and successful, counter-insurgency operations were conducted by the SAP, for a number of reasons. As in Rhodesia, Pretoria wanted to portray the conflict as policemen versus armed criminals. Secondly, the security police controlled an excellent informer network. Thirdly, the army had little COIN experience at this time and certainly lacked an efficient intelligence-gathering apparatus. The SAP stifled PLAN's first forays: there was little effective insurgency between 1969 and 1970. In 1971, however, PLAN began its long love affair with the landmine. Then in December 1971 SWAPO organized a widespread strike. Attacks on 'collaborators' with the 'Boers' were increased. In the first Ovamboland homeland elections of August 1973 only 2.3 per cent dared vote, in the face of the SWAPO boycott. (In 1975, however, Pretoria claimed a 55 per cent turnout in fresh elections.)

From February 1972 martial law effectively operated in Ovamboland. Floggings and torture became commonplace. The various churches increasingly stepped

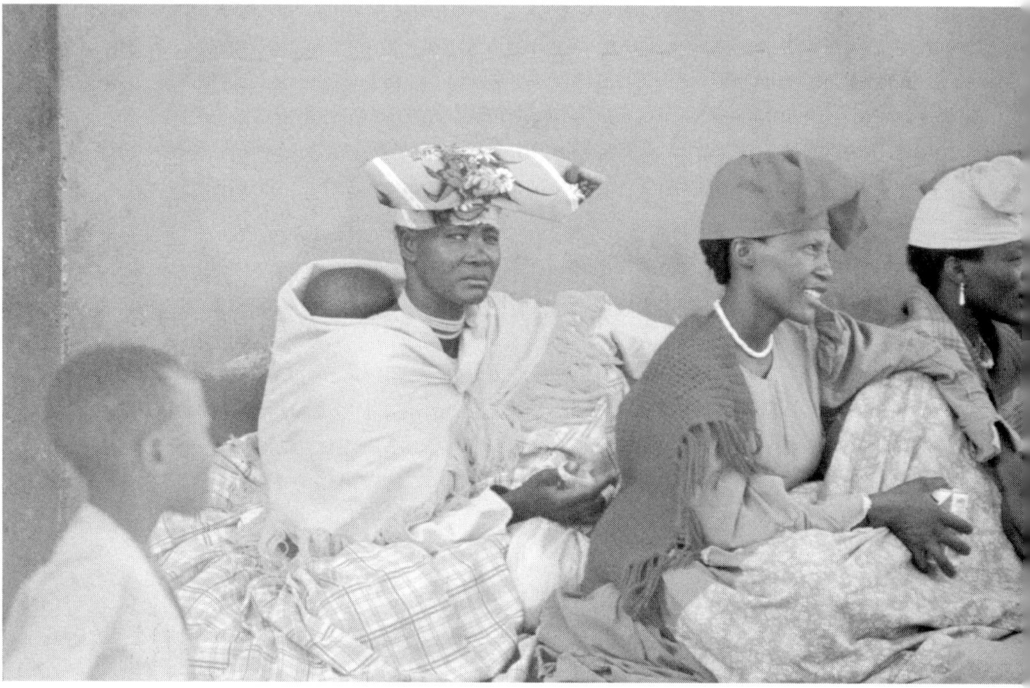

The population has many distinct ethnic groups. A picture of Herero women in traditional dress taken by the author

in to denounce excesses by the South Africans, although often similar outrages by SWAPO went apparently unnoticed by the anxious clerics. In December 1973 the UN General Assembly voted to recognize SWAPO as the 'authentic' representative of the Namibian people, a gesture that was to bedevil the UN's claims, later, to be able impartially to monitor elections in the territory. Pretoria of course felt disinclined to recognize the authenticity or the impartiality. By mid-1974, according to South African sources, the security forces had lost eleven men, the majority of them policemen killed by mines.

In 1974 the army took over command of the 'operational area' in northern Namibia. The SAP was clearly overstretched. And the army was determined to dominate the COIN programme in a more subtle fashion. Hearts and minds were needed, the army top brass had decided. Above all, the scene was shifting dramatically in Portuguese Africa. After the Lisbon coup, Portuguese troops began to move out of southern Africa very rapidly. Suddenly, SWAPO was offered an inviting 1,000-mile border to cross. The MPLA and Eastern bloc advisers provided arms, bases and training. By mid-1976, PLAN strength was perhaps 2,000 trained cadres; by 1978 it was approximately 10,000.

SWAPO was shaping up to be a more deadly adversary. The Portuguese scuttle was SWAPO's first real breakthrough in ten years of relatively fruitless campaigning. As with the Zimbabwean guerrillas in 1975-76, however, internal fratricide ravaged SWAPO. Dissident leaders, such as Andreas Shipanga, were imprisoned and PLAN insurgents in Zambia mutinied. The usual African cocktail – tribal, ideological and personality clashes, stirred up by 'imperialist' agents – was blamed. And, on the ground in southern Angola, PLAN and UNITA, once on/off allies became bitter enemies. This suited the SADF, which expanded its infrastructure along the entire border. Troop levels were augmented, especially after the South African withdrawal from Angola in March 1976. The figures for South African troop levels varied widely according to the ideological flavour of the analyst, but the anti-apartheid sources suggested that the number went from 15,000 in June 1974 to 45,000 in 1976 and reached 100,000, it was claimed, by the early 1980s.[5] This last figure, issued by leading anti-apartheid sources, was too high, especially bearing in mind – unlike the US army in Vietnam – the very lean ratio of combat troops to logistic tail in the SADF. Whatever the precise figures, after the abortive invasion, Pretoria's defence planners grew increasingly concerned about the SWAPO-Cuban-MPLA axis.

For the next decade and more, Pretoria's strategy was primarily to prevent any kind of SWAPO military success against the SADF. The 'demonstration effect' would have been a dangerous encouragement to the stirring black masses inside South Africa. Thus the SADF tried hard to destroy SWAPO's military options by enfeebling PLAN and the MPLA/Cuban infrastructure behind it, and at the same to create 'moderate' internal rivals to SWAPO's growing political ascendancy inside Namibia. But, like Topsy, the war in Angola just grew and grew, and South Africa's allies in Windhoek looked more and more like puppets. Pretoria simply failed to keep Namibia on its twin-track route to Pretoria-guided independence. South African policy began to wobble on both international and Namibian fronts, as well as being sucked into the black hole of endless and intensifying conflict in Angola, The result? The dirty little war in this last, almost forgotten, colony became South Africa's very own Vietnam.

*Chapter 6*

# Mozambique (1964-1975)

The initial search for Namibia's sovereignty was a long odyssey into the mirages of the desert. By comparison, Mozambique's march to freedom was short and not particularly sharp. Peace did not follow independence, however. As in Angola, civil war was to accompany the hasty imperial scuttle. Unlike Angola, only one nationalist movement, FRELIMO, inherited power.

FRELIMO emerged in 1962 from three groups that were themselves influenced by a kaleidoscope of tribal, religious and ideological sentiments. Even within the core of FRELIMO intense rivalries surfaced between the military and political wings. Small groups of FRELIMO cadres were trained in Algeria from 1963. In 1964 some of these men set up training camps in southern Tanzania. Soon instructors arrived from Cuba, China and Eastern Europe. A few of the most industrious trainees were sent to study political warfare at the Komsomol School in Moscow and the guerrilla warfare centre at Simferopol in the Ukraine. At the opening of hostilities FRELIMO had 250 trained and equipped insurgents.

On the night of 25 September 1964 FRELIMO launched its first major assault, on a Portuguese administrative post at Chai in Cabo Delgado near the border with Tanzania. During the early years of the war FRELIMO found it very hard to break out of its ethnic support in the northern provinces of Cabo Delgada and Niassa, even though Portugal's grip had always been weak away from the coastal towns. Major tribal rebellions inland had been common as late as the 1920s. The entire European population, concentrated largely in Beira and the capital, Lourenço Marques, numbered only 27,000 in 1940, although subsidized waves of poor white immigrants had pushed the total to 200,000 by 1970. A few settled in military-style *kibbutzim* in the rural areas but most preferred the sheltered employment and racial privileges of the urban fleshpots on the coast. This sudden surge of settlers made Mozambique the fourth largest white 'tribe' in sub-Saharan Africa, after South Africa, Angola and Rhodesia.

Yet the colony was different from the Afrikaner and Anglo-Saxon racial oligarchies, mainly because Mozambique had precious little autonomy. Lisbon's rule was rigid. The neo-fascist Portuguese dictatorship brooked very few reformist experiments in Mozambique. And the feared secret police, with its extensive urban informer networks, made sure Lisbon was obeyed. The secret police were

Guerrilla infiltration routes into Mozambique

sometimes dubbed 'animals officered by intellectuals'. Forced labour continued in various forms until the 1960s and on roadworks until 1973. Most crucially, the Mozambican economy was run for the benefit of the mother country. The settlers, therefore, did not have an effective, political, economic or moral basis when, later, they tried their own half-hearted (and half-baked) UDI.

Mozambique was one of the poorest colonies of one of the poorest states in Europe. FRELIMO recognized the superficiality of the settler economy by dubbing it 'shopkeeper colonialism'. The colonists did not exert much economic control – they served or managed foreign and metropolitan enterprises. The settlers were usually poor and unskilled, often illiterate peasants or shopkeepers. The colony survived largely by servicing its richer and more powerful neighbours, Rhodesia and South Africa. Trade, transport fees, tourism and black miners working in South Africa made Mozambique tick, albeit with typically Iberian *mañana.* Two years before independence South Africa took over from Portugal as the main suppliers of goods to Mozambique. Although Pretoria watched the

Lourenço Marques, the colonial capital of Mozambique

growing FRELIMO insurgency with alarm, it knew that ultimately Mozambique was critically dependent upon South Africa whatever the pigmentation of the rulers in Lourenço Marques.

In 1964 the FRELIMO president, Dr Eduardo Mondlane, predicted that the war would last 'maybe ten or maybe twenty years, even then it will be a negotiated settlement like Algeria'. It was to be a long haul but by the end FRELIMO claimed to have 10,000 guerrillas under arms. The insurgency grew slowly, partly because of the isolation of the first in-country bases in the far north and the multiplicity of tribes and clans. Mozambique comprised a population of around seven million, made up of nineteen tribes from nine major ethnic groups speaking seventeen different languages. The Portuguese successfully manipulated this demographic hotchpotch: the Muslim Yao tribe, for example, was susceptible to colonial blandishments because it feared a FRELIMO ban on its faith. The insurgents' military operations consisted largely of mine laying and hit-and-run attacks known as *flagelaçao* (whipping bursts). FRELIMO's tactics were undermined by divisions over strategy. Three main approaches were debated: firstly, risings in the main cities; secondly, emulating the Cuban/Guevara line by deploying small groups of guerrillas in the countryside as a 'focus' to trigger off mass insurrection; and, thirdly, a Maoist protracted war. The military wing, later dominated by Samora Machel, a former hospital orderly, got its way when the last option was adopted. Various factions still wrangled over such issues as the correct role of female cadres, traditional chiefs, the churches and socialism. The disputes, never fully resolved, resurfaced as causes of the post-independence civil war.

In February 1969 Mondlane, who had left his job as assistant professor of anthropology at Syracuse University, was assassinated in the Dar es Salaam FRELIMO HQ. A bomb had been put in a book delivered to him, an ironic end for such a bookish guerrilla chieftain. The source of the bomb has been blamed on internal rivals with, perhaps, the connivance of the Portuguese secret police. Later, a PIDE agent claimed responsibility.[1] Mondlane was not only the country's first black PhD but also the first Mozambican recipient, in 1963, of a CIA donation ($10,000).[2] It was briefly, and bizarrely, mooted that his white wife, Janet, who hailed from Indiana, USA, and had been living in Chicago, could take over as interim leader. A white American female guerrilla boss might have done wonders for FRELIMO's image in the salons of the West but little to induce conservative black peasants to join the cause. Instead, the diminutive Machel succeeded Eduardo Mondlane.

When Machel took command, FRELIMO claimed to control around 20 to 25 per cent of northern Mozambique, nominally liberated zones with a crude infrastructure. A new front was opened in the strategically more important Tete province, adjacent to the Zambian border. FRELIMO could rely upon sanctuaries in, and aid from, Zambia and Tanzania. Zambia, however, was vulnerable to counter-sanctions because of Portuguese control of rail transit routes.

The Portuguese tried to contain FRELIMO activity in the north, which had little economic significance and where, by 1960, fewer than 2,500 whites had settled. Approximately 50 per cent of the black inhabitants of the area, 160,000 peasants in Niassa and 270,000 in Cabo Delgado, were herded into *aldeamentos,* the Portuguese version of strategic hamlets. To counter landmines placed on dirt roads, 870 miles

Samora Machel (left) and Eduardo Mondlane, in the early days of the struggle.

per annum of tarmac roads were under construction by 1972. Major offensives, such as Operation GORDIAN KNOT in 1970, commanded by General Kaúlza de Arriaga, tried to sweep away the guerrillas' main bases. De Arriaga was not just a general but also a professor, politician and writer. His counter-insurgency had been thought out. Up to 50 per cent of de Arriaga's troops were assigned to the social aspects of containment, such as building schools and clinics. The number of blacks in primary schools rose from 427,000 in 1964 to 603,000 by 1972, for example. The Portuguese offered few significant political reforms but they did try hard with propaganda. In one year, 1972, planes dropped over five million pro-government pamphlets. Persuasion and bribery often worked. And, as in Rhodesia, a large number of captured guerrillas were 'turned' and used in elite units such as the *Flechas.* Many Africans volunteered for military service: 60 per cent of the 60,000 troops in the country were black. Dramatic high-level defections from FRELIMO to the Portuguese also boosted white morale. Racism in Mozambique was never as rigid as in its white neighbours. Class was often as significant. A well-to-do black was usually more acceptable in polite European society than a down-at-heel white. The Portuguese army worked hard at disseminating the various icons of the pro-Western, pro-Christian, anti-Marxist crusade. This was particularly true of elite black units where sometimes up to an hour a day was dedicated to politicization. General de Arriaga, who did not discourage his own personality cult – his nickname was the 'Pink Panther' – introduced a political programme (called 'mentalization') for his white troops.

Nevertheless, outside the elite black and white units, army morale was low, especially among white conscripts, who had to serve for at least four years. A dissident Portuguese officer noted, 'The soldiers don't know what they are defending. Before they are sent off to Africa they don't even know where Mozambique is. They are also victims of the war.'[3] Except for unusually strongminded and highly political commanders (such as General António de Spinola, who served in Angola and Guinea-Bissau) military strategy was dictated in faraway Lisbon. Marcello Caetano's dictatorship was out of touch with the 'Overseas War'. There was little co-ordination with, and between, the African colonies. In particular, the intense hostility between the regular army and the secret police was allowed to fester.

No one in Lisbon wanted to admit that the imperial wars made no sense, even though they were consuming 40 per cent of the national budget; the police clamped down hard on dissidents, even in the armed forces. Lisbon was equally prickly about criticism from Salisbury and Pretoria. On an ad hoc basis the Rhodesian security forces, with and without Portuguese permission, had been operating deep inside Mozambique during the late 1960s. An unofficial 'Council of Three' representatives from Mozambique, Rhodesia and South Africa began to meet regularly after February 1971 to co-ordinate military policies. In 1973 General de Arriaga disclosed a gentleman's agreement that allowed the Rhodesians to operate up to sixty miles inside Mozambique. The Rhodesians, especially the deep-penetration units such as the Special Air Service, were often loath to work with the Portuguese army, not least because of its reluctance to engage with the enemy. On patrols, Portuguese soldiers, particularly conscripts, would often make as much as noise as possible to warn off FRELIMO. The Rhodesians, however, often soldiered effectively with the much more aggressive elite units in both the police and the army. Co-operation with the *Flechas* often bagged Zimbabwean as well as FRELIMO insurgents working in tandem. Such successes paved the way later for the Rhodesian creation of the Mozambique National Resistance Movement, the nemesis of FRELIMO's rise to power.

One important symbol of South Africa's involvement was the giant Cahora Bassa dam in Tete province. It turned out to be the biggest white elephant in southern Africa's economic history. It only made sense to sell the electricity to South Africa but constant sabotage was to make the supply lines inoperative for over a decade.

Cahora Bassa dam – the biggest white elephant in southern African history.

As the dam was being built in the early 1970s, it was reportedly guarded by over 15,000 troops. FRELIMO kept up a nominal pressure on the dam and then moved southwards to the Umtali-Beira rail and road corridor and the beginning of the white commercial heartlands. By 1973 FRELIMO was deploying 122mm rockets for stand-off bombardments and, by 1974, SAM-7 missiles. FRELIMO's penetration into white farming areas shook the confidence of the settlers, who complained bitterly about the army's failure to protect them. As in Algeria, the relationship between the army and the settlers was often poor. In particular, white civilians accused the officer corps of fighting a comfortable 'air-conditioned war'. General de Arriaga in August 1973 tried to bolster white confidence by asserting that what FRELIMO could do to the army was 'what a mosquito could do to an elephant'. Yet by 1974 morale and efficiency had waned dramatically in the security forces. In May 1974 General Costa Gomes admitted that, in the Mozambican capital, the army had 'reached the limits of neuro-psychological exhaustion'. Tired and dispirited, yes, but not defeated. FRELIMO was winning almost by default.

The generals did not want to be blamed for another defeat such as the 1961 fiasco when India marched into the Portuguese enclave of Goa. In the early 1970s the African colonies were not yet lost and they were not the sole cause of the April coup in Lisbon. The 'discreet dictatorship' had simply run out of steam, as had the Falangists next door in Spain. The administration and the economy, with an inflation rate of 72 per cent in February 1974, were beginning to fall apart as Portugal struggled to catch up with the rest of Community Europe. At least nine coups had failed during the more than three decades of harsh authoritarianism under António de Salazar, and his successor Caetano had suffered three coup attempts. The fascist ideal of the so-called *Estado Novo* and the theories of 'Pluricontinentalism' – that the Portuguese empire was a unified state that spanned multiple continents – had obviously had their day. The rebel Armed Forces Movement (MFA) was going to launch a better-organized coup of its own.

An accelerated promotion scheme for graduate officers had enraged the traditionalists, even though a chronic shortage of young officers persisted. The new scheme helped to radicalize the junior officer ranks. To political rigidity, social backwardness, and economic decline was added the explosive bruised national pride and wounded professional vanity in the armed forces. One of the revolutionary sparks was General de Spinola's famous book *Portugal and the Future*. In it he wrote, 'We must begin by divesting ourselves of the notion that we are defending the West and the Western way of life.' As with France in Algeria, Portugal was not making an economic profit by holding on to its African obsessions, especially as the wars were expanding. Mozambique, for example, contributed only 20 per cent towards the local war effort. The colonies were a patent anachronism of Europe's oldest empire led by its oldest dictatorship. Something had to give.

And so, after so many years, in so few hours and with very little bloodshed, the dictatorship and empire collapsed as the MFA moved on Lisbon. De Spinola played the revolution's Neguib but no Nasser emerged. The MFA set about democratizing Portugal and its African 'provinces' (called 'states' after 1972). The army had not been tainted by Gestapo practices, unlike the French paras in Algiers or the Portuguese secret police. Nor had there been the bitterness spawned by urban terrorism. Suddenly, Lisbon seemed full of optimism … and flowers. Hence the most popular name for the coup of 25 April 1974 – the 'Carnation Revolution'.

The MFA ordered its troops to fight on in Africa, but the revolutionary impact replicated Russia in late 1917. Since most soldiers refused to fight, an undeclared ceasefire prevailed in many areas. On 7 September 1974 the new Portuguese government signed an accord with Samora Machel, paving the way for a provisional multi-racial administration in Lorenço Marques. Independence was set for June 1975. On 8 September 1974 diehard whites attempted a counter-coup. This feeble but bitter UDI lasted about as long as the generals' *putsch* in Algeria. In Mozambique the Portuguese army, with FRELIMO assistance, quelled the rebellion. A white exodus began. In October a spate of racial bloodletting erupted again. By June 1975 more than half the whites had fled: within a year only 10 per cent remained. The towns were full of scavenging stray dogs, once pampered pets now abandoned. Farmers killed their cattle rather than leave them. Mechanics sabotaged their machinery. The few whites who stayed did so for a number of reasons. Some were financial prisoners; others were ideologically committed to socialism. The latter often rose to senior positions in the government. FRELIMO had always insisted that it had been fighting to rid the country of colonialism, not whites. The remaining skilled whites were desperately needed. Few blacks had been trained to take over the reins, at any level. As Joseph Hanlon noted, at independence, of the 350 train drivers, only one was black.[4]

So what did Pretoria make of FRELIMO's victory by default? During the war South Africa had provided material and financial support for the Portuguese but had carefully avoided getting too involved (although claims were made at the time that up to 1,000 SADF troops had fought inside Mozambique).[5] Some discussions took place in military and intelligence circles about backing the white diehards and propping up a white-ruled southern Mozambique. After all, at the beginning of 1975 the whites still numbered around 200,000. FRELIMO influence had hardly touched the south, a region of considerable importance for Pretoria's transport routes, that stood right alongside South African territory. The Mozambican capital, renamed Maputo, was just an hour's drive from the eastern Transvaal. The idea was dropped as Mozambique slid into anarchy. Some Portuguese last-ditchers who fled to South Africa indulged in a number of OAS-style activities against FRELIMO and its white sympathizers.[6] Pretoria appeared to turn a blind eye to these ultras, for a while.

The South African military option was ruled out. No pretext could be manufactured, as in Angola. And it bears repeating that Mozambique, unlike Angola, was very dependent economically upon Pretoria's goodwill. Even with the Portuguese gone, the giant Cahora Bassa dam still only made sense by dealing with Pretoria. Over 100,000 Mozambican miners worked in South Africa. They were paid in gold at the official price that Mozambique could resell at the free market rate. The deal originally had been maintained as a kind of subsidy to the Portuguese war effort but by 1974 the gold price was three times the official level. So this became a vital component of Mozambique's foreign exchange earnings. FRELIMO could simply not afford to bring home the miners. Massive unemployment already racked the economy. And most of the miners came from the south where FRELIMO had secured little initial popularity. The economic ties cut both ways of course: Maputo was the most convenient port for the bustling Witwatersrand. The mine labour and transport arrangements, codified in the Mozambique Conventions that went back as far as 1875, suited both countries. After a decade of war and massive dislocation caused by the flight of nearly all the skilled personnel, FRELIMO was desperate for peace and for time to rebuild and consolidate its hold on power. Pretoria, initially helpfully, sent technical advisers to keep operational the port and rail facilities in the south.

Samora Machel: the new president of Mozambique

So a *modus vivendi* was possible between 'fascism' as Machel termed apartheid, and the newly triumphant revolutionaries. The economic leverage gave Pretoria the self-confidence to act with military restraint. Economic self-interest transcended, it seemed, ideological rivalry. Yet it was not quite that simple. Pretoria was worried that Machel might be pushed into the waiting arms of the Russians. Both China and Russia had supplied FRELIMO's army, the FPLM (*Forças Populares de Libertação de Moçambique*) during the war and after. Some Chinese instructors remained. Moscow was still angling for naval facilities, although Machel was politely aloof on this score. Soviet naval bases in the Mozambique Channel was the last thing Pretoria wanted. Better, then, to play along with Maputo for the time being, especially as Machel had not yet closed his borders with Rhodesia.

The softly-softly approach could not mask the psychological damage. Angola was so far away. Geographically, Moscow is nearer to London than Luanda is to Cape Town. Few South Africans had ever visited Angola but Mozambique was a place for regular holidays. 'LM' radio was a youth cult for whites. LM played the Beatles when the ultra-conservative South African Broadcasting Corporation (SABC) banned their records. Cheap prawns and wine were plentiful, so was sex, especially the multi-racial variety, well-suited to the conservative Afrikaners who needed to taste sin before they could persuasively condemn it at home. Suddenly the Rolling Stones and the Beatles were replaced by martial music, then African voices attacking neo-colonialism. The glorious Mozambican beaches were soon deserted by South Africans whose youngsters reluctantly turned back to the turgid SABC.

Another domino had fallen but Pretoria had to grin and bear it. Both Mozambique and South Africa wanted the compromise to hold. Almost overnight, however, the lucrative tourist trade evaporated – 30,000 prostitutes in Maputo were suddenly out of work. To the chagrin of Johannesburg business magnates, Pretoria impetuously reduced the number of Mozambican mineworkers and started to divert trade from Maputo to South African ports farther south, despite the extra costs. In Rhodesia, the powerful Central Intelligence Organization was busy creating a Frankenstein's monster: the Mozambican National Resistance Movement, or RENAMO as it was more often called. With Pretoria's help this guerrilla group was to ravage the FRELIMO dominion. In March 1976 Machel closed the border with Rhodesia. Direct Rhodesian raids and proxy RENAMO sabotage were about to bring Mozambique to its knees. The agony was only beginning – Mozambique was now entering the very heart of darkness.

*Chapter 7*

# Rhodesia (1965-1980)

The collapse of white power in Rhodesia had a tremendous impact on the Afrikaner psyche. As with the Portuguese colonies, the loss of Rhodesia diminished the defence perimeter of the white-ruled laager. The defeat of Ian Smith's rebellion, however, meant much more psychologically to white South Africa. Afrikaner racism, in particular, extended to the Portuguese who were often seen as idle, incompetent and poorly disciplined. Many Portuguese soldiers were conscripts from the metropole; they could pack up and go home. Rhodesia was supposed to be different. In Rhodesia, it was claimed, a new nation had been

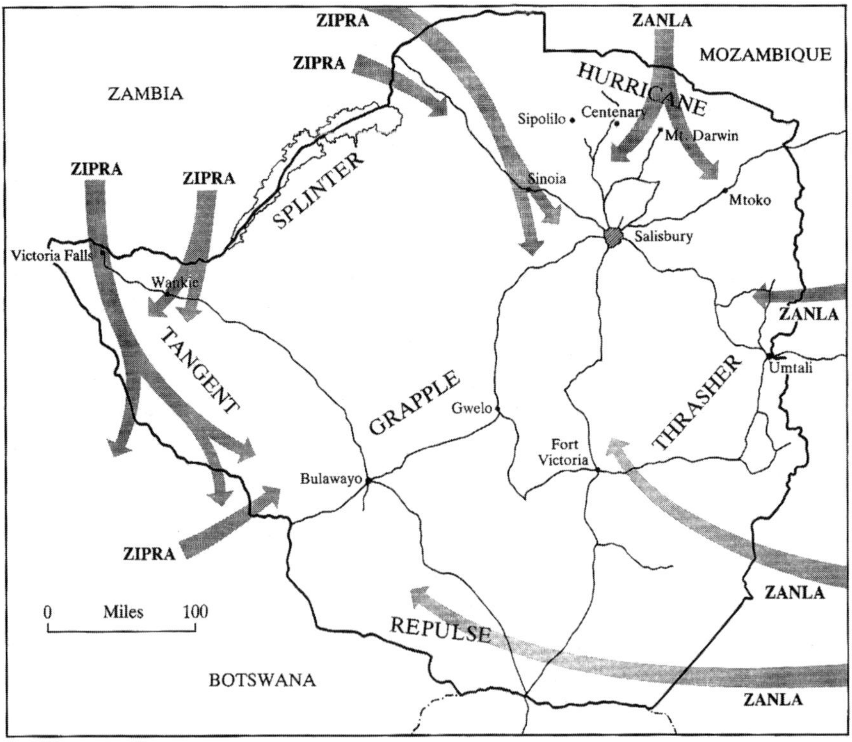


Guerrilla infiltration routes into Rhodesia

formed, although critics said it was a heavily armed white suburb masquerading as a country. Afrikaners assumed that, if pressed, and unlike the Portuguese, white Anglo-Saxons would fight black 'savages' and win. Such was the mood of much white popular opinion in South Africa until the very late 1970s.

Nonetheless, government circles in Pretoria exhibited a deep-seated ambiguity about the Unilateral Declaration of Independence (UDI) on 11 November 1965. The republic's premier, the dour Hendrik Verwoerd, cautioned Smith against the revolt against the British Crown. Pretoria, like the rest of the world, refused to officially recognize the Rhodesian regime. On the other hand, the South African government had a vested interest in proving that sanctions did not work. After the fall of Lisbon's empire, South African businessmen made huge profits from the captive Rhodesian market, although generous voluntary support was donated by various South African bodies, such as the Friends of Rhodesia. Historically, there had often been bad blood between the two white supremacist states: the infamous Jameson Raid had been launched with help from Rhodesia, which had also fought on the 'wrong side' in the Boer War (1899-1902). And then, in 1922, the colony disdained the offer of union with South Africa. Some 20 per cent, however, of Rhodesia's whites had Afrikaner roots. Many nationalists in Pretoria looked upon these Afrikaners 'as Hitler regarded the *Auslandsdeutsche*'.[1] This kith and kin factor, plus the South African origins of many English-speaking Rhodesians, forged a strong emotional bond, which was augmented by the large annual influx of South African tourists. Many middle-class white Rhodesians regarded it as natural to study at the often excellent, albeit segregated, English-language universities such as Cape Town, Durban and Rhodes (in Grahamstown). Ultra-rightists within the Afrikaner secret society, the *Broederbond,* and the *Herstigte Nasionale Party*, which had broken from the ruling National Party in 1969, insisted the Zambezi and not the Limpopo was the natural northern military boundary. Military co-operation between the two states had preceded the rebellion: joint exercises between their air forces, for example, had taken place as early as 1961.

After UDI, Salisbury's white supremacist policies shifted ever closer to the apartheid model – although, right until the end of the Rhodesian war, black-white relationships were always much better in the north compared with the south. Both white communities were deluged in a tidal wave of internal propaganda. Both gloried in verbose rhetoric about defending their Christian civilization against godless communism, the convenient depository for all demands by blacks for equal rights. In Rhodesia, however, a quarter of a million whites were outnumbered 25:1 by blacks; in South Africa the ratio was 5:1 (depending on how 'blacks' were designated). Writing in the mid-1970s, the Oxford historian Robert Blake commented, 'Apartheid south of the Limpopo is a religion, north of it a dubious and impractical expedient.'[2] Despite the racist ties, Pretoria understood that, in the long term, white rule in Rhodesia was impracticable – not least for South African interests. The best solution for Pretoria was the peaceful transition to a pro-Western 'moderate' black ruler, preferably one who was beholden to South Africa.

Hence the greatest paradox of the Rhodesian war: Ian Smith broke away from Britain to avoid black rule and then, with the onset of the guerrilla war, became completely dependent upon a South African regime that was even more determined than Britain to establish a black premier in Salisbury. Above all, Pretoria dreaded the possibility of a victorious Marxist army marching through the well-tended garden suburbs of Salisbury and Bulawayo, a precedent that it feared might be repeated in Pretoria and Johannesburg. Rhodesia transformed itself from a self-governing British colony into an occasionally truculent but inevitably subservient sector of Afrikaner imperium. Ian Smith became, in effect, the leader of almost another South African homeland. Pretoria cynically manipulated its Rhodesian satrapy by providing just enough military support to allow Smith time to reach the long-elusive 'settlement' with black 'moderates'. This policy totally backfired and, by extending the duration of the war, boosted the tally to at least 30,000 lives lost on all sides.

Ian Smith and the leading acolytes of his Rhodesian Front (RF) issued their illegal declaration on the eleventh hour of the eleventh day of the eleventh month of 1965. It was timed to coincide with Armistice Day to stress Rhodesia's contribution to the two world wars. Proportionately they lost more whites than any other part of the empire. UDI was also couched in the language of the American declaration of independence two centuries earlier, to arouse white American sympathies. The RF insisted that this was an act of justified defiance against a crass Labour government, not a rebellion against the Crown. Indeed, most white Rhodesians who were not of Afrikaner stock were royalists. RF propaganda made a point of ensuring the signatories of UDI were pictured with Queen Elizabeth dominating the backdrop.

Ian Douglas Smith

UDI was gross folly in many ways, not least because it prompted the internationalization of what had previously been largely a bilateral domestic tussle between London and Salisbury. Without UDI, any British government, Labour or Tory, would have left the whites in Rhodesia largely to their own devices, provided some kind of polite constitutional verbiage about *eventual* black equality was agreed upon. That was the purpose of the series of Anglo-Rhodesian talks from 1966 to 1971.

In 1965, however, whites in 'Southern Rhodesia' (to give the colony its official designation) were in an obstinate and beleaguered mood. Their confidence had been

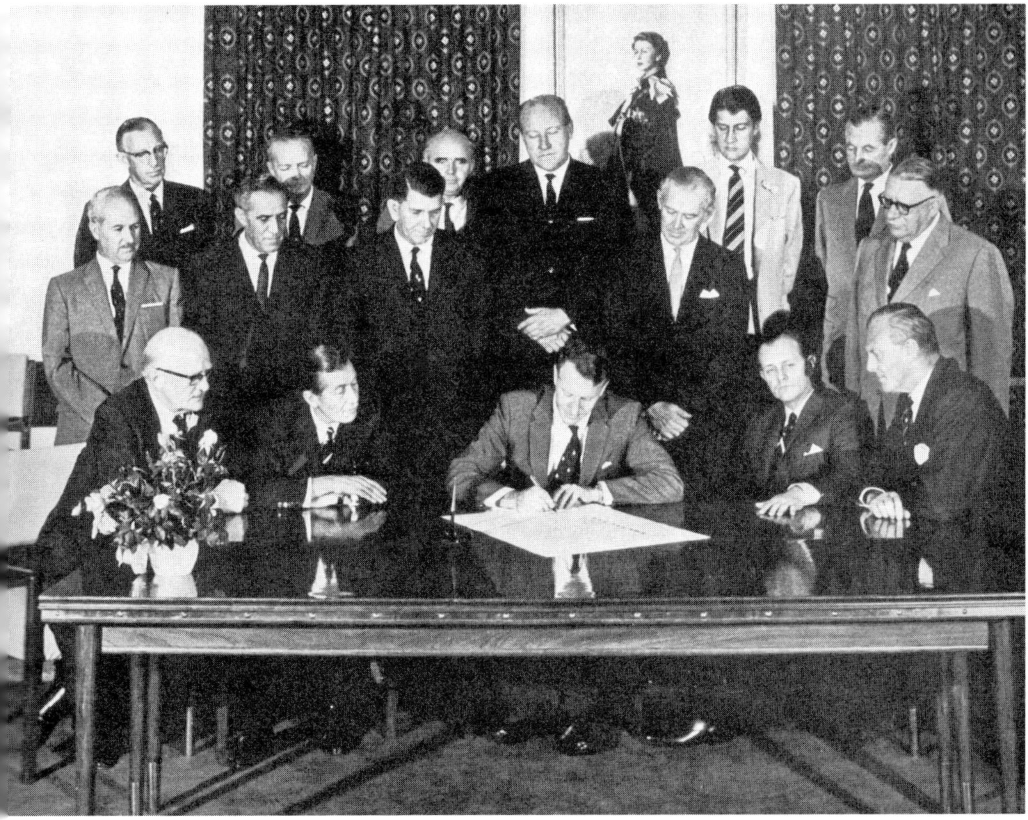

UDI was signed at 11 in the morning on 11 November 1965, under the picture of the Queen

shaken by the recent savagery against whites in the former Belgian Congo, the break-up of the Central African Federation because of the rise of black nationalism and the British refusal to grant Southern Rhodesians independence along with the other members of the federation (Northern Rhodesia as Zambia and Nyasaland as Malawi). The effectively self-governing administration in Salisbury also worried about the depletion of their armed forces in the federal re-allocation as well as the rise in white emigration because of the political uncertainty. The RF believed that a dramatic move could stop the rot.

UDI was a huge military bluff. 'Except for one or two senior members of the British South African Police (BSAP) and a few South African hotheads in the depleted Rhodesian Light Infantry (RLI), white Rhodesians would not have resisted a rapid British show of force.' That was the opinion of the most informed man in Rhodesia, Ken Flower, the genial Cornish director-general of the Central

Intelligence Organization, during a series of one-on-one conversations (1979 to 1987) with me at his isolated hilltop home in Hogerty Hill, on thc outskirts of the capital. 'A pipe band and a detachment of Royal Marines marching through Salisbury would have done the trick,' admitted one very senior Rhodesian defence official after the war.[3] The bluff was never called, partly because of parallel reticence within the British armed forces, especially in the air force, to resort to force. Despite this reluctance, if Prime Minister Harold Wilson had decided to send in his troops, no doubt the British armed forces would have complied … after a few resignations. Wilson, however, threw way his best cards by renouncing force at the outset. He opted for sanctions instead. Threatening 'to throw the book' at the RF, he simply flicked a few pages … one at a time. Sanctions were a gesture, never a concerted policy. Until 1974 they boosted rather than undermined the rebel economy.[4]

Wilson was torn by what he termed his 'four constituencies': the Tories, the Commonwealth, the UN and South Africa. The inevitable compromises that ensued gave Wilson's policies 'that madcap flair', a phrase used by Robert Good, the American ambassador to Zambia. The end result was an impasse: no force, no confrontation with South Africa and no 'sell-out'. The inherent contradictions

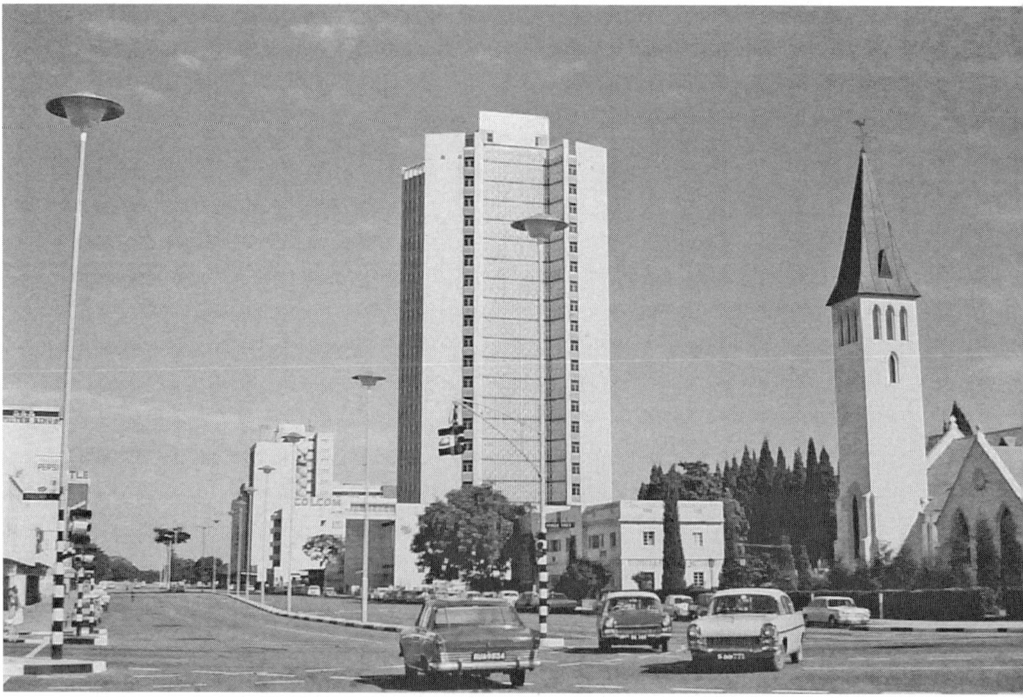

Salisbury, Rhodesia's elegant capital city

meant a gradual imposition of half-hearted leaky sanctions and growing RF resistance. Thus ensued a long diplomatic melodrama punctuated by angry encounters on Royal Navy ships, foolish estimates and silly superlatives. These negotiations gave Ian Smith credibility at the time and respectability abroad. Wilson boasted that UDI would last 'months if not weeks', while Smith promised that black rule would take a thousand years. At the same time, Ambassador Good noted that UDI 'was to be a middle-of-the-road revolution led by businessmen, a double contradiction and a shockingly bad estimate'.[5] Pretoria played a subtle game until 1978 when Prime Minister P.W. Botha risked all to back the internal settlement, with Bishop Abel Muzorewa as the chief 'useful idiot', to deploy Lenin's term.

Few of the key players in the Rhodesian saga foresaw the main elements of the unfolding Greek tragedy. Not only was black rule inevitable but it was almost inevitable that, once they were allowed to get away with UDI, Rhodesian whites were unlikely to accept their fate without a considerable struggle. That struggle was bound to be prolonged if, firstly, the black nationalist movement were to become divided and, secondly, international pressures, especially sanctions, were not comprehensively applied. Pretoria circumvented easily the feeble sanctions and the black nationalists spent as much time fighting each other as combating Smith's troops. So the war dragged on for fourteen years.

## *The course of the war*

The war can be divided into three stages: from UDI to 1972, the small Rhodesian security forces were engaged in a winning war; from 1972 to 1976, it could be described as a non-win war; and from 1976 to late 1979 the Rhodesians became engulfed in a losing war. If the Lancaster House talks in London had not intervened, military defeat was around the corner for white Rhodesia.

### **The opening round (1965-72)**

Politically-motivated strikes and isolated attacks on whites had predated UDI. After 1965 the main nationalist movements, the Zimbabwe African National Union (ZANU) and the Zimbabwe African People's Union (ZAPU), had hoped that their dramatic, if forlorn, military gestures would, firstly, encourage a general African insurrection and, secondly, prompt British armed intervention. From 1966 to 1968 both nationalist movements launched guerrilla forays. In April 1966 a small group of ZANU insurgents infiltrated from Zambia into Rhodesia and split up into three teams. They planned to cut power lines and attack white farms. A white farmer and his wife were murdered in May near Hartley (I shall use place names as they were generally described at the time). The most significant contact, however, had taken place earlier near Sinoia on 28 April. A seven-man ZANU squad, who had called themselves the Armageddon group and some of whom were originally trained at Nanking military college, was wiped out by the security forces who suffered no casualties. The Zimbabwean government of the 1980s apotheosized this military fiasco as the central event of the liberation war, partly to stress that they began their war before their old rival, ZAPUU. The date is commemorated as *Chimurenga* day.[6]

In fact, all seven 'heroes of the revolution' involved in the debacle were being fed by police Special Branch and the political commissar, according to the Central Intelligence Organization, was a Rhodesian agent. The tame guerrillas were supposed to lead the security forces to arms caches and nationalist sympathizers. Instead, because of an administrative cock-up, they were all killed, very inefficiently. An air force gunner in an Alouette expended 168 rounds, from a hastily rigged MAG 7.62mm, to shoot dead one guerrilla running across open ground in daylight. The regular and reserve policemen involved in the hunt were mostly armed with First World War-vintage rifles and Second World War revolvers. According to one eyewitness, 'It was little more than a baboon shoot, the police reservists congregating like farmers (which most of them were) around every kill and exposing themselves unbelievably to enemy fire.' A history of the Rhodesian Air Force commented thus on its first kill in the war: 'It was a very unconvincing and unprofessional action. Fortunately for the police, the guerrillas were too confused to take advantage of the inexperience of the hunters.'[7] Another Rhodesian commander described the official response as a 'shambles'. Racially arrogant, the Rhodesians always overplayed guerrilla incompetence, terming it disparagingly the 'K factor' ('kaffir' factor). Indeed, the military performance of the guerrillas, especially in the early part of the war, was appalling. Both sides, however, learned from their mistakes. In the end the Rhodesians often met fierce resistance and came to repent their initial underestimation of the enemy.

In 1967 and 1968 the pace of guerrilla activity quickened. The nationalists dabbled in urban warfare. Explosives were smuggled in through the borders in cars and lorries. Usually they were discovered. ZANU sent a white woman activist to leave bombs in Salisbury's major hotels, but the plot failed. At the same time, a small number of white nationalist sympathizers at the University College of Rhodesia were active in encouraging grenade attacks. Academics rarely succeed in practical revolutionary tactics; nevertheless the grenades on campus sent the Rhodesian Front into paroxysms of anger: the university just managed to retain its shaky multi-racial independence of government

Far more important than academics' activities were the conventional incursions. In August 1967 a combined force of ninety guerrillas from ZAPU and the South African African National Congress (ANC) entered Rhodesia near the Victoria Falls. They intended to move into Tjolotjo Tribal Trust Land (TTL) to establish recruiting bases. Later the ANC forces planned to infiltrate through Botswana and head for Soweto township in Johannesburg. The guerrillas were on a suicide

Rhodesian Alouettes, the core of the Fire Force concept (Group Captain Peter Petter-Bowyer)

mission, however. They had been told they would be welcomed by the local people, but the tribesmen in the sparsely populated shrubland of north-western Rhodesia were suspicious of the insurgents. Soon the bush telegraph brought the news to Rhodesian intelligence. In the first major operations of the war, forty-seven of the insurgents were killed by the security forces in three weeks. More than twenty were captured and the survivors, many of them wounded, escaped into Botswana, where they were imprisoned. Subsequently they were released into the care of Zambian authorities.

The failure of this joint ZAPU/ANC sortie had many consequences. The involvement of South African insurgents prompted Pretoria to send police units to aid Rhodesian operations in the Zambezi valley. (A number of army and air force units were included; the 'police' label was used to discourage international accusations that South Africa had intervened militarily in a British colony.) The initial South African contingent was about 2,000 men, though by 1969 it had reached 2,700, only a thousand short of the Rhodesian regular army. In the beginning Rhodesian troops regarded their South African allies with near contempt and disparagingly dubbed them 'clumpies' because of their clumsy bushcraft. Rhodesian units were forced to operate behind the South Africans to fill in the gaps created by their allies' inexperience. Rhodesian commanders thought that the South Africans were more of a liability than a help, and so were reluctant to allow South African troops to join in the fray. But the government insisted that Rhodesia had to accept the help for political rather than security reasons. Pretoria initially gained much more than the Rhodesians as the South African troops acquired valuable experience. For the following seven years Pretoria provided vital manpower support for Rhodesia's anti-guerrilla campaign. John Vorster, the South African premier, explained that he had sent his men in order 'to pull our own chestnuts out of the fire'. He also included his own 18-year-old son in the contingent. Later on in the war, Salisbury was to become totally dependent upon South African military largesse, particularly the loan of helicopters and their crews. Equally vital was South African economic subvention, which eventually amounted to approximately half of the annual Rhodesian defence budget.

A second manifestation of the ZAPU/ANC forays was the scope of the southern African planning by the insurgents. It was not merely a series of guerrilla pinpricks, but a concerted strategy. In the long run, the strategy of forming an alliance with other guerrilla groups was valid, yet in the short term the tactics were disastrous. Large-scale conventional incursions proved futile against highly-trained, mobile troops, backed by total air supremacy. It was not exactly a turkey-shoot, however. In the fighting of August and September 1967 the Rhodesian security forces lost their first man killed in action in the country since the Shona and Ndebele uprisings of the 1890s. But the guerrillas suffered severe casualties. Even worse were the ensuing splits in the nationalist movements, already strained by tribal, ideological and personality clashes. ZANU praised the courage of the insurgents, but castigated the alliance with the ANC as a 'gross blunder'. The ANC, said ZANU, should be pinning down its enemy in South Africa, not encouraging Pretoria to bolster the northern frontier of white rule to the detriment of the Zimbabwean nationalists. Besides, the ANC, argued ZANU, was superfluous: the four million Zimbabweans without external aid could easily overcome the 200,000 whites. The ANC's South African rival, the Pan-Africanist Congress, condemned the conventional tactics as 'a criminal act of manslaughter'. ZAPU retaliated against the rebuffs from ZANU and the PAC and hinted darkly that ZANU agents had tipped off Rhodesian intelligence.

Despite the recriminations within the nationalist ranks, the guerrillas kept coming. In early 1968, 123 guerrillas of both ZAPU and South African insurgents crossed the Zambezi near the Chewore River. During a three-month period they set up Viet Cong-style base camps containing considerable amounts of medical equipment, food and arms. Because of the heavy rains Rhodesian security force patrolling was light. A game ranger, however, stumbled upon the guerrilla presence, and on 18 March the security forces went in and destroyed the guerrillas' six base camps. In a running battle lasting nearly a month more than sixty-nine insurgents were killed for the loss of six of the Rhodesian forces. The remaining guerrillas were either captured or chased across the Zambezi back to Zambia.

In July a ZAPU/SAANC tandem force tried again. Three groups totalling ninety-one men slipped across the Zambezi. Once more they were spotted by Rhodesian security force patrols. Despite their sometimes fierce resistance the guerrillas were routed, although in one contact a South African policeman was killed. He was the first South African policeman to die in a direct contact with the guerrillas in the war in Rhodesia. By the end of 1968 more than 160 insurgents and twelve security force members had been killed.

ZANLA propaganda poster

The 1967-68 incursions had failed. Instead of large formations, lone guerrillas were subsequently sent into Rhodesia to acquire intelligence and to prepare for a more thorough process of infiltration. The slackening tempo of the war lulled the Rhodesian government into a false sense of complacency and lazy assumptions of military supremacy. Indeed, some Rhodesians even believed the war was over. Rhodesian intelligence, however, had accurately assessed the growing guerrilla strength. What they did not know was where the insurgents would strike, and when. For it was not the end of the war; instead it was the prelude to the coming *Chimurenga.* Although ZAPU forces were slow to revise their strategy, the leaders of ZANU moved quickly to re-appraise the conduct of the war. They argued that the ANC and ZAPU had ignored the first two stages of classic Maoist guerrilla warfare. By jumping to the third conventional phase they inevitably handed the tactical advantage to the well-equipped units of the security forces.

ZANU turned to the obvious source of help to remedy its deficiencies: Chinese instructors. ZANU had sent its first contingent of five men, led by Emmerson Mnangagwa, later to be made Zimbabwe's president in 2017, to China for training in September 1963. The first instructors at ZANLA's training camp at Itumbi in southern Tanzania did not arrive until 1969, however. Initially a few chosen ZANLA cadres were sent to China or Cuba; later the majority were trained in Mozambique or Tanzania. In the latter stages of the war, basic training for some recruits was provided inside Rhodesia. Training was divided into two phases. The first consisted of physical education, political indoctrination and training on basic infantry weapons. The second phase involved tactics (ambushes, patrol formations, and so on). Further specialized instruction was then given to the more able students.

The administration of the war was also improved. In April 1969 exiled ZANU leaders in Lusaka set up an eight-member war council, the *Dare re Chimurenga.* One of the *Dare*'s first moves was to try to persuade the FRELIMO forces operating against the Portuguese in Mozambique to allow ZANLA to operate from their territory. As the 1966-68 incursions had proved, the inhospitable terrain and the Rhodesian *cordon sanitaire* along the Zambezi had made guerrilla transit from Zambia hazardous. Mozambican rebel leaders, however, were reluctant to accede to ZANU's requests because of FRELIMO's special relationship with ZAPU, which was regarded as the major Zimbabwean nationalist movement.

For the white Rhodesians things looked decidedly rosy by the end of the 1960s. In economic and military terms UDI seemed a success. The new confidence encouraged an upswing in the influx of white immigrants. In stark contrast, morale in the guerrilla movements was low and manpower was in short supply. ZAPU and ZANU began to 'conscript' black Rhodesians living in Zambia. Sometimes Zambians were also press-ganged, much to the annoyance of the Zambian government. What really angered the Zambian president, Kenneth Kaunda, was the constant squabbling between ZANU and ZAPU. Foiled by the Rhodesian army, the guerrillas began to turn their guns on each other. ZANU and ZAPU, in the camps in Zambia and Tanzania, quarrelled over strategy and tribal affiliations. Occasionally the bickering erupted into pitched battles.

Political and tribal animosity was exacerbated by poor administration in the guerrilla camps. In 1970 James Chikerema, a ZAPU leader, described his movement's camps as representing 'the depth and height of decay, corruption, nepotism, tribalism, selfishness and gross irresponsibility on the part of the military administration from top to bottom'. In October 1971 Chikerema tried to reconcile the ZANU-ZAPU splits by forming the Front for the Liberation of Zimbabwe (FROLIZI). The Front was shortlived and ineffectual. In March 1972, Kaunda and other OAU leaders compelled the rival nationalists to unite under the banner of a 'Joint Military Command'. But there was little to command. And, like most shotgun unions, the marriage was brief and acrimonious.

From 1969 to 1972 isolated guerrilla attacks caused Salisbury only occasional concern. In January 1970, for example, guerrillas attacked Victoria Falls airport and a nearby South African camp. Infrequent sabotage attempts and sporadic landmine blasts scarcely dented an assertive white nationalism that believed its rule would last 1,000 years. Despite the failures to unite with ZAPU, ZANU was determined to set its own house in order. One of the weaknesses had been the lack of military expertise of the *Dare re Chimurenga.* Often a political decision would be made to satisfy the pressures from the OAU, and the guerrillas in the field would suffer. The combat commanders did their best to modify rash political strategies and instead concentrated on laying the foundations of a classic Maoist protracted struggle. In 1973 Josiah Tongogara, the able ZANLA commander, joined the *Dare* and injected a stiff dose of military pragmatism. The key to the successful infiltration was FRELIMO support. The Mozambicans had consistently urged ZAPU to operate from Mozambique, but had met with evasion. ZANLA eventually prevailed upon FRELIMO to be allowed to operate from bases in Mozambique and to use FRELIMO weapons and supplies. (ZANLA guerrillas, however, had to pretend to be acting as a part of FRELIMO.) From their new logistic base, weapons were transported into north-east Rhodesia and then cached. ZANLA skilfully enlisted the support of local spirit mediums who assisted in the politicization of the local people. The guerrillas constantly hammered home the theme that the liberation war of the 1970s was a continuation of the *Chimurenga* struggle of the 1890s. In the north-east, government administration had always been poor, and the tribal population, especially the KoreKore people, had a tradition of sullen non-co-operation with the authorities. Soon large columns of guerrillas with tribesmen acting as porters were winding their way into Rhodesia from Mozambique's Tete province.

Josiah Tongogara, ZANLA's leading commander

Rhodesian intelligence had got wind of the ZANLA build-up, although not its extent. Although Smith may have given some credence to the comforting (and totally erroneous) reports from the Ministry of Internal Affairs, his Cabinet received regular, and accurate, briefings from the top intelligence advisers. Although Rhodesian intelligence chiefs tended to ignore Internal Affairs sources, hardliners in the cabinet, such as Desmond Lardner-Burke, took them seriously. When intelligence men warned of the impending strikes, Lardner-Burke would complain of repetition of security lectures that were 'all gloom and doom that never materialized'. Thus Salisbury failed to mobilize its troops against a ZANLA force which had expanded its politicization programme and strengthened its logistic links with Mozambican insurgents.

Rhodesian intelligence was also aware of the deteriorating grip of the Portuguese on Mozambique. Ken Flower, head of the Central Intelligence Organization, visited the Portuguese premier, Marcello Caetano, twice in Lisbon. The permanent Rhodesian representative in Portugal, however, was feeding Salisbury with all sorts of poor intelligence; he chose to believe the confident propaganda put out by the Portuguese generals. When Salisbury finally voiced its concern, Lisbon rebuked the Rhodesians for undue alarmism. Since UDI, Rhodesia and Portugal had co-ordinated their strategies to include joint cross-border sweeps. When the Rhodesian authorities expressed their dismay at the FRELIMO successes in Tete, Caetano rapped Salisbury over the knuckles:

> Some of our neighbours with less experience than we have, do not conceal their fears and in this way play the game of the enemy. They have been told more than once there is no reason for their great fright.

Even as late as 1973, the Portuguese were inflicting military reverses on FRELIMO, but politically the metropolitan base for the war was crumbling. FRELIMO would soon be able to augment its logistic support for ZANLA.

The Rhodesians were also gradually building up the size of the regular army. (The length of national service had been increased in 1966 from four-and-a-half to nine months.) They were taking extra precautions, yet their mood was one of complete confidence. In 1972 they were unaware of the scope of the ZANLA infiltration from Mozambique in the east. To the north along the Zambezi, the Rhodesians had totally outclassed their opponents in direct combat. It was to take six years for ZAPU to recover from the defeat of its conventional sorties. The ZAPU/ANC alliance had been knocked out in round one. In round two the Rhodesian army was taken by surprise. In December 1972 ZANU launched its offensive.

**Round Two 1972-76**

'The enemy's rear is the guerrillas' front.' This was particularly true of South African pressure on Rhodesia from 1972 to 1976. John Vorster undermined Rhodesia almost as much as the combined efforts of the insurgents and the OAU did. Pretoria's leverage, however, was not applied until the second part of round two. The guerrillas struck the first blows. ZANLA troops had built a widespread underground infrastructure in the north-east of Rhodesia; the local spirit mediums had been won over and the peasants politicized. In November 1972 security forces intercepted a large ZANLA column in the Mzarabani Tribal Trust Land, which stood between the white farming area of Centenary and Mozambique. Suddenly the scope of the infiltration began to dawn on the politicians in Salisbury. In December it was announced that national service would be increased from nine months to one year. But the expansion of the armed forces could not avert the first wave of the new offensive.

On 21 December 1972 ZANLA attacked the isolated Altena farm in the Centenary district. According to Rhodesian sources, this attack was meant to be part of a simultaneous assault against five farms, but the Altena group misread their instructions and struck twenty-four hours prematurely. The ZANLA version is different: Rex Nhongo was the operational commander in charge of twenty-one men in the Nehanda sector, the ZANLA name for the area. He ordered the Altena attack in order to divert the security forces which were closing in on other guerrilla groups in the Mtoko region. The de Borchgrave family, who lived at Altena, moved to the adjoining homestead, Whistlefield farm. Two nights later ZANLA launched a rocket and grenade raid, which wounded de Borchgrave and his daughter. In the morning a relieving security force vehicle detonated a landmine. A white corporal was mortally wounded and three other soldiers were injured. On 28 December another three Rhodesian soldiers were killed in a landmine blast. Other attacks on farms followed. The guerrillas had infiltrated into a wide arc from Sipolilo, west of Centenary, to Mtoko in the east, and southwards towards the Chiweshe and Madziwa TTLs. The real war had started. Operation HURRICANE was set up to repel the guerrilla drive. But the response was slow and unsure; the Rhodesian war machine had grown soft with complacency.

Guerrillas were filtering in from Mozambique and Zambia. Rhodesia mounted more raids into Portuguese territory. The Zambians should also be taught a lesson, argued Ian Smith, and on 9 January 1973 Rhodesia closed its borders with Zambia, except for copper shipments, which brought large revenues to Rhodesia Railways. Kaunda was unmoved. Although Smith rescinded the order, the border stayed closed from the Zambian side. Portugal and South Africa were incensed; both governments wanted to use Zambian exports via Beira and South African ports as leverage to induce Zambian moderation. Now that incentive was removed and Rhodesia had to contend with another front along the entire Zambian border.

External diplomacy had failed. So the Rhodesian government tried to wipe out internal support for the guerrillas. Collective fines were imposed on the affected areas; tribesmen were hit where it hurt most: their cattle were impounded. In February 1973 all facilities – shops, clinics, schools, churches, businesses and mills – were shut down in the Chiweshe TTL. Other areas were also 'closed' while the Rhodesian army swept them. 'Inform on the guerrillas or your schools and shops will stay shut' was the message. Although intelligence began to improve, these collective measures embittered the peasant farmers.

Even more counter-productive in psychological terms was the establishment of protected villages. Whole communities were uprooted and put behind the wire. Although militarily effective, it was a propaganda gift to the insurgents. So were the 'no-go areas' and the 'freefire' zones along the Mozambique border. As the curfews were extended, the inevitable increase in innocent civilian deaths made guerrilla recruitment easier.

Still, guerrilla movement was seriously hampered by these measures and in some cases ZANLA had to resort to abduction. On 5 July the first large-scale exodus of schoolchildren took place. Two hundred and ninety-five pupils and staff were marched from St Albert's Mission in the Centenary area. Rhodesian security forces intercepted the column and all but eight were returned. Although many young men left schools to join the guerrillas voluntarily, the abduction attempts increased in the following years. The insurgents' manpower problem was minor compared with the Rhodesian government's limited resources of combat soldiers. White draft-dodgers were hounded. Coloureds (the term for mixed-race Rhodesians) and Asians (who had previously been exempt) were conscripted. Call-ups were extended to include more age groups; pay and conditions were improved for the regulars in the police and the army. Inevitably the drain of white skilled labour from the economy and the accelerating pace of emigration diluted the efficacy of the war-strained economy. Some RF MPs and businessmen argued that a large permanent standing army would be more cost-effective. The consensus

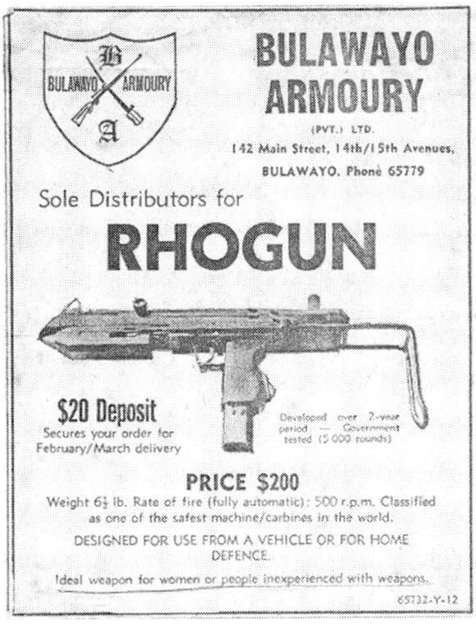


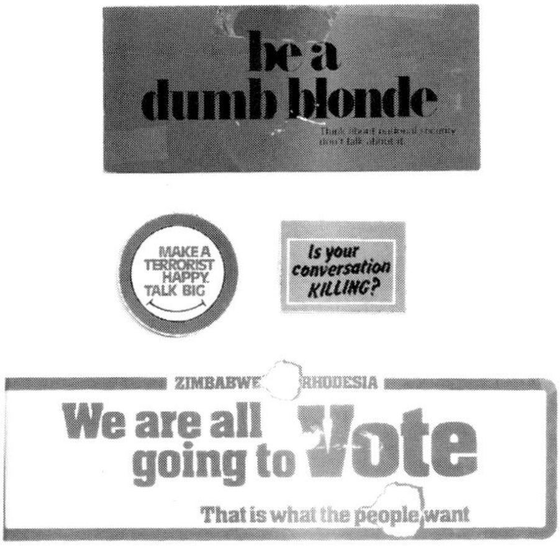


*Above left*: Rhodesian whites were well-armed but not a militaristic society

*Above right*: Rhodesian propaganda stickers

in the Operations Co-ordinating Committee (a joint war council) was against building up a large standing army. It felt that the rural police reserve, which knew its own areas, was more effective. The government still maintained publicly that the insurgency was a 'temporary emergency'; it was not necessary to plan for a protracted war, a long war of attrition which would bleed Rhodesia dry.

While insisting that there was not really a war, the government began to mobilize its full resources. From 1974 the regular army was expanded, partly by encouraging foreign recruitment. A second battalion of the Rhodesian African Rifles was formed. The haphazard call-up system was improved. At the same time a serious attempt was made to wage a psychological counter-offensive. Something had to be done about winning 'the masses'. As in Vietnam, the carrot and the stick were tried. The Ministry of Internal Affairs rushed through a programme of rural development schemes. Tribespeople were offered large rewards for pointing out guerrilla hideouts or the location of weapons caches. Then there was the stick. The augmented security forces were concentrated to clear areas where guerrilla support was widespread. From mid-1974 the PV (protected village) programme was put into top gear. In the following two years about 240,000 Africans were dumped into protected or 'consolidated villages'. Like the experiments in Mozambique, Angola, Algeria and Vietnam, the system produced only patchy results. Sometimes the rural population benefited from the amenities in the villages and felt relieved that they had been removed from intimidation by both sides in the war. Often, the conditions in the PVs were deplorable.

In 1974 Operation OVERLOAD removed tens of thousands of tribesmen from the Chiweshe and Madziwa areas and placed them in PVs where conditions were primitive and disease-ridden. The Rhodesians, like the Americans in Vietnam, forgot that hearts and minds also live in bodies.

Yet the short-term gains were impressive from the Rhodesian point of view. By the end of 1974, Rhodesian intelligence estimated that only seventy to a hundred hardcore guerrillas remained inside the country. The insurgents could perhaps have faced total elimination within a few months, if the security forces had kept up the pressure. But then the international factor ruptured Salisbury's COIN campaign. It went by the name of 'détente'.

Detente was precipitated by South African reactions to events in Lisbon: the Portuguese army became a debating society, not a fighting force. The war effort in the three African 'provinces' collapsed. A month after the coup the revolutionary junta in Lisbon asked Salisbury to halt all pursuit raids into Mozambique. A few days before Mozambican independence, according to the CIO agents running the operation, six former Portuguese Air Force pilots flew six Alouette III helicopters into Rhodesia, and were handsomely rewarded in US dollars.

Nevertheless, the *cordon sanitaire* around white-ruled Southern Africa was disintegrating; the sinews of white supremacy were raw and exposed. The new Mozambique and South Africa were groping towards an accord. Vorster did not want to disrupt his 'outward policy' of detente with black Africa. But Smith's Rhodesia was getting in Pretoria's way. South Africa wanted a moderate and pliant black regime to replace Smith and a long war in Rhodesia would produce a hardline Marxist regime inimical to South Africa. Mark Chona, Kaunda's top aide, and Hendrik van den Bergh, South Africa's intelligence chief, had been working secretly to force a compromise in Rhodesia. The war was destroying Zambia's economy, and Kaunda was tired of the rival Zimbabwean nationalists fighting in his country. Peace would suit both Kaunda and Vorster. As a result of tremendous pressure on Smith from Pretoria and equally blunt tactics by Kaunda and Julius Nyerere, a hurried and uneasy coalition of nationalists agreed to accept a ceasefire starting on 11 December 1974. A number of senior black political detainees were released and constitutional talks without preconditions were scheduled. As a quid pro quo for Kaunda's arm-twisting of the nationalists, Vorster promised to remove South African forces from Rhodesia.

The ceasefire did not work: the Rhodesians pulled back only some of their forward groups and failed to release all the detainees; the guerrillas continued to infiltrate. For example, on 16 December 1974 a group of guerrillas led by Herbert Shungu sent an emissary to a South African police camp with an invitation to discuss surrender terms. The South Africans walked blithely into a trap and were ambushed on the high-level Mazoe bridge. Six of them were killed. Despite the failure of the ceasefire, Pretoria was determined to maintain the pressure.

Disregarding the anger in Salisbury, the South African foreign minister, Dr Hilgard Muller, announced on 11 February 1975 that the SAP had been removed from their forward positions. On 1 August the remaining '200' SAP were ordered out of Rhodesia. (Secretly, under the codename Operation POLO, more than fifty helicopter pilots and mechanics remained to run the Rhodesians' vital chopper force.) Vorster had played his part by leaning on Smith. Now Kaunda nudged the nationalists to agree to a conference at the Victoria Falls bridge in August. The talks proved abortive, except for the unexpectedly good personal accord reached between Vorster and Kaunda. Black and white Rhodesians seemed light years away from settling their differences.

The ceasefire had been a major psychological setback for Salisbury. The nationalists spread the message on the bush telegraph that the whites had been defeated and were surrendering. Ian Smith's comments on the ceasefire were:

> We were on the brink of dealing a knock-out blow. We had them on the run; of this there is no doubt .... In a sense we dropped our guard and as a result we lost a bit of ground. This not only affected us militarily but, more important, psychologically.

The nationalists, however, were not in a position to take advantage of their propaganda success. The year 1975 was a bad one for their liberation struggle. In the previous December the 'Nhari rebellion' had erupted within ZANLA. Thomas Nhari, a senior member of the general staff, kidnapped senior ZANU men in Lusaka as well as taking over the Chifombo camp on the Mozambique-Zambian border. Tongogara's wife and children were also held captive and tortured. Nhari, as an ex-ZAPU man, had been trained in Russia. One of his complaints was the lack of sophisticated weapons reaching ZANLA. The disgruntled cadres that followed him also complained about the lack of supplies and poor administration. Eventually Nhari's men were brought to heel and the leaders, including Nhari, were executed, but only after the deaths of between fifty and sixty ZANLA personnel. Then in March 1975 the charismatic leader, Herbert Chitepo, was assassinated in Lusaka. In a Zambian-sponsored 'international' inquiry that followed, the blame was placed upon ZANLA and a number of leaders, including the unfortunate Tongogara, were tortured and imprisoned in Zambia. Chitepo's death was a major setback for ZANLA and the war effort was forced into low gear for a year.

Who killed Chitepo? Although much initial evidence pointed to ZANLA infighting, the Zambians had a major axe to grind. They were embarrassed by Chitepo's outspoken criticism of their policy of detente with South Africa. Salisbury also gained from Chitepo's death. Years later, former agents in the Rhodesian CIO admitted to organizing the murder. Two former British SAS men, Alan 'Taffy' Brice and Hugh 'Chuck' Hind, set up the operation in Lusaka. The Welshman planted an explosive device in the wheel arch of Chitepo's blue VW Beetle. (The CIO later sent Brice to London in late 1979 to assassinate Mugabe at the Lancaster House talks.)

Zambian pressures forced the remaining members of ZANLA to flee to Mozambique. Zambia became the sole stamping ground of Nkomo's ZIPRA troops. The emasculation of the ZANU leadership disrupted the logistic network to the men in the field; food and supplies ran short. The gaolings and the deaths in the Nhari rebellion had diluted the efficiency and numbers of ZANLA's combat commanders. The less experienced replacements soon fell victim to increased security force activity in Rhodesia and the expansion of the PV programme. ZANLA morale sagged and the casualty rate rocketed. According to Rhodesian intelligence, 'in December 1975 there were only three groups of ten terrorists each operating in Rhodesia'. That was only a slight exaggeration.

ZANU was also short of funds. The OAU had insisted on funnelling its financial support to the African National Council, the nationalist umbrella organization headed by Bishop Abel Muzorewa. Zambia had removed its diplomatic backing for ZANU after Chitepo's death. ZAPU, on the other hand, was given Kaunda's total endorsement; and ZIPRA continued to get a cornucopia of Russian arms through Lusaka. ZANLA had only a shaky base in Mozambique. Samora Machel, the Mozambican president, personally distrusted Robert Mugabe; Machel still viewed ZANU as a fractious offshoot of ZAPU and questioned ZANLA's support in the eastern parts of Rhodesia. Although Machel had kept Mugabe and his colleague, Edgar Tekere, under loose house arrest, he grew to respect Mugabe's commitment to the armed struggle and to appreciate his support both among the fighting cadres and the *povo*, the 'masses' in the countryside.

Gaining the total support of FRELIMO was only one of Mugabe's problems. Some sections of ZANLA had grown tired of the infighting between ZANU and ZAPU and the mismanagement which grew to alarming proportions in 1975. The idea of a 'third force' evolved to try to heal the nationalists' splits by co-ordinating the military wings, thus bypassing the fractious politicos. The Zimbabwe People's Army (ZIPA) was formed, led by Rex Nhongo from ZANLA and Alfred 'Nikita'

Joshua Nkomo, the leader of ZAPU/ZIPRA

Mangena of ZIPRA. The OAU and the front-line states initially welcomed this merger. Soon ZIPA began to act as an independent force. ZIPA wanted to separate from ZANU to form a revolutionary political party which would represent a total commitment to the armed struggle; a separate ZIPA delegation turned up at the Geneva conference, held later in 1976. FRELIMO, however, locked up some of the ZIPA leaders and others returned to the ZANLA fold. The ZIPRA elements left Mozambique to try to rejoin their comrades in Zambia and Matabeleland.

Although ZIPA's influence was temporary, it did launch a fresh offensive into Rhodesia. In Tete, ZIPA concentrated on mobilizing the masses; in Manicaland it adopted a strategy of sabotage, and in the south the guerrillas tried to destroy part of the new railway line to South Africa via Rutenga. The fresh onslaught began on 21 January 1976 when a group of ninety ZIPA guerrillas crossed the border south of Nyamapanda. The following morning four were killed and one was captured. Like so many captured guerrillas, he provided the Rhodesians with a wealth of information. He explained that this unit was part of a three-pronged assault. But the second wave, against the Melsetter area abutting the Mozambique border, did not take place until five weeks later and the third assault in the south-east did not occur until seven weeks later – three months after the planned 'simultaneous' incursions. This delay gave the security forces time to deploy more troops. Extra call-ups stretched the numbers to about 20,000 on active service. In February 1976 Operation THRASHER, based at Umtali, was established to monitor the eastern border and, in May 1976, Operation REPULSE, with its HQ at Fort Victoria, was set up to counter guerrilla infiltration in the south-eastern lowveld.

In March 1976, the Rhodesian government appeared to be on top of the war. Ian Smith was conducting a cosy series of talks with Joshua Nkomo about a settlement – a settlement that as far as Smith was concerned would never include black majority rule. To most whites the war seemed restricted to the border areas. In the towns and cities, where the vast majority of whites relaxed in comfortable suburban cocoons, life seemed perfectly normal. The army was doing well; the police informer network was flushing out guerrilla sympathizers; the blacks in the armed forces and the police (who outnumbered the white members) were loyal. Salisbury clearly felt able to fight a long war, with blacks and whites fighting side by side against what it called 'international communism'. It was only a question of time before the West came to its senses – or so the argument ran.

International factors were about to influence the course of the war, though not in the way Rhodesian whites expected. The power most immediately concerned was South Africa. When the Nkomo-Smith talks broke down at the end of March 1976, Pretoria was determined to push Salisbury towards an urgent settlement. Despite military successes in the Angolan civil war, the South African army had been forced by political constraints to retreat. The Cuban-backed MPLA had claimed a huge victory. For Pretoria the long-dreaded nightmare had become a reality. More than 20,000 Cuban combat troops were positioned in Angola. They would be bound to aid the attacks by SWAPO into South African-ruled Namibia/South West Africa. Pretoria did not want any escalation of the Rhodesian war into Mozambique which might suck Castro's men into another country contiguous to South Africa.

FRELIMO-ruled Mozambique was totally absorbed in consolidating its independence. The exodus of Portuguese whites had left the country in chaos. Mozambique was dependent upon Rhodesian tourists and food and transport revenues. Although Samora Machel was anxious to avoid all-out war with Rhodesia, his commitment to the guerrilla struggle was unequivocal. But the escalation of hostilities made war between Rhodesia and Mozambique inevitable. On 23 February 1976 the Rhodesian Air Force strafed the village of Pafuri, a mile beyond the south-eastern tip of Rhodesia. Four days later Mozambique seized two Rhodesian train crews. Then Smith repeated his errors of 1973 when the Zambian border was closed. He halted all Rhodesian rail traffic through Maputo. In retaliation, on 3 March, Machel cut all links and put his country on a war footing. One-sixth of Rhodesia's rolling stock, as well as massive amounts of sanctions-busting exports, were caught inside Mozambique. Rhodesia was now completely dependent upon the two railway lines to South Africa. This was a leverage Pretoria would soon employ.

The war began to creep towards the centre of the country. At Easter 1976 three South African tourists were killed when travelling on the main road to South Africa. Convoys on the main routes south were then inaugurated. The railway line via Beit bridge was sabotaged. Then the other rail artery, the Bulawayo-Botswana line, came under attack. Some ZIPRA members of ZIPA who had fled from Mozambique rejoined their comrades operating from Botswana and Zambia. Under intense OAU pressure from mid-1976, ZIPRA forces began to infiltrate across the north-western Zambezi and the north-east of Botswana. In August 1976, Operation TANGENT was opened to counter the new ZIPRA moves.

The Rhodesian government was more concerned about FRELIMO support for ZANLA incursions from Mozambique. Rhodesian intelligence reported that about 900 guerrillas were preparing to cross into Rhodesia in August from the Nyadzonya camp. Smith's commanders wanted to launch an Entebbe-style raid and wipe out the guerrilla concentration. This would also bolster sagging white morale. Smith was wary; Vorster had warned him not to raise the tempo of the conflict and thus risk the entry of Cubans into the Rhodesian war. On 5 August a group of about sixty guerrillas attacked a security force base at Ruda, north of Umtali. No casualties were caused, but it was unusual for the guerrillas to hit a base in such numbers. Three days later four territorial soldiers from Umtali were killed in a mortar attack in the Burmah valley, south of Umtali. A fifth Umtali man died in pursuit operations. For a small, close-knit community such as Umtali the loss of five local men was a major blow. The townspeople demanded action against the guerrillas ensconced across the border only a few miles away.

Selous Scouts column preparing to enter Mozambique (Peter Stiff archives)

Smith had the support of the other hawks on his war council. The target would be Nyadzonya about 40 kilometres north-east of Umtali. On 9 August Operation ELAND comprising a convoy of vehicles containing eighty-four Selous Scouts crossed the border. The column was made up of seven armoured Unimogs and four Ferret armoured cars (pre-UDI donations from the British). Two of the Unimogs were armed with Hispano 20mm cannon scavenged from retired Vampire aircraft. The Selous Scouts, including many blacks, particularly a turned ZANLA commissar, Morrison Nyathi, and an attached SAS member who spoke Portuguese, were dressed as FRELIMO soldiers. The vehicles, too, were disguised as Mozambican. After deploying some of the force along the route, seventy-two men, led by a South African, Captain Rob Warraker, drove coolly into a major ZANLA base containing over 5,000 personnel. The SAS man ordered, in abusive Portuguese, the gate to be opened. It was 8.25am. Dropping off a mortar unit at the entrance, the Scouts drove onto the parade ground, where excellent intelligence had accurately predicted that the inhabitants would be assembled. While the SAS man and a Shona-speaking Scout harangued the assembly with revolutionary clichés, the ZANLA cadres began to swarm around the Rhodesian vehicles. Eventually, as those pressed right against the vehicles realized that whites were inside, Warraker gave the order to fire. Initially at point-blank range, three twin MAG machine guns, one 50 Browning machine gin, one 12.77mm heavy machine gun, two Hispano-Suiza 20mm cannon, three .30 Brownings on the Ferret armoured cars and the personal weapons of the Scouts opened up. Carnage ensued. Hundreds were shot, burnt or drowned while trying to escape in the nearby Nyadzonya river. The commander of the Selous Scouts later wrote that the raid was 'the classic operation of the whole war … carried out by only seventy-two soldiers … without air support … and without reserves of any kind'. ZANLA, however, insisted that Nyadzonya was a refugee camp and later held up the raid as the worst atrocity of the war. It seems that, although nearly all the personnel in the camp were unarmed, many were trained guerrillas or undergoing instruction. According to ZANLA documents captured later, 1,028 were killed (without a single security force fatality). ZANLA had been totally surprised.

So was John Vorster when he heard the news. He immediately terminated Operation POLO, the codename for the South Africans who had secretly stayed on in Rhodesia after the official withdrawal in August 1975. Helicopter pilots, mechanics, and liaison officers were summarily withdrawn. The Rhodesian Air Force's strike capacity was cut in half. Worse followed. Although the closure of the Mozambique border had caused genuine congestion on the two railways to South Africa, artificial choke-points soon developed, particularly when it came to vital supplies such as arms and oil. Vorster was angry; the cutbacks in pilots, petrol and bullets made sure Smith knew it. And there was more. On Vorster's instructions, the Oxford-educated Dr Muller, the foreign minister, declared that South Africa supported the principle of majority rule in Rhodesia. The unsayable had been said. Politically Vorster had pulled the rug from under Smith.

The Soweto disturbances, which began in June 1976, had prompted Vorster to compromise over Rhodesia and Namibia. Henry Kissinger, the American secretary of state, knew that the key to compromise in Rhodesia lay in Vorster's hands. He was the only one who could nail Smith to the ground once he was down. Kissinger promised Vorster concessions on American anti-apartheid policy if he delivered Smith's head on a platter. During a series of talks in Pretoria in September Vorster did just that. In an angry encounter Vorster read the riot act to the Rhodesian premier: agree to majority rule or we will cut off your supplies. On 24 September, on Rhodesian television, Smith conceded the principle of majority rule. He announced that in return for majority rule (which he did not define) the war and sanctions would end and a 'trust fund' would be established for development. This was all part of the Kissinger package. Smith added, 'The alternatives to acceptance of the proposals were explained to us in the clearest terms which left no room for misunderstanding.' This was Pretoria's mafia style at its worst.

There was certainly room for misunderstanding in the Geneva conference which followed Smith's surrender. The nationalists were supposed to discuss the mechanics of the rapid transition to majority rule. But the various parties, the

Robert Mugabe and Joshua Nkomo formed the Patriotic Front

UANC (United African National Council, led by Bishop Abel Muzorewa), ZANU (Sithole), as well as Mugabe's ZANU and Nkomo's ZAPU (which had coalesced to form the Patriotic Front), all claimed to be the sole leaders of the African masses.

Smith expected the conference to fail. The moderates within his party realized that unfettered white rule was ending and that the best game plan would be to compromise with the most conservative of the black nationalist groups. Other RF MPs went around their constituencies explaining that the Kissinger package would buy time. Even if the two-year transition was accepted, the whites would still control the security apparatus. And, if things did not work out in two years' time, after that period of grace from sanctions and war Rhodesia would be in a much stronger position to finish off the guerrillas for good – with South African backing and perhaps even a wink from the West.

All the nods and winks in the world could not hide the fact that Smith had reversed the original war aim of the whites: to prevent black rule. Morale in the army slumped. Some of the younger army officers began to mumble about a military coup and Special Branch was kept busy monitoring these white, right-wing radicals as well as trying to keep tabs on the black guerrillas.

The guerrillas had planned to launch an offensive to coincide with the Geneva conference; it did not come off. Three days before the conference started the Rhodesians hit bases in Mozambique. In the north-east, in Tete province, six camps were destroyed. Eighty tons of war material were captured. Most of it was destroyed but eight tons, mainly anti-aircraft guns, anti-tank guns, mortars and heavy machine guns, were brought back to Rhodesia. In the south of Mozambique, camps in Gaza were hit and the main railway to Maputo was sabotaged. The guerrillas, however, suffered few casualties. The camps had received advance warning and so they had been evacuated. This became a frequent pattern which angered military commanders in Salisbury. They conjectured that a senior Rhodesian intelligence source was leaking information, either to the South

The Hawker Hunter was the work horse of the Rhodesian Air Force offensive capability

Africans (who, they suggested, might be tipping off ZANLA), or directly to Mozambique. Nonetheless, the raids in August and November had pre-empted the guerrilla offensive planned for the rainy season of 1976-77.

When the Geneva conference ended without any result, South Africa loosened its arm lock on Rhodesia. Salisbury would get enough arms to hold off the guerrillas until a settlement could be reached, but not enough to obliterate them, which would have brought in the Russians and their East German and Cuban proxies. Smith had clearly dispensed with international diplomacy and moved towards an 'internal settlement'. When the chairman of the Geneva conference, Welsh Labour peer Ivor Richard, tried to resuscitate the talks in early 1977, the idea of involving the guerrillas in the transitional security arrangements shocked Smith and his commanders. To them the internal route to black rule looked much safer. Most of the whites backed Smith's rejections of the British modifications of the Kissinger package. As P.K. van der Byl, the colourful defence and, later, foreign minister, said so dramatically: 'If this new proposal was to be imposed on us, it is better to fight to the last man and the last cartridge and anyway die with some honour than die in front of one of Mugabe's people's courts.'

The easing of South African pressure had ensured that the security forces were not down to the last cartridge, but nonetheless the full-scale war was about to begin. From 1965 to 1972 the guerrillas had managed to apply pinpricks to white rule. In the second phase, from 1972 to 1976, there had been a large degree of African political mobilization, particularly in Mashonaland, but the government had managed to contain the burgeoning conflict with the reluctant and erratic support of South Africa. In the following three years, 1977-79, the war would grow to engulf the whole country and to destroy the Rhodesian government's resolve to fight on.

**Towards all-out war (1977-79)**

After the debacle at Geneva, the Rhodesian government concentrated on finding an 'internal solution' to the war. Pretoria would continue to provide the arms to attack guerrilla camps in Mozambique and Zambia, and later Angola. This would 'buy time' to negotiate with moderate black leaders, who would be suitably awed by the still vigorous white military power. Such was the thinking in Salisbury. It meant that the Anglo-American proposals of September 1977, touted by Andrew Young, the American ambassador to the UN, and Dr David Owen, the British foreign secretary, were doomed.

The Patriotic Front was neither awed nor keen to negotiate an end to the war. By April 1977 the Rhodesian government conceded that about 2,350 guerrillas were active in the four operational areas: 500 in Hurricane, 1,000 in Thrasher, 650 in Repulse and 200 in Tangent. New operational areas were opened in central Rhodesia (Grapple), the Salisbury area (Salops) and Lake Kariba (Splinter). As the numbers of guerrillas increased, so did the extent of the penetration and disruption of the government infrastructure. Schools, clinics and mission stations were forcibly closed. In the south-east in May 1977 the government admitted that 22,000 tribesmen in four administrative areas had refused to pay their taxes. All over the country African councils in the rural areas could not function; local council buildings were looted and burnt. Stock theft and attacks on white farms mounted. In August 1977 the railway line to Sinoia was sabotaged on the outskirts of Salisbury. The most devastating guerrilla attack in 1977 was the bomb planted on 7 August at a Woolworth's store in Salisbury: eleven people were killed and more than seventy injured. Nearly all the casualties were black. ZIPRA infiltration increased across the Botswana border; the new tempo of Nkomo's effort brought a massive upswing in recruits, many of them schoolchildren, who crossed clandestinely into Botswana. They were then flown to Zambia for training.

Also, ZANLA raids grew more daring. On 18 December at 10.45pm about sixty ZANLA guerrillas attacked the Grand Reef security force base near Umtali. The troops were watching a film show in the canteen. The show came to an abrupt end as rockets crashed onto the area. The guerrillas had seen one Rhodesian Light

Infantry unit leave, but they had not noticed the arrival of another RLI Fire Force which returned fire. The guerrillas then disappeared into the night, after killing one African and injuring six whites at the base. A vociferous section of the RF demanded total war on the guerrillas: it wanted a full-scale call-up and urged that, while a large regular army was being created, the security forces should destroy all guerrilla bases in the front-line states. Some hardliners in the RF hatched a plan to appoint a military junta under General Walls, after putting Smith under house arrest. Later twelve RF members, nicknamed the 'dirty dozen', hived off from the ruling party to form the Rhodesia Action Party. (They were all defeated in the August 1977 general election.) But the dissident RF men had a point: the Rhodesian effort was poorly organized. A new War Council was set up to co-ordinate the various ministries directly involved in the war; it also included the service chiefs. A National Manpower Board was established to oversee white conscription. The most important development was the creation of a Combined Operations Centre (ComOps) in March 1977 which took over the role of the OCC and the National JOC. ComOps now co-ordinated the activities of the various Joint Operations Commands which remained the HQs of the respective operational areas. ComOps was thus the national JOC for day-to-day administration and also a think-tank for long-range strategic planning. It was headed by Lieutenant General Peter Walls, the Rhodesian-born, Sandhurst-trained, former C.-in-C. of the Rhodesian Army.

ComOps HQ was appropriately situated in Milton Buildings next to the prime minister's office in central Salisbury. By late 1979 the political-military balance

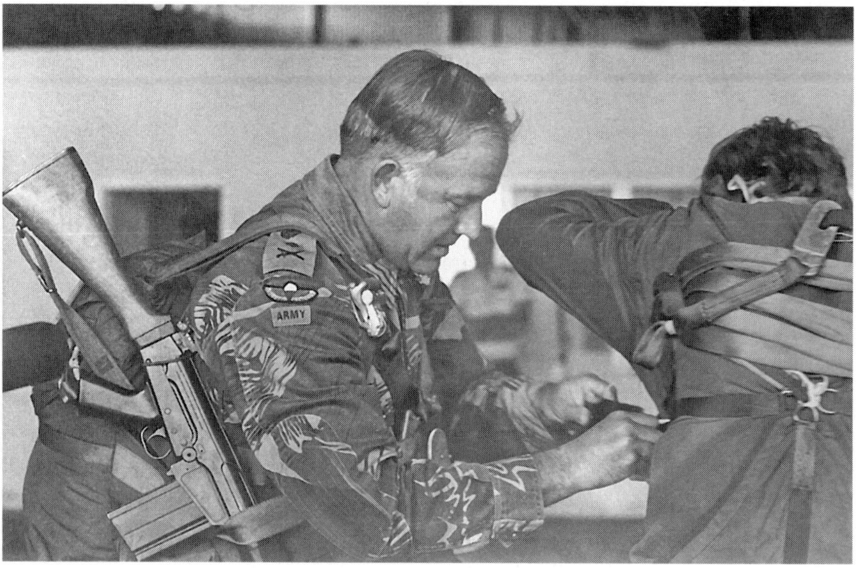

Lieutenant General Peter Walls was popular with his subordinates as a hands-on commander

had swung heavily towards Walls. By then, real power in Rhodesia lay in the hands of Walls, not Smith or Muzorewa. Ken Flower, who headed the CIO, also wielded tremendous power behind the scenes. By this time Smith and Walls were hardly on speaking terms because of disagreements over strategy. Both men were strong-minded and Smith found it easier to get on with Walls's deputy, Mick McLaren. The two ex-airmen spent hours talking about aircraft, often of the Second World War variety. (After the Rhodesian war ended, Walls was asked why he hadn't persuaded Smith of the importance of providing a political strategy for the war. Walls maintained that as a 'simple soldier' he was not in a position to dominate the political leadership, especially a stubborn man like Smith. Bearing in mind the position of the army in the last stages of the war and Walls's personal influence, it is difficult to accept Walls's conventional interpretation of civil-military relations. Perhaps Walls, a former member of the Black Watch, had fully imbibed the Sandhurst principles of civilian dominance.)

Besides changes at the top, in April 1977 – despite an outcry from the business community – conscription was extended to the 38-50 age group and exemptions were severely reduced. The maximum call-up for those under 38 was increased to 190 days a year; those older than 50 were asked to volunteer for police duties. In September the government encouraged national servicemen to stay on for another year by offering Rh$100 a month bonus. The bottom of the barrel was being scraped; the only alternative was to boost the number of black soldiers. Black doctors had already been drafted and apprentices were next on the list, but largescale black conscription was unnecessary as hundreds of volunteers flocked every month to join the Rhodesian African Rifles. The RAR was augmented with a third and a projected fourth battalion. In addition, the PV programme was stepped up. In June 1977, according to the Ministry of Internal Affairs, more than 145 PVs and forty consolidated villages had been completed; another thirty-two PVs were scheduled for construction by the end of the year. The Catholic Justice and Peace Commission asserted that 203 PVs had been erected and that, in August 1977, 580,832 people were living 'behind the wire', often in squalor. Dawn-to-dusk curfews had been imposed on most TTLs and 'no go' areas had been extended along the Botswana and Mozambique borders. The government was trying to pull out all the stops. As Roger Hawkins, the minister of combined operations, put it: 'Until now it has been accepted as basically a police operation with military support against criminals. Now it is to be a military operation, mainly by the army, with police support.'

Hawkins also admitted that 'our greatest problem before was lack of decision'. Decisions were now made. The most significant was to escalate the cross-border raids. ComOps personnel had been impressed by the various film versions of the Entebbe raid; in particular, they wanted to experiment with a Dakota fitted out with communications equipment to act as the 'command module' for future raids. And the SAS were arguing for a '1,000-kill' raid. In May 1977, Mapai, about 95 kilometres from the Mozambique-Rhodesia border, was captured by security forces. It was not a successful raid. In spite of the scale of the operation, only thirty-two guerrillas were killed, although large quantities of equipment were seized. But a Rhodesian Dakota was shot down and the pilot killed at the Mapai airstrip. The raid was prolonged to three days to salvage the plane. ComOps privately blamed the military failure on a tip-off; politically the Mapai raid was a disaster. An irate Vorster phoned Smith to tell him to pull out his troops. Pretoria was still not convinced of the validity of Smith's plan to bomb his way into a constitutional settlement. South Africa did not want an endless war; it was looking to its own military needs (in November 1977 the UN imposed a mandatory arms embargo on the apartheid state).

But then South Africa changed tack. For a number of political reasons, including the need to project a tough image to sidestep the ultras' HNP challenge in the November elections, the National Party government began to support the internal settlement plan in Rhodesia. Bishop Muzorewa's UANC looked like going along with Smith; so did Ndabaningi Sithole's wing of ZANU. On 25 September 1977 Smith had flown to see Kaunda in Lusaka to encourage the old warrior Nkomo to return. With his options widening, Smith had in effect rejected the Anglo-American settlement by late September. The Rhodesian government particularly loathed the idea of integrating the guerrilla armies with the Rhodesian security forces during a transition period monitored by a British Resident Commissioner (Field Marshal Lord Carver) and a UN-appointed military supremo (General Prem Chand). Perhaps a show of force before negotiating with Muzorewa and Sithole would work. And this time Pretoria nodded its assent. (On most occasions, until the last few months of the war, the Rhodesians did not consult Pretoria officially in case it disapproved. Salisbury wanted to avoid having to disregard South African advice, though the SADF liaison officers in Salisbury co-ordinated any military support required.)

On 23 November the Rhodesians launched their biggest operation to date. The Rhodesian army, with a crucial SAS core, hit the ZANLA HQ near Chimoio, about 90 kilometres inside Mozambique (roughly opposite Umtali). Three days later a second assault wave overcame Tembue in Tete province (220 kilometres from the Rhodesian border). The assaults, codenamed Operation DINGO, were classic examples of vertical envelopments. At Chimoio ninety-seven SAS and forty-eight RLI parachutists landed on two sides of the base, while forty heliborne RLI troops were dropped on the third side. The fourth side of the trap was, in theory, to be sealed by fire from heavily-armed Alouette K-cars, after the initial bombing strikes. Chimoio was estimated to hold at least 9,000 ZANLA and Tembue 4,000. Practically the entire air force (forty-two helicopters, eight Hunters, six Vampires, three Canberras, six Dakotas and twelve Lynx aircraft) was deployed for air strikes and to transport 185 Rhodesian troops. It was almost impossible to airlift more than 200 troops at one time. Normally, a 3:1 superiority is required for attacking an entrenched enemy; the Rhodesian attackers were massively outnumbered. The element of surprise and air power were supposed to fill the gap. During Operation DINGO, ComOps claimed that the Rhodesians had killed more than 1,200 guerrillas for the loss of one Rhodesian soldier and eight injured. According to ZANU sources, the guerrilla figures were much higher; probably nearer 2,000, many of them women and children. The Chimoio complex contained schools and hospitals, as well as military training sections.

The slaughter at Chimoio was to have a big impact on the collective psyche of the ZANU leadership. The mass graves were continually conjured up in political speeches and poetry, particularly after Mugabe's accession to power. After a week's protest, however, the most important leader still in Rhodesia, Muzorewa, decided to return to his negotiations with Ian Smith. Eventually, in March 1978, Smith reached an accord with Muzorewa, Sithole and a pliant Shona chief, Senator Jeremiah Chirau. These four men, nicknamed the 'gang of four', hoped to bring about a kind of majority rule that would end the war and pre-empt a military victory by the forces of the Patriotic Front. It was essentially a formula for white survival: 'Give them the parliament and we keep the banks and tanks.'

The Patriotic Front rejected the March Agreement as a sham, another UDI. Nkomo called the three internal black leaders 'small nuts in a big machine'. Nevertheless, Nkomo still kept back the bulk of his army. During 1978 he never deployed in Rhodesia more than 2,000 guerrillas; 8,000 to 10,000 remained in bases in Zambia. ZANU in Mozambique had repaired much of the damage caused by interparty dissension. 1978 was declared the 'Year of the People' in which ZANU intended to achieve a mass political mobilization of the peasantry before 1979, the 'Year of the People's Storm', the final onslaught on the Rhodesian government. ZANLA troops entered Rhodesia in groups 100-strong; by June 1978 at least 13,000 ZANLA troops were deployed in the country. They were assisted by locally trained recruits and thousands of *mujibas* (young unarmed local volunteers).

In Salisbury, Muzorewa and Sithole, now members of the four-man Executive Council (Exco) which in theory controlled the transitional government established in March 1978, promised that the war would wind down. They argued that, as majority rule was in sight, the guerrillas would have no reason to fight on. Both men claimed to represent large groups of ZANLA guerrillas but Smith was soon to find out that the two nationalists had deceived both him and themselves. During the rest of 1978 only a few hundred genuine guerrillas responded to the government's amnesty offer.

The internal solution was not working. The war escalated. The main reason why the guerrillas refused to heed Salisbury's call was the fact that behind Sithole's and Muzorewa's rhetoric all real power was still firmly in the hands of the whites. The obvious example was the running of the war. On the same day that the Bishop,

Bishop Abel Muzorewa, the leader of the so-called 'internal settlement' (Allen Pizzey)

Sithole and Chirau were sworn into government, Smith quietly created his own unofficial war council, which had six members: Walls, as head of ComOps, the army and air force chiefs, the commissioner of police, the director-general of the CIO and sometimes civilian ministers. The streamlined war council had been set up in September 1976 to co-ordinate the ministerial control of the war; in March 1977 the formation of ComOps had improved the central command. Smith's personal council primarily aimed at excluding the black co-minister of defence. They were considered unreliable and prone to security leaks. (The first black minister of defence, John Kadzviti, a Sithole man and former guerrilla, shortly after his appointment fled the country to escape a murder charge brought by the British South African Police.) Smith was officially excluded from the conduct of the war. In fact, however, he worked closely with the service chiefs.

The new administration tried to improve its image. Most of the political detainees were released, executions of political prisoners were suspended and the ban on the political wings of both ZAPU and Mugabe's ZANU was (temporarily) removed. In spite of the military repercussions, many of the PVs were closed, especially in the Mtoko, Mrewa and Mudzi areas. (Some were in regions where the government tacitly admitted it had lost effective control.) This was done to satisfy the UANC's clamour to end the PV programme, which it knew was unpopular with the tribespeople. The main weakness, however, was the tardy removal of racial discrimination. Smith seemed to regard the tempo of removal of racial inequalities as an exchange for winding down the war. The black leaders had not kept their side of the agreement, Smith argued. In turn the black leaders argued that white intransigence over the race laws had undermined their efforts to persuade the guerrillas to come home. Lacking real power, the three black internal members of the Exco did look like stooges.

Many white soldiers regarded the settlement as an opportunity to Africanize the war under effective white leadership. With blacks in a semblance of power, a tougher policy against the front-line states might be more acceptable to the world. White conscripts continued to agitate for blacks to be conscripted as well. Muzorewa opposed this move (except for blacks already affected – apprentices and doctors). But in September Exco announced that blacks would be conscripted in spite of the massive problems of training this posed for the army. Skilled men were needed in the field; few could be spared as instructors. The light had just dawned upon Muzorewa and Sithole: both leaders belatedly realized that they should flood the army with as many trained political followers as possible. Black Rhodesians, who comprised nearly 80 per cent of the armed forces in 1978, could well hold the balance of power in the future. It would be just as well to have some soldiers already committed to their respective parties.

Meanwhile, the security forces were determined to show that a black-white coalition in Salisbury did not imply a softly-softly approach to the war. Sometimes excesses resulted. At a village in the Gutu district in May, security forces fired upon a night-time *pungwe* (rally) organized by ZANLA troops. At least fifty black civilians were killed and twenty-four were wounded for the loss of one guerrilla. Despite protests from Muzorewa, such incidents of indiscriminate firing continued. Casualties caused by the guerrillas also mounted. By mid-June fatalities within the country were 100 a week, against three a week in the first five years of the war. Guerrilla attacks became more determined and cruel. On 23 June twelve missionaries – eight adults and four children – were raped, hacked and bludgeoned to death at the Elim Pentecostal Mission in the Vumba mountains near Umtali. (ZANLA denied responsibility, and blamed the Selous Scouts. After the war, regular ZANLA troops were proved to be guilty of the abomination.) In July the first major gun battle took place within the Salisbury city limits. The spiralling conflict continued to hit the white core: emigration was edging up to 1,500 a month and taxes were increased. On 20 July the government announced a compulsory national defence levy of 12.5 per cent extra income tax to help to cover a record budget deficit.

Salisbury was also perturbed by international events. In July 1978 the US Senate voted against lifting sanctions. Despite continuing South African backing, Rhodesia under a black-white coalition appeared to be the same pariah it was under unadulterated RF rule. And the Russians were meddling in southern Africa again. The Soviets and the Cubans were accused of encouraging an invasion from Angola of the Shaba province of Zaire. The bestial slaughter of whites in Kolwezi sent shivers down white Rhodesian spines, as they prepared to hand over to blacks. Black rule might come in parliament, but the whites were determined to control law and order and the security forces. Rhodesian intelligence sources began to fear that the Cubans would step up their support of ZIPRA, which could be given the means to launch a conventional sortie into Matabeleland. Vassily Solodovnikov, the Russian ambassador in Lusaka, was portrayed by the CIO as the *eminence grise* behind an invasion threat. BOSS had got wind of the plans and so had the CIO. The CIO head, Ken Flower, rushed off to London. The traditional intelligence links between the rebel state and Britain (as well as the USA) had, like oil, proved too slippery and vital to succumb to the moral dictates of sanctions. London tried to calm the Rhodesians; the British were more afraid of Smith renouncing UDI and handing back to them a Rhodesia which was portrayed by the world's media as completely wartorn. This thought terrified London more than any conceivable Red plot. The British fears were groundless because Smith would never willingly have renounced UDI. He had a pathological distrust of the British. (Although the CIO did have some grounds for alarm, as there was evidence of a conventional build-up, the Russians were playing a waiting game and were planning a long-term strategy. The year 1978 was vetoed. When the Cubans suggested a conventional sortie in mid-1979, ZIPRA rejected the plan even though ZANLA had also made extensive preparations for a conventional incursion. The Russians expected the war to last much longer and were gearing up for a big move in July 1980 or July 1981, depending on military developments.)

Lord Richard Cecil

In April 1978 the first (and only) Western war correspondent was killed. It was a sad irony, but it happened to be Lord Richard Cecil, a descendant of Lord Salisbury, the British prime minister who had lent his name to the Rhodesian capital. My regular squash partner in Salisbury, Richard was a former Grenadier Guards officer who had a distinguished record in Northern Ireland; he was shot while making a film of the war. Oddly, his rifle was inoperative and he could not defend himself when a guerrilla literally popped up in front of him. Because of his unusually good contacts with the Rhodesian army, he had caused some resentment among other journalists. He also carried a gun, which contradicted the professional ethics of journalists, who claim neutrality. Some journalists did nevertheless carry firearms for self-protection. The insurgents rarely asked for press cards before opening fire.

By mid-1978 Smith knew that his internal experiment was not working. The transitional government was being torn apart by party bickering among the blacks; even some of his own trusted supporters had been involved in a scandal over the theft of defence funds. The war was worsening and no one, not even South Africa, wanted to recognize the beleaguered state. Could Nkomo be brought into the internal settlement? Could ZIPRA and the security forces together wipe out ZANLA? Certainly Zambia and Angola, and perhaps other African states, would recognize a Nkomo-led Zimbabwe.

On 14 August Smith flew to State House, Lusaka, in a Lonrho company jet. Nkomo and Smith talked again, and later Brigadier Joseph Garba, a former Nigerian commissioner for external affairs, tried to involve Mugabe. The ZANU leader refused. The secret Nkomo-Smith talks did not blossom into a military alliance, however, because on 3 September 1978 ZIPRA guerrillas shot down an unarmed Air Rhodesia Viscount with a SAM-7 missile. Of the fifty-three people on board, eighteen survived the crash, but ten of them, including six women, were massacred by ZIPRA guerrillas. Nkomo said that ZIPRA had shot down the plane, but had not murdered the survivors. During a BBC interview the ZAPU leader incensed Rhodesians by chuckling over the Viscount incident. One RF MP, Rob Gaunt, captured the mood of the whites when he said:

> I believe we have done our utmost in this country to be reasonable and the time, I fear, is now upon us when all Africa is going to see their first race of really angry white men.

Smith called Nkomo a 'monster'; clearly a ZAPU-RF deal was out of the question. In a subdued speech (Walls had persuaded him to tone it down) Smith declared martial law in certain areas of the country. Although ZAPU and ZANU were later re-banned, Special Branch allowed senior ZAPU personnel, such as Josiah Chinamano, to leave the country before arresting the lower-echelon party members. Perhaps when the storm had died down, Nkomo and Smith could try again.

The whites called for a massive retaliation against Zambia. Initially, however, the Rhodesians hit Mozambique. In late September Rhodesian forces launched a four-day airborne attack against ZANLA bases around Chimoio. The area had been extensively attacked in the previous November in Operation DINGO. It had been rebuilt, but dispersed over a much wider area. The Canberras went in low with their Alpha anti-personnel bombs, followed by the Hunters with Golf bombs which were designed to explode above ground. The Rhodesian troops, including South African Recce Commandos in D Squadron of the SAS, spent three days clearing ZANLA from the trenches. Nine FRELIMO T-54s were driven off when they came to the rescue, and four Soviet armoured cars were destroyed. The Rhodesians lost no aircraft, but many were hit by ground fire. The Rhodesians suffered one trooper killed in 'friendly fire' during an air strike; a South African serving with the SAS was killed in a separate incident. Salisbury claimed that large quantities of ammunition had been destroyed and several hundred guerrillas killed. Zambia seemed to have had a reprieve. In early October Kaunda had opened the Zambian border, which had been closed since 1973. The British-owned Benguela railway through Angola was useless because of action by South African-backed UNITA rebels and the TAZARA line through Tanzania was clogged by mismanagement. Kaunda had no choice but to use Rhodesia to get his copper out and food and fertilizer in.

Then Rhodesian security forces swept into Zambia. Previously Salisbury had launched raids only in the border areas of Zambia. On 18/19 October 1978 Chikumbi, 19 kilometres north of Lusaka, was bombed. Mkushi camp, north-east of the capital, was also bombed and occupied by heliborne troops for two days. Via 'Green Leader', the lead pilot of the Canberra bombing force, Rhodesians controlled Zambian airspace during the Chikumbi raid, and in effect prevented any hostile Zambian air activity for forty-eight hours. Using a Zambian airstrip (Rufunsa, near the Rhodesian border) as a forward staging base, Rhodesian aircraft created panic in the camps they hit.

During the Green Leader raid the security forces suffered minimal casualties. The Rhodesians claimed more than 1,500 ZIPRA killed as well as a small number of Cuban instructors. In fact, the bulk of Nkomo's 10,000-strong army in Zambia was unscathed, although hundreds of refugees living in and near the camps were killed. From the gunners' sights it was impossible to distinguish innocent refugees from young ZIPRA recruits.

The three-day assault demonstrated the efficacy of Rhodesian firepower and the superior security force training and leadership. Perhaps better weapons could help to fill the gap? Nkomo rushed off to Moscow to ask for further military aid and Kaunda asked Britain to improve on the air defence weapons it had already sent. Besides new equipment such as AA guns, the British Aircraft Corporation sent instructors and a maintenance team to refit the Rapier SAM system which had fallen into disrepair.

The raids into Mozambique and Zambia had boosted white morale, but they had done little to deter the rainy season offensives of both ZANLA and ZIPRA.

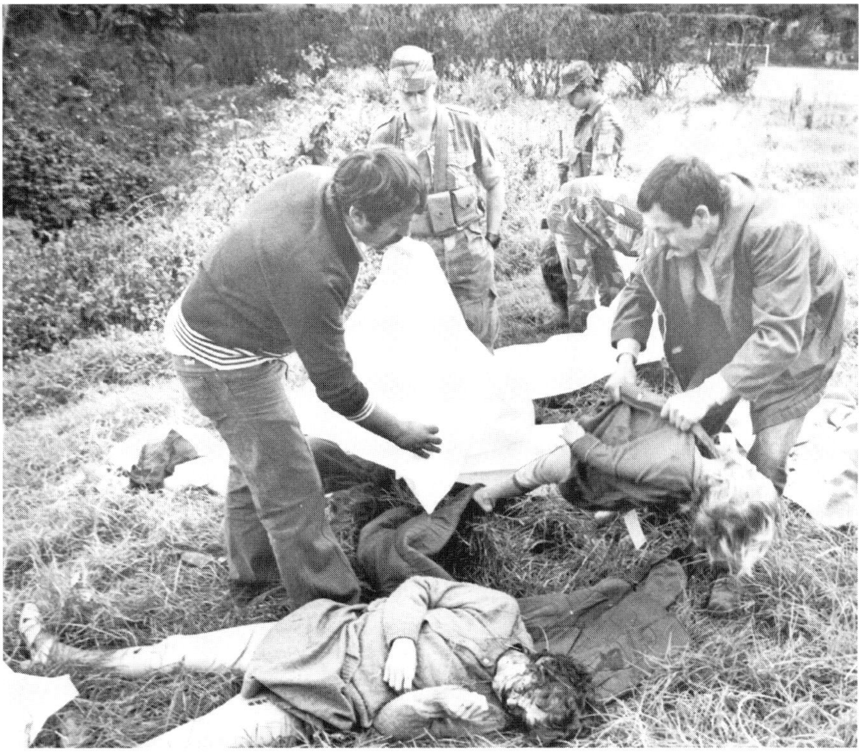

On 23 June 1978, twelve men, women and children were variously raped, hacked and bludgeoned to death by ZANLA at the Elim Pentecostal Mission near Umtali

On 23 October General Walls admitted: 'We have not only had a hard job containing them [the guerrillas] but in some areas we have slipped back a bit.' By December 1978 three-quarters of the country was under martial law. The generals, not a squabbling Exco, held uncertain sway. Courts martial had been set up which could impose the death penalty for acts of terrorism without the right of appeal to higher courts (though sentences were subject to a reviewing authority). The government claimed that more than twenty-two 'frozen zones' (encompassing 7 per cent of Rhodesia) were being policed by auxiliaries, the guerrillas who had come 'onside' and accepted the internal settlement. In fact, only a small proportion were converted guerrillas; the vast majority had either been unemployed or were UANC or ZANU (Sithole) supporters who had been trained in Uganda, Libya and the Sudan. By late 1978 the UANC and ZANU (Sithole) had about 1,000 armed guerrillas each. By late 1979 *Pfumu reVanhu,* as they had become known, had swollen to nearly 20,000. Most were loyal to Muzorewa. In spite of the brief training and supervision provided by Rhodesian whites, the auxiliaries turned on each other as much as they

*Pfumo reVanhu*, an auxiliary force loyal to Muzorewa (Allen Pizzey)

fought the PF. Often looting rather than battle was their main pre occupation. A measure of their military capability was that Selous Scouts often dressed up as auxiliaries to entice the guerrillas into attacking a supposedly 'soft' target. The RF was creating the conditions for its greatest fear: civil war. Five armies were active in Rhodesia by December 1978: ZANLA, ZIPRA, the security forces and the separate armed followers of Sithole and Muzorewa.

From Salisbury things looked decidedly ugly. The internal elections had been postponed from December 1978 to April 1979 because of the security situation. The internal 'solution' had impressed relatively few guerrillas; even UANC supporters were disgruntled. Moreover, few of the 25,000 Africans affected by the October call-up seemed ready to take up arms against their brothers in the PF. With whites emigrating and blacks reluctant to be conscripted, who would protect the Salisbury government in the future? The war was edging closer to the city suburbs. On 11 November, while Smith was celebrating the anniversary of UDI, guerrillas launched an attack on the exclusive Umwinsidale suburb of Salisbury. On 11 December guerrillas fired rockets and tracers at the central oil storage depot in the heart of Salisbury's industrial sites. Only five guards armed merely with truncheons had been protecting the vital depot. ZANLA forces (although ZIPRA claimed the honours) created a fire which lasted six days and destroyed 25 million gallons of fuel.

The Rhodesian government entered 1979 in dire straits. This was to prove the crucial year. ZIPRA forces were committed in greater numbers; Rhodesia was now safer for them than Zambia. ZANLA, which stopped active recruiting because numbers were too large to train, had infiltrated beyond the Bulawayo-Plumtree railway line. The cities were being surrounded and ZANLA believed they would fall like 'ripe plums' as Mao had foretold. Despite the frictions, in some areas ZANLA and ZIPRA were co-ordinating their strikes. ZANLA was preparing to establish formal liberated zones and to defend them with a locally-trained people's militia. The groundwork for the initial crude structure of administration was being laid.

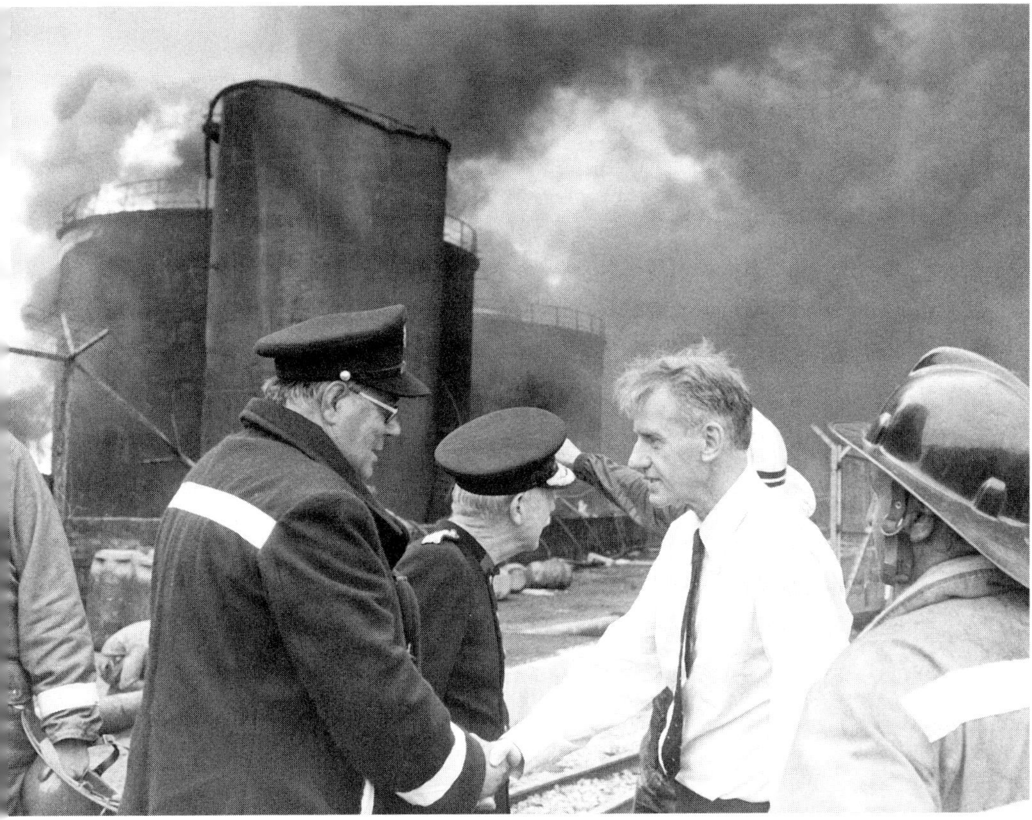

The great fire of Salisbury. Ian Smith thanks the South African fire chief for his help

South Africa also feared the worst. During the white referendum of January 1979 that preceded the April poll, Smith admitted that if things went wrong South Africa had made 'a very generous agreement' to help Rhodesian war widows and the war-wounded. (A year before South Africa had secretly offered Rhodesian special forces, and their families, the option to move south to join the SADF.) Pretoria was also preparing to construct refugee camps in the northern Transvaal. And, like the British, South Africa had considered contingency plans for the military evacuation of Rhodesians if a wholesale carnage against whites was to take place. Against such a scenario of fear, the whites still said 'yes' (85 per cent of the 71 per cent poll) to Smith's plan to elect the first black prime minister of 'Zimbabwe-Rhodesia'. How could Salisbury expect the PF guerrillas to believe that white rule was really over and to hand in their arms, if the unborn republic was to have such an ugly compromise name so redolent of white chicanery?

In the same month as the referendum, blacks had massively boycotted conscription. On 10 January only 300 out of the scheduled 1,544 blacks turned up at Llewellyn Barracks in Bulawayo. Also, 415 of the expected 1,500 whites failed to show up. Two days later whites aged 50 to 59 were told they would have to serve for forty-two days a year. Even 'Dad's Army' would have to be deployed for the coming general election.

On 12 February 1979 ZIPRA shot down another civilian Viscount aircraft. Air Rhodesia Flight 827 from Kariba to Salisbury was hit by a SAM-7. Fifty-four passengers and five crew members were killed as the plane came down only 50 kilometres from the spot where the first SAM victim had crashed. Nkomo claimed that the intended target had been General Walls, who was aboard a plane which took off just after the ill-fated Viscount. The alleged attempt to kill Walls was probably a post-hoc rationalization: ZIPRA had intended to shoot down a plane just before the referendum. The emotional white backlash might have produced a 'no' to Smith's plans and this would have disrupted the internal settlement to the benefit of the PF.

A feeling of sullen, resigned anger pervaded the white community, which retreated further into its laager. The roads were unsafe even for convoys; now the sky was dangerous too. Air Rhodesia flights were reduced and old Dakotas with heat-dispersion units around the engine exhausts were introduced on passenger runs. South African Airways cut back its flights and stopped its Jumbo jets from landing at Salisbury airport.

On 26 February the Rhodesian Air Force launched a retaliatory raid deep into Angola, the first major raid on that country. Four Canberra jets struck at a ZIPRA base at Luso, situated on the Benguela railway and 1,000 kilometres from the Rhodesian border. Thanks to excellent intelligence work, the Rhodesian pilots avoided the British-maintained air defence of Zambia and the Russian-manned radar tracking system in Angola. In this audacious raid 160 guerrillas were killed and 530 injured. The Soviet MiG-17s at the Russo-Cuban air base at Henrique de Carvalho (320 kilometres to the north) did not have time to retaliate. The guiding hand of South Africa was evident, however. The SADF was unhappy about the SWAPO threat to South West Africa and the UN's indifference to guerrilla incursions from adjacent Angola. Rhodesia could act as a cat's paw for the SADF, and SAAF Mirages could provide some emergency protection for the Canberras if things went wrong in Angola, despite their limited combat radius (a factor which also inhibited the Russian MiGs). All four Canberras returned safely. Ironically, on the same day as the raid ZIPRA did shoot down a Macchi jet-fighter north-west of Lusaka, but this plane belonged to the Zambian Air Force. ZIPRA troops were jittery, as the Rhodesian Air Force had made two big raids into Zambia in the week before the Luso sortie. Rhodesians were in a tough mood in February; as one ComOps spokesman discussed the cross border strategy he said: 'If necessary, we'll blast them back into the Stone Age.'

Special forces had already attacked Zambian oil depots, with little success. On 23 March 1979, however, the SAS, with South African Recce Commando support, hit the Munhava oil depot in Beira. RENAMO was given the credit, a frequently used device for Mozambican coastal raids. But the raiders arrived in Mark 4 Zodiacs, courtesy of ships from the South African Navy. (The navy also regularly supplied and transported RENAMO leaders by submarine.) The oil depot went up in flames and the desperate Mozambicans turned to the specialist unit of firefighters in Alberton, near Johannesburg. The South Africans helped in the arson plot and then basked in the applause for their good neighbourliness.

The Rhodesian strategy had always relied upon sound morale and leadership. But by 1979 the prospect of black rule, even by the internal leaders, had sapped white resilience. Grit had been transformed into mechanical resignation. Worse was the infighting within the RF and the UANC. The senior officers of the army were at loggerheads over military developments. An incident in January 1979 exacerbated their strategic (and personal) schisms. On 29 January a bugging device was discovered in Colonel Ron Reid-Daly's office. As Reid-Daly was then head of the elite Selous Scouts, this had serious security implications (though no one was actually monitoring his calls, because the Director of Military Intelligence, Lieutenant Colonel John Redfern, said he had actually 'forgotten' about it after the Selous Scout monitoring plan was devised in August 1978). All Selous Scouts and SAS operations were immediately suspended. Two days later Reid-Daly launched a personal attack on the army commander, Lieutenant General John Hickman. The occasion was a crowded RLI mess during the drunken celebrations of the regiment's birthday at Cranborne Barracks. An angry Reid-Daly used more than soldier's language to describe his commander. Later described as being 'overwrought and emotional', Reid-Daly turned to Hickman, the guest of honour and began, 'I want to say to you Army Commander for bugging my telephone, thank you very much.' Raucous cheers followed. Everyone assumed Reid-Daly was joking. Reid-Daly repeated his words, and the company went silent. Reid-Daly concluded, 'If I ever see you again, it will be too soon.' The two antagonists immediately squared up for a fight, but senior officers managed to separate them. Reid-Daly was court martialled for insubordination and given a minor punishment. He then resigned. But the Reid-Daly/Hickman row had dredged up many murky facts about the army. There followed a welter of accusations and counter-accusations of gunrunning and poaching. (Most prominent was the accusation that the Selous Scouts were using the no-go areas, from which other army units were excluded, to poach big game rather than hunt guerrillas. In some no-go areas on the Mozambique border guerrilla bands would seek refuge in Selous Scouts-patrolled areas and use them as a haven from patrols by other security forces.)

After another embarrassing incident involving too much alcohol, a lady and then wearing just his underpants while on parade, General Hickman was summoned to the ministry of defence at 7.45am on the following Monday. The co-minister of defence, Hilary Squires, had a file on his desk which contained the full details. The minister, who had a puritanical streak at the best of times, sacked Hickman on the spot. At 7.50 the general was out of a job. (Hickman, who had earned the MC in Malaya, later sued, and won, a case for wrongful dismissal.) After Hickman's departure, the ministry of defence needed a 'Mr Clean'. The two choices as Hickman's successor were either Major General Derry McIntyre or Sandy MacLean. McIntyre, although popular with his men, also had a reputation as a playboy, a man who was often described as 'a cross between a cavalier and a hooligan'. MacLean had a stable family background and, on the technicality that he was twelve days senior, was appointed the new army commander.

Hickman's decision to contest his dismissal publicized the problem in the army. Then Reid-Daly sued Hickman (and the minister of defence and combined operations, Muzorewa, the directors of army military intelligence and counter-intelligence, the director of military police, and other senior officers). As the court case dragged on to an inconclusive end, the normally publicity-conscious Hickman dropped out of sight. The death from wounds of his 19-year-old son also severely affected him. A bitter Reid-Daly went to South Africa, where he dabbled in a number of security firms and then, after helping to write his own account of the war, became briefly the head of the Transkei's army.

In spite of the scandals surrounding two of Rhodesia's best-known soldiers, Lieutenant General MacLean tried to give the impression that it was business as usual, for the army had to organize a massive security screen for the April one man-one vote, election. More than 70,000 men were involved in the country's biggest mobilization. The security forces were determined to prevent any PF disruption of the polls, but sometimes the preventive countermeasures were heavy-handed. The security forces also took the offensive across Rhodesia's borders. On 13 April the SAS led a major assault on the ZIPRA military command HQ in Lusaka (the Selous Scouts had done the initial reconnaissance in the city). The raiders tried to smash through the main gates in a Land Rover, but the padlock held and the vehicle had to be used a second time to batter through them. By this time the ZIPRA guards were alerted and the SAS were pinned down by a RPD light machine gun. The delay gave time for Nkomo, who was thought to be in the building, to escape. ComOps said that it wanted to destroy the ZIPRA nerve centre, but an SAS source later admitted that the aim was to kill Nkomo. The ZAPU boss maintained that he had been at home and that he had escaped through a lavatory window (despite his extensive girth). So complete was the destruction of the building that the ZIPRA leader could not have escaped. He must have been elsewhere, allegedly tipped off by a British mole in CIO. Rhodesian troops wearing Botswana Defence Force uniforms also sank the Kazangula ferry which was said to be carrying ZIPRA military supplies from Zambia into Botswana daily. At the same time commandos spirited away ZAPU men from Francistown in Botswana and took them back to Salisbury. Not a single Rhodesian soldier was killed in the dramatic attacks which were executed with total efficiency and accuracy.

ComOps regarded the April election as its crowning success. Never had a ruling minority done so much to hand over (apparent) power to a dominated majority. As one critical history, *Rhodesians Never Die*, observed about the two elections which marked the end of white rule: 'Rhodesia buried itself with considerable integrity and maximum bureaucratic effort.' Some Rhodesians, and most of the hundreds of foreign pressmen in the country, expected the April internal elections to be wrecked by PF attacks. Instead, the security forces inflicted a high kill rate on the ZANLA forces which had concentrated in the Chinamora, Mhondoro and other TTLs in the Salisbury area. Security forces were deployed near all the static and mobile polling booths; for the first time the auxiliaries were mobilized in a major supporting role in the rural areas. Eighteen of the 932 polling stations were attacked, but none were closed. In a 64 per cent poll (if the population estimates were correct) 1,869,077 voters took part. Even some guerrillas took part. In some areas ZANLA actively encouraged the peasants to vote, although in most cases the PF tried to discourage any involvement in the election. The diminutive bishop, Abel Muzorewa, won fifty-one of the seventy-two black seats and so became the first African premier of the country. The election was a success comparable to that in 1966 in war-torn South Vietnam. It proved that the PF was nowhere near 'imminent victory' and that the security forces were still powerful enough to mount a huge logistic exercise. If, as the PF claimed, the turnout was the result of intimidation, it showed who effectively controlled the population at that time.

Rhodesians believed implicitly in Margaret Thatcher's promise, when leader of the opposition, that she would recognize the April poll if the Tory group of observers said the election was fair. The group, headed by Lord Boyd, did indeed submit a favourable report, but the new British prime minister reneged on her commitment. She was swayed by a Foreign Office confidential paper outlining the possible repercussions of recognizing Salisbury, plus personal pressure from Lord Carrington, her foreign secretary. This was a catastrophic setback for Muzorewa. Many Africans rightly interpreted it as lack of faith. If a Conservative British administration would not go along with the internal settlement, who would? And the plain answer was – nobody. The internal settlement's goal had been to bring peace, recognition and the removal of sanctions. The only tangible result was an escalation of the war. When the bishop became prime minister on 1 June 1979 he assumed the additional portfolios of defence and combined operations. By then ZANLA forces numbered more than 20,000 in the country. Could Muzorewa survive Mugabe's 'Year of the People's Storm'?

The PF felt that military victory would come within one or two years at the latest. But what if Western nations recognized Muzorewa and channelled into Salisbury a vast array of military assistance? That would set back the war by years. By mid-1979 ZANLA had amassed a large reserve of conventional weaponry, although the variety of calibres and spares was proving a major problem. ComOps was aware of the arsenal at Mapai, not far from the ZANLA

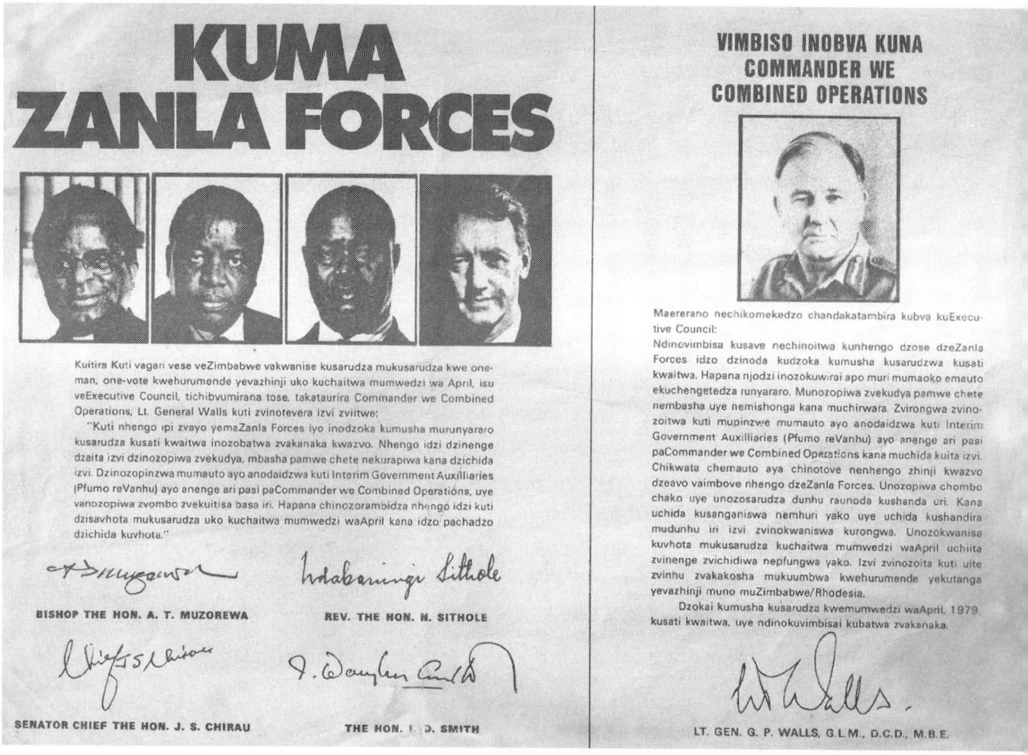


The 'gang of four' offered amnesty to insurgents who wanted to leave the Patriotic Front

base which the Rhodesians had hit on a number of occasions. The weapons seemed to be set aside for a special purpose which eluded Rhodesian intelligence. The arsenal had been intended at one time, May 1979, to support Operation CUBA. This was a Cuban scheme to set up a provisional government within a liberated area of Rhodesia. Many Eastern-bloc and Third World countries would have recognized it and thus have pre-empted Western recognition of the Muzorewa administration. Mapai could have supplied such a venture in the Chiredzi area, apparently ZANLA's choice. ZIPRA did not want anything to do with the plan and the Cubans withdrew their support. The open terrain in the Chiredzi area and its proximity to South Africa would have made a joint ZIPRA/ZANLA/FPLM/Cuban army an ideal target for a Rhodesian and South African conventional counter-attack. The other area mentioned in Operation CUBA, the north-east, would have been far more viable.

As it happened, the Cuban fear was unwarranted; not even South Africa risked recognizing Muzorewa. But Pretoria did pour equipment, pilots and ground troops into the very area set aside for Operation CUBA. And with the promises of bonuses and security of pensions, many whites in the civil service, security forces and police were persuaded to stay for another two years. Yet after the brief euphoria of the April election, the whites grew disenchanted with Muzorewa's ham-fisted management of the new coalition government. Even his own UANC split with the departure of James Chikerema's Zimbabwe Democratic Party. Then the bishop talked of encouraging skilled whites to return, but demanded a levy of $20,000. His biggest failure was his 'campaign for peace'. Muzorewa launched his amnesty programme at the same time as he authorized the RLI to wipe out groups of mutinous auxiliaries. Sithole's men were particularly unruly in the Gokwe area. In this area and others a total of 183 auxiliaries were killed. One group was gunned down by troops hiding in the backs of troop carriers; another was lured into a schoolhouse for a supposed meeting to thrash out discipline problems and obliterated in a strike by Hunters. Undoubtedly the government needed to control the more lawless bands of *Pfumo reVanhu,* but to kill so many of what the PF considered to be the bishop's own force – just before the amnesty launch – was catastrophic timing. Few PF guerrillas were impressed.

The Amnesty Directorate had been set up on 7 June 1979. It was headed by an Ulsterman, Malcolm Thompson, the man who had masterminded the administration of the April election. The amnesty call included the exhortation to phone a series of numbers across the country. Most of the numbers were UANC offices. A group of journalists tried to phone these offices in the early evening; most of the numbers were unobtainable because the offices were unmanned. The security force aspects of the amnesty were much more professionally executed. Besides the radio and TV campaigns, trilingual leaflets were scattered across the country. The air force helped with 'skyshouts'. Aircraft would suddenly swoop down on a guerrilla camp. As the guerrillas ran to escape the expected bomb run they were deafened by the blast from enormous tannoys which delivered a dramatic and simple message: 'You are about to be killed by the security forces. Give up and live.' Despite many possible personal doubts about the internal settlement, guerrillas were severely punished by political commissars for listening to amnesty broadcasts. They could be executed for reading an amnesty leaflet.

The internal leaders had promised peace after the March Agreement in 1978. Then they said the war would end after the one man-one vote polls; then after the installation of a black premier ... . Eventually few whites believed anything Muzorewa or Sithole said. Many emerged from their cocoons of total reliance on 'good old Smithy'. After the April election the disenchantment in the army, particularly among the Territorials, was widespread. The bickering among the internal nationalists, which threatened to destroy all the hard work the part-time soldiers and policemen had done, undermined their loyalty. A number of white police reservists refused to guard Muzorewa's house the week after the April poll. They pointed out that the prelate had many bodyguards while their own families went unprotected. No disciplinary action was taken against the policemen. The real bone of contention was still white conscription. Why should the bishop call up 59-year-old whites, possibly hostile to the UANC, when he refused to conscript his youthful black followers? Only a handful of blacks had been called up. The whites began to feel that their taxes and skills were running the country and yet they were being compelled to fight for a black administration that could soon steal their rights and property. Another issue was the loyalty of the so-called 'new Rhodesians', the roughly 1,400 foreign mercenaries and volunteers in the regular forces. On the night of Muzorewa's election victory, Captain Bill Atkins, an American Vietnam veteran who had been in the Rhodesian army for two years, said:

> A good proportion of the foreign professionals [in the army] will stay – we're not mercenaries. If we find that we're working with a guy we disagree with, we will leave. We're not here for the money. If they [the new Muzorewa administration] back away from the war, as the Americans did in Vietnam, then we'll leave.

No amount of reluctant military support from South Africa, white Rhodesians or foreign levies could replace some kind of international diplomatic support for Muzorewa. The PF rejected the new leader as a puppet. As one ZANU official put it, 'At least the leader of a so-called Bantustan in South Africa can fire his own police chief.' But Muzorewa could not. Behind the facade, the whites were in control. Even Ian Smith was still there in the cabinet as a minister without portfolio. But the PF regarded him as the minister with *all* portfolios. And the new Tory prime minister, Margaret Thatcher, was still reluctant to recognize Muzorewa. At the Commonwealth Conference in Lusaka in August, Mrs Thatcher secured the agreement of her fellow premiers: an all-party conference would try for one last time to cut the Gordian knot of the Rhodesian impasse. Muzorewa was bitter and Salisbury's *Herald* newspaper thundered: 'Is Mrs Thatcher really a Labour Prime Minister in drag?'

The Lancaster House conference opened on 10 September and staggered on until just before Christmas. Both sides struggled to inflict military reverses on their opponents, both to influence the course of the three-month conference and to be in a commanding military position if diplomacy should once again fail. As during the Geneva conference the guerrillas talked and fought, but this time there were four times as many guerrillas in the country as in 1976. Within forty-eight hours of Muzorewa's accession to power he had authorized raids into his neighbours' countries. Later, on 26 June, the Rhodesians hit the Chikumbi base, north of Lusaka. Simultaneously five choppers dropped assault troops into the Lusaka suburb of Roma where they stormed into the ZAPU intelligence HO. During the fighting thirty ZAPU cadres and one SAS captain were killed. Five hundred pounds of sensitive documents were seized. What had happened to the 150 tons of British air defence equipment which had been sent to Zambia in October 1978 and the Rapier missiles which the BAC team had repaired? Was it plain incompetence, or were the Zambians afraid of protecting PF targets in case Salisbury decided to hit directly at Zambian military installations?

On 5 September, five days before the Lancaster House marathon began, Rhodesian forces hit ZANLA bases in the area around Aldeia de Barragem, 150 kilometres north-west of Maputo. This was part of a new strategy: instead of just targeting PF military bases, Salisbury escalated its strikes to include the economic infrastructures of both Zambia and Mozambique. The attacks on economic targets, especially dropping bridges, were a small part of the ComOps 'final solution' plan. The highly secret proposals estimated that both Mozambique's and Zambia's economic structures could be destroyed within six weeks. The techniques to be used would have escalated the war gravely and almost certainly brought in the major powers. ComOps demanded a clear political green light for total war on Zimbabwe-Rhodesia's neighbours. If Muzorewa had been recognized after a possible breakdown of the Lancaster House talks, then the plan might have been put into action. Instead only small parts of the scheme were used. It was then poorly organized. Major setbacks resulted and Walls was privately criticized by senior commanders for undue interference, particularly regarding the choice of targets. Some of the final raids were not planned by Walls or the CIO chief, who often had the final say, because both men were in London for most of the Lancaster House talks. Several raids had to be publicly supported by them even though they had been carried out against their better judgement.

In September the Rhodesians tried to destroy much of the transport system in Mozambique's Gaza province, and beyond. More bridges were destroyed by SAS and South African Recce Commandos. Then Salisbury stopped the rail supplies of maize to Zambia through Zimbabwe-Rhodesia. In October and November vital Zambian road and rail arteries were hit. The aim was two-fold: to stop the infiltration of PF guerrillas and supplies, and to induce the front-line states to pressurize the PF into accepting a more conciliatory line towards the Salisbury delegation in London. Such a strategy was not without its costs. ZIPRA had improved with the aid of Cuban, East German and Russian instructors. And FRELIMO had added a stiffening to ZANLA forces. In Zambia the regular army was too small and ineffective to give much conventional support to ZIPRA in its defence against Rhodesian raids, but in Mozambique the position was quite different. The ZANLA bases there were well defended.

The Rhodesian raids were now no walkover. In the three-day Operation URIC (Operation BOOTLACE for the South Africans) in the first week of September the Rhodesians were determined to stop the flow of both ZANLA and regular FPLM soldiers infiltrating across what the Rhodesians nicknamed the 'Russian Front'.

The target was Mapai, the FRELIMO 2 Brigade HQ and a control centre for ZANLA, a very heavily defended forward base 50 kilometres from the border. Conventional military thinking dictated that in addition to air support, two infantry battalions supported by artillery and tanks would have been required. As ever, the Rhodesians would make do with far less, relying on the shock of air power, surprise and courage. The aerial order of battle included eight hunters, twelve Dakotas (half SAAF), six Canberras (of which four were South African), ten Lynxes and twenty-eight helicopters, including the newly-acquired, but worn-out Cheetahs (Hueys) along with a majority provided by the SAAF: Pumas, Super Frelons and Alouettes. A Mirage and Buccaneer strike force was on cockpit readiness in South Africa, and a battalion of paratroopers, with Puma helicopter transport, was on standby at a base near the Mozambique border. The command Dakota, the Warthog, was equipped with an advanced sensor system capable of locating and monitoring the guidance systems of ground-to-air missile installations and identifying surveillance radar systems. The crew included an intelligence officer and four signallers for communications with friendly forces. The plane was piloted by John Fairey, a scion of the famous British air pioneer. The SAAF had its own AWACS aircraft, a converted DC-4, nicknamed Spook. This was the largest single commitment of the SADF in the war.

The Canberras normally carried the cylindrical Rhodesian-designed Alpha bombs. But these had to be released in level flight, at an air speed of 350 knots, 300 metres above the ground. When they struck they bounced four metres into the air and exploded, sending out a deadly hail of ball bearings. The flak at Mapai was so heavy that they would have been blown out of the sky if they tried a low-level attack. So the SAAF supplied conventional bombs which were dropped from 20,000 feet. A heliborne force of 192 troops went in after the bombers. In all, the raiders numbered 360 men in the field, from the SAS, Recce Commandos, RLI and the engineers. They met very fierce opposition. The fire from the 122mm rockets, mortars, recoilless rifles and machine guns from the entrenched ZANLA/FPLM enemy was intense, the heaviest the Rhodesians had ever encountered. All they had, besides airpower, were 82mm and 60mm mortars, RPG-7s, light machine guns and their personal weapons. Soon the battle developed into a grim face-to-face encounter in trenches. The defenders stood and fought, and showed no intention of running from the airpower, as they had so many times previously. General Walls, in the Warthog above the battle, wanted a victory not a defeat to accompany the politicking at Lancaster House. Nor did the South Africans want to commit their reserves and so not only risk defeat but also reveal the extent of their cross-border war with Mozambique.

Two helicopters were shot down. The first was a Cheetah, hit by an RPG-7. The technician was killed but the badly wounded pilot was extricated by a quick-thinking SAS sergeant. The second to be downed was an SAAF Puma; the three air crew and eleven Rhodesian soldiers were killed when an RPG-7 rocket hit the chopper. One of the dead was Corporal LeRoy Duberley, the full-back of the national Rhodesian rugby team. The remains of the wrecked Puma were later golf-bombed in a vain effort to destroy the South African markings. Seventeen soldiers were killed in Operation URIC. Walls called a stop to the operation. This was the worst single military disaster of the war. And, for the first time, the Rhodesians were unable to recover the bodies of their fallen comrades. As a book on the Rhodesian SAS later noted, 'For the first time in the history of the war, the Rhodesians had been stopped dead in their tracks.' The RLI and the SAS were forced to make an uncharacteristic and hasty retreat.

The Rhodesians had underestimated their enemy. They were outgunned. Their air support had proved unable to winkle out well-entrenched troops and they were even more vulnerable when the aircraft – even when the whole air force was on call – returned to base to refuel and rearm. Combined Operations had decided to use more firepower. Surveillance from the air was stepped up by deploying the Warthog. The South African Air Force became heavily involved in these last months, both in the fighting and as standby reserves, as in the case of Operation URIC in September 1979. Super Frelon and Puma helicopters were difficult to pass off as Rhodesian equipment, but the Canberras and Alouettes also on loan were practically indistinguishable from their Rhodesian counterparts, except when they were shot down. The combined Rhodesian-South African efforts were approaching all-out war in the region. But, at the end of the climactic raid on New Chimoio, one Selous Scout admitted: 'We knew then that we could never beat them. They had so much equipment and there were so many of them. They would just keep coming with more and more.'

The political warfare at the conference table was almost as bitter as on the real battlefields in southern Africa. The PF haggled over every step of the negotiations. Muzorewa had conceded easily. But Ian Smith had to be brought into line by the toughness of Lord Carrington, the conference chairman, as well as by a series of lectures from Ken Flower, General Walls and D.C. Smith, his RF deputy. David C. Smith had played a pivotal role. Bishop Muzorewa had not wanted to include Ian Smith in his delegation to London, but David Smith had talked the bishop into it and said that he himself would not go if the RF leader were excluded. Ian Smith's presence was counterproductive for the Salisbury team, however. The RF chief did his best to undermine the bishop's leadership. Gradually the PF was pushed into a diplomatic corner. The British had bugged all the hotel suites, especially the PF's, and knew exactly how far to push the guerrilla leaders. The Rhodesians realized that their hotel was bugged and sometimes used an irritating device which made squawking noises to hide conversations. More often they talked about confidential matters out-of-doors. Lord Carrington told the PF he would go ahead and recognize Muzorewa if the conference broke down. None of the front-line states wanted the war to continue and they exerted a continuous leverage on the hardline PF coalition. Josiah Tongogara, who had more influence over ZANLA than did Mugabe, believed that a political compromise was possible. Nyerere also urged moderation and persuaded Britain that more than 'metaphysical' force was needed to set up a ceasefire monitoring group. Samora Machel was also a vital ally of Carrington. In spite of Mugabe's threats to go back to the bush, Machel privately told him that he wanted peace, and without Mozambique as a sanctuary ZANLA would collapse. Machel told Mugabe: 'We FRELIMO secured independence by military victory against colonists. But your settlers have not been defeated, so you must negotiate.' Angola, Nigeria and Zambia, for different reasons, wanted a speedy end to the conflict; there had been too much suffering for far too long.

If the guerrillas had not been put in a stranglehold by their backers, especially in Mozambique, and had walked out of the conference, Lord Carrington had warned that he would go for the 'second-class solution': recognition of Muzorewa. Paradoxically, the very success of the military raids, especially on the economic infrastructure (including the SAS-Recce Commando raid on Beira harbour on 18 September), was probably politically counterproductive. The raids raised the morale of the white hardliners in Salisbury, but it ensured that the front-line states kept the PF sitting around the table. A tactful lull in the externals might well have prompted Mugabe to go for the unconditional surrender option, and walk out, and thus force Carrington to hand the baton to Muzorewa.

On 12 December Carrington took a gamble and sent Lord Soames as the new British governor of Rhodesia. It was a highly risky venture, 'a leap in the dark' in Soames's own words. Final agreement on the complete process of drafting a new constitution, a return to British rule, a ceasefire and a new election had not been reached. But the rebellion was over. As soon as Lord Soames stepped down on Rhodesian soil, the revolt against the British Crown was quashed and sanctions were removed. But the civil war went on.

Walls had long predicted privately that the war would end in a military stalemate, and so it was. On 21 December 1979, after an epic of stubborn last stands, all parties to the conference signed the final agreement. On 28 December the ceasefire creaked uncertainly into life. By 4 January 1980 more than 18,000 guerrillas had heeded the ceasefire and had entered the agreed rendezvous and assembly points inside Zimbabwe-Rhodesia.

Just as the ceasefire began, one of the main architects of compromise, Josiah Tongogara, was reported killed in a motor accident in Mozambique. As the most prominent soldier on the ZANLA side, his voice of moderation – especially regarding relations with ZIPRA – would be sorely missed. Because 'motor accidents' had been staged throughout the Rhodesian saga as a means of removing opponents, ZANU went out of its way to try to prove the incident an accident, even to the extent of sending a white employee of a Salisbury funeral service to

Maputo to embalm the body. A strong suspicion of murder lingered at the time; nevertheless, no firm evidence of his murder has surfaced. For once in the long Rhodesian saga of assassinations, a road accident may have been just a simple road accident. Some contemporary sources suggested that Tongogara was killed by a small group of professional assassins from Eastern Europe. Senior ZANU men had agreed to his removal because of several general factors, including his desire to work closely with ZIPRA and his emphasis on encouraging whites to remain in the country. But the specific reason may have been his alternative plan, discussed privately during the Lancaster House talks, if the conference had failed. He argued that the three main armies (ZIPRA, ZANLA, the Rhodesian security forces) could guarantee a peaceful, five-year transition to civilian rule. A council of four parties (the RF, UANC, ZANU and ZAPU) would provide the administration, with a council of the military leaders acting as a watchdog. During this period the armies would be integrated. Then, after five years, or sooner if the integration was completed, elections would be held. Sir Humphrey Gibbs, the former governor, was suggested as a compromise candidate for the transitional presidency. ZIPRA apparently went along with the plan, but the constitutional conference reached agreement before Walls could be consulted by Tongogara. With hindsight such a plan appears bizarre, but it certainly paralleled Tongogara's public demands for conciliation.

Certainly some reconciliation would be needed to rebuild the devastated country. The long war had exacted a sad toll. More than 30,000 people had been killed (though some historians have offered a lower figure). Operation TURKEY had destroyed a vast acreage of peasant crops to prevent food reaching the guerrillas. The International Red Cross estimated that 20 per cent of the seven million black population was suffering from malnutrition. More than 850,000 people were homeless. The maimed, blinded and crippled totalled at least 10,000. The Salvation Army reckoned that of the 100 mission hospitals and clinics which served the rural population, fifty-one were closed, three had been burnt to the ground, and most of the others were badly damaged and looted. About 483,000 children had been displaced from their schools; some had gone without schooling for five years. Half the country's schools had been closed or destroyed. Finding a real peace was only half the problem; a massive reconstruction programme would have to follow.

Many outside observers and most whites in Rhodesia expected the fragile truce to erupt once more into fullscale war which a British governor with only 1,300 Commonwealth troops would have to contain. Ninety-five per cent of the country was under martial law when Soames arrived. Extra regular troops had entered the conflict. FPLM soldiers from Mozambique were fighting alongside ZANLA. On the other side, the South African army's commitment had grown. By November 1979, South Africans were operating in strength in the south-east, particularly in the Sengwe TTL and along the border. They were supplied by air from Messina and their HQ was at Malapati. They were using artillery bombardment to create guerrilla movement, a technique the Rhodesians could not afford with 25-pounder shells costing $150 each. By December the SADF was operating north of Chiredzi. The aim was to put one battalion, each with a company-sized fire force, into each major operational area, making the total commitment five battalions. The news of South African involvement was deliberately leaked to boost sagging white morale.

If the ceasefire collapsed, more foreign regulars would be sent to fight in the civil war, a war that could have engulfed southern Africa. A grave responsibility rested on the man at the epicentre of the storm, Lord Soames, who had no previous experience of African affairs. As the London *Observer* warned: 'A bomb disposal expert would be the best British Governor to send to Zimbabwe-Rhodesia. The country lies ticking, a black and white booby trap with many detonators.' Would the ceasefire hold?

A Rhodesian T-55. These tanks were originally destined for Idi Amin's Uganda. Courtesy of the South Africans, they wound up in Salisbury to considerably boost Rhodesia's conventional power. They were displayed at the end of 1979 and during the elections as psychological reassurance for the whites

### *Ceasefire*

Nobody in Rhodesia really believed the ceasefire would hold. Despite the mountain of pessimism, the British governor and his staff were determined to try to make it work. No British government for fifteen years had dared to contemplate sending British troops to Rhodesia. Now a predominantly British Commonwealth force was being sent into the middle of a war with only light arms and the responsibility of having to defend itself against attacks from the guerrillas or the security forces or both. It was a high-risk venture. The fact that it succeeded can be attributed mainly to the personality of the new governor and the courage of the Commonwealth Monitoring Force.

Soames was an excellent choice as the Empire's last pro-consul. As one Foreign Office insider said of the well-fleshed, ex-Etonian and Sandhurst man, 'He's large, noisy and impossible to ignore.' His Churchillian connections (he had married Churchill's daughter, Mary) appealed to the old-fashioned patriotism latent in many white Rhodesians and his blunt patrician manner earned him the respect of the African leaders. As one of Nkomo's senior aides told me, 'We Africans get on with old fashioned Tories better than modern Labour politicians.' Soames lifted sanctions, opened the closed borders, put an end to secret trials and released dozens of political prisoners. But could he stop the rival armies rupturing the ceasefire and, even more difficult, could he ensure that elections be held amid the barrage of intimidation and violence?

The Commonwealth force was the key to peace. The force, 1,300 strong and led by Major General John Acland, was made up of 159 Australians, seventy-five New Zealanders, fifty-one Kenyans and twenty-four Fijians, with the rest British troops from thirty-five different units. Their task (code-named Operation AGILA) was to supervise the movement of PF guerrillas from the various rendezvous points to the sixteen assembly points (APs) and then to make sure they stayed there. By 6 January 1980, 15,730 guerrillas had assembled. Their numbers ranged from thirty in one AP to 6,000 in others. By 9 January more than 20,634 had gathered and the numbers gradually increased to about 22,000. Small groups of Commonwealth troops camped near the APs to give a reassurance that the Rhodesian Air Force would not bomb the area. Even though most APs were turned into fortresses by the guerrillas, Commonwealth troops were told not to make their own defensive measures obvious. Although they were supposed to be merely a 'psychological barrier', in areas near some APs British troops began to dig deeper slit trenches.

Another danger was the presence of land mines. Tens of thousands of mines were laid by the Rhodesians along 750 kilometres of the border. Some maps of the minefields were incomplete; even in well-mapped areas the rains had shifted many of the devices. Twenty-five security force engineers were killed and ninety-one lost limbs while putting the mines down. During the ceasefire the guerrillas sometimes helped to point out their mines in the vicinity of APs and their access routes, but the random nature of guerrilla plantings would cause tragedies long after the end of the war

Although the Rhodesian commanders had warned that most of the Commonwealth groups would be 'taken out' on the first night, remarkably few incidents ensued. By and large, the Commonwealth force, particularly the British members, worked with tremendous tact, courage and good humour to persuade the guerrillas that the ceasefire was not a trick. Besides reassuring the guerrillas, the Commonwealth force became responsible for feeding and housing 22,000 people. Everything from film shows to panties (for the hundreds of female guerrillas) had to be provided. Rations were issued on a scale equivalent to an African soldier in the Rhodesian army. It was a logistic nightmare. Meat, 450 tons, was bought from South Africa and ninety tons was airlifted for immediate distribution. Eighty per cent of the goods were provided locally, but the initial demand for 23,000 of everything (from toothpicks to sets of knives and forks) meant purchases from Britain, Hong Kong, America and South Africa.

Food, clothes and entertainment were crucial. Many of the guerrillas were angry and bored. They did not want to stay cooped up for two months until the election results were announced. Many of them wanted to get out and join the guerrillas who remained outside the APs. Of the 22,000 in APs, about 16,500 were ZANLA and 5,500 ZIPRA. But many of these men were not guerrillas: a large percentage were *mujibas* or, in some cases, just camp followers. At least 7,000 fully-trained ZANLA troops remained outside. They had been ordered to stay out and organize for the election even if (as happened) their commander, Rex Nhongo, should order them via TV and radio broadcasts to go to the APs. More than 500 fully-trained ZIPRA troops also remained operational outside the APs. In addition, thousands of guerrillas were still in Mozambique and Zambia; many of these were infiltrating across the border after the 4 January deadline for assembly of guerrillas in the APs. ZANLA infiltration and political harassment were escalating, and the removal of Rhodesian security forces to their bases had also led to a massive upsurge in banditry and crime. The increasing violence threatened to swamp the fragile ceasefire. The small groups of Commonwealth troops around the fourteen APs (two were disbanded) were extremely vulnerable, even though British troops were in reserve in Kenya and RLI Fire Force troops were ready to spearhead rescue attempts for endangered Commonwealth troops.

On 6 January Lord Soames authorized the redeployment of the security forces with the order to use minimum force. As well as the regular units, more than 15,000 auxiliaries were included. Soames was forced to rely upon the security forces and the police, as well as the civil service, if he was to effectively administer the transition. From the viewpoint of many African states, as well as guerrillas, this was bound to encourage a pro-establishment bias during the run up to the election. Soames was further criticized for allowing South African troops to remain in the Beit bridge area. (Officially they were removed on 30 January; unofficially some regular SADF troops donned Rhodesian uniforms. Mugabe insisted that 6,000 South African troops were still operating in the country. Three thousand, he said, had just been disguised as Rhodesian troops and 3,000 had been serving for some years as volunteers.) The other major criticism was of Lord Soames's deployment of the auxiliaries, who often acted like thugs in the TTLs.

After a few weeks it looked as though, from a military perspective, the ceasefire was a success. The guerrillas were being fed and clothed, although they were still jittery about possible attack, especially from the air. Occasionally they would overreact. In one incident the guerrillas surrounded the entire 'Echo' AP with machine guns, RPG-7s and mortars trained on the Commonwealth troops. And, on the other side, in spite of military skirmishes with 'unlawful' guerrillas (those who had not moved into APs or had strayed from them) Soames appeared to have the Rhodesian security forces under control. But this was an illusion; towards the end of the war, the Rhodesian military had begun to act as a state within a state. It was only the personal contacts between Smith and his service chiefs which kept the fiction of political supervision intact. With 95 per cent of the country under martial law, military dominance was inevitable. Soames was in fact at the mercy of the Rhodesian high command.

The key figure was still Walls. A confidential memo in the files of the Foreign Office's Rhodesia section described him as the right man in the right job at the right time, 'One of the more comforting aspects of the Rhodesia complex.' Walls had earned the respect of the Brits at the Lancaster House conference by backing Ken Flower's reading of the riot act to Ian Smith when the RF leader was the odd man out in the Salisbury delegation's acceptance of Carrington's initial proposals. In the end, Walls, not Soames, was to prove the final arbiter of war and peace in Rhodesia.

Another key figure for British intelligence was Derry McIntyre, one of the most popular senior officers in the army. MI6 had fingered him as the man who might be sufficiently daring, able and charismatic to lead a coup. Many of the Commonwealth soldiers showed true grit during the exigencies of the ceasefire, but some of the officers were playing fast and loose with the Rhodesian women. The most egregious example was the British commander himself, Major General Sir John Acland. The unconventional Scots Guards officer was foolish enough to seduce, over a game of bridge, Major General McIntyre's attractive wife. The understandably irate Rhodesian general intended to personally shoot, with his service revolver, the offending British commander This could have collapsed the very delicate peacekeeping exercise, and possibly spark general war in the region. McIntyre was eventually dissuaded from an almost justifiable homicide.

Nevertheless, he was completely distracted at a time when a coup was highly possible. Whether Acland was acting under orders in the service of his Queen or whether he was dangerously indiscreet is not known. Experience of the British officer corps might suggest the latter, especially considering Acland's record for impulsive behaviour during his long (and distinguished) career.

Behind the scenes, the security forces worked to ensure a Muzorewa victory. The auxiliaries were busy in the village 'teaching people how to vote'. And the army illegally distributed anti-Mugabe leaflets. Security force members, mainly Selous Scouts, were also responsible for a number of 'dirty tricks' including attacks on churches (while leaving false evidence of ZANLA complicity) and the destruction of the pro-Mugabe Mambo Press in Gwelo. The security forces denied any involvement, particularly the planting of a massive bomb which nearly succeeded in killing Mugabe when he was on a visit to Fort Victoria on 10 February. Mugabe had led a charmed life. The CIO at the very last minute had aborted an attempt to assassinate him in London during the Lancaster House talks. At least nine other Rhodesian attempts on his life were foiled or aborted. The last one was scheduled for 2 March 1980, when the SAS planned to use a SAM-7 Strela to shoot down a plane carrying Mugabe and twenty-two members of his central committee as it came in to land at Salisbury airport. Some SAS operators objected to killing the crew as well. ComOps cancelled the plan at the last minute. The dirty tricks and assassinations, which came under the code name Operation HECTIC, were poorly planned, partly because of constant infighting and vacillation in ComOps.

Meanwhile, ComOps lambasted Mugabe's dirty politics and mass intimidation, while denying any underhand measures of their own. Long after the war many senior commanders denied the secret chemical and biological warfare, especially poisoned clothing and food, which perhaps killed as many insurgents (and innocent people) as conventional warfare.[8] After independence, many senior Rhodesian military leaders were surprised, and disgusted (or pretended to be), when they found out about some of their own side's undercover adventures. Some Rhodesian commanders tried to dissociate themselves from the dirty tricks perpetrated by the CIO and SB. The SB's head, Mike Edden, was on the ComOps staff, and the Selous Scouts, like the SAS, were directly, though sometimes separately, controlled by ComOps. Chief Superintendent 'Mac' McGuinness ran the SB element of the Selous Scouts and kept a lot of information close to his chest. Information was also compartmentalized because of the unadulterated mutual loathing of BSAP Commissioner Peter Allum and CIO boss Ken Flower. It is difficult, however, to absolve the service commanders, who were also part of ComOps, of complicity in at least some of the atrocities of the secret war, especially in the final days.

One of the unexpected aspects of the pre-election turmoil was that nobody tried to assassinate that fine, fat target of a man, Nkomo. Like Mugabe, he was protected by men from Scotland Yard, as well as his own bodyguards. A South African organization had put a price of R100,000 on his head, but because of the Viscount massacre many whites would have happily *paid* to despatch the ZAPU president. Like Mugabe, Nkomo had also led a charmed life: he had escaped a number of assassination attempts arranged by the Rhodesians. Besides the attack on his HQ in April 1979, a contract to kill Nkomo had been given to a single assassin by Rhodesian agents. Ironically, Nkomo was also in continuous contact with Rhodesian intelligence through most of the war, in a fascinating London-Salisbury-Lusaka triad of conspiracy. Tiny Rowland, head of Lonrho, was the key figure in this triangle. Nkomo had also established close ties with British establishment figures in the early sixties. During his long years of detention in Rhodesia, senior members of the UK Liberal Party were negotiating with Kenneth Kaunda to help to spring Nkomo by using a small group of Israeli mercenaries. Jeremy Thorpe, the controversial Liberal leader, told me the fine detail, after the war.

As election fever spread in February, intimidation on all sides mounted. It was clear that the bulk of violence originated from ZANLA, and Soames warned that ZANU(PF), the Mugabe party, would be banned for campaigning in areas where intimidation was rife. One ZANU(PF) candidate, the fiery Enos Nkala, was prevented from campaigning after uttering particularly bloodthirsty threats to voters. Walls urged Soames to ban ZANU(PF) completely because a large army of guerrillas, led by commissars, was active outside the APs and were making clear to the Shona peasantry that they could vote for only one man. The governor was unresponsive. After all, Lord Soames said, with a refreshing lack of political correctness, when he arrived in Salisbury:

> You must remember this is Africa. This isn't Little Puddleton-on-the Marsh, and they [black Africans] behave differently here. They think nothing of sticking tent poles up each other's whatnot, and doing filthy, beastly things to each other. It does happen, I'm afraid. It's a very wild thing an [African] election.

### *Elections*

The election was to be held on the last three days of February 1980. What worried the Commonwealth troops were the possible reactions of the guerrillas in the APs if their respective leaders did not become prime minister. Would the 16,000 pro-ZANLA men march out of the APs with guns blazing if either Muzorewa or Nkomo won the election? Every one of the Commonwealth contingents wanted to withdraw before the election results were announced on 4 March. Eventually General Acland persuaded the Ceasefire Commission, made up of representatives of the security forces, ZIPRA and ZANLA, that small security force detachments should replace Commonwealth troops in the APs (small police units had already been positioned). This would act as an insurance against air attacks and be the first step on the road to the integration of the three armies once a new government was installed. British officers at Government House drew arms and prepared to defend themselves at dawn against the Rhodesians. 'It was shades of the Indian Mutiny,' according to one historian.

As a final piece of old-style security, Lord Soames requested that 570 British policemen should stand near the polling booths in their regular uniforms. And so it was that 2,702,275 men and women, in the middle of African rainstorms, voted under the watchful eye of British Bobbies, traditional helmets, boots and all. If the estimate of the population was correct, it was a 93 per cent turnout. Senior Rhodesian intelligence officers had predicted that Muzorewa would win at least thirty seats. Indeed, both Walls and Peter Allum, Commissioner of the BSAP, had spent the last days of February on a morale-boosting tour to tell their men that Muzorewa would win, and that there was no chance of a Marxist takeover.

In 1979 I had been elected by my colleagues to represent the foreign correspondents in the Salisbury Press (Quill) Club. Many hundreds of foreign hacks – the locals called them 'vultures' – flew into the country. I was stringing for *Time* and travelled around the country with Peter Jordan, the daredevil staff photographer for the magazine. We went in a vehicle that could cross any terrain, a hire car, by ordinary saloon deep into the bush to report on a Muzorewa rally and ignored security force warnings not to go any further. 'You *oiks* are mad – we wouldn't go in there with our [mineproofed] vehicles.' We were soon seized by guerrillas. Splayed over the bonnet with AKs at our backs, we offered all our cigarette bribes in one go. I cursed inwardly as I thought of the Shona classes I had missed at the university. I stuttered in my weak Shona and I mentioned that we were on our way to meet the Bishop, personally. Which was true. The hostile insurgents had decided to switch from Mugabe to Muzorewa just the day before. They reluctantly let us go. The Bishop flew into the isolated gathering of voters with heavy security in an Alouette. The always affable cleric greeted us warmly. Peter and I were then invited to jog with the Bishop and I asked him, 'If you are so popular, why did you fly into the isolated area while we risked driving in?' He had sufficient political nous to offer a non-committal reply. Peter and I debated his electoral chances. We gave him far fewer votes than Mugabe. In the press club sweepstake only one well-informed hack got it almost right, David Martin of the London *Observer*.

Not predicting the total defeat of Muzorewa was a major intelligence failure. Most of the security elite failed to predict Mugabe's win because they did not want it, and because they did not want to believe, or could not interpret, the evidence which was all around them. In the last year or so of the war, but especially in early 1980, Rhodesian intelligence was swamped by data. 'Never had so much intelligence been collected to so little point,' was the postwar verdict of Professor Ray Roberts, the University of Zimbabwe historian.

Right from the start, the interpretation of the war, that it was a non-political criminal issue to be dealt with primarily by the police, was misguided. As late as 1977 the police had an equal voice with the army in all decisions. Ian Smith tended not to listen to military advice but for too long heeded his secretary for internal affairs, Hostes Nicolle, who represented the old Native Department tradition, and who, it was said, 'could misunderstand Africans in three [indigenous] languages'. By the war's end, the much-vaunted Rhodesian flair for innovation and invention had produced a command structure of Kafkaesque proportions. The creation of ComOps tended to increase rather than diminish inter-service and inter-departmental rivalry. Military Intelligence, Special Branch, CIO and the Selous Scouts often conducted their own wars inside and outside the country. They all had different notions of what kind of war they were fighting and accordingly disparate methods of countering it. ComOps was universally dubbed 'the Muppet Show' by servicemen and women.

Very few experts, except ZANU(PF), expected any one of the nine contending parties to win an overall majority of the eighty black seats in parliament. Despite a multi-million dollar campaign, backed by Rhodesian businessmen and South African funds, as well as the loan of a small fleet of helicopters, Muzorewa's UANC won only three seats – fewer seats than he had choppers. Nkomo's Patriotic Front (ZAPU) won twenty seats, mainly in his Matabeleland base. The rest of the fifty-seven seats went to Robert Mugabe's ZANU(PF). It was the first time in Africa that a Marxist had been voted into power. The most right-wing prime minister in recent British history, Margaret Thatcher, had inadvertently created the conditions for the first electoral triumph of Marxism in African. The internal settlement had merely hastened genuine black rule by allowing Muzorewa to play Kerensky to Mugabe's Lenin. Although ZANU(PF) had actually predicted fifty-seven seats some weeks before the election, Mugabe was obviously stunned by the extent of his triumph. ZANU(PF) had been so long geared for war that the ZANU boss worried that his party might not be ready for the reins of government. Hence his request that Soames stay on for at least six more months.

ZAPU was shattered. In Salisbury in the early hours as the election results came in, Nkomo's second in command whispered in my ear, 'You give them one man-one vote and look what they do with it.' The whites were panic-stricken. Some had their petrol tanks full ready for the 'Beitbridge 500', the 500-kilometre drive to the South African border. Other whites prayed for a white security force coup. Contingency plans did certainly exist under the name of Operation QUARTZ. The most persistent version of the conspiracy was based on Mugabe being defeated. This could have happened because of an elaborate plan to stuff the ballot boxes with Muzorewa votes. A few (highly deniable) nods and winks came from Britain's Secret Intelligence Service (MI6) and Pretoria. Rhodesian intelligence believed in the Brits adhering to ABM: Anybody But Mugabe. Ken

Flower, however, firmly vetoed the subversion of the democratic process. But if Mugabe had been defeated fairly, and resumed the war, the Rhodesian army would have wiped out ZANLA in the APs and (perhaps) joined forces with ZIPRA to finish off the rest. Then a Nkomo-Muzorewa-white alliance would have run a pro-capitalist Zimbabwe.

QUARTZ, then, was a plan for a *counter-coup*, not a coup. Mugabe's party would have lost the election or been proscribed by Lord Soames because of the massive intimidation. Mugabe would have led ZANLA back to the bush to continue the armed struggle. The first military stage of the operation involved SAS and the Rhodesian Armoured Car Regiment, with their new T-55 tanks, surrounding buildings occupied by returned PF leaders. The SADF provided a range of sophisticated monitoring systems. The ZANLA leadership element was specifically targeted for destruction; ZIPRA would be allowed the chance to surrender if trapped in the same locations. At the same time, the Air Force, the RLI and Selous Scouts would wipe out ZANLA assembly points. South African forces would assist where necessary. ZANLA's ambitions would be set back twenty years. QUARTZ was a military plan, but it contained elements of political sensitivity, especially the need for ZIPRA to at least acquiesce initially, and later co-operate, in backing a Nkomo-Muzorewa-Smith coalition. It must be repeated, however: QUARTZ was dependent on Mugabe's return to the battlefield. Many of the NCOs and junior officers, who had got wind of, or were involved in, the contingency, may have misinterpreted the deployment as a pre-emptive coup. Many wanted one.

So, despite a massive display of troops and armoured vehicles around the main government building, road junctions and communication points just before and after the announcement of the election results on 4 March, no coup materialized. Some British newspapers reported, erroneously, that Walls had vetoed a planned coup three hours before it was due to be triggered off. The misinformation may have leaked from Whitehall, not Salisbury. British intelligence was certainly suspicious about a Rhodesian *coup de main.* And Muzorewa was approached by ZAPU officials on 1 March to discuss a possible coalition. Then, on 2 March, as the extent of the Mugabe landslide was becoming apparent from leaks, Muzorewa was asked by some whites to consider backing a coup. He refused. The most powerful military leader, Walls, also refused to countenance a rebellion. He made it clear to ComOps staff that Rhodesia would not 'copy the rest of Africa'. However much he might have questioned the validity of the electoral process, he clearly recognized that the political consequences of a pre-emptive coup would have been disastrous.

Many whites expected one but it did not happen. In fact the country had been much closer to a coup on other occasions. During the 1974-75 detente period there had been rumblings within the RF party of a coup to depose Smith because he was *delaying* a settlement by his hardline stance. Then, during the Kissinger period, some rumours had circulated of a coup from the right to *slow down* the pace of change. In the period 1977-78 some young army officers talked of a military government which would wage an effective all-out war. In the end, the British convention of military subservience to the civilian authority was formally observed. Despite being at the peak of its deployable size and readiness, and augmented by South African forces, the Rhodesian military reluctantly accepted Mugabe's electoral triumph. A rapid exodus of South African troops and equipment followed. Special Branch shredded its files and the Central Statistical Office destroyed its more sensitive information, particularly the records of Rhodesia's illegal trade with Eastern-bloc nations and African states (and the Vatican). Bulk files were burnt in Salisbury crematoria. Many of the cabinet papers were spirited away to South Africa.

Walls had kept his promise to Machel. Just before the election he and Ken Flower had flown to Maputo (and brought back two large boxes of prawns, a delight Rhodesians had been denied since 1976. I spent an indulgent Christmas meal at home with Flower and his family). Machel promised to abide by the results of the elections if the Rhodesians promised not to launch a coup if Mugabe won. Despite Mugabe's threats to go back to war during the election campaign, it was clear that Machel did not favour a resumption of hostilities. At most he would have offered Mugabe a quiet exile if he lost the election. A Rhodesian coup could not have worked against the massive vote for Mugabe. Even without intimidation he was clearly the favourite son of the masses. Above all, the people wanted peace. A coup, with South African support, could have precipitated civil war, even if such countries as Zambia had recognized a coalition which included Nkomo.

And yet recent evidence, particularly in works written and published by Peter Stiff, a former officer in the BSAP and prolific writer on southern African militaria, points to an elaborate but separate South African plan to thwart Mugabe's win at the polls. A week after the elections, the Rhodesian security machine had been wound down, and the elite troops had been confined to barracks, but the South African forces had mobilized the powerful Battlegroup Charlie near the border. South African and ex-Rhodesian special forces were preparing a series of roadside bombs (disguised in electricity sub-stations and traffic light control boxes) placed in Jameson Avenue in Salisbury. The intention was to detonate them by remote control on 17 April when a VIP motorcade was due to pass on the day before the independence celebrations. The prime targets included Lord Soames, Mugabe and Prince Charles. The killings were expected to trigger off a mass ZANU reaction to the death of their leader, especially from Rufaro stadium where the *povo* were due to celebrate their freedom. Mass revenge on white Rhodesians would replicate the worst days of the Congo. The hog-tied Rhodesian forces and the tiny British monitoring force could have done little. So the South African battlegroup would cross the border to 'restore order'.

The British could hardly object to a humanitarian intervention, especially after the shock of the death of the heir to the throne, nor did they have the military reach to protect the numerous white British passport holders. Pretoria would have installed a temporary administration of Muzorewa and Nkomo, whose regular ZIPRA formations would also move rapidly into the country to spell an end to ZANLA. With ZANLA men and supporters running riot in the country, they would be considered unfit to govern. Zambia would welcome the re-birth of Nkomo's power, while the other front-line states, utterly exhausted from the war, would do little more than protest. Mugabe would have been cheated of his victory, and thousands of whites would have been murdered, but Pretoria would have kept the Marxists from power, and installed, finally, a pliant black administration which was beholden to South Africa. CIO's Danny Stannard got wind of the plot and the foreign special forces in the country were forced to flee. The South African invasion force stood down. Such was Stiff's interpretation of

Robert Mugabe's victory completely altered the politics of southern Africa (IDAF)

a very febrile few days in Salisbury. Certainly, Pretoria's frenetic military activity fitted this interpretation and more recent revelations from long-retired Rhodesian and South African intelligence officers confirmed some of Stiff's story.[9]

### *Independence*

Once again Mugabe survived the machinations of his numerous enemies. He had been portrayed as a 'black Hitler' for so long in the Rhodesian media. When I met him, in January 1980, in the garden of a rented house in the leafy Salisbury suburb of Mount Pleasant, he seemed to be the most intelligent leader, black or white, I had ever met in Africa. This Catholic Marxist, who apparently despised the white settlers but loved the British royal family and the Irish priest who had helped to educate him, was obviously a cold but complex man. He seemed to embellish his pronounced BBC Home Counties accent. He also minced when he walked, which I thought odd in a guerrilla chieftain. I was not sure whether he would bring peace or more war.

On 18 April 1980 Zimbabwe became independent with Mugabe as premier. The Rhodesian albatross slipped off Britain's neck. Soames, the amiable Tory, had accomplished his 'mission impossible' and handed over a British colony to a Marxist guerrilla leader. The new black leader took over a white-constructed dictatorship with the panoply of secret courts, secret hangings and emergency powers. Would Mugabe now turn those weapons the other way? If he did, and the whites fled, what good would peace be to an economically prostrate country?

After the first tidal waves of shock, some whites responded to Mugabe's calm calls for reconciliation with comments about a 'miracle'. As one right-wing white businessman said, 'The war's over and we've got a strong leader. There's no mucking about with a coalition that could have triggered off a civil war.' Mugabe appeared on television to ask for understanding between the races. 'Let us deepen our sense of belonging,' he said, 'and engender a common interest that knows no race, colour or creed. Let us truly become Zimbabweans with a single loyalty.' Some whites accepted Mugabe's call, while many prepared to quit Zimbabwe. Others could not because the financial restrictions on emigration grew even tighter.

Under the averted gaze of the British, the SADF flew out or drove out much of their loaned equipment, although some Rhodesian officers, keen to appease the new government, backtracked on an agreement to return 800 brand new MAGs and the Eland armoured cars. The majority of white regulars in the armed forces and the BSAP (renamed the Zimbabwe Republic Police) left. Some joined the South African Police, but afterwards found the strong Afrikaans orientation uncongenial. The RLI was officially disbanded with some dignity on 17 October 1980; its last deployment was an anti-poaching operation. ZANLA commanders detested the Selous Scouts (who quickly disbanded with very little ceremony), but

Mugabe asked the SAS commander, Lieutenant Colonel Garth Barrett, to stay on as a form of Praetorian Guard. Barrett politely refused. Many SAS men joined the Reconnaissance Commandos based at Durban, South Africa; others went to assist the training of the Territory Force in South West Africa. The regiment's silver was presented to 22nd SAS Regiment in Hereford. The specialized vehicles and weapons, as well as records, were transported back to South Africa, along with a very large consignment of ivory. A few SAS men joined the British equivalent (despite the fact that some Rhodesian SAS operators had warned off some of the British SAS men on duty in Rhodesia during the ceasefire and election period). Some RLI men returned to conventional British regiments. Few of the turned black guerrillas in the Selous Scouts went south, despite being invited by the SADF, even though many were murdered soon after independence. Morrison Nyati, the turned Scout who had been a guide at the raid on Nyadzonya, was flayed alive. Twenty-eight volunteer black Scouts joined their white colleagues in Phalaborwa, in South Africa. Colonel Ron Reid-Daly, former commanding officer of the Scouts, was appointed to (though never formally took up) command the Transkei's army. White members of the Rhodesian forces were in action against SWAPO guerrillas in Namibia within months of the ceasefire north of the Limpopo. Overall, Rhodesian tactical skills and some soldiers were quickly absorbed into the SADF, though the strategic implications may have been conveniently ignored, at least for the time being.

Black Scouts who remained (or survived), along with remnants of the RAR and RLI, became the nucleus of the newly formed special forces unit of the Zimbabwe National Army, 1st Parachute Battalion. It was commanded by Colonel Dudley Coventry, a former SAS commander. The ZNA took time to find its feet, but one immediate change was evident at ComOps HQ: the magnetic markers and arrows on the maps showing ZANLA bases in Mozambique and ZIPRA deployments in Zambia were cleared away. The new locations were of South African bases. The change of enemies was dramatic.

## *Why Rhodesia lost the war*

Lancaster House saved the Rhodesians from almost certain defeat, despite their operational ingenuity. The history of the Rhodesian armed forces was one of tactical brilliance and strategic ineptitude. Rarely in military chronicles have such thinly-stretched troops, hampered by manpower, training, equipment and financial constraints, achieved such consistent success in the field. On a technical level the achievements of the security forces will be studied in military colleges for a long time to come. (When I was a founding member of the directing staff of the newly established UK Joint Services Command and Staff College from 1997 to 2000, a surprising number of officers chose to write their MA dissertations on Rhodesian counter-insurgency.) There were relative failures in Rhodesia, for example the PV programme and projects such as the auxiliaries which could have been either very successful or disastrous, if the war had gone on. Some of the pseudo-guerrilla activities of the Selous Scouts and the sheer bravado of the external raids will continue to fascinate military specialists. The most notable development was the rapid deployment of heli-borne troops, usually consisting of RLI and RAR soldiers, to hunt guerrillas. This 'fire force' concept contributed to most (approximately 12,000) of the conventional kill rate inside Rhodesia.[10] The Rhodesian obsession with successful operational techniques, however, created a fatal blindness to the strategic political imperatives required to counter a protracted insurgency. The Salisbury government for long insisted it was waging a campaign against violent criminals rather than fighting a civil war. External communism, not internal nationalism, was blamed. The flamboyant foreign minister, Pieter van der Byl, appeared convinced that 'This is not a racial war, but black terrorists and white-skinned communists on one side and a multi-racial army of black and white soldiers fighting should-to-shoulder on the other.' Rhodesian politicians proved more adept at explaining why Africans should not support the guerrillas than at explaining why they did.

The initial aim of the war was to prevent the passing of power to *any* black government, no matter how moderate. An admission of racism, if only within the high command and cabinet, might have produced a more coherent policy. Yet no clear political programme, beyond a vague preservation of the status quo, was ever articulated. Rhodesian officers prided themselves on being *apolitical.* In starkest contrast with the guerrillas, there was very little or no political indoctrination in the Rhodesian armed forces; no school of political warfare was established. Rhodesian grand strategy, such as it was, was shot through with a fatal negativism. There was little faith in far-reaching reform as a war-winner. Such a recognition, of course, would have undermined the very reasons for the war being fought at all. White Rhodesians struggled long and hard against the only thing which could have avoided a war – African participation in national politics. To change horses in midstream was extremely difficult but the Rhodesians did try it. The war drifted from a confrontation with the principle of black majority rule to a war for the sort of black government white Rhodesians were prepared to live under. Yet once the principle of having any kind of majority rule government was conceded, the Rhodesians' war aims became increasingly confused and their strategy consequently weaker.

Faced with the inner weaknesses of their strategies, the Rhodesians resorted to more and more desperate measures. The policy of winning hearts and minds was largely abandoned in the field just as the first moves towards a political strategy of a moderate black government were coming to fruition. Perversely, it was considered that black participation in the political process would permit tougher, war-winning operations. Martial law was introduced, the punitive destruction of villages and livestock of those who were accused of aiding the guerrillas became routine and a more aggressive external strategy was adopted. Also the use of chemical-biological warfare was stepped up. One senior officer in ComOps admitted to me at the height of the war in 1979:

> We relied 90 per cent on force and 10 per cent on psychology and half of that went off half-cocked. The guerrillas relied 90 per cent on psychology and only 10 per cent on force.

The insurgents, on the other hand, had a clear vision of their purpose: to break the back of white supremacy and establish a black majority government. This gave the guerrillas remarkable stamina and their cause the strength to weather numerous political crises and consistent military defeat in the field. The apparent simplicity of the guerrilla objectives masked enormous confusion and conflict as to how to achieve them. At times, dissension among the nationalists was far more potent than the firepower of the Rhodesians in delaying majority rule. The divergences in ideology, tribe, clan, training and deployment contributed towards the divisions within the Patriotic Front. For ZANLA, the works of Mao, Marx and Lenin were the staple fare of political education. Nkomo's army paid little attention to Maoist doctrine but did in practice use Chinese revolutionary tactics. The Soviet connections meant that Castro's Cuban experience was more important to them. ZANLA was dominated by Chinese theory diluted by FRELIMO experience. Despite these important influences, nationalist objectives tended to dominate all political thinking. ZANLA recruits were educated in the 'national grievances'. Issues such as land alienation, education, health and welfare discrimination, political oppression, low wages and social inequalities were the fundamentals of the recruits' political diet. Nkomo's cadres were steeped in the history of the chicanery used by the British South Africa Company to destroy the Ndebele state in the 1890s while the Shonas in ZANLA were taught the history of their first *Chimurenga.*

While such nationalist propaganda was heavily laced with the jargon of scientific socialism, some bizarre contradictions intruded. A most glaring example was the guerrillas' embrace of traditional religion, charms against Rhodesian bullets and the reliance on spirit mediums. One of the second-order effects of the many poisonings of both humans and cattle as a result of the government's secret chemical-biological campaign was to lead to many literal witchhunts that caused the deaths of many innocent women. Historically, poisoning had always been associated with witches and wizards. While the PF talked of modernizing a society whites were trying to freeze, its military wings in the TTLs were destroying nearly every vestige of modern advances such as animal dip tanks, schools and clinics. Marxist doctrine had a strong emotional appeal for the guerrillas in that it offered them a straightforward explanation of what had happened in Rhodesia and a model for the solution to their struggle. Yet, despite the presence of some convinced Marxists in the ZANLA leadership, the adherence of both wings of the

PF to anti-capitalist dogma was largely pragmatic: despairing of their efforts to involve Britain in the 1960s, they felt obliged to look to the communist bloc for guiding principles in the same way as they begged for arms. Despite being clothed in the ferocious Asian garb of a people's war, the guerrillas accomplished what the Marxists would have termed a 'bourgeois nationalist revolution'.

The guerrillas waged a far more effective psychological war than their opponents.[11] The vast majority of whites made the cardinal error of believing their own mindlessly optimistic propaganda, proof of the old adage that people will usually believe what they want to hear. Blacks tended to ridicule RF propaganda aimed at them. While Rhodesians viewed hearts and minds as adjuncts to the more important business of killing guerrillas, the nationalists placed a major emphasis on psycho-military campaigning. Guerrilla propaganda was simple and effective. White Rhodesians were generally contemptuous of African culture and, although there were training courses on 'African customs' for most soldiers and policemen,

ZANLA propaganda poster, especially for women. Female cadres did take part in combat

an unbridgeable gulf of misunderstanding existed. The insurgents, however, were in close touch with aspirations of Africans and in their propaganda they used skilfully their intimate involvement with the civilian population. Although guerrillas disseminated printed material, including dramatic posters of the social realist school, the major medium was the spoken word. On the international front, the insurgents gained the support not only of the Eastern bloc and the third world, but much of the Western press. In particular, the guerrillas managed to create the impression that atrocities, especially against 'refugee' camps, were a Rhodesian monopoly. Ultimately, it was on the propaganda fronts, both internally and externally, that the guerrillas created the political conditions for victory.

Despite being outnumbered by 25:1 and without a single country's official recognition, some whites insisted that the war had been winnable. They asserted that détente in the mid-1970s was mere appeasement, that the nationalists released from detention should have been indefinitely imprisoned or hanged, and that the guerrilla bases in the front-line states should have been obliterated in the early 1970s. 'War is war,' argued the diehards, 'so why didn't we bomb Lusaka or do a "dambuster" on the Cahora Bassa dam and knock out Mozambique in one single blow?' Such an escalation depended on the wholehearted support of Pretoria that was never forthcoming. Any successful long-term containment of the guerrillas would have required diplomatic recognition and military aid from the West. Yet this would never have been given to a white-dominated government. If a plausible political solution, perhaps an assertive Muzorewa administration in 1976, had been gracefully conceded by the RF then Anglo-American military backing might have led to a defeat of the PF, if the guerrillas had fought on. But the RF always gave far too little, far too late.

Sanctions also played a role in the rebels' defeat, albeit a secondary one to the pressures of guerrilla war. For some years economic constraints were merely nuisances: the shortage of razor blades, ladies' stockings and good whiskey resulted and, as Flower lamented in his memoirs, the Salisbury Club ran out of port for the first time since 1896. Oddly, the thing that Rhodesians seemed to ask of intending visitors to the beleaguered state most often was, 'Please bring some chocolate Smarties. *Please*.' By the late 1970s, sanctions were biting. They did play a part in winding down the morale of the whites and prompting emigration, a key factor in undermining military strength. Most of the consequences of sanctions, halfheartedly and hypocritically applied as they were, were unintended. While privileged whites suffered a loss of perhaps ten Rhodesian dollars a year, most of the hardships were shifted onto the poorest blacks, particularly in the TTLs and front-line states. Sanctions polarized the political spectrum: whites became more intransigent; but similarly black peasants became radicalized as they slipped more deeply into poverty. The incomplete sanctions against Rhodesia generated international credibility and legitimacy for the liberation movements, and far more radicalized peasants, a far cry from making the whites bend the knee in a few months as Harold Wilson had predicted.

Pretoria, particularly in 1976, played a vital role in bringing Salisbury to heel. Getting 'good old Smithy' as white supporters called him, to agree to a firm commitment to majority rule was like nailing jelly to a wall. Only John Vorster managed that. The war, sanctions, propaganda and Pretoria crushed the rebellion among whites in the north. I have spent some time explaining why white Rhodesia's illegal republic collapsed because its downfall was to have a very major impact on the even more recalcitrant whites in the south. It was to take a decade before the Afrikaners started to deal seriously with their question of majority rule.

Rhodesians fought not only an unwinnable war but, politically, they fought it in a most unwinnable way. Applying the implicit lesson for his homeland, South Africa, the charmingly eccentric writer Denis Beckett aptly summarized the war:

> Shades of Vietnam. Side A has overwhelming firepower, radio communications, a monopoly of air support, and all the access to public propaganda. Side B has nothing but rifles and boots, and even operational commands are conveyed by written scraps foot-slogged through the bush. Side A's propaganda machine makes much of 'winning the hearts and minds of the people'. But its soldiers in the field think this is a lot of pious nonsense and place their faith instead in the Nixonian amendment: 'When you've got them by their balls, their hearts and minds will follow.' Side B is perceived by the majority of the population as liberators … . And it all comes to its inevitable end. Side B in the seat of government struggling desperately to restore a shattered economy. Side A writing books in the past tense from distant places, its former officers all blaming each other for their failure.[12]

When Denis Beckett wrote these lines in late 1982, he wondered which domino would fall next – Namibia and then South Africa? Pretoria had now to man a defence perimeter on the Limpopo, not the faraway Zambezi. A new front for ANC infiltration was opened up in the northern Transvaal. Zimbabwe had the strongest economy and army in the region, after South Africa. And it was now led by a battle-hardened Marxist who was a dedicated enemy of apartheid. Mugabe became a hero to the black youths in South Africa. White power looked even more fragile in the apartheid state; so did its economic leverage. A Muzorewa-led Zimbabwe was supposed to be a central satellite in P.W. Botha's proposed 'Constellation of States'. Mugabe instead helped to set up a rejectionist front. Mugabe's accession to power emphasized the basic tenet of pan-Africanism: that Africa could not be truly free until the whole continent was purged of white supremacy. The searchlight was now on Pretoria. The final battle lines had been drawn.

# PART III

# DESTRUCTIVE ENGAGEMENT

# *Chapter 8*

# Battle Lines Drawn

As the white-ruled colonies collapsed, the black-controlled successor states formed a front-line alliance against apartheid: the friendly buffers became deadly enemies. The *cordon sanitaire* was transformed into guerrilla sanctuaries and mini-Ho-Chi-Minh trails. This book's previous section was concerned with Pretoria's attempts to *stabilize* colonial rule; the next chapters detail South Africa's determination to *destabilize* her neighbours. Some engagement existed but it was often a deliberately destructive relationship.

Mugabe was a central figure in redrawing the new battle lines. They extended in the west from the Cunene and then Limpopo rivers to the east along the borders of the Kruger National Park, past Swaziland and then on to the rolling green hills of Northern Natal's Zulu heartlands. Despite the fences and security force patrols, rough terrain and wild animals, this was a very long and convenient border for guerrilla infiltration, although most of the ANC's fighting power was resident *inside* the Republic of South Africa. After Zimbabwean independence in April 1980 an anti-apartheid curtain fell, dividing black- and white-ruled Africa. To be sure, this was often a flimsy transparent divider, riddled with SADF bullets and the unctuous hypocrisy of black presidents-for-life spewing forth praise for democracy and demands for sanctions while begging for food and petrol from the pariah. A little like the Cold War division in Europe, though based more on race than ideology, two rival military coalitions faced each other: the black front-line states versus the SADF and its Namibian and homeland cohorts. These military formations were partnered by two economic alliances. On the one side stood the Southern African Development Coordination Conference (SADCC) which became the Southern African Development Community (SADC) in 1992. Its rival was Pretoria's planned co-prosperity sphere, the Constellation of Southern African States (CONSAS). Both blocs were much looser than the NATO/EEC and Warsaw Pact/COMECON groupings but the parallel did extend to the fact that, like the Warsaw Pact, the front-line states' and South Africa's armies performed dual functions: external deterrence and internal control. Both southern African variants operated more or less sophisticated protection rackets as well as waving aloft the national flags.

The European analogy should not be stretched. The SADCC was not intended to emulate the EEC or the later European Union, or even the failed federations of central and east Africa. Yet the Manichean passions and paranoia of the Cold War were more than replicated in southern Africa. From the north, the black Armageddon was striding down to devour Christian capitalist civilization; from the south, racist Boers rained destruction on the dignity of man in the whole subcontinent in order to stall the inevitable liberation of the enslaved majority. The front-line states accused South Africa of destabilizing the region by military, economic and political measures, a charge that Pretoria vehemently denied, despite the mountain of contrary evidence. Pretoria's critics said that it was practising a form of the Brezhnev doctrine, the Soviet policy of enforcing compliance in Eastern Europe. Pretoria defended itself by claiming the historical analogy was more the Monroe doctrine, which Washington deployed to ensure order in Latin America. More effectively, Pretoria accused the front-line states of harbouring SWAPO, ANC and PAC 'terrorists' dedicated to the destruction of law and order, harming both blacks and whites. The front-line states, insisted Pretoria, were therefore guilty of the primary destabilization. Moreover, the front-line states, while decrying imperialism and colonialism had invited in Cuban, East German and Russian forces to threaten South African borders. This was the new socialist imperialism. And the harsh rhetoric and calls for more sanctions imperilled the granary and industrial powerhouse of a region beset by drought and man-made disasters. Both sides cried justice in a noble cause. The trouble for Pretoria was that few outside its borders were listening to the special pleading.

Pretoria's relationship with its neighbours was important because it had long been a tenet of South African diplomacy that the road to the West ran through Africa. Membership of the 'West' and the 'Free World' depended upon at least some kind of rapprochement with the southern members of the Organization of African Unity. In the 1960s Prime Minister Vorster promulgated his 'outward policy' and later, in the mid-1970s, his 'détente' initiatives, centred on resolving the Rhodesian impasse. These moves were intended to form a 'commonwealth' of economically interdependent states, regardless of ideological differences. Yet the diplomacy produced very few results. Only the eccentric, right-wing dictator of Malawi, Dr Hastings Banda, endorsed full diplomatic ties with Pretoria. And he was well paid for his troubles. The rest of Vorster's diplomacy crashed in the aftermath of the Portuguese collapse, Soweto 1976, and Pretoria's Information scandal. The late 1970s were dedicated to internal diplomacy: the Bantustans and the 'internal settlements' in Namibia and Rhodesia. Then Mugabe's victory completely derailed Pretoria's diplomatic efforts.

From 1980 to 1984 the sword and economic blackmail largely replaced polite diplomacy. *Machtpolitik* replaced summitry. Anxieties about the deepening wars in Angola and Mozambique did, however, prompt a brief respite in 1984. A non-aggression pact was signed with Samora Machel and a limited agreement on troop withdrawals was reached with Luanda. Both agreements were hailed as

The SADCC states versus the Constellation (until 1989)

diplomatic breakthroughs by South Africa but the practical effects were shortlived. The temperature soon plummeted. The civil wars raged on in Mozambique and Angola. Pretoria's relations with its neighbours slipped below zero in October 1986 when Michel died in a plane crash in the Lebombo mountains, just inside the South African border. Pretoria was accused, probably unfairly, of assassination. Despite a host of conspiracy theories, it was probably pilot error by the Russian crew. The South African government, distracted by internal crises, did not return with gusto to its diplomatic offensives until late 1988. The optimism radiating from the initiatives to secure Namibian independence made the rejectionist front in southern Africa totter as P.W.Botha sallied forth on tours of Malawi, Mozambique and Zaire. Mugabe, as ever, was unmoved. In his view the Botha peace gesture was a temporizing sham, a breathing space before renewed bouts of military destabilization. The basic problem was apartheid. As Joseph Hanlon, an authority on the region, put it so succinctly, 'The South African government will continue to sjambok its neighbours as long as it sjamboks its own people.'[1]

### *The front-line states*

The concept of the front-line alliance went back to the 1969 Lusaka Manifesto, drafted largely by Julius Nyerere and Kenneth Kaunda, which supported the liberation war against colonial rule in the south. In 1971 the Mogadishu Declaration advocated an intensified armed struggle. During the mid-1970s Angola, Botswana, Mozambique, Tanzania and Zambia formed a loose coalition to co-ordinate their policies on Rhodesia. (Nigeria, as one of the most powerful black states, became an honorary member.) Practical military aid was provided by Zambia, Tanzania and Algeria and funds were co-ordinated by the OAU's African Liberation Committee, based in Dar es Salaam.

Ideological cohesion was impossible, except for an apple-pie and motherhood commitment to anti-colonialism, because the Commonwealth states, particularly Botswana and Zambia, shared – paradoxically – Pretoria's concern about a 'Marxist saddle' (Angola, Mozambique and potentially Zimbabwe) straddling southern Africa. Hence Kaunda and Vorster worked together in 1974 and 1975 to try to prevent the Rhodesian war spiralling into a major East-West confrontation. Neither politician wanted a repetition of the calamitous great power and UN intervention in the Congo during the 1960s. This was partly the reason why the front-line states forced Mugabe and Nkomo to form the Patriotic Front. It was bound to be an unworkable, short-term shotgun marriage especially as Zambia, Angola and (reluctantly) Botswana backed Nkomo's ZIPRA forces, while Tanzania and Mozambique aided ZANLA. Russian and Chinese involvement, especially arms supplies and training, compounded the problem. Moscow sponsored the 'charmed circle' of so-called 'authentic' liberation movements (ANC, ZAPU, SWAPO and earlier the MPLA) while China assisted – in the Russian perspective – the 'splinter' groups (ZANU, the PAC and earlier the FNLA and UNITA). Crudely, the formula – for those with a taste for alphabet soup – was: China/PAC/ZANU/Mozambique/Tanzania versus the USSR/ZAPU/ANC/Zambia/Angola.

This was, very approximately, the position in the late 1970s although the divisions were never watertight partly because Moscow supplied weapons, directly or indirectly, to *all* the movements.

Rhodesia wonderfully concentrated the minds of the front-line presidents because the war threatened the very survival of the regimes in Zambia, Mozambique and perhaps Botswana. Namibia was different. The SWAPO war affected only one other foreign state immediately: Angola. And Namibia did not directly involve the black Commonwealth states and Britain in the way Rhodesia did. Moreover, the Patriotic Front deployed much more impressive guerrilla forces than SWAPO, whose poor leadership was frequently derided by the front-line presidents. After Sam Nujoma spoke at one front-line summit, Machel is reported to have ridiculed SWAPO's war effort. 'Don't tell me how many white farmers you have ambushed. How many South African *soldiers* have you killed?'

The front-line states, however, were in a weak position to criticize SWAPO's performance. The Zambian army's reactions, for example, to the major Rhodesian raids of 1978 were uniformly farcical. The Zambian Air Force had apparently no idea how to operate or maintain the Rapier air defence system provided by the British. When they were helped to get it working, they managed only to shoot down their own planes. Further, Kaunda found himself in the same invidious position as King Hussein when he hosted the Palestine Liberation Organization. In 1970 the Jordanian king bloodily asserted his sovereignty but Kaunda's Fred Karno's army, of under 9,000 men, was no match for the better-trained (by Cubans and Russians) and better-armed ZIPRA forces of 12,000-15,000 troops. It was rumoured in Salisbury at the time that there was Zambian government complicity in the devastating 1978 Rhodesian attacks on ZIPRA bases. Perhaps the Rhodesian security forces 'did a Hussein' on behalf of Kaunda. Certainly, ZIPRA soldiers often acted in Zambia as if they were a state within a state, and Kaunda's police and army dared not act. Not until ZIPRA left the country in 1980-81 could Kaunda pretend to be master in his own house.

Despite the military deficiencies, political fissures and mounting economic problems, the front-line alliance did notch up some successes. As outriders for the OAU, the front-line states did act as a buffer to discourage direct Soviet penetration and American meddling. Both superpowers were forced on occasion to defer to the front-line decisions on Rhodesia and Namibia. No formal bureaucratic machinery cemented the front-line alliance: a group of sometimes like-minded dictators conducted their own personal foreign policies, a little like the Concert of Europe in the early nineteenth century. But they took risks that would have made Metternich blanch. Their alleged backing of the hare-brained Cuban plan to invade Rhodesia in 1979 was very dangerous. That could have provoked a massive overt SADF entry into the war and chronic superpower tension. And in mid-1979 they were prepared to blast the Commonwealth out of the water, or least try to get Britain kicked out of an institution it had set up, if Margaret Thatcher had recognized the 1979 Rhodesian elections. Instead they helped to engineer the Lancaster House settlement, in which Kaunda, Machel and Nyerere acted out the roles of honest brokers. Machel, especially, put in a vital last-minute performance by dictating to Mugabe: the Mozambican leader threatened to cut off the life-support systems to ZANLA if Mugabe did not compromise. The most Mugabe would get if he disobeyed his ally would be a small house for his permanent Mozambican exile. Machel knew that Mozambique was buckling under the pressure of Rhodesia's final desperate all-out blows.

Rhodesia had been the 'hole in the doughnut'. In 1980 independent Zimbabwe was the most developed country with the best economy and battle-hardened armed forces in the region, second only to South Africa. Zimbabwe soon became the core state of the SADCC, established at Arusha, Tanzania, in 1979. SADCC's purpose was to reduce the front-line states' reliance on Pretoria's economic muscle. It was not seen initially as a common market because, compared with their joint trade with South Africa, their inter-bloc commerce was minimal. The SADCC was primarily an attempt to co-ordinate transport, food production and general commerce. Because the South African Transport Services (SATS) dominated the regional rail network and access to the best ports, SADCC's rival (though barely functioning) transport links were the keys to liberation or domination. SADCC grew to embrace nine member states: from the original front-liners (Angola, Tanzania, Zambia, Mozambique and Botswana), the new boy Zimbabwe and the latecomers, Malawi, Swaziland and Lesotho.

The SADCC was immediately, and correctly, perceived as an enemy by Pretoria, a direct rival to its plan to create a constellation dominated by South African capital. P.W. Botha specifically called it a 'counter-constellation'. Could the new organization threaten South African hegemony? Lesotho was surrounded by South African territory and all its foreign trade went via its giant, literally all-embracing, neighbour. Sanctions and war had locked Zimbabwe into South Africa's grip. Malawi was heavily dependent upon Pretoria's trade and development loans. Botswana, Lesotho and Swaziland (the three original British protectorates) had been deliberately embedded in the South African economy from the start and they were still tied into a customs union and rand monetary zone. Especially in Botswana, white businessmen and women ran much of the domestic economy. South African personnel kept Maputo's power, port and railway access functioning. The Zambian economy, left largely to its own devices, had become a shambles, except for pockets of white-run agriculture and, of course, the mines. They were run, like many mines in the front-line states, by the giant Anglo-American corporation. As one SADCC senior official noted laconically: 'SADCC does not have to worry about regional co-ordination of mining: Anglo-American already does it.'[2] Admittedly, Angola and Tanzania remained relatively aloof from South Africa's economic tentacles but Angola's dwindling resources were committed almost entirely to the civil war and Nyerere's socialist dogmas had reduced Tanzania to an economic basket case. Moreover, their rail and road routes were closed by war or disrupted by poor maintenance. More insidiously, both black and white business people throughout the region were used to dealing with Johannesburg. It had not been called the City of Gold for nothing. The original gold wealth had built the foundations for the most dynamic entrepôt in Africa. Better goods came from there, often more cheaply and certainly more quickly than from Europe. The old habits of the colonial era died hard. FRELIMO authorities often found it more convenient to chat in Portuguese to white exiled Mozambican or Madeiran businessmen in the Transvaal to get supplies for the party elite. The patterns of kickbacks and bribes were well-established. Hence much of the foreign aid donated to the SADCC ended up in the vaults of Johannesburg's banks. Sweden had to ban Mozambique from using its aid to buy goods in South Africa. SADCC's chances looked slim. Nonetheless, it did survive and grow, despite Pretoria's best attempts to strangle it at birth.

The success of sanctions against apartheid depended on the success of SADCC. As long as the front-line states traded with or via South Africa, Pretoria could manipulate its neighbours. The opportunities were limitless, South African goods were, for example, re-labelled in Swaziland and exported from there. Dummy companies were set up; false destinations were put on export licences. It was almost bound to be a re-run of the Rhodesian sanctions farce. Transport, it bears repeating, was the lynchpin and, in particular, the Benguela railway through central Angola to Zambia and Zaire, and the road-rail-oil pipeline from Umtali (Mutare) through Mozambique to the port of Beira. If the SADF kept these access routes to the Atlantic and Indian Oceans cut, and they usually were, courtesy of UNITA and RENAMO, then Pretoria could survive, probably, even the most comprehensive sanctions, short of an effective naval blockade. That was the bottom line.

There's always one: Dr Hastings Banda of Malawi was the odd man out

Military planners in Pretoria asked themselves a fundamental question. Should the SADF destroy these rival routes completely or should South Africa revive the front-line economies, and these routes in particular, and thus entice the SADCC into an unofficial constellation? (Indeed, some South African ultra-optimists even talked of *merging* SADCC and CONSAS.) Was it to be military destabilization or trade leverage? Pretoria tried both, often simultaneously. And how would the front-line states react, especially their zealots? With cool economic pragmatism or a passionate ideological martyrdom? They, too, tried both.

### *The Constellation strikes back*

The Constellation scheme was formalized in November 1979 at the Carlton Conference in Johannesburg. Named after the hotel in which the conference was held, the event was heralded by the South African press as the marriage between big business and the National Party newly committed to the free enterprise ethic. A pro-capitalist constellation of forty million consumers would do very nicely for both the hawks in the party and the 'liberal' multinationals based in the country. Two potential hiccups were obvious: Namibia and Zimbabwe-Rhodesia. The pro-Pretoria Democratic Turnhalle Alliance (DTA) administration in Windhoek and Muzorewa sitting uneasily in Salisbury were billed as the up-and-coming stars in the constellation. Again, the optimists ranged farther – maybe Zaire and Zambia might join too. Mugabe's rapid membership of SADCC pricked the balloon. Instead the constellation became a mere rump of South Africa and its homelands. Nonetheless, the *idea* behind the constellation, economic hegemony, but by now more indirect means, continued to animate the Afrikaner leadership.

Mugabe's victory astounded Pretoria's planners. They had trusted the much-vaunted diplomatic skills of the British Foreign Office that had given them the nod and the wink of the inevitable triumph of their own rumoured ABM (Anybody But Mugabe) plan. While Mugabe preached reconciliation with the Brits and his own white settlers, the rising volume of his anti-apartheid rhetoric incensed Pretoria. This helped to spark a more aggressive policy towards the front-line states. Pretoria launched its own version of a total onslaught. Initially, Pretoria teased with primarily economic tactics, such as slowing down fuel supplies aimed at trying to keep Mugabe in line. But co-ordinated commando raids on the Lesotho capital on 9 December 1982 (in which forty-two people were killed) and on a fuel depot in Beira, causing £15 millions of damage, marked a new military phase of the South African destabilization onslaught.

Despite its convenience as shorthand for Pretoria's misdeeds, 'destabilization' was always something of misnomer when it was in vogue in the 1980s. Elements of *re*-stabilization, for example economic aid to Mozambique, especially for the transport infrastructure around Maputo, no matter how self-interested, were part and parcel of the process. The policy was also called 'destructive engagement' partly because some left-wing critics saw the official Washington policy of 'constructive engagement' as somehow a mischievous endorsement or accompaniment to SADF aggression. Joseph Hanlon was more blunt: he called this second front of apartheid a 'beggar your neighbours' plan.[3] Amid the diplomatic debate certain strategic ambitions were clear.

Obviously first and foremost the survival of the white regime was the self-evident goal, as were the territorial imperatives of regional hegemony and the psychological demands for status, particularly after the rebuffs of the SADCC and Mugabe, the personification of cold, calculating evil for white conservatives. More general aims included a desire to replace the colonial *glacis* with a cordon of instability so that the front-line states would be too weak not only to succour ANC and SWAPO guerrillas but also to impose or even urge sanctions. The resulting chaos induced by military options and economic blackmail, on top of drought, famine, floods, bureaucratic bungling and endemic corruption, would convince South African blacks that 'majority rule doesn't work', especially the Marxist variety. The mailed fist would confirm the 'invincibility' of the security forces. This would not only show local blacks that the government had not gone soft – that Mugabeism would be stopped at the Limpopo – but would also demonstrate to the West that Pretoria was willing and able to act as an independent regional superpower, with or without nods from Washington.

There were specific goals as well. The most important were military. Crucially, the ANC and SWAPO insurgents had to be pushed as far north as possible. Guerrilla sanctuaries would not be tolerated in contiguous states. Later, this operational goal turned, perhaps haphazardly, into the strategic ambition of foisting non-aggression pacts on those adjoining states from which the ANC insurgents infiltrated. Other operational goals emerged, such as the initial need for combat experience and the capture of massive amounts of communist weaponry, as well, occasionally, as capturing real live Cubans and Russians. White communist PoWs were used to justify to the white electorate the propaganda claims of a total onslaught by foreign Reds. Attempts were made to persuade neighbouring states to allow SADF personnel to enter their territory to assist in regional security (for example to protect the Cahora Bassa power lines) or to provide civil aid during national calamities such as mine disasters (South African *civilians* had frequently assisted in such cases). Except for a projected deal to protect the Cahora Bassa power lines with SADF men working in Mozambique, in uniform or dressed as private security officials, the possibility of SADF troops being officially invited into the front-line states was unlikely.[4]

Political goals included attempts to persuade the front-line states to recognize the nominally independent homelands. Even more forlornly, Pretoria hoped that more governments would follow Malawi's example by exchanging ambassadors. (Four states, Mozambique, Swaziland, Zimbabwe and Lesotho, did exchange trade representatives.) Like the desperate hunt for diplomatic recognition, Pretoria's attempts to lean over the fence to persuade the neighbours to tone down the volume of their anti-apartheid rhetoric largely failed, except in the case of Lesotho where a South African blockade helped topple the noisy and erratic regime of Chief Leabua Jonathan. Some of the economic aims were to maintain water and electricity supplies by manipulating the captive markets, not least with the monopoly power of South Africa's transport network.

There was a big difference between capturing markets and creating chaos, argued the South African business community. Why spread anarchy which could blow back into South Africa? The long-term cost-benefit analysis of a captive regional market required more trade, not scorched earth. Beggaring your neighbours was not only bad for local businesses but it also discouraged much-needed Western investment in South Africa. Who would want to risk their capital in the middle of a battle-zone? Here economic pragmatism collided with Afrikaner pride, especially that of the soldier-imperialists in the State Security Council. To some hawks, military means became an end in themselves. Foreign critics tended to single out senior officers such as Major General Pieter van der Westhuizen, a military intelligence specialist, who was tasked with the military destabilization programme, particularly the control/liaison with forces such as RENAMO. The military option became holy writ and opponents, the 'cocktail diplomats' in the South African department of foreign affairs, were sometimes detested as much as the communist enemy. It was not unlike the feeling inside the UK Ministry of Defence HQ ('Main Building') in Whitehall during the height of the Cold War, when references to the enemy sometimes meant not the Russians, but the Foreign Office. It was largely a joke in London, but the mutual dislike – even hatred – in Pretoria was very real.

Militarization of policy-formulation could have been one straightforward explanation for the contradictions inherent in Pretoria's destabilization policy. But this was not a sufficient explanation. Nor could it be in a complex matrix where 'aggressor and victims are linked by direct dial telephone, railways and extensive trade'.[5]

Destabilization was very costly. Joseph Hanlon had suggested as early as 1986 that Pretoria's policy had already cost, directly or indirectly, 100,000 lives, £10,000 million worth of damage and had made one million homeless. Another respected source put the figure for 1980 to 1986 at $25-30 billion in the SADCC countries — $400 for every man, woman and child in the whole region of southern Africa.[6] Everybody was suffering from the fat-cat profit-mongers in Johannesburg's elite northern suburbs to the starving Mozambican peasants I had seen wearing bark to hide their nakedness in the bush in Sofala province in 1986. What was it all for?

Deon Geldenhuys, an extremely polite young Afrikaner professor at the Rand Afrikaans University in Johannesburg, was often (inaccurately) accused in the

A destroyed hospital in Caia, Sofala province, Mozambique. The town was completely stripped when the author took this picture in June 1986

early 1980s of being the architect of the beggar-your-neighbour policy; Kissinger and Metternich were some of the epithets used. He was not a Svengali whispering in the ears of the State Security Council members. In fact he was summoned to the council and his views were pilloried, not least because he was what was then termed a '*verligte*' (literally an enlightened one, a reformer). He was also frozen out of some government research contracts. Some military top brass did use his academic studies as *ex post facto* rationalization for the destabilization policies. Certainly, South African leaders were unusual in the way they paid so much attention to the work of academics – to utilize or ban their theories.[7]

Geldenhuys had initially suggested that destabilization was an end in itself. The British columnist, Simon Jenkins, opined in *The Economist* in July 1983: 'South Africa's policy towards its southern neighbours seems governed not by consistency but by some arcane Afrikaner intuition. From time to time, an incipient black nation needs to be taught a lesson to emphasize who is regional boss.' Crude racism and instinctive reactions to perceived threats and actual anti-Boer rhetoric may well have been significant factors. P.W. Botha – who enjoyed his nickname of the 'Great Crocodile' – was so angry when Mugabe, in a bitter speech, called the Afrikaner leader a racist – that the prime minister ordered immediate punishment. Locomotives, borrowed from South Africa and desperately needed to shift Zimbabwe's record 1981 harvest, were abruptly recalled.

Whatever the causes of Afrikaner destabilization, some opponents within the South African establishment certainly criticized the militarization of the country's foreign policy. They argued publicly and in secret committees that economic cooperation and re-stabilization worked better than knee-jerk retaliation. It became like the Kremlinologists who used to spend their careers reading between the lines of arcane statements from Moscow. So it was with the apartheid critics and foreign and South African academics who studied Pretoria's stop-go aggression. It was couched not just in dove/hawk dichotomies as in the West. No, the runes of the foreign affairs department were read and contrasted with the SADF/police or State Security Council hardliners' effusions versus the *verligtes* in the National Party and cabinet. In particular the debate was crystallized into the swings of the power pendulum between the so-called 'forward' and 'laager' strategic schools within the military elite as well as the more general debate between economic versus military options discussed endlessly within the media. South Africa suffered strict censorship, but it had to allow some media freedoms – to prove it was in the vanguard of the West's war on communism. Despite what the critics said about South Africa, it probably did have the freest press in Africa. The press bulldogs could bark loudly and often, but they couldn't really bite. Investigative journalism was hobbled, especially in the realm of security and prisons. So destabilization was extensively reviewed locally. The media would cover the events which led to National Party politicians making the peace with Mozambique in 1984 while the military, or elements within it, would disagree and quietly continue to arm the RENAMO insurgency in the same country. Two leading authorities on destabilization, Phyllis Johnson and David Martin, insisted in 1986 that 'Given the authoritarian nature of the South African regime, such an argument is, at the most charitable, ill-informed. At another level, it may be disinformation.'[8] Yet the same study considered in detail the splits between the South African government and the SADF over military aid to RENAMO in the Gorongosa documents (which I discuss in a later chapter). The two anti-apartheid critics clearly accepted the damning documents as fact, although Pretoria insisted that some or all of the papers were forgeries (depending upon various official statements). Unless one assumes that very damaging documents were intended to be found, which makes no sense, the Gorongosa papers suggested, *prima facie,* that on the important issue of supporting RENAMO major differences of opinion over the destabilization programme persisted. As I was one of the very few people to trouble to visit regularly both SADF HQ in Pretoria *and* RENAMO HQ in or near the Gorongosa forest – I say 'trouble' as I travelled hundreds of miles cross-country on a motorbike during the height of the fighting – it did seem to me that support of the rebel movement had caused many splits in Pretoria's civilian and military/intelligence elites. Johnson and Martin's view that the alternation of carrot and stick in Mozambique were not the result of domestic friction, but rather a calculated oscillation, an explicit variant of good cop/bad cop method of interrogation, seemed naïve even at the time.

This school of thought assumed a consistency and mastery of political and military strategy over a long period in numerous operations that few governments in the world have ever displayed. Over such vital issues as intervention in the Angola war in 1975 and in Rhodesia in the 1970s (before the formal theories of destabilization were developed) and, later, the abortive Seychelles coup in 1981 and the debate over RENAMO, there had been well-documented evidence

AFONSO DHLAKAMA
Presidente da Resistência Nacional Moçambicana e
Comandante Supremo das forças da RENAMO


A RENAMO propaganda poster

of genuine disputes within not only the intelligence and military leadership but also within the National Party, especially in cabinet. Had all this been for show, clever disinformation over the destabilizing decade just to fool apartheid's many enemies? If this is true, then the Afrikaner leaders deserved a whole barrowload of Oscars. In the 1980s, the style of the Botha regime was predominately reactive. Circumstances and chance, not Machiavellian prescience, were the real dictators in southern Africa. Joseph Hanlon commented thus on the Nkomati accord in 1986: 'it seems that the State Security Council went into Nkomati not so much intending to violate it, but simply with no commitment as to how to abide by it.'[9] And this pact was the main fruit of Afrikaner diplomacy in the decade of destabilization until a deal over Angola led to a settlement in Namibia in 1988-89.

Pretoria was both building structures for peaceful co-existence and waging war. A 1980s Marxist would have commented on the inevitable and terminal contradictions of capitalism at bay in southern Africa. The contradictions of a race war (or class war, *pace* Marxism) could be explained by a combination of reasons. This was the most accurate, if tamest, explanation. It was cock-up as much as conspiracy. The pace of destabilization varied in that tumultuous decade from country to country. The military instruments – raids, assassinations, sabotage and support for the allies, or proxies, such as UNITA and RENAMO – were interlaced with economic manoeuvres. The on-off transport diplomacy could be positive or negative – train routes could be blocked or opened. Sometimes it appeared to be dictated by a whim, for example Prime Minister Botha's choking off supplies to Zimbabwe when he felt Mugabe had pushed Pretoria too far. If sometimes the carrot and stick techniques seemed maliciously whimsical, at other times military adventures could be timed with … military precision. For example, the May 1986 raids on three Commonwealth front-line states were intended to scuttle the peace plans proposed by the Eminent Persons' Group. Covert destabilization, as opposed to open warfare in Angola, was most intense in the period 1980-84, especially in late 1982 and early 1983. It had been suggested that the SADF, never slow to emulate their Israeli mentors, were directly encouraged by the Israeli Defense Forces' aggressive forward policy and, in particular, the invasion of Lebanon in 1982.

Although the army of anti-apartheid experts assumed that destabilization was the work of prescient devils in Pretoria concocting a hell-brew with precise measures, the truth is both more mundane and complex. Through the fog of war, accompanied by angry phone calls, racist bigotry, patriotism, ignorance, fear and doubt, a competing group of frequently highly competent Afrikaners, all committed to white survival and/or supremacy, plotted and prayed. They won some points and lost some, depending on a combination of time, skill and chance. It was like wars everywhere and in all times, with the important exception that many Afrikaners felt that, unlike their black opponents, they could lose big only once. Unlike the period after the war of 1899-1902, they could not lose and hope to live and fight another day. Unconditional surrender was not an option. That fear fuelled a ruthlessness and a determination that made 'destabilization' a word almost as dreaded in the region as 'apartheid'.

Some hardliners in the police supported Nkomati because they could see the advantages of ejecting the ANC insurgents, *Unkhonto we Sizwe*, from Mozambique. At the same time some more *verlig* officers in the SADF opposed the accord because they felt that RENAMO had been betrayed. Doves and hawks could agree, however, on the dangers posed by the Cubans. P.W. Botha was the flag-bearer for the forward military school, especially to deter the Cuban forces in Angola. And yet he was also keen on economic measures, albeit he still believed in the hopeless CONSAS. Botha understood the lesson of the Portuguese: over-extended on the colonial periphery, the centre had collapsed in Lisbon. So despite the often hamfisted crisis management, some of the goals were shrewdly calculated. The Cuban threat, for example, kept Washington onside in Pretoria's campaign to portray itself as a crusader-in-arms in Ronald Regan's war on the Evil Empire. This limited congressional sanctions in the short term and secured military backing from America in the shooting war in Angola. Pretoria had managed to get some support for UNITA although RENAMO was not included in Reagan's laundry list of backing guerrillas who would fight Marxism in Latin America, Africa or, most dramatically, in Afghanistan.

### *Destabilization after Nkomati*

The uprising that began in 1984 in South African townships was initially reasonably well-covered by the foreign TV cameras, before Pretoria imposed a blanket censorship. Western camera teams could rarely gain access to much bloodier wars in the neighbouring states, however. Destabilization had been shrouded in mystery. This was not true of the very well-publicized jewel of South African diplomacy, the Nkomati accord. This was signed amid the glare of world publicity. Few observers could miss the irony of a smiling Machel, the victim, in a field marshal's uniform tailored in London, standing next to the dour P.W. Botha, the architect of destabilization, dressed in a rumpled civilian suit. Presumably both believed they had upstaged each other. The South African leader craved international respectability. Above all, Pretoria wanted formal recognition of its position and legitimacy by its black neighbours. True, Pretoria had signed a secret pact with Swaziland in 1982, but it was evident that Pretoria had an outcast's passion for status. Nkomati bestowed it. Destabilization had proved its point: even the most anti-apartheid front-line president loved power more than he hated Pretoria. With a gun to his head, Machel had to smile and shake hands. Economic blackmail and RENAMO had helped to bring Machel to heel. Mozambique's Marxist regime was forced to beg from the racist capitalist, the ultimate humiliation for African socialism. This was intended as a lesson in 'de-Marxification' for the restless masses in South African townships. Nkomati was one mighty punch in the solar plexus for SADCC and the Western sanctions' campaign.

Grandstanding as a regional peacemaker almost immediately after Nkomati, P.W. Botha set out on a rare official visit to Western Europe. He was received with a coolness bordering on disdain but the South African media hailed his 'grand tour' as the best diplomatic days since Jan Smuts bestrode the Western stage. Gone were the days of being a political leper, the regime now strutted as though its status as a regional superpower had been formalized … finally. No longer was South Africa a gazelle among a world of lions. The fashionable comparison in Pretoria was that South Africa in its region was now like the USA in the Caribbean. Didn't Washington restore order in Grenada by invading it? Force brought peace there, purred South African diplomats smugly. And Washington had sought advantage from its proxy's – Israel's – invasion of Lebanon. So what was the difference between Israel being allowed, even encouraged, to arm the Christian militias there and South Africa sending weapons to the anti-Marxist RENAMO? Pretoria even pressurized Washington to help ease the arms embargo on South Africa so that the government could reinsure its new status as a now respectable ally of the Reagan doctrine. So P.W. Botha got his way with the contested new constitution at home and seized the high ground on regional diplomacy.

Hubris inevitably preceded a fall. Suddenly everything began to come apart at the seams. The war in Angola began to take off while South Africa's continued backing of RENAMO was revealed by an understandably irate Machel. Most dramatically, from August 1984, the domestic 'unrest' erupted into continuous insurrection. As Joseph Hanlon observed, 'The diplomatic gains of Nkomati were lost on the streets of the townships.' Then it was downhill fast: the states of emergency, renewed broader sanctions, the collapse of the rand after Botha's disastrous Rubicon speech, setbacks in the conventional warfare in Angola and an almost total collapse of Nkomati as RENAMO grew into an uncontrollable monster.

The West became entangled in a web largely of its own making. The bigger states tried to balance their South African trade with aid to the front-line states. Vacillation and inconsistency characterized Western policy. Washington armed UNITA, while trying to pose as an honest broker in Namibia and Angola. The US eventually imposed tougher sanctions on Pretoria but cut aid to Zimbabwe, while initially refusing it altogether to Mozambique. The European Community helped all the SADCC states, especially Mozambique, while politely applying mild sanctions on Pretoria with no clear objectives. Scandinavia piously demanded mandatory sanctions, while Margaret Thatcher denounced the very principle of sanctions. Thus she and her foreign secretary, Sir Geoffrey Howe, were regularly insulted by Mugabe and Kaunda, yet Britain was the only Western country that trained the Zimbabwe and Mozambique armies to fight RENAMO.

Destabilization had travelled to the West. Confusions over policy reigned there almost as much as in the capitals of the frontline states. No one knew how to handle the rogue elephant on the rampage. Above all, the front-line alliance was nowhere nearer co-ordinating its military forces or strategies. The involvement of Tanzanian and Zimbabwean troops in Mozambique had not crushed RENAMO. Often military co-operation backfired, as FRELIMO resentment of Zimbabwean 'imperialism' grew apace. There was little practical basis for forming a joint military high command. Some of the states were ambiguous about military support for the ANC. Angola, Tanzania and Zambia, those conveniently farthest removed from the SADF's reach, risked allowing ANC military bases. The others, officially, permitted only diplomatic or humanitarian representation. And trade, of course, continued almost unabated: loans and credits were doled out from South Africa, which carried on overt or secret trade with at least forty African states.

As the fires of insurrection spluttered out in the townships in 1986, Pretoria began slowly to re-assert its regional status. The desire of nearly all the southern Africa states to wind down the Angolan war provided the opportunity for P.W. Botha to play the peacemaker again. The roles of Presidents Mobuto of Zaire and Denis Sassou-Nguesso of the Congo were also important. Although ideologically at odds, neither wanted the Angolan conflict to spill over again into his own country. A number of francophone conservatives also pushed for peace, and specifically talks between UNITA and the MPLA. In September 1988 President P.W. Botha

*Above left*: Regional peacemakers: General Mobutu of Zaire

*Above right*: President Denis Sassou-Nguesso of the Congo

leaped on board the peace train. His foreign minister, Pik Botha, secretly shuttled around a number of African capitals while his party leader paid official visits to Malawi, Mozambique and Zaire. As ever, Mugabe remained deaf to Pretoria's overtures but elsewhere the unity of front-line states wobbled noticeably.

## *Conclusion*

For eight years following Zimbabwe's independence, South Africa had bribed, blackmailed, seduced and thumped her neighbours, as well as traded with them. Despite the long 'unrest' crisis of 1984-86 and the bruising economic pressures, the apartheid regime was still, in regional terms, a colossus. For all its contradictions, destabilization had kept the growing *Umkhonto we Sizwe* (MK) infiltration at bay. The formal political attitude of the front-line states was that the civil war in South Africa was not an anti-colonial struggle but rather a campaign for majority rule where whites, as Africans, would have a permanent place in the sun. During Nkomati, FRELIMO officials had explicitly stated that the ANC was involved in a civil-rights struggle, not a guerrilla war to overwhelm a colonial regime.

Pretoria had taken up the cudgels of the Reagan doctrine with a vengeance. The South African-backed UNITA and RENAMO had given the socialist-trained MPLA and FRELIMO more than a run for their Eastern-bloc money. Russian, Cuban and East German advisers found it difficult to cope with a new breed of pro-Western guerrillas fighting established pro-Soviet regimes with the techniques of classical revolutionary warfare. The SADF hoped that the expected Russian scuttle from Afghanistan was perhaps a pointer to the future of Reagan's counter-revolution in Africa as well as Asia. The *Mujahedin* did defeat a superpower and, by then taking on America, changed the face of world politics and the nature of war. Neither UNITA nor RENAMO, however, looked like they were going to make it all the way to the Finland Station. Even their supporters in Pretoria did not expect them to take over Luanda or Maputo anytime soon. Even the thought of keeping in power Jonas Savimbi or Afonso Dhlakama, the RENAMO chieftain, if they ever won, was daunting. The MPLA and FRELIMO would have gone back to the bush and the Soviets would have found themselves in the happier position of once again trying to subvert governments, not fighting insurgents. Of course the Soviets could not know that Afghanistan had indeed been their Vietnam and that the humiliating withdrawal from Afghanistan was the straw that broke the camel's back. The USSR itself was about to implode, but the strategists in southern Africa could not have known that in the dramatic years that immediately followed 1988-89 and the onset of a peace of sorts in the region.

The ruling National Party was trying to shed direct rule of blacks by its homelands policy. The idea of permanently propping up a diva such as Savimbi or the less than charismatic Dhlakama, whose policies had been compared with Pol Pot, was not an enticing prospect. Pretoria wanted economic, not actual, *Lebensraum*. By 1988, except for a few hardliners, the Pretoria consensus was that their friends in the bush in Mozambique and Angola would have to go it alone. They had now become an embarrassment to the settlement in Namibia and the restoration of the spirit of Nkomati with Maputo.

Apartheid's critics had always insisted that UNITA and RENAMO were mere pawns of South Africa while Pretoria had assumed, or at least said, that the ANC and SWAPO were largely puppets of Moscow. It would be inaccurate to draw an exact parallel, of course, between the long history of a movement such as the ANC and a bastard organization such as RENAMO, born in double original sin from Rhodesian and South African parentage. Nevertheless, whatever the debate about the nature of their birth, in maturity RENAMO, and also UNITA, developed an independence of their mentors. SWAPO's unilateral policies could have and almost did derail the Namibian settlement. And like Frankenstein's monster, RENAMO outgrew its handler's leash and threatened to act against Pretoria's interests in Nkomati Mark 2. In short, neither superpowers nor the regional states could simply shut down completely the guerrilla players in the drama, although they could severely curtail their activities. This raised the question of whether Pretoria could simply turn off the destabilization tap, if it decided to do so.

Even regime change in Pretoria could not suddenly stop the chaos that had been unleashed. Pretoria had tried to control the front-line states with, as the bottom line, a naked and sometimes foolhardy display of power. It did confirm South Africa's status as the regional superpower, even though its actual achievements, the Nkomati and the later Angolan and Namibian agreements, were finessed by the influence of a real superpower, the USA. The front-line states were forced to modify their behaviour towards South Africa but not, with very limited exceptions, their political attitudes. Pretoria did not manage to install a ring of conservative client states as substitutes for the bygone colonial regimes. Even in the late 1980s, the destabilization battles on all the economic, military and political fronts were likely to be Pyrrhic victories for the SADF. And in the big Angolan battles, as I shall explain in the next chapter, it is hard to use the term victory at all. All that the machinations across Angola, Zimbabwe and Mozambique and elsewhere had created was chronic instability – as intended. But instability was infectious, not least for white South Africans. Famine, death, roving bands of desperate refugees, destruction and, above all, bitterness and hatred stalked the region. Mugabe's view was that comprehensive sanctions, despite the increased suffering, were worth it to end more quickly the agony caused by the root cause: apartheid. The carrot and the stick were beginning to look the same to the masses of numbed victims. The South African scholar Sam Nolutshungu put it so aptly: 'For those within its range, there is no more safety in submission than in resistance.' Pax Pretoria had bloodily stored up the anger of an entire subcontinent.

*Chapter 9*

# The Big Battles: Angola (1976-1990)

Destabilization in Angola was different. Because Pretoria lacked economic leverage, blunt military force was the chosen instrument. Subtle railway diplomacy elsewhere gave way here to a series of major incursions that led to large conventional battles.

Angola was considered a serious threat because oil made the country relatively wealthy by local standards. The mineral potential could not only have fuelled Angolan development but also the regeneration of all the front-line states, especially if the Benguela railway could function again. (This was to be a distant dream; the whole railway was officially re-opened only in 2015, reconstruction courtesy of the Chinese.) Left alone, an oil-rich Angola might (perhaps) have matured into an alluring multi-racial 'Brazil in Africa', a model for South Africa's blacks. For Pretoria's hawks, however, the military challenge was immediately paramount. Angola played host to the entire range of Afrikaner demons: the ANC, SWAPO Cubans, East Germans and Russians. Often, they were convenient demons. The presence of nearby real-live communist troops, especially Cubans, was used partly to justify Pretoria's endless filibuster over Namibia, not least to entice the Americans for whom Castro was the apex of their own demonology. Although legally distinct issues, the removal of Cuban troops became 'linked' to Namibian independence. This had suited Pretoria and Washington (and, arguably, Moscow).

Castro's latter-day *conquistadores* allowed South Africa to square the circle: continual SADF operations inside Angola ensured that the Cubans stayed but Castro's men made it impossible for the South Africans to quit Namibia, argued Pretoria. The Reagan administration went along with this self-serving rationale and indeed went further by arming UNITA, thus forming an implicit alliance with the apartheid state. It took almost eight years for Reagan's foreign policy advisers to come to the realization that the fundamental obstacle to peace in the region was not winkling out the Cubans from Angola but cajoling the SADF out of Namibia. Meanwhile, the diplomatic impasse and the spiralling conflict had enabled Moscow to demonstrate its commitment to the cause of African liberation. At the same time, Angola's red armies were providing ample daily evidence of the total communist onslaught to the increasingly paranoid Afrikaner leadership. It was more difficult to calibrate precisely the benefits to Washington of American's military dalliance with both Savimbi and the Great Crocodile in Pretoria while simultaneously carrying on a half-hearted sanctions war on South Africa's economy.

While it was abundantly clear that Pretoria's policy in Namibia was to hang on to the territory for as long as possible, mainly for its military advantages, South Africa's grand strategy in Angola was less discernible. The options ranged across a wide spectrum, including:

- replacing the MPLA with UNITA;
- forcing both into a coalition government;
- establishing a secessionist tribal state in southern Angola;
- forming a great Ovamboland in southern Angola *and* northern Namibia;
- and simply keeping the MPLA government on the defensive.

The specific military strategy was more apparent. To prevent a Marxist axis in Luanda and Windhoek, the SADF tried to ensure:

- widespread destruction of Angola's infrastructure;
- the containment of the ANC and SWAPO by destroying their bases and pushing them ever northwards;
- and the subvention of UNITA. If UNITA could not win, then at least it could constitute a military buffer against the Cuban/Russian/FAPLA/SWAPO socialist alliance.

Officially, the SADF stated that its 'hot pursuit' and 'pre-emptive' raids against SWAPO bases in Angola were intended to deter guerrilla infiltration into Namibia. For years, military aid to UNTA was hushed up. SADF action was always characterized as anti-SWAPO sweeps. As the UNITA versus SWAPO war grew after 1983, however, it became increasingly difficult to maintain this fiction. Technically, the SADF was fighting two distinct wars: a largely successful counter-insurgency campaign against SWAPO over the fate of Namibia, and the conventional war of attrition in south-eastern Angola to project and, later, protect UNITA.

### *An invisible UNITA*

Just before Savimbi led his tattered remnants into the bush in March 1976, UNITA issued a final communiqué from Gago Couthino. It said that seventeen Cuban soldiers had been executed by an all-woman firing squad. Five of the soldiers had been accused of rape.[1]

It might have been a touching feminist gesture but it was poor PR for the guerrilla leader who was later to excel in the arts of media manipulation. For seven months after this, Savimbi disappeared. According to his (initially sympathetic) biographer, Fred Bridgland, Savimbi led 1,000 followers on a 3,000-kilometre trek through central Angola. At the end of his own version of Mao's long march, seventy-nine supporters, including nine women, were still with him.[2] At the nadir of his fortunes, UNITA strength tottered at around 200 armed guerrilla (according to John Marcum[3]), although Savimbi claimed over 2,000. Nonetheless, UNITA still retained a sizeable popular tribal support. Even the MPLA admitted that at least 350,000 peasants, and possibly as many as a million, in Bie and Huambo provinces, fled into the bush, encouraged no doubt by MPLA revenge for earlier UNITA atrocities.[4]

Savimbi had not thrown in the towel: low-level insurgency continued. Attacks on the Benguela railway particularly distracted FAPLA resources in the period 1976 to 1978 when twenty out of twenty-five diesel locomotives were destroyed. The line was virtually closed. UNITA, however, was on its own as SADF supplies had petered out. By the end of 1978, from Luanda's perspective, the civil war was effectively over. It was merely a case of mopping up stray armed bands. Some Cuban troops were sent home. The remaining combat soldiers assumed largely guard and training functions. The SADF was still fighting a war against SWAPO, it was true, but Luanda hoped that increasing international support for the MPLA would deter the Afrikaner hawks. Relations with Zambia were thawing, for example. Deeply immersed in the Rhodesian war, Kaunda was desperate to secure supplies via the Benguela route. The Luanda government also reached out a

Presidents Neto and Castro

neighbourly hand to the ever-mercurial Mobutu – but only after a few sharp blows. In 1977 and 1978 the Katangese gendarmes in exile had been unleashed from their Angolan bases. They committed unspeakable atrocities in Zaire's Shaba province, particularly during a massacre of white civilians in Kolwezi. French and Moroccan troops restored order and tried to entice back the Zairian troops who had fled into the forests. Thereafter, a somewhat chastened Zairian president made a a reluctant peace with the MPLA … for a while.

The MPLA leaders grew over-confident and more self-indulgent, as they sat back to taste the spoils of power. In the African way, 'it was their time to eat'. The ruling central committee took incautious steps. In particular, revolutionary zealots tried to construct, almost overnight, a by-the-book Marxist state, even though the concept of the class struggle had very little relevance to Angola in the late 1970s. The leading academic authority on Angola, John Marcum, summed up the MPLA's follies thus:

> Lacking the educated cadres that would in any case have been essential to realize their vision, the MPLA leadership embarked on a programme of economic centralization and agricultural collectivization. They imposed restrictions on organized religion and rejected the legitimacy of such issues as the under-representation of rural sectors and ethnic groups (notably Ovimbundu) in positions of political influence. The result was ambitious, maladministered, alienating governance by a largely Luanda-centred *mestiço* and ethnically Mbundu elite propped by an influx of Cuban, Soviet, East German and East European advisers and technicians.[5]

An alien ideology backed by foreign troops: this was perfect propaganda fodder for Pretoria and for a slowly recuperating UNITA. Savimbi could claim that the MPLA had substituted one white imperialism for another. To win over the Angolan peasantry in any hearts-and-minds contest, the MPLA needed peace, organizational skills and funds on top of political moderation. Luanda could counter, with some justification, that it was UNITA and SADF depredations that prevented reconstruction. The MPLA leadership did not win over the bulk of the disaffected peasantry, particularly the Ovimbundu, UNITA's natural constituency, and, more dangerously, it provoked Pretoria by establishing ANC training camps in the north and a large military infrastructure for SWAPO in the south.

A vengeful SADF top brass was preparing to move back in force. Cross-border raids had never ceased; now the army was gearing up to do the job properly, not as in 1975 when the 'politicians' had hog-tied South Africa's offensive capability. The decision to go to war with independent Angola was apparently taken in December 1977 in surprisingly peaceful surroundings, an unpretentious seaside cottage at Oubos, near Port Elizabeth.[6] It belonged to the prime minister, John Vorster. To this unlikely war conference he had summoned his senior officers. His generals advocated a largescale operation against the reinforced SWAPO bases in southern Angola. Vorster was reluctant to give the green light. After all, the recent invasion of the same country had destroyed his detente policy and had undermined his own government, especially the row over the secrecy of the 1975 invasion. Despite the later opposition of the department of foreign affairs, the ailing Vorster succumbed to the hard-line option. It was a decisive step in the rise of the South African military. The immediate outcome was Operation REINDEER in May 1978 (discussed in more detail in the next chapter on Namibia). This operation and the others that followed dwarfed the 1975-76 intervention.

Despite the renewed tempo of SADF activity that continued throughout 1979, the MPLA appeared confident. In August the Benguela line was re-opened (temporarily) for the first time since 1975. The MPLA held its first (one-party) elections, albeit in only a few regions of the country. The party predicted rapid social transformation.

Such optimism was naive because UNITA was expanding. Despite all the pious denials from Pretoria and Jamba, Savimbi's provisional 'capital' in the extreme south-east of Angola, SADF aid was also expanding. According to the UNITA chieftain's main biographer, at the end of 1979, 'South Africa's support for Savimbi, which since early 1976 had varied from non-existent to the unpredictable, had become a substantial commitment.' This now included weapons and military instructors. Nor was Pretoria the sole donor. During 1979, 500 UNITA officers were trained secretly in Morocco. Senegal provided more open political backing. Money came from Saudi Arabia and the Gulf states. And Mobutu, as usual, was playing a double game. Despite the official rapprochement with Luanda, he was giving covert aid to UNITA. Savimbi now publicly proclaimed that he *controlled* one-third of Angola. In 1979 that was an exaggeration, although his *range of operations* probably extended to at least a third of the country.

The highwater mark of the MPLA's tide of success in this period was in 1980. Military and diplomatic pressures began to mount against the new socialist leader, Eduardo dos Santos, who had taken over after the death of Neto in September 1979. He was to rule his country for thirty-seven years and turn the government into a family business. Another man who did the same for the same period was Robert Mugabe. And it was his first victory in 1980 that shook the ruling Afrikaners to the core. Mugabe's electoral triumph made Pretoria even more adamant about preventing a similar outcome in Namibia. In June 1980 South African launched Operation SCEPTIC (more commonly known as Operation SMOKESHELL) against SWAPO bases in southern Angola. One British military historian described this as South Africa's 'biggest combined land and air operation since the Second World War'.[7] This was just the beginning. The SADF's confidence and boldness grew apace once Ronald Reagan had replaced Jimmy Carter in the White House.

Eduardo dos Santos took over after Neto's death in 1979

Savimbi was soon welcomed in Washington. UNITA joined the Nicaraguan 'Contras' and the Afghan *Mujahedin* as 'freedom fighters' sponsored by a new administration dedicated to clawing away at the peripheries of the Soviet empire.

*Savimbi's resurrection*

From 1980 onwards South African military strategy fused the anti-SWAPO and pro-UNITA wars. Simultaneously, the Reagan administration's diplomacy transformed the 'Namibian problem' into the 'Angolan problem'. Gradually, Pretoria shifted from insisting that the SADF would withdraw its troops from *Namibia* only if the Cubans went home to the much more ambitious demand that South Africa would quit *Angola* when Castro's men left too. Thus, the stakes were dramatically raised; both 'problems' became much more intractable and, at the centre of the conundrum, Savimbi rose Houdini-like from his political grave.

Nearly all Western military experts who had closely observed UNITA guerrillas in action, especially in the period 1980-90, confirmed that Savimbi's soldiers were of excellent calibre. They were generally competently led by their officers, well-trained and disciplined under fire. Yet UNITA's renaissance was only partly due to its fighting qualities; Pretoria's helping hand was crucial. This aid came in various packages. Training, intelligence and supplies were provided first. Also South African and Portuguese businessmen traded with UNITA: smuggled diamonds, poached ivory and rare wood were some of the contraband.

Help with communications was also vital in a sprawling, rugged country like Angola, which is five times the size of Britain. Savimbi's main base, Jamba, hugged the border with Namibia in the desolate south east. The Portuguese used to call this area 'the end of the world'. Savimbi's well-camouflaged 50-mile-wide capital was very isolated. Savimbi had to rely on two main supply routes, via Zaire, courtesy of the CIA, and via Namibia thanks to the SADF. Most visitors, especially journalists like me, chose the easy route from Wonderboom airport near

Pretoria, flying in an old Dakota that dropped to treetop level in the final stages of the journey to avoid stray SAM-7s. Travelling to Jamba in the mid-1980s, guests would be met by extremely well turned-out UNITA officers, searched and then offered the unique opportunity to have their passports stamped with 'Free Angola'. Most declined as it would have invalidated their passports for travel elsewhere in Africa. Driven in a captured Russian truck along empty dirt roads, signalled forward at deserted intersections by immaculate military policemen wearing spotless white gloves, guests reached an officers' mess, where they were indulged with South African wines and beers. This was a comfortable, and perhaps Potemkin, war for the majority of the media who avoided, or were kept from, the front. A self-publicist of genius, Savimbi garnered acres of favourable coverage in the more conservative outlets in the West. The message, though, eventually palled. It was always the same: 'next year in Luanda'.

Such ambitions rested upon South African military assistance in two fields: sabotage and invasion. Frequently, highly professional SADF Reconnaissance Commandos ('Recces'), the premier army unit, would enter Angola to destroy installations, leaving behind false evidence of UNITA complicity. (They did the same in Mozambique and gave the credit to RENAMO.) Many of these operations were skilfully accomplished by 4 Recce based at Langebaan in Cape Province. This unit specialized in airborne assaults. (Some of the incursions came via the navy's three Daphné-class submarines, however.) Special forces hit Lobito oil terminal (August 1980), Luanda oil refinery (November 1981) and destroyed the road and rail bridge over the Giraul river near the port of Namibe (November 1982). Limpet mines were attached to Angolan and Eastern bloc ships in harbour. Way up north, Cabinda, the oil lifeline for the MPLA, was the most obvious target, however. It was here that one of South Africa's most daring covert later missions was to backfire dramatically. Inland, particularly in the north, sabotage was sometimes the work of genuine UNITA special forces.

More important for UNITA's expansion were the continuous minor raids and occasional full-blown conventional assaults from the SADF's occupied zones in the centre of southern Angola. These sorties hammered SWAPO and increasingly FAPLA as well. SWAPO units tended to hug Angolan bases and sometimes wore identical uniforms. Such raids distracted FAPLA attempts to crush Savimbi's resurgence. Enmeshed in the south, FAPLA could not prevent UNITA cadres pushing ever northwards, across the Benguela line and on to threaten communications both to Luanda and the important diamond-mining centres to the northeast.

According to President dos Santos's new year message in January 1982, in the first eleven months of 1981, there had been fifty-three SADF troop operations, more than 100 bombing raids and 1,600 reconnaissance flights. On its own, FAPLA could not counter the big conventional air and ground attacks. After the three-week incursions of June 1980 (Operation SCEPTIC) there followed Opcration PROTEA in August/September 1981. During PROTEA, several Soviet military personnel were killed and one warrant officer was taken prisoner. Thousands of South African troops occupied a 33-mile-deep strip of Cunene province, including Ngiva, the provincial capital. The SADF was to sit tight there for over three years. FAPLA, not SWAPO, became the main antagonist. UNITA troops were very thin on the ground in Cunene province but the SADF christened its occupied zone 'UNITA-liberated territory'. Operation DAISY came next, in November 1981. A mechanized ground force, backed by Mirages, Canberras and Buccaneers, made the deepest penetration since the 1975 adventure. During 1981 the SADF kept piling on the pressure in the south, as UNITA troops moved into northern provinces such as Malanje and Cuanza Sul.

UNITA not only claimed SADF successes as its own; it also seized hostages for its propaganda machine. In March 1983, for example, UNITA captured eighty-four Czechs and Portuguese working on a construction project in central Angola. Savimbi sought indirect international recognition by insisting that official representatives of the foreign governments concerned should personally receive back their nationals in Jamba. It was ironic that President Reagan was building up his military sponsorship of Savimbi at a time when UNTA was regularly bagging hostages; the taking of hostages was one of the prime definitions of terrorism in the Reagan lexicon.

Southern Angola was sinking into anarchy as various armies marched across the flat wastelands. The innocent man-in-the middle, as usual, suffered most. In three weeks Operation PROTEA generated 80,000 peasant refugees. In 1983 President dos Santos estimated that that the total cost of South African 'aggression' was US$10 billion. The Luanda government was spending perhaps as much as 50 per cent of its overall budget on the war.

An overstretched FAPLA and a rampant SADF boosted the resurgent UNITA's expansion into central and northern Angola. The crunch came at Cangamba in August 1983. This was the first major conventional assault by UNITA in the history of the civil war – and it went all wrong. Savimbi's troops had performed well as guerrillas but even conventionally trained UNITA soldiers could not match FAPLA … without SADF intercession. Though accounts of the battle vary, apparently only SADF air strikes saved Savimbi from a total rout. FAPLA claimed that over 1,000 UNITA soldiers were killed, including a large proportion who were blown up in their own minefields as they retreated in panic. That was the FAPLA version.

Cangamba was a significant escalation and this suited some hawks in Pretoria. The generals had clearly adapted to the lessons of the 1975-76 debacle. They had jettisoned the previous penny-packet commitments: the size of troop deployment, firepower on the ground, especially better artillery, and concentrated air strikes, were rapidly increased. That pushed up costs in treasure and in young conscripts' lives. In August 1982, for example, a SAM-7 missile brought down a Puma helicopter ferrying twelve soldiers during fighting in Cunene province. The twelve, none older that 22, were killed along with the three-man crew. This was the highest SADF death toll in a single accident in more than sixteen years of fighting in Namibia and Angola. Angolan troops now more than stood their ground against the SADF. Battletrained and well-stocked by the Russians, FAPLA was becoming more aggressive. The cross-border war was no longer a pushover for the marauding South Africans. And their defence planners worried that Cuban combat troops and Soviet advisers would step up their front-line involvement. The South African army had killed or captured a handful of Soviet soldiers but it was not proven that they been performing combat duties.

Some defence hardliners in Pretoria still believed that the war could be won in one short, sharp blow. It seemed as though South African military intelligence was once again trying to outdo the Israelis in flamboyant tactics. It was rumoured in intelligence circles that a second grab would be made for Luanda. In 1983 hawks in the State Security Council discussed in detail a project for a rapid thrust towards the Angolan capital to install Savimbi. A number of hardliners, including the defence minister, General Magnus Malan, were determined to reverse the verdict of 1976: the next time – with enough force – the SADF could seize Luanda. As usual, the cover would be a big drive on SWAPO. The FAPLA HQ at Lubango was the immediate target. Then, if all went well, would come the quick thrust to Luanda. It is not clear what SADF military intelligence had to say about the Russian SAM-9 sites and the elite Cuban tank squadrons defending the road to the capital. A contingency plan existed, however, in case the Cubans shifted troops to Mozambique to open up a diversionary second front. The SADF might have combined with RANAMO to make a real or feint assault on Maputo, the capital.

Threatening to invade *both* capitals of South Africa's Marxist neighbours was too much even for hawks inside the SSC. The chief of the army, General Jannie Geldenhuys, an intelligent moderate, questioned the feasibility, and indeed the sanity, of this proposal. Geldenhuys threatened to resign and go public. Although P.W. Botha usually sided with his ultras, in this case the Great Crocodile opted for Geldenhuys and caution. This at least was the security gossip in Pretoria, and it was augmented by the Russians publicly warning Pretoria to be cautious. In November 1983 Soviet diplomats at the UN met secretly with the South African ambassador. He was told bluntly that the Russian missile system, Cuban-piloted MiG-23s and Cuban-manned tanks, plus all the Soviet reinforcements required, would be deployed if the SADF tried to move on Luanda.

Invading two capitals was too much for General Jannie Geldenhuys. (SADF)

Nonetheless, on 3 December 1983, the SADF launched a big push – Operation ASKARI. SWAPO vanished into the bush, and the SADF was confronted with combined and determined Cuban and FAPLA forces. In a fiercely contested encounter three miles north-east of Cuvelai, the SADF suffered twenty-one killed. The biggest single losses occurred when a Ratel-20 was cornered in a minefield and then knocked out by a T-54 tank.[8] Although Cuban and Angolan losses were, as usual, much higher than South Africa's, the very stiff resistance surprised Pretoria and vindicated Geldenhuys's caution. Bad weather and the Soviet missile system had challenged the SADF's accustomed superiority in the air.

Enough was enough. ASKARI had been a major disappointment for the SADF. Their conventional opponents had dug in their heels. SWAPO guerrillas were still a nuisance and Savimbi was just as far from Luanda. The Russians were leveraging up the costs of South Africa's war, already running at an estimated $4 million a day. Perhaps it was time for a bit of diplomacy. The Americans, certainly, were eager for a foreign policy success in Angola and Namibia: in 1984 Reagan was trying for a second term of office. So far, years of constructive engagement with South Africa had produced little but frustration.

### *The Lusaka accord*

Both FAPLA and the SADF needed a breathing space. The South Africans, fighting on a 250-mile 'front', were over-extended. The Angolans were straining to contain the South Africans; UNITA had taken the opportunity to again consolidate its operations in the north. It was the same old story and the protagonists were all tired. Thus American diplomatic pressure on South Africa coincided with battle-front incentives. Pik Botha's department of foreign affairs, for once, was given its head to try a diplomatic assault on Angola (and Mozambique). Pretoria needed to break out of its isolation, especially as it was planning its new constitution at home and P.W. Botha was planning a major tour of Western Europe, a rare event for the pariah state. Some of the generals, however, opposed any deal with Marxists merely to placate what they dubbed 'Pik's cocktail party friends'.

In February 1984 an agreement was signed in Lusaka between Pretoria and Luanda. The SADF was to withdraw in stages from its three-year occupation of Cunene province. The MPLA promised to end SWAPO's incursions from this zone. A Joint Monitoring Commission (JMC), comprised of SADF officers and FAPLA, supervised the withdrawal. UNITA was not involved in this local ceasefire. The Angolans and their white enemies on the JMC got on well. It was the not unusual phenomenon of professional soldiers' natural empathy surfacing in the absence of their political masters. On a few occasions they even fought alongside each other against stray bands of SWAPO and UNITA who opened fire on JMC units.

The Lusaka accord was a temporary *truce,* not a non-aggression pact (such as the ensuing Nkomati agreement between Maputo and Pretoria). The SADF's withdrawal slowed down and then stopped after the exit from Ngiva. It was to take over a year to complete a (temporary) exodus from a 25-mile-wide strip between Ngiva and the Namibian border. Optimists prayed that the Lusaka agreement would lead both to peace in Angola and also a rapid settlement in Namibia. It was not to be. Separate talks between SWAPO and South Africa broke down in May 1984. Pretoria once more upped the stakes. The South African government insisted that there could be no peace in Namibia unless UNITA was included in a settlement in Angola. The war in southern Angola was now recharged.

A single incident now mightily embarrassed Pretoria and laid bare the raw sinews of destabilization. It was called Operation ARGON and it happened on 21/22 May 1985 near the Malongo oil terminal in the Cabinda enclave. It would be easy to write a whole book about the enclave, its separatist movements and Western intelligence chicanery. Because of its mineral wealth, independent or as part of Angola, it seduced many, not least the Americans who co-operated with the MPLA-run Sonangol oil company. After a hot, muggy, overcast evening, an alert FAPLA foot patrol clashed with a 4 Recce commando unit which had arrived in Gemini inflatables from a navy submarine, the SAS *Johanna van der Merwe.* The team, comprised of seven white Recce commandos and two black Angolans, had managed to reach the beach, despite numerous difficulties, not least the very shallow water, mudbanks, oil installations and civilian fishermen, plus lots of heavily-armed FAPLA who were both sober and professional. Six of the nine-man team escaped despite three being badly wounded, two were killed and one, Captain Wynand Petrus du Toit, was shot three times and taken prisoner, after a ferocious firefight. After he had received good medical treatment from Cuban doctors, who held off the interrogators, du Toit was paraded at a press conference in Luanda. He admitted that their targets were the US-operated Gulf Oil complex, which was also sometimes guarded by Cubans. The Recce commando admitted that they were planning to put two limpet mines on each of the five huge oil tanks. In addition the saboteurs carried UNITA propaganda material and a small tin of paint to daub 'Viva UNITA' on the road. The unfortunate officer also admitted that he had taken part in other operations for which UNITA had been credited. Pretoria lamely tried to argue that its commandos had been on a reconnaissance mission to gather intelligence on SWAPO and ANC bases in Cabinda. The army's most elite unit, very lightly armed, would hardly have carried such an interesting array of sabotage and deception material to gather information on non-existent insurgent bases. In fact this was the third submarine operation to hit Angolan coastal targets: Operation NOBILIS successfully attacked ships in Luanda harbour and Operation BOUGAINVILLEA blew up railway rolling stock in Lobito port. In the third, botched, submarine op, the very best of the SADF's soldiery had been caught out and had confessed (though not to everything). A writer, sympathetic to the MPLA, summed up the impact of the du Toit escapade:

> That one incident shattered the credibility of 'constructive engagement', destroyed the peacemaking image the apartheid regime was trying to create for itself, and called into question all the Unita claims over the years. Had it not been for the action of that FAPLA patrol, the Angolan economy would have been deprived of its main foreign exchange earner and of the fuel needed to keep everything going, including the armed forces. Headlines would have declared that Unita was in control of Cabinda province and about to make its long-announced but continually postponed assault on the capital. One can only speculate as to what the reaction of the foreign oil companies operating in Angola would have been, or the reactions of their governments.[9]

The American government's response was, however, to propose the repeal of the Clark Amendment, which had previously prevented official US military aid to Savimbi. At the same time, the US was buying $600 million-worth of Cabinda oil every year. Ironically, then, Gulf Oil was effectively financing the MPLA to pay the Cubans to protect its installations against capitalist-backed UNITA guerrillas (and South African imposters). Nevertheless, Washington claimed to be the 'honest broker' in Angola. The US refused to recognize the Angolan government even though it was a valuable and reliable trading partner. US trade with Angola was the fourth biggest in black Africa. The American commercial connection was much larger with South Africa, however.

The diplomatic web was intricate. Israel, for example, in the early 1980s had assisted in the training and equipping of the Zairean army with CIA approval. Some of this support went allegedly to UNITA as well as to attempts to revive the FNLA (minus Roberto) and insurgent secessionist movements in Cabinda. In 1983 a (temporarily) revived FNLA launched a short-lived offensive in the north. It soon collapsed. In 1985 UNITA absorbed some of the FNLA remnants and began a more substantial northern campaign. A UNITA Kimbundu officer, Colonel Antonio Dembo, established a force in the Dembos forests, north-east of Luanda.[10] This was a blow to the MPLA for it was in this region that the Marxist party had founded its ideological and military 'focus' for the start of its war against the Portuguese. The northern campaigns and sabotage by UNITA and the SADF were, however, diversions from the main killing fields of the south. From mid-1985 onwards the SADF and Savimbi's army were sucked into a series of conventional battles, the largest in Africa since the Second World War.

## *The conventional wars*

The Soviet Union and its allies had gone to great lengths to build up FAPLA. The East Germans had created an elaborate SAM system and air force training had been carefully supervised. The key figure here was Iko Carreira, something of a Renaissance man. Of Italian and Portuguese parentage, he had defected from the colonial army to join the MPLA. Much later, after a stroke, he typed impressive novels with one finger. An obituary in Britain's *Guardian* newspaper in June 2000 described him as 'brave, multi-lingual, and worldly'. Certainly in the 1980s he was utterly without illusion about the costs the MPLA needed to pay for its survival. He said in 1984: 'Savimbi, we can beat him; the South Africans, we can beat them; but the CIA and the Americans, that's the unknown quantity for us.' In the early 1980s, Carreira went to Moscow for military training, the first African general to take the Soviet Union's advanced officer course. Returning home two years later, he became air force commander (although he had once commanded all FAPLA forces); he was the technical specialist with whom the Soviet leadership dealt when supplying Angola with their most advanced fighter planes, especially to guard the capital. In 1983 alone, Moscow delivered approximately $800 million in military equipment. The USSR's party boss for just over a sickly year, Konstantin Chernenko, fought back his terminal illness to give a forcible warning in March 1984: 'No one has the right to turn back the pages of history in southern Africa.' Soviet resolve was hardening in Angola (as well as Afghanistan).

Iko Carreira: something of a Renaissance man

In late August 1985 the Angolan army launched Operation PARTY CONGRESS against UNITA strongholds around Mavingo and Cuito Cuanavale. Soviet officers assisted, reportedly serving at regimental level. South African military intelligence, which had intercepted cockpit conversations in Russian, declared that Soviet pilots were flying Angolan MiG-23s and helicopter gunships. The SADF always had to underplay the prowess of Angolan black forces, *pour discourager* their own black locals at home. It was much more convenient to play up the devious skills of Cuban pilots and the quality of advanced Russian kit. FAPLA captured Cazombo, and UNITA fell back towards Mavinga. Even Jamba was threatened.

In mid-September, after finally pulling out entirely from southern central Angola, as dictated by the Lusaka deal, the SADF intervened decisively with air strikes and a mechanized battalion, the 32nd Buffalo Battalion. The South African Air Force (SAAF) also transported UNITA reinforcements in its C-130 Hercules aircraft. Savimbi's men had been wrongfooted and found themselves badly positioned to withstand the main assault. Defence Minister Malan even stated publicly that South Africa was helping UNITA, albeit with 'humanitarian aid'. For three consecutive days in late September, with its then mastery of the air, the SAAF bombed and strafed advancing FAPLA units. The SADF eventually stopped and then turned the FAPLA offensive. UNITA had been saved to fight another day. The 1985 offensive had almost succeeded in overwhelming Savimbi's war. Luanda was bound to try again.

On 24 October 1985 UNITA officially joined the Reagan list of endangered species in countries such as Afghanistan and Nicaragua. In November Reagan officially approved a covert aid package of $13 million to the Angolan 'contras'. In January 1986 Savimbi was received in Washington amid a blaze of publicity. Within two months Stinger ground-to-air missiles and TOW anti-armour weapons were passing through Kamina air base in Zaire into Savimbi's hands (and, no doubt, Pretoria's). As in Afghanistan, the Stingers were to prove lethal to low-flying aircraft. Savimbi now had the capacity to deter the MPLA's helicopter gunships and the MiG-23s that had caused so much damage to UNITA in the 1985 offensive before the SAAF intervened.

The first six months of 1986 witnessed an arms build-up on both sides. Both camps expected that a make-or-break battle would come in the dry season. Castro pledged that his support for FAPLA would continue until apartheid had

Mig-25s flown by the 'internationalists'

been dismantled. What was required was better air defence for FAPLA air and ground forces. For six months a sea and air bridge poured in Soviet arms, including new SA-6, SA-8 and SA-13 systems. Pretoria could not compete with the latest Russian radar systems which were sited at Lubango, Menongue, Luena and Cuito Cuanvale. The Russians were trying to dominate all Southern Angolan airspace. South African intelligence claimed that there were twenty-seven Mig-25s, twenty-three Mig-23s, seventy Mig-21s and ten Sukhoi 22s in Angola. This tally was probably exaggerated. A range of combat and transport helicopters was also imported. Angolan pilots were flying the helicopters and the MiG-21s although the more advanced aircraft were still being flown by the 'internationalists', foreign communists.[11] Large numbers of T-62, T-55 and PT-76 tanks were airlifted in, as well as BTR-60 armoured personnel carriers and BRDM-2 armoured cars.

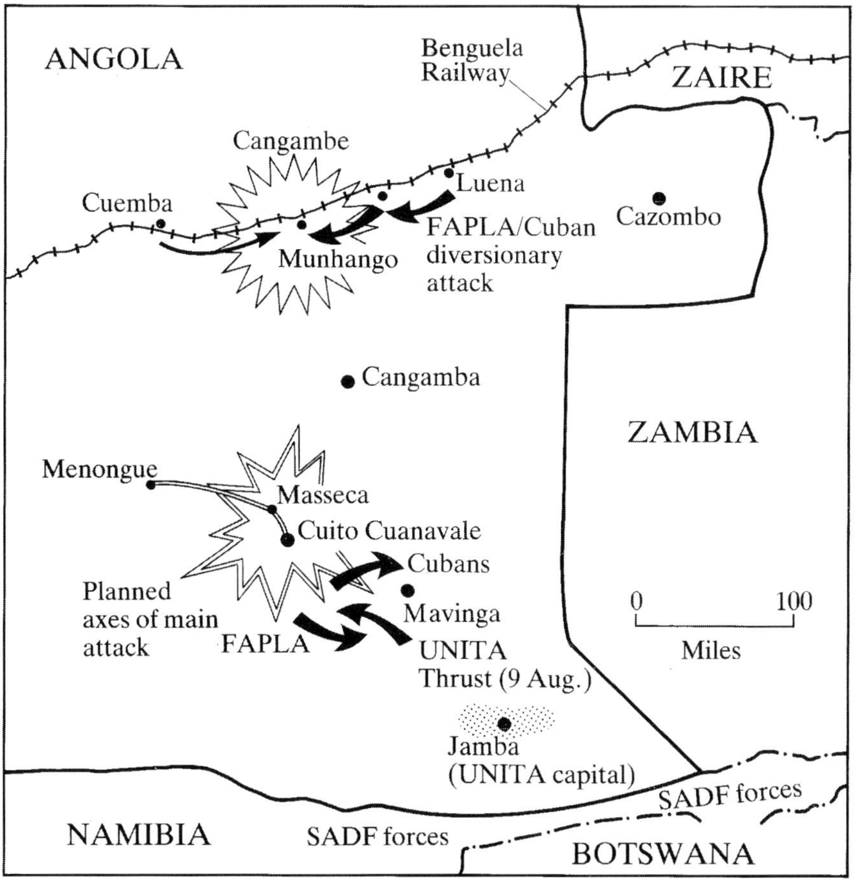


The fighting in southern Angola in August 1986

I attended a UNITA intelligence briefing in Jamba on 21 August 1986. Savimbi put the total balance of manpower as follows:

80,000 FAPLA
45,000 Cubans (35,000 combat troops)
7,000 SWAPO
4,000 Russian and East German personnel
2,500 Portuguese
1,200 ANC MK troops
Plus weary remnants of Katangese gendarmes.

This estimate was exaggerated. FAPLA would probably have numbered around 50,000 (including 24,000 conscripts and 10,000 members of the militia serving at any one time with the regular army). Not all the forces allied with MPLA would be in action, of course, against UNITA. SWAPO in 1986 would probably have committed about 3,000 to fighting alongside FAPLA against UNITA as a form of 'rent' for the MPLA's support of the war in Namibia. In short, perhaps 20,000 pro-Marxist troops were directly involved in the 1986 offensive in the south.

On the rival side, UNITA claimed to field 28,000 regulars and 30,000 part-time militia. For all its skills in irregular warfare, UNITA had little with which to counter a largescale conventional assault. It boasted an array of captured T-34s and T-55s and various armoured personnel carriers but they were not in general use. UNITA's main bases, highly organized with well-camouflaged schools, hospitals and clinics, bristled with a variety of anti-aircraft weapons such as the ZU-23-2 23mm guns. I had first worked with the *Mujahedin* in Afghanistan in 1984 and saw daily what Soviet air supremacy could do. I had witnessed constant attacks by subsonic and supersonic bombers as well as the cavalier use of Hind gunships, the most deadly machines to be at the wrong end of. The Afghan rebels cried out for a proper man-portable air defence system (MANPADS). Then, in 1986, the US Stinger changed the course of the war and portended the end of the Soviet empire. It was also introduced into southern Angola. Man-portable, weighing 15.7 kilos and slightly longer than 1.5 metres, the Stinger was an ideal guerrilla weapon. It could reach 1,500 metres in altitude and was equipped with a highly accurate infra-red guidance system that permitted it to be fired at a target from any angle. Here finally was a weapon that could counter the awesome Hinds, the Mi-24 flying tanks. The Stinger had an 8-kilometre range compared with the 3-kilometre range of UNITA's existing stock of (often unpredictable) SAM-7s. By July 1986 UNITA officers were claiming a strike rate of eight in ten with their new Stingers against one in ten with the SAM-7s. UNITA also claimed to have US TOW anti-tank missiles and some Redeye ground-to-air missiles. In addition, the SADF had donated numerous small arms, mortars and logistical supplies, especially fuel. Some of it was from Armscor but a lot was equipment captured from SWAPO and FAPLA.

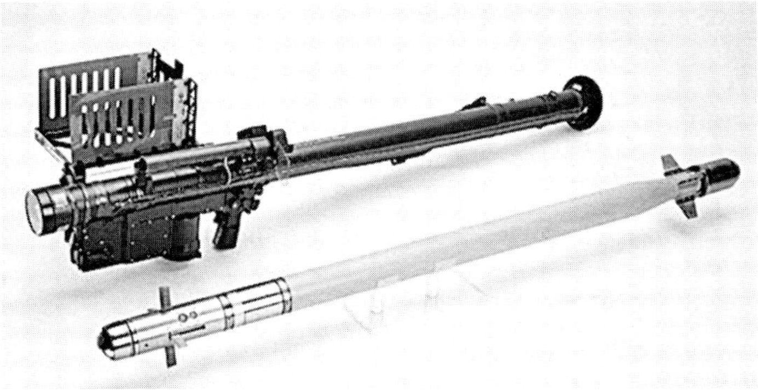

The Stinger: UNITA claimed a strike rate of eight in ten aircraft

Everybody expected big things from the much bigger arsenals. The Russians had wanted to launch a major offensive in March 1986 but the Cubans insisted that FAPLA had not fully recovered from the 1985 battles. In late May 1986 two FAPLA columns left Luena heading towards Munhango, UNITA's last salient across the Benguela line, and another towards Lumbala. UNITA intelligence decided that this was 'deception movement'. In June 1986 the main FAPLA thrust was accurately predicted as emanating from Cuito Cuanavale to the south of the feint. Brigadier Peregrino Chindondo, UNITA's chief of military intelligence, explained to me in Jamba that the FAPLA thrust was developing along two axes: a cautious advance from the south of Cuito Cuanavale to engage UNITA's anticipated main counter-attack, while a rapid Cuban push from the north-west would fall on Mavinga. The Russians, according to Chindondo, had augmented their airpower in nearby Menongue, the main Soviet/Cuban air base in the region; twelve extra MiG-21/23s had been added to the eleven already stationed there. Four extra Sukhoi-22s complemented the existing four.[12]

On 9 August 4,000 UNITA regulars foiled the planned FAPLA/Cuban pincer by a pre-emptive assault on Cuito Cuanavale. On the next day UNITA cut, temporarily, the road to Menongue. On 11 August UNITA claimed to have destroyed Cuito's air base. Savimbi's troops withdrew from the town after damaging the surrounding military installations. FAPLA maintained that this battle for Cuito was against SADF forces, although Savimbi insisted, to my face, it was a UNITA success. Well he would do, wouldn't he? UNITA also claimed to have brought down twenty-two aircraft, including MiG-21s, Mig-23s, and a Mi-8 and Mi-25 choppers.

UNITA officials also claimed that their enemies had deployed chemical weapons. One officer gave me an eyewitness account. 'The leaves of some of the trees became totally dark, the sand became very, very dark as well …. The smoke was yellow and green.' Savimbi told me that he had personally directed the fighting at Cuito Cuanavale. And he added, 'They threw grenades which didn't explode in the normal way. They gave out smoke and our soldiers felt dizzy. They couldn't fight so they dropped their weapons. Some became blind.' In the absence of concrete scientific evidence, however, these reports had to be treated with scepticism. Observers of many concurrent wars, such as Afghanistan, noted how often guerrilla spokesmen harped on the same theme of the enemy's use of chemical weapons. They perhaps thought it was the kind of information that Western journalists wanted, or ought, to hear.

At a press conference in Jamba on 21 August 1986, Savimbi was ebullient about containing the recent offensive that experts had predicted would overwhelm his forces. There was an extra Patton-like swagger to the bearded warlord, who also carried a pearl-handled Colt revolver slung low over one hip. Savimbi did not openly admit that the American Stingers had turned the tide of battle for him but he hinted to the same effect very broadly. 'We have got all we asked President Reagan to give us and it has arrived in a very quick manner.' Artistic appreciation of that generosity was displayed in the massive mural of Savimbi and Reagan together, which dominated the central parade ground of his HQ. The UNITA president said that the recent offensive was as good as over. 'The Russians have only a month left … September. After September, it is the rainy season again. Their tanks willl be dead, useless.' He admitted that in the 1985 campaign three factors had threatened UNITA's survival: 'Air power, armour and Soviet advisers. But we are in a position of challenging their air power and armour.' Thank you, Stinger and TOW, was left unsaid.

Mural of Reagan-Savimbi bromance – picture taken in August 1986 in Jamba by the author.

So FAPLA had not won the 1986 fighting season. UNITA lived to fight another day and had even re-opened its northern campaign. The war had also threatened to spill over into Zambia again. The MPLA government was negotiating with Zaire and Zambia to re-open the Benguela railway. Paradoxically, Washington showed great interest in this project, while simultaneously arming UNITA which kept it closed. It was rumoured that as a prelude to a diplomatic dance to resuscitate the railway, Kaunda, Savimbi's old friend, would allow FAPLA to open up a new front in the north-east from Zambian territory. With characteristic rhetoric, Savimbi dismissed this threat. 'There is a difference in having soldiers for parade and having soldiers for fighting. Mine are seasoned soldiers for fighting, those in Zambia are for parade.' Savimbi was spot on: the Zambia army was a complete shambles; even putting on a good parade was beyond their skill set.

As soon as the rains brought the conventional war season to an end, the Soviets set about rebuilding FAPLA's offensive capabilities yet again. The 1987 campaign was partly planned by Soviet officers. As in Afghanistan, Russian officers found it hard to adapt their conventional, often hidebound, experience to the dictates of guerrilla warfare: the revolutionary arteries of the Red army had grown sclerotic. In both Angola and Mozambique the guerrilla victors in the independence wars had become ossified conventional forces. In Angola, the setpiece Warsaw Pact-style offensives compounded this tendency. In contrast it could be said that the SADF had shown not only how to contain communist tactics of insurgency, especially in Namibia, but also how to wage a potent counter-revolution. In one sense Pretoria's generals had become the true exponents of the Reagan doctrine, especially in the destabilized neighbouring states. Hence discomfited Soviet generals were forced to witness their Marxist counter-insurgency tactics being emasculated and their clients besieged by the new guerrilla 'liberators' backed by the SADF.

This argument could only be taken so far: so far as Pretoria's white supremacists could afford the high costs of their military counter-revolution. The money spent in Angola might have been better used for more effective containment, or reform, at home. It could have been argued that every gun, truck and military radio given to UNITA was one less weapon to repress the domestic black struggle against apartheid. The massive destabilization efforts ranging from Luanda to the Seychelles and farther afield, distracted a great deal of the apartheid government's intelligence, in both senses of the word. From this (narrow) perspective, Pretoria's forward military policy nicely dovetailed with the goals of the South African Communist Party. Counter-revolution could therefore have played into the hands of the revolutionaries.

The FAPLA campaign in 1987 was a case in point. That year's fighting raised the stakes for South Africa and, more dangerously, raised the spectre of the great powers imposing a settlement in Angola and Namibia that was inimical to Pretoria's interests. The South African government assumed that an escalation in Angola would cause East-West *collision*, not collusion. Once again, Pretoria was wrong.

The SADF's analysis of the MPLA's strategy was often simplistic and contradictory. On the one hand, the MPLA was portrayed as a willing tool or dupe of the Cubans, who were themselves puppets of the Kremlin. (Although, in 1988, Pretoria tried a different tack: the 'radical' Cubans were said to be preventing the 'moderate' Russians and MPLA from settling the conflict.) On the other hand, the MPLA was sometimes depicted as an independent actor. In this version, Pretoria's analysis liked to stress the so-called 'peace party' within the MPLA that wanted a settlement with UNITA (usually minus Savimbi) which was in contention with the hawks who wanted each year one more chance to win on the field of battle. Many warring factions in the much-purged and coup-ridden party did exist but a general consensus on hostility to UNITA was pervasive. Whatever was actually discussed in the central committee of the MPLA in 1987, the knock-out option triumphed once more.

In my much later discussions with senior Russian officers who worked in southern Africa in this period, it became obvious how much the South African and Western intelligence experts played up the Russian roles. Actually, the South African and Western intelligence analysts actually didn't know what the Soviets were doing, but they could never adnmit that. So it became Chinese whispers, ignorance feeding off ignorance. It was also all tinged with racism. It was assumed that Russian or Cuban generals had to make the decisions because black senior officers, whether in Zimbabwe, Mozambique or Angola, were usually incompetent.

In July 1987 the offensive of 1986 was repeated on a grander scale. Two thrusts, one from north at Lucusse and another from Cuito Cuanavale, moved on Mavinga. The battlegroups advanced very cautiously, sometimes at the speed of two to three miles a day, under extensive air cover and heavy armoured support. UNITA initially avoided direct contact; instead the guerrillas severely harassed the supply and communications lines of this ponderously mobile Siegfried Line. Preliminary encounters developed along the Lomba river north of Mavinga. By September perhaps as many as 15,000 FAPLA troops were engaged in a fierce conventional battle with approximately the same number of UNITA regulars.

Both sides banned battlefield media coverage by independent journalists and tried to dramatize their enemy's losses while minimizing their own. Estimates of FAPLA dead ranged from 1,000 to 4,000; UNITA's were less. Savimbi also claimed four Russians and twenty Cubans killed. At the end of September UNITA asserted it had destroyed fifty-two tanks, 111 vehicles, twenty-one armoured vehicles, three MiG fighters, eleven helicopters and a Sukhoi -22. Although this claim was no doubt exaggerated, Savimbi's new American arsenal had certainly exacted a heavy toll. Also, both the SADF's new G5 and G6 howitzers were reported in action. In the air, advanced Israeli electronic countermeasures were deployed in SAAF Mirages. Israeli Seeker drones were said to have been able to jam Angolan radar connected to AA missile batteries. Repeating the techniques by which the Israeli Air Force destroyed the advanced Soviet air defence system deployed in 1982 in Lebanon's Bekaa valley, a SAAF-converted Boeing airliner was used as an airborne electronic warfare centre to direct air strikes into Angola within range of FAPLA missile screens. Soviet mobile SAM-8 launchers and one SAM-13 launcher were wiped out. The SAAF did admit that one of their Mirages was shot down by a SAM-8 missile.

On the ground, SADF casualties were far more serious. The South Africans fought on two fronts. In what Pretoria denied was a move to distract the enemy flank during the UNITA/FAPLA battles, the SADF attacked a SWAPO complex near Cuvelai in south/central Angola. The SADF insisted that it was merely pre-empting the annual SWAPO rainy season offensive. In October twelve SADF and one South West African Territory Force soldier were killed. At the same time, on the eastern battlefront, another eleven SADF soldiers were killed. Such high white casualty figures could not be hidden. Defence Minister Malan admitted for the first time that the SADF was actually fighting alongside UNITA, although Savimbi conceded only that the SADF was running a field hospital near the Mavinga front. Malan added that direct Russian and Cuban intervention had forced South Africa either to accept 'the defeat of Dr Jonas Savimbi or halt Soviet aggression'. The very last thing Savimbi needed was the SADF trumpeting that it had saved him (again). After years of subtly trying to build up UNITA's credibility, it was strange of Pretoria to upstage Savimbi, especially at a time when his forces were performing creditably. One explanation could have been straightforward. Pretoria was anxious to emphasize the dramatic confrontations with professional white communist troops to justify and explain the high October casualties to a concerned white electorate. It would have been politically far more difficult to explain away all the deaths at the hands of black insurgents such as SWAPO in the Namibian war, which Pretoria had claimed was as good as won.

It was also rumoured that Pretoria was lying about white fatalities. The SADF strongly denied this. It was, after all, difficult to hide so many deaths in the relatively small white society, which still had tattered remnants of a free press. The number of whites seriously wounded was impossible to assess. Even more difficult to obtain were full details of the blacks killed and wounded in both the South African and South West African armies. Reports about 'rebellions' and a 'mutiny' in 101st and 102nd SWATF Battalions filtered out. Soldiers from these battalions, some manned by 'turned' SWAPO insurgents, fought alongside UNITA during the climactic battles around Cuito Cuanavale. A large number of these black Namibians refused to continue fighting in Angola. It was reported that they objected to wearing UNITA uniforms and acting as cannon fodder to reduce white SADF casualties.

For FAPLA the knock-out blow had degenerated into a slogging match. The socialist alliance had not totally mastered South African airpower, so crucial to a FAPLA victory in the south. Pretoria's enemies could lose and fight again; the

SADF could not risk one major reverse. The Russian could easily re-equip their allies but it was much more difficult for the SAAF to replenish its ageing inventory. It was alleged that Pretoria had secretly bought some Mirages from Argentina to replace its losses in Angola. Pretoria did admit to having lost three planes during the most recent FALPA offensive. But the real losses could have been higher. On the ground, white casualties were mounting and so was the cost of the electronic cat-and-mouse game in the sky. Previously, the rains had brought a respite from conventional war, when mud became the real enemy. Then getting to a battle was often more difficult than winning it. The SADF could half-relax and deal with the rainy-season infiltration of their weakest opponents, SWAPO. This time, there was to be no let-up.

### *A town too far?*

The proverbial fog of war still surrounds the details of the 1988 battles. The war in Angola, however, had definitively changed. FAPLA dug in around Cuito Cuanavale. The fighting there was described by Castro as the 'turning point of African history', while the Angolans dubbed the town as 'the Stalingrad of the South African army'. Both are exaggerations. The fighting around Cuito was undoubtedly bitter. It had some operational value because of its airstrip, its role as a major supply base and the control of the major bridge over the Lomba river. But it also, like Stalingrad, became more a symbol of the contest of wills. The SADF said they did not intend to capture it, rather contain its potential threat. As General Kat Liebenberg, chief of the South African army, put it: if Cuito had been captured, 'we would have been in the position of the dog that caught the bus'. It would have been too difficult to supply and defend, let alone the repercussions capture would have had on the secret diplomacy going on. Briefly, it did look as though the town would fall to the SADF so FAPLA and the Cubans pumped in reinforcements. In mid-January 1988 the FAPLA air force chief of staff, Alberto Neto, announced that the South African-led siege of the town had been lifted. He said that 6,000 South African troops had been trying to envelop Cuito and admitted that their artillery (presumably the G5 howitzers and the self-propelled G6s) had been effective. The 46-ton G6 could fire accurately up to a range of twenty-five miles – six miles farther than NATO's 155mm artillery. The mobility, 'to shoot and scoot', was vital in such difficult terrain, bad weather and risk of Soviet retaliatory air strikes.

The Russians had continuously upgraded their air defence network. Mobile radar systems (of seven different types) based in twenty-three sites formed a series of overlapping arcs that covered nearly the whole country. The offensive arm consisted of fighters, including the MiG-21s and MiG-23s, with defensive punch provided by six anti-aircraft systems and four calibres of anti-aircraft guns. As back-up, field units deployed three forms of shoulder-launched weapons. This network often worked, as the SAAF could regularly attest. In February, Pretoria admitted that another one of its Mirages had been shot down. Cuban pilots, once reluctant to engage (and sometimes under orders *not* to engage) the highly skilled South African pilots, now became eager to get stuck in. Faced with a massive air defence network, superior Russian aircraft and bolder aviators, an unaccustomed wariness was detectable among SAAF pilots. From 1986 Stingers had reportedly given a new technological edge to UNITA, though few observers had seen them in use. Low-flying attacks had been deterred. But Soviet electronic countermeasures at local level and the national air defence system eventually swung the air war back in Luanda's favour. Cuito Cuanavale was the operational centre of the most south-eastern arc of the radar defence. To regain air superiority, particularly over UNITA territory, the SADF had to smash a hole in the FAPLA cordon and eliminate that key component of their air defence system.

The Angolan air force also intervened more confidently its defence of the 'African Stalingrad'. The contested skies prompted the SADF to switch to artillery rather than aerial bombardment of the besieged town, sometimes from extreme range. There was some anxiety too that Russian Frog ground-to-ground missiles, with a range of forty miles, were about to be introduced to deal with the SADF's superior artillery. Pretoria's other alternative, a fullscale infantry offensive, was ruled out because of the risks of even higher casualties. Hundreds of white soldiers might have been killed.

In March 1988 an audacious SADF operation was reported, 400 miles inside Angola, far to the north of the main battleground. This looked like a disinformation feint. The SADF was too heavily engaged in fighting FAPLA in Cuito Cuanavale. At the beginning of April Pretoria admitted that it was using tanks in the battle. It was a response to a FAPLA claim that Angolan troops had captured an unspecified number of SADF tanks. Pretoria conceded that just one tank had been hit by a mine. Thirteen Olifant tanks had first engaged on 9 November 1987 when they knocked out two T-55s within minutes. In reality, the damage had been far greater for the SADF which began to withdraw from the FAPLA front. The South Africans had just endured their heaviest fighting since the battle of El Alamein, the last time they had fought alongside (British) tanks. The Cubans were jubilant: a 'disaster' had been inflicted on the racists. The SADF had not been defeated but it could no longer afford the costs of trying to win … or even contain the Eastern-bloc forces. The South African army had inflicted very heavy losses, thousands of Angolans and Cubans killed, but had lost forty soldiers themselves, mainly young white conscripts in the battles round Cuito. The SADF had also lost a handful of planes and tanks. Far more important, it had lost the game of technological leapfrog with the Russians, which it was bound to do if Moscow persisted in re-supplying the MPLA. For so long the SADF had strutted with arrogant impunity, deploying its superior forces whenever and wherever Pretoria had so chosen. At Cuito Cuanavale the SADF had been bogged down in the mud and trenches; 1988 was

Flanders very briefly revisited. More prophetically, it was like the German retreat after the Russian victory at Stalingrad. It was certainly a long way from Pretoria's blitzkrieg of 1975.

It was time to talk again. And it was General Malan who publicly suggested a possible opening to Moscow. The Afrikaner leaders must have reckoned: after the planned rush to depart from Afghanistan why not a Russian exit from Angola too? The arch-enemy of Russia's supposed total onslaught on Afrikanerdom, in effect, bestowed the first formal recognition of not only Moscow's power and influence but also its legitimate stake in the region. From Pretoria's perspective, Reagan was on the way out; even that old-time conservative crusader had let South Africa down. Imposition of new sanctions had already removed much of the US moral and economic leverage. Indeed, anti-Americanism was much more virulent in Afrikaner circles than any Russophobia.

The bitter conventional battles between 1985 and 1988 had altered the military balance in the region. Despite the relative decline of SADF power, the attrition on both sides dictated prudence. Over 2,700 Cubans lost their lives in the period 1975 to 1991. Could either side ever win militarily? And at what cost? These were questions the superpowers were not prepared to ask, let alone answer, in public. Their thinking converged, however, at the Reagan-Gorbachev summit in Moscow in June 1988; they agreed that the war would end soon. So it was that in London, Brazzaville, Cairo and New York, with superpower prodding, the Angolans, Cubans, and South Africans met face to face. SWAPO and UNITA were excluded.

The first meeting was in London. At the coffee station in the conference rooms in Brown's Hotel the three key generals, Jannie Geldenhuys, Rosales del Toro (Cuba) and the ex-footballer, Antonio dos Santos França 'Ndalu' (Angola), bonded early during the first breaks. An added bonus was the incredibly proficient and equally beautiful translator who sat on the arm of Fidel Castro's chair. The top South African diplomat admitted that 'it was much nicer to focus on her than on the grisly if kindly and courteous Fidel.'[13] While the generals bonded, the diplomats, whom the military inevitably called lounge lizards, sacrificed their livers for their countries. The head of South African National Intelligence Service, the youthful academic-looking Dr Niel Barnard, helped out at crucial moments in acting as the interpreter of what the notoriously irascible state president, P.W. Botha, might go along with. Another academic was the highly effective American facilitator, Dr Chester Crocker, the Assistant Secretary of State for African Affairs. Crocker managed to massage endless memos and egos, not least Castro's. Honour demanded that the Cuban leader, in spite of and because of, his military losses would be allowed to claim a military victory … as long as he agreed with the details of the settlement. It was this propaganda contribution to a grand strategic understanding that has misled historical assessment of the fight around Cuito

Cuanavale. Both historians with insider access to the SADF and those who fought there agreed that there were no attempts to take the town, let alone hold it, as it had little strategic value. As the American scholar Jeffrey Herbst put it at the time, the SADF could not 'afford a victory, much less a defeat' at Cuito. The final battle symbolized a standoff that made the main combatants realize that military victory was not possible at a price they were prepared to pay.

A little after the fighting one of the most political of South African generals, Constand Viljoen, expressed the opinion of the top brass: 'There is absolutely no doubt who won the military war. We never lost a major battle. Our victory in Angola had a direct bearing on the collapse of the Soviet Union.'

That was a longterm, and accurate, view. At the time, in 1988, the burst of diplomacy was supposed to stop the Angolan war escalating into superpower conflict. Namibia might take a little longer, it was thought, but most believed that the Angolan battles could be wound down a ratchet or two. Even the most stubborn Afrikaner could see the sense in negotiating a deal before Reagan left office. Yet in June 1988 even a formal ceasefire seemed elusive as a force of Cuban troops 3,000-5,000 strong (Pretoria said 10,000) erected a 300-mile-wide front right along the edge of the south-western border of Namibia. The SADF called up extra citizen force reserves. On 27 June a combined FAPLA-Cuban air and ground attack near the Calueque hydro-electric scheme resulted in the deaths of twelve SADF troops (and much higher Angolan and Cuban casualties). Was Castro trying to gain advantage during the itinerant peace conferences, manoeuvring to stall the peace process until a Democrat might win the US presidential race, or spoiling to inflict a final bloody nose on the SADF before bringing his men home as heroes? Whatever his motives, a powerful force of confident Cuban troops stood along the Namibian border. This was April 1976 all over again. Thirteen years of fighting in Angola and what had Pretoria achieved?

The US-USSR convergence of interests, the costs to South Africa in lives and rand, the loss of SAAF air superiority and war-weariness on all sides prompted a ceasefire in August 1988. Thanks mainly to superpower midwifery, the main contestants – after ten rounds of talks – signed a final agreement in New York in December 1988. The South African foreign ministry had been given a new lease of life. The energetic director-general, Neil van Heerden, played a prominent role abroad and at home in his attempts to soothe the worries of the hawks. The New York accord meant the end of two of the three wars in the region (the fighting in Mozambique still raged). Yet the SADF's counter-insurgency war with SWAPO and the conventional war with FAPLA and the Cubans were over, or so the agreement stipulated. The accords did not cover the UNITA-MPLA conflict but it was implicitly assumed that the New York accord would lead to a Savimbi-Luanda deal. In exchange for dumping UNITA, Pretoria got its pound of flesh: the ejection of an estimated 6,000 MK guerrillas from Angola. That understanding was a crucial demand of the South African hawks. The hardliners were forced to drink the 'poison of peace'.

The December 1988 agreement was a turning point at least as crucial as the Lancaster House settlement over Rhodesia. Above all it established a timetable for Namibian independence. On 1 April 1989 the UN transition would begin. On 1 July the SADF was scheduled to reduce its troops in Namibia from 50,000 to 1,500. Elections were also scheduled for November 1989. The last 25,000 Cuban troops, monitored by the UN, were set to quit Angola by July 1991. Castro's *Afrikakorps* had weakened the SADF, but Castro had vowed to stay until apartheid was crushed. In that he had failed. The Afrikaner generals lived to fight another day – but not for long. The loss of Namibia proved a mortal blow to Pretoria's hawks.

Would the unexpected outbreak of regional peace also be a mortal blow to the most stubborn of local warlords, Jonas Savimbi? UNITA had lost its major support, although the CIA stepped up its supplies from Zaire. The Americans tried to get Savimbi to move north, a long way from his tribal base. Not only were Savimbi's supply lines in jeopardy, so was his image. In 1989 a series of reports about his ruthlessly dictatorial rule surfaced in the Western media. Even his once faithful biographer, Fred Bridgland, gave credence to reports of Savimbi burning some of his rivals as witches. Savimbi was clearly in trouble, yet somehow he managed to fight on in the region for more than a decade.

Since both the MPLA and UNITA were losing the military support of their immediate allies – the Cubans and the SADF – OAU members, especially in francophone states, put pressure on both sides to negotiate an end to the civil war that had gone on for fifteen years (on top of nearly fifteen years of anti-colonial struggle). Savimbi was encouraged to go into exile to his external main base in Morocco but, of course, he refused. In June 1989 President Mobutu brokered a ceasefire agreement at his Gbadolite palace, the so-called 'Versailles in the jungle'. It was the first time that the MPLA president, Eduardo dos Santos, had met Savimbi since 1975. The new ceasefire was broken almost immediately, but a start with reconciliation had been made.

The Angolan peace agreement had helped to derail the war train in the region; in particular, the OAU had tried to broker a RENAMO-FRELIMO settlement. And yet the core issue of apartheid power still festered. This applied especially to Namibia as it struggled to grasp its independence.

*Chapter 10*

# Namibia: From Afrikaner Colony to Independence (1976-89)

Namibia was not formally an Afrikaner colony, of course. Rather, it was a territory illegally occupied by South Africa. Pretoria not only kept a large army there, in contravention of the original mandate, but the SADF also used the vassal state as a forward base to send its legions into Angola, Zambia and Botswana. If Namibia fitted a little awkwardly into the mould of 'colonial' war, it also differed from the destabilization regime imposed on the front-line states. And yet it was a fulcrum for that destabilization and a crucial part of the defensive *glacis*. Indeed, as far as many Afrikaner conservatives in both Namibia and South Africa were concerned, SADF power in the territory was *the* key to survival of the entire white laager. It had long been a cliché of southern African politics to assume that when the real thumbscrews were applied – to stave off heavy-duty sanctions or even a great power naval blockade – Pretoria would have to free either Namibia or Nelson Mandela. Major events in 1988-89 – the war in Angola, international diplomacy and concerns for the health of both Namibia and Mandela – forced Pretoria to make existential concessions on both.

*The bush war – early days*

After the 1976 retreat, Pretoria desperately tried to consolidate its position on the Angolan/Namibian border. Economically, South Africa struggled to keep the Cunene river hyrdoelectric project alive. And, on the military front, Pretoria attempted to sanitize the border. Politically, the Namibian anti-SWAPO front had to be built up.

The northern section of Namibia was fortified during 1976. White Namibian reservists in the citizen force and commando units were activated. Small towns such as Ondangwa and Ruacana were transformed into sprawling stockaded garrisons. A string of new military bases was established and airfields were constructed for the expanding fleet of helicopters and fighter jets sent from South Africa. Thousands of Ovambo villagers were moved as a kilometre-wide, freefire zone was instituted along the defoliated 'cutline', the Angolan/Namibian border.

Despite its messy internecine fighting SWAPO did its best to exploit its alliance with the Cuban and MPLA forces. It built up its People's Liberation Army of Namibia (PLAN). During 1976 the number of guerrilla attacks and skirmishes was more than three times the total for the previous ten years.[1] PLAN insurgents began to probe the white farming areas south of the Ovambo homeland. On 30 June 1976 defence headquarters in Pretoria claimed that twenty-six guerrillas had been killed in the previous twenty days. At the same time, South Africa proclaimed martial law in the 'operational area' of Ovamboland. Meanwhile, Lusaka complained to the UN that SADF forces in Caprivi were repeatedly violating Zambian territory in the operations against PLAN.

Anti-apartheid groups in exile and the UN estimated that Pretoria had placed between 45,000 and 50,000 SADF personnel in Namibia. Besides the police and army stood two squadrons of Impala II and Mirage jets, plus helicopter squadrons. This was the heavy metal backing the army and police counter-insurgency. Behind this SADF shield, Pretoria tried to sharpen its blunt political sword, the internal option. That had two edges: firstly, Namibianization of the indigenous forces. Ethnic units had already been established: the 'Bushman Battalion' (1974) and units from the Ovambo, Kavango, and East Caprivi peoples (1975). White reserve units were beefed up. From 1977 onwards multi-ethnic units were formed. The goal was to establish a Namibian army loyal to Pretoria. Secondly, credible politicians had to front the internal show. That was more important than the first cutting edge. During 1975 a gaggle of politicians had been meeting at the old

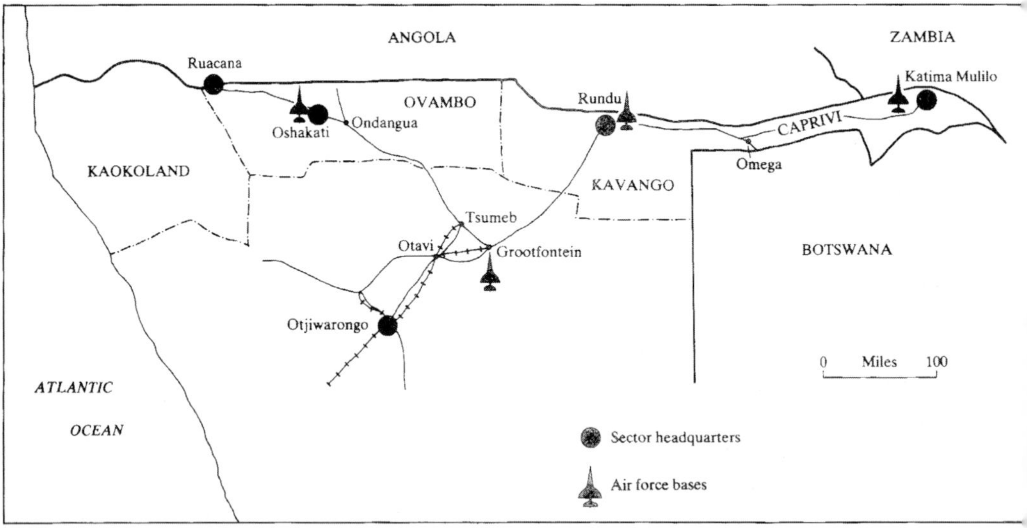


The SWA/Namibia operational area

German Gymnasium (Turnhalle) in the capital, Windhoek. From the Turnhalle conference evolved the skeleton of the internal political 'settlement'. It was decided that South West Africa – Namibia was not a popular name with many of the Turnhalle delegates – should become an independent, unitary state but the old apartheid system of the three-tier government would remain. Some of the more obvious and obnoxious aspects of discrimination, such as bans on mixed marriages and petty apartheid in restaurants, would have to go, and soon. Shibboleths, such as separate schools, would not. This the three-tier government would ensure. The tiers – local government, black homelands and white areas, and, on top, an administrative tier comprising a national assembly and ministerial council – would depend on consensus in this council. The council would represent all eleven ethnic groups but each group, and, most crucially the whites, would have a veto. And behind the clumsy complex, bureaucratic facade, Pretoria and the SADF ruled.

In the real world outside, two UN resolutions, 385 and 435, provided the parameters for an international settlement. Resolution 385 was adopted with Western support on 30 January 1976. This insisted that South Africa should withdraw its administration and that UN-supervised elections should lead to Namibian independence. Further details enshrined in Resolution 435, about the timing, the size and the deployment of UN monitoring forces, and the electoral and constitutional process, became the grist for a decade of haggling. The UN faced one massive obstacle: until Pretoria had little other economic or military alternatives, it would stall, with every trick in the diplomatic book, on a UN-style electoral transfer to independence because SWAPO would almost certainly win that election. Hence followed ten years of chicanery, of Namibianization as futile as American's Vietnamization, because Pretoria adamantly rejected what it called the 'red flag in Windhoek'.

Washington did not want any more red flags flying either. During Henry Kissinger's whirlwind safaris to Africa in 1976, he embroiled Pretoria in his plans to set up pro-Western black moderates in Salisbury and Windhoek before it was too late. The internal settlements in both states were carefully manipulated by Pretoria once Kissinger left office. By March 1977 the dominant figure in the Turnhalle conference as not a pliant black, but a tough white, Dirk Mudge, who was the former deputy leader of the National Party in Namibia, hardly a bleeding-heart liberal. He bore a passing resemblance to Ian Smith – was a second UDI hovering in the background? In the same month, the five Western members, at the time, of the UN Security Council – Britain, Canada, France, West Germany and the US – formed an ambassadorial 'contact group'. These important trading partners of South Africa, despite their economic clout, were to be strung along for years. As long as Pretoria was seen to be talking to the contact group about the UN route, serious sanctions could be put on the back burner. That suited both sides perfectly.

The Turnhalle in Windhoek

Meanwhile, South Africa dug in. In August 1977 military activity in the whole of the vast territory was centralized in Windhoek. Previously operations had been decentralized, first to the SAP, then to the regional control of the SADF in the large military base at Grootfontein. This unification of command and control was a sensible efficiency move but it also prefigured the establishment of the South West African Territory Force (SWATF) and the enhancement of the Windhoek politicians' self-image as leaders with their own army, just like Sam Nujoma and his PLAN. Later (theoretical) control of the newly (re-)established SWAPOL – the South West African Police – was also devolved to Windhoek as were various administrative functions previously transferred to Pretoria. In fact, the (South African) general officer commanding the SWATF, when it was formally inaugurated in 1980, doubled as the commander of all SADF forces in Namibia. Pretoria's generals still ran the show, although Namibianization of the army did mean that more black and white locals became potential cannon fodder on the Angolan front line.

A prime political component of the entrenchment of South African power was the appointment of Judge Marthinus Steyn as adminstrator-general on 1 September 1978. While the Turnhalle politicians continued to squabble, Steyn repealed some apartheid social legislation, such as the hated pass laws. He maintained much of the anti-terrorism legislation, however. Namibian nationalists were not appeased. Middle-of-the-road political parties such as the Namibia National Front and the influential black Lutheran Church leadership edged further away from the Tunrnhalle politicians grouped in the Democratic Turnhalle Alliance (DTA) and sidled towards SWAPO's position. During the second half of 1977 larger combat units of PLAN fighters infiltrated Ovamboland. The SADF admitted that the security forces were involved in an average of 100 clashes a month. PLAN's strength then stood at an estimated 2,000 guerrillas in Angola, 1,400 in Zambia and 300 operational inside Namibia.[2]

For all the patent weaknesses of the internal option, it did confirm some self-awareness on behalf of the hawks in Pretoria. They had made a startling U-turn. Integration with South Africa, permanent direct rule and Bantustan balkanization had all been tacitly dropped. It is hard to imagine now but those were once the dominant Afrikaner leitmotifs. The skeleton of Namibian independence had taken on real flesh, even in the corridors of power in Pretoria. True, the ever-changing blueprint still implied indirect South African rule of a putative independent, confederal, white-dominated Namibia and, yes, *de facto* SADF control was intended. Nevertheless, the idea of some kind of independence greater than, say, the Transkei – and that automatically meant excluding SWAPO in power – began to percolate through the Afrikaner establishment.

Throughout 1978 Pretoria bargained with the contact group about a transition deal. The issue of Walvis Bay compounded the complexities. SWAPO insisted that the area, the only deepwater port on the 1,000-mile coastline, was an integral part of Namibia. It had never been part of the German colony. It had been controlled by the British and later annexed to the old Cape colony in 1884 and hence, with some justification (even after Namibian independence) was claimed as South African territory. It had important strategic roles, not just maritime, and it later became a tourism centre because its unique waters attracted wild life such as flamingos, whales and dolphins. Like Gibraltar, Hong Kong and the Falklands, it was a small colonial legacy that was destined to divert much diplomatic energy.

Clemens Kapuuo, a Herero chief who was a founder of the DTA and a prominent non-SWAPO contender for leadership of the country, was gunned down

Both Pretoria and SWAPO tended to talk and fight at the same time: the more summitry, the more bloodshed. PLAN was very active in 1978: hit-and-run attacks were stepped up in Ovamboland. In one incident, 119 mission school students were abducted across the Angolan border. Such abductees (and volunteers) were usually offered the same bait – university scholarships abroad that often ended up as military conscription 'for the duration'. In February 1978 the Ovambo minister of health was assassinated. A month later Clemens Kapuuo, a Herero chief who was a founder of the DTA and a prominent non-SWAPO contender for leadership of the country, was gunned down. Administrator-General Steyn was then given sweeping powers of arrest and detention.

In May 1978 the SADF launched the first major planned incursion into Angola to destroy SWAPO bases: Operation REINDEER. The cabinet in Pretoria intensely debated the potential risks.[3] The doves warned of more sanctions, while the generals persuaded a vacillating Vorster. REINDEER consisted of the three sub-operations: an airborne force, roughly a battalion, struck a PLAN base codenamed ‘Moscow’, near Cassinga, some 160 miles inside Angola; a mechanized force attacked the ‘Vietnam’ camp, some eighteen miles north of the border, near Chetequera; and a heli-borne force swept through a series of small bases east of Chetequera.

The military had invested considerable political capital in the success of Operation REINDEER. The head of the army, Constand Viljoen, flew into the thick of the fighting, in the tradition of Boer war chieftains. The SADF’s toughest commander, Colonel Jan Breytenbach, known to his men as the ‘Brown Man’ because of his deep tan, led the Cassinga attack. PLAN fought back hard. The Cassinga fighting on 4 May involved female guerrillas in combat. It also involved a dogged fight-back by a male insurgent who had stationed himself under a bus. This action was described by a South African journalist, Willem Steenkamp, who also happened to be a citizen force officer. He explained how SADF elite paratroopers had trouble dislodging the PLAN fighter:

> After offering a spirited resistance he solved the problem himself by running out of ammunition, after which Swart [a SADF paratrooper] says ‘he threw his rifle out and said “You can’t shoot me, I’m a prisoner!”’ Legal niceties tend to blur in a fighting situation, however, and the exasperated paratrooper shot him dead in the same instant.[4]

Windhoek, the capital, was not usually directly affected by the war. Note the charming narrow sloping roofs – designed originally for heavy snowfalls (Author)

The belated intervention of FAPLA and Cuban forces almost overturned the operation. According to a semi-official South African account:

> Had the opposing armour been handled less ineptly, the operation could well have turned into a costly and embarrassing disaster. As it was, enemy tanks were actually on the landing zones as the last of the force was lifted out by Pumas.[5]

The almost unchallenged South African airpower was crucial. Canberra and Buccaneer aircraft had bombed the main bases before the infantry and armour went in, and helicopters were on standby for evacuation. Considerable amounts of equipment were captured as well as valuable intelligence documents. Pretoria claimed that 1,000 PLAN insurgents were killed and 200 captured. SWAPO counter-claimed that most of the dead were non-combatant refugees. In SWAPO and some UN chronicles, Cassinga was rated as a massacre, the moral equivalent of Vietnam's My Lai.

Certainly, Operation REINDEER was a severe military setback for PLAN. Previously SWAPO had thought that its bases deep inside Angola were safe from SADF depredations because of the political and military cover provided by their hosts. From now on, PLAN – literally – went underground. The classic Soviet-style bases with parade grounds, formal buildings and elaborate trench systems, all too visible from the air, were transformed into Vietnam-style heavily camouflaged base areas.

The SADF changed its operational style too. Invaluable lessons had been learnt. The line separating disaster from victory had been thin, even though only six South Africans had been killed in REINDEER. It was, for example, the *first* real

Sam Nujoma cradles a survivor at Cassinga: SWAPO propaganda poster

parachute attack (consisting of almost all reservists) carried out by the SADF and 'probably the largest of its kind in Africa since the Second World War' in the opinion of war correspondent Willem Steenkamp. Whether it was bigger than the Suez paradrop in 1956 is arguable. It was the *last* large SADF paradrop. Dropping troops into the thick of battle from lumbering transport aircraft needed re-appraisal as the Angolan-based forces developed missile screens.

REINDEER was also significant because it marked the SADF's entry into large-scale semi-conventional warfare. It was a precedent for the expansion of the war into Angola with sophisticated conventional incursions. New weapons were tested, notably in the field of artillery and armoured personnel carriers. Penetrations grew deeper and contacts with Angolan and Cuban forces became commonplace. REINDEER confirmed the shift from a small counter-insurgency war in the 1970s to the big conventional battles, backed by superpower arsenals, of the 1980s. REINDEER also had important political ramifications in Pretoria. The 'wets', to use the later 1980s Thatcherite term, had lost. Despite the preachifying by the foreign ministry about sanctions devils, no hellfire had descended. The hardliners thus began to win nearly all the strategic battles inside the 'deep state' – to use a term from the twenty-first century – that was entrenched in Pretoria. The defence minister, P.W. Botha, was winning his political battles too; he needed a fillip after the failures in Angola in 1976.

SWAPO regrouped. An attack was planned on the Caprivi's capital, Katima Mulilo. This strategic crossroads bordered on Angola and Zambia in the north and Botswana in the south, while Kasangula, at its extreme eastern tip, is the point where Zambia, Botswana and Zimbabwe intersect. This is perhaps the shortest border in the world – Botswana and Zambia touch for just 45 metres. Katima was, therefore, a handy international flashpoint to retaliate for Cassinga. At precisely 11.15am on 23 August 1978 a 122mm Redeye rocket landed on Katima's military base. More than twenty others followed in quick succession. Then the Zambian army joined in PLAN's rocket attack with a few 82mm mortar shells. One of PLAN's rockets smashed into an SADF barracks. Ten South African soldiers were killed and ten were wounded, more than had died in Operation REINDEER.

REINDEER had been a bombshell that landed smack in the middle of the contact group's credibility. The Western diplomats regrouped too. On 30 August Secretary-General Kurt Waldheim presented the official peace plan. It called for a UN force of 7,500 troops, with civilian back-up, to ensure elections which were to be held within one year. The UN would monitor a sequence of events: the end of hostilities, repeal of apartheid laws, release of detainees and return of refugees, then free and fair elections, adoption of a new constitution and, finally independence. This was later formalized as UN Security Council Resolution 435.

Then came the big shake-out in the South African government. On 20 September 1978 John Vorster announced the cabinet's decision to go it alone in Namibia;

an internal election would be held before the end of 1978. The apartheid warrior also announced his retirement. But who would take over from Vorster? The premiership was decided by a vote of National Party MPs. There were three main contenders. Foreign Minister Pik Botha was popular among the white electorate but his strength in the party caucus was small compared with his main rivals, P.W. Botha and 'Connie' Mulder. In the final round of voting Pik Botha gave his support to his namesake. I was standing outside the parliament building in Cape Town on 28 September while the caucus was making its final decision. Despite looking like a slightly seedy, second-hand car salesman, with his slicked-back hair and pencil moustache, the large crowd outside kept chanting 'Pik, Pik' – even after P.W. Botha's victory had been announced. Pik had always been a dove over Namibia, now the Great Crocodile – and to mix animal metaphors, the arch hawk – was in charge.

The internal settlement plan, a slap in the face for both the UN and the contact group, caused a serious problem for the Western powers: the African states now bayed for a sanctions showdown. Pik Botha signalled the cabinet's new hard line in mid-October when the foreign ministers of the contact group travelled to Pretoria for urgent talks. With the SADF chief of staff next to him, the South African foreign minister said: 'If it comes to a choice between the friendship of the world and internal stability [especially in Namibia] then we shall have to choose internal stability.' The internal option was now rammed into top gear.

In the December 1978 poll the DTA, led by Mudge, won 80 per cent of the poll in a 75 per cent turnout. The DTA took forty-one of the fifty seats. Critics alleged that the result was rigged as part of Pretoria's master plan, which included a Rhodesian replay the following year. SWAPO in Namibia and the Patriotic Front in Rhodesia/Zimbabwe boycotted both respective elections. In both cases lavish election rallies, with free food, drink and T-shirts (and lots of helicopter travel), were funded by South Africa. In both cases the voting turnout was exaggerated. The Pretoria-flavoured internal parties both won landslides, although neither result was recognized by *any* government except the one that had manipulated both exercises. And yet both elections, and in particular the one-man-one-vote Rhodesian poll of 1979, approximated to the Western models more closely than 90 per cent of other, internationally recognized,

Pik Botha in his prime, but he still looked like a second-hand car salesman

elections in Africa. Whether either elections were 'free and fair' in the context of civil war was irrelevant, however. Without SWAPO (and the PF) neither made diplomatic sense.

The hard men in Pretoria probably understood that. South Africa had already gone a long way towards accepting the UN position; so had SWAPO by giving up its claim to power without first competing in an election and by making concessions over the status of Walvis Bay. Pretoria wanted to 'buy time' for the DTA to build up credibility as a rival to SWAPO when the day of reckoning, UN elections, finally came. But was Pretoria buying or losing time? South Africa's international position was weakening. The sanctions bandwagon was picking up speed. And South Africa's oil supplies were as shaky as its main supplier, the Shah's Iran. Nevertheless, to Pretoria's blinkered eyes, the December poll in Namibia was a triumph. Now it was time to do the Namibian waltz again with the Western Five, while trying to bring off another internal coup, in Rhodesia.

Anti-apartheid critics continued to accuse South Africa of total insincerity in its negotiations. In this perspective, Pretoria's hawks-versus-doves split on such issues as destabilization in general, and Namibia in particular, was merely a good-cop-versus-bad-cop technique to mislead foreign opponents, especially the ever-hopeful right-wingers who were always looking for 'change' in South Africa's hard line. But such divisions in Pretoria did exist, as revelations about support for RENAMO were later to confirm. Most Afrikaner leaders did intensely dislike being treated as pariahs, whether it was being denied visits by international rugby teams or proper diplomatic status. Pretoria desperately wanted to be accepted by the Western world, to which it believed it naturally belonged. So a genuine rationale always existed for a Namibian settlement. Nor did Pretoria want real sanctions, though in the late 1970s they were not considered a major threat, more an irritation. And yet the South African government did not want to leave Namibia, for political and military reasons as well as the fact that the territory's large deposits of uranium, diamonds, phosphates and other minerals made a substantial contribution to the South African economy. Time was needed to denude these mineral deposits. In short, a balance of genuine desire for rapprochement was always mixed with cynical filibuster. South African diplomats, often the clumsiest representatives of an unsaleable regime,

Dirk Mudge: The DTA leader

became Machiavellian princes over Namibia. It was partly a matter of longevity and local knowledge. Foreign diplomats changed jobs and foreign ministers came and went, according to whim and electoral fortune, but Pik Botha – the longest-serving foreign minster in the 'Western' world – was always there. So was a group of his able lieutenants.

Given a background of genuine desire for an improved entente with the contact group, the hawks-and-doves typology had to be understood as a crude generalization. A kaleidoscope of sometimes multi-coloured views rattled around the Afrikaner leadership. They only *looked* as if their ideas and personalities were frozen in stone. And there were contradictions. For example, a hawk on defence, such as P.W. Botha, was also considered to be a relative liberal [sic] on the question of restoring the franchise to the so-called coloured community. Even the doves, traditionally associated with the foreign affairs department, would give an instinctive hardline response when security bottom lines were threatened.

The doves were put on the back foot in February 1979 when Prime Minister P.W Botha lambasted the Western contact group and Kurt Waldheim (long before the secretary general was publicly shamed because of his Nazi past). The Great Crocodile lashed out because they had agreed, behind South Africa's back, he said, to allow SWAPO to have its own bases *inside* Namibia during the projected ceasefire period. He also said that that the UN Transition Assistance Group (UNTAG) would not now, as previously agreed, be required to monitor the restriction of PLAN troops in bases outside Namibia. Negotiations were put on ice for five months. In March 1979 Pik Botha returned to his boss's pet project in a major speech: a constellation of southern African states. Pretoria would solve its regional disputes without meddling and ignorant foreigners. This 'sub-continental solidarity' would include seven to ten African states south of the Cunene/Zambezi line. It would be a military pact as much as a political and economic alliance. Pretoria's new Maginot Line would envelop both Namibia and Rhodesia, but ruled by moderates. As if to enforce this defence perimeter, the SADF launched a series of raids into Angola and Zambia in the same month. And SADF troop levels in Namibia were boosted from 20,000 to 30,000, according to London's respected International Institute for Strategic Studies.

Once more the internal option was cranked up. The DTA-dominated National Assembly in Windhoek was given extra powers over fiscal affairs. As a sop to the restive right-wing, internal political representatives of SWAPO endured another crackdown. Over half the country and 80 per cent of the population were placed under some form of martial law. Nevertheless, a rash of right-wing extremism broke out: neo-fascist white supremacists compiled a death list that targeted black church leaders. The *bittereinders* also complained about the removal of some protection for white local affairs. Mudge, however, made it clear that retention of apartheid laws and the constant intervention of Pretoria undermined his credibility.

The DTA boss was beginning to prove too independent for Pretoria's liking. The breeze of UDI flitted across the desert sands. Administrator-General Steyn appeared to go along with Mudge on the necessity of curbing exclusive white control over the best amenities. The puppets were roaring. And worse, the military were becoming averse to Steyn. In August Professor Gerrit Viljoen, a 'super-Afrikaner' and head of the *Broederbond*, replaced Steyn. Viljoen was the right hard man to sort out the Afrikaner recalcitrants in the territory. P.W. Botha – in a typical authoritarian flourish – did not consult his own department of foreign affairs on such a sensitive appointment.[6]

In August 1979 South Africa and the Western Five resumed talks. President Neto of Angola had proposed a demilitarized zone extending for thirty miles on both sides of the border as part of the transition. This idea was taken up during the important Commonwealth conference in Lusaka held in the same month (and focusing on Rhodesia). SWAPO was pressurized into dropping its demands for bases inside Namibia, while the front-line states, not the UN, would offer to monitor SWAPO's bases in Angola and Zambia. Pretoria gave a cautious nod. The war in Namibia ground on, however. PLAN now had an estimated 8,000 troops, but was losing ninety a month in battle (according to Pretoria). The insurgents knocked out the Ruacana power station and large parts of Namibia were blacked out.

From the August Commonwealth conference through to the Lancaster House talkathon to the February 1980 elections, attention in southern Africa was focused on Rhodesia. Above all, the British government was determined to throw off the UDI albatross; the USA was absorbed in presidential elections. The sanctions threat wound down. Pretoria, buoyed up by the high gold price, egged on the DTA, and further Namibianized the war effort, while confidently expecting that Bishop Muzorewa would score another victory in the second round of the Rhodesian elections.

*Mugabe won. Pretoria was shattered. So how on earth could Mudge, a white former National Party leader, do what Muzorewa, once an internationally accepted black nationalist, could not?*

The ghost of the hapless bishop was destined to haunt Windhoek for years. So Pretoria resumed negotiations with the West, particularly on the details of the DMZ. In a 60-mile wide, 700-mile long DMZ, 7,500 UN soldiers would not be sufficient, argued Pretoria, which wanted to retain forty SADF bases in the Namibian section of the DMZ.

SWAPO was cock-a-hoop over Mugabe's ascendancy and geared up its campaign. In May 1980 a PLAN mortar attack destroyed several military planes at Ondangwa. White civilian and military casualties mounted, while armed convoys were needed on the northern roads. The operational zone edged closer to the capital. Anti-apartheid groups accused the SADF of terrorist tactics in retaliation: 'Evidence of indiscriminate brutality, including barbarous torture and mutilation, was coming to light.'[7]

Operation SMOKESHELL, June 1980 (SADF)

There was no mistaking the ferocity of Operation SCEPTIC (also called Operation SMOKESHELL) launched on 9 June 1980. SWAPO leaders had declared 1980 the 'year of action'. They got it with SCEPTIC, the South Africans' biggest ground and air operation since 1945. The target was a well-entrenched, sprawling (65-square-kilometre) PLAN base in southern Angola, codenamed 'Smokeshell'. A South African officer described a section of the taskforce as it prepared to cross the border:

> Early on the morning of June 8 Battle Group 61 began to form up in order of march. It was an awesome sight to the young troops. Drawn up in lines were scores of huge Ratels, homely high-reaching Buffels, Eland 'Noddy cars' (as the mechanized force infantrymen had taken to calling the little vehicles) with their long 90mm guns, 140mm artillery pieces hooked on to massive tractors, Unimog ambulances, ungainly recovery vehicles festooned with cranes and cables, fuel bowsers grunting along like pregnant elephants; there had been few such concentrations of war machines on the border in anyone's experience.[8]

SCEPTIC was originally intended as a short, if big, punch raid. It grew, however, into a massive three-week operation. SWAPO had dug in well. PLAN deployed its light AA guns, especially 14.5mm single and 23mm twin guns, in a ground-defence role. One ZU-23-2 knocked out several Ratel infantry combat vehicles. After a brief artillery barrage, three South African mechanized groups swept in. The infantry normally remained in their Ratels, de-bussing only to deal with stubborn opposition. Close air support was provided by Impalas firing cannon and rockets. Helicopters were used as additional transport and for casualty evacuation. The SADF, according to the South African version, clashed with two semi-mechanized PLAN columns. Ground armoured vehicles and SAAF air strikes destroyed several BRDM-2 Scout cars and BTR-152 armoured personnel carriers. A FAPLA mechanized column also entered the fray. The Angolans brought down at least one chopper. Pretoria claimed to have blown up fifty tons of enemy equipment and captured approximately 250 tons, including SAM missiles. For the loss of seventeen men, the SADF also claimed 360 PLAN killed. Pretoria said it had wiped out PLAN's nerve centre. Whatever the precise truth, SCEPTIC had been a serious military setback for SWAPO.

It was time to pump up the DTA again. On 1 July 1980 a council of ministers, with Mudge in the chair was sworn in. Now Mudge & Co. had the authority to administer twenty government departments, including a local department of defence. The new department's first act was to promulgate a law establishing compulsory military service from 1981. On 1 August the South West African Territory Force was formally inaugurated. Mudge now had his own army. On 1 September control of the police passed to the National Assembly.

The monotonous rhythm of South African diplomacy in the territory jangled the nerves: bash SWAPO, boost Mudge and then talk to the UN. Pretoria, however, continued to make the (not unreasonable) point that so long as SWAPO activities were (partly) funded by the UN and SWAPO was recognized as the *sole* authentic representative of the Namibian people, how could the UN claim to be impartial monitors of an election? South Africa raised the stakes by insisting that in future talks the DTA should be represented and separately from the Pretoria delegation. This proposal made little headway. At home the DTA was failing too. In second-tier elections the diehard whites won more seats than the 'liberal' DTA. These polls were seen as a test of white opinion. If the multi-ethnic DTA had won, it would have shown that the majority of whites were ready for the principle of one man, one vote in a unitary state. They were not.

Pretoria also raised the stakes by hinting that it wanted UNITA involved in any international settlement. This gambit was possibly part of a rumoured 'separate deal' with Luanda. Mudge had called the Lancaster House agreement a 'fiasco' and Pretoria heartily agreed. So why not an 'international' fix that excluded the troublesome Commonwealth, UN *and* Western Five? A bargain with fellow Africans – the Angolans? Pretoria would dump UNITA if the MPLA dropped SWAPO. UNITA would be afforded some regional autonomy in central and southern Angola, the Cubans would be progressively removed and Pretoria would help with rebuilding the economy, the Benguela railway in particular.

Ratel

Casspir Mk 3 (SANDF)

And somehow the Angolans were led to believe that the facilitators of the Lancaster House agreement, the Thatcher government, were prepared to back this bilateral deal.

From one perspective, resolving Namibia was simple – get rid of South African control and everything would 'come right'. Namibia had always been much more complicated than that – even for those fighting for 'liberation'. With at least forty competing Namibian political parties and eight different armies involved in the conflict, plus a host of international bodies and concerned, but usually self-serving, foreign governments, it was bound to be. Behind the web of international intrigue what was the real nature of the conflict in the heartland of the struggle, northern Namibia?

## *The nature of the war*

SWAPO's war varied according to the terrain and ethnic affiliation. The SADF throughout most of the 1980s had restabilized the Caprivi. Kaokoland, because of its barren deserts and minimal population, was used as an occasional infiltration route and for mining the main (gravel) roads. Kavango, partly because of its relative economic development and tribal factors, was less politicized by SWAPO than Ovamboland, PLAN's natural stamping ground.

The SADF always claimed that SWAPO had remained stuck in the initial 'terrorist' stage of insurgency, but large groups of trained guerrillas regularly infiltrated into the white farming area, often displaying great military skill, particularly in anti-tracking procedures. Tactics included regular ambushes of SADF patrols, frequent attacks on bantustan officials, sabotage of installations and railways, and occasional bombings in urban areas. Despite the difficulties of carrying mines long distances, PLAN specialized in mine warfare, including the techniques of tunnelling under or lifting sections of tarred roads. Anti-personnel mines were often laid alongside anti-vehicle mines to hamper mine-clearance. The SADF, with its panoply of sophisticated mineproofed vehicles, usually escaped heavy casualties. The civilians suffered, however. In 1980, for example, 220 Ovambos were killed and 256 injured by mines.[9]

SWAPO often avoided direct assaults on the SADF. Stand-off bombardments with mortars and rockets became another speciality. PLAN's arsenal comprised the usual Eastern bloc medley of AK-47s and RPG-7s. The SKS carbine was deployed because it could fire rifle grenades. Besides 60mm and 80mm mortars as well as 122mm rocket launchers, some insurgents, especially in PLAN's special forces, carried SAM-7 missile AA launchers. From the mid-1980s the Dragunov sniper rifle made an appearance.

In response the SADF counter-insurgency strategy was extensive and expensive. In the 1980s the cost of the war reached perhaps R4 million a day. On average the estimate of troop levels by the mid-1980s was 20,000 to 30,000 SADF personnel plus 22,000 SWATF when the Namibian forces were said by Pretoria to have taken over 50 per cent of the SADF's manpower deployment. With logistic back-up and police forces, especially during preparations for big operations in Angola, the tally of 'occupation' forces could have reached 100,000, a ratio of one man in uniform for every fourteen Namibians.[10] By 1988 Pretoria claimed over 11,000 PLAN killed for the cost of approximately 700 members of the security forces. Both sides claimed that their enemies cooked the figures. The SADF tended to discount the very high 'accident' figures in the operational areas as well as black SWATF casualties. The SADF estimate of 11,000 PLAN killed seemed high as SWAPO deployed a standing force of between 9,000 and 16,000. Either SWAPO was able to maintain morale and troop levels at a remarkable level or Pretoria had overestimated the body counts. In total the war cost at least 20,000 Namibian lives, directly or indirectly. And perhaps 10 per cent of the roughly 1.4 million population went into exile. Pretoria had erected a massive defence structure which many of the top brass were loath to jettison in order to build another Siegfried Line a thousand miles to the south along the Orange river.

The SADF created a mirror image of itself in the SWATF – with minor changes in insignia – except that in Namibia the army had far more blacks. A black officer

On horse patrol with the SA army, 1985 (author)

corps was trained at the military college in Okahandja. The militia-based area force was similar to the South African commando structure. The mobile conventional troops, composed of motorized infantry and a parachute battalion, comprised a reaction force similar to the SADF citizen force. And there was a standing formation which included six infantry battalions and special forces. The SWATF was supposed to be a unified, multi-ethnic army but white elitism and residual tribalism of the original ethnic battalions undermined, to some extent, efforts to totally integrate the Namibian army. The selective conscription also tended to reinforce ethnicity. In theory, after 1981 all males between 16 and 25 were liable for call-up (as well as men aged 17 to 54 for commando duties, although this was not extensively applied). In practice, conscription was not applied in Ovamboland. Many Namibians, however, were prepared to volunteer for military service because of the pay and privileges. Often the security forces provided the only form of paid employment in the Caprivi and parts of Kavango. Perhaps as much as 44 per cent of the total buying power in Kavango was generated by the resident SWATF 202nd Battalion. Some SWAPO supporters crossed the border to avoid conscription, while others were said to have joined the SWATF in order to infiltrate it and gain military experience for later use with PLAN. SADF instructors, however, claimed repeatedly that their security screening weeded out nearly all these fifth columnists.

Besides ethnic and ideological tensions, traditional inter-service rivalry also intruded, not least between the army and the police. Except for some specialist units, the police and army did not usually share bases. The role of the police became increasingly important partly because the UN proposals for demilitarization *excluded* police forces. Their size and capability were therefore boosted by Pretoria. Besides a conventional SWAP COIN unit, various other police units were active. A Task Force was set up to counter guerrillas outside the operational area, particularly insurgents who came via Botswana. Two units, the Home Guards (Special Police) and above all *Koevoet,* became notorious because of their numerous alleged atrocities against civilians. Some army officers were openly hostile towards units such as *Koevoet* because they felt their activities undermined the SADF's hearts-and-minds programmes. Senior officers such as Generals Constand Viljoen and Jannie Geldenhuys made their concerns known very clearly in Pretoria.

The problem was *Koevoet* was deemed a major COIN success. *Koevoet* was called 'crowbar' because 'the crowbar prises terrorists out of the bush like nails out of rotten wood'. In its ten years of existence it comprised on average of 250-300 white officers and NCOs and around 900 blacks. With support and admin staff, the unit stood at around 3,000. It was set up by Colonel Hans Dreyer, an SAP officer based in Natal but who served with British South Africa Police in Rhodesia. He worked with the BSAP's PATU (Police Anti-Terrorist Unit) as well as the army's Selous Scouts, although some heritage can be traced from the Portuguese *Flechas*. Dreyer brought in some ex-Rhodesians after Mugabe's victory and he recruited some Angolans from the FNLA. Most of the fighting troops were Ovambo, however, and the dominant language was Oshiwambo. Some of the Ovambo were volunteers but many were 'turned terrs' who had been captured and given an offer they could not refuse. *Koevoet* was organized into forty to fifty-man platoons, equipped largely with mine-resistant Casspir vehicles and Wolf Turbos for conducting patrols, a Duiker fuel truck and a Blesbok supply vehicle (both variants of a Casspir). They rotated one week in the bush for one week at camp. There were three *Koevoet* units based in Kaokoland, Kavango, and Ovamboland.

South African counter-insurgency took on many forms from terror to hearts and minds. At the strategic level, Pretoria's intelligence services did everything possible to divide the SWAPO leadership. Agents in Lusaka probably played a major role during the 1970s mutinies and faction-fighting, in the same way that the Rhodesian Central Intelligence Organization turned ZANLA against ZIPRA and their often frustrated Zambian hosts against both guerrilla armies in residence. SWAPO dissidents such as Andreas Shipanga and leaders of CANU (the Caprivi African National Union), which had merged with and then left SWAPO were wooed into the internal fold. Pretoria had hoped to split SWAPO by releasing Herman Toivo ja Toivo in 1984. The intelligence chiefs expected serious friction between him and Sam Nujoma, but were disappointed. Amnesties were offered to guerrillas. They were never very successful: in 1985, for example, four PLAN members did take up the offer. I was asked to sit in on their interrogation just after capture and they appeared genuinely willing to 'cross over to the dark side'. Captured guerrillas were sometimes turned and took part in a variety of pseudo ops for *Koevoet,* often in PLAN uniforms. The security police were frequently successful in buying their way into the pockets, if not necessarily the hearts, of a large number of Ovambo informers. Some of these agents became wealthy by local standards. The foolish ones became conspicuous spenders who purchased *Cuca* shops and new cars in Ovamboland and were then eliminated by PLAN, while the wise informers invested discreetly in real estate in Windhoek.

The counter-insurgency, especially *Koevoet's* pseudo operations, attracted a great deal of media attention and criticism. Both Namibian and South African churchmen regularly condemned their exploits and accused them of indiscriminately murdering civilians for bounty money (*kopgeld*, literally 'head money'). The *Koevoet* fighters were indeed paid bounties which may have partly explained their high tally: 3,225 insurgents killed or captured during their 1,615 contacts. The Bar Council in Windhoek complained that few cases of alleged *Koevoet* crimes reached the courts. When they did, sentences were often derisory.

The activities of 32nd (Buffalo) Battalion, a special infantry unit made up of former FNLA guerrillas, led by white Portuguese, South African and ex-Rhodesian officers, were condemned as much as *Koevoet*. Deserters from the battalion offered journalists lurid accounts of atrocities against Ovambo civilians, particularly in southern Angola. A South African military expert, however, commented: 'Among those who know the business, 32 Bn is widely regarded as the premier light infantry unit in the world today.'[11]Providing intelligence and reconnaissance for the major operations in Angola, as well as constant search-and-destroy missions against PLAN forward bases and camps, the Buffalo Battalion and *Koevoet* accounted for thousands of kills; whether they were *all* PLAN insurgents is a moot point.

The SADF, usually with great efficiency, also conducted the more traditional COIN operations. Its small-unit ground patrols and high-speed, cordon-and-search operations with helicopters, sometimes called 'Hawk Ops', were often models of military precision. The topography of Ovamboland, particularly its flatness, discouraged the use of standard measures such as observation points, although imaginative use was made of patrols on horseback and motorbikes. For both political and sound agricultural reasons, the concept of strategic hamlets was not applied as it was in Rhodesia and Portuguese Africa.

Like their colonial counterparts, the SADF emphasized civic action and psychological warfare or Psychological Action (PsyAc) as it was called. Besides obvious functions such as protection of convoys and administrative infrastructure, the SADF became a small-scale welfare state in the north. Sometimes idealist young national servicemen, especially graduates, went into the schools, hospitals and the local civil service (although SWAPO accused the SADF of attacks on mission hospitals and schools). The SADF's PsyAc mixture of genuine idealism and cynical manipulation largely backfired, however. Often local blacks resented job competition from paternalistic whites in uniform. The PsyAc showcase, the Omega Bushmen base in Caprivi, for example, provided employment for Bushmen, many of whom had suffered a great deal from rival ethnic groups in Angola (sometimes they had been hunted like wild animals). The Bushman culture, critics maintained, was being destroyed by the militarization and racism of their South African mentors. The bogus anti-SWAPO cultural and nationalist tribal movements, such as Etango in Ovamboland, largely comprised members of the security forces and their relatives. Often civic action, or 'social upliftment', as the SADF liked to call it, was simply a means of propping up crumbling Bantustan structures. The SADF largely took over the running of the health services in the north and made genuine improvements but the major reason for the collapse of the medical services (besides SWAPO attacks) was the inefficiency and the corruption of the ethnic administrations and their ten separate health services. Like all COIN, it all came down to the political strategy, or lack of it.

*Constructive relations (1981-84)*

Pretoria's political strategy for Namibia grew much tougher at the beginning of 1981 for two reasons. Firstly, Prime Minister P.W. Botha called an election for April 1981. Election time always meant banging on the military drum. Secondly, Ronald Reagan entered the White House. In Reagan's words, South Africa was 'a friendly country … a country that strategically is essential to the free world in its production of minerals that we must all have'. This was the sweetest music to Afrikanerdom. Dr Chester Crocker, the new assistant secretary of state for Africa, dealt a new set of cards – the linkage of Cuban troop withdrawal to Namibian independence – much to the chagrin of other members of the contact group. In early January all the Namibian poker-players, including for the first time the DTA, met face to face. Mudge demanded the removal of the UN's pro-SWAPO bias and an end to its funding of its activities. South Africa had manoeuvred its pipsqueak ally on to the international conference tables. In Pretoria's worldview, the DTA had been transformed into a legitimate and credible player.

In March senior SADF officers, including intelligence officials, visited the US for the first time in years. In the same month two other allied delegations pitched up separately in Washington: Savimbi, plus entourage, and the DTA. The 'polecat' was tacitly becoming a partner in Reagan's goal of rolling back Soviet influence in Africa. Major General Charles Lloyd, the SADF commander in Namibia, started to warn of the build-up of Soviet weaponry in Angola, especially an air defence including radar and missile systems. He said that South Africa had to prepare to defend itself against a conventional war with Cuban and Angolan regulars. It soon came.

On 24 August 1981 the SADF launched a massive attack 120 miles into southern Angola. Operation PROTEA involved a series of incursions by mechanized columns moving from bases at Ruacana and Ondangwa. The targets were the new radar installations, AA sites and PLAN strongholds. Serious encounters with FAPLA ensued. Two T-34/85 tanks were knocked out by Ratel-90s in one engagement. Two Russians were killed and one captured. Pretoria claimed that PLAN was directed by Russians though it was more likely they were attached as advisers to FAPLA. The SADF claimed over 1,000 FAPLA and PLAN killed. They captured many tons of modern equipment plus eight T-34 tanks. The SADF had lost one helicopter and ten men. In November, Operation DAISY, although smaller, penetrated farther than any incursion since the 1975-76 invasion. The Angolan air force clashed with South African Mirages and a MiG-21 was shot down.

Operations PROTEA and DAISY had inflicted serious reverses on the enemy and Pretoria decided it was time to parley again. By the end of 1981 the South African government said it was prepared to take the UN route again and even to accept a UN peacekeeping operation. Pretoria had to make some kind of diplomatic obeisance to Washington's notions of constructive engagement. After the military engagements came the political constructiveness. The US argued that only by working with Pretoria could the SADF be reined in and the Cubans would then leave. It was always the proverbial chicken and egg: so long as the SADF occupied southern Angola, Luanda was forced to turn to its Cuban protectors. Washington could never answer the question: who would protect Luanda if Castro's men left? At one stage the French – increasingly out of step with the contact group – suggested that their troops, with Portuguese help, could replace the Cubans.

Pretoria was making polite noises but no real concessions. Nevertheless, off centre-stage, the right-wing Conservative Party, a breakaway from the National Party, was accusing P.W. Botha of being a 'liberal', a terrible swear-word in conservative Afrikanerdom, and of selling out the whites in Namibia. To make matters worse, the DTA looked as if it were on its last legs. The alliance had suffered defections to the right and, more important, to the left, when its Ovambo president, Peter Kalangula, quit. The ruling National Party had to sell its internal option to the West, the Namibians and to the South African (white) electorate. Nobody wanted to buy the DTA, however. In January 1983 the DTA administration gave up the ghost. Mudge resigned as chairman of the council of ministers. Willie van Niekerk, a gynaecologist whose previous claim to fame had been a treatise on hermaphrodites, took over direct rule as the new administrator-general. He tried to resuscitate the internal option. After a number of still-births, he coaxed into life the Multi-Party Conference (MPC), a disparate group of eight fractious parties, including the Afrikaner nationalists and DTA remnants. The new gambit did not take off. The Thirion Commission report of September 1983 further lambasted the three-tier structure in Namibia for its corrupt and bungling management.

Encouraged by the mess in the Augean stables that Windhoek had become, SWAPO pressed on with its war. In February 1983, as part of the annual rainy season offensive, 1,600 PLAN combatants infiltrated Namibia. Knowing that the Namibian policy was on the ropes, Pik Botha had secretly met Angolan government leaders in the Cape Verde islands the previous month. The talks were complicated by UNITA's resurgence. The anti-SWAPO war was being sucked into the vortex of the general conflagration in Angola. Washington pestered Pretoria to pull pack its troops from southern Angola and to arrange a thirty-day ceasefire. A few days after Pretoria had offered a ceasefire (on 6 December 1983), the SADF began the massive Operation ASKARI inside Angola. PLAN's and FAPLA's capability was weakened before a ceasefire was to be implemented. Operation ASKARI led to serious engagements with FAPLA and Cuban armoured units in which the SADF lost twenty-one men, their highest total for a single operation since the beginning of the war.

On 30 January 1984 a delegation from the SADF military intelligence directorate, led by its head, Major General Piet van der Westhuizen, met the SWAPO leadership in Lusaka, at a discreet meeting convened by Kaunda. The Zambian president had recently asked P.W. Botha to give Namibia its independence as a 'Christmas present'. The next day in parliament Botha announced that the SADF had begun its withdrawal from Angola as a first step towards a formal ceasefire. The prime minister conceded publicly that Namibia was costing too much in blood and treasure. On 16 February the ceasefire was formalized with Luanda. Pretoria showed further flexibility by releasing Andimba Toivo ja Toivo in March, as well as other political prisoners and guerrillas captured at Cassinga in 1978. Kaunda also organized a three-day meeting between the MPC and SWAPO, but the talks hit a dead end. SWAPO maintained that Pretoria was trying to get around UN Resolution 435 and to seduce the insurgents into joining the internal fold, just as Ian Smith had tried to entice Joshua Nkomo and ZAPU into coming back home to Salisbury.

Pretoria, meanwhile, had cracked down on opposition in Ovamboland, alleging that 800 PLAN fighters were moving south through Kaokoland. Over a thousand SWAPO supporters were rounded up. And the already strict press censorship was tightened in the territory. It was the carrot and stick again – talk and thump. Pretoria now started taking linkage to its logical extreme: a straight SWAPO-MPC deal tagged on to a UNITA-MPLA settlement, cutting out all the non-African troublemakers. In June 1984 the South African government offered SWAPO a token role in the interim government in Windhoek. 'We are being offered nice cars and nice apartments and asked to play the part of South African puppets,' replied a SWAPO spokesman. In July the administrator-general met Nujoma face-to-face in the Cape Verde islands. Pretoria wanted PLAN to stop fighting while the Cuban issue was sorted out, but Nujoma was prepared to agree to a ceasefire only if South Africa went ahead immediately with the UN settlement plan. It was deadlock once more.

### *Steps to a settlement (1985-88)*

The Angolan war and the domestic insurrection inside South Africa consumed the attention of the SADF and Pretoria for two years – 1985 and 1986. Namibian independence took even more of a backseat as conventional battles raged in south-east Angola and the South African townships went up in flames. To some extent the internal politicians in Windhoek were left alone to ponder their predicament. Leaders such as Mudge evinced a certain smug self-satisfaction: Namibia, certainly south of the operational area, was a haven of peace compared with Big Brother's troubles. Perhaps Windhoek's experiments in social engineering could act as a guide for the future South Africa?

The ruling Multi-Party Conference looked back at the mistakes of the DTA. It had failed because of its collaborationist ethic, its obvious dependence on Pretoria. It had never been an anti-colonialist or nationalist movement but at most a civil rights movement. The MPC would therefore take a more nationalistic approach, a more robust stance towards Pretoria, as it concerned itself with social reforms in the area of health and education. Yet it still lacked credibility. For, unlike the DTA, it was an *appointed*, not an *elected* administration. In June 1985 the MPC became the 'Government of National Unity'. Of course it squabbled right from the start. Ministers started suing each and attacking their own government. Some of the ministers were determined to shake off the stultifying embrace of Pretoria. But they knew that they owed their careers, if not their heads, to the protection of the SADF. And the war went on.

**Inside Namibia: a snapshot in October 1985**

Namibia at war was a strange, beautiful, almost surreal place: images flashed by of Vietnam, Rhodesia and, occasionally, the savagery of the Congo. Yet, for the casual foreign visitor, it was a place that worked: unusually for Africa, for example, the roads were as good as the beer. The game parks were well run, so were the hotels, with their odd mixture of German efficiency, Afrikaner hospitality and African good manners. The clarity of the light made it a photographer's dream. The overwhelming sense of natural grandeur and of space harmonized with the champagne quality of the air. Because of the war and the country's isolation, it was almost untouched by one of the great scourges of the twentieth century: packaged tourism. Away from the northern war zones, Namibia was usually the quintessence of primeval tranquillity. Enchanting classical German building, relics of the

Ovahimba women in their plaits and mud

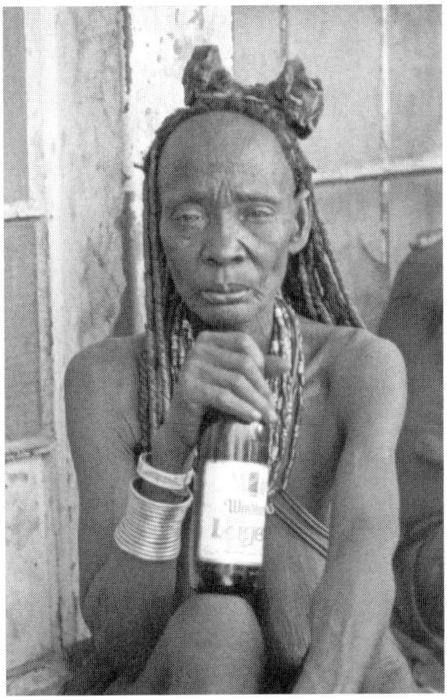


An Ovahimba woman enjoying the fruits of modern civilization, Opuwa, 1985

Second Reich, looked as though they had been plucked from Rhenish forests and planted in the desert. Brechtian characters strolled along the sand-scoured, melancholic streets of picturesque little towns such as Lűderitz and Swakopmund. Life was very pleasant for a visitor, especially if he or she were white.

There were so many lyrical paradoxes and brutal contradictions – much deeper than the simplistic political picture of illegal, repressive South African occupation. It was that too, but Namibia was so much more. Cameos of the territory, word-pictures from Namibians speaking out loud, gathered during one month might be able to provide a more realistic impression. I used to visit the territory regularly but I have chosen to add here some verbatim sketches from my diary of October 1985 because I spent a continuous month travelling throughout the country. Also, because I was working with an Afrikaans-speaking film crew, I gained unusual access to the military zones, travelling along the entire front line from Caprivi to Ruacana. I conducted all the following interviews in both English and Afrikaans (and in African languages with civilian translators; the exception was the interviews with the San).

> *First, a cramped Hercules transport aircraft, full of national servicemen reading comics, travels from Pretoria to Windhoek. Then that old war-horse, the Dakota, comes in flying low over the flat scrubland just in case a SAM-7 missile is waiting. The Dak touches down near the Omega base. It is hot, very hot, in the Caprivi strip. The Bushman troops (201 Battalion) at Omega are unerring trackers. Their white South African officers confirm they are*

*also very reliable under fire. Off-duty, however, they can be erratic, explains the camp doctor, as he points to a corporal nursing a wound in his rear. 'He was shot with an arrow by a Bushman who refused to work after drinking too much.' A lively discussion follows on the San's cultural survival. A white officer who speaks one of the 17 highly complex local Bushman dialects, is defensive: 'The army is not turning the Bushman into a war machine; it is preventing their extinction.' Another officer adds: 'We are not trying to Westernise the vulnerable Bushman culture. We just want to make him a better Bushman.' The army, he said, encourages Bushman troops to spend a day a week with their children teaching them the old customs and fieldcraft.*

*Travel to Oshivelo, and then Ondangwa, where the white civilians and soldiers' families live in stockaded areas, each with a trim, little sandbagged bomb-shelter in front of their bungalows. At the air bases, artists are evident. An Alouette gunship has 'I'm Noddy' painted on its Browning. On a Buffel APC someone had carefully painted 'Boswell Wilkie Circus' on the sides, but 'Road Runner' tops the logo list. Oshakati has the best collection of propaganda posters to inspire bored troopies: 'Think: it might be a new experience'; 'Winners Never Quit'. Warnings about mines abound everywhere. And always the unofficial scrawl,* Min dae *[a few days left of national service]. This not* Apocalypse Now, *though. There is no 'fragging'. Morale is generally high. And despite the posters warning of the dangers of drugs, this army is not 'dropping out'.*

*Ovamboland, utterly flat. The rains are beginning: the sandy soil smells rich and fecund. The ubiquitous* Cuca *shops, always grandly named, often apparently selling nothing, except information perhaps. A BMW might be parked outside. The huts and villages are often very poor and scruffy, a sharp contrast with the regimented tidiness of the army bases. The ordinary soldiers are suspicious of foreigners; some are told not to talk to writers and journalists, even if they are South African. After a few hours, relaxed, they talk like young soldiers anywhere. 'Ag, man, the army is all hurry up and wait.' They admit to boredom, that the army doesn't give them jobs that match their skills, a comment that is echoed by the many graduate conscripts.*

*The officers, particularly the regulars in the PF, permanent force, are also suspicious. Justifiably. The SADF is castigated in the media throughout the planet. The drinks flow in the mess, so does the frank talk, usually in Afrikaans. English is often the language of formality, of reserve. The SADF is bilingual but Afrikaans is the dominant language. Slangy Afrikaans is the language of combat, fear, orders, prayer and laughter for the troops. The talk is of war, sex and sport. Universal clichés of men-at-war. Firstly, always the war. 'SWAPO is good, so we have to be too,' says a keen citizen force 'camper' [reservist]. More beers. A graduate officer admits: 'We might be winning the war here but we might also be losing it at home.' A* Koevoet *T-shirt emblazoned with 'Our business is killing and business is good'. An army captain comments on the*

On patrol with motorbikes on the Ovambo/Angola border.

The army found horse patrols very effective. Both pictures taken by the author while on patrol with the army in October 1985

*reputedly poor relations between the army and the police. 'We have the odd punch-up, especially with* Koevoet, *but here the relationship works because the police do what the army tells them to do. In South Africa, the townships are in a mess because the police do their own thing, and cock it up. The army must bring them under control.'*

*Along the Ovambo/Angolan border by road, in Buffels, then patrolling in a Puma helicopter. Always dust, the real enemy of the chopper, not SAM-7s. Then patrols with the SWATF units on motorbikes and horses. 'PLAN doesn't hear us coming until it's too late' is the theme. 'The terrorists are dead scared of horses, you know.' The motor-cyclists act as outriders for the convoy. The enemy here is camel thorn – punctures, not mines.*

*Foot patrols, searching kraals. Automatic fire; brief contact. Later, capture of four PLAN insurgents. They are not terrified. They are not mistreated. They know they are destined for a long captivity, unless they join the SWATF. Better training, food, money, medical attention, entertainment. Why not? Two of the captives, however, quietly explain that they are committed to SWAPO ideology and that they would never fight for the 'puppets in Windhoek'.*

*Ruacana, overlooking the big hydro-electric project. Because of the war less than 10 per cent of the potential electricity power is produced by the region, despite the chronic underdevelopment. The base commander plays Elvis Presley tapes in his civilian pick-up truck, chews on a pipe and calls his wife 'Corporal'. 'Corporal' is proud of her involvement in the new 'tourist wing' at the base, right next to the mess. Very few tourists can enter the area but the small wooden building, a mile from the border, is used for official visitors. In this case my film crew. The commander complains about the new restraints on fighting in Angola [following the Lusaka accord]. He says plaintively: 'Now we are supposed to wait for the bastards to come and hit us first.' The next night SWAPO obliges with a stand-off bombardment. The Ruacana base is hit by 122mm rockets, mortars and a recoilless rifle. The new tourist wing is partially destroyed. Two SADF officers are slightly wounded. The commander is angry and embarrassed. He tries to hide the damage. An angry reaction force caught up with the attackers and, reportedly, killed eight PLAN fighters a few miles inside Angola. In the mess afterwards, one of the officers admits to me, 'I'm here in the operational area because this is the one place I can kill kaffirs legally.'*

*The atmosphere is more relaxed at Opuwa, the midget capital of Kaokoland. During a patrol in Buffels, the soldiers provide water and tobacco to the primitive, handsome Ovahimba people. Only a few thousand of these 'cattle people' are left in the deserts of Kaokoland. They daub themselves in fat and ochre. The women plait their hair and look like red Bo Dereks. Most are almost untouched by civilization, though a few less noble savage ladies are to be found drinking and smoking pipes outside a tiny store next to the SADF base. A black SWATF major takes me and some of his drinking friends to his girlfriend's hut. It is a corrugated iron square. Although inside is immaculately tidy, the tiny hut has no windows at all. The major's lady, Dorca, explains why: 'I want no windows,' she says slowly in broken Afrikaans, 'SWAPO come and shoot me otherwise.'*

*The discussion in the Opuwa mess is hearty and sophisticated. A graduate in law from Stellenbosch university, doing his two-year army stint, explains why he no longer believes in a political strategy for the SADF. 'When I was at Stellenbosch [the Afrikaner Oxbridge], a student asked P.W. [Botha] during his speech there, about the political future for the blacks in South Africa. He replied, in as many words: 'Shut up and concentrate on your job, studying, and leave me to my job, politics.' We all felt insulted by that. The more conservative officers disagreed with the law graduate. They spouted the 'Africans-are-generally-happy-here-we-only-need-to-kill-the-small-amount-of-communist-troublemakers' philosophy. They were talking specifically about Namibia.' 'Same applies to South Africa,' they said. 'If they are so happy, why not give them the franchise and let them vote happily for the National Party?' responded the law man.*

*'Ag, man, be serious.' The variety of opinions, often openly expressed, ranging from brutal racism to liberal concern, suggests that this is not a brainwashed war machine. Moreover, standards of military professionalism are high. And so, generally, is morale. There are exceptions. For example, some coloured troops refused home leave because they fear reprisals in their own communities in South Africa because they are serving in the army.*

*Away now from the operational area. Okahandja, the training school for the SWATF. Namibia is not a polite word here among the officer instructors. 'We are fighting for South West Africa. We are not prepared to die for Namibia.' This is the fundamental paradox of the war: why should young South African conscripts fight and die to* defend *one sort of majority rule in Namibia while they are fighting and sometimes dying in South Africa to* prevent *the same principle being applied at home? One SWATF officer from the local German community admits: 'I'm HNP in my heart but in my head I know there has to be change.' [HNP is the Herstigte Nasionale Party – the very right-wing splinter of the National Party.] A change perhaps to a professional regular army in Namibia or South West Africa, if you prefer. To avoid the political problems of conscripting Ovambos and other SWAPO supporters? The German-speaking officer replies coolly: 'A regular army? And what if it turns against us?'*

*Windhoek. The airport is named after J.G. Strydom. You can usually characterize a developing country by its main airport. This is clean, efficient and ultra-modern with all the international signs awaiting independence. Yet it is named after the Afrikaner apostle of apartheid. Typical South African hamfisted PR. A local official says: 'That's a little thing. You know, this independence thing takes time.' A masterly understatement. Another misnomer is the grandiloquently titled Government of National Unity, which can't even agree on the name of the country. The new administration reeks of Muzorewa's defeat. The rationale is to buy the time that the bishop never had. The same white Rhodesian clichés: 'preservation of standards' and 'respect for different cultures' permeate the conversations. The new black ministers have a taste for blonde secretaries and black Mercedes. One, Moses Katjiuonga, 43, a former Maoist with an American accent, and now the leader of SWANU [South West Africa National Union], admits: 'If things go wrong this time, we should blame ourselves, not Pretoria.' But Andreas Shipanga, the head of SWAPO-D [Democrats] and minister of nature conservation, mining, commerce and tourism, wants to pass the buck: 'This country has become a pawn of superpower rivalries.' The ever-affable Shipanga has the shakes. The tough-talking Dirk Mudge emphasizes the major reforms made despite the fact that A-G-8 [residual segregation laws that can be repealed only by Pretoria's diktat] blocked other necessary changes. There's a multiracial cabinet and one man, one vote. The hated Group Areas Act is gone, he says. Windhoek is fifteen years ahead of South Africa.' In a somewhat setpiece tone, he insists: 'As a result of these reforms we have relative peace. We have a war on our border but no women and children protesting in the streets.'*

*Many Namibian whites indeed feel that their country is being used as a social laboratory, as a litmus test for the fainthearted in the south. A Windhoek restaurant owner, who still refuses – illegally – to allow blacks into his establishment, says very bluntly: 'The* huigelaar *[two-faced] Botha clan is using South West as a playground to see if it [multiculturalism] works. If it doesn't, they will shoot the kaffirs.' Social engineering clearly has its limits in Windhoek. Squabbles about what race can use what facilities still abound. As one very senior, and also very exasperated, white civil servant puts it: 'Instead of fighting over the rules, we should be playing the game.' Competing with SWAPO not with each other, he explains.*

*Intelligence briefing, defence HQ, Windhoek, Just before the rainy season offensive, 'only forty SWAPO terrorists active in the operational area,' explains a senior SADF intelligence officer. (He concedes that the rains will make the number grow considerably.)*

*My question: 'Is it cost-effective to have such a massive and expensive machine running around after forty guerrillas on the border here when South Africa itself is said to be infiltrated by hundred of ANC insurgents?'*

*Answer: 'No comment. I was not briefed to reply to such a question.' Abrupt end of briefing.*

*Windhoek is seductive, with its dusty, small-town charm and graceful buildings. Afternoon tea with the administrator-general, Louis Pienaar and his wife, an ultra-courteous couple. Pienaar suggests that South Africa could leave suddenly – 'like a thief in the night'. Pretoria is sick of the shenanigans of the Windhoek politicians. The feeling is reciprocated. Yet Windhoek's most famous character, Johannes Smith (Smitty to his admirers), says fiercely: 'The Boers will never leave in the twentieth century.' Smith runs the* Windhoek Observer *almost singlehandedly. He is the local Cassandra and the scourge of the Establishment. Many read his paper avidly, sometimes banned for carrying nudes on the back page, for his political and social column, 'The People Hear'. My South African editor friend, Denis Beckett, had affectionately called Smith's weekly effusions, 'one of the most libellous gossip columns of modern times'. Smitty is what might be called a South West African nationalist in his dislike of Pretoria. A highly articulate white lawyer, Anton Lubowski, is a conventional pro-SWAPO Namibian nationalist. He is concerned with human rights. Politely and patiently, he explains that SWAPO has already accepted that the constitution for the future Namibia would be based upon the International Declaration of Human Rights. He claims that the internal government's bill of fundamental human rights is flawed as it specifically excludes the existing 'inhumane' security legislation.*

*Lighter moments intrude. It is the* Oktoberfest, *full of Germans, some in* Lederhosen, *guzzling quarts of lager. Then a desert journey to Lűderitz, where quaint* hoch Deutsch *is still spoken by some whites and blacks. Apparently the Kaiser's birthday is still celebrated here. Finally, Windhoek to Keetmanshoop, thirteen hours by train. One goat joins the train and some AWOL soldiers, accompanied by military policemen, leave. In the compartment is a scholarly SADF colonel who is researching ethnology. He tries, unsuccessfully, to explain what makes up Namibia.*

What made Namibia tick economically was mineral wealth, particularly the uranium and the diamonds. Described as a 'political timebomb' for the Government of National Unity, the Thirion Commission, which had previously revealed the worms in the administrative woodwork, in 1986 published its report on the mining industry, concentrated in the monopoly held by Consolidated Diamond Mines, a subsidiary of De Beers. It was alleged that a systematic 'scorched earth' policy had been stripping the territory of its diamond wealth before independence and illegally stockpiling the diamonds outside the country.[12]

The SADF had better news for the embattled leaders in the Windhoek Tintenpalast (Ink Palace), the seat of government. The commander of the SWATF, Major General George Meiring, insisted that SWAPO's war effort had been ground down. PLAN had paid a heavy rent to fight alongside FAPLA. The additional attritional effect of combat with the SADF and SWATF had led to the deaths of over 10,000 PLAN fighters, according to General Meiring. He said: 'SWAPO losses over the last twenty years are unparalleled in the history of modern revolutionary warfare.' Nevertheless, despite their losses, SWAPO fighters were often hero-worshipped, especially by young black Namibians. In the first legal SWAPO rallies inside Namibia during 1986, crowds of up to 10,000 were reported.

So SWAPO was far from beaten, militarily or politically. During early 1987 PLAN slipped through the security forces' cordons into the white farming areas around Etosha, about 120 miles south of the border. The last time they had managed this, in 1983, they had created havoc, killing a number of white farmers and soldiers in fierce contacts.

Like the DTA, the Government of National Unity was slipping into a rapid decline. Pretoria had stamped on its efforts to wrest real power; and its nominal army, the SWATF, was rocked by disaffection among its black troops, who were reluctant, in some cases to fight, not least alongside UNITA. The crunch came in 1988. South Africa had power in Namibia and SWAPO had the bulk of popular support. Neither could come to terms with each other … until the escalation of the Angolan war forced the great powers to step in.

### *The endgame in Namibia*

The internal parties had always faced an obstacle race of horrifying complexity with the odds heavily in favour of the obstacles. The men in the Tintenpalast – and some of the ministers had shown great spirit in trying to beat Pretoria at its own game by working within the system – might have gained some credibility if the war had been stifled. As in Rhodesia in 1979, only the guerrillas could guarantee peace, however. In February 1988 a massive 25-kilo bomb exploded in a packed First National Bank in Oshakati, killing eighteen people and injuring thirty-one. SWAPO denied responsibility for this tragedy, the bloodiest, if not the biggest, blast in the history of the war.

War weariness and sheer exhaustion had set in on both sides. The Angolan wars had begun in 1961 and the SWAPO campaign in 1966. By 1988 the SADF found itself fighting on three fronts: a PLAN insurgency inside Namibia, a series of direct clashes with the Cubans on the Namibian border and the conventional battles in support of UNITA in the south-east. The MPLA and its allies claimed to have snatched air superiority from the SAAF, even though in air-to-air dogfights the South Africans claimed a 9-1 superiority in aircraft shot down. On the ground the combined numbers of Cuban manpower and sophistication of Russian weaponry were pounding away at the SADF. With a strangled economy, Pretoria could no longer afford the military, political and economic costs of the Namibian millstone. The internal option had reached a dead end. South Africa's Namibian policy was in tatters but so was the entire Angolan infrastructure. Washington had effectively vetoed Angola's access to the World Bank and the International Monetary Fund. Angola's economic crisis, incomparably more critical than Pretoria's, grew even more desperate as the Luandan government, which earned 90 per cent of its export earnings from oil, watched in horror as world oil prices fell. And, most importantly, Moscow was cutting back on its foreign adventures, most notably in Angola and Afghanistan.

Battlefield attrition and the convergence of superpower self-interest in Angola provided the proverbial window of opportunity for Chester Crocker to finesse his eight-year campaign of constructive engagement. As I outlined in more detail in the previous chapter on Angola, starting in London in May 1988, representatives from Angola, South Africa and Cuba huddled together to find a way out of their own maze. Crocker was usually in the chair and the Russians nudged the Cubans if they started to become too revolutionary for the new apostles of *glasnost.* For seven months they haggled in Cairo, New York, Geneva and, most frequently, Brazzaville to implement Resolution 435, the 1978 proposals that they had all in principle agreed on. The end state was obvious: how to stop the Angolan war before it sucked in the superpowers, now eager for cosy détente. That meant getting Cuban troops out of Angola and the SADF out of Namibia. In the end, despite much scorn from both left and right, Crocker's linkage was finally working. With ruthless determination and diplomatic skill, the Georgetown professor had the Holy Grail – Namibian independence – within his grasp, and before Reagan handed over to George Bush.

A ceasefire came into effect in Angola on 1 September 1988. UNITA forces were excluded from the negotiations – Savimbi's private war was destined to run into the twenty-first century. Nevertheless, the core of the settlement process was a *de facto* non-aggression pact between Angola and South Africa. In the haggling over the transition in Namibia it was agreed that Cuba would withdraw its troops over twenty-seven months, while the SADF would reduce its strength to just 1,500 troops in two bases in Namibia. UN-monitored elections would ensue and independence would be achieved by the end of 1989. In late December 1988 Pretoria ratified the final deal. As Pik Botha put it, 'The hard nut has been cracked.' After 100 years of colonial rule, this looked like the real thing, even to the most jaded of Namibians. The London *Times* editorialized on 26 December 1988: 'The agreement, if implemented, deserves to be hailed as the most important diplomatic breakthrough in Africa since the colonies first began to emerge into independence some 30 years ago.' Many in the SADF were unhappy but P.W. Botha had carefully – and unusually – consulted with his generals and intelligence chiefs at nearly every stage of the peace process. The Great Crocodile knew that Ronald Reagan, his chief protector against US sanctions, was leaving the White House.

All the main antagonists could make plausible claims to success. Cuban troops could return home with honour. Pretoria had kept its promise to prise out Castro's intruders and could soon extricate itself from a painful war. The Russians could shed an imperial burden. SWAPO looked set to win the elections. Washington could wave a diplomatic triumph. And Angola could begin the mammoth task of rebuilding a devastated country. Savimbi, however, remained perhaps capable of toppling the whole edifice. Pretoria's hard men would not yet throw him to the wolves but nor would they allow him to be a spoiler of their urgently required exit strategy.

The very first day of the UN-managed transition – ominously 1 April 1989 – justified the fear of the pessimists. The Cubans had pulled back and the South African troops had returned to their bases in preparation for demobilization and the move south, back to the republic. Suddenly, in direct contravention of the UN agreements, over 1,000 PLAN insurgents poured over the borders. No UN blue helmets were in place to stop or dissuade them. SWAPO's flagrant breach of the agreement seemed inexplicable. The party stood to win the forthcoming election – all it had to do was sit back and wait. Instead they provided a wonderful opportunity for Pretoria to renege on the whole deal. Various explanations have been offered. Sam Nujoma had an arrogant and impetuous streak. The military and political wings of the party were at loggerheads. Perhaps local commanders had simply misunderstood the details of the transitional arrangements. Whatever the reasons, with UN blessing, and after the intercession of Mrs Thatcher, who had flown into Windhoek on 1 April (the 'African Queen', as she was dubbed, was touring southern Africa) the SADF mobilized. This was a replay of Lord Soames's use of Rhodesian troops in January 1980 to counter ZANLA excesses. It was a bizarre twist of fate: SADF troops were hunting SWAPO guerrillas with UN consent. 'It feels strange to be in the right for once,' said a senior South African officer. 'I'm not sure we can handle it.' In a week of savage fighting perhaps 375 guerrillas were killed for the loss of twenty-six South African dead and 120 wounded. SWAPO's catastrophic diplomacy and UNTAG's belated and inadequate deployment had achived the impossible: they had placed South Africa on the side of the angels.

The UN's unique honeymoon with Pretoria did not last longer than the invasion crisis. The South African government, with some justification, threatened to pull out of the whole exercise. It stalled but did not ditch the process. Rows with the UN peackeepers ensued, inevitably, but the same troops needed mineproofed vehicles to protect them from SWAPO landmines. UNTAG was forced to lease SADF Buffels and Casspirs, built by Arnscor in defiance of the UN bans. This was a further irony: the UN was forced to shop for equipment it had prevented others from buying. Soon more deepseated problems, not least about the role of *Koevoet,* emerged. The UN fielded some heavy hitters, such as the former Finnish president, Martti Ahtisaari, to smooth the transition. During the year of the transition, the UN had to deal *inter alia* with the return of refugees and the release of political prisoners, let alone supervise the electoral process over such a vast territory. But the major powers wanted it to work. Of course Pretoria did not want SWAPO to win and so pumped in vast sums of money to the splintered opposition parties. In the November 1989 election – which the UN deemed free and fair – SWAPO won 57 per cent of the vote. On 21 March 1990 Sam Nujoma was made president of independent Namibia. The South Africans withdrew from Walvis Bay in 1994. The new SWAPO government had much to do, not least to rebuild socially and materially after the long war. And its new army had to do some real soldiering, not least in suppressing the discontent in Caprivi and later to fight in the future big war in the Congo.

At independence day celebrations in Windhoek many optimistic foreign dignitaries wondered if a new dawn of détente was breaking over the region. Pessimists, however, asked whether Pretoria would start to destabilize its new neighbour, the country it had ruled since 1915. Would Pretoria raise another rebel Namibian army as it had with UNITA? The SADF was still supporting the RENAMO insurgents in the destabilization saga on the Indian Ocean side of the region, in Mozambique. The civil war was far more savage than its predecessor, the anti-colonial struggle against the Portuguese.

Sam Nujoma (left) and Herman Toivo ja Toivo celebrate independence

## *Chapter 11*

# Mozambique: The civil war (1976-1992)

FRELIMO might have inherited the political kingdom at independence in 1975 but unfortunately the departing whites took nearly all the keys of that kingdom: the money, the expertise and, in some cases, even the machinery. FRELIMO had initially to quash an attempted white coup, encouraged by Rhodesia, and a series of military revolts within the party, caused partly by friction between a sometimes envious military wing and the pork-barrelling politicians. Amid the economic, political and military chaos, President Samora Machel insisted that he would adopt the Soviet model. Unlike the MPLA, Machel had assumed power without massive Soviet and Cuban military assistance because FRELIMO had not been challenged by any significant rival liberation movements. Nevertheless, Machel's first state visit outside Africa, in May 1976, was to the USSR. In Moscow he declared his intention to transform his country into the 'first fully Marxist state in Africa'. FRELIMO would be fashioned into a Russian-inspired Marxist-Leninist 'vanguard party' – despite the fact that Machel had led a largely Maoist-style war, with limited support from the peasantry and the tiny, urban working class. Mozambique soon received a variety of tanks, armoured vehicles, SAM systems and, later, combat aircraft and helicopters (which were largely obsolete, except for the aircraft). The initial influx of 200 Soviet instructors helped to transform the guerrilla force into a conventional army. Other Eastern-bloc allies, notably the East Germans, shaped the internal political system, especially the propaganda and security organs.

Thirty days after independence, Machel proclaimed the immediate nationalization – with little or no compensation – of all private educational institutions, hospitals, clinics, funeral parlours and legal practices. In the countryside, although Mozambique did not boast a single agronomist, a Marxist 'villagization' scheme, similar to the disastrous Tanzanian experiments, was set in motion, despite the opposition of much of the peasantry. The secret police rounded up thousands of opponents and placed them in gulags for 're-education'. Some were executed. The rapid nationalization of all facets of life created chaos, all of which

Samora Machel opted for the Soviet model

was blamed on the departure and/or sabotage of the whites. The white exiles, however, said that they left *because* of the massive upheavals. Everybody was blamed by FRELIMO except itself: the Portuguese, then the Rhodesians and finally the *bête blanche*, South Africa, although – as the disorder became endemic – Machel had the grace, later, to blame also the rushed implementation of his socialist policies. In 1980 he warned his former guest, Robert Mugabe, not to repeat the Mozambique example. The key was keeping white expertise in the country, Machel said.

FRELIMO's hasty revolution was perpetually under fire. The party had to fight three wars in succession: an anti-colonial war against the Portuguese army, then a bitter struggle against the Rhodesian forces, and – most savagely – after 1980, a double-barrelled war against RENAMO and the SADF.

At independence in 1975 most Mozambicans expected peace although the new government believed – with some justification – that the South Africans were weighing up options to topple the revolutionary regime. Pretoria had toyed with a UDI-style white-ruled puppet administration in the south alongside the South African border. Gradually, the intelligence chiefs moved away from the political difficulties of a direct military overthrow of FRELIMO and shifted to stirring up the chaos and/or offering economic inducements. Because of the fear of SADF intervention, the soon-to-be Mozambican foreign minister, Joaquim Chissano, stressed as early as 1974 that Mozambique would become 'a base for revolutionary change in Africa', but qualified his statement by adding that he meant a 'revolutionary base in *ideas*'. The *povo* (masses) in South Africa would have to act as their own saviours, he explained. Nevertheless, Maputo had to prepare its armed forces for a possible conventional thrust from South Africa and, more immediately, to resist the large-scale Rhodesian offensives which began in August 1976.

## *Mozambique versus Rhodesia*

Machel closed his borders with Rhodesia on 3 March 1976. The new president was committed to support ZANLA's insurgency because it was the same kind of war against colonialism that FRELIMO had waged. ZANLA had fought side-by-side in the contacts with the Rhodesians and Portuguese. Machel supported the austere intellectual Robert Mugabe but the down-to-earth and ill-educated Mozambican president found it easier to communicate with the far more easy-going fellow soldier, Josiah Tongogara, the ZANLA commander. The tightening of the sanctions noose and the ZANLA-FRELIMO military alliance led in early 1977 to the eastern front's domination of the course of the Rhodesian war. Salisbury responded in two ways: pre-emptive and retaliatory raids on joint FRELIMO-ZANLA forces and the 'creation' of a secret anti-government army, RENAMO – the Mozambican National Resistance Movement. Much ink has been spilled on the origins of this rebel force. It is true that it was founded in double original sin: fashioned by the Rhodesian Central Intelligence Organization and then nourished by apartheid South Africa's military intelligence. And yet it also became a genuine popular symbol of resistance to the excesses of the Marxist government in Maputo. UNITA in the west had more credibility from the start. Savimbi had usually been portrayed, even by his detractors, as originally a genuine nationalist leader. Depending on which version, he later collaborated allegedly with the Portuguese, and unquestionably with the Afrikaners after 1975. RENAMO, however, always had a bad press and its long-term leader, Afonso Dhlakama, struggled for any international credibility.

The godfather of RENAMO was Ken Flower, the wily ex-police chief who ran the Rhodesian CIO for two decades. From the early 1970s he had tried to persuade his Portuguese counterparts of the need to establish a pseudo-guerrilla force in Mozambique. Although he had an excellent personal rapport with the BOSS chief, Hendrik van den Bergh, Flower kept the South Africans informed but they played little or no part in setting up RENAMO.[1] After the Portuguese collapse,

The godfather of RENAMO, Ken Flower. A very rare picture of the camera-shy spy chief (left), taken by the author in the author's Salisbury flat, 1980

the CIO and the BSAP Special Branch collected together a number of black and white Mozambican soldiers and policemen of varying degrees of professionalism and thuggery. A small band of about forty *Flechas,* led by Angolan-born Colonel Oscar Cardosa, joined the Rhodesians, who already had collected a nucleus of disgruntled white Mozambicans who were trying to form an anti-FRELIMO political front. What the CIO needed was a black military leader. During 1976 disaffected FRELIMO soldiers crossed the border. One potential rebel leader, André Matsangaisse, arrived in mid-1976.[2] He said he was a junior officer who was disillusioned with the army. (FRELIMO said he had been cashiered for the theft of a Mercedes and had then escaped from the 're-education centre', Sacuze prison in Sofala province.) In June 1976, a radio station called *Voz de Africa Livre,* Voice of Free Africa, started broadcasting from Gwelo in Rhodesia. The station, operating in Portuguese, attacked the 'communist tyranny' in Mozambique. Voice of Free Africa was directed by a colourful character called Orlando Cristina; he advocated a 'pure' non-communist Mozambican nationalism. (FRELIMO accused him of being a long-term agent of the colonial secret police.) Cristina had worked for Jorge Jardim, a wealthy Portuguese businessman with close ties to the former dictator, António de Salazar. Jardim was said to have donated some of his personal fortune to help run RENAMO and to fund its weapons supply.

This force had various names, initially MNR (Mozambique National Resistance) and later *Resistência Nacional Moçambicana* (RENAMO). Its first major base was at an old tobacco farm outside Odzi, not far from Umtali. This base was commonly referred to by locals as 'the funny farm'. Other camps in Rhodesia followed as the propaganda beamed from Gwelo and the poor conditions inside Mozambique generated a flow of anti-FRELIMO refugees. The Odzi camp was controlled by an officer from the CIO's Mozambique desk, Eric 'Ricky' May, who brought in former SAS personnel to run the embryonic army. In April Matsangaissa led a daring raid on his former prison at Sacuze and released 500 prisoners. More than half agreed to follow him back to Rhodesia to join RENAMO. In June Afonso Dhlakama arrived in Odzi after interrogation by Special Branch for one month in Umtali. He became second-in-command to Matsangaissa. The SAS thought highly of the first RENAMO commander as a fighting solder, while the CIO, however, reckoned Dhlakama lacked fighting spirit and charisma. Indeed, when I conducted the first ever TV interview with him at his secret Gorongosa HQ, in November 1986 (after a week travelling cross-country on a motorbike to reach him) my first impression was of a timid bank clerk. Dhlakama told me that he been conscripted into the Portuguese colonial forces but that he had defected to join FRELIMO in the closing stages of the anti-colonial war. He explained further that he had quit FRELIMO because he supported the more moderate nationalism of Machel's predecessor, Eduardo Mondlane. FRELIMO claimed that Dhlakama had been thrown out of the party because he was a 'petty criminal' – a common epithet for the party's ideological opponents. Much of RENAMO's simplistic 'philosophy' – Mondlane's

FRELIMO was described as 'good', 'real' and 'nationalist' while Machel's was 'communist', 'evil' and 'totalitarian' – seemed to have been concocted by CIO case officers and, by the style of it, late at night after too many whiskeys. The white Mozambican dissidents associated with Cristina were also involved in creating a makeshift political platform for the radio station. Right from the start the Rhodesians kept the political elements separate from the fighters in Odzi; for years afterwards RENAMO officials blamed the Rhodesians as the original cause of the continuous tensions in the 1980s between the (mainly white) external leadership and the black military command inside Mozambique. The CIO was suspicious of Cristina's ties with Jardim, whom Salisbury suspected of betraying their sanctions secrets. With the increasing support of the Rhodesian SAS, the CIO concentrated on building up RENAMO's military potential. Flower initially implied that RENAMO was designed primarily as a unit to spy on and disrupt ZANLA operations, 'the eyes and ears of our intelligence in Mozambique'. In a secret CIO document, he wrote:

> The undoubted success of the [RENAMO] movement also signified that FRELIMO in Mozambique (as between MPLA and UNITA in Angola) lacked that essential measure of support that they needed from the population: or the Portuguese had acted too hastily in transferring power to a liberation movement which could not establish popular support through free elections.[3]

This passage raised a number of questions. The first is about the initial ambitions for RENAMO. Was it merely to disrupt ZANLA or was it intended actually to topple Machel? SAS officers apparently assumed that they were helping RENAMO to overthrow FRELIMO. One history of the regiment claimed that RENAMO spontaneously engaged ZANLA.[4] FRELIMO later claimed that nearly all the '350' RENAMO/SAS 'attacks' between 1976 and 1979 were led and organized by white Rhodesians. This FRELIMO figure understates the number of military engagements and exaggerates Rhodesian leadership. Although the CIO was surprised by the rapid success of its protégé, the Rhodesian war ended before FRELIMO's grip on power was severely challenged. After the war, some CIO officials maintained that if more money had been pumped into what had been a shoestring operation, then

Bob MacKenzie, an American officer who served in the Rhodesian SAS and who was heavily involved with RENAMO

FRELIMO might have been overthrown and, therefore, the war on the eastern front might have been won.

The second, more important, question is the extent of the Mozambican dissidents' independence. RENAMO apologists insist that the Rhodesian role was limited to finance and training. According to an American right-wing history of the movement:

> The Rhodesian government had every reason to provide a sanctuary for RENAMO, as the Mozambican government was providing a sanctuary to Marxist guerrillas trying to overthrow it. But the fact remains that the Mozambican National Resistance was created, and its activities were conducted, by Mozambicans.[5]

RENAMO naturally tried to play down considerably the contribution of the Rhodesian SAS. It did, however, concede that the spectacular destruction of the Beira oil storage depot in March 1979 was led by an SAS captain, Bob MacKenzie. Captain MacKenzie was one of the most colourful of the characters involved in the Rhodesian war. He had been 70 per cent disabled as a private in the US Army in the Vietnam War, but later managed to pass the very tough induction course for the SAS. He subsequently joined the SADF's special forces, and died a heroic, if pointless, death in Sierra Leone in 1995. He was also a regular contributor to the *Soldier of Fortune* magazine. Most of the early spectaculars in Mozambique claimed by RENAMO were in fact SAS operations, although often they would benefit from logistical and scouting support from RENAMO troops. Most of the big RENAMO targets were decided by the CIO and Special Branch.

An acceptance of Rhodesia's crucial role does not mean that the standard orthodox view – that the CIO recruited mercenaries and criminals to spread random terror and disorder in Mozambique – is correct. Whatever their unholy origins, the guerrillas did come to represent a groundswell of popular hostility to FRELIMO rule. And RENAMO's early forays did encounter widespread sympathy from the peasantry in central Mozambique. That support might have been offered for a wide number of reasons, from clan loyalties to ideological convictions, from resentment against FRELIMO who sacked traditional chiefs to peasant dislike of villagization, and because of old religious affiliations among disaffected Catholics and Muslims. In short, the initial and inchoate Mozambican resistance was undoubtedly cynically fostered by the CIO but it also fed on very real discontent among blacks inside the country. But any RENAMO claims to have developed an organized internal resistance inside Mozambique and to have established an effective external political network *before* the CIO set up the Odzi base are not credible.

By 1978 RENAMO guerrillas numbered about 500 trained men. Initially they operated in the Manica province of Mozambique. Their targets were FRELIMO bases and convoys, the capture of weapons and attacks on 're-education centres'

During a Rhodesian raid on Mozambique this FRELIMO APC was destroyed

to gain recruits. RENAMO also tried to establish an infrastructure among the peasantry in Manica and Sofala provinces. The guerrilla strength doubled in 1979. A central internal HQ was built in the Gorongosa mountains, an area where Matsangaissa had operated as a FRELIMO insurgent. ('The' Gorongosa base was a very movable feast – it was also called later Casa Banana and it shifted around according to the rhythm of the war.) The RENAMO commander, along with 200 Mozambican insurgents, plus a dozen SAS men, consolidated their positions on the Gorongosa plateau. Another 200 RENAMO troops, led by Lucas Mushlangu, with no SAS back-up, set up another permanent base at Gogoi in the Sitatonga mountains of southern Manica. From January 1979 the SAS had augmented its initially small contribution. In particular in the last three months of the war, in Operation BUMPER, the SAS escalated its commitment as part of Rhodesia's all-out final offensive against Mozambique (and Zambia). The CIO and the Rhodesian Combined Operations HQ grew optimistic about their little counter-revolution – or the 'second war of liberation' as RENAMO dubbed it.

A young RENAMO soldier (taken by author in central Mozambique)

Then RENAMO came unstuck. On 17 October 1979 Matsangaissa was killed while personally leading a foolhardy frontal assault – against his SAS companions' advice – on the FRELIMO garrison in Gorongosa town at the base of the mountains. Dhlakama was rushed in by chopper to take over command. FRELIMO claimed that Mushlangu had challenged Dhlakama and the matter was settled in a gunfight. The RENAMO version is that 600 guerrillas voted for Dhlakama at the new Sitatonga base. Dhlakama was later to be confirmed as the 'president' and commander in chief. Yet in late 1979 Dhlakama had taken charge of a small army that was about to face annihilation. The Lancaster House settlement in London caught RENAMO in a vice between the large forces of Mugabe and Machel. The Rhodesian sanctuary, so vital for guerrilla operations, was about to disappear. Who would back RENAMO now? Enter, centre stage, South Africa.

A very rare early picture of Afonso Dhlakama, with the author, in Gorongosa base

### *The Pretoria connection*

Mozambique's war against Rhodesia had caused massive dislocation in the central provinces, the loss of thousands of Mozambican lives and, according to UN estimates, the sanctions blockade on Salisbury had cost Maputo £250 million. After nearly two decades of conflict and with his ally, Mugabe, in power, Machel looked forward to peace and social reconstruction. He assumed, in particular, that RENAMO 'banditry' would wither away. Machel was quite wrong.

Flower had been trying to get Pretoria to contribute towards a larger RENAMO force after it was up and running successfully. BOSS was sympathetic but Prime Minister Vorster refused to back the insurgency because of the harm it might have done to his détente policy. P.W. Botha was much more interested. From 1978 he opened up the coffers to Rhodesia's military needs. South African weapons and vehicles (initially motorbikes) were also provided to RENAMO in 1979. A frequent visitor to the Odzi base was Colonel Cornelius (Charles) van Niekerk, of South African military intelligence (SAMI or 'Sammy' to its friends). The colonel had been a military attaché in Nampula in the early 1970s. His job had been to monitor the limited involvement of the SADF in Portugal's counter-insurgency campaigns. Apparently he spoke both Portuguese and the local language in Nampula, Macua. Van Niekerk soon became a central figure in the RENAMO story. His first role was as the liaison officer with the Rhodesian operation and Ricky May specifically. Later he became the main contact between Dhlakama and Pretoria. Flower and General Peter Walls had arranged directly with the SADF chief, Magnus Malan, that 'compromised' units of the Rhodesian army such as the Selous Scouts and some of Muzorewa's auxiliaries, could be transferred to South Africa, to avoid possible reprisals. Flower ensured that RENAMO was included. Pretoria took over the Salisbury connection, lock, stock and barrel. The RENAMO leadership was quite happy to adopt its new benefactor – Dhlakama had nowhere else to go.

Van Niekerk – 'Commander Charlie' was his nickname, used widely by RENAMO leaders – was technically working under the SAMI's Directorate of Special Tasks. He was designated DST-2 (Eastern Section). The SADF initially code-named this Operation ALTAR and it later became the more covert Operation MILA. South Africa's intelligence chiefs did not expect RENAMO to actually win and take over power. But officers such as Commander Charlie broke a golden rule of spycraft: you never fall in love with your operators. As one senior South African intelligence officer later admitted, 'We fell in love with RENAMO and that became the be all and end all of our operation.'

Some estimates put RENAMO at 2,000 men in March 1980, although Flower told me at the time that the figure was closer to 1,000. Some were sent directly from Odzi back to Mozambique. Cristina moved the radio station from Gwelo initially to the SADF special forces' base near Phalaborwa, in the eastern Transvaal, and started to broadcast with the claim that Voice of Free Africa was now operating *inside* Mozambique. SADF transport planes also moved RENAMO personnel and equipment to Phalaborwa from where – according to contemporary opponents of the organization – Dhlakama and his HQ staff were shifted to a new base on the edge of Letaba river, one kilometre from the Kruger national park. It was founded on the former Letaba Ranch, which SAMI called Zobo City. The initial training was done by an ex-Rhodesian Light Infantry soldier who was promoted into the SAS and who then joined the South African Recce commandos: Captain David Scott-Donelan was in charge of training RENAMO officers some time later for specialist roles as well as setting up a course for female guerrillas working as nurses and combatants. RENAMO sources insisted, however, that Dhlakama's HQ remained inside Mozambique during the transfer. Further, RENAMO has always insisted that Dhlakama had stayed in the bush throughout the 1980s, except for occasional diplomatic forays to Europe and Pretoria.

During the sensitive handover period, members of the Rhodesian SAS simply drove RENAMO's and their own South African-supplied vehicles in a convoy though the main Zimbabwe-South African border post at Beit bridge. The final SAS commander, Lieutenant Colonel Garth Barrett, had asked General Pieter van der Westhuizen, the director of SAMI, to allow his men to stay together to form a new regiment of the South African Reconnaissance Commandos. Eighty per cent of the SAS, 127 men, including Barrett and Captain Bob MacKenzie, a fervent advocate of RENAMO, joined the Recces. Only a handful stayed on after their year's contract expired. According to my conversations with Barrett and a number of his men, they disliked the excessive regimentation of the SADF with its Afrikaans orientation and they disagreed with the SADF tactics, especially when the SAS were used as cannon fodder.

The transfer of Rhodesia's extensive borrowed equipment from South Africa plus the move south of the elite and threatened units all took place with the knowledge and tacit acquiescence of the British colonial authorities. Flower made a point of telling the governor's staff of the transfers. It has been suggested that this was churlish repayment for Machel's assistance to the British at Lancaster House, but in practical terms the British could have done little. Rhodesia was a powder keg in March and April 1980. If Lord Soames had insisted on handing over RENAMO to a probably grisly fate at the hands of FRELIMO, there could have been the repeat of the controversy over the betrayal of the pro-German Russian forces, especially the Cossacks, by the British in 1945. Stalin slaughtered most of them. In Rhodesia the British were glad to turn a blind eye – no one in 1980 foresaw the consequences of saving RENAMO.

Amazingly, Mugabe kept Flower on as director of the CIO. Although he informed the new premier of the broad outlines of RENAMO operations, the intelligence chief did not, or so he told me, hand over *details* of the bases and the new South African administration. Later, Pretoria accused the long-serving spymaster of betraying RENAMO operations when the insurgents suffered serious reverses in 1980 and 1981. South African intelligence retaliated by leaking stories that Flower had always been a British agent who had sold out both RENAMO *and* Rhodesia. Flower vehemently denied both allegations and suggested that the SADF had incompetently managed both RENAMO and their SAS advisers, a view shared by some of the SAS personnel involved. I must declare an interest here: I had a good personal relationship with Flower and his two daughters, who remained friends long after the spymaster's death. Even when I returned to British government service after the Rhodesian war I could not discover anything that indicated that Flower was a British mole. It was true that he visited Washington, London and other capitals regularly. As the longest-serving intelligence director-general in the Western world, such visits would be expected, and useful to Rhodesia (and then Zimbabwe). A better explanation for some of the cock-ups after the 1980s was the shake-up of the three main South African intelligence services, initiated by P.W. Botha after the Information Scandal. This demoralized many of the former BOSS agents, who had been very successful. BOSS was renamed DONS and later NIS; previously it had been the dominant agency working in the neighbouring states. The ascendancy of military intelligence under P.W. Botha disrupted the spy network throughout southern Africa.[6] My own view was that the army intelligence people were often smart and energetic but they sometimes lacked political nuance as well as proper experience in the field.

While the SADF was rebuilding RENAMO at bases inside South Africa, FRELIMO attacked the demoralized RENAMO cadres inside Mozambique. Rebel bases near Gorongosa were overrun and, in Operation LEOPARD in June and July 1980, the stronghold at Sitatonga was captured, along with supplies of South African military equipment. Hundreds of RENAMO guerrillas were killed, captured or deserted. Dhlakma fled with a few hundred followers 90 miles south to a small base, Garagua, on the Save river. This was the nadir of RENAMO's fortunes. Without South African help, the movement might have been obliterated.

In October 1980 Pretoria determined to resuscitate its secret ally. According to Martin and Johnson's account, Dhlakama and a South African military delegation led by the ubiquitous Colonel van Niekerk hammered out a new strategy. Pro-FRELIMO sources say that while the Rhodesians had encouraged RENAMO to adopt a hearts-and-minds approach so as to gather intelligence from a supportive peasantry, now the SADF ordered a scorched-earth policy of straightforward destruction and destabilization.[7] There were certainly differences of emphasis between the two white supremacist strategies but it would be inaccurate to dismiss entirely the attempts by a revived RENAMO to politicize the *povo*, the peasant masses. Externally, too, Pretoria tried to improve RENAMO's almost invisible image. Cristina became secretary-general of the political wing and a third-generation Mozambican of Goan ancestry, Evo Fernandes, opened up RENAMO's first European mission outside Lisbon. Fernandes had been connected to Jorge Jardim as well. When Jardim died in 1982, Fernandes apparently obtained funds from his former employer, the conservative millionaire industrialist Manuel Bulhosa, whose oil refinery in Maputo and other assets had been nationalized by FRELIMO.

The second prong of the revival was military. According to RENAMO, the relocated radio station had caused a big upswing in recruitment. The movement now claimed 10,000 men under arms, no doubt an exaggeration. This tally was boosted by the infiltration of newly-trained (and re-trained) men from the South African bases. RENAMO had fresh objectives. In Gaza province they tried to create a buffer to prevent the re-invigorated ANC thrust into South Africa. (This paralleled the buffer function of UNITA in southern Angola to stop SWAPO infiltration into what was then South West Africa.) RENAMO also tried to establish control in parts of Inhambane so that it could be re-supplied by sea rather than expensive airdrops. Submarines were used for transporting RENAMO VIPs and special forces on operations but large replenishment ships such as the SAS *Tafelberg* were used for major shipments. The South Africans also played a part in encouraging the rebels to wage an urban terror campaign in Beira and Maputo. Crucially, RENAMO began to concentrate on the road and rail routes that crossed the country – shots across the SADCC's bow.

As RENAMO cadres fanned out across the countryside they found a welcome in some areas. Although much of RENAMO's political programme was a flimsy concoction of Rhodesian and South African propaganda, the simple message of Mozambican nationalism versus Soviet colonialism did strike a chord. The guerrillas attracted dissident and disillusioned FRELIMO officials, villagers exasperated by Marxist collectivization, youngsters seeking adventure and, more often, food. Muslims and Catholics alienated by the government atheism crusade were attracted as well as traditionalists for whom RENAMO's restoration of *regulos* (chiefs) meant a welcome return to the old ways. In central Mozambique, the guerrillas often shared the same Shona culture, with its emphasis on spirit mediums and ancestor worship. When the guerrillas were not destroying or mutilating, which they did, they could choose to show a reforming front, by being all things to all men. They often looted FRELIMO stores and co-operatives and distributed some of the goods to the peasantry. The Robin Hood tactics worked well in the short term but the peasants soon realized that the guerrillas could not restock the pillaged shops. As in all bush wars, perhaps the majority of the *povo* cursed the military outrages of both sides and tried to keep their heads down. Although some Mozambicans joined RENAMO willingly, many of the

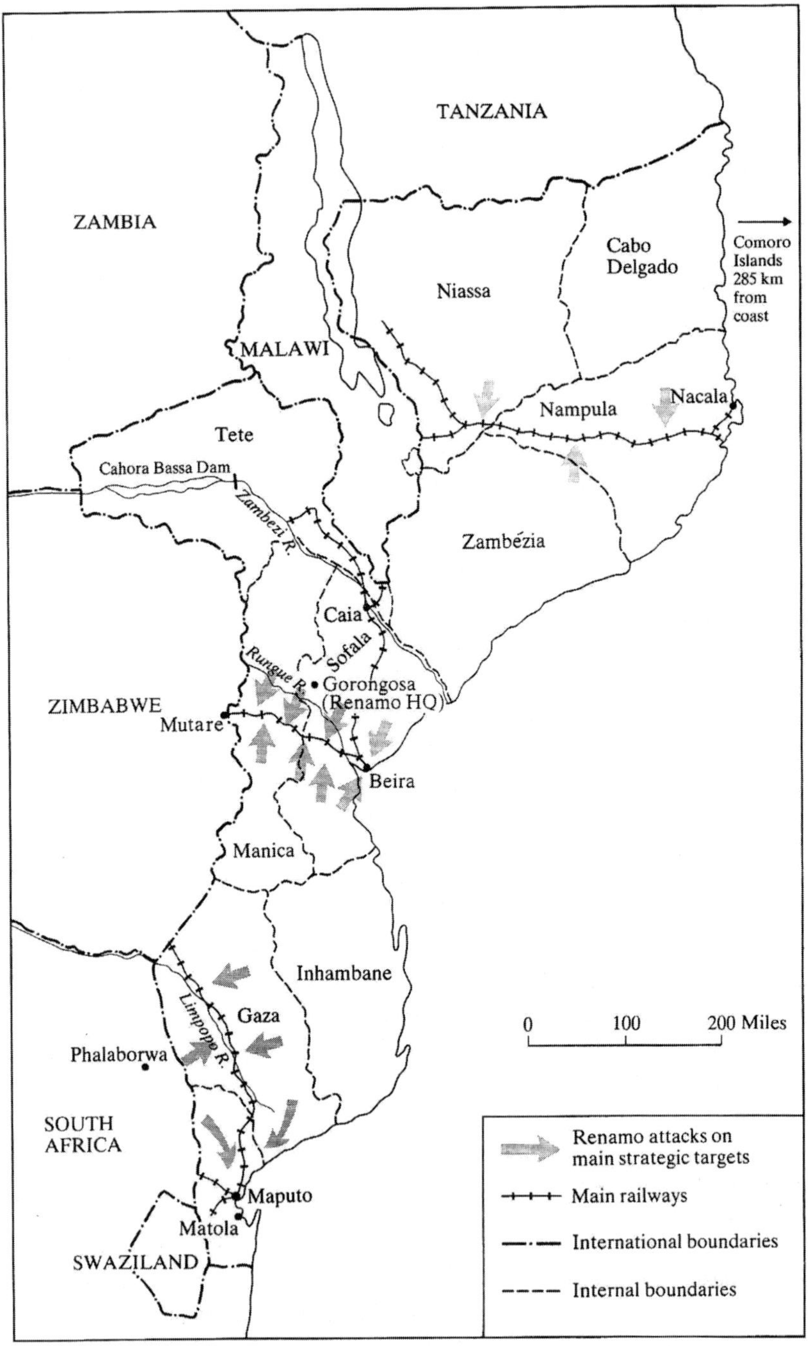


RENAMO attacks in Mozambique

rank-and-file soldiery appear to have been press-ganged into military service. Desertion could be severely punished.

FRELIMO reacted slowly to the RENAMO resurgence. The ruling party seemed to have believed its own propaganda about isolated bands of criminal bandits. It was not until late 1981 that FRELIMO began to realize the extent of Pretoria's connivance and that the SADF-RENAMO axis posed a serious threat to the survival of the Marxist regime. In effect, FRELIMO had a fullscale civil war on its hands. Machel appointed experienced guerrilla commanders as regional governors, not the Soviet-trained heavy weapons specialists. FRELIMO tried to construct a lightly-armed highly-mobile COIN force without dismantling its conventional deterrence against the SADF invading the country as it had done so recently in Angola.

Besides arming RENAMO, the SADF stormed into Mozambique. On 30 January 1981, in the first SADF raid on Mozambique, Recce Commandos crossed the border in vehicles painted in Mozambican army colours and drove fifty miles to Matola, a suburb of Maputo. The command vehicle was a captured BRDM. Some of the other captured vehicles (from FAPLA and PLAN) were too rusted and damaged. Eventually two South African Magirus Deutz heavy trucks were repainted and fitted with heavy guns. They set up roadblocks on the Matola-Maputo road. With pinpoint accuracy the raiders destroyed three houses on the tree-lined streets of the quiet neighbourhood. Thirteen ANC members were killed (the SADF claimed thirty) and one innocent passer-by. FRELIMO reported that in one house the ANC fought back and killed two of the attackers, both permanent force sergeants (in fact three NCOs were killed). One soldier threw a grenade into the window of the house while he was lying beneath the sill and pressed against the wall. Unfortunately for him, and contrary to the detailed intelligence report on the house, the window had a metal grill. The grenade bounced back and exploded, catching the ammunition on his chest webbing. After another raider was killed and one went missing, the commandos escaped, leaving, unusually, one SADF body. FRELIMO blamed this audacious raid on information supplied by CIA agents in their general staff. Actually, the raid had all the hallmarks of the daring Rhodesian incursions that also deployed Mozambican vehicles during the 1976-79 period. This was not surprising. Rob Hutchinson, the missing man, later announced dead, was a former member of the Rhodesian SAS and before that the Royal Marines. Most of his companions were ex-Rhodesian SAS too. According to Colonel (now Commandant) Garth Barrett, the unit's commanding officer, the SAS taught the Recces 'all they knew' about 'externals' (cross-border raids). The ex-SAS comprised the spearhead of this first Israeli-type raid on Mozambique. The Rhodesian connection extended further: the information about Zimbabwean troop movements in Mozambique and FRELIMO intelligence in general was leaked via South African agents in Zimbabwe's special branch and the CIO, which had retained some of the key personnel from the UDI period. Most of the white security experts in Zimbabwe were loyal to the new Mugabe government, yet such were the snakes and ladders of southern African sabotage that the ex-Rhodesians on one side of the fence were able to provide intelligence for their ex-countrymen in the service of the SADF. This was particularly true of RENAMO intelligence and counter-intelligence.

The Matola raid (officially Operation BEANBAG) was 6 Recce's first and last operation. It had been a success, despite the loss of three soldiers and one body left. Some key MK personnel had been killed and captured and the raid had narrowly missed hitting the MK chief of staff, Joe Slovo. The surprise attack on the outskirts of the capital caused uproar in FRELIMO and internationally. A number of the local FRELIMO commanders who had not reacted quickly enough were sent to re-education camps and others disappeared. The East Germans, whom Machel trusted, had persuaded him that the raid was a result of heavy CIA penetration in Mozambique. There was a big shake-up in FRELIMO's counter-intelligence operations in the search for alleged CIA agents (although some of the key reconnaissance had been done by a white ex-Rhodesian and former SAS member living in Maputo). FRELIMO's efficient propaganda machine went into top gear and showed (fabricated) pictures of various abandoned SADF steel helmets with swastikas painted on them. The raiders were accused of slicing off the ears of the MK dead. Maputo's *Tempo* magazine compared the barbaric methods of the South Africans with that of the Nazis or the US Army in Vietnam.

The raid, however, had further disillusioned many top SAS operators. The first version of BEANBAG had been aborted after the convoy crossed from Koomatiport at night. The vehicles broke down and the radios failed at the start of the bundu-bashing before the tarred roads. The op was delayed for two months. Commandant Barrett was incensed that two of the South African doctors in his unit refused to cross the border. Another (and only) doctor on the op had volunteered. The Rhodesians had a reputation for high levels of front-line medical support; the South Africans were by comparison deficient. The second attack was delayed by a last-minute prayer meeting by an Afrikaner padre. Barrett was incensed. Not only did it delay the operation by more than a (crucial) half-hour but the thirty-minute sermon was extremely denigrating about black soldiers, despite the fact that Barrett's command included three black Portuguese-speaking operators. True, the raid included a typical bit of Rhodesiana; the mascot dog which joined the raid was called P.W. Botha. One of the team, a driver who claimed to have Rhodesian army experience, was an imposter. He had acute shellshock and had to be restrained when the fighting began. Even one of the experienced ex-SAS trooper 'lost it' on the way back, and threw some of the equipment out of the truck, when the convoy refused to turn around to go back for the missing trooper (even though he was presumed dead); in Rhodesia the SAS protocol was never to abandon one of their own, dead or alive, on the battlefield. The Rhodesian military experience had been useful to the SADF both in special forces' training and in building up the SWATF, but too often the old Anglo-Afrikaner differences would flare up. So often was the Boer war refought – even in the 1980s.

Other SADF raids ensued. Three were launched before the second SADCC annual conference on 19/20 November 1981 in Malawi's commercial capital of Blantyre. All were aimed at the railways and port facilities servicing landlocked Malawi. This was a general warning to the SADCC and Malawi's membership of it in particular. One of the raids was a failure. On 14 October a FRELIMO patrol came across a group laying mines on the Beira-Umtali (Mutare) railway. During the firefight a mine exploded, killing the saboteurs. One of them was later identified as Alan Gingles, a Sandhurst-trained soldier who had joined the Selous Scouts and subsequently enlisted with the SADF. Two weeks later two vital bridges over the Pungwe river were blown up. The bridge carrying the road and oil pipeline was destroyed and the one carrying the railway was damaged. All traffic between Zimbabwe and Beira was cut and the Recce Commandos were blamed. The bridges were expertly sabotaged, so it probably was the work of the SADF. The rule of thumb in such matters in intelligence circles was that if the job was botched, it was RENAMO; if it was done properly, it was the Recces.

On 7 December 1981 the ex-SAS/Recce backing for RENAMO could not prevent FRELIMO forces over-running the Garagua HQ. It was almost deserted, however, as informers inside FRELIMO had tipped off the rebel leadership. Nevertheless, RENAMO activity expanded elsewhere. In February 1982 Machel toured Inhambane and Gaza provinces to try to raise morale and to encourage the peasantry to oppose the rebels. But within weeks some of the areas were inaccessible to FRELIMO. In the early 1980s much of the territory held by RENAMO was in relatively uninhabited parts of the country but the rebels could still interdict road and rail. Authorities on Mozambique such as Joseph Hanlon insisted that there were no attempts to set up classic 'liberated zones'.[8] This was true of the early 1980s but gradually, as rebel influence spread, a crude infrastructure of sorts was developed with primitive schools, clinics and barter trade. In my travels cross-country for hundreds of miles on foot and motorbike in a number of provinces, I witnessed these zones in 1986. A pattern was established, dictated often by weather: insurgent gains during the rainy season were followed by dry-season government counter-offensives. Towns were won and then lost again.

Nonetheless, RENAMO's emphasis – no doubt with Pretoria's prodding – was on military action. And yet some of the targets appeared to contradict South African interests. The rebels destroyed electricity pylons from the Cahora Bassa project. This caused supply problems in the Transvaal even though Mozambique contributed less than 12 per cent of South Africa's supply. RENAMO claimed that this demonstrated its independence of Pretoria, though it may simply have been a SAMI cock-up.

A second contradiction was Malawi's entanglement with RENAMO. During the 1980s and increasingly in the early 1990s there was no doubt that various elements in the Malawian army and intelligence service supported RENAMO. (They also helped me to gain covert access to rebel bases in Mozambique.) The CIA also used Malawi as a conduit to its limited relations with the rebels. How much the ageing dictator, Hastings Banda, knew is uncertain. Like General Pinochet in Chile, Banda was an absolute dictator who claimed to know where very leaf fell. Banda was a paranoid mix of his three lives: peasant, Europeanized doctor and then 'king'. Many of his authoritarian foibles were Ruritanian or puritanical (he banned short skirts on women and long hair on men) but he liked to keep on good terms with Britain, his home for many years, and the Church of Scotland, his spiritual home, as well as South Africa, because he didn't think much of nearly all other black politicians. So it was strange that RENAMO was hitting road and rail links with Malawi, which had good diplomatic relations with Pretoria. Various rationalizations were offered at the time. The simplest was that Pretoria was using RENAMO attacks to remind an increasingly eccentric and gaga Banda that his membership of SADCC would carry penalties. That would not explain why some Malawian security officials helped the rebels. Strong cultural/tribal ties persisted between the rebels in Zambézi and Tete provinces and southern Malawian communities. Another rationalization was that Pretoria manipulated its economic leverage over Malawi to force Banda to provide sanctuary to RENAMO guerrillas in southern Malawi. An even more convoluted theory was that Banda supported the notion of a separate 'Rombezia', an area from the Ruvuma river, the northern Mozambique border with Tanzania, to the Zambezi. Jorge Jardim, formerly the Mozambican consul in Malawi, apparently encouraged Banda in this madcap scheme. In the early 1960s Banda had tried to persuade Julius Nyerere that much of the Rombezia area was historically a part of greater Malawi (with a slice donated to Tanzania). Elements in RENAMO had originally advocated such separatist tribal designs. So Banda's quirky territorial ambitions might well have partially explained the paradoxes. Whatever the inspiration, the reinforced Malawian connection probably played a part in RENAMO's August 1982 offensive. The insurgents consolidated their position in Zambézia and Gaza provinces. RENAMO sources stressed the agreement on 15 August with Jimo Phiri, the leader of a small anti-FRELIMO guerrilla group called *Africa Livre*, which had ties with Malawi. (Phiri later opted out of the RENAMO embrace.)

RENAMO claimed 1,500 military engagements in 1982, including a spectacular assault on Beira harbour on 9 December. In fact the Recce Commandos blew up the oil storage tanks with limpet mines after landing by sea. Damage was estimated to be at least £10 million. An immediate fuel crisis hit Zimbabwe. The government-controlled South African TV service revelled in showing extended lines of frustrated Zimbabwean motorists pushing their cars in miles-long queues at petrol stations. Earlier in the year, on 17 August, South African agents were blamed for the assassination of a well-known anti-apartheid author and academic, Ruth First, the wife of Joe Slovo, the South African Communist Party leader. She was killed by a parcel bomb in her office at Eduardo Mondlane University.

On 23 May 1983, in retaliation for the devastating ANC car-bomb explosion in central Pretoria, SAAF jets bombed Matola and Liberdade suburbs of Maputo. FRELIMO asserted that the victims were three workers in an innocent jam factory, a soldier guarding a bridge, a child playing and an ANC man cleaning his car. The SADF counter-claimed that forty-one ANC, seventeen Mozambican soldiers and six civilians had been killed. The SAAF was embarrassed by reports from Western journalists who had inspected the jam factory. Pretoria's version was that, except for a Mozambican SAM-3 missile site, the jets hit carefully chosen ANC facilities. The SAAF had limited the strike to rockets and cannonfire because bombs were felt to be too inaccurate. Impala Mk IIs were deployed because, being slower, they could be more accurate than the more advanced Mirages.

While the SADF, almost unopposed, flaunted its military superiority in the skies above Mozambique, on the ground FRELIMO launched a number of successful counter-offensives against RENAMO, especially in the southern Gaza and Maputo provinces. Captured rebels were regularly paraded and publicly executed. In late 1983 RENAMO conducted its own series of offensives. One, Operation BLACK SEPTEMBER, led to the capture of twenty-four Soviet technicians in Morrua in Zambésia. By the end of 1983, RENAMO claimed that its 'zone of active operations' – not control – extended throughout Mozambique, except for the two northernmost provinces (Niassa and Cabo Delgado), western Tete and southern Maputo.

SADF air raids, captured Soviet personnel and RENAMO's creeping domination of the rural areas left the Russians in an awkward position as guardians of FRELIMO's revolution. Pretoria's destabilization posed a serious test for Soviet prestige and resolve. Moscow sent some of its top generals to review the situation in Mozambique and Soviet warships docked at Maputo to wave the red flag. After the Matola commando raid, the Soviet ambassador to Mozambique warned Pretoria that the USSR would come to the aid of FRELIMO if the SADF interventions continued. The introduction of Cuban troops was mooted, a suggestion that drew a counter-warning to Maputo from the US state department. But nobody wanted the 'Angolanization' of the Mozambique war, especially the Russians. Moscow was bluffing because its interests in Mozambique were limited. Except for the MiG-21s, Mi-24 gunships and SAM-7s, Soviet weaponry sent to Mozambique was out of date. FRELIMO had noticed this. And there was growing dissatisfaction with the quality of the socialist bloc advisers. The East Germans were good at tapping phones but they could not stop RENAMO. Soviet economic aid, and especially during the calamitous 1983 famine, was deemed by FRELIMO to be totally inadequate.

To survive, Machel needed better allies. In April 1982 Mozambique had signed a treaty of military co-operation with Portugal. The old enemy returned to help train elite sections of the Mozambican army. Zimbabwe and later the UK agreed to provide officer training for the army. In a direct slight to the East Germans, Maputo recognized West German's rights in West Berlin partly in exchange for a food aid agreement. This opened the door to additional aid from the European Economic Community. In 1984 Mozambique renewed links with China and joined the IMF and World Bank. All of these steps seemed to justify the US state department's 'weaning theory': Western aid would seduce Machel away from the Russian embrace. The Western press started to print, possibly apocryphal, stories of Machel's growing distaste for the Russians. During a tour of development projects in Mozambique, Machel was told that one section was being built by the Russians, another by the East Germans and Romanians. 'But the only trouble is,' Machel is reported as saying, 'they all want to be paid in US dollars.'[9] RENAMO's right-wing adherents in the US, most notably in the Heritage Foundation, argued that the weaning theory was nonsense: that FRELIMO was irremediably Marxist. Aid should be given to anti-Marxist rebels as part of the Reagan doctrine, they said. Nevertheless, Mozambique did take steps to dismantle the most negative aspects of its Soviet-inspired economy, allowing a measure of decentralization in agriculture and economic planning. Foreign investment was encouraged, although few takers came forward because of the war and FRELIMO's bureaucratic inertia.

In October 1983 Machel toured Western Europe. He was hungry for Western investment. In London he reportedly had a secret meeting with Anglo-American's chairman, Harry Oppenheimer. Later, Machel had a highly publicized meeting with Lonrho's Tiny Rowland. Rowland was a big man in many ways – especially in Africa. Rowland was born Roland Walter Fuhrhop in 1917 during the First World War in a British internment camp for aliens outside Calcutta. Despite his family's (and his) internment in both world wars, Rowland ended up a friend of MI6 as well as a notorious corporate raider, media magnate and good friend of African politicians, from Nkomo to Mandela. Rowland agreed to fund various projects in Mozambique, some of which required the protection of private security firms that were not unconnected with British intelligence. Washington boosted its famine relief although military aid was blocked by congressional conservatives. Machel indeed looked like changing horses in mid-gallop.

It was Pretoria's sword, not Western food, that made Machel put on the mantle of a born-again capitalist. His economy was in absolute chaos. On top of war, drought and floods, Pretoria had tightened its economic blockade. Foreign exchange earnings had dwindled partly because South African trade through Maputo in 1983 was down to 16 per cent of its 1973 levels. This was partly because of the derelict state of the harbour and partly because of economic blackmail. Legal migrant workers had been reduced from 118,000 in 1975 to 45,000. In short, no amount

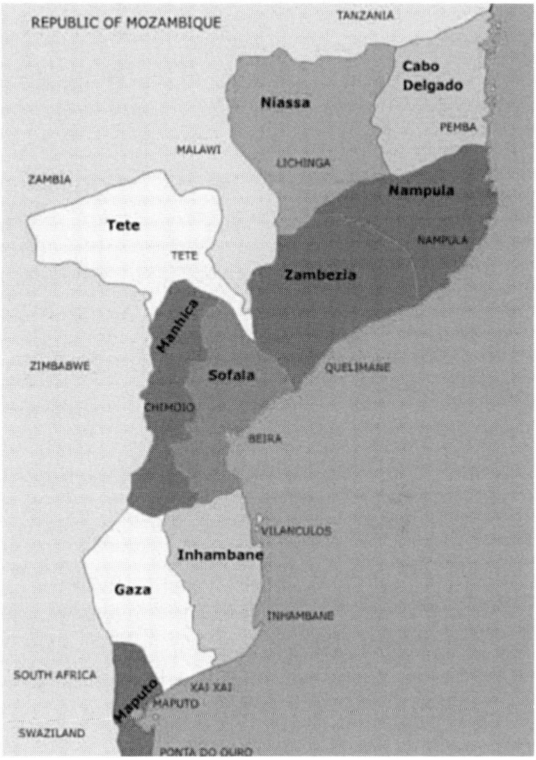


Provinces of Mozambique

of Western or Eastern charity could compare with benefits of the release from Pretoria's stranglehold.

It all depended upon what Pretoria really wanted. The complex debate within the security establishment boiled down to the 'minimalists', who thought that destabilization could change Mozambique's political behaviour, and the 'maximalists', who believed that the time was right to overthrow the FRELIMO government. In support of the maximalist view, Zimbabwean intelligence had presented a secret report to Mugabe which argued that Pretoria was capable of toppling Machel in forty-eight hours. Pretoria soon had eyes on the report. Magnus Malan explicitly warned that South Africa might find it necessary to initiate a replay of Israel's recent invasion of Lebanon to get rid of ANC 'terrorists'. Yet the minimalists on the State Security Council asked what RENAMO could do in Maputo if Machel fell. The minimalists, led as ever by Pik Botha, doubted whether RENAMO 'had the capacity to run anything more than a Mercedes and a few atrocities'.[10] The foreign minister was attempting to draw FRELIMO into a formal pact with Pretoria but he complained that 'South African military intelligence was a trickier negotiating opponent than the

FRELIMO Marxists'. The debate within the SSC grew red hot. At the same time the RENAMO secretary-general, Orlando Cristina, was assassinated in April 1983 at a 'farm' near Pretoria. It was probably a training centre for the rebels. The official statement talked of 'an unknown gunman', but the versions varied from enemies within RENAMO to FRELIMO secret police or even SAMI action. Evo Fernandes, who took over, was said to be hostile to a pact with FRELIMO. Washington was decidedly not. Chester Crocker became directly involved with the SSC debate. When Magnus Malan was presented in the SSC with the American-sponsored outline of a Maputo-Pretoria pact, he is reported to have said 'This piece of paper is not worth my signature.' The final decision on a treaty with Machel was clinched when the Americans persuaded the chief of police, Johan Coetzee, the former head of the security branch, that FRELIMO would be made to stick to an agreement to eject the ANC. Coetzee's conversion swayed a sceptical P.W. Botha.

After some haggling with Maputo, the two heads of state met in almost a circus atmosphere alongside the Nkomati river on 16 March 1984. With cameras whirring, 1,500 guests lunched sumptuously along the white VIP railways carriages that had been used for the abortive Rhodesian conference at Victoria Falls nine years earlier. Behind the polite, if bizarre, *coup de theatre* stood the simple truth: Pretoria had put a gun to the desperate Machel's temple, and said, 'Kick out the ANC, or else'. Or as Joseph Hanlon put it at the time, 'FRELIMO was screaming, "Of course, I love you, just don't hit me again."'

The Nkomati accord, signed on 16 March 1984

Both sides pledged to curtail the activities of their protégés, the ANC and RENAMO – without naming them. A joint security commission was established to monitor the agreement. Nkomati was a victory for Pretoria and a clear defeat for the front-line states, as well as the anti-apartheid activists worldwide. The apartheid chieftain had sat down over lunch with the Marxist Machel, so surely now it was OK to trade or play rugby and cricket. Pretoria had broken out of its diplomatic quarantine and the ANC – and MK – were unceremoniously turfed out of Mozambique (except for a small political representation). The ANC leadership was shattered at the abrupt, almost brutal, way its comrades had been booted out. Oliver Tambo, the ANC president, somehow managed to sound a conciliatory note at a press conference in London:

> The South African regime had decided to destroy Mozambique, to kill it as a state, and the [FRELIMO] leadership was forced to decide between life and death. So if it meant hugging the hyena, they had to do it.

Moscow reacted very coolly to the hyena's triumph. The front-line states, while sympathizing with Machel's dilemma, were outraged by the success of Pretoria's blatant blackmail. Machel put on a brave face and prayed, no doubt, that the shame of Nkomati would at least buy him a breathing space. And it all depended on whether the Afrikaners would keep their word. Some did and some did not.

The old divisions surfaced after the temporary façade of Nkomati bonhomie. According to RENAMO sources, the head of military intelligence, General van der Westhuizen, against the express wishes of both Pik Botha and Chester Crocker, had ordered a massive re-supply of military equipment for the rebels just before the Nkomati signing. Much of this golden handshake was Soviet weaponry captured in SADF raids on SWAPO camps in Angola. Some was dropped by air near the Gorongosa base. This assistance was supposed to keep RENAMO going for at least six months' fighting. After Nkomati, however, RENAMO maintained that all aid from South Africa stopped, except that Colonel van Niekerk still faithfully remained at his liaison post. The Voice of Free Africa was stilled, however. Trying to put a bold face on things, RENAMO spokesmen said that it would now prove conclusively that the movement could wage war without holding hands with the SADF. Privately, Dhlakama was incensed about the way Pretoria had behaved. The RENAMO president told me personally that he was informed about Nkomati less than a week before it was signed. And yet supplies continued to reach RENAMO after Nkomati, according to captured documents.

These documents (essentially three diaries and files of military papers) were captured by FRELIMO from the rebel Gorongosa HQ in August 1985. They revealed a serious rift within the South African security establishment. Although RENAMO protested that the documents were forged, there is little doubt that they were essentially genuine. General van der Westhuizen is quoted in the Gorongosa documents as saying: 'We, the military, will continue to give them [RENAMO] support without the consent of our politicians in a massive way so that they can win the war.' The whole South African cast appears in the documents but the most frequently mentioned is Colonel van Niekerk ('friend Commander Charlie'). The documents indicated the SADF bugged private conversations between the 'treacherous' Pik Botha and FRELIMO officials. Obviously the foreign ministry was totally at odds with the hardliners in military intelligence.

The Gorongosa papers indicated that at a very high level – although P.W. Botha's position was studiously ambiguous – the SADF kept the supply lifeline open long *after* the Nkomati deal. FRELIMO appeared to have kept its side of the bargain. The ANC's military wing, *Umkhonto we Sizwe,* did shut up shop in Mozambique. Like RENAMO, the ANC suffered only a temporary setback. By 1985 both insurgencies were more active than before Nkomati. Pretoria said that although the ANC had sought new infiltration routes, Mozambique was still being used. In sum, both signatories breached the 1984 agreement but Pretoria's transgressions were greater and more calculated.

Before Nkomati the SAAF would use their C-130 Hercules aircraft – although they were deemed too large and vulnerable to land. Afterwards, military intelligence would hire smaller civilian aircraft such as the reliable old Daks, flying out of Wonderboom airport north of Pretoria. Frama Inter Trading Company, later known as Wonder Air, was usefully deniable for the government.

Boosted by the continuous logistical support, RENAMO went on the offensive. The rebels were credited with blowing up Maputo's power station, one month after Nkomati. The capital was without electricity for a week. The rebels pushed into the north of the country for the first time, where cordial ties were established with the largely Muslim tribe, the Macondes. They had once formed the bulk of the FRELIMO force before independence but they had become alienated by the government's religious intolerance. The Muslim factor was to prove invaluable later in building up RENAMO's international links. By the end of 1984 the movement claimed over 15,000 troops whose 'zone of operations' spread through all ten provinces while it had 'consolidated control' over all the rural areas in seven provinces.

With South African help, RENAMO started to build up an international network of right-wing allies. Besides its military constituency and revanchist sympathy among the 600,000 to 700,000 members of South Africa's Portuguese community (amounting to perhaps 15 per cent of the registered white electorate) sections of both the government and military in Portugal had links with the rebels. RENAMO had friends in high places in Bavarian politics and somewhat superficially the CIA. Rumours circulated that some of the Irangate money during the Reagan presidency had trickled both into UNITA *and* RENAMO. Intelligence information, in some cases deliberately leaked by Pretoria, indicated that Saudi Arabia and some other moderate Islamic states, such as Oman and the United Arab Emirates, plus other members of the so-called 'Safari Club', originally put together by King Hassan of Morocco to help Savimbi, provided some money to RENAMO. The Muslim funds channelled by ex-Rhodesian sanctions-busting firms and ex-CIO executives in Holland bought weapons (and other supplies) on the European arms market and passed them down the ancient Arab trade route from Oman, Somalia and Zanzibar to the Mozambique coast. The Comoro islands, just 190 miles off the northern coast of Mozambique, had close ties with Pretoria after mercenaries, with Rhodesian help, overthrew the government in 1978 and restored as president a pliant conservative, Ahmed Abdallah. Many of the RENAMO air supplies were said to come from these islands. And, elsewhere in Africa, Zaire was not unfriendly and a RENAMO representative was established in Kenya. Pretoria helped RENAMO officials to travel by providing excellent forgeries of Swazi and Kenyan passports.

RENAMO was stronger inside Mozambique and it had made its first tentative steps towards international recognition. For the rebels' allies in Pretoria it was time to take the next logical step: to persuade FRELIMO to recognize RENAMO. Mozambican government officials met secretly with Evo Fernandes in May 1984 in Frankfurt. In June and July Pik Botha and General van der Westhuizen talked to FRELIMO officials in Maputo. From 1 to 3 October the Mozambican government delegation met face-to-face with RENAMO, led by Fernandes. (Dhlakama was also in Pretoria, but apparently took a back seat.) The 'Pretoria Declaration' called for a ceasefire and a tripartite commission, with the SADF, to monitor it. In its view, Pretoria had secured, a second, albeit minor, diplomatic victory by forcing FRELIMO to implicitly recognize the rebels, not least by meeting them around a conference table. The ceasefire was supposed to lead to a political settlement. Neither materialized, however. Possibly manipulated by hardline revanchists in Portugal, Fernandes adopted a tough, even arrogant, stance towards FRELIMO. The rebels demanded a power-sharing arrangement with Maputo, while FRELIMO conceded only an amnesty for those who surrendered. But why accept an amnesty, if RENAMO was increasingly more confident of actually *winning* the war?

Pik Botha was bitter at the failure of the Pretoria summit. In particular, he blamed the revanchists in the Portuguese government and intelligence community who were hostile to FRELIMO because of the seizure of Portuguese property, as well as ideological reservations. The foreign minister was stonewalled by Lisbon when he complained but a clampdown on Portuguese activists inside South Africa was ordered. In December 1984 Pik Botha flew secretly to Malawi, Somalia and the Comores in an attempt to stamp out pro-RENAMO sentiments. President Botha, meanwhile, had made the SADF chief, Constand Viljoen, personally responsible for clamping down on dissident pro-RENAMO elements within the army and especially in military intelligence. Viljoen acted swiftly. Although none of the senior officers implicated were touched, some of the lower ranks were shifted sideways, posted away from Phalaborwa or dismissed. RENAMO's liaison officer in Pretoria was literally locked out of his office. The US state department applauded these gestures but they wanted more: for Pretoria not only to rein in RENAMO but actually provide military aid to FRELIMO. Was Washington suggesting, in particular, that SADF regular troops should assist Machel? Did Chester Crocker want to make the SADF 'his Cubans'? With some scorn the South African top brass pointed out that while America was maintaining an arms embargo, the SADF was unlikely to act as a cat's paw for Washington. Operations in Mozambique would have required, especially, the deployment of large helicopters, and South Africa was desperately short of these. In the end, the SADF was prevailed upon to provide £1 million in vehicles and radio equipment for FRELIMO.

Thus Pretoria found itself aiding both sides in the civil war. Cynically, that could have maximized chaos. Yet there was also genuine assistance when South African experts regularly repaired communications infrastructure ravaged by RENAMO action. The radios donated to FRELIMO also made sense: it could facilitate a ceasefire and, if that meant a political advance for RENAMO, it was a bonus for Pretoria. Playing both sides against the centre was not the deal struck at Nkomati, however. By early 1985 Machel had realized that the Afrikaners were acting in bad faith. The resurgent RENAMO was, to quote a senior FRELIMO official, 'unpicking the social fabric'. FRELIMO held the cities but, throughout the country, RENAMO owned the night.

Machel turned to his neighbours. The Tanzanians offered to send troops. In July 1985 Britain granted funds to enlarge the officer training scheme at Nyanga, Zimbabwe, to include Mozambicans. The Zimbabwe National Army (ZNA) expeditionary force in Mozambique had mushroomed from 1,500 in mid-1984 to 12,000 in 1985. That figure soared to perhaps 18,000 during major offensives. Even to some supporters in Pretoria, the RENAMO war was getting out of hand. The tame beast had become viciously uncontrollable. In March 1985 a 'Mafia-style syndicate' was unearthed in the Portuguese community in Johannesburg, according to media reports. It had been allegedly smuggling money and supplies to the rebels. Acting on Mozambican information, the army found a 'dozen' SADF pro-RENAMO members who were 'purged'. At least that was the official version.

On 28 August 1985 Zimbabwean paratroopers, backed by Mozambican troops, stormed into the RENAMO main HQ, 'Casa Banana', at Gorongosa. RENAMO sources said that, facing a heli-borne assault by 12,000 ZNA and 8,000 FRELIMO, they had retreated in good order, with small losses. Two of the Soviet officers who had co-ordinated the assault were killed, RENAMO claimed. Left behind, however, apparently thrown down a latrine, were the diaries of Major Joaquim

Vaz, secretary to Dhlakama. On 16 September, Machel told Pik Botha in Maputo about the diaries. The Afrikaner was reported to be furious when he found out that he had been called 'treacherous' by General Viljoen and that the SADF were still bugging his conversations. Two weeks later, to coincide with Machel's surprisingly warm welcome by President Reagan in the White House, some of the captured documents were made public by Colonel Sergio Vieira, the minister of security, at a press conference in Maputo. It was all there in telling detail: weapon supplies, Pretoria's economic targets in Mozambique, the SADF's construction of an airstrip at Casa Banana, submarines picking up RENAMO VIPs, and the record of three visits by deputy foreign minister, Louis Nel, *without* the knowledge of his boss, Pik Botha. That really set the cat among the pigeons in Pretoria. As Mozambique-watcher Joseph Hanlon observed, 'There can be no stronger indication of continued high-level support for a surrogate army than for a deputy foreign minister to illegally enter a foreign country to talk to that army's leader.'[11] The strains between the department of foreign affairs and the SADF and their respective supporters in the cabinet and in the SSC reached breaking point. Viljoen and Pik Botha gave contradictory press conferences. Eventually a compromise line was formulated: yes, there had been 'technical' violations of Nkomati, but – no, no – destabilization was not intended. What Louis Nel had been trying to do was to set up a 'Camp David-style' settlement but the army did not want to tell Pik Botha in case the foreign minister would not let his deputy go to the RENAMO HQ as it would have been deemed too dangerous. That took some swallowing – even in Pretoria.

And, once again, where did the president stand? He was, without question, an authoritarian figure and the military was his main constituency. Could he really have been unaware of the military shenanigans? Yet he had committed himself publicly to Nkomati, the touchstone of his regional foreign policy initiatives in 1984. Some of the hawks who had conspired to continue RENAMO's alliance were promoted, not punished. Van der Westhuizen, for example, was moved up to the powerful position of secretary of the SSC.

The captured RENAMO documents had highlighted the in-house squabbles among the Afrikaner leadership. They had also given the diplomatic initiative to Maputo, leaving Pretoria back in the dock of world opprobrium. That was the moral position; the military position was different. Despite the presence of 12,000 ZNA troops and 2,000 Tanzanians (and the promise of 5,000 Nigerians) the FRELIMO armed forces in the countryside started to disintegrate. Some were FRELIMO by day and RENAMO by night. RENAMO held, or ran riot in, vast swathes of territory while FRELIMO dug in in the cities. And even the few major cities were more scrapheaps than modern conurbations. Alistair Sparks, the veteran South African writer, and not unsympathetic to Mozambique's plight, noted in 1986 that Beira was a 'city of 300,000 people with no electricity, water, telephones,

FRELIMO PoWs in Caia, captured by RENAMO in the 1986 offensive. Not well fed, but not badly treated, they told me. (Author picture)

food or goods in the shops'.[12] Adopting classic Maoist tenets, RENAMO hoped that once the rural areas were fully consolidated, the FRELIMO-held cities would fall like the proverbial ripe plums. Such was the economic collapse and FRELIMO's poor military performance that by 1986 Mozambique could hardly be called a state any more.

This boded well for RENAMO; 1986 had been a good year for the rebels. On 14 February the Gorongosa HQ was recaptured. In October the movement launched its biggest offensive to date. For the first time it seized and held towns in Zambézia, Tete and Sofala provinces. It seemed that RENAMO was trying to dominate the central provinces in order to divide the country in two and to gain permanent access to the sea. In one of the large captured towns, such as Caia in Sofala province, RENAMO could have proclaimed a provisional government. If the town was not recaptured, probably by Zimbabwean forces, that could have boosted the rebels' drive for international recognition.

Pretoria continued to administer the usual medicine. In early October Pretoria announced that all the estimated 70,000 legal Mozambican workers (nearly all miners) would be forced to leave when their current labour contracts expired. The ejection of these legals (and perhaps as many as 140,000 illegal workers) would cost Maputo at least £25 million per annum in lost foreign exchange earnings. This indicated South Africa's determination to retaliate against Western sanctions by punishing its neighbours, even those, like Mozambique, that were too weak to vote for them in world bodies. The move was also intended as a warning to Maputo about ANC activity in the country. Six SADF personnel had just been injured in a landmine explosion inside the republic but next to the Mozambique border. This time it was economic jabs, not jets.

At the same time Mugabe and Machel exerted pressure on President Banda to cut his links with RENAMO. Regional media, all fed by one source, the official Mozambican news agency, was full of largely inaccurate, or, at best, simplistic stories that Banda had caved in to front-line diktat and had pushed 10,000

RENAMO insurgents out of southern Malawian bases, which had been staffed by South African (and even Israeli) advisers. And, *voilà*, the October offensive. RENAMO, however, had secure bases aplenty in Mozambique; they simply did not need such military sanctuaries inside Malawi. Nor was Banda a man to be dictated to. It seemed more likely that Banda had refused 'the offer he could not refuse' (presumably with Pretoria's advice). On 19 October a Soviet-crewed Tu-134 jet, with Machel and other FRELIMO VIPs on board, crashed on South African territory. In the wreckage, the South African police found evidence, they said, that Machel and Mugabe were planning an internal coup against Banda. RENAMO hung on to its Malawian connection.

Joaquim Chissano, the 47-year-old foreign minister, was elected to replace Machel in FRELIMO's darkest hour since independence. The tall, slim, elegantly-dressed Chissano was a sharp physical contrast to the short, rough-and-ready Machel. He was as collected as Machel was turbulent. As Chissano assumed the presidency, the war was lapping around the edges of the capital.

## *November 1986: a cameo of the war*

The Mozambican civil war was not a media event. The FRELIMO government did not offer much freedom to report from its side, and the sheer inaccessibility of the guerrillas, poor international connections and their bloodthirsty image discouraged reportage from their side. Nevertheless, in November 1986, I and a former policeman who spoke Shona, travelled hundreds of miles, on foot, in dug-out canoes and on captured FRELIMO motorbikes through RENAMO-controlled provinces in central Mozambique. The main purpose was to conduct the first TV interview with Afonso Dhlakama at his Gorongosa HQ. I quote verbatim from my contemporary diary to give a first-hand impression of what the country was like. We entered covertly from Malawi.

> *The entry: dug-out canoes wobbling through swamps. Hippos grunt. Then a long march, sometimes waist-deep in water. A kingfisher darts down to seize a fish and lily-trotters hop dementedly. Drier land. Eventually contact with a RENAMO agent. Expectations of Khmer Rouge. Instead a genial figure in blue jeans, a purple tea-cosy hat and clean check shirt. His jeans are tucked into his socks as he pushes a bicycle along the bush path, while carrying the ubiquitous symbol of RENAMO rank, a transistor radio in a gaudy bag, made of curtain material. Unlike the smartly dressed officers in Savimbi's 'Free Angola', the man in the tea-cosy does not want to stamp any passports.*
>
> *A small transit camp. Our communication is in basic Portuguese and broken Shona. Fed ground corn (sadza) and chicken, three times a day, the same food precisely for weeks, except for captured FRELIMO canned food, usually Russian fish and tinned Australian cheese. The insurgents operate a*

*hand-cranked generator for their communications, probably an old Mortley-Sprague but difficult to get near radio hut. The defensive lay-out of the base is exactly the same as the ZANLA camps of the 1970s.*

*A signal is sent to the main RENAMO base in Zambézia province. It is 40 miles away, well-hidden among mountains and forest. It holds abut 500 ragged troops and perhaps two to three thousand camp followers (as well as a much bigger army of rats). The camp is made of wood and thatch, with bits of looted furniture indecorously adorning the primitive style. I had just visited UNITA's Jamba HQ, the Las Vegas of guerrilla bases. But this is very crude. With one generator occasionally providing power. The base has a small clinic with virtually no medicines; the top motorbike mechanic doubles as the doctor. Nearby there is a school, where the teacher has one book, a FRELIMO textbook, with pages containing Marxist propaganda torn out. The camp commandant and rebel governor of the province is Commander General Calistu Meque, a dangerous eccentric. His whimsically autocratic manners are reminiscent of Shaka Zulu's not-so-gentle court. We are told about the reasons for RENAMO's fight. There are complaints about harassment of religion and traditional chiefs, and forced communization of the land. They talk too of free elections and the end of Marxist tyranny. But this is also Shona territory. The old ways, the spirit mediums, the need for polygamy, and lobola (bride price) are also discussed.*

*The insurgents are clearly under formal discipline. The worst infringement of the code is to intimidate the povo, the peasantry. Most guerrilla armies have similar codes. This one is similar to ZANLA's and that was breached as much as it was observed. Male soldiers are not supposed to smoke or fraternize with the large number of female cadres in the camp. Both sexes volunteer, or are press-ganged, for the 'duration'. Morale appears high but military standards are decidedly low. The rebels wear rags; the officers wear a bizarre array of Rhodesian, East German, Tanzanian, Zimbabwean, Portuguese and FRELIMO camouflage dress. Weapons are generally in a terrible condition, rarely cleaned. They have Malawian or homemade beer for the officers but no oil for weapons. Some of the officers keep their AKs in good condition. These are second-generation guerrillas: FRELIMO perhaps absorbed, say, 30 per cent of the expertise of their Eastern bloc instructors during the 1960s. In turn, RENAMO soldiers, many of whose officers are ex-FRELIMO, have adapted a percentage of that original training, which has been beefed up by Rhodesian and South African advisers. During the whole journey of hundreds of miles we see, however, no direct evidence of South African involvement, except the radio network, which had been donated, apparently, before Nkomati. We see no white or black South African troops. Indeed many of the villagers seem to be astounded at the sight of our white faces.*

*The zany general puts on a weapons and training display. The rebels on parade are hardly the brigade of guards but they do not behave like unruly bandits. RENAMO rolls out for its guests a galaxy of ill-assorted hardware, ranging from old German Mausers to Russian AGS-17 grenade-launchers, which are rare in Africa. They have some SAM-7s but they do not know how to operate them. They ask us to demonstrate. Half-guests, half-hostages, we manage to politely refuse, feigning ignorance, at least in the case of my colleague, a weapons expert. Thus, the Zimbabwean gunships and the FRELIMO air force, when the latter manages to fly, are a major problem for the rebels, who have no effective defence against air attacks. Otherwise, boasts General Calistu, 'Zimbabwean troops run away just like FRELIMO when we attack them. They always call up air support.' RENAMO claims that it captures all its weapons. FRELIMO says that the rebels' arsenal is largely comprised of SADF donations of Russian weapons seized in Angola.*

*Two hundred miles south, travelling cross-country in a convoy of three small Japanese motorbikes. Two-up. The rebels drive with great speed and little skill (which is disturbing as two of the bikes lack brakes). Usually villagers rush out to greet us. They bring corn and water. We pass a religious college – people wave Bibles at us. There seems to be little starvation, although the peasants are dressed in rags, sometimes even in bark. Long columns of porters pass us, going north. They are carrying bags of ground corn on their heads for sale or barter in Malawi. This is no PR fix: we stop and go where we want (or where the bikes break down). The peasants do not appear cowed. In this raw, primitive, regressive society, there appear – on the surface – to be few local problems with hearts and minds.*

*We hop from base to base in what RENAMO calls liberated zones. We pass abandoned Portuguese stores, farms and once pretty little colonial towns, painted in light, pastel shades. Everything now is utterly deserted. A beautiful, isolated, desecrated cathedral arches towards the heavens. Blasphemous graffiti despoil the walls. On the road nearby a bright red tractor stands gutted. A derailed passenger train is strewn across an embankment. The carriages are overgrown by fast-encroaching bush. Once this part of Mozambique teemed with wildlife. We see only four deer, a few monkeys and many tree-snakes during the entire trip.*

*Then the majestic Zambezi river. A half-finished bridge stands to attention on either side. A large sub-station for the Cahorra Bassa hydro-electric scheme mourns its crippled and useless state. Bits of the transformers decorate the roofs of villagers' huts, though hardly any part of Mozambique has regular electricity. Petrol is king here. For the RENAMO*

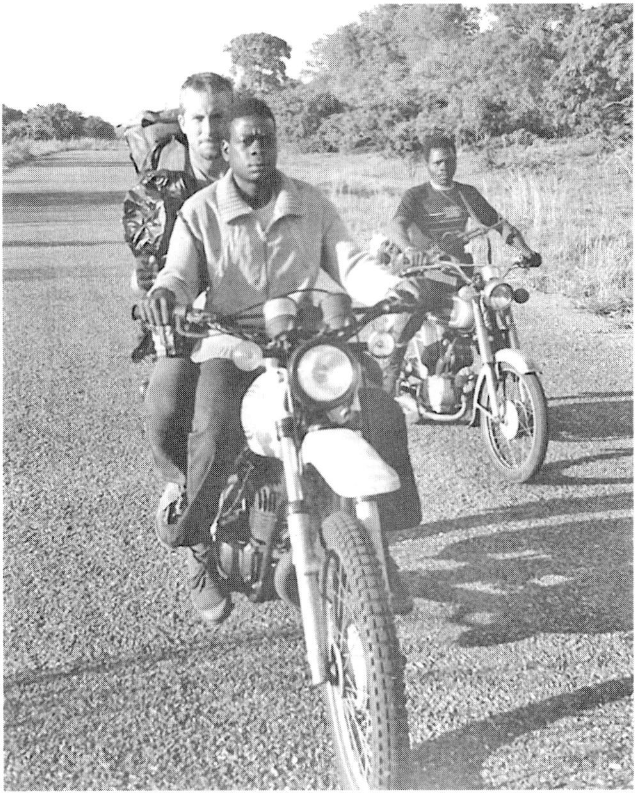

Travelling on small bikes, two up, this time on a rare bit of tarmac. Tim Lambon is cradling the camera (Author, 1986)

*elite's motorbikes and for boats to cross the wide, surging Zambezi. Everything is cannibalized to keep the few machines and motors running. 'This is something out of Mad Max,' comments my companion. On the other side of the fast-running river, crossed in a captured FRELIMO inflatable, bikes and all, are heavy plant, worth millions of pounds. Massive cranes bend, as if – in pain – they were left marooned like the Martian machines in H.G. Wells's* War of the Worlds.

*Caia, a largish small town in Sofala province. It has a big airstrip but no sign of air activity at all. The town was recently captured from FRELIMO. Caia is absolutely empty, as though giant vultures had picked clean its carcass. A child's tin rocking horse and a 1930s typewriter are the only artefacts I see left behind in the flight or pillage. It is as if a neutron bomb had been dropped. Indeed the whole of Mozambique seems to inhabit that dread feeling of a post-apocalypse film. RENAMO camps outside the town. Is this a Khmer Rouge addiction to the ideological purity of the countryside or prudent fear of Zimbabwean air force gunships? Hundreds of FRELIMO prisoners are also camped outside the town. They look hungry and miserable. RENAMO says they would be freed, after a time. Those who wanted to enlist could. None would be kept against their wishes. That seemed dubious. As did the RENAMO officers' explanation that the town had been ravaged by retreating FRELIMO troops, not the advancing RENAMO.*

*The motorbikes race now on tarmac roads in broad daylight to reach the edge of the Gorongosa forest. We camp at a satellite of the main HQ, from where RENAMO sends out its forces to disrupt the Beira Corridor. We are to meet Mozambique's Scarlet Pimpernel, Afonso Dhlakama. Is he a nationalist committed to an African variant of Western social democracy, as RENAMO propagandists imply, or the most vicious mass-murderer since Hitler, as FRELIMO insists? Is he a Mozambican patriot or a puppet of Pretoria? These thoughts pass through our minds as we are introduced to an unprepossessing, chubby-faced young man, dressed simply in a blue shirt and dark slacks. There is no Savimbi-style posturing with fancy six-guns. He is sitting quietly and alone at a plain table in a grass hut.*

*He is 33, and looks like a younger version of his arch-enemy, Robert Mugabe. Dhlakama, too, is Catholic-trained. He is a family man with three children. He is confident, quietly spoken and relaxed. Obviously intelligent, he speaks a very precise Portuguese, although he understands some English. Unlike most politicians and generals, he is prepared to listen. He discusses international affairs and he questions why everybody rates his movement as the most cut-throat of the world mafia of insurgencies. He offers us a 'Coke', the most ubiquitous capitalist symbol in Africa (although not in Mozambique) and suitable rival accompaniment to the Russian AKs that surround us.*

*The conversation goes on for two whole days. Dhlakama vehemently denies that he receives military support from Malawi or South Africa. He emphasizes in almost Maoist terms his self-sufficiency. 'We have no complex theory. Our strategy is simple. It is based on the support of the people.' He claims to control 85 per cent of the country. He denies any part in the grand scheme to destabilize southern Africa. He has no contact with UNITA, he says, and proceeds to criticize Savimbi's current overtures to FRELIMO, which followed the condolences Savimbi sent after the death of Machel.*

*'And the plane crash?' I ask.*

*'Looks like an accident to me,' says the unlikely-looking warlord.*

*The West, he maintains, particularly America, has no idea of what is really happening in Mozambique. 'The people are now independent but they are not free. Here in Mozambique everything is done by force. People are taken by force to live in communal villages, their children are sent to Cuba, without their parents' consent. We believe independence has nothing to do with this sort of thing. The ideals which drove us to take up arms against the Portuguese haven't yet been fulfilled.' He launches into a tirade against Chester Crocker and the US state department 'who have been doing a good job of promoting the cause of the Marxist FRELIMO'. He also accuses Pretoria of betraying him.*

*And what of the Vaz diaries, which said that Pretoria was still helping him? He insists they are forgeries. The RENAMO president then changes the subject.*

*RENAMO is winning, he insists. 'We are not the desperadoes, it's FRELIMO that's desperate .... All the aid money is used to buy weapons to keep them in power, not sent to those who are dying of hunger .... They spend their days watching the ports along the coast, hiding and waiting in Maputo for the arrival of a boat from the US bringing food and everything else that's necessary for the survival of FRELIMO which is surrounded in the city of Maputo. In fact, FRELIMO survives only in the big cities.' The war can be won militarily, he asserts, but paradoxically he concedes that negotiation is possible, especially if there were to be a military coup by some FRELIMO generals who are tired of fighting a no-win war.*

*The 'president' claims that he has 22,000 trained regulars, while he is also building up a part-time force which currently stands at 7,000. So RENAMO is doing well on the ground but what about its atrocious external image? 'The Marxists have traditionally been brilliant at propaganda,' he admits. He also admits to the fact that he needs to jack up RENAMO's external political representation. He adds quickly that he doesn't get money or supplies from external sources.*

*We leave Dhlakama. His off-the-record remarks seem to confirm his naivety if not his integrity. We are utterly cynical about some of his claims. But the fact remains that we saw no evidence of South African involvement and no evidence in Malawi of bases, although there were refugee camps for over 800,000 Mozambicans. After travelling for hundreds of miles, we did see basic organization and infrastructure. We saw food being grown. We witnessed no cruelty to the peasantry although RENAMO is hardly likely to stage a quick atrocity for the benefit of Western journalists and their cameras.*

*On the harsh return journey, we stay at camps where no sentries are posted. The camps lack basic defence perimeters which even a lowly SADF corporal would insist upon. The Viet Cong would have made mincemeat of this lot, we think. We conclude that RENAMO guerrillas are doing so well militarily not because they are any good but because FRELIMO is so bad. The journey to 'Free Mozambique' had been instructive but we left as sceptics, still wondering about the amazingly coincidental congruence of RENAMO's and Pretoria's strategies.*

*The Chissano era*

Joaquim Chissano, a popular choice with the party, swore that he would continue on Machel's path. Given the deteriorating military situation and limited political options, the new leader had precious little room to manoeuvre. Almost immediately, he was impelled to devalue the currency by 420 per cent to secure World Bank and IMF loans. On the diplomatic front, Chissano tried to improve the chronic relations with Malawi. In December 1986 both countries signed a security agreement. Malawi promised to stop RENAMO using its territory as a sanctuary, and to allow FRELIMO troops the right of hot pursuit inside the country. Malawian troops – about 500 by June 1987 – were sent to guard the Malawi-Nacala railway. Mugabe also obtained permission from Banda for ZNA troops to cross Malawi's territory to get at RENAMO bases in Zambézia.

The neighbourhood fences mended, Chissano ordered an immediate offensive against the rebels, despite and because of growing pressure within the military high command that talks, brokered by the Catholic Church, should be held with Dhlakama. In February and March 1987, Zimbabwean and Tanzanian forces captured the towns that RENAMO had seized in Zambézia in 1986. FRELIMO believed that RENAMO could no longer use the province as a base to declare a provisional government of 'Free Mozambique'. Maputo claimed that 2,200 rebels were wiped out in this counter-offensive. Many of the significant military gains of 1986 were eliminated by the surprisingly successful government counter-blow.

Gleams of hope punctured the dark gloom in Maputo. Western aid increased: the USA handed over food and economic assistance worth £40 million, although the pro-RENAMO right-wing forces in Washington, led by Senators Jesse Helms and Bob Dole, tried to cut all aid to Chissano. British aid was more precisely targeted at military efficiency. At the official level, 480 field-grade Mozambican officers had so far been trained by the British Army in Zimbabwe. The UK also gave £750,000 to Malawi to buy non-lethal equipment for its troops guarding the Nacala railway. Mozambican units, trained by ex-British SAS personnel at Manica, also protected the line. That was the public British connection. Various small private armies were also set up and, allegedly, paid by Lonrho and the UK government, and then supplied by Hall and Watts (Defence Sales) and in some cases trained by Defence Systems Ltd, a polite employment agency for ex-SAS soldiers. Foreign projects such as Lonrho's cotton plantations at Montechoeria needed to

President Joaquim Chissano tried to mend fences

be protected against RENAMO; otherwise foreign investment would have withered away completely. Yet it was an unflattering commentary on FRELIMO's military performance that ex-SAS men were needed to help secure these projects alongside thousands of Malawian, Tanzanian and Zimbabwean troops, plus all the hundreds of Eastern-bloc advisers still in place. The various armies did manage to keep the main routes open, most of the time, especially the Beira corridor. RENAMO hit the corridor but less often, and it was rapidly repaired, usually by Zimbabwean staff. In particular, the Lonrho-owned oil pipeline was promptly and expertly patched up after RENAMO sabotage. Nevertheless, the protection of the corridor cost much in lives and money. Fortified bunkers were built all along the route; convoys were hit frequently. Between 1981 and 1986 over 200 Zimbabwean railway workers were killed and 600 injured trying to run the RENAMO gauntlet. And, at the end of the line, Beira was still a scrapheap, not a modern port.

What was Pretoria doing about RENAMO reverses? In May 1987 the SADF was reported to have provided a 'heavy' re-supply to its secret ally. The South African Police also lent assistance. An estimated 250,000 Mozambicans had already entered the republic illegally in search of food, security and work. The

RENAMO forces marching in central Sofala province (1986, author).

desperate illegals were wonderful recruitment fodder. Arrested, usually in the eastern Transvaal, because they did not have the correct papers and, faced with the alternative of starving to death if they were forced to return home, they would be given small amounts of cash and offered an interesting job. RENAMO would not be mentioned until the luckless migrants were in a rebel training camp. Then they were threatened with death if they tried to desert.

On 19 July 1987 the massacre of nearly 400 peasants at Homoine in Inhambane province provoked another crisis in the Pretoria-Maputo détente. RENAMO was blamed but the rebels insisted that the atrocity was the work of mutinous government militiamen. RENAMO also alleged that the ZNA had established a special pseudo unit under the command of Colonel Lionel Dyck, which was raping, pillaging and murdering in the name of RENAMO. In 1986 Dhlakama had declared war on Mugabe. Partly because of the early 1987 counter-offensive by FRELIMO, some RENAMO units had taken refuge in the mountains along the Zimbabwean border. Foraging, as much as political, raids blighted the eastern Zimbabwean highlands. Other atrocities continued in Mozambique, sometimes in the same locations. Maputo continued to damn Pretoria. It looked like the final nail in the Nkomati coffin. Neither side wanted the pact to die, however. Surprisingly, the agreement was revived and even the joint security commission, defunct since 1985, was resuscitated. Lisbon was actively involved. The Portuguese government, largely bearing the burden of debt on the construction costs of the huge Cahorra Bassa scheme, hinted that South Africa's sanctions-busting centre in Portuguese territories such as Madeira and other facilities in the Azores might be in jeopardy.

Chissano's moves had been adroit. Within a few months he had stopped RENAMO's advance and repaired some of the broken fences with Malawi, South Africa and the West. He now felt confident enough to purge his armed forces of the more complacent veterans of the liberation war, some of whom were talking to RENAMO about a negotiated settlement. He appointed younger officers, loyal to himself, who were committed to defeating the rebels.

Despite the formidable array of opponents, RENAMO refused to accept Maputo's continuous amnesty offers and fought on for victory, or at least a power-sharing arrangement. Externally, its position had not improved. RENAMO still depended not only upon 'a South African father who wavers on his alimonies but a Portuguese mother who continues to nourish the unacknowledged offspring'.[13] RENAMO enthusiasts in the US and UK kept sniping at Reagan's and Thatcher's diplomatic dance with Chissano. An American conservative, writing in London's *Sunday Telegraph*, observed: 'Renamo is in fact the world's fastest-growing anti-communist insurgency. A mere 2,000 guerrillas eight years ago, it now numbers 20,000, an increase that makes it twice the size of Marxist-Leninist Frelimo when the Portuguese packed their bags in 1975.'[14]

Yet no matter how well RENAMO performed militarily, it was plagued by the South African alliance and its poor external representation. These plagues were not unrelated. Elements within RENAMO wanted to ditch Pretoria but this was opposed by Evo Fernandes. And, in Washington, the SADF versus foreign affairs ministry was mirrored by the CIA versus the state department. Some Africa experts in the CIA wanted to 'wean' RENAMO away from Pretoria, whereas Crocker's team desired a more straightforward clean-hands relationship with Maputo. Fernandes wanted to keep Pretoria close, whereas other RENAMO leaders wanted to set up a central network elsewhere, including a radio net. Washington and Lisbon were suggested. In April 1988 Fernandes was assassinated in Lisbon. The CIA, Portuguese secret police, and RENAMO opponents were all put in the frame. One elaborate conspiracy had *all* of them involved in eliminating the poor man. (Later reports suggested it was done by FRELIMO agents.) The fratricide within RENAMO was undermining the determined efforts of the ultra-right especially in the USA, largely co-ordinated by an energetic young American, Tom Schaaf, to present a credible internal front organization.

In April 1988 the Gersony report, a damning indictment of RENAMO, compounded the external activists' problems. Robert Gersony, an independent consultant, prepared the report for the US state department's bureau for refugee programmes. Taking evidence from Mozambican refugees in six countries, Gersony concluded that 100,000 innocent people had been killed and that 90 per cent of the attacks had been caused by RENAMO. The report's methodology was suspect but it still caused immense political damage to RENAMO in the USA. RENAMO called for an independent enquiry into Homoine and offered to prove that Zimbabwean gunships had strafed Red Cross centres; but no one was listening. Roy Stacy, the former US deputy assistant secretary of state for Africa, accused RENAMO of committing 'one of the worst holocausts' since the Second World War; another Western diplomat described the rebels as 'starving wolf-packs, who kill, first and foremost to eat'. Other reports emphasized the 'instrumentalized' children who had been kidnapped and programmed to kill by RENAMO. This would add to the future misery: Mozambique had just *one* trained psychiatrist for a population of 14 million. Who would help heal a traumatized generation?

RENAMO always argued that they were not assassins without faith or law. A British journalist, Nicholas della Casa, was freed by the guerrillas in December 1988, after being held captive for eighteen months. He told me: 'In my view the population of RENAMO-held areas regarded the guerrillas in much the same way as the population of Dorset regards NATO soldiers: occasional grumblings, but no real resentment.' Nick was a good friend, if a very eccentric one who had travelled with me in war zones, but this was surely masterly understatement, although he had been well-treated during his captivity. Very few commentators, however, dared to travel in RENAMO-controlled territory, but that did not stop them discussing in great detail the conditions they had never seen. The rebels said that FRELIMO's murderous incompetence and ZNA pseudo-gangs were largely responsible for outrages against civilians. RENAMO's protests went largely unrecorded in the world press, however.

In June 1988 the defence ministers of Mozambique, Tanzania, and Zimbabwe met at Quelimane to co-ordinate a massive offensive against the rebels. In August four combat groups, of about 2,000 troops each, launched a combined onslaught in central Mozambique. RENAMO melted into the bush and lived to fight again. The central purpose of this attack was to clear completely the main communications routes, especially the Beira corridor, which had been annexed *de facto* by Zimbabwe. In 1989 Pretoria made overtures to Maputo and P.W. Botha met Chissano. Pretoria began to deliver lots of equipment, including vehicles, radios, medicines, mine detectors and uniforms, to help FRELIMO protect the Cahora Bassa power lines and to repair 520 sabotaged pylons. As a result of the concurrent peace deal with Angola, Pretoria moved to extend this to a peace of sorts in Mozambique. By 1989 the SADF hawks were finally listening to their master's voice. RENAMO suddenly became a taboo subject in security circles in Pretoria. Then the master fell ill. P.W. Botha was a sorcerer who had conjured up a semblance of unity in the SSC and cabinet. Would peace or more war result from the decline in the health and power of the Great Crocodile?

Britain, Kenya and Portugal helped behind the scenes while FRELIMO still talked of amnesty but RENAMO wanted a government of national unity and free elections. Could the great powers do in Mozambique what they had done in Angola and Namibia?

Meanwhile, half of Mozambique's population was starving. Millions had become refugees internally and in the neighbouring states. In 1990 messianic militias sprouted, often literally putting the fear of God into both government and rebel soldiers. Like the later Lord's Resistance Army in Uganda, these militiamen claimed that bullets aimed their way would be turned into water. The best-known group, called *Naprama,* routed professional fighters with mere spears. Everyone had lost in the civil war. It had become a war of attrition, a soldier's war, crushing civilians and it was grinding on into a survivor's war; would anyone be left standing? The country was prostrate. Perhaps the only winners were the hawks in Pretoria who believed they had bought time. RENAMO had been a useful tool to control FRELIMO. The SADF had backed both sides, thus earning Mozambique an unusual accolade: 'a South African-backed Soviet surrogate', as RENAMO dubbed it. Other ironies abounded. The right wing in the US often supported RENAMO, yet it had been omitted from the Reagan doctrine's laundry list even though a secret CIA document described RENAMO 'as a self-sustaining fighting force' in 1990. The 'weaning' theorists in the state department also had a point. In the aid game, the West could always outdo the Soviets. Thus economic largesse, even if it was cat-called 'neo-colonialism', played to America's strong suit, just as weapons supplies, as in Angola, played to Russian strengths. Another paradox involved Zimbabwe. Cecil Rhodes had dreamed of providing Rhodesia with a corridor to the sea, hence his sponsorship of the railway to Beira in 1899. The Marxist Mugabe made the British colonial dream a reality: the Zimbabwe National Army became the fat controllers, albeit disputed by RENAMO, of the Beira corridor. FRELIMO troops were considered more of a hindrance than a help. Senior ZNA officers made it clear they wanted to place all local FRELIMO units under their own command, restrict them to base or disarm them. The ZNA was convinced (correctly) of RENAMO penetration of FRELIMO at all levels, and therefore tended to mount operations without informing FRELIMO. A Zimbabwean soldier lamented, 'First we were told to guard the pipeline. Now we seem to be fighting the whole war.'[15] Zimbabwean businessmen developed a similar disdain for FRELIMO's curious management techniques, a compound of the worst of Portuguese bureaucracy and East German central planning. In turn, the Mozambicans, not unnaturally, grew to resent what they saw as Zimbabwean imperialism. Rhodes could rest comfortably in his grave.

Peace was breaking out all over the region. By 1990 it did not look like the war in Mozambique could be won by either side. It was a military stalemate. Yes, foreign states, especially South Africa, had stirred the pot. Nevertheless, the country had appeared to be in the grip of an indigenous and massive peasant revolt. It would be incorrect to overemphasize the clash of Marxist revolution versus a pro-Western counter-revolution. The melange of ethnic, cultural, religious, racial, linguistic and ideological differences would be too complex to allow for such a trite generalization. Widespread disaffection with FRELIMO rule had long been evident but RENAMO was just one (very major) manifestation. On the other hand, RENAMO's flimsy rhetoric about social democracy, elections *et al*, did not prove to be a convincing explanation as a motor of revolt.

Pretoria had extricated itself from the quagmire in Angola and Namibia. For over a decade the mayhem in Mozambique had distracted the front-line states from their jihad against apartheid, precisely what Pretoria had intended. But apartheid, as we shall see, was being eroded from within the Afrikaner-dominated republic.

### *A road to peace?*

For once, I was back in my native Wales, contemplating my first Christmas at home for twenty years. It was December 1991. I took an unexpected phone call.

'President Dhlakama will give you a TV interview. He wants to discuss the ceasefire and settlement. Can you fly in next week?'

'Fly in? You mean no bikes?'

'No, a light plane. Low under the radar, straight to Gorongosa.'

'Sounds good but it's Christmas soon.'

'We will get you in and out before Christmas day.'

Afonso Dhlakama in December 1991, taken by author during the RENAMO peace congress in Gorongosa

Within a few days I was in a Piper Aztec with 'Pilots for Christ' emblazoned on the side. Flying from Malawi to central Mozambique the pilot, who had qualified that year, started to circle a tiny strip that had been made between very tall trees. It looked like a footpath, not an airstrip. The pilot didn't add to my confidence by praying fervently as he attempted to land.

I was one of two journalists asked to attend the national congress to discuss the brokered peace talks and planned election. Local ceasefires were holding in some areas, and FRELIMO had ditched Marxism, it said, and had changed the constitution to allow a multi-party system. The independence of Namibia, the release of Nelson Mandela and above all the collapse of the USSR meant FRELIMO had lost its main foreign ally and had little immediate alternative but to talk to RENAMO.

Dhlakama talked with me for many hours again in his old Gorongosa HQ. He was now dressed in smart suits and boasted female bodyguards like Colonel Gaddafi. His English had expanded to match his girth so I did not have to struggle in Portuguese. The warlord still had a touching faith in British influence. 'London is the key to peace,' he insisted. He also asked me why the Conservative government was spending so much money training a still-Marxist army in Zimbabwe while they couldn't afford to maintain some of their own famous regiments. A good question, I thought. His obsession with London was to pay off; he was invited there eventually and I visited Dhklama over the years, especially when the FCO thought he had a chance of actually winning a free election.

Our two-man team filmed the pre-congress cabal of RENAMO delegates. Dhlakama was in a dress uniform which made him look like a chief scout. Around him were old traditional chiefs in 1930s demob suits, a white hunter in safari gear, tense academics, some thugs, *mestiços* … an apparent attempt to balance the classes and tribes of the old Mozambique. I didn't know whether I was witnessing a historical milestone in southern African history or a remake of *Al Capone.*

Robert Mugabe has been much maligned, not least for his genocide of Ndebeles in the 1980s, but he played a crucial role in making a deal in Mozambique. For some reason both Dhlakama and Mugabe bonded. Both spoke Shona, were Catholics and had been guerrilla leaders. Most importantly, Mugabe adopted an almost paternal affection for Dhlakama. The Zimbabwean president's authority and revolutionary credentials were vital in bringing FRELIMO on board. On 4 October 1992, the General Peace Accords, negotiated by the lay Catholic Community of Sant'Egidio, with the support of the United Nations, were signed in Rome by Chissano and Dhlakama. A UN peacekeeping force (UNOMOZ) of 7,500 arrived in Mozambique and oversaw a two-year transition to democracy. Dhlakama had long promised me the first TV interview in the presidential palace. He did well, not least in rigged elections but he did not secure the presidency. I visited him in Maputo when he was leader of the opposition but I declined to visit him again in Gorongosa when he went back to war two decades after the Rome peace deal.

## *Chapter 12*

# Zimbabwe (1980-1990)

### *Fighting Apartheid*

Zimbabwe was certainly part of apartheid's second front (the struggle inside the country by the ANC was considered the first). Each destabilization campaign was distinct. Zimbabwe was of special interest to Pretoria, because historically Pretoria had treated Rhodesia as almost part of the South African *reich*. Before 1923 Rhodesia was encouraged to join the southern republic. Many military strategists in South Africa had long regarded the Zambezi, not the Limpopo, as the true border of white imperium. Mugabe's victory was a worst-case scenario for Pretoria.

Mugabe had seen firsthand what damage had been inflicted on the front-line states during his war of liberation. On taking power in Zimbabwe, Samora Machel, his former host, had warned him not only to keep white expertise but also to avoid a full-frontal war with South Africa. Mugabe cut formal diplomatic and sporting ties with the apartheid state; that was the least he could do to satisfy pressure from the Organization of African Unity but he privately assured Pretoria that he would not allow any of the South African resistance movements to operate militarily from Zimbabwe.

Nevertheless, Pretoria soon began to apply a tourniquet to Zimbabwe's lifeblood. The Rhodesian war had locked Zimbabwe into the South African economic system. Roughly 90 per cent of its exports passed through the apartheid state. The transport nexus worked both ways: Zimbabwe was a main route for South African trade with Zaire, Zambia and Malawi. Some sort of *modus vivendi* was necessary. Mugabe initially suppressed ZANU-PF hotheads who were screaming for their *Chimurenga* to immediately march south. 'We've got to sup with the devil or starve,' said one of Mugabe's closest aides, 'but if we starve, many other African countries starve with us. And that's where South Africa knows it's got us cornered for a long time.'

Pretoria was soon to serve up a varied destabilization diet: economic pressures, particularly in 1981 and 1982, support for Zimbabwean dissidents, and not just in ZAPU, selective assassinations, sabotage and anti-Mugabe propaganda. Pretoria, however, stopped short of direct and continuous military intervention. Zimbabwe was a member of the British Commonwealth where British military instructors, admittedly

Railway diplomacy

a small number, trained a large and battle-hardened military force. Washington might have encouraged Pretoria's legions to fight Cubans and Russians in Angola but the US would not countenance a similar riposte in Zimbabwe. Covert, albeit deniable, dirty tricks were another matter. Pretoria had all the best cards: economic dominance, a large potential fifth column of whites inside Zimbabwe and a reservoir of revanchist whites attached to, or integrated in, the South African Defence Force.

Pretoria insisted on holding Mugabe to his promise not to harbour active ANC insurgents. They had to be thrown out of the country. Mugabe quietly returned around 300 to Zambia. It was not enough to satisfy the South African government.

In July 1980 South African railways began to withdraw its technicians and engineers lent to the *ancien régime*. 'Inexplicable' bottlenecks in the ports and on the railways followed. 'The notoriously drunken stationmaster in Messina' – the small railway town near Zimbabwe's main border post at Beit bridge – became a legendary figure in this blackmail scenario.

Pretoria also took a close interest in the mutinies in the half-integrated Zimbabwe National Army and how the white-piloted aircraft, fixed- and rotory-wing, played such a crucial role in containing them. Stirring up ZIPRA and removing the white air force component were obvious means of leverage. Although some of the Afrikaner doves praised Mugabe's reconciliation moves, the hardliners in military and intelligence circles thought that the post-independence ZIPRA-ZANLA battles indicated that Mugabe was ripe for toppling. Mugabe was concerned that once again South African agents might try to assassinate him.

Pretoria withdrew more locomotives. On 16 August 1981 a mysterious explosion destroyed the armoury at Inkomo barracks near Harare. At the time it was blamed on vengeful ex-Rhodesian and South African infiltrators. Actually, it was ZNA incompetence – untrained troops had made a cooking fire near gas containers and explosives. Despite the reality, the Zimbabwean government ran with the rumour that South African saboteurs were everywhere. Many of the incidents were sabotage, not accidents, however. On 18 December 1981 a blast ripped through the new ZANU-PF HQ in Harare. One senior South African officer warned, 'If it came to a showdown, we could wring Mugabe's neck like a chicken.'

A part of the neck-wringing was being conducted in the Transvaal, not far from Zimbabwe's southern border: the SADF was training recruits for Super-ZAPU, including some genuine ZIPRA. To appease their guilt at the apartheid connections, the disgruntled black soldiers used to quote an old African saying, 'In order to cross a river you sometimes have to ride on the crocodile's back.' Many ZIPRA soldiers were fiercely loyal to their former military commanders, especially Lookout Masuku and Dumiso Dabengwa, and less to their political boss, Joshua Nkomo. The detention of the generals at Chikurubi maximum security prison in Harare prompted a major exodus from the ZNA, and a small one into the arms of the waiting South Africans.

Three sometimes rival groups of dissidents ranged across the vast swathes of empty Matabele bush: bandits feeding on the anarchy; genuine ZIPRA rebels held together by a disciplined command structure, with support from sanctuaries in Botswana, and perhaps only titular loyalty to Nkomo; and Super-ZAPU, supplied from South Africa. The Central Intelligence Organization was also alleged to be running pseudo-gangs pretending to be super-ZAPU or the real ZIPRA. Mugabe lumped them all together as disorganized bandits contaminated by the devil in Pretoria. He claimed that 5,000 dissidents were waiting to invade, in a replay of the Bay of Pigs adventure in Cuba.

In March 1983 a broadcasting station, Radio Truth, started pumping out anti-Mugabe propaganda. It said it was operating from inside Matabeleland. In fact, the radio station was a South African Broadcasting Corporation installation on the outskirts of Johannesburg. Pretoria denied any connection. The denials were unconvincing at the best of times; then on 25 November 1983 the tapes of the theme music of RENAMO's *Voz de Africa Livre* were accidentally switched with that of Super ZAPU's Radio Truth. Mugabe had further proof that the propaganda stations were broadcasting from South Africa, not Mozambique and Matabeleland.

As the previous arms caches were used up or seized by the ZNA, Pretoria supplied weapons to both ZIPRA and Super-ZAPU. The ferment in southern Zimbabwe suited Pretoria for a number of reasons. It undermined Mugabe's policy of reconciliation and hastened the exodus of whites, especially farmers. More white farmers were now being killed than during the war that ended in 1980. This weakened the Zimbabwean agricultural economy and discouraged international investment. Attacks on foreign holidaymakers also hit the tourist industry. Secondly, the *Gukurahundi* campaign of genocide concentrated the ZNA's attention in Matabeleland and not in Mozambique, where South Africa was bolstering the anti-Marxist rebels. As a bonus, the saturation of ZNA forces in southern Matabeleland discouraged ANC penetration into the Northern Transvaal province of the white republic.

The North Korean-trained 5 Brigade conducted extensive massacres (called the *Gukurahundi*) in Matabeleland

On 27 July 1982 Pretoria aimed a precise blow at Zimbabwe's military machine. A quarter of the air force was sabotaged at Thornhill base near Gweru (Gwelo). Thirteen fighters and trainers, including Hawk Mk 60s recently purchased from Britain, were blown up. Six white officers, including an air vice marshal, were detained, tortured with electric shock treatment, sexually abused, acquitted, re-detained and eventually expelled from the country. The six officers were completely innocent. The airmen had cherished their shiny new British machines, so long awaited during the lean sanctions years. Their treatment caused a furore, especially in the right-wing media in the UK. The Thornhill raid was a South African special forces' operation, assisted by some former members of the Rhodesian SAS. The audacious attack virtually eliminated the jet strike capability of the Zimbabwean Air Force and prompted a mass exodus of the remaining white pilots and technicians.

The airmen's trial also cast a poor light on Mugabe's claims that Zimbabwe was a beacon for human rights and judicial probity in both southern Africa and the Commonwealth. John Cox, one of the officers jailed, called the trial 'one of Africa's finest examples of a comedy of errors – incompetence compounded by greater incompetence … that was to make the Goon Show look serious'.[1] Cox, a Briton, said all this only after he had returned safely to Winterbourne, near Bristol, England.

A month after the Thornhill attack, three white soldiers from a much larger SADF raiding party were killed on the wrong side of the Zimbabwean border. The three were ex-Rhodesians who had served in the RLI and SAS. Pretoria was eventually forced into admitting that a raid had taken place, but said it was an 'unauthorized freelance operation' to rescue political prisoners in south-eastern Zimbabwe. The number of these unauthorizd and freelance operations grew apace, and the diplomatic lie became laughable. Undeterred, former SAS soldiers continued to attack Zimbabwe's alternative oil supplies by hitting pipelines in Mozambique. By December 1982 the combined strangulation of South African and Mozambican sources meant that Zimbabwe was down to two weeks' supply of petrol.

American pressure on Pretoria forced a curtailment of these raids but South Africa had made its point: the tap could be turned off whenever it suited the apartheid regime. With US mediation, South African intelligence chiefs had a series of high-level meetings in Harare to set up a liaison committee to prevent what one Zimbabwean minister termed 'nuclear war by accident'. The SADF's Major General Pieter van der Westhuizen, the head of military intelligence, travelled discreetly to Harare for talks with the ZNA chief of staff, General Sheba Gava. Separately, Niel Barnard, the youthful head of the National Intelligence Service, also made a secret trip to Zimbabwe. As far as overt raids were concerned, an uneasy truce followed.

The covert intelligence war did not, however, cease. From 1980-1984 various South African intelligence agencies had run a sophisticated penetration of Zimbabwe. For example, duplicate keys of nearly every cell-block in prisons and police stations, duplicate keys of the Zimbabwe Republic Police Special Branch and CIO vehicles and the architectural plans of security installations such as army bases had been sent to Pretoria. A clever ploy but the hoard was lost by bungling spooks in Pretoria. That debacle and the unintended deaths of so many white farmers made the Afrikaner spymasters think again. Some of the farmers had been killed by genuine ZIPRA dissidents, not under Pretoria's control, although others were probably murdered by turned dissidents acting in a pseudo role under the command of the ZNA. Harare was applying the lessons learned from the Selous Scouts in the previous decade. It was likely that Major General H. Roux, of South Africa's Directorate of Special Tasks, pulled the plug on many of the dirty tricks in 1984, although a number of minor operations continued, especially against the ANC. And of course South African military intelligence continued to monitor the communications traffic of the ZNA.

The South African engagement in Matabeleland wound down before the 1985 election but it soon became clear to even the diehard strategists in Pretoria that Nkomo's chances of electoral triumph (let alone Bishop Muzorewa's) were nil. Despite whites continuing to vote for Ian Smith or other white conservatives, the chimera of a white-Nkomo-Mzuzorewa government had finally been interred. Pretoria had to deal with Mugabe as the undisputed leader. Pretoria shifted some of its focus to Mozambique as ZNA troops poured into the country to swamp RENAMO, Pretoria's anti-Marxist ally.

South Africa was not finished with Mugabe. In May 1986, the SADF openly attacked Harare, as part of its military assault on three Commonwealth countries in the region. The ambition was to sink the Commonwealth Eminent Persons' Group's peace drive. Air strikes were conducted against ANC facilities in Zambia and Botswana. The ground strike in Harare would be more clandestine and well-planned. The first target was 16 Angwa Street in downtown Harare. Operatives working under the general codename of Operation BARNACLE – part of the destabilization programme – had already bugged the offices, which controlled MK operations in the region. The other target was an ANC safe house in a four-bedroomed suburban house in Ashdown Park, a leafier northern suburb. The attack on the premises, Operation KODAK, had been allocated to 5th Reconnaissance Commando in late 1985. On the night of 18 May 1986, three Pumas flew in at a height of 35 metres to stay below the radar while keeping radio silence. They established a small rural communication base, with a commander and a doctor, and some indigenous help with transport. Switching from a decrepit van, they hired saloon cars, carrying their weapons in golfbags, to fit their tourist cover. They drove to Harare. Using an aluminium ladder to scale a wall, one team planted in the office three school satchels, containing 1.5-kilo bunker bombs. The team that hit the office was made up of three operators, two blacks and a white. The attack on the safe house, which was supposed to contain an armoury, was to be dealt with by six men, both black and white. The second team went in with all guns blazing and killed one occupant and seized documents. They escaped the same way they came in, with no problems en route, but dropping spiked caltrops to slow down any pursuing vehicle. The one hiccup for the special forces was a severe complaint from their quartermaster that they had left behind the expensive aluminium ladder. Pretoria had made its political point – it could penetrate the very heart of Harare, to hit ANC targets, and get away with it unscathed.

The government mouthpiece, the *Herald*, responded with banner headlines: 'Racists Bomb Frontline Capital'; the editorial lambasted the 'Boer Vampires'. Mugabe publicly lost his temper when he talked of 'killing Boers'. Sanctions were immediately discussed in the Zimbabwean cabinet but the economic pragmatists won the day. Mugabe later returned to the subject of imposing sanctions on South Africa though soon the war in Mozambique and the dramatic changes impelled by the release of Nelson Mandela were to alter Zimbabwean dynamics.

The cold war between Harare and Pretoria, sometimes interrupted by real fighting, lasted just over a decade. Nkomo's shotgun marriage with Mugabe and the resultant tense peace in Matabeleland, as well as the exodus (and occasional arrest) of some of Pretoria's intelligence assets in Zimbabwe had diminished the undeclared war between the two states. Occasional raids and sabotage from South Africa continued, but less frequently. The excuse was still the same: 'crazy gangs' of ex-Rhodesians were trying to rescue friends and relatives off their own bat. Yet it was strange, nearly a decade after their defeat, that ex-Rhodesians were still so bitter, so well-organized and so well-financed that they could attempt sophisticated missions without the knowledge of the generally well-informed South African intelligence system.

The SADF had fought well in the second front in Angola and Namibia, although often the Afrikaner intelligence agencies had not matched the professional skills of their combat troops. And the SADF was nuclear-armed. Those in Harare who expected the Afrikaners to fight as long and hard as the white Rhodesians were surprised when Nelson Mandela, the ANC leader, and the South African president, F.W. de Klerk, managed to negotiate a relatively peaceful transition to majority rule. The two lawyers eventually finessed a legal deal that held – just.

The electoral victory of Mandela in 1994 would transform southern African politics. Mugabe's war with apartheid would end. The Zimbabwean leader had supported the PAC, not the ANC. The PAC's attachment to black consciousness and Maoist inclinations, plus its wariness of Moscow and trade union affiliations, had appealed to Mugabe. But it would be hard to ignore the psychological challenge as well: Mandela replaced Mugabe as the liberation hero of the region and the continent. Mandela's secular sainthood in the West was a feat Mugabe could only dream of. It became apparent from Mugabe's surliness and even public sulks at major African events, when Mandela was inevitably feted, that the Zimbabwean leader resented his relegation in the pantheon of African idols.

*Zimbabwe's war in Mozambique*

FRELIMO had done much to install Mugabe as Zimbabwe's leader. Yet Mugabe's backer was constantly under fire itself. FRELIMO had to fight three wars in succession: against the Portuguese, then the Rhodesians and finally the SADF-RENAMO axis. When Mugabe took over in April 1980, the CIO handed over control of RENAMO to South African military intelligence. The disruption of oil pipelines, railways and road bridges, especially along the crucial Beira corridor, was almost always the work of the South African Reconnaissance Commandos, often with a former Rhodesian SAS element. If the job was botched it was RENAMO – if it was done properly, it was the work of the Recces.

Sometimes the SADF role was overt. On 23 May 1983, in retaliation for a car-bomb explosion in Central Pretoria, South African jets bombed alleged ANC safe houses in the Matola and Liberdade suburbs of the Mozambican capital, Maputo. After this public humiliation of its ally, the USSR warned Pretoria directly that Soviet and Cuban troops might enter the war, as they had done in Angola. This was the time of the Reagan doctrine, when the US was prepared to support resistance against Russia's 'evil empire'. Despite much lobbying in Washington, RENAMO never managed to get on Reagan's list of worthy insurgents. This was partly because of its terrible reputation for atrocities, some of it invented by FRELIMO. As the RENAMO leader, Afonso Dhlakama, told the author in 1986, 'Marxists are always good at two things – propaganda and the secret police.'

Supporting RENAMO was a useful policy for the hawks in Pretoria – it deterred FRELIMO's support for the ANC and it kept Zimbabwe dependent on South African transport routes. The Zimbabwean security interest focused on three main alternative routes. Firstly, the Beira Corridor: a rail, road, oil and electricity powerline linking the port of Beira to Mutare on Zimbabwe's eastern border. This 320-mile corridor became the responsibility of both ZNA and Mozambican troops. Secondly, the Tete corridor was a 150-mile stretch of road between Nyamapanda on the Zimbabwean border to Zobue town on the Mozambique/Malawi border. Protecting the Tete strategic bridge was the specific responsibility of the ZNA 1st Mechanized Battalion which was deployed to Tete in 1985. Finally, and of least importance, was the Limpopo corridor, a derelict rail link from Chicualacuala on the Zimbabwean/Mozambican border running 300 miles to Maputo. The Zimbabweans began to upgrade the railway in 1987. Disrupting these alternative routes made Harare almost totally dependent on Pretoria's borders and good will.

Pretoria's intelligence community was divided between the maximalists and the minimalists. The maximalists believed that it was the right time to overthrow FRELIMO and replace it with RENAMO. Mugabe had received a top-secret report from his own intelligence in 1982 that Pretoria was capable of toppling his main ally, Samora Machel, in forty-eight hours.

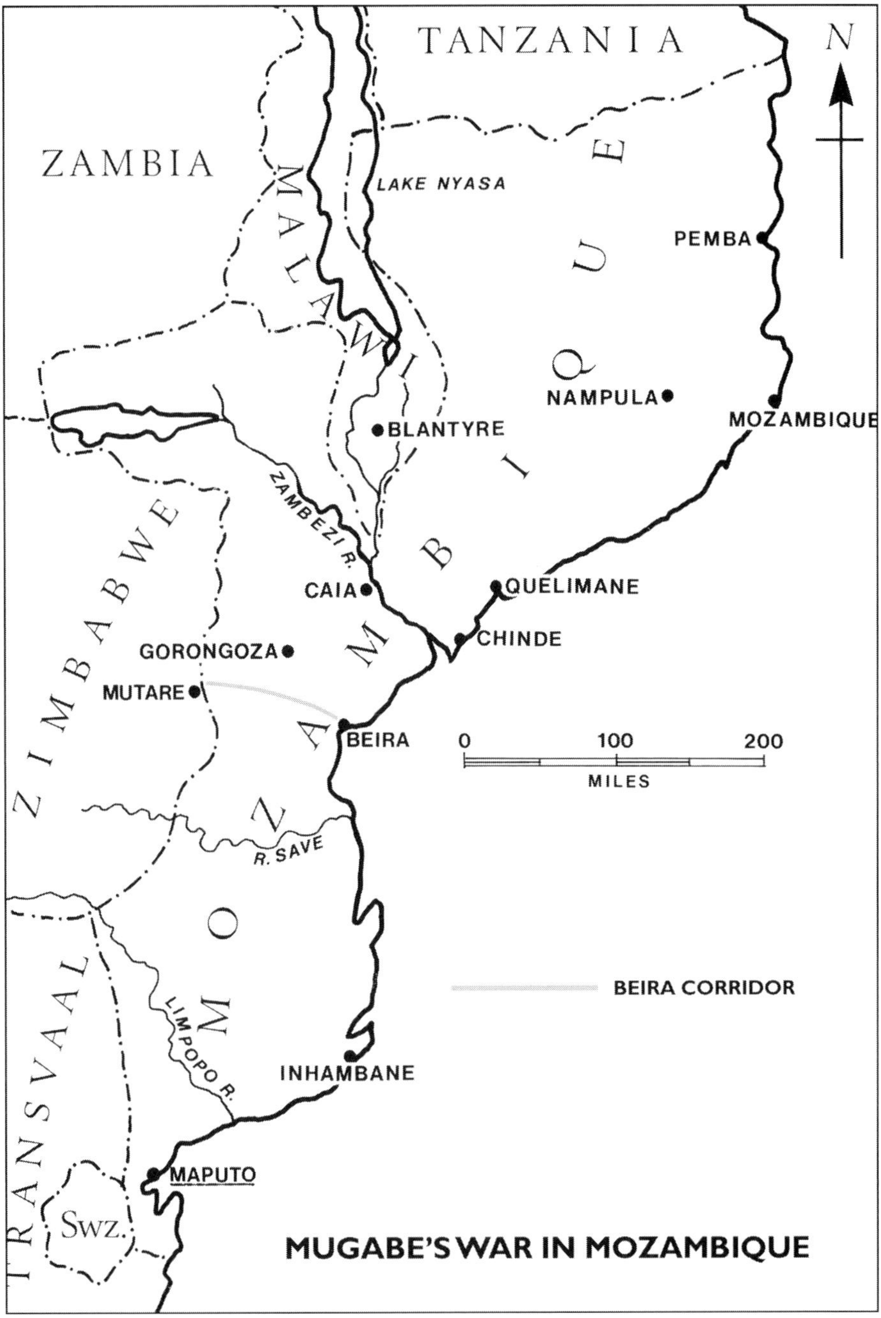


Mugabe's war against RENAMO, especially the control of the Beira corridor

The minimalists had their way, after the South African president, P.W. Botha, was persuaded. Machel and P.W. Botha met in a circus atmosphere alongside the Nkomati river on 16 March 1984 and signed a deal. The Nkomati agreement was simple: both sides would ditch their rebel friends, the ANC and RENAMO, although the pact did not mention either of them explicitly. RENAMO's support was scaled down but not stopped. Both Machel and Mugabe were still under the cosh.

Within a year both men realized that Pretoria was acting in bad faith, despite being aware of the conflicting opinions within Pretoria about RENAMO. Mugabe owed Machel a great deal. The two men had signed a military pact in October 1980. Since 1982 Zimbabwean troops had helped Machel with 500 troops initially sent to guard the Beira corridor, but the focus of the ZNA then had been on the perceived internal challenge from ZAPU. By 1985 Mugabe felt that this domestic matter had largely been resolved. Now he had to fully respond to Machel's urgent requests as FRELIMO faced an existential threat from a revived RENAMO.

In contravention of Nkomati, the SADF's logistical and communications support had enabled RENAMO to expand nationwide. But the particular focus was Beira, one of the few half-functioning southern African ports not in apartheid hands. It was also Mugabe's lifeline. The leaders of Mozambique, Zimbabwe and Tanzania needed to co-ordinate militarily. They concentrated on the main trade corridors, not just Beira, but also the northern transport link, the Tete Corridor. Tanzanian and a small number of Malawian troops helped guard the trains. In July 1985 the British granted funds to enlarge the officer training scheme in Nyanga, Zimbabwe, so as to include Mozambicans. (And unofficially ex-SAS troops were hired to protect Western business interests in Mozambique.) But the major rescue component was Zimbabwean. Its expeditionary force mushroomed from 1,500 in mid-1984 to 12,000 by the end of 1985. That figure soared to 18,000 during major offensives against RENAMO.

In December 1984 the ZNA deployed 800 troops, including its SAS, 3 Brigade and the Para Group, to hit the RENAMO HQ in Gorongosa. Since RENAMO was always moving its main base, and had set up various dummy HQs to confuse the enemy's air observation, the raid was not a success. Perhaps that was not a surprise as it had been code-named Operation LEMON, military slang for a screw-up. Also RENAMO had been tipped off. Zimbabwe intelligence did not know whether it was penetration of the CIO by the South Africans or a slip-up by the notoriously inept, cruel and recently purged Mozambican secret police. On 28 August 1985 Zimbabwean paratroopers, backed by Mozambican troops, stormed the real RENAMO main HQ called Casa Banana, in the Gorongosa game reserve. RENAMO claimed that they had to flee the helicopter-led assault of 12,000 ZNA and 8,000 FRELIMO. That was their, probably exaggerated, estimate. RENAMO also claimed to have retreated in good order. It was certainly a major action, dubbed Operation GRAPEFRUIT. The ZNA deployed three infantry battalions, combined

Zimbabwe's airpower was crucial in the war in Mozambique

with SAS and commando groups as well as gunships using old Rhodesian fire force techniques.

The ZNA's protection of the Beira corridor was initially static – erecting bunkers along the road and rail line. The ZNA soon moved to a forward defence, by searching out the rebels. FRELIMO never did this. The ZNA commanders, many of them experienced ZANLA officers, had little time for their old comrades. Usually, they planned operations without even telling FRELIMO, partly because their allies would often tip off their friends and relatives among the rebels.

In his fine book on Mugabe,[2] Africanist scholar Stephen Chan recounted an incident when a Zimbabwean unit received one of the advance warnings of a RENAMO attack, but decided to hold its ground. 'RENAMO clearly thought it was a FRELIMO group it was attacking. The Zimbabweans held the attack, then countered. Then spent hours weeping over the boy soldiers they had killed.'

RENAMO did recruit or press-gang a large number of boy soldiers. The fact that teenagers could outfight most government soldiers, if not the ZNA, suggested to

Mugabe's intelligence advisers that Pretoria's assessment of the rottenness of Machel's regime was accurate. Without ZNA stiffening and training, the demoralized FRELIMO soldiers would usually run from any fight. But the rebels respected the ZNA, especially their use of airpower. The Zimbabwean air force's combat ability had been seriously depleted by the destruction at Thornhill but it did use airpower, especially helicopter gunships and replacement Hawks, to strike at RENAMO. The rebels did not possess effective anti-aircraft capacity; they did have a number of SAM-7s but rarely knew how to fire them. Generally, they tried to take cover if the Zimbabwe Air Force pressed their attacks.

By this time, FRELIMO was so fragile that it was forced to beg for help from the Russians *and* from Mrs Thatcher in London. At one stage even Pretoria helped FRELIMO with communications, while still supporting RENAMO. Mozambique had become a donors' republic, a Soviet surrogate state, assisted by Pretoria and right-wing British Tories, let alone a country propped up by Mugabe. Mozambique was a sorry mess.

Things could not get worse for Machel and Mugabe but they soon did. On 19 October 1986, flying home from a front-line summit, Machel's plane, piloted by Russians, flew into a mountain, just inside South Africa. Someone had apparently moved a homing beacon. Pretoria vehemently protested its innocence but Mugabe took the death of his friend as a clear warning of his own endangered position. As chairman of the Non-Aligned Movement, Mugabe had just hosted a summit in Harare and he had waxed lyrically to his audience about the need for sanctions against apartheid.

Mugabe took Machel's death as a clear warning from Pretoria. Machel was honoured in the USSR, however, with a commemorative stamp

Mugabe's intelligence advisers noted another major South African re-supply to RENAMO. Even more alarming for Harare was the information that Pretoria may have had a role in bringing together Dhlakama and Ndabaningi Sithole, Mugabe's old rival. Dhlakama literally declared war on Mugabe and moved RENAMO troops into the Eastern Highlands of Zimbabwe. Sithole had a tribal base in southern Manicaland among the small Ndau group, a tribe that was over-represented in the RENAMO high command. The ZNA had to resort to old-fashioned protected villages in response to RENAMO depredations. RENAMO was operating regularly inside Zimbabwe, though it may have suited Mugabe to play up the duplicity of Sithole and his ZANU-Ndonga party. The ZNA COIN operation was called Operation NDONGA CHIRENJE (DESTROY NDONGA).

Mugabe also asked the US for help during a visit to Washington (US DoD)

Mugabe had more than repaid his debt to his dead comrade, Machel, who was replaced by the far more urbane former foreign minister, Joaquim Chissano. Mugabe had (eventually) got on well with the rough-and-ready Machel, but he would now engage intellectually with Chissano. Zimbabwe had expended much blood and treasure in Mozambique. The Zimbabwe Defence Force (ZDF) may have suffered as many as 1,000 major casualties in Mozambique from 1982 to 1991; the number of fatalities was unknown because Harare imposed a news blackout on combat injuries and deaths. Unlike the Rhodesians, the ZDF did not, or could not, always reclaim their fallen comrades, so the figure could be higher than even vague estimates. A major cause of death was the frequency of air crashes either because of aged equipment such as the venerable Alouettes, poor maintenance or pilot error.

For all this cost in men and materiel, could Mugabe reap any long-term dividends, besides immediate, if disrupted, access to the sea? Indeed he could. Mugabe had larger ambitions: to bring peace to Mozambique, for national and personal reasons. Mugabe had finished off ZAPU, the war with apartheid was ending, so could he emerge as the regional peacebroker?

Chissano's economic and military position was untenable, though he still refused to negotiate directly, as equals, with Dhlakama. Mugabe ordered another offensive against RENAMO in February 1990. But it took two years of intense diplomacy to extend various ceasefires into a final peace agreement in 1992. The Catholic Church and the Italian government played a busy role at the numerous series of talks in Rome. In typical Italian style, the host government bought new Armani suits for RENAMO, lean men as bushfighters but now grown to be fat-cats from too many diplomatic lunches. The Italians also purchased tickets for both Mozambican sides for a World Cup football match in June. Both sides joined in cheering for the African team, Cameroon, against Argentina. The Kenyans, Malawians and, in the background, the South Africans also played a constructive role in the Rome peace agreement. The Americans were busy too, talking about 'tidying up' southern African problems in tandem with the Mandela-de Klerk process. But the cement that finally got the Mozambican antagonists to fix a permanent peace was undoubtedly Robert Mugabe.

Malawi's Hastings Banda had originally arranged a personal meeting between Dhlakama and Mugabe. The Zimbabwean leader may have been struck by the fact that Dhlakama, especially before his fat-cat days, looked just like a young lean Mugabe. The two men soon ignored their host and talked warmly in Shona. They struck up a rapport that lasted, even though Mugabe was said not to have liked the RENAMO chieftain initially. Nevertheless, Mugabe did imply publicly that he was prepared to replicate Thatcher's comment on Gorbachev: 'he is a man we can do business with.' During various meetings, Dhlakama managed to play it right as far as respecting the older man's intellectual and liberation credentials; in turn, Mugabe was once again the kindly teacher with a pupil whom he might occasionally concede was a little like his younger self. The Portuguese had tutored Dhlakama well in the arts of diplomacy. And Tiny Rowland was also at hand to lend advice – and jets.

Mugabe's meetings with Dhlakama helped Chissano with his hardliners who wanted to fight on. It became clear to Mugabe that, despite all the alleged atrocities, RENAMO had much genuine popular support among the *povo*. Mugabe patiently and cleverly engineered the personal meetings between the two Mozambican leaders in Rome in early August 1992. Once more in Rome, on 4 October 1992, the two men signed the deal, which led to peace in Mozambique after over thirty years of conflict.

Mugabe made a formal speech. 'It is not the day of judgement. It is the day of reconciliation. Today is not the day when we should examine who was right and who was wrong. Today is the process of peace. We cannot escape that process.' Here was Mugabe as the prince of reconciliation again; his Mozambican peace speech had strong resonances of his statesmanlike broadcast to the new Zimbabwe just after he had won the 1980 election. A well-qualified and close observer, Professor Stephen Chan, dubbed Mugabe's astute diplomacy 'a Roman triumph' and asked whether this was to be his last.

## *Chapter 13*

# Fellow Front-liners

*Lesotho*

Lesotho, the size of Belgium, boasts, or laments, some unusual claims to fame. For example, it is the only country in the world where the entire area is more than 1,000 metres above sea level. It also has one of the world's highest AIDS rates. Its dramatic mountain scenery and usually friendly inhabitants attracted a little tourism and a lot of foreign aid. It is still one of the three remaining independent African kingdoms, although today's constitutional monarchy has had a lot of ups and downs. Lesotho also had the shortest railway line on the continent, 1.5 kilometres to be exact. Its most distinctive feature, however, is that it is one of only three countries completely surrounded by another state. Unfortunately for Lesotho it was for years the often hostile apartheid-ruled South Africa. (The other enclaved states, the Vatican and San Marino, have not recently been threatened by their big brother, Italy.) Lesotho's coat of arms proudly proclaimed its aspirations: *Khotso, Pula and Nala (*peace, rain and prosperity). Sadly, it missed out on all three during the apartheid period. And even though it was later twinned with Wales, it did not enjoy a matching rainfall.

In 1868 King Moshoeshoe asked to become 'like a flea in the blanket of Queen Victoria'. It was not quite a 100-year itch, for the Basutoland protectorate became independent in 1966 when London set a precedent for Pretoria's bantustans. The country's dictatorial ruler, Chief Leabua Jonathan, established a pattern for the bantustan rulers, including a penchant for bowler hats. The difference was that Lesotho could, and did, join the UN and the Commonwealth and so received aid when Pretoria turned on Jonathan. Initially, the National Party government funded the chief, a former herdboy who had later worked as a clerk in the New Modderfontein gold mine in the republic. Like the tinpot dictators in the Transkei and Ciskei, he was particularly averse to free elections. He aborted the 1970 elections when he looked like losing them to his rivals in the Basotho Congress Party, led by Ntsu Mokhehle. Jonathan thereupon declared 'a holiday from politics', one of the more imaginative and honest dictatorial phrases to emerge from Africa. Pretoria went along with this quite happily because the Congress Party was deemed to be dangerously socialistic.

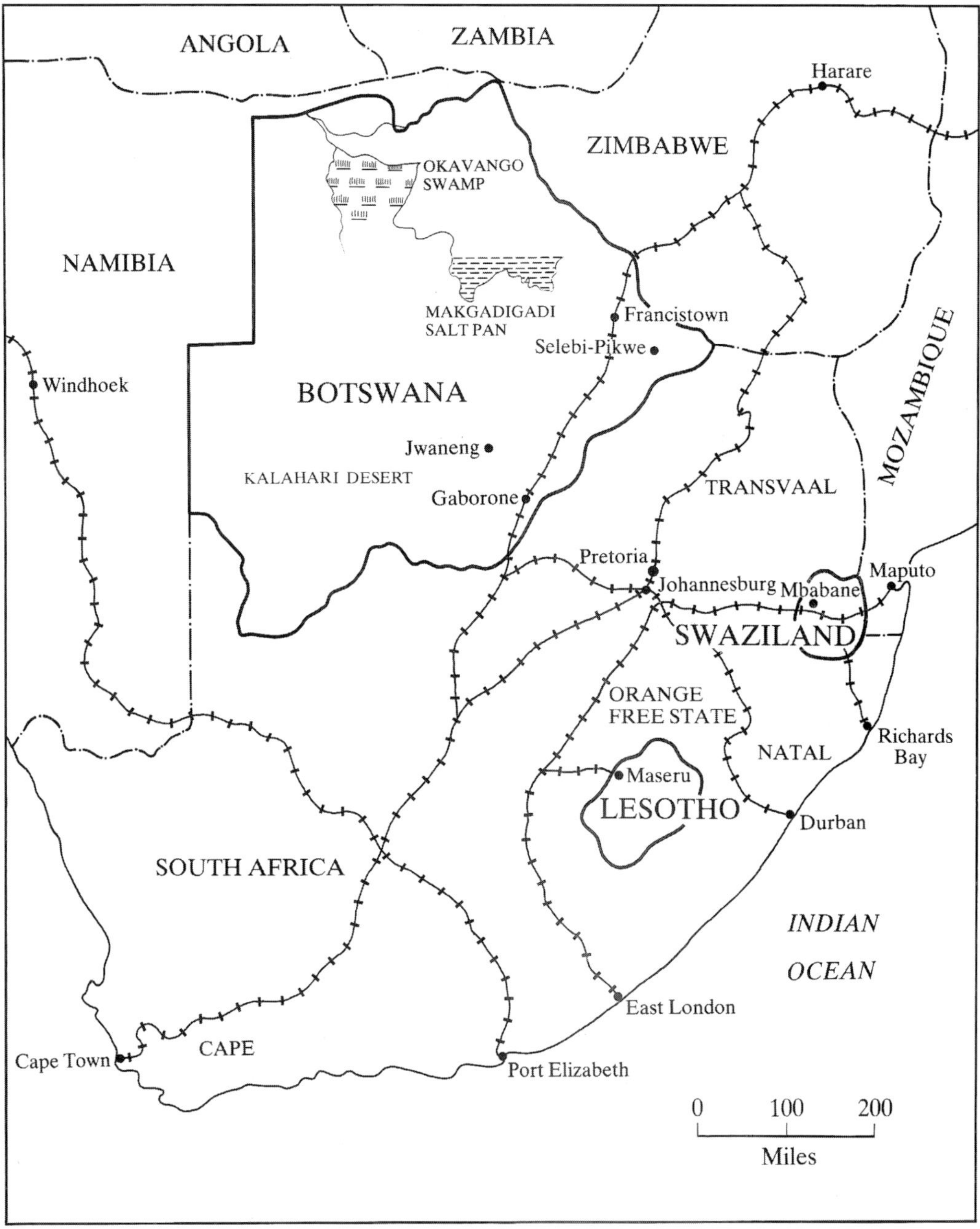


Hostage states: Botswana, Lesotho and Swaziland

The three former British protectorates were essentially captive states

In 1971 Jonathan began to distance himself from Pretoria and started to indulge in anti-apartheid tirades, partly because he thought it would bring in more aid money. But his position was weak; more than half of the kingdom's able-bodied men worked in South Africa, and the economy and transport systems were controlled by South Africans. In 1974, after a bloody rebellion, some members of the Congress Party went into exile, including Mokhehle. Despite his earlier affiliations to the Pan-Africanist Congress, Mokhehle decided 'to ride on the back of the devil' – Pretoria.

In 1979 the Lesotho Liberation Army (LLA) was founded, funded, armed and trained by South Africa. The attacks began in May 1979 and increased in 1981, as Jonathan became even more outspoken. What really incensed Pretoria was Jonathan's invitation to communist states, particularly Russia, China, North Korea and, finally, Cuba to open embassies in Maseru, the capital, as well as the use of Lesotho as a base for MK as well as ANC civilian refugees. Just as Jonathan was, first, a protégé of Pretoria and then an antagonist, so Mokhehle switched from being an opponent of South Africa to becoming head of the LLA, an SADF-SAP surrogate force, which killed and sabotaged from 1979 to 1986. The LLA raids, launched from South African territory, did not lead to a popular uprising against Jonathan, even though the Congress Party would have won the aborted 1970 elections, and Mokhehle retained his personal following in Lesotho. Jonathan manipulated historical Basotho enmity towards the 'Boers' to tar the LLA, justifiably, with a pro-apartheid brush. Jonathan used the LLA as an excuse to suppress ruthlessly all his domestic opponents.

Then came the big raid, the first large-scale direct attack by the SADF on one of the former British protectorates. It came on the eve of Human Rights Day, 9 December 1982. It was a major operation and carefully planned.

Operation LATSA, the running of the Lesotho Liberation Army, was controlled by the Special Tasks Division of Military Intelligence. By 1981 Ricky May,

Chief Leabua Jonathan famously declared 'a holiday from politics'

formerly a CIO and BSAP Special Branch officer and old RENAMO hand, had been made a colonel in the SADF. The LLA's training was done at an SAP security branch base just over the Lesotho border in the QwaQwa homeland and a camp near Bergdale, Natal. The LLA cadres were also trained in Transkei under the auspices of former Selous Scouts commander, Colonel Ron Reid-Daly, at Port St John. Also involved were Captains Bob MacKenzie and Peter Cole, both ex-Rhodesian SAS and ex-6 Recce Commandos. The MK had built up a major infrastructure in Maseru, led by the charismatic Chris Hani. Pretoria had deemed Hani's men to be responsible for a number of attacks in South Africa.

Seventy experienced SF operators were drawn from 1st and 5th Reconnaissance Regiments. Around 80 per cent were black, though the command elements were white officers. Their training had begun in August 1982 in Bloemfontein. For months they worked on mock-ups of the houses they were going to attack in Maseru's sprawling and poorly designated suburbs. Despite their bloodthirsty reputation, the Recces usually took extreme measures to avoid killing innocents, especially women and children. During the months of training the Commandos would practise with different coloured T shirts, representing acceptable targets and non-targets. During the assault if a soldier shot at a 'civilian' target he would be fined. When they got it right, beers were given as rewards. There were bound to be some accidental hits during these big externals. It was easy to point a gun but a trained operator could remain 'selective' only if there was no movement or until fired on. Afterwards returning fire became instinctive.[1]

The attack was delayed on a number of occasions for political reasons. When it came, the seventy SF soldiers, augmented by some local guides and back up, entered on foot, after crossing a river; some had gone by car earlier posing as tourists, and then some with Puma helicopters in support. The MK often fought well; many had weapons and in one case a big box of grenades which kept the Recces at bay. The Lesotho Paramilitary Force intervened and caused some South African casualties; the SAAF had four Impalas bombed up and ready to go. But hitting a foreign capital was avoided when Pretoria's top brass talked to their counterparts in Maseru and got the small but keen Lesotho security forces, more than over-excited at shooting down a Puma, to cease fire, not least to avoid a bombing raid.

The ANC played down the damage to its Maseru infrastructure and Chris Hani had left the capital just before the raid. Twenty-seven coffins, draped in the gold, black and green ANC flag, were given a semi-state funeral, attended by King Moshoeshoe II, on 19 December 1982. In the face of an international furore, Pretoria said the ANC was about to launch attacks on South Africa and its homelands, the Ciskei and Transkei.

The smaller the country, the more intricate the domestic politics. Lesotho indulged in endless debate about whether to appease Pretoria, as well as the undue influence of the communist embassies. The Catholic Church, royalist parties who supported the rusticated king, and internal opposition parties all plotted to oust Jonathan. And Pretoria encouraged them all. The South African government wanted Lesotho to recognize the nearby homelands, especially the adjacent Transkei, and to sign a pact similar to the Nkomati agreement: an end to the subvention of the LLA for the ejection of the ANC. In Maseru, I interviewed Desmond Sixishe, the suave information minister, who mocked the idea of a security pact: 'There is no need for a non-aggression pact between an elephant and an ant.'

Foreign aid donors eventually persuaded Jonathan to hold elections. In 1985 he went through the motions, although the opposition parties were effectively disbarred. Information minister Sixishe waved away critics of the de facto one-party state by saying, 'If people *choose* to vote for one party …'. Nevertheless, splits within his own ruling party continued to undermine Jonathan. In particular, his North Korean-trained Youth League began acting like Maoist Red Guards, much to the disgust of the more conservative officers in the country's security forces whose prestige was already dented by the failure to curb the excesses of the LLA, let alone direct SADF assaults.

In late 1985 Jonathan's twenty-year dictatorship was approaching its final crisis. Pretoria continued to fund an alliance of Basotho opposition parties and to manipulate payments from the customs union which embraced the three former British protectorates. Pik Botha dangled funding of the massive Highlands water project in front of Maseru if it played ball. Jonathan did try to mend his fences with Pretoria and King Moshoeshoe II but it was too late. Events were getting out of hand. On 9 December 1985 the SADF attacked several houses in Maseru and killed six ANC members and three Mosothos. Pretoria then gave a list to Lesotho and demanded that all ANC members on it be expelled or handed over. On 1 January 1986 Pretoria imposed a severe but not total blockade of the landlocked country. Cars and trucks were subjected to intensive searches and some took three or four days to get through the border posts. The blockade was a catalyst for the simmering conflicts inside Lesotho, particularly between (and within) the army and the Youth League. After a complicated series of manoeuvres, the army commander, Major General Justin Lekhanya, toppled Jonathan in a near-bloodless coup on 20 January. Lekhanya pushed the king back into the political limelight to give the new regime local credibility. The general had already made a pilgrimage to Pretoria to explain his conservative views on the ANC. So the South African hawks were happy. After the coup, wild scenes of jubilation erupted on the streets of Maseru to welcome the end of the blockade, the Youth League rampages and the bowler-hatted Jonathan.

The coup was interesting for a number of reasons. It was the first full-blown military coup in a southern African state. More significantly, it was a classic demonstration of the utility of sanctions. By direct, almost comprehensive, sanctions, Pretoria forced a state to rapidly change its political stance, an apt lesson for the UN. Nevertheless, the coup was very much a family affair: Jonathan's executive power passed nominally from Jonathan to his uncle, the king. As one regional observer noted, 'While South African footprints can be seen all around the coup, it would be a mistake to conclude that Pretoria engineered the military takeover.'[2] Nevertheless, Pretoria pressed home its advantage.

The new military government included a number of civilian ministers, some of whom had been linked to the ANC. And the Oxford-educated king was known to have liberal views. Nonetheless, Lekhanya and his ruling military council tipped their hats politely in Pretoria's direction. ANC members were periodically rounded up and expelled at short notice (though not usually to South Africa). The influence of the remaining communist embassies was curtailed. The new military government publicly opposed sanctions and disinvestment. The LLA was wound down and Mokhehle returned home. The Highland water scheme was set in motion. The so-called kingdom in the sky had been brought down to earth. It was back in Pretoria's fold.

Ironically, it was the government of the secular saint, Nelson Mandela, that sent in the South African army again, in October 1998. Under the aegis of the Southern African Development Community, South African troops and the Botswana Defence Force went in to quell civil unrest following a disputed election. Botswana's troops were welcomed but the South Africans were met with stiff resistance from Lesotho's security forces. The unprepared and now far less professional South African troops suffered quite a bloody nose; they were surprised by the hostility and looting that followed their intervention. Parts of Maseru were destroyed.[3] This was the first time the ANC government had intervened outside its own borders. Too many old memories had been revived.

### *Swaziland: the conservative kingdom*

Swaziland is the second smallest country in Africa and can fit at least seventy times into South Africa, which surrounds it on three sides. After independence from Britain in 1968, King Sobhuza became not only the longest-reigning but also the most absolute monarch in the world. With a skilful mixture of modern and feudal statecraft, he beat the white settlers, imperial bureaucrats and black radicals at their own games. His initial alliance with Swazi whites against the African socialists was tactically astute. The king compensated for his kingdom's vulnerability, a country small in size and few in numbers defending a coveted location, by asserting traditional values. Tradition meant conservatism in land tenure, in resource husbandry and, above all, government. The survival of the monarchy and country became fused in the public mind. The monarchy brought stability to the country, despite its sensitive position locked between the apartheid republic and revolutionary Mozambique.

When the king died in 1982, after ruling for sixty-one years, both Swaziland and its monarchy looked vulnerable. The ANC 'presence' in the country became a live question as the SADF pounded into Botswana, Lesotho and Mozambique. Despite the cordial relations between the Swazi police and the SAP, Sobhuza had limited the crackdowns on the ANC. He did this for a number of reasons but mainly because he was trying to maintain Swazi credibility in the OAU and Commonwealth. That meant some distancing of the kingdom from Pretoria. As Sobhuza's personal grip on power began to wane in his final years, his technocrats encouraged him to join the SADCC. But in the same month that Swaziland signed up, a South African trade mission, a *de facto* embassy, was opened up in Mbabane, the capital. Swazi foreign policy was always a balancing act between its anti-communism and the need to be seen to oppose apartheid. When Swaziland became a SADCC member, Pretoria felt that it had to woo back the kingdom, which it considered, like Malawi, to be a natural conservative ally. In February 1982, not long before the king's death, Pretoria had signed a secret security agreement with Swaziland. Although it was made public in 1984, after the Nkomati pact, the Swazi arrangement was somewhat different. Swaziland did not need the kind of military pressure, such as RENAMO, that had induced Mozambique to come to heel. There was often a meeting of minds in the security elites in both Mbabane and Pretoria. So, unlike Nkomati, the 1982 agreement allowed the SADF and SAP to operate against 'international terrorists' *inside* Swaziland.

After Sobhuza's demise, Swazi politics fell into total confusion. Would the security pact hold, especially if the radical socialists came to power as a reaction to the long autocracy? Unlike Lesotho, there were no political parties for Pretoria to manipulate. And not even the most subtle Africanist in the South African foreign ministry could fathom all the nuances of the ever-changing feudal cabals that controlled the interregnum. For, technically, Swaziland was not a monarchy but a dyarchy. All power was supposed to be shared between the hereditary male ruler, called the 'Son of the She-Elephant', with his mother – yes, the 'She-Elephant'. This created a problem with a king in his eighties. So a Queen Regent reigned after Sobhuza but she was deposed and another of Sobhuza's many wives took her place. The regency was riddled with Byzantine intrigue, tales of witchcraft, massive corruption and various assassination attempts. Personality clashes within the remarkable ruling clan, the Dlamini, as well as ideological rivalry between the modernizing technocrats and the traditionalists inside the royal council, the *Liqoqo*, threatened the survival of the conservative monarchy. Eventually, the traditionalists triumphed and in April 1986 an English public-school-educated-19-year-old youth became King Mswati III.

Thereupon nearly all the bickering ended. The world's youngest ruling monarch inherited much of the nation's awe of his late father. Nor was the young king troubled by the complex array of formal opposition forces that delayed the

Swazi warriors at the coronation of King Mswati III (author)

king of Lesotho's return to grace. The elaborate coronation marked the official confirmation of the traditionalists' emphasis on absolute monarchy. P.W. Botha and Pik Botha sat alongside Samora Machel and Prince and Princess Michael of Kent, representing the British Queen. Maureen Reagan stood in for her father, a hereditary representative from the most elective of institutions, the American presidency. Quite by accident, the Americans got it right: sending a favoured daughter is a mark of respect in the local Nguni culture. The world's media were in attendance too, not least because all unmarried Swazi young women, black and white, were expected to dance topless in front of the king as part of the celebrations. It made for good TV, whereas my fully-dressed TV interview with the king was cancelled at the last minute, even though I had been coached on how to depart the monarch's presence by retreating on all fours.[4]

The vulnerable Swazi monarchy was back in the saddle but no one knew which advisers in the king's coterie called the shots. As ever, Pretoria's main concern was to keep out the ANC. Pretoria had been active on this score during the regency. In 1982 Sobhuza had been offered a straightforward swop: South African land in exchange for keeping out the ANC. This had been the sweetener for the security agreement. Regaining foreign-owned land in Swaziland had been the *leitmotif* of Sobhuza's long rule even though the economy had ended up largely in South African hands. But large Swazi irredentas still existed in South Africa. The king had always talked of 'bringing all his children together'. Although ethnically related to the Swazis, these territories had become part of existing South African homelands. The chief minister of KaNgwane, Enos Mabuza, one of the more progressive Bantustan leaders, wanted none of it. 'We have no wish,' he said, 'to be part of a medieval monarchy that rules by decree.' The KwaZulu leader, the mercurial Gatsha Buthelezi, was also extremely hostile to the deal and took the issue to the supreme court. Although the proposal would have given the landlocked kingdom direct access to the sea, it would also have more than doubled the existing Swazi population. The country's social and employment structures would not have coped. Such a transfer would have reinforced the apartheid doctrine of stripping blacks of their South African nationality. Moreover, the deal would have contradicted a basic OAU tenet that sanctified former colonial borders.

Pretoria had got what it wanted, a security agreement; once the king was dead the land deal was quietly dropped. Swaziland continued to co-operate with the SAP's monitoring of ANC activities, especially after the Nkomati accord forced some ANC personnel to take refuge in the kingdom. In 1984 over 300 ANC members were deported from Swaziland. Also, the SADF entered the country on a number of overt hot pursuits as well as secret operations. A complicating factor was RENAMO which set up bases in the mountainous border area. Occasionally, during actions to root out the ANC, the Swazi security forces fought with RENAMO by mistake.

Another important South African propaganda aim was to encourage Swaziland to oppose sanctions publicly, which it did. The cheerfully eclectic Swazi economy had been almost totally dependent upon its big white neighbour. The kingdom's trade faced both ways: to South Africa via the customs union and to Europe via the Lomé agreement. In the mid-1980s Swaziland began to benefit enormously from sanctions evasion, especially the relocation of firms such as Coca-Cola, which had divested from South Africa, and from the relabelling of South African products. The Israeli embassy's flag fluttered proudly in Mbabane, and the most arresting new building was the Pagoda-style Taiwanese embassy. Swaziland pragmatically paid lip-service to the radical OAU creeds, while heartily trading with the three main pariahs in the world.

Occasional attempts to de-link from the South African connection met with the usual mix of economic harassment, including border 'delays'. As with Lesotho's Highland water scheme, attempts to improve the domestic economy often involved South African capital. In February 1986 Swazi railways, which until then had the world's only all-steam system, opened up a new southern link that was plugged in at both ends to the South African rail network. It made economic sense but also meant that the SADCC rail route through Maputo, sometimes sabotaged by RENAMO, became less important.

If Lesotho returned to the South African fold in 1986, Swaziland never really left. It did flirt briefly with a more rebellious stance at the end of the 1970s when it rejected membership of South Africa's constellation plan. Like the other royal mini-state, Lesotho, its economic options were always few. Probably the Swazi monarchy thought it needed Pretoria to survive. Swazi policy had always been pragmatic. Because of its feudal, royalist structure the conservative ruling elite were worried about the triumph of African socialism in the region, especially in South Africa. The end of sanctions did not help the Swazis' brass-plate economy.

And yet the monarchy survived. It even started to experiment with secret voting for the bicameral parliament, the *Libandla.* Swaziland remained tied to the South African economy and currency. Peace in the region did help tourism; the country has some charming resorts and national parks. And yet Swaziland's economy has not developed to cover the many social problems, including the world's highest HIV and AIDS rate and one of the world's lowest life expectancy.

*Botswana: an African success story*

Botswana is big: the same size as France or Texas. It is, however, 80 per cent desert or semi-desert. Like Lesotho and Swaziland, it is ethnically homogenous. Its population in 2018 is around two million, making it one of the most sparsely populated countries in the world, though it has many more cattle. It is a country of stark, often unspoilt, beauty. In the centre lie the exquisite Okavango swamps, in the north the nature reserves teaming with wild life, and to the south and east large cattle ranches. Most of the inhabitants live in the south along the South African border. Independent from Britain in 1966, it was then surrounded on three sides by South Africa and SADF-controlled Namibia. And yet, for all the poor examples set by its black and white neighbours, Botswana developed as one of the few economic and democratic success stories on the continent.

Despite its domination by the South African economy – in the 1980s, 85 per cent of imports originated or passed through its white neighbour – Botswana attempted to distance itself from apartheid. During the 1970s President Sir Seretse Khama tried to prevent the fighting in the Caprivi, southern Zambia and Rhodesia from spilling over his borders. Botswana did suffer from minor SADF incursions in the north-west and from Rhodesian raids in the east. Sir Seretse was lionized in a 2016 movie, *A United Kingdom*, but he certainly displayed great leadership, not least in walking a tightrope in the region. He became a prominent member of the

The former British protectorate of Bechuanaland became the successful state of Botswana

front-line states, although his economic and geographical position forced him to mute some of his criticisms of his white neighbours. After Zimbabwe's independence, the main refugee camp in Botswana's Dukwe area continued to serve as a recruiting ground for both ZIPRA and Super-ZAPU dissidents. Botswana joined the SADCC and, in 1983, the organization's HQ was defiantly established in the capital, Gaborone, a few miles from the South African border.

Sir Seretse Khama and his wife Ruth, lionized by Hollywood. As president he set a moderate multiracial course in a dangerous region

During the 1980s Pretoria's concern, as ever, was to deter the infiltration of ANC insurgents. Sir Seretse's immediate successor, Quett Masire, continued to honour the 'open-door' policy for South African refugees but refused to allow guerrillas to operate from the country. The ANC, however, did use Botswana as an entry point for operations in the Transvaal. Botswana argued that if the SAP and SADF, with all their resources, could not monitor and prevent ANC infiltration, how could the tiny Botswana Defence Force (BDF), especially across such vast ranges of bush? Pretoria replied that Botswana was not trying, or not hard enough. Every year Pretoria would present Gaborone with a list of ANC suspects that it wanted expelled or handed over. Botswana would ask for proof that the ANC refugees were involved in military operations. Pretoria also wanted Botswana to sign the usual non-aggression pact, as well as to recognize the homelands, especially the Tswana bantustan, Bophuthatswana. Gaborone always refused.

Botswana was in a much stronger position than either Lesotho or Swaziland to resist Pretoria's untender traps. Besides owning vast herds of cattle, it had found lots of diamonds. Like South Africa and its then diamond partner, the USSR, Botswana produced about 30 per cent of the world's supply. Jwaneng, in the southern Kalahari, became in the 1980s the world's most valuable diamond mine. This piece of nature's bounty helped generate Botswana's amazing 11 per cent growth rate in the first half of the 1980s. By 1989 Botswana's foreign reserves had overtaken South Africa's gold and foreign exchange reserves. As in the oil-rich states, this new-found wealth was not spread evenly. The resulting disparities and discontent were not, however, manifested in a strong opposition party. Rival political groups did challenge the dominant Botswana Democratic Party. The BDP had been in power since independence, making Botswana *de facto* a one-party state. Yet the rival parties secured only a few seats in parliament. Nevertheless, Pretoria did meddle in internal party politics by encouraging elements in the

Botswana National Front to advocate a non-aggression pact. And Pretoria also had good connections with the senior members of the small defence force. Pretoria's stirring of the pot led nowhere because the ruling party seemed genuinely popular, especially in a society not divided by tribe. Masire's government also made capital out of playing David to the apartheid Goliath. Although Botswana was not entirely free of political thuggery and corruption, there were no political prisoners.

Another problem for Gaborone was the manipulation by South African capitalists of Botswana's mineral windfall. De Beers, the diamond arm of Anglo-American, effectively controlled the sale of Botswana's precious stones. De Beers, however, needed Botswana, to preserve its marketing monopoly, as much as Botswana needed South African investment and industrial expertise. Yet, like the Highland water scheme in Lesotho and the Swazi rail extensions, Pretoria was quite happy to use major projects, such as the development capital required for the extraction of soda ash in the huge Sua Pan salt lake, to force the Gaborone government to make political concessions. Botswana did try hard to de-link. In 1976, for example, it left the rand monetary zone but its trade and transport dependence kept it a hostage, though not a helpless one. The richer the middle class in Botswana became the more they spent on regular shopping sprees in the malls of Pretoria or Johannesburg, just as the most radical relief agencies and NGOs in black southern Africa found themselves shopping in the pariah state.

Pretoria found it almost as easy to handle Botswana as the tiny royal kingdoms. The same old siege machines were wheeled out: border 'delays', withholding of customs dues and manipulation of capital investment. 'The best-managed economy in Africa,' as the Johannesburg *Financial Mail* put it, was lightweight armour against Pretoria's pressures. Until 1985, however, both countries practised peaceful co-existence, to their mutual economic benefit.

The Recce Commando raid on multiple targets in Gaborone on 14 June 1985 ruptured the cosy pattern. Three weeks after the highly publicized military fiasco in Cabinda, in Operation PLEXI, the SADF commandos fired rifles, mortars and grenades for just under an hour in the capital city. South African intelligence had amassed endless files on ANC MK personnel and the Botswana authorities had been reluctant to act. Fourteen people were killed in the Gaborone attack and many documents were seized. Some were MK and others were innocent civilians. The Recces drove out of the capital in one big convoy, managing to get lost while trying to cross the border on a dirt road where the fence had been cut for them. The Botswana Defence Force had been encouraged to stay out of the raid but, when they did try to follow up, the Recce Commandos' caltrops punctured the late pursuers' lead vehicles. The SADF Cabinda raid, involving US oil interests, had annoyed Washington. Now the American ambassador in Pretoria, the ex-journalist Herman Nickel, was recalled. In Washington the state department summoned the South African ambassador-designate to warn him, 'If you want to bring the wrath of God on your head, I couldn't think of a better way of doing it.' The British foreign office, deploying more diplomatic language of course, called the attack on a fellow Commonwealth state 'indefensible'.

In May 1986 the indefensible was repeated when the Recces attacked Gaborone again during their triple assault on Commonwealth states to destroy the Eminent Persons' Group peace initiative. There was a scruffy hotel at Mogaditsane, about three miles west of Gaborone, less than a mile from a large Botswana Defence Force base. South African intelligence had worked out that three rooms in the hotel were rented on a permanent basis for use by MK. A straightforward helicopter assault was planned, deploying two Pumas, with twelve Recces in each, plus two Alouette gunships with 20mm cannon and a command Cessna with sky-shout facilities. Botswana had no effective air force but, just in case, SAAF impalas were on standby. At first light on 20 May 1986 the Cessna circled the BDF bases. The sky-shout blasted out a pre-recorded message in a replay of the famous Rhodesian Green Leader raid which instructed the Zambian military to stay out of the fray.

> Soldiers of the Botswana Defence Force. South African troops are attacking ANC positions close to your base. These ANC gangsters infiltrate into our country to murder innocent women and children. We regard the soldiers/people of Botswana as our neighbours and friends. We have no fight with you. For your own safety, please do not interfere. Our only objective is to eliminate these ANC gangsters. Greetings to our fellow soldiers.[5]

One Recce, 'Julius', the assault group commander, was blinded in one eye by shrapnel from an RPG-7 fired by his own men when they devastated the three ANC rooms. One, probable, ANC target was killed and the BDF claimed three injured when an Aloutte responded to a burst from BDF ground fire. In terms of MK material and men this was not the Recce Commandos' most glorious hour. They had spent under five minutes on the ground, but they had been surprised by the sudden arrival of lots of curious local civilians. The diplomatic fallout was immense, however.

Botswana had always been one of the most easygoing countries in Africa. The sense of friendliness and lack of tension were almost palpable. As the confrontation intensified, roadblocks and security checks spread throughout southern Botswana, as they had elsewhere along the racial fault line in southern Africa. ANC activity increased as did overt SADF incursions and dirty tricks. Tourism, an important money-spinner, suffered as Pretoria issued a number of warnings about the potential dangers in Botswana for South African holidaymakers.

On 28 March 1988 the SADF once again attacked the outskirts of Gaborone, destroying an alleged ANC base and killing four people. Botswana officials insisted that the victims were genuine refugees and innocent Batswana. General

Magnus Malan, however, congratulated the SADF for a 'surgeon's incision against the ANC, with minimum force, to achieve maximum advantage'. This time the BDF investigated why the security forces did not react. A scapegoat was of course found, a corporal who failed to order his patrol to fight the invaders was sentenced to fifteen years in prison for cowardice. Botswana felt obliged to join the local arms race. The 3,150 members of the BDF were to be better equipped and trained. In April 1988 Botswana announced that it would spend more than $130 million on modernization in the next two years. The defence budget had already risen from $8million (1986-87) to $27.29 million (1987-88). Britain then agreed to sell nine secondhand Strikemasters to boost the air force's almost non-existent combat role. British military advisers also assisted the BDF. By the late 1990s the Americans assumed most of the responsibility for training the BDF, especially its officer corps. The BDF joined various UN missions, including Operation RESTORE HOPE in Somalia (1993-94) as well as providing peacekeepers in Mozambique. It performed particularly well in the operation to restore peace in Lesotho, in 1998, despite the poor performance of its ally, the South African army.

At independence Sir Seretse Khama made the conscious decision to avoid building an army to concentrate instead on development. When the BDF was established in 1977 it was more concerned with anti-poaching and aid to civilians during natural disasters. It grew dramatically in the final period of apartheid destabilization. Botswana remained a success story due to its mineral resources as well as conservative fiscal administration and pragmatic foreign policies. It was a diamond in a continental desert of mismanagement.

### *Zambia*

Besides being largely an economic wreck, Zambia was also a political paradox. President Kenneth Kaunda, always known as KK, ruled from independence in 1964 to his ousting in 1991. In public he was a scourge of apartheid, yet in private he was often the main black interlocutor with Pretoria. He took over as the chairman of the front-line states from Nyerere in 1985 and played host to the ANC HQ and to the large SWAPO facilities in Lusaka, yet his mining-based economy was largely run by Anglo-American. A South African defence white paper termed Zambia 'a Marxist satellite' but Pretoria's doves regarded him as a useful 'moderate'.

Kenneth Kaunda: tried to be all things to all men

Zambia's political dilemmas stemmed primarily from the vast chasm between Kaunda's emotive rhetoric, always accompanied by the waving of his handkerchief, and the country's desperate economic performance. The economic woes stemmed from various causes but they included gross corruption and mismanagement, harassment of the small yet vital Indian business community, the aftermath of Rhodesian UDI and sanctions, the closure of the Benguela railway and, most important, the collapse of the world price of copper. Kaunda blamed nearly all his misfortunes on Rhodesia and South Africa. That was politically useful though not entirely accurate.

The Rhodesian war did a great deal of damage, particularly in 1978 and 1979 when the Soviet Union supplied a squadron of MiG-21s, as well as military advisers and equipment for the lacklustre Zambian army. Then, with the political defeat of the Soviet-backed Joshua Nkomo, an ally of Kaunda, the Russian connection was wound down. South African military forays in Zambia had been limited mainly to operations in Zambia adjacent to the Caprivi Strip. After 1975 the SADF trained and assisted a dissident group led by Adamson Mushala for seven years. Originally supported by the Portuguese army, South African military intelligence helped the group, never more than 200 fighters, to destabilize Kaunda's rule both in the name of national opposition to the one-party state and in the name of Barotse tribal separation. Mushala was killed in 1982 but dissidence continued until an amnesty in 1990 as part of Kaunda's reluctant move to multi-party politics. During the last Rhodesian offensives into Zambia, the SADF simultaneously moved into the Western province in some strength. The spillovers from both the SADF's pro-UNITA and anti-SWAPO campaigns disrupted the area throughout the 1980s.

The SADF was restrained for a number of reasons: the amount of South African mining involvement, the trade with and through Zambia, and Kaunda's diplomatic usefulness. On a number of important public occasions Kaunda provided a means for Pretoria to break out of its diplomatic cocoon: in 1975 during the Victoria Falls conference, in 1982 during the P.W. Botha-Kaunda summit and during the separate South African talks in Lusaka with Angola and SWAPO in 1984. And, often, Kaunda worked secretly behind the scenes as a mediator. Initially to the South African government's annoyance, a series of meetings in Zambia between South African business and opposition leaders and the ANC was fixed up by KK. Lusaka was also the venue for a major ANC conference as well as front-line and SADCC summits. There were often gala occasions. Despite the shabby surroundings, the fleets of new Mercedes and flowing wine would have added some tone, except for the fact that all these luxuries were provided by South Africa. When the Zambian shops did have any quality goods for sale, they were often from the despised republic but nobody bothered to disguise the 'made in South Africa' labels.

By 1986 Kaunda seemed to have despaired of his role as regional mediator and his ability to persuade Pretoria to see reason. The SADF raid on alleged ANC bases and offices in Lusaka on 20 May 1986, at the same time as raids on Gaborone and Harare, may have been the last straw. SAAF Impalas had flown low, avoiding Russian and British aid defence systems, and pounded the facilities using bombs and cannon. Kaunda's position hardened dramatically at the Commonwealth summit in London in August where he committed Zambia to applying sanctions, without any contingency plans or discussions with his ministers. Anti-white paranoia about 'foreign agents' resulted in numerous cases of arrest and maltreatment of tourists and visiting businessmen, which further strained relations with Zambia's major aid donors. This was made even worse by Zambia's repudiation of its IMF agreements. The repudiation was precipitated by widespread food riots in December 1986 after the government had been forced to drop food subsidies as a precondition for the desperately needed IMF loan. The riots, mainly on the northern copperbelt, were eventually put down by the army, with some loss of life. Zambia was in no position to feed itself properly, let alone impose comprehensive sanctions on the regional superpower. But Kaunda also felt obliged by his promise to Maputo by sending a token force of troops to help anti-RENAMO operations in Tete province.

KK managed just to see out the period of apartheid destabilization. And yet his role as an anti-apartheid activist and mediator with South Africa were perhaps his raison d'être. Remove apartheid and his national utility was also removed. The sacrifices demanded by the Rhodesian war against the nextdoor enemy were often met with some sense of national purpose. But once Ian Smith was replaced by Robert Mugabe things got worse, not better. In 1980 and 1986 KK faced serious rumours of a military coup. Zaire, Nigeria and Tanzania may have neglected essentials such as transport and agricultural reforms but they were never foolish enough to run out of beer. Zambia managed to run out of that politically sensitive commodity regularly in the 1980s. The Zambian army, however, was always supplied with cheap and plentiful supplies of beer. Nevertheless, in October 1988 there were once more rumblings of a coup. His long-term ally, Julius Nyerere, had retired with some dignity, even though he had destroyed his own economy. Julius tried to persuade his friend Kenneth to do the same. It was clear the Zambian leader would go only kicking and screaming. KK had survived perhaps because, for all his lachrymose bluster, he was no real military threat to Pretoria. In the end the discontents among his own technocrats, unions and the professional classes as well as more passive hostility from the peasantry forced KK to hold multi-party elections in which he was thrashed by the new opposition. And the army made sure there was no backsliding. KK was jailed for a while but later remerged as an elder statesman.

### *Malawi: the odd man out*

Malawi was *in* the front line but not *of* the front line. It was a very conservative state with formal diplomatic relations with South Africa even though it was separated from the outcast by more than 400 miles of Mozambican territory. Malawi was conservative because His Excellency the Life President *Ngwazi* Dr Hastings Kamuzu Banda was ultra-conservative. Malawi was Banda squared: small, disciplined and notably intolerant. He ruled as a modern African monarch, dressed in black homburg, three-piece suit and thick spectacles. Pictures of the *Ngwazi,* or conqueror, were everywhere. The highly eccentric and very old president had lived away from his homeland for over thirty years, mainly in England where he worked as a successful general medical practitioner. He was also an elder of the Church of Scotland. Banda often harked back to the colonial era and appeared to believe that, in non-political roles, whites were often more qualified than blacks to hold key positions. This anachronistic viewpoint was also epitomized in the founding of the well-known Kamuzu Academy. The academy was an Eton in the bush, complete with white teachers. Banda argued that an educated man should know European history and Latin and Greek; he gave speeches in English which were rendered into the vernacular by a translator.

Malawi's relations with South Africa, though basically cordial, vacillated. During the 1970s Malawi was the darling of hardnosed economists. The growth rate was 6 per cent per annum and the country exported food. South African aid and loans had helped, although Pretoria predictably dangled funds for big projects in return for political concessions. South Africa had provided soft loans for the building of Banda's new capital at Lilongwe and a railway to Nacala, the port on the Mozambique coast. Banda was always grateful, in particular, for his new capital, as Western donors had refused to assist in the grandiose scheme. In 1967 Malawi and South Africa had exchanged ambassadors. Malawi was the only African country to do so. In 1970 John Vorster paid a rare visit and Banda reciprocated the following year. The life president also established diplomatic relations with Taiwan and Israel. All three pariahs, but especially South Africa, helped train Malawi's four security-related organizations: the army, police, special branch and the Young Pioneers. The heads of each service were handpicked by Banda, who ruled with an iron fist. Opponents disappeared or were 'accidentalized' in car crashes. Banda maintained his autocracy by keeping his opponents divided, in jail or in exile. He also dished out favours, money and properties judiciously, especially to the active women's section of the sole legal political movement, the Congress Party. In this he was astute, for women were traditionally the backbone of African society and agriculture, a fact which tends to be underplayed in male-dominated African politics. In 1981, for example, Banda simply appointed thirteen extra women to parliament, making the total number thirty-four. In a 128-member parliament this probably gave Malawi one of the highest percentages of female parliamentarians, not only in Africa but in the rest of the world.

Although South African companies were well-represented in the economy, as were South African and Rhodesian managers, the financial structure was never dominated by apartheid capital, partly because a small number of parastatals, directly controlled by Banda, supervised most of the economy. Malawi was sometimes dubbed 'capitalism without capitalists'. This worked for a while because of the retention of white expertise, and, a rarity in Africa, an efficient and honest civil service modelled on the British system. By the mid-1970s the rigidity of parastatal control and poor weather conditions caused a rapid decline in agricultural production. In 1976 a coup attempt, led by the head of Special Branch, Focus Gwende, was ruthlessly crushed. As Special Branch had close ties with Pretoria, this might have been a factor in the cooling of relations with the South African government. When Malawi joined the SADCC, Pretoria tried to woo back its fellow conservative with more loans. The stick was also applied. The SADF used RENAMO to cut Malawi's transport links through Mozambique. Strangely, Malawi also had ties with the rebels (discussed in the chapter on the civil war in Mozambique). As Joseph Hanlon noted, Malawi 'was an agent for its own destabilization'.[6] One of the reasons was that, as Banda started losing his mental facilities, various factions were vying to succeed him; some favoured RENAMO, while the younger technocrats did not. In 1987 Malawi's position started to shift, not least through pressure from Mozambique and Zimbabwe. Malawi's small but competent army sent troops in to Mozambique to protect the Nacala line. During Margaret Thatcher's visit to Malawi in March 1989, she offered £720,000 to equip Malawian forces operating in Mozambique and a team of Royal Engineers to help with mine clearance on the Nacala railway.

As apartheid collapsed simultaneously with the end of the Cold War, the aged and senile anti-communist dictator had less value. As in Zambia, Banda was forced to give way to multi-party elections after a referendum in 1993. The army skilfully defanged the Young Pioneers and generally finessed a relatively peaceful transition during the 1994 elections. As with KK, Banda faced prosecution, not least for the disappearance of some of his opponents. And yet, as in many transitions from authoritarianism, the defeated old leaders from the independence period were usually treated leniently, despite their many crimes. Fittingly, the Conqueror was conquered by death in a Johannesburg clinic in 1997, probably aged 99.

Dr Hastings Banda, an anachronism among black leaders

### *Adventures elsewhere*

Destabilization was primarily aimed at the frontline states. All suffered in varying degrees from the cutting edge of South Africa's military and economic power. Mozambique was torn apart by the RENAMO war, while Tanzania was relatively unscathed because of its geographical distance and minimal trade with South Africa. The blockade of SADCC southern routes actually benefited Tanzania because it forced Zambia and Zimbabwe to make more use of facilities at Dar es Salaam.

Pretoria's adventurism extended far beyond the frontline states, and beyond Africa. The long arm of the SADF and its agents reached London where, for example, Pretoria was blamed for the bombing of an ANC office on 14 March 1982 or to Paris where an ANC representative was assassinated. Sweden's former prime minister, Olof Palme, was killed in Stockholm on 28 February 1986, allegedly by an ex-Rhodesian special forces operator under the control of South African military intelligence. Pretoria considered Palme an enemy because of his involvement in the channelling of large ANC funds.[7] South African secret money also went into European and US media in an attempt to buy influence. Pretoria's slush fund bought into news agencies and publications such as the *Washington Star*. Domestically, the *Citizen* newspaper was purchased.[8]

Africa was the main battleground, however. With its Rhodesian and French allies, Pretoria meddled in many continental wars. South Africa provided clandestine military and diplomatic backing for both the Biafra and Katangese secession movements. White South Africans were prominent among the mercenaries who fought for Moise Tshombe as leader of Katanga in 1960-63 and as Congolese prime minister in 1964-65. The Congo wars spawned a hard core of mercenaries who were employed on and off by Pretoria for twenty years. Some were used in Zaire where Pretoria and the CIA cultivated ties with the venal Mobutu, particularly for supply routes for UNITA. One of the best-known Congo veterans, 'Mad Mike' Hoare, came out of retirement in Durban to lead the November 1981 coup attempt in Seychelles. Hoare was past his prime and, although his fifty-odd member team included experienced ex-Rhodesian and serving SADF soldiers, the coup was poorly planned and financed. The precise extent of Pretoria's involvement was deliberately fudged. Yet military intelligence knew all about it and middle-ranking SADF officers provided small arms. There was some opposition and cautious distancing at senior military and political levels but if it had worked no doubt the top brass would have taken all the credit.[9] In parliament Magnus Malan dismissed the opposition's outrage at the government's handling of the aftermath of the bungled coup, when Hoare's men were jailed for hijacking an Air India Jumbo aircraft to get back to Durban, by saying, 'If the government wanted to take over the Seychelles government or cause its downfall, it could have used the best army in Africa to do the little job in a jiffy.'

A successful coup, engineered partly by Rhodesia and South Africa, did take place in a jiffy in the Comores. In the early morning light of 13 May 1978, another ageing ex-Congo mercenary, Bob Denard, accompanied by a pet German shepherd and thirty other dogs of war, waded ashore at Itsandra beach to claim possession of the republic of the Comores on behalf of the deposed ex-president, Ahmed Abdallah Abderemane. The inhabitants of the islands, a former French protectorate, greeted Denard as a liberator from the repressive and manic rule of Ali Soilih, who was shot 'trying to escape' two days later. Soilih once had a vision of being assassinated by a man with a dog, so he ordered all the dogs on the island to be killed. Hence the reason for Denard taking his pet to war. For more than a decade Denard ruled the islands behind the powerless façade of President Abdallah.

One of the four main islands had opted to stay French: Mayotte (Mahore) hosted a French Foreign Legion battalion. The Comores were considered to be of strategic importance because they sat astride the main sea lanes of the Indian Ocean. South Africa was reported to have established a powerful communication and listening post on the main island, Grande Comore, that monitored not only shipping but also eavesdropped on radio traffic through much of east Africa. Pretoria was persistently accused of using the Comoros islands as a staging post for supplying RENAMO and for selling arms to Iran. With some reservations, the French cooperated with South Africa in funding Denard's 'presidential guard'. The cost, about £2 million, was part of a wider operation, agreed between King Fahd of Saudi Arabia and CIA chief William Casey, to support anti-communist movements worldwide. The French, and their friends in Morocco and Gabon, were also involved not only in the Comores gambit but other ventures in Equatorial Guinea, São Tomé and Principe, as well as UNITA territory, all with South African connections. French influence in the Comores was embodied in the deputy commander of the presidential guard, Commander Charles (alias Rogér Ghys, a French protégé despite his Belgian origins). After a protracted struggle with Denard, Charles was pushed out of the islands in October 1987, leaving Pretoria for the moment, as the main influence.[10] Besides its military and sanctions-busting utility, South Africa expanded the tourist infrastructure of the islands. South African aircraft, painted in the livery of the Comores, as well as South African Airways, established regular flights to the new apartheid dependency.

After the death of the president in highly questionable circumstances, French pressures forced Denard to quit the island in late 1989. He took refuge in South Africa. Pretoria's meddling had left a sad legacy: unstable presidents who sometimes indulged in extreme Islamism and thus encouraged other islands in the archipelago to want to return to French rule. The islands suffered twenty major coups or coup attempts following independence in 1975. Bob Denard made another attempt in 1995 but the French stopped him. The post-apartheid world was a different place.

### *The meaning of destabilization*

South Africa's muscular foreign policy had been both crude and subtle. It gave ground when necessary, as (eventually) in Namibia, but then it would consolidate as in Mozambique, or go on the offensive as in Lesotho. Whatever the internal disagreements within Pretoria's governing elite about the means, the desired end was always the same: the creation of a circle of compliant states in southern Africa. These states were simultaneously meant to be military and political buffers and conductors of economic domination. As Joseph Hanlon noted, South Africa was defending 'not merely a set of racial taboos but an economic system'. The SADCC survived the South African campaigns but the main front-line states were always too weak economically and too dependent on Pretoria to really push for total sanctions on the apartheid regime. Despite the flood of rhetoric from presidential palaces, trade went on. Economic reality usually triumphed; the front-line states needed to eat and drink, and sometimes the basics, not just fine South African wines. So Pretoria did well on the economic front, though its regional wars also drained the coffers. And what did military destabilization achieve? Few of the major political goals. True, two states signed non-aggression pacts but no homelands were recognized, nor were they ever likely to have been. And South African political refugees were rarely handed back to Pretoria. And no one sent ambassadors to Pretoria except for wayward Malawi.

Domestically, the SADF raids bolstered the ruling National Party's tough-guy image despite the opposition Conservative Party's criticisms of the government as too *soft* on its neighbours. At the same time, the Pax Pretoria did reinforce the tendency in South Africa to try to fix political problems with military 'solutions'. For all the frenetic military activity the ANC grew in stature during the 1980s. Nonetheless, the settlements in Angola and Namibia did push MK bases farther away from the heartland of white power. In this sense, destabilization as an Afrikaner 'counter-revolution' did roll back the externally based ANC guerrillas. It was, however, a military counter-revolution without a political content. It depended on tanks and blockades, not ideas. Meanwhile, the trainloads of food, soap, and cooking oil for the masses, as well as expensive consumer goods for the elites, continued to roll north. The more Marxist-oriented front-liners confirmed the old cliché: the misery of being exploited by capitalists was nothing to the misery of *not* being exploited. Pretoria made the valid point: ironically, just as southern African countries increasingly started to embrace private enterprise, private capital was fleeing the continent.

Destabilization had been a key element of Pretoria's regional policy, and yet there had not been much public debate inside the republic about the scale of the damage it had caused. Few South African whites, cocooned in their cosy, censored little world realized that on the other side of the front line, destabilization was a venomous hate word. The red blood of the massacres in Mozambique or Angola had taken on a hideous monochrome. Harvey Tyson, the editor of the *Star,* Johannesburg's main English-language daily, tried to explain destabilization to his local readers:

> What if Botswana sent an army unit to Pretoria to blow up a building; Swaziland sent in secret police to grab some AWB [the neo-Nazi *Afrikaner Weerstandsbeweging*] plotters; Zimbabwe landed troops at Port Elizabeth where they blew up the petrol tanks, and Mozambique dropped military equipment and equipped mercenaries to capture White River, Nelspruit and Middelburg? ... And what would you call Captain Wynand du Toit's excursion into northern Angola? If it were Cuban troops scouting around Saldanha, we'd call it more than destabilization – we'd cry invasion.[11]

Joseph Hanlon tried to do the same for a British audience:

> Suppose a foreign power trained Welsh guerrillas, aeroplanes dropped arms and other supplies into the Welsh mountains, submarines came close to the coast to land instructors and pick up men for training, commandos came ashore and blew up British Rail bridges, and a pirate radio station broadcasting in Welsh called for an uprising. All this and more has been done in Mozambique. This example is, of course, hypothetical; there is no war in Wales. But because the Welsh nationalists have more support in Wales than the MNR [RENAMO] has in Mozambique, it is perhaps reasonable to ask what would happen if a foreign power were to support them. In this case Britain is rich and powerful and would be able to quell a substantial guerrilla insurgency in the Welsh hills, were one to be organized; by comparison, Mozambique is poor and weak and hasn't much chance against the South African-backed MNR.[12]

Hanlon continued his analogy by noting that Britain and Spain had 'indigenous dissidents'. He asked what would have happened if substantial international support were given to the IRA or the Basque ETA organization. It is also true that the great European conflicts are full of examples of one nation nourishing rebels in another rival state. And yet the engine for destabilization in southern Africa was different: the preservation of a uniquely racist system. In this important respect South Africa was not like other regional hegemons. It is now time to turn to the core of the subject: the war against the apartheid homeland. Destabilization in the front-line states and the defence of white supremacy were two sides of the same coin. Destabilization was apartheid exported. Pretoria had long evaded history. White rule was bound to end. But how?

# PART IV

# WAR IN SOUTH AFRICA

# *Chapter 14*

# Black Resistance

The African National Congress is the continent's oldest black nationalist party. It was founded in 1912, nine years before the Chinese communist party and two years before the Afrikaner National Party. Although the ANC stood head and shoulders above its rival resistance movements, the road to power was slow and erratic. Its political clout among the masses inside South Africa was not in doubt but its military campaigns were largely ineffective. Although it won in the end, the ANC was often called the most unsuccessful guerrilla army in the world. Of course guerrilla wars are not necessarily won on the battlefield. Possibly TV's Bill Cosby show, for both whites and blacks in the republic, had as much social impact as the armed struggle.

The ANC suffered from periodic crises of survival but each time it metamorphosed into a more militant force. One of the most contentious issues was the relationship with the South African Communist Party, founded in 1921. The SACP provided a vital organizational core and a crucial arms and training link with Moscow. This nexus, however, also alienated black nationalists both inside and outside the party, as well as potential allies in the West. Joe Slovo, a Jew of Lithuanian origins, was a leading figure in both parties. As chief of staff of the ANC's guerrilla army, *Umkhonto we Sizwe* or MK, he was responsible for much of the military strategy. The SACP espoused a two-stage theory of revolution. The party theoreticians argued that the National Party government represented an internal colonial force that oppressed blacks as well as the white working class, despite the latter's privileges. The first stage of democratization would be accomplished by an anti-colonial, multi-racial, nationalist revolution. The communist party would then act as the vanguard for real change, the second stage, a socialist government via a socialist revolution. As both parties overlapped in membership, the question of the primacy of nationalism versus socialism, plus the timing and nature of armed struggle, energized many of the debates about future planning. Obviously Pretoria played up the ANC's slavish affiliation to Moscow, rather than a genuine indigenous multi-racial change to democracy. Pretoria always conflated the *rooi gevaar* and the *swart gevaar* – the red and black dangers. The ANC's ideological differences impacted on ideology and military strategy. And for decades the question of whether Nelson Mandela was also a member of the SACP consumed endless scholarly effort. The upshot seemed to be that he was always a secret member. And, today, so what?

The ANC was founded in 1912

## *Petitions and pleas*

The first of the ANC's many battles was the opposition to the 1913 Native Land Act, which consolidated white possession of most of South Africa's land. Sol Plaatje's great classic, *Native Life in South Africa*, published in 1916, vividly captured the suffering of the black peasantry. Black rights were further eroded by the 1936 Land Act. Land hunger was always a prime ingredient of early ANC militancy. The ANC flag was striped green for the stolen land, as well as black for the people and yellow for the gold.

The ANC was originally led by conservative, black, middle-class figures. They supported, more or less, the Union of South Africa's war efforts in both world conflagrations in the hope that the British government and the emerging Commonwealth would intervene eventually on their behalf. As with the Rhodesian nationalists, their faith was misplaced. Neither petitions to London nor Pretoria worked. A younger and angrier generation formed the ANC Youth League in 1943-44. Its leaders included the eventual pantheon of ANC heroes, Nelson Mandela, Oliver Tambo and Walter Sisulu. In 1948 the advent of fullblooded white supremacy helped to push the ANC towards further organized defiance. Spontaneous peasant revolts in the rural areas had long been a feature of black anger. In 1950 tribespeople rose in rebellion in Witzieshoek; in February 1960 a peasant insurrection erupted in Pondoland. Rural resistance met with brutal police retaliation. In the cities the ANC launched better publicized and more organized defiance campaigns, based largely on Mahatma Gandhi's model of passive resistance.

The ANC became an omnibus national movement, not a party, which encompassed supporters from a variety of classes, tribes and races. 'Africanists' within the movement, however, were hostile to an alliance with whites, especially those in the communist party. On 26 June 1955 the ANC helped to organize a 'Congress of the People' at Kliptown, near Johannesburg. The ANC later adopted the Freedom Charter that emerged from this congress. This vaguely worded,

Utopian document became the moral constitution of the ANC and its political vision of a multiracial society. In 1958-59 the Africanists broke away to form the Pan-Africanist Congress (PAC). They advocated direct action against apartheid without, they said, the patronizing support of white liberals and communists. Even within the ANC there was still opposition to the 'pleading, cowardly and *hambe-kahle* [go-slow/go well]' attitude of the conservative, often middle-class, leadership. The ANC-PAC split reflected a continuing debate within the nationalist movements throughout Africa. Fundamentally, it revolved around the issue of a 'pure' African nationalist response versus the concept of a class, race and ideological alliance to overturn the colonizer/racial oppressor. This divergence was to widen dramatically in South Africa in the 1980s. The ANC was even accused of multi-racial collaboration with Pretoria, while the PAC and its allies were damned for reverse racism. Accusations of crude black racism were dispersed with the arcane, incestuous lexicon of neo-Marxist debates.

The ANC-PAC competition came to a head in 1960. The ANC had decided to hold, on 31 March, massive demonstrations against the hated pass laws, linked with a national campaign for a minimum wage. On 18 March, however, the PAC, led by Robert Sobukwe, pre-empted the ANC by announcing that an anti-pass campaign would begin on 21 March, linked to a demand for a slightly higher minimum wage than the one advocated by the ANC. In most cases the demonstrations passed off peacefully. But in Sharpeville in the Transvaal the police panicked, opened fire and killed sixty-nine protesters and injured 180. On 30 March, in Cape Town, 30,000 Africans marched on parliament. Troops and armoured cars were deployed around the legislature to deter them. (One of these units was led by a young captain called Magnus Malan.) After police promises to negotiate, which were reneged upon, the protestors were persuaded to disperse peacefully. This march, not Sharpeville, was the immediate pretext for the government's declaration of a temporary state of emergency. The ANC and PAC were banned; their leaders went underground or into exile.

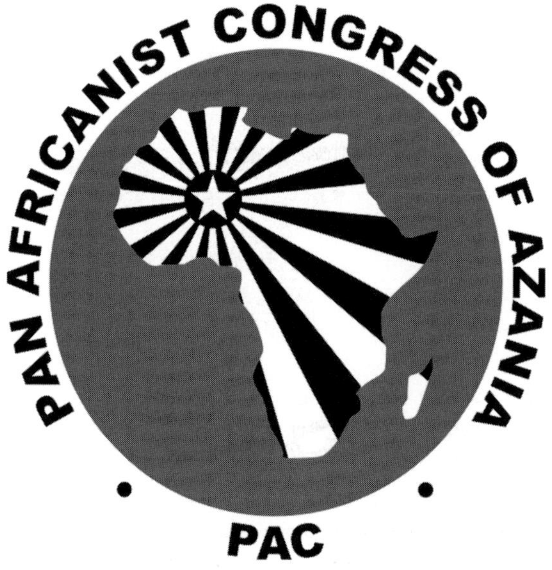

Pan-Africanist Congress emblem

### *The genesis of the armed struggle*

For nearly fifty years, from 1912 to 1961, the ANC had pleaded and protested, totally in vain. Black rights had been whittled way, not ameliorated. The days of passive resistance were over. On 16 December 1961 *Umkhonto we Sizwe* (Spear of the Nation) or MK, was set up as the military wing of the ANC. It was a symbolic day: Afrikaners commemorated the Battle of Blood River that day, their supposed covenant with God. Ironically, too, the armed struggle began five days after the president of the ANC, Albert Luthuli, received the Nobel Peace Prize. Could peaceful methods ever have worked against such an obdurate regime? Luthuli warned in 1957 that the road to freedom 'was sanctified with the blood of martyrs – in other words, no cross, no crown'.

Black politics was to produce numerous martyrs but no original military tacticians: no local Giap or Guevara emerged to lead the armed struggle. In January 1962 Nelson Mandela did leave South Africa secretly and visited a number of African countries where he received some rudimentary military training. Few of the ANC or PAC leaders had enjoyed the benefits of formal and extended military instruction, and it showed.

The decision to wage civil war was not taken lightly, despite the sustained fury inspired by Pretoria's legalized tyranny. It took decades for the ANC to become a revolutionary party. It was always, as Anthony Sampson described it, 'a baffling mixture of purpose and muddle, radicalism and conservatism, Christianity and communism'.[1] Some black leaders welcomed the armed confrontation; others lamented it and hoped that this necessary evil would be brief and that the Boers would soon come to their senses and negotiate. In the first phase of the ANC insurgency (1961-65) operations were limited almost entirely to sabotage attacks avoiding the loss of life. In retrospect, the decision to opt for a sabotage campaign, which developed eventually into a people's war, seems an almost inevitable progression. At the time the more militant leaders were influenced by the recently successful guerrilla campaigns in Cuba and Algeria. The ANC debated four possible forms of military action: sabotage, guerrilla warfare, terrorism and open revolution. Sabotage was chosen because, in Mandela's words, 'It did not involve loss of life and it offered

The South African Communist Party helped to form an organizational core of the ANC resistance; one of the reasons for the PAC split.

the most hope for future race relations.' Nonetheless, other peaceful stratagems *might* have worked, even in the 1960s, if they had been properly implemented. As it was, the first phase of the ANC's warfare was a fiasco. A much better organized and sustained nationwide campaign of civil disobedience might have been more effective, especially if it had been accompanied by a 'populist' strategy of strikes. Gandhi's *satyagraha* campaigns, first developed when he lived in South Africa, did eventually work on the Indian subcontinent. Both the British *Raj* and the Afrikaner pigmentocracy rested upon the same risky political levitation act. Awe, more than military power, kept the ruling minority suspended above the masses. The population ratio of underclass to rulers, it is true, was much greater in the *Raj* than in South Africa. And Gandhi's peaceful resistance targeted the British overlords precisely: he made them feel uncomfortable in their cherished field of moral rectitude. The Afrikaners defended their status quo in a different moral universe. Moreover, the demands for self-rule in the *Raj* were much better organized; the ANC failed to design a mass mobilization properly or even the small-scale sabotage campaign. MK gradually improved. Nonetheless, the decision to opt for an armed struggle meant that the resistance movements were attacking the government at its strongest point, the means and will to deploy the mailed fist.

The PAC attempted an even more apocalyptic approach. Unlike the ANC, it wanted to kill whites from the beginning. It set up a military wing, *Poqo,* meaning – like Ireland's Sinn Féin – 'ourselves'. With little overall political direction, *Poqo* tried to inspire a spontaneous grassroots insurrection against white rule, a Mau-Mau-style night of the long knives, which was nearly every white African's secret fear. And yet spontaneity presumably should have included an element of surprise. Potlako Leballo, the mercurial PAC leader, spoiled the effect by announcing the 1962 uprising in advance at a press conference in Maseru. No nationwide rebellion ensued, although a number of pro-government chiefs were murdered in the Transkei and, notoriously, on 22 November 1962, 250 blacks carrying axes, pangas and homemade weaponry went on a rampage in Paarl, in Cape Province. Two whites were killed there and five others in the Transkei. A police crackdown, however, soon crushed *Poqo*. The PAC was criticized – not least by the ANC – for its theory of spontaneous combustion, both on tactical and moral grounds. Although effective insurgency usually demands thorough political preparation, the PAC's early strategy was perhaps, in some ways, justified by the spontaneous aspects of the Soweto rebellion of 1976 and the 1984 unrest that caught the ANC almost completely unawares. Because of *Poqo's* failures in the 1960s and chronic infighting within its exiled leadership, the PAC increasingly lost ground in the liberation struggle.

The initial phase of both the PAC's and the ANC's armed struggle was emasculated by the SAP. Some of the leaders set about rebuilding their banned parties in exile. The ANC turned to Moscow for more help while the PAC received funds from China and, for a while, allegedly from the CIA.[2] The PAC made some unhelpful friends: FNLA, UNITA and COREMO (a FRELIMO splinter). The ANC made much better progress on the cocktail circuits abroad, and in their choice of allies. The small disciplined, largely white, communist party proved itself to be a true heir of Lenin in its clandestine activities. In contrast, the ANC leaders blundered around in the twilight world of illegal politics. Their amateurishness was exhibited by the Rivonia fiasco. Mandela had been operating underground for seventeen months, despite some close shaves. On one occasion a black security policeman recognized him but the policeman winked, gave the ANC thumbs-up salute and passed on by. Mandela spent some of his time at the Liliesleaf farm in Rivonia, a white middle-class suburb on the outskirts of Johannesburg. He read a great deal during this period, especially Clausewitz. On 5 August 1962 he was captured near Durban, possibly after a tip off from CIA sources. While Mandela was in prison, on 12 July 1963, the security police pulled off the most spectacular coup: the MK leaders, including Walter Sisulu, Denis Goldberg, a white civil engineer, and Govan Mbeki, were all caught in one place, the Rivonia farm, with a mass of incriminating documents. One of Clausewitz's truisms, never underestimate your enemy, had been studiously ignored. As a biographer of Mandela commented:

> undoubtedly some men in the political collective at Rivonia had become over-confident of their security as, disguised, they functioned from the unreal world of 'underground'. Always referring to the government as 'fascist' they never operated as though it was; a failing that would continue to weaken the liberation movement.[3]

The ensuing lengthy trial of the Rivonia men and Mandela, all charged in essence with treason, allowed the ANC a political platform. Mandela, who had set up a legal practice in Johannesburg with Oliver Tambo, spoke with great power from the dock. Facing possible capital punishment, he said:

> During my lifetime I have dedicated myself to this struggle of the African people. I have fought against white domination, and I have fought against black domination. I have cherished the ideal of a democratic and free society in which all persons live together in harmony and with equal opportunities. It is an ideal which I hope to live for and to achieve. But if needs be it is an ideal for which I am prepared to die.

No one was hanged then, but the life imprisonment of Mandela (then aged 44) and his colleagues, plus the police round-up of many other underground ANC personnel, decapitated the movement. The MK leaders were taken away

WOMEN ARISE AND ACT!
UMKHONTO
WE SIZWE

MK poster for women revolutionaries

to the bleak Robben Island off Cape Town. The prison acquired a romantic notoriety like Alcatraz and Devil's Island, although Mandela might not have found his labouring in a quarry so romantic. His speech in court and the twenty-seven years spent behind bars transformed him from a partisan prophet into an international secular saint. But MK needed generals in the field, not martyrs in jail. The armed struggle collapsed into a decade of torpor.

*Poqo* advocated an explicitly murderous policy while the ANC's sabotage concentrated on destroying property not people. Both had failed to elicit mass response. Isolated acts of resistance, sometimes involving white radicals, continued. A member of the tiny African Resistance Movement, John Harris, placed a bomb in the concourse of Johannesburg station. Despite the ARM's commitment to damaging only property, one of the fifteen injured in the explosion later died. Harris was duly executed, the only white insurgent ever to be executed in South Africa.[4] One of the best-known whites to take part in the liberation struggle was the communist leader, Bram Fischer, an Oxford-educated QC and scion of a very distinguished Free State Afrikaner family. He had helped to defend Mandela at the Rivonia trial, even though some of the documents seized at the Liliesleaf farm were in his handwriting. He was a leading member of the SACP who went underground but he was caught and sentenced to life imprisonment in 1965. Fischer was treated particularly badly by the Afrikaner guards in prison. Fellow prisoner Denis Goldberg, interviewed in 2018, said that the guards had tried 'to break Bram not least by making him clean latrines with a toothbrush…. This man could have been prime minister of the country if he had wanted'.[5] He was released from prison in 1975 shortly before his death from cancer. Fischer's politics incensed conservative Afrikaners: even his ashes were denied to his family.[6] Later, books and films lionized the modest Afrikaner rebel. In her famous post-apartheid book, *Country of My Skull*, Antjie Krog wrote, 'He was so much braver than the rest of us, he paid so much more; his life seems to have touched the lives of so many people – even after his death.'[7]

Bram Fischer: a noble Afrikaner and revolutionary

The continued involvement of whites in the resistance, from communist revolutionaries such as Fischer to parliamentary liberals such as Helen Suzman, did much to prevent the South African struggle from descending into a stark black-versus-white cataclysm. These whites were reviled by large sections of the white population but in the long run all South Africans would owe a debt to the courage and stoicism of the dissident individuals who looked beyond their skin colour. In the short term the ANC's multi-racial approach helped its restructuring after the Rivonia fiasco. The first phase of the armed resistance had stalled because of, in the words of a military history of the movement, 'a lack of bases, inadequate organization and discipline, logistical deficiencies, insufficient international support, poor political mobilization, shortage of funds, vulnerability to the regime's counterespionage and counter-insurgency tactics …'.[8]

### *The second phase*

The second phase of the resistance, essentially from the Rivonia period to the Soweto uprising in 1976, was spent regrouping ANC forces and strategy. The leadership's long exile in the front-line states often proved demoralizing. Although both the ANC and PAC were recognized equally by the OAU, the PAC's bloody internecine feuds almost led to the OAU stripping the movement of its funds and recognition. To a lesser extent the ANC was also prone to internal wrangling. One of the causes was the disastrous ANC participation, along with Zimbabwean insurgents, in the incursions into Matabeleland in 1967-68. They were wiped out by the Rhodesian army. In 1968 Portuguese troops ambushed and killed a small PAC raiding party trying to infiltrate through Mozambique.

The ANC tried to expand in four directions: its underground inside the republic; the preparation for mass mobilization; the armed struggle; and international diplomacy. Until 1976 the ANC made better progress in the final aim, especially procuring contacts in Africa and in the Eastern bloc. At the Morogoro conference in Tanzania in 1969, the ANC streamlined its military structure and dedicated itself to mobilizing its domestic constituency, especially among the youth.

The ANC remained a broad church of resistance politics, despite increasing dependence on the Soviet arsenal and the South African Communist Party. Although there were revolts by, and purges of, Africanist and Trotskyite elements in the movement, the ANC tried to keep to the middle of the road. Despite Pretoria's barrage of accusations that the ANC was a mere tool of the KGB, the ANC's political culture remained moderate and multi-racial. One example was the ANC President Oliver Tambo's signature on the protocol of the Geneva convention, which legally bound the ANC to avoid attacks on civilian targets and engage in 'humanitarian conduct of the war', the first time a guerrilla group had ever done so. Pretoria, meanwhile, treated all captured ANC insurgents as common criminals, sometimes hanging them.

The ANC's successes, getting guns and training from the East and with cocktail diplomacy in the West, did not immediately threaten white supremacy. The ANC leaders seemed to sit back and let other people's battles create a more favourable environment for their own war. FRELIMO's victory allowed the ANC to shift its operational base to Maputo and the SADF's withdrawal from the Angolan civil war in 1976 inspired a mood of expectancy among South Africa's restless majority. Yet it was a majority whose intellectuals seemed more in tune with a creed of 'black consciousness' that owed few debts to the ANC. In early 1976 the ANC was out of touch – at best a resistance movement in waiting.

In the aftermath of Soweto, the Johannesburg *Sunday Times* described the situation as 'riots looking for a place to happen'. It did happen on 16 June 1976 in Vilakazi Street, about a mile from the Soweto stadium where thousands of schoolchildren were set to congregate to protest against the use of Afrikaans as a medium of instruction in their schools. The children in Vilakazi Street never reached the stadium. They were confronted by a small group of heavily-armed white policemen. Tear gas was fired, rocks were thrown and then shots rang out. The first to die was Hector Pietersen, aged 13, and shot in the back. That was the start of it. Within the first week 176 people had been killed; within a year the total reached at least 600 blacks. For eighteen months the country was rocked by strikes and riots. The catalyst was the blandly named but formidable Soweto Students' Representative Council, and the various imitations that spread across the country. This was a children's crusade: the young puritans closed down the illegal shebeens, smashed the township official liquor outlets and ordered a boycott of Christmas, even Christmas cards.

The ostensible cause of the uprising was instruction in Afrikaans. That in itself was a considerable historical irony. The secret and powerful Afrikaner *Broederbond* had been born out of the frustration caused by Lord Milner's imperial policy of Anglicization. Decades later the arrogance of power had dispelled the lessons of these old injustices created anew. Now Afrikaans was being forced on blacks who regarded it as the language of apartheid. Relatively few teachers were qualified to instruct in the language. The youth wanted better education via the medium of a universal tongue, English. But the language question was the detonator, not the cause, of the explosion. Behind the riots festered the bitter rage at the inferiority

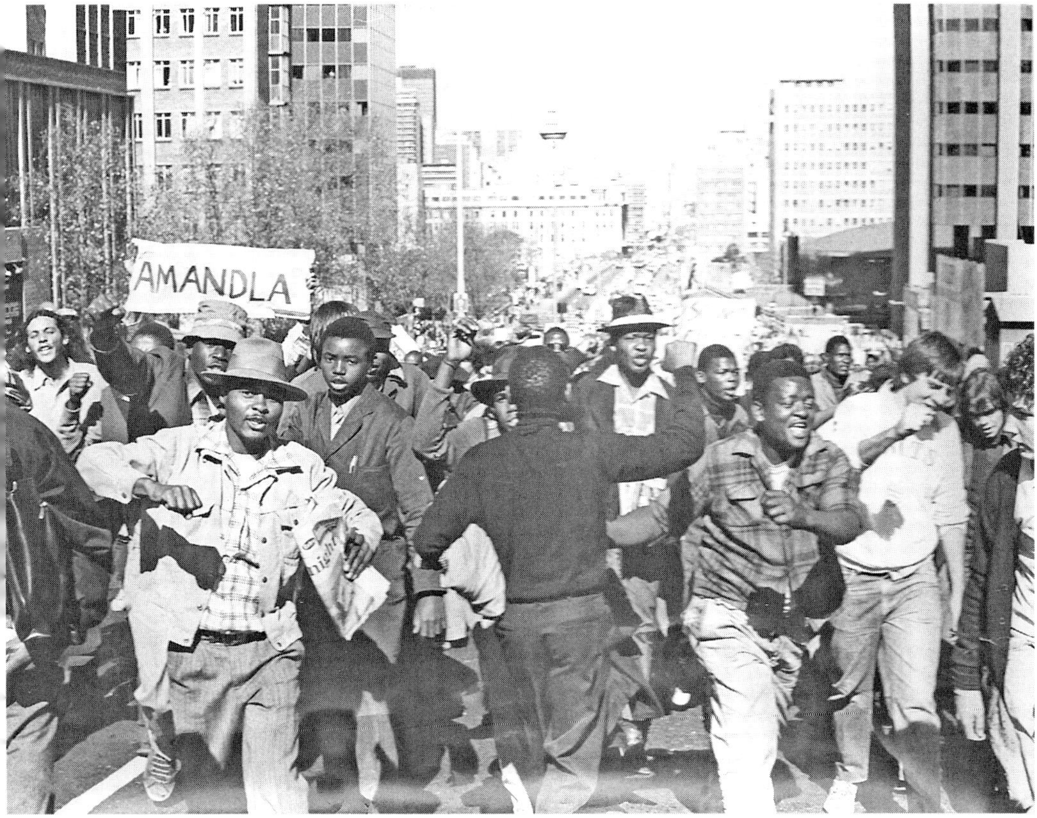


The Soweto uprising 1976 (*Beeld*)

of the children's segregated education and the anger at their parents for not doing something about it. Besides the general and specific hostility towards apartheid, poverty also fuelled the rebellion. A survey in 1976 indicated that 43 per cent of the householders in Soweto, a few miles from the richest city in Africa, were living below the Poverty Datum Line.

Soweto shattered the complacency of the white rulers and the docility of the black majority. It would never be the same again: the iron certainty of apartheid began to bend. Anxious pragmatism began to replace ideological conviction. Nonetheless, the intellectual motivation behind the organizers of the revolt, the black consciousness movement, was apparently crushed by late 1977. Its chief symbol was Steve Biko. Without being anti-white, he argued that blacks must be responsible for their own liberation and rejected white involvement in the anti-apartheid movement. No matter how well-meaning white tutelage of the struggle might be, liberals all too easily assumed that blacks merely wanted to become incorporated into a social

Steve Biko: his brutal murder would haunt Pretoria for years

system hog-tied by white cultural and economic values. Biko wanted first for blacks to secure their own psychological emancipation after hundreds of years of conditioning to see themselves as inferior. Biko's charisma, intelligence and previous extensive contacts with white journalists made him an international figure after his murder by the police in September 1977. The callous manner of his treatment by the security police was exacerbated by the fact that South African politicians, most notoriously the police minister, Jimmy Kruger, were seen to dance on Biko's grave. That was a serious error of judgement. Biko's death would haunt Pretoria for years to come, not least because of Richard Attenborough's *Cry Freedom* film on the young martyr.

The core organizations of the black consciousness movements were SASO (the South African Students' Organization) and the BPC (Black People's Convention). Despite their attachment to Frantz Fanon's radical philosophy, especially as

MK attack on SASOL plant, 1980

articulated in *The Wretched of the Earth*, the black consciousness organizations tried to stay within the bounds of the law. In the beginning, Pretoria seemed to have encouraged the movement, as it appeared to tie in with its own ethnic ambitions to divide and rule. Moreover, Biko's outlook, despite the historical ties with Africanists in the PAC, distanced itself from both the PAC and ANC. Again this suited Pretoria. After the Soweto rebellion continued to spread, the security police had fewer reservations about clamping down on Biko and other black consciousness leaders. Thousands of black youngsters fled the country. Perhaps 75 per cent joined the ANC. Logically, the black consciousness activists should have enlisted with the PAC. The ANC, however, was the only liberation movement capable of absorbing and training the enraged new Soweto generation.

### *The third phase*

The third phase of rebellion emerged in the years 1977 to 1983. This so-called period of 'armed propaganda' was intended to mobilize domestic political support while continuing to hit dramatic targets from time to time. Rioting and strikes, particularly in the Western Cape in 1980, were supported by the demonstration effect of military raids. One of the most spectacular raids took place on 2 June 1980. Three skilled MK teams hit the showcase SASOL oil-from-coal plants. These vital strategic installations were heavily guarded. The ANC magazine, *Sechaba,* exalted in the 'sea of flames, the fires of freedom, the most beautiful fire which symbolized the largest act of sabotage in South Africa'. In August 1981 MK launched a 127mm rocket attack on the SADF complex at Voortrekkerhoogte, a little like the IRA mortaring Sandhurst. In December 1982 MK attacked South Africa's only nuclear power station, at Koeberg, causing $22 million-worth of damage. In May 1983 an ANC bomb exploded (prematurely) near the Air Force HQ in Pretoria, killing eighteen people and injuring nearly 200.

The ANC conducted numerous small operations. According to Gavin Cawthra's sympathetic account of the ANC, between January 1977 and October 1982 there were, *inter alia*, thirty-three attacks on railways, twenty-five on industrial and power installations, fourteen on administrative buildings, thirteen on police stations, three on military bases and nineteen clashes between guerrillas and army units.[9] Many of the operations were linked to particular local issues: an attack on a railway installation during a rail strike or the bombing of a township administration building during a rent boycott, for example. Between 1976 and 1986 the frequency of bombings, raids, and political assassinations rose dramatically.

By the mid-1980s the ANC was beginning to look more like a government-in-waiting. It had its HQ in Lusaka, military training and educational centres in Tanzania and Angola and diplomatic missions throughout the world. The senior officials of the so-called 'external mission' of the ANC tended to shun PLO-style camouflage uniforms; executive suits were the norm. It was still a coalition of differing viewpoints trying to influence millions of blacks in a country a thousand miles to the south. About 60 per cent of the personnel were involved in the fighting wing, the MK; the rest worked in agriculture, education and political activities. By the mid-1980s the various estimates averaged out at a figure of 10,000 externally-trained guerrillas, based outside the country, mainly in northern Angola, and perhaps 500 to 2,000 externally-trained men active in South Africa. (The PAC had perhaps 500 insurgents in various African states). Increasingly, the external guerrillas were considered to be an officer corps, both as instructors for internally-based cadres and as the nucleus of a post-apartheid army. The annual MK budget was estimated to be $50 million.

The breakdown of the ANC's arsenal commonly used inside South Africa was hand grenades, explosives and small arms, although in 1985-86 limpet mines and land mines were also deployed regularly. The most common weapons found in caches by the SAP were the Czech Skorpion 7.65mm machine pistol and the Russian Tokarev 7.62mm and Makarov 9mm pistols as well as the ubiquitous AK-47. Later, RPG-7s and SAM-7s were introduced.

In his excellent study of the ANC's military campaign, Stephen Davis, writing in 1986, summed up the MK's predicament:

> Few national liberation movements have waged guerrilla wars under conditions as difficult as those with which the ANC grapples. Pushed by South African power to command posts five hundred to a thousand miles from the target frontier, the Congress attempts to control a nationwide anti-apartheid revolution with limited resources, outdated weaponry, restless soldiers, and perilous channels into and out of the Republic. Yet its exiled bureaucracy had imperfectly but doggedly adapted to the hostile strategic environment of the subcontinent.[10]

One of the most important ANC assets was its sanctuary status in the front-line states. It was especially dependent upon the goodwill of the outer arc of sanctuary states, Tanzania, Zambia and Angola, and the unofficial collaboration of the transit states, particularly Botswana, Mozambique and Zimbabwe, to enable the Ho-Chi-Minh trails to function. Sometimes the front-line states would intercept MK guerrillas and send them back to Zambia. Botswana was especially vulnerable to SADF pressure to do so. Even when the neighbouring states tried to bend to Pretoria's diktats, few of them possessed the security infrastructure to stop all the infiltrators, often disguised as ordinary travellers. 'It's very easy to cross from Zimbabwe to South Africa,' confirmed Eddison Zvogbo, Zimbabwe's minister of legal and parliamentary affairs. 'We're not paid by South Africa to be their policemen.' Mozambique could not afford to take such a cavalier attitude. After the Nkomati agreement, MK was unceremoniously ejected. Sometimes the squabbling of the ANC politicians and the behaviour of the occasionally mutinous guerrillas antagonized their hosts. Generally, however, the hosts displayed a political and often personal commitment to the ANC leadership that transcended these problems. When a drunken ANC driver allegedly drove into, and accidentally killed, the Tanzanian prime minster, Edward Sokoine, in April 1984, just outside Dar es Salaam, the government hushed it up.

Other guerrilla organizations had suffered from similar problems while in exile. And they had become the government in the end. The ANC leadership, however, recognized that South Africa was different; not least in that it was industrialized and devoid of any large areas of jungle or thick bush and was not suited to classical African insurgency. Nor had the other insurgencies encountered such a resolute and well-armed incumbent power – who regarded themselves as indigenous Africans, not colonialists. After hundreds of years the ruling Afrikaners felt they had nowhere else to call home, unlike the neighbouring Portuguese and most Rhodesians. Thus the ANC tried to redefine the traditional notions of a people's war. It encouraged a 'gathering of forces' for a *cumulative* destruction of the Afrikaner edifice. The military campaign, co-ordinated by the exiled movement, was only one element of the struggle. Equally important were the underground cadres working permanently *inside* South Africa and the legal but severely harassed internal allies in the churches, schools, unions, civic associations and political groups opposed to apartheid.

## *Political allies*

The exiled ANC, PAC and black consciousness movements were related to a complex array of domestic forces. Two of the most important were the United Democratic Front (UDF), founded in 1983, and a supporter of the Freedom Charter and, secondly, the Azanian People's Organization (AZAPO). The latter was founded in 1977 and subscribed to the more racial Azanian Manifesto drawn up by the National Forum. The black consciousness, Africanist viewpoint was expressed primarily via AZAPO and the National Forum, whose target was 'racial capitalism'. Its declared means of change was as a workers' struggle. Although much of its rhetoric was socialist and 'workerist', critics alleged that AZAPO was a workers' organization in name only. In township politics ideological disputes were sometimes a matter of political etiquette rather than a formal difference of belief systems. Nevertheless, AZAPO and UDF rivalry had often seemed to match that of their mutual hostility to the apartheid regime.[11] Both black groups waged their private civil war in the black ghettoes. But the UDF, often viewed as the overground of the ANC, tended to catch the imagination of the media and perhaps the majority in the townships.

The UDF was fashioned deliberately as a loose coalition of anti-apartheid groups. Some of its approximately 600 affiliates sported such intriguing titles as the Deepawali Cheer Society, the Seventh Avenue Social Organization and the Johannesburg Scooter Drivers' Association. Some of the affiliates were large union or student bodies; some were mere dial-a-quote groups that did not extend far beyond an executive committee but were always good for a punchy quote for journalists with pressing deadlines. The bizarre battery of organizations should be understood in terms of the abnormal politics of South Africa. Because democratic politicking was so circumscribed, nearly all aspects of township life, including those not normally associated with political affairs, became politicized. These included religious sects, burial societies and gangs, especially prison gangs. I spent many months running with these gangs, especially some of the 80,000 gang members on the Cape Flats, when I made a documentary film on the subject in the 1980s, with Marie Bruyns, the country's leading TV producer.[12] The loose and hydraheaded UDF was deliberately designed to allow the front to survive the constant culling of its top echelons by the police. Others would spring up to replace them. The UDF struggled to stay legal, despite the banning and imprisonment of its leaders and the curtailment of its foreign funds. It acted as a 'strategic transmission belt' to cross-fertilize nationwide the successful tactics adopted at local level.

The UDF and the smaller AZAPO, besides their links with banned external resistance, functioned though their own domestic networks and via sympathetic bodies in the various legal student, church and union movements. All these groups were founded on the politics of refusal: no collaboration with the regime. On the other hand, a number of black organizations were tactically committed to working *within* the apartheid system. The most prominent of these was Chief Mangosuthu Buthelezi, the leader of the Inkatha Freedom Party (IFP) and the jigsaw-puzzle empire of the KwaZulu homeland. He assumed the colours and sometimes the rhetoric of the ANC of which he was once a member. The ANC encouraged him to set up the IFP in 1975 but the mercurial chief broke away from the Congress in 1979. The ANC later mocked his concept of 'loyal resistance' and accused him of trying to hijack the revolution. 'He has left the nation and joined the tribe,' asserted Dr Nthato Motlana, the highly respected Sowetan leader.

Chief Mangosuthu Buthelezi

Chief Buthelezi built up his largely Zulu power base in Natal and claimed the membership of his IFP was 1.5 million. If this was ever true, and he did have a large tribal base, the membership was partly founded on force and intimidation as much as Buthelezi's charisma and pro-Zulu and royalist rhetoric (although the Zulu king and his first minister were often at loggerheads). An Inkatha card was often the only means for a black to secure employment, a house or a scholarship in Natal. Partly because he was lionized by the white business community and the South African Broadcasting Corporation, because of his anti-sanctions stance, the chief became the black man that the ANC, UDF and AZAPO could all agree to hate. Although the Zulu leader had called for the release of Mandela and there was often pub talk of the two strongest tribes, the Afrikaners and Zulus, doing a direct deal, Buthelezi had realized that the white embrace could turn him into Muzorewa Mark II. The banned external movements insisted that it was impossible to work within the system. How could reform work within a system that was based upon the principle of exclusion? Only the armed struggle, they argued, could force the government to surrender or at least retreat to the negotiating table. Along with the Indian and coloured leaders, Buthelezi cooperated with the tricameral parliament set up by the government in 1984. They all maintained that apartheid could be destroyed by working from the innards of the beast. But was this merely playing Pretoria's game, being coopted as junior allies in an upmarket form of racial domination? Had Buthelezi become, in the phrase of the time, a 'Gucci freedom-fighter', or, in Lenin's phrase, a troublesome but 'useful idiot' for Pretoria?

Black resistance, then, had taken many forms, from the most servile and pro-capitalist toady in the homelands, those sophisticated tribal concentration camps, to the most radical PAC spokesperson who claimed that only guerrilla warfare in all its forms could usher in the dawn of a socialist Azania. (The ANC rejected the title 'Azania', derived, they said, from an Arabic term of abuse for the peoples of east/southern Africa. The Romans, however, used the name, politely, long before the Arab conquerors. The PAC, which favoured the name, apparently wrote a polite letter to a bemused and ailing Evelyn Waugh, the author of *Black Mischief*, for enlightenment, as he called his imaginary country Azania in the 1932 book.) Regardless of what they wanted to call their new freed country, all the main movements pretended to occupy the vanguard position in the crusade against white supremacy. The black spectrum stretched from '*Ja-Baas*' collaboration with Pretoria to pathological rejection of all whites. The PAC called for a 'one-bullet, one-settler' policy. Even the most dedicated and most moral opponents of racial injustice disagreed enormously as to how far the armed struggle should go. Some felt that eventually Pretoria would have to settle for a 'transfer of power' in a national convention; others shouted for total victory on the battlefield.

By 1984, the Orwellian nightmare had begun to assume a tangible form in South Africa: from the blasphemy of the 'necklace' (a burning, petrol-filled tyre placed around the neck of an alleged collaborator) to the doublespeak of frenzied government propaganda. At the beginning of that ominous year the armed struggle was just over twenty-two years old, and white power was as firmly entrenched as ever. The first phase of the civil war had ended in the debacle of Rivonia. From the Sharpeville massacre to the June Soweto uprising sixteen years had elapsed. On the cusp of each crisis capital and whites had fled. They had panicked but the security forces had not. Each wave of resistance was absorbed, diluted, pushed back and pumped underground. Each time that 'dreadful calm'– to use novelist Nadine Gordimer's phrase – had returned to white society. The second phase of revolt, from the Rivonia aftermath to 1976, had helped to mobilize and polarize blacks. After Soweto the third phase lasted until 1984; the cycle of revolt had been reduced to eight years. And yet the ANC had no real master-plan: the leadership in Lusaka was always slow in keeping up with, let alone controlling, the events forged in the crucible of volcanic anger in the townships. From 1984 to 1986 blacks in the urban areas, and in the countryside this time, rose up once more. During those heady days for blacks, the radicals liked to suggest that Soweto in 1976-77 was like Russia's failed but preliminary revolution of 1905. Hyped up by foreign media, the events of 1984-86 took on the appearance of the beginnings of another 1917. It was not to be. The year 1984, however, did mark the genesis of a crucial fourth phase of the deepening civil war.

## *Chapter 15*

# States of Emergency

For the first half of 1984 P.W. Botha's imperial presidency was riding the crest of a wave. He had toured Europe after the signing of the Nkomati pact. At home his victory in the 1983 referendum enabled him to proceed with his new 'dispensation', the tricameral parliament for whites, Indians and coloureds. New local authorities had also been set up for blacks. Black councillors were supposed to handle the complex township administrations with neither a popular base nor adequate funds. On the other hand, the UDF, AZAPO, civic and student organizations as well as black labour unions had formed a popular front, of sorts, to ensure boycotts of both the national tricameral and black municipal elections. The turnout for the Indian and coloured polls was poor and for the earlier black councils disastrous. Political conviction and intimidation both contributed to the electoral boycotts. The politics of refusal grew apace, for co-operation meant stark collaboration to the resistance movements. Instead of repressive domination, Pretoria was offering 'cooptive domination' in the words of Frederik van Zyl Slabbert, an opposition MP.

There was precious little wrong with the old Westminster system perhaps; all it needed was the extension of the franchise, equally, to blacks. But no, P.W. Botha had insisted on taking the Gaullist route, although the 'Mussolini option' was a more common description. As with Hitler in 1933, Botha tried to gather up the business community in his drive against the perceived Bolshevik menace. Most senior businessmen agreed to hold hands with P.W. After all, this was 'a step in the right direction', wasn't it? The tricameral parliament, however, was *not* a step in the right direction: it was a declaration of war on the black majority. Approximately 75 per cent of the population was officially excluded from this new parliamentary system.

This arrogant exclusion was a major cause of the revolt of 1984-86. Also, the new black councils, with Pretoria's typical shortsighted parsimony, were left to raise most of their finance from rents and service charges. Rent increases for a hardpressed underclass led almost inexorably to more rent boycotts. The economy was not in good shape. Inflation was then 12 per cent, drought ravaged the countryside and Pretoria was forced to import grain from Zimbabwe for the second year running. In addition to poor economic conditions and political anger at the national and local political changes introduced by diktat, the widespread disaffection with low standards of education was becoming more acute. Expenditure on African education per head was still only a seventh of that spent on white education. This 'gutter' education led nowhere except to unemployment lines, menial labour or, for the more spirited, the guerrilla bases abroad. This was the argument of the Congress of South African Students, which helped to organize school boycotts throughout 1984.

The revolt of 1984 was not, however, merely a children's crusade. Entire communities were sucked into the maelstrom of rebellion: parents, teachers, unionists and churchmen. But as the turmoil grew a cumulative, but definitive, objective emerged: the overthrow of apartheid.

The proverbial spark came on 3 September, the very day on which the new constitution came into effect and P.W. Botha was sworn in as 'state president'. Residents in Sharpeville, Bophelong, Boipatong, Sebokeng and Evaton townships in the Vaal Triangle (the industrial area on the Rand which included Johannesburg, Pretoria and Vereeniging) protested about rent increases and other charges. Protest turned to riot. Mobs attacked local authority buildings and homes of black councillors and policemen. The deputy mayor of Sharpeville was hacked to death on his front doorstep. Shops were looted. Police action resulted in twenty-six killed. Their funerals were transformed into venues for mass protest. In September black organized labour flexed its muscles too. Over 40,000 mineworkers went on strike (their first legal one). The violence spread rapidly throughout the Transvaal.

In October Pretoria sent the army into the townships. The SADF had often worked with the police, for example in providing manpower for extensive roadblocks, and the police fought alongside the army in Namibia. This was different. The troops went into the townships in large numbers like an alien occupying force. The first major incursion was Operation PALMIET. On 23 October a combined force of 7,000 police and troops poured into Sebokeng, searching all 19,800 houses. Most of those arrested were charged with very minor offences; none was charged under security laws. The increasing use of the SADF plus accusations of police brutality raised the temperature of the revolt.

In November students and unions organized a mass two-day general strike or 'stay-away'. Perhaps as many as 500,000 workers struck and 250,000 students boycotted classes. They demanded a withdrawal of the SADF and police from the townships, the resignation of black councillors, a freeze on township rents and bus fares, and the release of political prisoners.

Vicious attacks on black officials, some corrupt, some genuinely committed to community service, escalated in the townships. Many officials fled to the rural areas; others, such as policemen, gave up their gutted homes and moved with their families into tents in fortified army or police bases. The black radicals, the 'young lions' of the revolt, echoed the ANC line: the townships were to be made

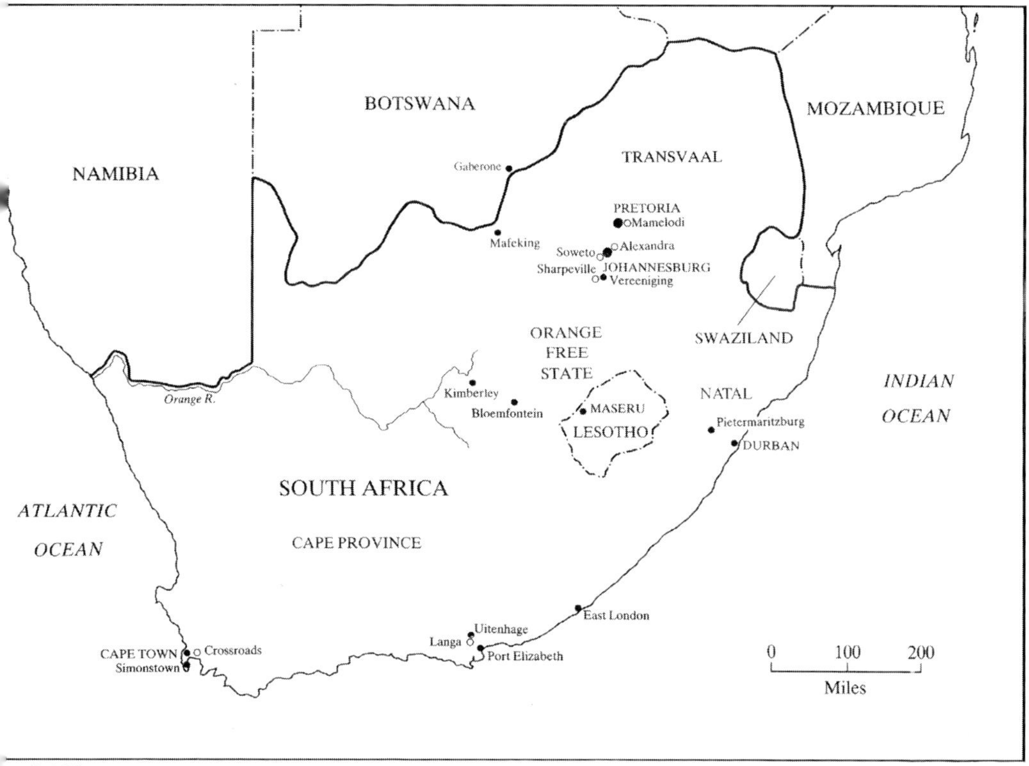


South Africa

Main areas of 'unrest'

'ungovernable'. They talked romantically, and unrealistically, of establishing 'liberated zones'. Pretoria reacted predictably with more strongarm measures, locking up union, students and community leaders. The years of carefully nurtured labour relations looked like collapsing in ruins. In an unprecedented rebuff to Pretoria, the major business organizations, including the *Afrikaanse Handelsinstitut* (the Afrikaner chambers of commerce), issued a manifesto condemning detention without trial and calling for political rights for blacks, open trading areas, the abolition of influx control and an end to forced removals. They wanted industrial peace but the price was a political settlement. Anti-apartheid groups, especially in America, took up the local businessmen's (admittedly self-interested) call. The disinvestment lobby expanded rapidly; more and more US municipal authorities, colleges and churches decided to sell their holdings in companies with South Africa stock. In December a number of prominent Americans, including twenty-three congressmen, were arrested in Washington for staging protests inside the South African embassy.

Then the 'unrest', in Pretoria's parlance, began to really take off. The focus of insurrection kept shifting. For the first few weeks the action was in the Vaal Triangle, then it moved outwards to the East Rand. Beginning in 1985, the turmoil switched to the Western and Eastern Cape; then slid into Natal and then back once more to the Transvaal. There appeared to be a subconscious realization that each region should take it in turn to keep the momentum up and thus prevent a repeat of the early burnout of the attempted national effort of 1976-77.

The cycle of insurrection fed on itself, as one area emulated the tactics of another. It was all recorded, faithfully and otherwise, on TV, thus stimulating further pressure, especially from the USA. There Bishop Desmond Tutu, the winner of the 1984 Nobel Peace Prize, whipped up the sometimes prefabricated moral fervour of the chattering classes. American pressures on South Africa duly encouraged the radicals in the townships. TV cameras, ravenous for blood and guts, also fed this cycle. The South African government believed that TV sometimes created rather than merely recorded the grim events. Pretoria's almost total ban on non-SABC coverage of the unrest was not, therefore, surprising, although the year or so it took to implement the ban was. It was a cynical gesture that seemed to work. Perhaps Pretoria had adequately sized up the attention span of Joe Public in America. Yet in 1985 apartheid was the moral fad of the year in the USA. The clamour even influenced the re-elected Ronald Reagan. At the end of 1984 America had joined a unanimous summons by the UN Security Council for a voluntary embargo on the *purchase* of South African arms.

Opposition in Washington and other world capitals was energized by the Langa massacre on 21 March 1985. On the twenty-fifth anniversary of the Sharpeville massacre, members of the South African Police opened fire on a crowd of people gathered on Maduna Road, between Uitenhage and Langa township in the Eastern Cape. Without warning, police in two armoured vehicles shot dead twenty and wounded twenty-five blacks among an unarmed crowd, many of whom were attempting to flee. They had been marching to the funeral of earlier victims of police action. An official enquiry found that the police had acted without provocation. This massacre was a tipping point in both the domestic rebellion and world condemnation of apartheid.

Perhaps, just perhaps, until the Langa massacre, the new state president's reforms, if far-reaching enough, might have made some immediate political impact. In January 1985 some 'concessions' had been granted. Laws which banned inter-racial sex and multi-racial political parties were repealed. Black and white could now share a bed and a political party but not a house, because the Group Areas Act forbade that. (A black woman could not live with her white husband in a white area, but a white man was generally allowed to 'move down' to live with his black, Indian or coloured wife in her respective group area. The real problems came with schools and hospitals.)

Nelson Mandela made the same point when President Botha offered to release the ANC leader if he renounced violence. In February 1985, via his daughter Zindzi, Mandela said:

> What freedom am I being offered when I must ask permission to live in an urban area? What freedom am I being offered when I need a stamp in my pass to seek work? What freedom am I being offered when my very own South African citizenship is not respected. Only free men can negotiate. Prisoners cannot enter into contracts.

After Langa any 'contract', any deal, in the near future between the ANC and Pretoria looked unlikely. P.W. Botha's strategy had always been a Jekyll and Hyde concoction. From now on repression took command of the milder persona of reform.

The UDF persevered with the boycotts, stay-aways, rent strikes, marches and other peaceful, if often illegal, demonstrations. At funeral services, one of the few legal outlets for the outpouring of personal and political grief (before they were also generally restricted), ANC and Russian flags were openly displayed, along with wooden replicas of AKs. The cutting edges of the insurrection were arson and the murder of suspected informers and black councillors and policemen, perceived to be the main, and available, local representatives of apartheid. The 'necklace' became a trademark of the young 'comrades' in their war on collaborators. After Langa, forty-six councillors in the Eastern Cape resigned. By June, some 240 councillors had quit, leaving only five out of the thirty-eight new town councils functioning. Not all violence was directed against apartheid officials. Often UDF and AZAPO supporters became embroiled in their own bloody feuds. Naturally, Pretoria made much of the black-on-black violence, touted as a visible symbol that blacks were not fit to rule the country. Much of the inter-black rivalry was entirely spontaneous but the police later fuelled indigenous animosities by encouraging conservative vigilantes in the Cape and Buthelezi's Inkatha in Natal to take on the comrades at their own game.

Meanwhile, South Africa was going up in flames. That at least was the overriding image sometimes conveyed in the compressed, often breathless, reportage on TV screens in Europe and America. In contrast, little of the violence, except the occasional necklacing to emphasize black barbarity, was shown on SATV, the local state broadcaster. Helen Suzman, at one time the only liberal opposition MP in parliament, made the point that if the local whites could see just a little of the barbarous police behaviour shown on foreign networks then 'tens of thousands of decent white South Africans' would raise their voices in angry protest. Maybe she was right, but that didn't happen. If the media sometimes exaggerated the revolutionary violence, the government had to err in the other direction to show that it was entirely in control, especially to a white electorate tempted by the hardline solutions advocated by the increasingly assertive far-right Conservative Party. On 21 July the president declared a state of emergency, the first in twenty-five years, in thirty-four magisterial districts in the Eastern Cape and in the industrial areas of the Witwatersrand. The security forces already possessed extensive powers of arrest and detention which exempted them from potential prosecution for any act carried out in 'good faith'. To the comrades this appeared to be a licence to kill. By the end of the year over 1,000 blacks had been killed, many by police action. Over 7,000 people had been detained, usually without trial.

In America the demands for a harsh sanctions bill became irresistible. Far more serious was the action of private bankers. In the 1960 emergency Chase Manhattan had been Pretoria's ally. On 31 July 1985, however, William Butcher, the conservative chairman of the bank, refused to roll over further loans to South African borrowers. The 'Butcher of the Rand', as he was called in desperate business circles in Johannesburg, well knew that his decision would start a chain reaction akin to a classic run on the banks. Nearly all the American bank loans were short-term; $14 billion was due over the following twelve months. South Africa's most serious financial crisis ever followed Butcher's knifing. Despite its fundamentally sound economy, in spite of the recession at the time, Pretoria's credit rating was lower than even the chronically mismanaged economy of Zaire.

To restore confidence, Pik Botha and other government officials had hinted strongly that the president was about to deliver an epoch-making speech at the National Party congress in Durban on 15 August 1985. As the crisis in the country mounted, so did the expectation that P.W. Botha would finally break the political deadlock. The least that was expected was the freeing of Mandela. Instead P.W. dug in his Achilles' heel. During a bleak performance watched on TV around the world, the president wagged his finger and contemptuously dismissed his critics in a much-revised (and apparently much-diluted) speech. He offered little beyond threats.

P.W. Botha's finger-waving in his infamous Rubicon speech

It was billed as the Rubicon speech. In one unintentional sense it was. Julius Caesar's crossing of the Rubicon river led to three years of civil war that eventually destroyed the republic. The Great Crocodile's posturing might have impressed some of his backwoods Afrikaner faithful but it alienated the vast majority of South Africans. If Langa had finally destroyed any hope of winning over 'moderate' blacks, the Rubicon fiasco finally switched off the English-speaking business magnates in South Africa. The influential *Business Day* described the president as a 'hick politician'. Not only was the content diabolical but so was the exaggerated and bellicose presentation. The mannerisms were like Botha's renowned comic impersonator, Pieter-Dirk Uys. The president stuck out his jaw, like Mussolini (and now Donald Trump), while uttering the tired clichés of the eternal irreconcilable himself, Ian Smith. His eyes betrayed the occasional flash of lunacy as he shot out his arrogant words. It was obvious that the president was totally oblivious to the PR disaster he was inflicting on his country.

Money talks loudest: the rand fell to an all-time low against the dollar. Foreign investors deserted in droves. The government suspended trading on the foreign-exchange markets and closed the Johannesburg stock exchange for five days. Pretoria then announced a four-month freeze on repayments of principal on foreign debts and introduced new exchange-control regulations. With a performance like Botha's Rubicon, market-led sanctions became much more important than official government-imposed strictures. Once again, Pretoria had shot itself in both feet. When, in September, Gerhard de Kock, the governor of the Reserve Bank, visited his erstwhile capitalist allies in Europe and America, cap in hand, he was treated like a leper.

On 9 September, to sidestep a tough sanctions bill from Congress, President Reagan announced a somewhat milder package that restricted Krugerrand sales in the US, new loans to the South African government and exports of computers and nuclear-related goods. Eleven of the European Community states introduced measures of their own the next day. The exception was Margaret Thatcher. But even she modified her opposition to sanctions somewhat at the October Commonwealth conference, which tightened up existing measures, and demanded an end to apartheid and the state of emergency, the release of Mandela and the lifting of the ban on the ANC. The Commonwealth also agreed to appoint an Eminent Persons Group (EPG) to secure these demands via dialogue with Pretoria and the main black political movements.

In South Africa, dialogue seemed impossible with Botha squatted on his imperial throne. The important Johannesburg business magazine, the *Financial Mail*, called for his resignation in September. Under the headline, 'Leave Now', the newspaper said:

> It's like watching a bad magician at work – the kind who embarrasses even the children at birthday parties. See him talk about the 'creation of structures to give effect to the foregoing principle'... see the rand plunge. Hear him growl 'Don't push us too far' and hear the applause from the ANC. See him pledge R1 billion to improve conditions in black areas and watch the flames over Guguletu.

> That's how the world perceives us – on the skids.
> The world is also frightened of the Nationalists' götterdämmerung stance: 'Don't push too far' … Or what? Or we'll impose martial law, wreck the economies of our neighbouring states, nuke Lusaka? What did the man mean? We, too, are disturbed by this bully-boy posturing, since the Nationalists have always shown themselves as people of their harshest words ….
> He played a gauleiter instead of a statesman – and the deathliness inspired by him and his waving hands is with us still. So all we have to say is: do it and go. And if you can't bring yourself to do it, go anyway.[1]

P.W. didn't go anywhere, but the despairing businessmen did: to Lusaka. A small group of senior South African businessmen and journalists, led by the chairman of Anglo-America, Gavin Relly, flew to Zambia in September 1985 for talks with the ANC. Critics of South Africa's unique marriage of 'economic exploitation and racial oppression' – racial capitalism – argued that 'for once the apartheid government and its paymasters were running scared and in different directions'.[2]

Whether Anglo was really a friend or foe of apartheid, no sensible businessman could stand by and do nothing to try to break what was seemingly an unending cycle of township unrest, government repression, disinvestment and sanctions.

Pretoria blamed nearly all the violence on the ANC and more particularly the South African Communist Party that was said to control it. Pretoria was wrong on both counts. The ANC was taken by surprise by the outbreak and the enduring scale of the revolt that began in 1984. It had not instigated it. And the SACP was an important restraint on the hotheads in MK who wanted to hit white soft targets. In June 1985, however, at its Kabwe conference, the ANC had adopted a strategy of 'people's war' that was intended to take the struggle into the comfortable and almost untouched white suburbs, at precisely the same time as the ANC was gaining ground, and respectability, in Washington and London. This was unfortunate timing too for the arrival in Lusaka of the white business leaders three months later.

Oliver Tambo said that he hated violence

On 13 September, at Kaunda's Luangwa Lodge, Relly, dressed in white floppy hat and an open-necked shirt, amiably discussed the rival virtues of socialism and capitalism with the ANC leadership, dressed impeccably in suits and ties. 'What we are concerned with,' Relly told the ANC leader Oliver Tambo, 'is not so much whether the following generation will be governed by white or black people but that it will a viable country and that it will not be destroyed by violence and strife.' Tambo argued that he hated violence but that without dismantling apartheid the civil war would inevitably escalate. Despite their disagreement over the need for nationalization, Relly confessed that 'it was one of the nicest days I've ever spent. A picnic among South Africans talking about their future together.'[3]

Despite P.W. Botha's temper tantrums about Relly's safari, capitalism's very own journey to Canossa prompted a stream of prominent whites to make the same pilgrimage. The president fulminated and promised to confiscate their passports. Nevertheless, Pretoria's propaganda obsessions and the visits to Lusaka by desperate (and curious) white liberals, churchmen, academics and businessmen had promoted the ANC to a government-in-waiting.

If the business community wanted to talk to some of the real representatives of South Africa's majority, Botha was determined to annihilate the liberation movements. Then the president could beckon those elusive moderates. The shadowy personages – never named, although Buthelezi, surviving black councillors and the homeland leaders were implied – were scheduled to participate in a national council. No one stepped forward, not even Buthelezi, who insisted Mandela's freedom was a pre-condition for serious talks. The roller-coaster of often savage repression and the occasional wilted carrot of reform had become mutually exclusive. As veteran journalist Stanley Uys noted, 'Botha's reformism in South Africa today is like a lift going up in a building that is coming down.' Every gesture of reconciliation by Pretoria was usually accompanied by a sharp kick in the groin. As Denis Healey, the British labour politician, acidly observed:

> In the week before Christmas, Mr Botha had invaded Angola yet again, sent his death squads into Lesotho to murder his opponents, has moved a great stride towards martial law itself and, finally, has arrested Mrs Mandela for the crime of living in her own house.

All this at a time when the president was trying to use seasonal goodwill to preach conciliation.

Yet Pretoria continued with its switchback strategy. The major reform of 1986 was the scrapping of the hated pass laws and influx control. Since 1916 more than 18 million Africans had been arrested for infringing these laws. More than any other law, Africans loathed having to carry this 'badge of inferiority'. In the 1960s such a reform would have inspired black jubilation. In the very different climate of 1986 it looked like a grudging concession to the liberation struggle – a quarter of a loaf. A few more crumbs were tossed. Despite the opposition of hawks, the partial state of emergency was lifted in March 1986. The harsh security laws on the statute book were still intact; so was the endemic violence. The lifting was a tactical move to appease foreign bankers and the conservative Western governments.

The end of the pass laws, albeit far too late, was a real reform, but the central issue of political power was totally obfuscated. Chris Heunis, the minister in charge of constitutional change, looked as if he had been appointed because of his ability to talk at great length in meaningless babble – far more meaninglessly than the average politician. Right from the start Pretoria had decided to emulate Humpty Dumpty when he said to Alice 'When I use a word, it means just what I choose it to mean – neither more nor less.' The act in question had been passed into legislation as 'The *Abolition* of Passes and Coordination of Documents Act (1952)' [my italics]. That act *tightened up* pass laws by changing the name of passbooks to 'reference books' but blacks kept to the old name. Then came a real classic, 'The *Extension* of University Education Act (1959)'. This forced established South African universities to kick out blacks. Another well-known example of doublespeak was 'The Prohibition of Political Interference Act (1968)'. This allowed only the National Party to interfere in black politics. Multi-racial white opposition parties such as the Liberal Party had to eject their black members or disband. All this was in the name of 'grand apartheid' (placing unwanted blacks in the homelands where a Sowetan had probably never been) and those who were privileged enough to work in 'white South Africa' (populated by a vast majority of non-whites) had to obey the rules of 'petty apartheid' which kept blacks out of white beds, cinemas, and, most obsessively of all, toilets. And so the babblespeak went on. There was much white talk of 'self-determination' for blacks. That was Pretoria's code for the denial of their political rights.

After 1984, P.W. Botha introduced his much-vaunted 'new dispensation' (translated as 'apartheid under a new name') Unfortunately, this new vocabulary, intended to confuse the world and the local blacks, did not confuse the white right wing at all. Hence Heunis. He made incoherency into an art form. Now the reformist language had to fool left and right, at home and abroad. That meant jettisoning English and relying on the subtleties of Afrikaans. Any problem could be brushed off as mistranslation. Black and white affairs were now divided into 'own' (an awkward translation of *eie*) affairs and 'general' affairs; that meant that Pretoria could interfere in everything, although coloureds and Indians could look after a small number of matters which were culturally specific. When dealing with the white conservatives, Heunis-speak became really esoteric. Power-sharing, in the tricameral dispensation, was paraded as nothing but a 'division' of power with a clever play on the Afrikaans word *magsdeling* (power-sharing) and *magsverdeling* (division of power). It didn't work: the right wing knew it meant 'giving kaffirs the vote', just as much as backs realized the whole thing was a wordy edifice to keep them from getting real power. In short, reformism meant sharing some power without giving up white control.

Opposition leader Frederik van Zyl Slabbert

No wonder the leader of the opposition, Frederik van Zyl Slabbert, cut through Pretoria's verbose Malice in Blunderland by resigning from parliament. For him, it had become a pointless talking shop. Not all liberal parliamentarians agreed. They pointed, for example, to Helen Suzman's public role, with parliamentary privilege, as a heroic scourge of apartheid. Van Zyk Slabbert decided to cooperate with extra parliamentary forces among the black majority.

Meanwhile, the more militant members of that majority were trying to finish off the remnants of civil administration in the townships. In its place the comrades started to construct their own area and street committees. This counter-system was a descendant of the embryonic 'M' plan, designed by Mandela in the 1950s. His plan for 'cells' as the basis of underground resistance was itself founded on the structure of the Zionist Irgun insurgents. Street committees were first set up in the Eastern Cape townships and Soweto. 'People's courts' were also established to enforce the comrades' often arbitrary rule. The levels of voluntary compliance and intimidation, backed by kangaroo courts, varied from township to township. Sometimes adults were terrorized by bands of feral youngsters, especially if they dared to break consumer boycotts. Often their victims were forced to consume all their 'illegal' purchases on the spot, sometimes fatal if they were everyday items such as cooking oil, washing powder, soap and paraffin. Parents also grew frustrated with the long school boycotts and the self-defeating demand for 'liberation before education'. Nonetheless, despite the fear and warweariness, the 'alternative structures' garnered a great deal of support across the social spectrum. But effective organization and discipline of the tenuously administered zones were difficult because of constant security force harassment and the arrest of each layer of leadership as it rose to the top.

The ANC in Lusaka was battling to feed trained men and women into the townships. The ANC designated 1986 as the 'Year of Umkhonto we Sizwe'. If this was more than a propaganda gambit, it was a misnomer. As the months of 1986 passed, the liberation mania began to dissipate. The severity of the repression, sheer physical exhaustion and frustration with the excesses of both disciplined comrades as well as roving bands of *tsotsis* (criminal thugs) and psychopathic Pol Pot-type elements, over two years, had taken their toll. A particular point of contention was the school boycott. Eventually, after due consultation with the leadership in Lusaka, the Soweto Parents' Crisis Committee urged a return to school. Sacrificing the education of a generation was not the best tool of liberation. As Zwelakhe Sisulu, the son of Walter Sisulu, warned, 'We are not poised for the immediate transfer of power to the people. The belief that this is so could lead to serious errors and defeats.' In short, chaos in the townships was not the same as people's power.

Yet the mood of weariness and questioning in the townships was not reflected in the international coverage of the 'imminent revolution' in South Africa. P.W. Botha was sometimes characterized as a second Shah of Iran, dead on his feet. The ANC still talked of 'turning every corner of our country into a battlefield'. And Winnie Mandela (literally) fuelled the sense of holocaust with her infamous statement, 'Together hand-in-hand with our boxes of matches and our necklaces we shall liberate this country.' In fact, the revolt, not the president, was dying on its feet.

The over-exaggerated sense of crisis – as journalists, including this one, ran out of extreme epithets to describe another extra turn of the screw applied by Pretoria – helped, however, to set up the conditions for the Commonwealth intervention. For the first five months of 1986 the EPG scurried around southern Africa trying to erect a bridge of compromise between Lusaka and Pretoria.

Despite Pretoria's hostility, the EPG reached the edge of an important breakthrough. In exchange for a commitment from the ANC to *suspend*, not renounce, violence, the South African government would have to release Mandela and other political prisoners and detainees, end the military occupation of the townships, lift the ban on the ANC and PAC and allow normal political activity. The alternative was more sanctions and further isolation.

In military terms, at least, the president in 1986 was not like Smith's Salisbury in 1976. On 15 May the president accused outsiders of 'meddling' in South Africa's affairs. Four days later he ordered SADF raids on purported ANC positions in Harare, Lusaka and Gaborone. Apparently military intelligence was dubious about the accuracy of its information on the situations in the Zimbabwean and Zambian cities. It offered the president instead precise and ripe targets in Mozambique but the president was intent on lashing out simultaneously at the three capitals of the Commonwealth states. The raids deliberately obliterated the EPG peace mission which was still in South Africa at the time of the attacks. The military actions embarrassed not only the EPG luminaries but also Pik Botha who heard about them on his car radio while travelling to his foreign ministry, or so his aides told me. The raids were entirely political. Militarily they made little sense. It was even rumoured in the intelligence community that the Zimbabwean CIO was tipped off by SADF military intelligence just to make sure key ANC officials got out of the way.

After the raids, Sir Geoffrey Howe, the British foreign secretary, visited southern Africa to try to rescue something from the Commonwealth mission. He was treated very frostily by President Botha, who told him bluntly that South Africa's problems would not be solved by *uitlanders*. Sir Geoffrey, famously mild-mannered, was even more humiliated by Kaunda who gave the diplomat a public dressing down about the Thatcher government's attitude towards sanctions. As Helen Suzman summed up the aborted peace mission, 'EPG got the raid; Sir Geoffrey got the finger.'[4]

The chattering classes in South Africa endlessly speculated about the motives for the raids, although the main reason seems to have been what the press dubbed 'Rambothaism', a tough policy to satisfy the clamour of the right wing, especially at a time when the ultra-right *Herstigte Nasionale Party* won its first seat in seventeen years, in a by-election. Thus a major world event, delaying a peace settlement in a subcontinent and killing tens of thousands, was influenced by a few thousand political Neanderthals. There was no doubt, however, about the repercussions of the raids: renewed isolation and more dollops of the sanctions brew. Yet the ruling National Party leaders pretended to be surprised at the harsh international reaction. As senior journalist Stanley Uys commented:

> Are the Pretoria politicians and the military chiefs trying to tell us they had not anticipated the consequences. A corporal with a lobotomy could have told them that the raids would wreck the mission.

They were raids against reason.

Black-white polarization escalated. The right wing praised the military operations while the EPG left and issued a damning indictment of Pretoria. The EPG report, published as *Mission to South Africa*, stated that Commonwealth intervention 'may offer the last alternative to avert what could be the worst bloodbath since the Second World War'. A smaller scale bloodbath, at the KTC squatter camp in the Crossroads area near Cape Town, was taking place at the time the EPG book was launched. For years the government had been trying to move squatters out of the area to a resettlement camp many miles way. Pretoria's new allies, black conservative vigilantes called *witdoeke* locally (because of the white scarves worn to identify themselves separately from the comrades), forced out, with machetes and fire, 70,000 people. Not only had the most stubborn squatters in the Cape been moved out, but more crucially the support base for the UDF groups too. In June a friend, George De'Ath, a freelance cameraman working for the BBC, died from head wounds received from axes and pangas deployed in the fighting between the *witdoeke*, the SAP and the comrades. He was the first foreign journalist to be killed while covering the South African civil war. The *Cape Argus* newspaper described the mood in the black communities in the area, 'You can reach out in front of you … clench your fist and squeeze fear out of the air.'

On 2 June 1986 the state of emergency, lifted in March, was re-imposed. Four days before the tenth anniversary of the Soweto uprising, the security forces arrested the remnants of the leadership of the internal resistance still at large. By the end of the year more than 23,000 people, including about 9,000 children, had been jailed for varying periods under the June decrees. The SADF smashed the pretensions of the liberated zones in the townships. Pretoria was back in charge. The new state of emergency totally swamped the internal resistance. The UDF, though allowed, just, to continue to exist, was reduced to a shadow of its former self. By early 1987 even the radical college students and schoolchildren had heeded Lusaka and gone back to their desks under the compromise slogan of 'education for liberation'. As the domestic turmoil began to subside, the festering resentment of the Commonwealth leaders about the treatment meted out to the EPG crystallized into a fresh round of efforts to punish and isolate Pretoria.

In June the British government first met the ANC at ministerial level and thus ended the paradox, where Margaret Thatcher was urging Pretoria to talk to the ANC, something she had refused to do herself. In October, after overriding the presidential veto, the American Congress imposed fresh sanctions. They barred new corporate investment in South Africa and fresh loans to the government. South Africa's iron, steel, coal, uranium, textiles and some foods were put off limits. Landing rights for South African Airways were ended. In September the European Community had adopted a diluted version of the new American measures. Japan also prohibited imports of South African iron and steel products. South Africa's main trading partners were lining up against her. The logical economic arguments *against* sanctions, and there were many, no longer mattered. Imposing sanctions was a question of standing on the side of the angels; it meant you were either for or against apartheid. It had become an almost purely emotional issue. The tide of opinion swept up even stonewallers such as Reagan and Thatcher.

### *The fourth phase of resistance (1984-86): a summary*

More than 2,000 South Africans had been killed in the unrest by the end of 1986; only a handful were white. The gentle rhythm of the sprinklers on the luxuriant lawns or the slurping sound of the automatic pool cleaners called 'Kreepy-Kraulies' in the comfortable white suburbs had scarcely missed a beat (or a slurp). Pretoria's toughminded security forces had once more overwhelmed the passionate, but inchoate, black resistance.

The centralized National Security Management System (NSMS) had erected a parallel shadow government throughout the country run mainly by the military. (See appendix.) The NSMS had played a major part in defeating the fourth phase of the resistance. It had picked up the original crude and vague total strategy doctrine, refashioned it into a subtle, workable form and then applied it at the local level, often with great ingenuity. This more sophisticated approach to counter-insurgency was generally associated with the army's domination of the urban containment strategy by 1986, although there were sympathetic elements within the SAP, notably the scholarly General Johan Coetzee. Originally, the somewhat simplistic 80:20 per cent ratio of political to military input had been the received wisdom. That became refined operationally as 30:20:50. This formula assessed black attitudes. About 30 per cent were reckoned to be moderates who would go along with the status quo, provided they were left alone to mind their own business. About 20 per cent were considered to be comrades and their supporters, who were resolved to overthrow white rule. The remaining 50 per cent were adjudged to be fence-sitters, waiting to see who would win.

The strategy could be summarized as coercion, co-option, divide-and-rule and WHAM (winning hearts and minds). After the putative 20 per cent of radicals had been stamped on hard, the NSMS set about wooing the supposed uncommitted and moderate/conservative 80 per cent of the township dwellers. WHAM/civic action was taken very seriously. Lieutenant General Charles Lloyd, who had developed the Namibian psychological operations, championed this approach on taking over as secretary to the State Security Council in 1987. Pretoria's 'psyops' was a refined version of the French civic action in Algeria. It failed there, and it did not work in Rhodesia or Namibia. Nevertheless, the policy did create a general sense of relief in the townships chosen for development (most notably Alexandra, in the centre of the plush northern white suburbs of Johannesburg), not only about new roads, schools, shops and houses, but that the reign of comrades was over. And yet it was always unlikely that good sewers could act as a substitute for the vote.

That was the public and acceptable face of the NSMS. The localization of the total strategy also had a much more sinister, and effective, manifestation: the rise of the vigilantes. The townships had always suffered, or benefited from, a rough-and-ready form of impromptu local justice. In 1983-84 I made a documentary film on the *Makgotla* vigilantes in Soweto. Apartheid South Africa was often termed a police state, but in comparison with Western countries it was very *under*-policed, in terms of crime, not politics. While the white liberals in the relatively well-policed northern suburbs of Johannesburg were demanding police powers be curtailed, the under-policed inhabitants of the Cape Flats and Soweto often said the SAP was too soft on crime, partly because they were chasing the ANC and ignoring *tsotsis.* Some vigilante groups did spring up spontaneously. They claimed that their traditional methods, usually a good beating with a *sjambok* (whip), worked better than the *soi-distant* and occasional whitemen's justice. The *sjambok* was used in traditional courts, for example, to discourage infidelity, hardly a vote winner in the white suburbs. This old-fashioned style of direct retributive 'justice' had derived from the more conservative rural system of chiefs sorting out their own tribal problems. It was anachronistic in the cities, especially as so many urbanized blacks had been politicized by the struggle. And the comrades, correctly, accused the NSMS of trying to take over the vigilantes. The vigilantes' titles varied according to the region and the popularity of, usually, US TV programmes or films: hence the frequency of 'A-teams' or 'Green Berets'. They represented a privatization of state repression. The *witdoeke* and A-Teams in Crossroads became the internal equivalent of external destabilization: the vigilantes in Crossroads were sometimes as ruthless as RENAMO. Vigilante forces played a deadly role demoralizing the UDF-ANC resisters in 1986. They were especially disruptive because they came from *within* the community. Liberal critics attacked the media obsession with analyzing this violence as 'black-on-black' conflict. 'This label has as about as much heuristic value as describing the Second World War as white-on-white violence,' said human rights activist Nick Haysom.[5]

There were constant allegations that the SAP supported, or at least turned a blind eye to, Inkatha's impis in their wars with the UDF; evidence mounted about police complicity with the vigilantes in the Cape and the Transvaal. Nevertheless, it should be repeated that some of the vigilante group had originally reflected a genuine conservative, tribal and generational backlash against the lawlessness of the comrades.

After 1986 vigilante violence became far more refined, professionalized and centrally organized. Black and white pro-ANC activists' were assassinated. One was a former university colleague of mine, David Webster. He was shot outside his Johannesburg home in May 1989. In a bizarre twist of fate, he was an expert on death squads. Webster was the sixty-first anti-apartheid campaigner to be assassinated after 1977. A Natal university lecturer Rick Turner, whom I visited secretly in his Durban home while he was under house arrest, was shot in January 1978 at his house a few days after my visit.[6] But only in one case was anyone charged for these assassinations. As more friends and acquaintances were killed, I began to question whether the SAP were slack, over-busy or complicit. The hit squads, the media inaccurately dubbed them 'Z squads', even operated in the front-line states and in Western Europe. Jeremy Brickhill, whom I liked and admired for his lonely and brave stand but did not agree with him, was the only white Rhodesian who took an active military role, in intelligence, with ZAPU. He survived, just, an assassination attempt in Harare. The death squads' Latin-American-style operations caused great anxiety in both black and white liberal communities, not least for the government's failure to do anything about their campaign of terror. This caused a crisis for not only the (low) credibility of the SAP but also for the (once high) reputation of the legal system. The state had imposed draconian legislation but it still chose to act outside its own sweeping laws, as the evidence mounted of government involvement – *direction*, of the death squads.

So how did these squads work and who was directing them? The ANC and PAC quite often indulged in murderous fratricide and occasionally foreign intelligence agencies were involved with the odd shoot-outs. But these were distractions from the main effort, co-ordinated by the NSMS. The dirty tricks multiplied in the late

1980s and spluttered on after the advent of the ANC government. Many of the revelations emerged after the war and during the confessions of the Truth and Reconciliation Commission. (An organigram of the death squads can be found in the appendix.)

The squads were controlled overall by the president and below him the NSMS and State Security Council. The SADF, National Intelligence Service and the SAP all had fingers in the pie. But secrecy, and rivalry, were maintained by the army's special forces, military intelligence and the SAP operating separate units throughout the country and sometimes aboard. So much secrecy was involved that sometimes even fulltime professional operators didn't know for whom they worked. The most infamous organization was the Civil Co-operation Bureau, a wonderfully Orwellian name. It was set up with the approval of Magnus Malan, the minister of defence, in 1988. After the war, the army tried hard to distinguish itself from the SAP black ops. (A little like the *Wehrmacht*'s attempt to set itself apart from the Waffen SS.) The CCB worked as the third arm of the so-called 'Third Force', along with the SAP's C10 (also called Vlakplaas from where it was based) and the Directorate of Military Intelligence and SF ops. General Malan, during his appearance at the TRC, compared the CCB to the British Special Operations Executive during the Second World War in that its job was to infiltrate, penetrate and disrupt the enemy and to gather information. He claimed that he never authorized any assassinations. The CCB was nominally a civilian organization and had formal business fronts. The fulltime operatives were drawn from the SADF, SWATF and SAP, although quite a lot of the dirty work was done by underworld types who probably did not know they were working for the government. The business fronts were known as 'blue plans' and they sometimes developed into major commercial concerns. One important CCB operative was Eben Barlow who went on to found the very successful private military company Executive Outcomes. Before that Lieutenant Colonel Barlow had been based in London at De Beers to assist in sanctions-busting operations. The 'red plans' included the actual operations, killing or maiming or blowing up enemy infrastructure. One of the planned CCB ops was to beat up, but not kill, the UN special representative Martti Ahtisaari in 1989. The UN official switched his itinerary at the last minute and escaped the beating that the CCB had organized for him. My friend Jeremy Brickhill survived but was seriously wounded in a car bomb on 13 October 1987 in Harare. The CCB also killed SWAPO activist and lawyer Anton Lubowski. The secret organization also planned to kill Winnie Mandela but called off the op.

Another separate part of the third force was an SAP unit headed by Eugene de Kock, who became infamous during the Truth and Reconciliation Commission. Although he got a very bad press and a sentence of 212 years, de Kock had a good record of early service in the SAP and SADF. Initially he was reluctant to become an officer because of his stutter, but he reached the rank of colonel, after

Many white conscripts disliked serving in the townships (Abe Berry, courtesy of the *Star*)

showing undoubted bravery and leadership in Namibia and Rhodesia. And yet he became the most despised face of apartheid, nicknamed the 'Prime Evil'. He was a founding member of *Koevoet* in Namibia and the organizer of assassinations and torture at the SAP CIO unit HQ in Vlakplaas, twenty kilometres west of Pretoria. De Kock later apologized to many of the families of victims who had been killed by his unit and finally was granted parole after implicating senior political leaders including the last white president, F.W. de Klerk.

The worst excesses of the third-force coalition were in the years 1987 to 1990. At the beginning of this period the security forces had gained an undoubted ascendancy over the domestic resistance. The reform ingredients had been ladled out at the national level, with the repeal of certain apartheid laws, and, at the local level, with the souped-up civic action. The townships sank back into a mood of sullen, resigned anger. The young lions had been beaten on the streets in their uneven battles but the ANC had won the propaganda war. Mandela had become famous internationally. How were the ANC leaders in exile going to deploy the international goodwill and domestic support to make the final surge against the ramparts of Pretoria?

The ANC strategy had four prongs: mass action, the political underground, international diplomacy and the armed struggle. Taking mass action first, it could be argued hat *kragdadigheid* (hardline attitudes) by intractable apartheid bureaucrats,

The fighting still continued on the Angola/Namibia border, 1987 (author)

not the ANC's revolutionary work, had precipitated the major phases of the rebellion. The classic examples were the Bantu education bureaucracy's insistence upon the use of Afrikaans in 1976 and the insensitive way the bureaucracy urged the black councils to raise rents in 1984. Once the mass revolts had been triggered, the ANC in Lusaka could not keep up with events. As Frederik van Zyl Slabbert said in parliament, 'It is not the external ANC that is radicalizing the internal situation. It is the internal situation that is radicalizing the ANC.' The ANC leadership might have optimistically termed rampaging mobs of school kids 'mass combat units' but very few ANC officers were involved in leading or organizing them. This largely spontaneous mass mobilization was of course useful in itself for the revolutionaries. The children, for example, turned the group areas to their advantage: the ghettoes became, in some cases, temporary no-go areas. And the younger generation were 'conscientised' (politicized) and educated by the struggle:

> The 1985 school boycotts afforded thousands of children the opportunity to learn the practical science of making petrol bombs; the street sociology of taunting armed soldiers; the pavement politics of pamphlet distribution

> and slogan painting; the geography of safe houses and escape routes; and the grammar and dialectics of undercover operations.[7]

The second aspect of the ANC strategy was the expansion of its underground structures inside the country. Ironically, it was constructed along lines not dissimilar to Pretoria's NSMS. The underground, however, lacked sufficient trained personnel and weapons. The security police constantly eviscerated the internal wing of the ANC, despite its tight cell structure. During the years of township turmoil, there were never enough leaders or hardware to match the ardour of the local comrades. 'Our aim of arming the people had a long way to go,' admitted Ronnie Kasrils, the senior MK strategist. 'Every stone-thrower wants a gun.' A strange kind of urban warfare emerged, therefore, where the rioters outpaced the radical organizations, where the masses led the supposed vanguard.

The third prong, the international front, was largely successful. Talks with senior UK and US representatives undermined Pretoria's (and Inkatha's) tarnished legitimacy as well as boosting black morale inside South Africa. Yet an obvious contradiction surfaced between the craving for international respectability in the West and the terrorism of the armed struggle, the fourth prong. Success in one area tended to weaken the other. Advances on the cocktail circuit boosted the ANC doves who argued for a negotiated settlement. The hawks preferred Molotov cocktails. As with the rise of the SADF in Pretoria, so too in Lusaka, hints about a 'creeping military coup' were dropped, associated in particular with the rise of the charismatic Chris Hani, officially number two in MK and also general secretary of the SACP. Men like Hani wanted to strike at soft targets inside the republic to shake the whites out of their awesome complacency. As Hani put it, 'We are prepared to see a wasteland if that is the price of freedom.' Yet the ANC was clearly divided on the issue of white civilian targets. The divisions were not only along the lines of older conservatives versus young hotheads, but also they were inspired by ideological and, possibly, regional differences between 'Jo'burgers' and 'Kappies' (similar to the liberal Cape/class clashes with the blue-collar/hardliners in the Transvaal within the National Party). Black and white politics always exhibited strong regional nuances, sometimes cutting across race, in that sprawling country. Typically, Pretoria explained away the ANC divisions purely in terms of African nationalists versus communists and tribal splits,

Chris Hani, SACP and MK leader

especially hostility to alleged Xhosa dominance. That accusation contained more than a grain of truth.

After the important Kabwe conference in 1985, when the ANC formally launched its people's war, MK tried to step up its campaign. Landmines were first introduced in November 1985. In 1976, according to Pretoria's figures, two MK incidents were recorded every six months. In 1986 five bombings, raids and assassinations occurred every week, although there were fewer 'spectaculars' such as the attacks on SASOL plants, Koeberg nuclear plant and the Air Force HQ. Yet the Lusaka hierarchy displayed a continuous ambiguity towards bombs that claimed civilian victims, such as the incidents in the Amanzimtoti shopping mall and outside the Ellis Park rugby stadium. Sometimes, the leadership claimed that their units had acted without orders: the Nkomati agreement had over-extended and disrupted the guerrillas' chain of command and communications. This made wildcat attacks more likely. Nonetheless, within the MK high command, elements were agitating for more strikes on white civilians, partly to maintain the battered morale in the townships, especially after 1987. Yet taking the war into the white areas, making whites specific targets, contradicted not only the basic tenets of a multi-racial struggle, a philosophy enshrined in the SACP's ideology but also the fact that a growing number of whites were joining the ANC and climbing its hierarchy. White veterans were to be found in the national executive committee. Targeting whites specifically was also impolitic, to say the least, at a time when visits to the ANC in Lusaka by white businessmen, politicians and, increasingly, sports chiefs had become so fashionable. A race war was the last thing the ANC doves wanted. At times, though, the ANC spoke with two tongues. In its radio broadcasts directed at a popular black audience the language was very strident:

> The regime's police and soldiers who have been massacring our people in millions over the years still return to their homes and spend comfortable nights in the warmth of their beds. They must be haunted by the mass offensive. We must attack them at their homes and their holiday resorts just as we have been attacking their bootlickers at their homes. This must now happen to their white colleagues. All along it has only been the black mothers who have been mourning. Now has come the time that all of us must mourn. White families must also wear black costumes. Domestic servants must play a leading role. They know where their employers keep their weapons and they are the ones who can devise plans of transferring the ownership of these weapons.

That was in 1985. Yet in the USA the ANC could describe itself as 'a community of love and justice on a pilgrim's road to freedom'. Joe Slovo, when he was the SACP boss, had tried to fudge the contradictions: he termed white civilian casualties 'diversions and blemishes'. Slovo, demonized by Pretoria, maintained that the government needed to blame all the bomb attacks on him, a white, because they could not admit that blacks were sophisticated enough to organize a sustained bombing campaign. 'Botha and Botha have done for me what Saatchi and Saatchi have done for Mrs Thatcher,' he joked. As the ANC stepped into the diplomatic limelight, Slovo dropped his Stalinist mantle and went public, after decades in the shadows. This coincided with a 1988 film about his tragic family life, *A World Apart,* written by his daughter, Shawn. Joe Slovo confidently asserted:

> We have moved a long way from being an agitational opposition to presenting an alternative government .... Before the government wouldn't talk to us at all. Now they say they will talk to us if we stop violence. That shows it has been effective.

In the 1960s the violence was almost a form of 'political graffiti'; then came a period of armed struggle in the 1970s. By the end of 1986 the ANC and SACP perceived three essential pre-revolutionary factors: a crisis in the enemy ranks; a clear demonstration that the masses were prepared to make the ultimate sacrifice; and the widespread recognition that the ANC was the alternative source of authority. In the early phases of the 1984-86 uprising there was a general feeling that an apocalyptic moment of change was at hand. In a novel interpretation of *Revelations*, Chapter 21, Pretoria's leaders would, as in a vision, sign a surrender document, perhaps in a railway carriage. By 1987 that ebullient mood had vanished. The ANC had ordered the townships to be made ungovernable. That invited chaos, as we have seen, not people's power. The security forces smashed the comrades and restored Pretoria's writ throughout the land.

Nevertheless, a comparison of the two insurrections, 1976-77 and 1984-86, would prove instructive. Soweto was quelled, with the deaths of hundreds of blacks, fairly rapidly by the police, on their own, with existing legislation. From 1985 the military had been required in large numbers to back the police, deployed under a state of emergency. The 1976 insurrection was largely a children's war that marshalled the support of an elite group of established community leaders. In 1984 working-class adults joined in, more or less willingly. If 1976 was an urban revolt, then by 1986 even the most remote *platteland* towns had become inflamed. The revolutionary climate in the 1980s was much more intense. The organization, which was often poor, was at least better than in 1976-77. Belatedly, the ANC tried to manipulate the internal and international dimensions of the revolt, although bodies such as the UDF and the powerful labour unions (not all of whom toed the ANC line) were, arguably, more influential. The sustained, better-organized unrest created embryonic alternative structures which, although eventually destroyed, gave the masses a taste of people's power. The flamboyant and extensive political exploitation of funerals was a new weapon used by the liberation movements to publicize their cause. Finally, marginally better weapons, especially limpet mines and landmines, and more AKs, were smuggled into the front line. According to Peter Magubane, a well-known photographer, raised in Soweto, who had covered the conflict since the 1960s:

> Things are getting tougher, more clinical. If there is a protest march or a funeral procession, you will find buckets of water placed at every house along the way. That's in case there is tear gas, so the marchers can wash it from their eyes and from their faces. That was not true at the time of the Soweto riots in 1976. The children have become more politicized. They have left the adults behind.[8]

The persistent assaults on black collaborators with the government reflected at total rejection of apartheid. The system was not to be reformed but destroyed. In the heady days of 1984-86 the majority smelt victory. The rulers had lost confidence in their ideology and the ruled were convinced they could win. The balance of confidence, if not the immediate balance of power, had changed.

Yet the immediate mood of black triumphalism had been blown away. Battle fatigue among the young militants, harsher and more sophisticated police tactics, led by the army, the detention of thousands of black leaders, a genuine backlash from moderate blacks, as well as vigilante activity, plus the end of the school boycotts, which took thousands of combatants off the streets, all helped persuade the radicals that the revolution was not imminent. After two years of pumping adrenalin around the body politic, a sullen cloud descended. All sides sensed a breathing space to prepare, soon, for the next phase.

On the long march to freedom there were many twists and turns. Pretoria's decapitation of the Black Consciousness movement in 1977 had promoted the fortunes of the ANC. After 1986 the ANC had made substantial diplomatic gains but may have suffered some loss of face in the townships. The ANC had been quick to grab the credit, largely unjustifiably, for the uprising but when it failed it also had to take some blame. Despite the military defeat of the comrades a belief in ultimate victory had been firmly planted in the popular psyche. As Tom Lodge, a former colleague at the University of the Witwatersrand, a political sparring partner and an eminent analyst of the ANC, concluded, 'In South Africa, the role of guerrilla warfare is likely to remain chiefly inspirational and psychological, important mainly to the extent that can help the ANC exercise political leadership over constituencies it is unable to organize directly.'

Tom Lodge was sympathetic to the ANC and yet he was implying that the armed struggle had failed as a military strategy. Many insurgents who managed to cross into South Africa found little to support them internally. Their capture rate was very high, if they survived arrest. In military terms MK cadres were very ineffective. Howard Barrell, who worked inside MK intelligence, wrote a very compelling Oxford doctorate on these failures. This highly competent intelligence officer and now academic colleague wrote in 1993:

> monitoring mechanisms and operational management in the ANC were abysmal. This was attributable to a number of shortcomings. There was no ANC leadership presence on the ground inside South Africa. Key officials often failed to attend meetings of the top operational organ, the Revolutionary Council (RC), and of its successor, the Politico-Military Council (PMC). Rank-and-file ANC members had almost no ability to reward good operational leadership and punish bad: members of the RC and PMC were appointed by the National Executive Committee (NEC); and ordinary ANC members were given only two opportunities to influence NEC membership – in 1969, the year the RC was set up, and 1985. Parallelism between political and military structures made the timeous exchange of mutually relevant information extremely difficult. Personality and inter-departmental rivalries undermined decisions that were taken from time to time to improve information flows between sections. Furthermore, long and poor lines of communication into and out of South Africa, as well as between ANC machineries in different countries, meant that good information on which changes to methods and strategies might have been based was often out of date by the time it reached ANC decision-makers in Lusaka or Maputo. Assessing strategy and deciding on improvements to it could, hence, be a highly speculative process.[9]

This was, frankly, polite academic-speak for saying the ANC could not organize a piss-up in a brewery, and this coming from a senior intelligence insider. And yet the ANC won.

## *The twilight of the imperial presidency*

The 'Great Crocodile' led his party into the May 1987 election with all his customary Teutonic charm. The campaign soon degenerated into a plebiscite on which party had the best security policy. As John Barratt, the ever-affable head of the South African Institute of Affairs, observed, 'The *swart gevaar,* the *rooi gevaar,* the *buitelandse gevaar* were combined into one really big *gevaar*.'[10] The National Party took 54 per cent of the vote and increased its seats from 118 to 123. Some observers interpreted this result as a vote for reform. The emasculation of the liberal opposition and the twenty-two seats won by the Conservative Party (up from seventeen), the first time since 1948 that the official opposition had been on the right, indicated the voters, especially English-speakers, had moved to the right, attracted by the security ticket. With its new reliance on the English-speakers, the

Nationalists probably no longer represented even a majority of Afrikaners. Botha now led a minority of a minority tribe.

As expected, Pretoria launched a raid on the ANC just before the election. Five people were killed in Livingstone, Zambia, in April, though Kaunda claimed that none of the victims had ANC connections. This was the only cross-border raid to be officially acknowledged by the SADF in 1987.

The electoral triumph of the National Party, despite a disastrous economic and political performance that would have caused it to be immediately thrown out of office in any Western state, plus the wind-down of unrest, brought a renewed confidence to the whites. Except for the liberal minority, South African whites seemed to be preternaturally, or was it desperately, inclined to be optimistic. Their peculiar political environment demanded constant psychological reassurance. They liked to feel good about themselves. 'There's nothing wrong with us; the world just doesn't *understand* us or the situation.' Hence the importance of international sports tours and the massive attention given to the visit of the most minor starlet, probably going to the glitzy Sun City entertainment centre. The fact that few people would watch them perform, although I enjoyed big acts such as the Beach Boys and Rod Stewart, didn't matter. The important thing was that foreigners 'came to see for themselves'. We are not alone. Township violence was off the world's TVs; therefore out of sight, out of mind. Even tourists were coming back; so were some of the whites who had panicked and taken the 'chicken run' to Australia and Britain. The economy had even begun to pick up a little. In short, by late 1987 the whites had relaxed back into their cyclical post-crisis complacency. 'It'll all come right.'

Of course, not all was well. In August 300,000 miners went on strike, the biggest strike, and costliest mine strike, South Africa had ever faced. It was more about politics than wages. The savage feuding between the UDF and Inkatha, both in Natal and in the hostels in Johannesburg, intensified, claiming hundreds of lives. Then Allan Hendrickse, leader of the majority Labour Party in the coloured House of Representatives, blocked the mechanisms of the clumsy tricameral system to demand the repeal of the Group Areas Act. Botha humiliated Hendrickse in a televised primetime speech on the tame SATV. The president had brought the Indian and coloured parliamentary majority leaders into his cabinet; now both were forced out. It was rumoured that the president would suspend all three parliaments and rule by decree.

Angry at the mild truculence of his junior allies in the constipated tricameral show, Pretoria made tentative gestures towards the ANC. In November Govan Mbeki, the frail 73-year-old former chairman of the ANC, was freed, without preconditions, after twenty-three years in jail. This was seen as a trial run for Mandela's release. At a press conference, Mbeki refused to renounce the armed struggle or the ANC. The government confined him to Port Elizabeth and banned him from making public statements. Mandela's release did not look imminent.

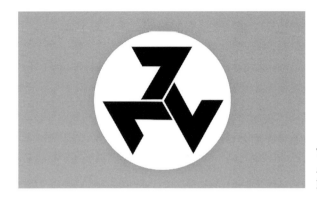

The ultra-right-wing Afrikaner Resistance Movement's logo

Meanwhile, MK tried to regain some momentum, even though the townships were relatively quiet. Pretoria claimed that 220 ANC personnel had been killed or arrested during 1987. The one spectacular came in July when the ANC detonated a bomb outside a military HQ in downtown Johannesburg: sixty-eight people were injured. As long as the ANC kept up its campaign and the Conservative Party bayed for tougher action, the president found it difficult to move with his stalled, if not moribund, reform programme. The rise of the right and the antics of the pathological Afrikaner fundamentalists in the Afrikaner Resistance Movement (*Afrikaner Weerstandsbeweging*, AWB) mesmerized Pretoria. Afrikaner interests, especially regarding security matters, always came first, reform and the rest of the world very much second.

In February 1988 Pretoria banned seventeen black organizations affiliated to the UDF and detained many of their leaders. An international outcry resulted from the bannings. If Pretoria crushed legal groups, what choice was there but to join the armed struggle? The government was unmoved. West German and British pressure did, however, manage to restrain further reactionary legislation. In the first case, the Foreign Funding Bill, which would have cut off foreign aid to anti-apartheid organizations, was amended. In Germany, in particular, the bill was seen to threaten the inflow of humanitarian aid. This caused offence to German public opinion at a time when *Cry Freedom* had captured the imagination of West German youth. Secondly, both London and Bonn demanded the stay of execution of the Sharpeville Six, six blacks who were accused of being members of a lynch mob. Pretoria was inclined to listen to both these foreign governments as their fingers were in the dyke against further EC sanctions. Another issue was the threat to *tighten up* some aspects of the Group Areas Act, while allowing a few 'grey areas' for mixed racial co-habitation. This was pushing the few remaining western sympathizers too far. The Germans threatened to withdraw their ambassador and more if the Sharpeville Six were hanged. As the London *Daily Telegraph* correspondent tartly observed, 'Suddenly, white South Africans were contemplating the prospects of no more air filters for their Mercedes.'

Pretoria backed down on the Group Areas Bill, the execution of the Sharpeville Six and the banning of foreign funds. Pretoria also showed some flexibility regarding imprisoned nationalist leaders. The aged and sick PAC leader, Zeph Mothopeng, was released on humanitarian grounds. What terrified Pretoria was Mandela dying in prison. That could have triggered off a cataclysm; but so could his release, the hardliners in Pretoria thought. Mandela had been moved to a five-star Cape Town clinic for medical treatment and it was made clear that he would not be going back to Pollsmoor Prison on the outskirts of Cape Town. Mandela was moved into a bungalow in the gardens of Paarl prison. The ANC leader had dedicated much of his time to horticulture in his long years of being entombed in grey concrete. He had been proud of his pot plants and now he was living in a rose garden. But it was not freedom.

President Botha still worried about his right wing. Some of the Conservative Party-controlled towns in the Transvaal had actually regressed to the segregationist policies of the 1960s. But in the October 1988 municipal elections the opposition Conservative Party had reached a plateau. So P.W. could look again at reform. It all depended upon getting some blacks into the government. Not one single African, 75 per cent of the population, was in central government: no MP, no cabinet minister, let alone a general. This was the Fabianism of the tortoise. Some black faces were desperately needed. Buthelezi was the obvious choice, perhaps the only one, for Pretoria. And he did have some credibility but he would not accommodate Pretoria while Mandela was in prison and the ANC was banned. Besides, he was seriously distracted by the UDF-Inkatha war that had caused more than 1,800 deaths by the end of 1988. The proposed national council, without Buthelezi, was dead in the water. The turnout for the black municipal elections was still abysmal despite the government spending a fortune on promoting them and prohibiting boycotts. The pro-voting campaign, which included cartoons of two civic-minded squirrels solemnly debating the electoral process, failed to persuade the vast majority of black votes to join the politicized squirrels.

Despite the muted factionalism in Lusaka and the rampant version in the townships at home, the insurgency continued. According to Pretoria, 330 guerrillas were killed or captured in 1988 but the ANC bombings, often of soft targets, claimed forty-nine lives. The SADF retaliated with a raid on Gaborone in March 1988. The ANC claimed that Pretoria was responsible for a covert operation in Paris on 29 March 1988 when Dulcie September was shot five times from the rear outside the Paris ANC office. Aged 52, she was the first ANC official to be killed outside Africa. In the same month, Albie Sachs, another veteran ANC activist, and later judge, lost an arm in a car bomb explosion in Maputo. In apparent response, 100 kilos of explosive packed in a stolen BMW exploded outside Ellis Park rugby stadium. This Beirut-style attack killed two white men and injured thirty-five other people, minutes after the final whistle of a top league rugby match. This was a blow to the very core of the Afrikaner male psyche: rugby; and it was the biggest

Albie Sachs, veteran ANC man, lost an arm in a car-bomb explosion in Maputo

bomb explosion in the history of the insurgency. Two months before, the SAP had seized the largest quantity of arms yet found by the police in South Africa, on a smallholding at Broederstroom, north of Johannesburg. The haul included a SAM-7 missile-launcher and one missile. Four of the five ANC operatives were arrested. All were white. Four of the men involved were South Africans and the sole woman was reported to be a Swazi who had taken out British citizenship.

The increasing attacks on soft targets coincided not only with the internal debate in Lusaka, but also a shift in the stance of the SACP towards the inevitability of successful revolution. Moscow's experts on Africa began to stress the possibility of a political settlement and the need to preserve the South African economy intact. Quietly and discreetly, relations between Pretoria and Moscow thawed, even though no formal diplomatic relations had existed since the mid-1950s. Relations between the two foreign ministries improved markedly during the lengthy talks to secure an Angolan settlement. *Glasnost,* it seemed, was even reaching into the dusty corners of the Union Buildings, the seat of the South African government.

Even before the dramatic fall of the Berlin Wall in November 1989, Moscow had tried to pull back from supporting so many military commitments. More national liberation struggles were directed against Soviet-backed regimes than against American ones. Moscow largely divested itself from Afghanistan, Angola, Ethiopia and cut back on the big handouts to needy outliers such as Cuba and Nicaragua. In South Africa, real revolution could have harmed the coy arrangement between Moscow and Pretoria to sell diamonds and gold. Both the USSR and the USA appeared to be converging on finessing a less bloody transition to black rule in the apartheid republic.

By 1989 President Botha had reached a political dead end. After a stroke in January he announced, eventually, his resignation as NP leader, though not as president. During ten years in power he had become an authoritarian bully, who terrified members of his own cabinet. His predecessors, such as Malan and Verwoerd, were essentially modest, unpretentious prime ministers, even if they were also racial bigots. Botha, though, had taken on the trappings of the great dictator. He had assumed an increasingly imperial manner, as he grew more remote from his immediate colleagues and party. To a lesser extent this had happened to his almost exact contemporary, Margaret Thatcher. Like all tyrants, Botha had tended to disdain criticism or advice. English-speakers had often found his finger-wagging bellicosity embarrassing and yet many white South Africans, who shivered with wicked delight every time he told the rest of the world to get lost, eventually deserted him to join the very right-wing parties. Nevertheless, he had displayed bravery in splitting his tribe when he rid himself of the infamous 'Dr No', Andries Treurnicht, the prophet of the Conservative Party. P.W. Botha had shown courage too in insisting that his countrymen had to 'adapt or die'. But temperamentally and intellectually he had lacked the will and the ability to proceed along the reform path he sometimes pointed to. After the whirlwind of protest raced through the republic in 1984 he had lost his way completely. Then followed the catastrophes: the Rubicon speech, the curt dismissal of the EPG peace mission and the public humiliation of Allan Hendrickse, the Labour leader, which lit up the tricameral parliament as a ship of fools.

As he partially recovered from his stroke in early 1989, he tried to use the SATV to resurrect his position in the party. This time on TV the hand that had jabbed defiance at the world shook visibly. The Great Crocodile had lost his teeth. Like many other African bosses he was mighty reluctant to give up his throne. The emperor with no clothes finally conceded that he would go, after the general election scheduled for September 1989. Political pressure from his party, led by rival F.W. de Klerk, forced the ailing president to quit in August. The old man left gracelessly, cursing de Klerk. Botha had served the National Party his whole life, so it was sadly ironic that the manner of his departure from power severely damaged the party he had served so faithfully.

Despite Botha's awesomely self-important public speeches, the departing president left no intellectual legacy. As his old parliamentary opposition rival, Frederik van Zyl Slabbert, put it in his book *The Last White Parliament*:

> His political philosophy is remarkably uncomplicated: if things go wrong, there must be an enemy responsible, and if they go right it is because of 'good Government'. The simplicity of the total onslaught philosophy appealed to him as Minister of Defence and he carried its logic into his office as Prime Minister and State President. If all else fails, Moscow must be responsible for what goes wrong, whether it be regional instability or domestic unrest, and those who not do accept this are the witting or unwitting tools of it.[11]

F.W. de Klerk: a Nationalist politician ready for change?

P.W. Botha's successor, F.W. de Klerk, was a brighter and more sophisticated figure. I had first interviewed him at length five years before his ascendancy and he seemed light years away from the Great Crocodile. He appeared to be a modern politician, ready for big change. But how would the military react to this new modernizing man? The constitutional structure and the total strategy rested on Botha's power and his personal relationship with the generals. F.W. de Klerk was not a part of the charmed circle of securocrats; nor did he appear to want to be. Civil-military relations looked set for a sea-change. The constitution had been designed to fit one man. So had its part-model, the Gaullist constitution, and that had survived the demise of its mentor.

As the prime icon of white rule crumbled so did the major black symbol of resistance at large in the country: Winnie Mandela. The 'Black Evita' was also rejected by her own people because of the scandals associated with her bodyguards, the tip of the iceberg of a long series of incidents in which Mrs Mandela had more than overplayed her position as a stand-in for her husband. She had become a local heroine because not even Pretoria could keep her in line, nor could the ANC. The Indian leader, Amichand Rajbansi, fell from grace too. In the last days of his Raj not even his NP allies could tolerate his mafia style of politics.

As South Africans geared up for another election, in which yet again blacks could not vote, parties across the political spectrum were in a state of flux. There were constants too. Disinvestment continued, although more slowly than at the beginning of 1989, Mobil being the latest to decamp. High inflation, low business confidence, the government's mounting deficit and the inability to raise foreign loans all contributed to the erosion of the formal economy. The political logjam remained: no credible black leader could talk to Pretoria until the ANC was unbanned. The state of emergency was renewed again in June 1989. Thirty-two organisations, from civic groups to student bodies and the UDF, were banned from carrying out any political activities. The refined National Security Management System continued its careful scrutiny of all political dissent throughout the country. And the shooting war went on. According to figures released in June 1989, in 1986 there had been 231 guerrilla attacks; in 1987, 235 attacks; and 245 in 1988. The emergency powers had not deterred an escalation in the number of MK assaults.

On the cusp of a new decade, it was clear that the security forces had driven the black internal opposition underground. That was a short-term success for the states of emergency. But could such severe repression in the ominously precarious garrison state last for much longer?

# *Chapter 16*

# The Garrison State

South Africa was frequently termed a 'garrison state', in which the military became increasingly dominant in a white society, including the business community, that was engulfed in a siege mentality, largely of its own making. Until F.W. de Klerk's presidency evidence had mounted of the republic's militarization, though theoretically no inevitable correlation exists between continuing military crisis and the likelihood of military intervention. Britain in 1940-41 was just one example of this caveat. South Africa's civil-military tradition had absorbed much of the British idea of *apolitical* armed forces, as well as the entrenched Boer/Afrikaner dislike of an independently-minded standing army. Since Clausewitz professional armies in the West have been expected to be subservient instruments of the political will of the state. And yet the military intervened in nearly every European state in modern history and, as far back as the time of President Eisenhower, American democracy had been threatened by a military-industrial complex. The politicization inherent in effective counter-insurgency, especially in the developing world, has often reversed the orthodox democratic norms of civil-military behaviour.

Although it had been suggested, in anti-apartheid circles, that the military were considering taking over in Pretoria in 1976, there is very little hard evidence of this. It is true that militarization began in earnest in 1978 with the premiership of Piet 'the Weapon' Botha, as some of his Afrikaner enemies dubbed him. Under Botha the parliamentary system had declined, including the power of the National Party which had ruled since 1948. And the liberalization of apartheid's economic strategies had as a 'necessary corollary' the limitation of the political rights of whites most vulnerable to the changes it was likely to usher in.[1] To summarize a complex academic debate at the time, the State Security Council and its nationwide shadow government was said to operate a sham democracy, even for whites, as the inner cabal of securocrats, military and civilian, undermined the privileges of poor whites to grant economic rights to blacks as part of a limited 'reform by stealth'. Meanwhile, real political power was kept in the hands of a small civilian-military elite.

Under the rule of P.W. Botha there was more than a grain of truth to the reform-by-stealth argument while the securocrats ran the real show. Often, however, military repression was a knee-jerk reaction by an imperial president who had run out of ideas. Still, he had some clever advisors, in suits and uniforms, though he usually chose to

Union Buildings, Pretoria, the seat of apartheid. Real power was kept in the hands of a small civilian-military elite

ignore them. Under Botha the SADF and SAP contained both hawks and doves as varying styles of racial domination. After the crushing of the 1984-86 revolt a fierce debate raged within the security elite. Until 1984 the grand reformist programme had rested upon measures to stabilize urban blacks (after the earlier Riekert Commission, attempts had been made to establish a conservative black 'insider' middle class and working class in the cities); the unions (via the Wiehahn Commission that had legalized black unions); and the political system (by 'extending democracy' by means of a tricameral parliament with a national council for blacks tagged on as an afterthought). Low-level protest and action and township organizations would be tolerated to an extent. But anything more than blowing off a little steam would be controlled by immediate repression: banning, detention and infiltration. During 1984 to 1986 the hawks appeared to be in the ascendancy; probably the annihilation of the EPG mission was a high watermark of the hardline position.

### *The National Security Management System (NSMS)*

After 1987 the reformists were resuscitated, but they came back with a more subtle approach. Yes, grand gestures were necessary. Talks with a declawed ANC were still mooted. More importantly, however, instead of a 'top-down' strategic emphasis, they planned to expand the grassroots approach developed during the last unrest. The top tier of the government's carrots, the national council, was not enticing anyone. Instead, the second and third tiers were to be augmented. This was all based on a simple economic determinism. Through the NSMS – and its network began to parallel the nine areas of regional economic development – a type of economic federalism was being built. Perhaps later the homelands, urban areas (as city sates), the national council and the tricameral parliament could have been tied up into a 'consociational' federal political system. Thirty years later, in 2018, all this seems arcane but it is important to understand what the pro-apartheid intellectuals were trying to do. It was not just hammer blows. The lesson of 1984-86 was that total strategy dictated from above just did not work. The apartheid reformers thought that grassroots civil action programmes might work far better. Under the NSMS umbrella, a national counter-insurgency system was erected. A government manual, *The Art of Counter-Revolutionary Warfare,* outlined this grassroots campaign. It was almost as if the first ANC insurgency proposals, the so-called 'M-plan', was written large and then put in reverse. The first step was the elimination of what remained of the comrades' alternative structures. This was largely done. The second stage, according to the manual, was the restoration of 'effective administration … an effective and well-motivated administration will deny revolutionaries the initiative'. The next step was to pump millions of rand into the townships, particularly the thirty-four most rebellious ones such as Alexandra, Mamelodi, New Brighton and Bonteheuwel. This was not just a question of new houses, post offices and pavements. The counter-revolution required better educational facilities, social clubs, sports grounds, clinics, career advice centres and the involvement of religious organizations. This was to be done on a person-to-person basis. The aim was social control and restoration of the ruptured informer network. The new 'loyal' infrastructure had to be able to defend itself. 'Self-defence' was the 'most important part of counter-organization of the masses'. Hence the recruitment of what the British in Malaya called 'special constables'; in South Africa *kitskonstables.* These 'instant police' would supplement the local black municipal police and the SAP as the first line of containment in an emergency (see appendix for summary of the various police forces). The pacified areas would transform 'hot spots' into what the manual defined as 'oil spots' that would gradually seep outwards to join other 'loyal' local areas to form swathes of satisfied customers, grateful for Pretoria's largesse.

That was the strategic plan. In many ways it was the direct application of the homeland principles to the cities: shift the burden of control onto allies in the black community – policemen, councillors, businessmen and vigilantes. Local black defence structures were vital to destroy the radical opposition. At the same time material advances would, it was hoped, create a stable, property-owning, middle-class nucleus with a stake in the system and opportunities for political advancement at municipal and regional levels. If this worked, then the homelands and semi-autonomous 'city-states', such as Soweto, could have been represented in the national council, with a few token blacks in the cabinet as well. Perhaps even some genuine nationalists from the ANC might have been enticed. This panoply of ambition was Pretoria's version of the Namibian and Rhodesian internal settlements. At the end of the day, this upmarket version of apartheid would still have left the whites in total control. Of course that was what the decades, the centuries, of struggle had been about.

This turbocharged version of racial domination was designed with the same missionary zeal and determination as the 1950s vintage model. The apex of the system was the State Security Council, which in turn controlled the NSMS, set up originally in 1979. It came fully into its own in the 1984-86 period. Later, officials tended to coyly drop the 'Security' part of the title. 'National Management System' sounded much more benign.

How did the NSMS work? The SSC had a secretariat and various committees that were plugged into conventional government bureaucracy. Indeed, at every level, from cabinet to local councils, a parallel NSMS organ had been created. At the main regional levels stood the Joint Management Centres (JMCs). Originally the JMCs corresponded to the (then) eleven SADF area commands, although the network was re-jigged to tie in with the nine economic development regions. Lower down the hierarchy were the eighty-two sub-JMCs which were supposed to cooperate with the Regional Service Councils then being set up. These councils were supposed to raise, from business levies, much of the 'upliftment' of the townships. At the bottom level 320 mini-JMCs worked with the local black, coloured and Indian councils, and other local bodies. Each JMC, sub-JMC and mini-JMC had three major committees dealing with firstly, intelligence, secondly, political economic and social matters and, thirdly, communications.

Political engineering on such a vast scale was much more sophisticated than anything the British in Malaya or the French in Algeria had attempted. This was not foreign territory from which Afrikaners could retreat 'home'. They were home. General Magnus Malan had experienced first-hand the French operations in Algeria. He had not only been on the losing side but he had also seen how the war had ripped French society apart. Above all, Charles de Gaulle sat in Paris, not Algiers. The Afrikaner securocrats had to travel only a few miles from their citadel in Pretoria

General Magnus Malan had first-hand experience of French operations in Algeria

to the surrounding townships to sample the revolutionary turmoil. In short, the NSMS strategy was an elaborate ploy to steal the thunder of the radicals – or freedom fighters, from the ANC perspective. The ANC had targeted the masses' main grievances as: lack of freedom of movement, health, education and housing. So Pretoria scrapped influx control and passes, while tightening up on movement into the cities by rigorous squatter and health regulations. Next it poured money into building new houses, clinics and schools. Nearly $2 billion was spent in 1988 on such measures in the thirty-four 'difficult' townships. And $8 billion was earmarked for 200 other townships in the following five years. Some of the money came from central government; the rest was to be raised by the Regional Services Councils (often unpopular, especially with white businessmen, because of the levies raised from them) and directly from private enterprise. The Urban Foundation was active in providing houses, for example.

The ANC damned the Pecksniffian programme as collaboration. But who in the townships would actually not want better roads, houses and libraries? One senior officer attached to the SSC argued:

> These people have their aspirations, of course, but tthey are really concerned about bread-and-butter issues – housing, schools, motor cars, 'the good life'. And if you want their support, you can *buy* it.

But could Pretoria afford a new generation of tanks for its border wars *and* then of tens of thousands of new houses for a black middle class, which was just as likely to lead a revolution as stop one? And would the small white tax base continue to support guns and butter, especially butter for blacks? The right wing continued to advocate cruder, cheaper forms of repression. Meanwhile sanctions were shrinking the economy. How could so many blacks be bought off or contained?

In the short-term the NSMS project may have achieved some limited successes, especially in the immediate aftermath of black disillusionment with the 1984-86 revolt. In that period it was essentially a military operation. The main JMCs were staffed by SADF generals and brigadiers with a sprinkling of senior police. The SSC staff was perhaps 75 per cent SADF/SAP, with the remainder from the National Intelligence Service and the department of foreign affairs. After 1987 the system was civilianized a little, especially at the lower levels, by bringing in civil servants, white businessmen, MPs from the Indian and coloured chambers of parliament and black councillors. Yet in essence the system was a policy of short-term military containment, not a long-term political solution. That appeared to be F.W. de Klerk's appraisal when he took over from President Botha. First, he shored up his own position in the party and then re-asserted political control over the military. He ordered cutbacks in defence spending and reduced national service to one year. More significantly he relegated the SSC and demilitarized the whole NSMS structure, by trying to turn it into a series of regional coordinating committees to maintain the task of upgrading black facilities. The new president faced opposition in military and police circles, partly for political reasons. De Klerk's changes were interpreted as an assault on the right's, especially the Conservative Party's, influence in the old system. The opposition was fuelled by the incoming president's determination to release political prisoners. But could the new broom really make a clean sweep in a white community which had been heavily indoctrinated by apartheid ideology for over forty years and, which, for a decade at least, had revelled in the glorification of the military?

## *White society*

### Conscription

One of the most important aspects of the militarization of white society was the growing length of time more and more whites served in the SADF and police. Conscription was the one case where apartheid fell more heavily on whites rather than on blacks. Unlike the Rhodesian army, the SADF spent a great deal of effort to (further) indoctrinate its conscripts in the fundamentals of the total onslaught. By the late 1980s Pretoria had distanced itself a little from the total red threat thesis, partly because it was proving counter-productive. Yet a whole generation of believers had already been indoctrinated. The white population at large seemed to have swallowed the total onslaught dogmas hook, line and sinker after many years of SABC propaganda.

A major critique of the doctrine surfaced in the anti-conscription movement, centred in the late 1980s on the End Conscription Campaign (ECC). This small, mainly middle-class, English-speaking group raised objections on moral, political and religious grounds. In 1988 the minister of law and order, Adriaan Vlok, silenced the ECC. But that did not stop a thriving South African export industry, the exodus of white graduates. (Students could defer military service until they had completed their education.) Nevertheless, draft-dodging was a minority taste, because young South African white males were programmed throughout their education to accept national service as a duty.

Besides the moral arguments against defending apartheid, some practical reasons were offered as to why a professional volunteer army would have been more efficient than a conscript force. Pretoria had regularly rejected this option, however. Afrikaners, like Americans, had displayed a historical antipathy towards large standing armies, not least because of their experiences in their respective wars of independence against the British. Both Afrikaners and Americans tended to prefer the concept of temporary militia forces. Paradoxically, most Afrikaners opposed conscription during the two world wars. Under apartheid they insisted, however, that it was a national duty – for whites. Moreover, a volunteer, well-paid professional army would probably have been largely black. Pretoria had always been very reluctant to arm too many 'natives'. Since the 1960s Pretoria had argued that national service was cheaper and safer politically. In the late 1980s the more recent twist to the worries about the army's political stability was the deliberate infiltration of the police and SADF by the right wing. A smaller professional army would probably have been more susceptible to political control by neo-fascists than a large conscript force, infused each year by thousands of young English-speakers who were often imbued with impeccable liberal values from their university education.

In the last days of apartheid, military planners not knowing the game was up, the concept of a larger volunteer army was discussed. The Rhodesians toyed with the idea of creating a large white-officered Askari-type army on the model of their successful Rhodesian African Rifles. Even the most patriotic white Rhodesian tended to become more and more annoyed when he saw blacks taking 'their' places in the civilian economy because constant call-ups made cheaper black labour more attractive. In South Africa there was usually no shortage of black volunteers because of economic factors; many whites went into the SADF very reluctantly, however, partly because of the financial sacrifices. There was nothing worse for a regular soldier than to serve next to a reluctant conscript. A dominant topic of conversation in the operational area was 'how much longer do we have to do?' The '*min dae*' attitude ('only a few days left') was very common, and demoralizing, on the border.

The debate continued about a larger professional force, perhaps one that could form the nucleus of a multi-racial force that could assist in the future transition and integration. The SADF was seen to defend not South Africa, but merely the whites, or perhaps just the National Party. Military reformers argued that a multi-racial volunteer SADF could have been the first step towards teaching the futility of the civil war itself. A *post-bellum* republic would have to finance an army, probably a smaller one; better that it be professional, competent and multi-racial, especially the officer class.

**Education**

'Christian National Education' was the fundamental basis of all white state schools. This tended to create a susceptibility to right-wing views and National Party or Conservative Party ideologies. Such intrinsic indoctrination was reinforced by cadet training programmes through the state educational system for boys and, sometimes, girls. Many schoolchildren, particularly in the Afrikaans-medium institutions, attended special camps, or *veld* (field) schools, during vacations. Apart from the 'youth preparedness' courses in schools, children were taught about 'terrorism'. Two young English-speaking high-school students from Johannesburg explained what they had been taught about the subject:

> Marie: It's like communism, you know. Russia's trying to take over South Africa for the strategic position, and the gold and all that and the blacks don't know any better because they're not properly educated, and if a communist is going to come to them and say, do this and that and the other and we'll give you a black government, they just don't know any better, the blacks don't, and they'll believe the communists…
>
> We build the schools and they just burn them down…
>
> Michelle: … you just have to go slowly and, listen, all our taxes go to their houses. OK, Soweto's nothing fantastic, but at least they've got a roof over their heads. They want all the facilities that we've got, but you can't all of a sudden just give them everything. They're not prepared to take it in stages.[2]

Those comments encapsulated many white adults' views as well.

**Propaganda**

The military ethos was propagated extensively in the media. The most faithful voice of official orthodoxy was found, not surprisingly, in the SADF's monthly magazine, *Paratus*, which was distributed widely for sale to the general public. In 1977 the SADF established its own public relations department on a fulltime basis. Unlike in NATO armies, where PR posts were often dumped on reluctant 'passed-over' captains or majors, some excellent regular offices served in PR in South Africa although there were also some failed journalists working in 'media operations' who liked to parade in officers' uniforms.[3] Because of the extensive censorship, including a minefield of legislation such as the Defence Act, Prisons Act, Internal Security Act and the Publications Act, it was often impossible to report on the security situation. Normally, only a handful of military correspondents could get close, with the SADF, to any combat in Angola or Namibia. Those who did, such as Willem Steenkamp (of the *Cape Times*) or Helmoed-Römer Heitman (a correspondent for *Jane's Defence Weekly*), had very close relations with the military. Indeed both Steenkamp and Heitman were citizen force officers.[4]

Via the obedient state-controlled electronic media and pro-government newspapers the SADF and SAP encouraged an emphasis on 'positive' and 'balanced' (that is, pro-Pretoria) aspects of the news. The SABC not only played down internal problems but also played up others' troubles, especially in countries that attracted white emigration. This message was echoed ubiquitously in private conversation: 'It's happening all over the world. Look at Northern Ireland. It's *worse* there. I'd rather stay here, thank you.' This type of propaganda was paradoxical: the government wanted it both ways. On the one hand, Pretoria claimed its troubles were not unique. 'We are a microcosm of the world issues everywhere.' Sort of Nigeria dumped on Australia. Yet, on the other hand, the official diplomatic line was, 'Our problems are uniquely complex, and

The South African press could bark but not bite (Andy, courtesy of the *Star*)

we require time for a uniquely South African solution.' It was ironic that the government's propaganda was internalized by the whites but usually scoffed at by the blacks, presumably the most important target. Whites often gave credence to the communist onslaught that many blacks regarded as probable liberation (if they believed in the theory). The Angolan war with real-live Russians and Cubans involved, and captured, added flesh to the abstraction. But for years Pretoria had whipped up a less tangible, groundless paranoia, a little like the rockets fired by the authorities of Oceania on their own people in *1984*. As the big shooting wars on borders subsided and Moscow and Pretoria started to talk and even flirt, then the total war was likely to be internalized. As Van Zyl Slabbert observed:

> Inevitably, as the external onslaught subsides, the internal onslaught will come under sharper focus – the enemy without will become the enemy within. I fear that the government has in any case managed to militarize the white population to such an extent that it won't matter much to the ordinary person who the 'enemy' is as long he is ready to fight. There, I believe, lies one of the greatest obstacles to evolutionary and negotiated change.[5]

One of Pretoria's prime weapons against its own electorate was ignorance. Blacks in the more closely-knit townships relied upon a very efficient news grapevine. Whites had to resort to a less effective gossip-machine which, in the twilight world of censorship, produced epidemics of alarmist rumourmongering. The media were not totally shackled, however. Pretoria's claim that the country had the freest press in Africa was not entirely off the mark, although Africa was hardly a good yardstick. South Africa's 'alternative' press, such as the *Weekly Mail*, and sometimes the more establishment-oriented English-language papers, such as the *Star, Cape Times*, *Financial Mail* and Ken Owen's blistering editorials and columns in *Business Day,* and even, occasionally, Afrikaans papers such as *Die Beeld*, would attack the government with some ferocity. It was said they were guard dogs who could bark but not bite. If they wanted to report in any detail on security matters, they had to play Russian roulette with the censorship laws. According to opinion polls, most whites relied upon (and trusted) SATV for news information. But the state-controlled-TV waged a 'scorched air' policy on truth. This produced a breast-beating angst in the liberal community, or emigration, and increasingly *verkramp* views on security among the silenced majority of whites. *Bittereinder* statements became common parlance. As one Afrikaner farmer's wife said stoically to me:

> We will never give up. We will fight to the last Afrikaner. We did not accept English rule and we will never accept Bantu rule. We don't mind sanctions. We will go back to oxwagons if they cut off our petrol.

Another white woman, of a once impeccable liberal business background, was ruthlessly candid: 'Let's be completely logical. We can hand over peacefully now, fight and lose, or we kill the lot of them.'

**Social trends**

Many overt signs of militarization were evident in white society. The SADF encouraged support groups such as the Southern Cross Fund to raise money for the 'boys on the border'. It also campaigned for proposals such as 'Ride Safe', a national scheme to give lifts to servicemen. And some of the radio request programmes were reminiscent of wartime Britain. And yet a sense of a 'white nation at war' did not emerge as it did in Britain in the early 1940s or like Rhodesia in the late 1970s.

An unobservant American tourist, say, could travel to South Africa, exchange his dollars at a bounteous rate, stay in an excellent five-star hotel in Johannesburg, visit the well-managed game parks in the eastern Transvaal, tour the exquisite wine farms of the Cape, swim from the resplendent Durban beaches and not notice a sign of warfare in 'your beautiful country'. He would have been unlikely to visit a township or the Namibian border. Nor would the hypothetical visitor know, or perhaps care, that one million whites possessed, legally, 2.5 million privately-owned firearms, often handguns kept in the glove compartments of cars. The visitor would have been unaware probably of the bizarre wave of Afrikaner working-class fathers and mothers who shot their own families, the so-called 'wipe-out' phenomenon. The rates for white suicide, divorce, alcoholism, drug abuse and even road traffic collisions were unusually high. On the other hand, the homicide rate for blacks in Soweto was ten times higher, proportionately, than in New York city. It was not all gloom and doom of course: many whites revelled in the Californian shopping habits and lifestyle. Despite the fact that many whites enjoyed a living standard that was the second or third highest in the world, South Africa was a society under great stress. It was partly due to international pressures, isolation and urban terror as well as the universal maladies of unemployment, inflation and rising mortgages. It was difficult to isolate the incidents of what is now called 'post-traumatic stress disorder' as a part of the war psychosis engendered by militarization and call-ups.

Afrikaners clearly preferred beer and *braais* (barbecues) to military parades. They were not Prussians. It was, however, hard to generalize about Afrikaners, let alone the other whites of different ancestry. The Greeks, Portuguese, English, Irish, Germans and French South Africans perhaps did not constitute any kind of nation, white or otherwise. Despite apartheid, which had worked to keep people apart, a Zulu middle-class doctor usually had more in common with a fellow white medical professional than either had with a Xhosa peasant or semi-literate Afrikaner railwayman from the backwoods. Afrikaner society was certainly more cohesive than other white 'tribes'. Yet Afrikanerdom exhibited many contradictions. An Afrikaner male considered himself to be a rugged individualist, or so he would insist, whose past had been nourished by adversity and the tales of Blood River; yet he was also a soft, urbanized, organization man, brimming with his, and her, religious, political and social structures. Take the Afrikaner on the extreme right, typically the most bellicose of his people. According to my friend Denis Beckett, then the editor of the famously iconoclastic *Frontline* magazine, who said in 1989:

> The CPs [members of the Conservative Party] are terrified of blacks, so terrified they can't see straight. They're a walking mass of schizophrenia. They spend half their time bragging about their relations with black individuals; the other half forcing everything from science to religion to fit the conclusions their terror motivates.[6]

The CP or AWB supporter would swagger and declare, 'If it comes to it, there's no problem. Each white will shoot five blacks,' and then lean over confidentially or assert boldly, depending on the venue and language, 'and we can do it – that's the problem solved.' At the other extreme, at the comfortable dinner parties of Johannesburg's plush northern suburbs, the same discussion would develop: the if, when and where of emigration and whether one could survive without a maid. The majority of whites, however, the local variants of Middle America or Middle England, had no intention of leaving the country they loved so much. They tried not to think too much about the future.

**The economy**

A type of military-industrial complex had surfaced in South Africa, as the earlier examination of Armscor suggested. The drive for military self-sufficiency distorted the economy. For example, in the late 1970s the SADF helped to persuade the government that South Africa needed its own diesel capacity. The country then started to produce diesel engines at about one-third more than an imported model. In fields where total self-sufficiency was not possible, Pretoria co-opted and compromised many firms by forcing them into security collaboration. The National Key Points Act, the various amendments to the Atomic Energy Act, the National Supplies Procurement Act and other legislation had required private companies to maintain secrecy about their production levels, sources of supply, trading partners etc., all of which compounded the siege mentality.[7] The position of the oil majors was especially sensitive. Even the major international car manufacturers were discouraged from publishing statistics of car sales and production.

**Partisan politics**

Under SADF regulations, permanent force personnel were not allowed to be members of political parties, nor could they take part in party political activity. The SADF offered itself as a professional non-partisan force, despite its frequent identification as the fighting wing of the ruling party. The SADF did on occasions publicly break its own rules about overt partisan behaviour. In 1980 details of a document, *Psychological Action Plan: Defence Force Budget Debate,* were leaked to the newspapers. The document outlined covert steps to manipulate the news media so as to nullify the parliamentary opposition's criticism of defence measures proposed by P.W. Botha. A parliamentary row ensued, the story was denied and some of the officers involved were quietly promoted sideways.

This incident was a minor one compared with the later dirty tricks organized by the SADF. In 1988 the SADF found itself in the dock over three major legal cases. Two involved SADF officers and men accused of murdering civilians, and stabbing to death a SWAPO leader in Namibia. The third was concerned with harassment of the End Conscription Campaign. The SADF was forced to admit that, *inter alia,* it had put up posters in Cape Town bearing the slogans 'ECC are yellow', 'ECC does it from behind' and 'ECC believes in fairy tales'. The SADF also used a helicopter to drop anti-ECC pamphlets over an ECC fair. In Cape Town's Supreme Court, in an affidavit, Lieutenant General Jan van Loggerenberg, head of the Air Force, confirmed such methods were necessary as South Africa was on a 'war footing'. Defending the ECC, in its application for an interdict restraining the SADF from harassment, Sydney Kentridge SC, said that the SADF had effectively declared martial law. 'These are the pretensions of a junta of South American generals in a country in which the army acts as an independent force .... There has seldom been a more dangerous assertion of power by the army,' maintained the eminent lawyer. As Kentridge noted, it was ironic that the SADF said it needed martial law and underhand tricks to deal with the ECC when subsequently it was restricted anyway under the emergency regulations.

After the involvement in fullscale conventional armoured warfare in the neighbouring states and the many gallons of blood spilt in the townships, such actions as dropping pamphlets by air, printing T-shirts and putting up posters, with homosexual innuendos, against the ECC, seemed almost benign. Yet the public airing in court of the SADF's views on the military situation in the country, as well as the publicity given to Kentridge's condemnation, was significant. Both the ECC case and the 1980 budget incident were rare documented evidence of the SADF's frequent manipulation of white political activity. Few scruples had been displayed, of course, about SADF intervention in black politics, at home and abroad.

### *Praetorianism in Pretoria?*

When F.W. de Klerk replaced P.W. Botha as president, military influence was dramatically downgraded but that did not end debate about a creeping or silent coup. Other analysts suggested that Afrikaner/Boer societies had always displayed illiberal and martial tendencies. Historians pointed to the previous 'age of the generals' when soldier-statesmen such as Generals Louis Botha, Barry Hertzog and Jan Smuts were not career soldiers and returned to their civilian roles when the military crisis had ended. In the late 1980s there was no precedent for a standing core of politically influential senior officers, nearly all Afrikaners. The SADF, however, did not represent a 'nation in arms' in the traditional French or even Israeli sense.[8] Notwithstanding the careful, if limited, incorporation of other races, the SADF was essentially an instrument of white domination. The military top brass were not unified by a single vision, beyond preserving if not white rule than at least white influence. The military and police had often disagreed with each other as this study has shown. The army had constantly criticized the SAP's heavy-handedness in the townships and in Namibia. The army complained of having 'to do the SAP's job for them' in the townships. An anecdote, repeated throughout army messes in 1986, illustrated this point:

> President Botha was angry that a crocodile was eating too many people. He instructed the SADF and the police to stop the croc. The SADF sends in a

> high-level aerial photographic unit with in-flight computers, then analyzes the pictures, puts in a ground-level reconnaissance crew and, finally, sifting through the data, plans a detailed operation and despatches a team of Recce Commandos to grab the crocodile and deliver it, carefully trussed up, to the president.
>
> The police, meanwhile, send out two constables who grab the first lizard they can find and beat it until it confesses to being a man-eating crocodile.

Military influence had grown, just like Topsy. There had been no conspiracy. Military intelligence had been unruly perhaps in its continuing support for RENAMO and there would be 'rogue' operations after 1990. But in 1989 there was no single alternative voice, no de Gaulle or even a de Spinola. Even General Magnus Malan was seen as an NP man, not the military's representative in the government. Secondly, the extensive NP *apparatchiki* were deeply hostile to any notions of Bonapartism. The ruling securocrats may have lost faith in the NP and its ideology, but most still wanted white rule. South Africa was an advanced industrialized country, not a banana republic in South America or Africa. The small regular officer class in the army knew it could not solve the political conundrums on its own, although perhaps a few senior policemen may have been tempted. Moreover, a military coup would have been a diplomatic disaster, too much for the pariah state to bear at the end of the 1980s.

It was indisputable, however, that military authority had grown. Even if military influence had always been part of the South African tradition, in 1989 there was more of it. Despite the many differences, the Rhodesian experience was instructive. In the end the senior military and intelligence chiefs forced the politicians to do a political deal to end the war, as outlined at Lancaster House. The British helped the Rhodesians to save themselves from their own folly. It was close, but there was no coup in Salisbury in March 1980. The British, and Clausewitzian, paradigm survived in the British colony: the verdict of the ballot box was not usurped by last-ditchers in the officers' mess or in smoke-filled rooms full of jilted politicians. In Rhodesia, growing military influence had been beneficial in the frenetic last days of white rule. South Africa in 1989 was not as desperate as Rhodesia had been in 1979; military defeat was around the corner for the rebel state. In stark contrast, the nuclear-armed apartheid republic was still the strongest state on the continent a decade later.

In the last days of the 1980s it was likely that very big changes and military threats faced the republic. What were they likely to be and would the security forces act as 'iron surgeons', either to extend the life of apartheid or to excise the cancer of white supremacy? Already some senior military intelligence officers were acting behind the scenes to help their political bosses see the futility of an endless war on the majority of the state's inhabitants. This was the mood that had helped F.W. de Klerk become president.

*Fighting on*

The intelligence planners looked at a possible prompt deal, dependent on the release of Mandela. He was still in prison but he was being treated by his warders as a president-in-waiting. At the time of writing in 2018 the end of apartheid and the victory of the ANC were in retrospect inevitable. In 1989 that was not the case. And so the ANC and SADF also had to prepare for a long haul. What were the major fronts likely to be?

**The conventional threat**

The SADF's withdrawal from Angola had altered the conventional war pressures on the republic. The Russians and Cuban were going home. Namibia's path to independence was likely to be smooth, not least because the country was so dependent economically on Pretoria's good will. Nor could the OAU cobble together a substitute for foreign communist armies. The forces of the OAU lacked a common military organization, military doctrine, leadership, joint training and a general staff. Only Zimbabwe had efficient armed forces and a common border. The Zimbabwe National Army, however, over-committed in Mozambique, had always assumed a defensive posture on its southern border.

The rugged terrain, two oceans, deserts and mountains provided defensible topographical boundaries for South Africa. If an invasion could have ever materialized, then South Africa, sixty times larger than Israel, had the room for manoeuvrability and in-depth defence, unlike the Jewish state. The new defence perimeter in the northern Cape was easier to guard than northern Namibia: largely open scrubland and desert in southern Namibia provided excellent opportunities for armoured thrusts and aerial interdiction of any invading columns. Still, the SADF had extensive land borders to defend. If Lesotho and the four independent homelands were to be included that amounted to about 14,000 miles of border to patrol.

The rebuilding of conventional reaction forces after the very heavy fighting in Angola would have been expensive. The cost would be great as would the actual procurement difficulties. One problem was getting new jet engines despite sanctions. Sixty per cent of the total 1989-90 defence budget (just over £2 billon) was scheduled to be spent through the special defence account (not subject to defence audit) which was generally used for secret arms purchases and for Armscor. The 20 per cent increase on the previous budget implied that intensive modernization, especially in aircraft and helicopters, was under way.

The standing forces also faced a number of manpower problems, ranging from the shortage of skilled technicians and the difficulty in retaining quality non commissioned officers due to more pressures associated with regular call-ups, especially for duty in the townships. The end of the most recent bout of township insurrection would have helped this. And the withdrawal from Angola and

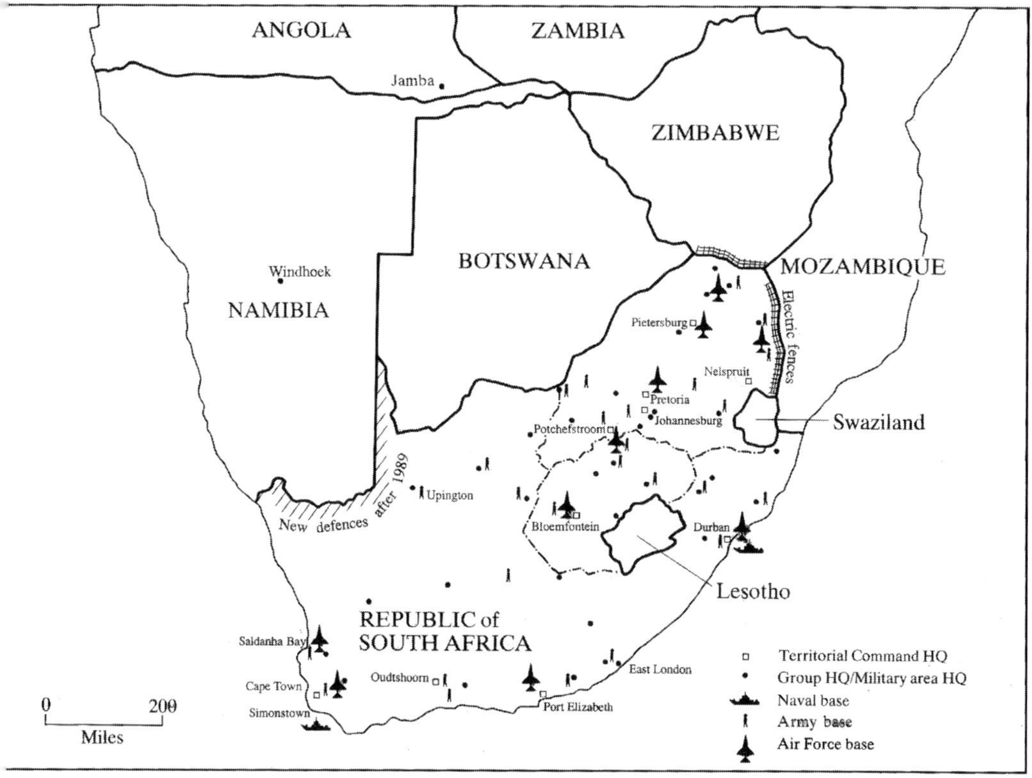


The new SADF defence perimeter 1989-1990

Namibia did not appear to have created major morale problems in the way the retreat from Sinai affected the Israeli army, for example.

A seaborne invasion was an alternative, albeit far less likely than assault by land from the north. A 1965 report, *Apartheid and United Nations Collective Action*, envisaged the possibilities of a fullscale naval and air invasion of South Africa.[9]

It estimated that 100,000 UN soldiers would be required, with possible casualties ranging from 19,000 to 38,000 men. In 1989 the SADF was very much more powerful than in 1965. Pretoria also had a nuclear deterrent. If the UN had managed to cobble together an invasion replicating a Normandy D Day landing it would have been 'as obsolete as a charge of the armoured knights at the battle of Agincourt'. Should such an impossible endeavour have succeeded then the task of actually occupying a country the size of South Africa would have been very daunting.

A naval blockade was more often talked about. The SADF, with its tiny navy, could not have matched the assets found in NATO and Warsaw Pact inventories, especially nuclear submarines and modern aircraft carriers. It would have been possible to block the five or six major South African ports. Britain's Beira patrol, to stop Rhodesian sanctions-busting, was largely a symbolic gesture by one state and it didn't work. A truly international blockade of South African harbours might have forced the obdurate Afrikaners to negotiate. Such elaborate gunboat diplomacy might also have curtailed the arguments about long-term damage of comprehensive sanctions.

**Guerrilla warfare**

Unlike Mozambique, Rhodesia or Angola, South Africa was not suitable for classical African insurgency. Except for a few areas, such as northern Natal, it was a developed country with few wild, inaccessible places. Nevertheless, the triumph of the bush struggles in the neighbouring black states had influenced the morale and tactics of the South African insurgents. Guerrilla warfare had never been infallible, even in backward and remote territories, let alone in more industrialized societies. There, partisans had succeeded only with the backing of conventional formations: Tito's forces with the Red Army or the South Vietnamese irregulars with the help of the North Vietnamese army. Mugabe's guerrillas relied heavily on the FRELIMO army in the last years of the Rhodesian war but the ANC in 1989 was not likely to have received the direct assistance of the front-line armies. Indeed, Pretoria's agreements with Luanda and Maputo had resulted in the removal, directed by the Angolan and Mozambican security forces, of ANC guerrilla facilities. Yet both the ANC and the PAC, which had adopted at times a Maoist line, attempted to fight their wars in the countryside as well as in the cities. The MK's deployment of landmines in 1985 was one phase of its rural strategy.

The SADF's containment policy had concentrated on the borders and the interior. According to General Johan van der Merwe, the head of the security police, 49 per cent of the insurgents who were killed or captured inside South Africa during the eighteen months prior to August 1988, had infiltrated from Botswana. A further 13 per cent came through Swaziland, 9 per cent through Lesotho, 5 per cent via Zimbabwe and less than 1 per cent through Mozambique. The entry point of the remaining 23 per cent was unknown; presumably they were too dead to talk. The Swazi route had been largely disrupted by the local Swazi police and Lesotho's access was curtailed soon after the 1986 coup.

The SADF had reacted in a number of ways to this infiltration: by punitive raids on the frontline sates, diplomatic and economic pressures, largescale patrols and the erection of physical barriers. Electrified high fences (known locally as Caftan) traversed sensitive sections of the Mozambique and Zimbabwe frontiers. In 1986 it was reported that the cost of the fencing, carrying a lethal 4,000 volts, was R130,000 per kilometre. According to the SADF, seventy people were killed on these fences in 1988. Many were refugees attempting to flee from Mozambique.

The fences were widely criticized but – unlike the Berlin Wall, which tried to keep people *in* – Pretoria's 'ring of steel' tried to keep people, including armed enemies, *out*. The weak point was clearly Botswana. Of the ninety-nine insurgents arrested or captured in the first six months of 1988, forty-seven had come through Botswana. The borders with Botswana were long, very thinly populated and presented inhospitable terrain. The SADF regarded the Botswana security forces as either lax or in cahoots with the ANC. Patrolling these borders used up extensive manpower and was very tedious, as were minesweeping duties in other parts of the Transvaal.

The second line of protection against infiltration was area defence. The farming areas in the northern Transvaal had suffered far more grievously from depopulation, debt and drought than from insurgency. But a zone depopulated by whites was an invitation for further guerrilla encroachment. Pretoria had tried to get whites back into border areas with various incentives, including offers of subsidized land and facilities for ex-soldiers (and ex-Rhodesians who seemed to cling nostalgically to the peripheries of the 'old country'). The paraphernalia of farm defence was very reminiscent of the Rhodesian war, including the MARNET (Military Area Radio Network), an updated version of the Rhodesian Agric-Alert. But, again, helping the farmers to fortify their homes and providing mineproofed vehicles was costly. (Under later ANC governments the attacks on white farmers rapidly accelerated; ten times more were killed than at the height of the war in Rhodesia. These defence systems were deployed extensively then in 'peacetime', especially the radio networks.)

Behind the farmers stood the commando system. Reservists in the countryside were often 'area-bound': they did their call-ups in their own areas because of their local knowledge and their obvious interest in protecting their own properties and families. They also guarded key points such as dams and power installations. Although many rural commandos were volunteers, expanding conscription had undermined the original 'spirit of voluntarism' that had been an important component of the ethos of rural commandos. Partly because of this, many of them were understrength.

Another weak point in area defence was the proximity of so many bits of the various homelands, which had their own autonomous security forces of very varying quality. Originally, homelands were seen as *the* solution to the apartheid dilemma, but they soon became part of the problem. Poverty, unemployment, acute soil erosion because of overcrowding, overstocking, land dispossession, corruption and repression had turned the four independent Bantustans into coup-ridden hotbeds of discontent. Even the 'model' homeland, Bophuthatswana, inspired a short-lived military coup, which was rapidly suppressed by the SADF and a highly embarrassed Pretoria. Likewise, the non-independent homelands had also become breeding grounds for radical discontent. In some white areas adjacent

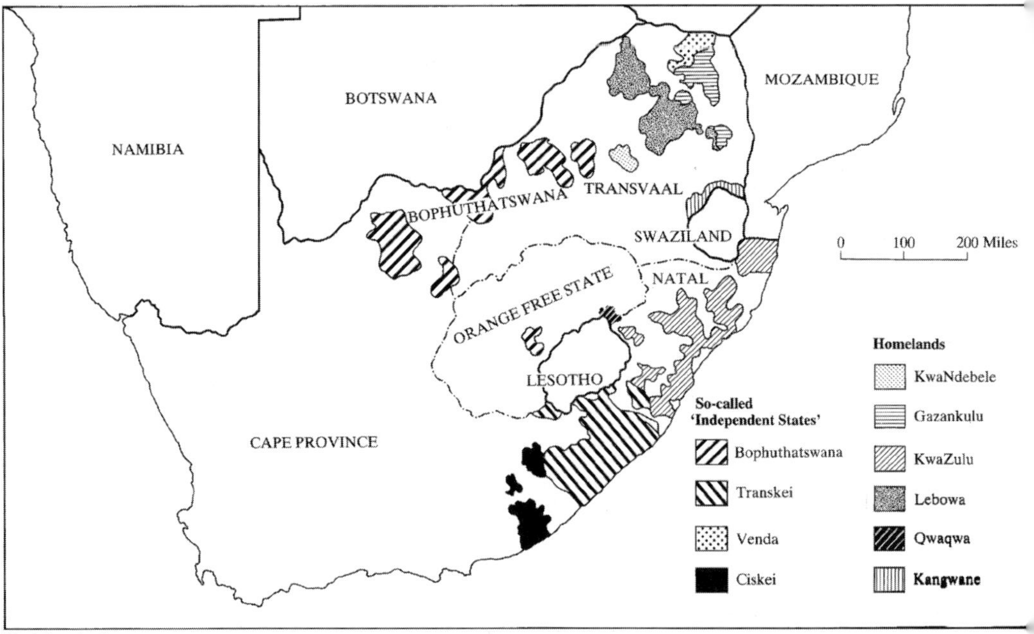

Black homelands

Policing internal borders was difficult with so many Bantustans

to homelands, and Lesotho, endemic crime such as stock theft, had distracted the security forces as much as possible guerrilla infiltration.

In theory, Ciskei or Transkei – when they were not threatening to invade each other – could have invited in, say, Cuban troops. After all, they were supposed to be sovereign independent states, even though no one had recognized them except their creator, Pretoria. The South African government would not have allowed them to enlist a single foreign soldier they didn't want (they had initially encouraged in ex-Rhodesians). Nevertheless, the homelands were already becoming mini-sanctuaries for insurgents (both local and foreign-trained cadres). And they were a lot nearer to Pretoria than bases in Angola or Mozambique. The police forces in the homelands were often more ruthless than their counterparts in the SAP but if guerrilla theoreticians such as Carlos Marighela were half-correct, then this repression was just feeding the incipient peasant rebellion.

In the countryside, liberated areas run by guerrilla warlords were not a feasible proposition. Yet in the 1984-86 unrest small towns and villages in the *platteland* (countryside) caught the epidemic of revolt. Trade union activists were also trying to organize and mobilize the (frequently) exploited and, so far, non-unionized farm workers. The ANC saw the countryside as part of the revolutionary struggle. The occasional landmine or town riot may not have compensated for the (apparent) romance of bush warfare, or a local Che Guevera to lead it, but the costs of containing the (very) low-level area war was a contributory strain on the SADF's manpower and treasury. Guerrillas rarely win wars. Their adversaries usually lose them. By 1990 this was not yet true of the *platteland,* as it was in the black townships and cities.

**Urban warfare**

The debate about hitting soft white urban targets ran and ran in the MK's planning committees. It would have savagely polarized the struggle and society, especially if white schools had been deliberately hit. (Parents and schools were nearly always on high alert for this, and the rumours spread like a bushfire about major attacks 'expected tomorrow' to tie in with some special ANC event.) It is often said that Londoners managed to survive the Blitz in 1940 but few had the option to emigrate. More than 1.5 million white South Africans had or could get foreign passports. They could have emigrated if MK had adopted a sustained policy of blasting the cosy white suburbs. Rhodesian towns and cities were largely untouched by urban warfare, partly because of good police intelligence. And yet white emigration was a key cause of the collapse of Rhodesia. The exodus of the South African intelligentsia, business managers and many other middle-class professionals had already weakened the South African economy. By 1988 the white migration rate had tailed off, however: immigrants outnumbered emigrants by 10,400 to 7,767, if the Central Statistical Service was to be believed. The brain drain had declined from its peak in 1986. The blazing necklace had been a good reason for anyone to check whether the passport was still valid. The official figures could have been misleading not least because many young people, with little capital, especially males of military age, leaving to 'go on holiday' or 'to study abroad', often did not bother to go through any cumbersome (and 'unpatriotic') emigration procedure. Although the ANC had recently urged its white supporters to stay inside the country, the exodus, particularly from the English-speaking communities, was continuing to peak and trough with the waves of revolt. The majority of whites, even those holding foreign passports, were often locked into the system; many were 'currency detainees' because of the restrictions on taking out foreign currency. Hence the frequent smuggling of gold Krugerrands and buying yachts, sailing them away and not returning to harbour. The determined, talented and highly educated would always find a way. Rhodesians could and did leave their country with nothing and made a new life, sometimes in Europe or sometimes 'Down South' in the republic. They became 'uhuru-hoppers' for a second time by going to Australia or the USA and, reluctantly, to the UK. This was all well and good if you were young and fit. The constant flow of whites leaving was a form of 'socio-economic suicide', according to one management expert. Unlike Algeria and Angola, the majority would probably see it through, they said, as long it was a second Belfast, not Beirut. Then, to use the local parlance, the proverbial 'chicken run' would become an 'owl run'.

Even if the urban insurrection had remained confined largely to the black areas, a scenario of barricades going up and revolution being built from within the ghettos was unlikely. Townships like Soweto were not the same as the urban jungle of Algiers; the small detached houses were laid out in stark, long, straight lines with streets wide enough for armoured cars to patrol and with little cover to prevent the deployment of helicopters. Most black townships had been designed with both military and political containment in mind. Riots in Soweto may have helped mobilize the masses and were bad for the government's PR but they were not the ideal means to take over nearby Johannesburg or Pretoria.

Urban counter-insurgency, however, was often demoralizing, sometimes dangerous and certainly exhausting for young conscripts. Fighting on your own doorstep against fellow countrymen was a far cry from the *skiet-en-donder* (action-packed) adventures of repelling Cubans on the northern borders. Before October 1984 an average of 1,500 men failed to report for duty at each call-up. On the first call-up after the troops were sent into the townships, this number rose by 500 per cent, according to the SADF's own figures (later retracted). Attendance at 'camps', the call-ups after two years national service, was also generally between 40 and 60 per cent. These figures did not indicate that all absentees were opposed on political grounds to call-ups, in the townships or elsewhere. Sickness, change of address, deferments etc. would have explained a large percentage. But there was still a perception that the rise of absenteeism and increasing opposition to the army's occupation of the townships were related. The increase in conscientious objection (despite the public obloquy and stiff penalties for those who failed to qualify for the narrow definition of religious objection that permitted alternative community service), confirmed this trend, as did the growth of South African resisters' groups in Europe.

Limpet mines were increasingly the favoured weapon of urban guerrillas. Their use in urban business areas in 1988 and 1989 rose dramatically. In the first eight months of 1988, for example, seventeen people were killed and nearly 200 wounded in bombings in restaurants, ships and cinemas. Such random carnage was difficult to prevent as contemporary Islamist terrorism has shown in Europe, with such actions supported by a tiny minority of the Muslim population. In South Africa the opinion polls indicated that Nelson Mandela was by far the most popular of all politicians. Thus MK operatives were swimming in an increasingly comfortable sea of urban fish with potential majority support, or, almost as effective, neutrality.

## Trade Union militancy

Before 1979 blacks were excluded from both economic and political power. No other work force in the history of industrialization had been so excluded for so long from the system it made possible. The Wiehahn Commission of 1979 had led to the incorporation of organized black labour into the economic, but not political, structure. The more radical unions were therefore bound to flex their new economic muscles to press for political incorporation as well. (Initially, some unions, rejecting Lenin's advice that all available political platforms should be exploited, opposed registration under the Wiehahn plan because they regarded it as collaboration.)

Throughout the 1984-86 insurrection, the major unions tried to mobilize their factories and mines to liaise with parallel movements in the townships. This caused a major rupture in the union movements between the 'workerists' (who wanted to concentrate primarily on shop-floor matters) and 'populists' (who emphasized primarily political and community questions).

The biggest union confederation was COSATU (Congress of South African Trade Unions) established as a 'super-union' amid much fanfare in November 1985. COSATU had identified itself with the ANC and UDF. Its main rival was NACTU (National Council of Trade Unions), a merger of CUSA (Council of Unions of South Africa), which had a workerist bias, and AZACTU (Azanian Confederation of Trade Unions), which supported the black consciousness/Africanist line. On the right, Inkatha sponsored UWUSA (United Workers Union of South Africa) which supported the 'free market' and attacked COSATU's espousal of sanctions and disinvestment. A large number of independent unions proliferated as well.

The ANC/PAC/Inkatha splits were compounded by the workerist-versus-populist debate which raged *within* the various affiliated unions of the confederations as much as *between* the big confederations themselves. There were also divisions along the lines of skills, religion, education, language, race, class, ethnicity, regions and migrants versus settled labour. Much, though not all, of this diversity was the product of apartheid's divide-and-rule tactics. Apartheid quite deliberately tried to create a tame 'insider' black class with residential rights (under the former notorious section ten of the pass laws) separate from the migrant workers. The latter were forced to live in abysmally cramped, single-sex hostels in mine compounds. Part of the reason was to discourage the unionization of mineworkers: migrant workers, the majority of the mine workforce, were easily sent back to their homelands or neighbouring states at the least sign of militancy. Migrant workers often felt alienated from, and betrayed by, the more comfortable workforce settled, with their families, in the townships. According to one migrant worker, 'Township workers have been corrupted by rich whites and blacks, by teachers and bad priests. They don't believe in the brotherhood of workers.'

Besides these difficulties, the black labour movement had to contend with state repression, the constant detention of union leaders, massive unemployment, which offered plentiful scope for scab labour, and the general poverty of resources in the organizational structures of unions, alleviated somewhat by a corps of white intellectuals working as union advisers. Nevertheless, by 1987 COSATU claimed

750,000 members. By the late 1980s perhaps 25 per cent of the workforce in the modern sector of the economy was unionized. COSATU had tried to reduce the fragmentation of its affiliates by forging the confederation into fewer large unions on the principle of one industry, one union. The merging pattern was of smaller better-paid union-protected labour in the modern, formal sector of the economy, a burgeoning non-unionized black economy and a growing army of urban unemployed and rural masses living at, or below, subsistence level. Despite its sympathies with the ANC, many in COSATU were wary of entanglement for ideological and practical reasons, to avoid being completely banned, for example. In the post-apartheid society COSATU had no wish to become a tame labour appendage typical of so many one-party states.

Despite police harassment, new political forms of industrial action were conducted by the unions, such as factory and underground sit-ins, sleep-ins, go-slows and overtime bans. Obviously, the most important weapon was the outright strike. Black strikes, once illegal, were typically of short duration and localized. Strike actions became longer and bigger. The most significant strike, in the economy's most vulnerable sector, was one called in 1987 by the country's largest union, the National Union of Mineworkers, led by the indefatigable Cyril Ramaphosa, the general secretary. Over 340,000 miners came out for three weeks. Led by Anglo, the Chamber of Mines – the toughest of the employer federations – eventually managed to force the NUM back to work, with very few union gains. Anglo initially dismissed 36,000 of the strikers.

Anglo-American, the biggest mineowner, was showing what critics called its 'multifacialism': on the one hand, displaying a liberal face, offering 'stakes' (shares) to its workers and yet maintaining a hostel system with built-in security measures to match many top-security prisons. The large force of mine police was described as a means of 'privatizing repression'. According to one source, the

Cyril Ramaphosa led the powerful National Union of Mineworkers. He later became the country's president

Gold Fields Company operated its own armoury of 6,000 shotguns, had patented its own rubber bullets and ran a mine-security training camp for other mining houses.[10] Despite their claims to be world leaders, wage and safety conditions in South African mines also left much to be desired. Anglo had encouraged a dialogue with the unions, but on the other hand, not surprisingly, rejected their pretensions to represent the political aspirations of their workers as well. Anglo was trapped in the dilemma facing all major businesses in South Africa: without political emancipation economic confrontations inevitably became politicized. It was the sole legal route for organized black pressure. And it was bad for profits. Anglo's reactions to the 1987 mine strike confirmed, to some critics, the conspiracy theory that Anglo and Pretoria were in bed together. 'Like distracted lovers, they may not always have enjoyed each other's company, but they were bonded by inseparable interests.'[11]

After the collapse of the 1984-86 insurrection, many blacks decided that unions could do a better job than the comrades. Certainly the unions offered an organizational backbone and discipline that mass protest lacked. And yet the unions had not put their own houses in order. The NUM, for example, was unable to stop the tribal factionfighting among miners that had little to do with politics. And ruthless intimidation had also been a hallmark of strike 'solidarity'. Nevertheless, the state could not simply ban the labour movements; they were too integrated into the economic structure. Sometimes the major employer organizations had to cajole Pretoria into releasing senior union leaders from detention because they were needed to ensure industrial peace. By 1989, however, the unions did not have the strength, will and organization for a sustained national strike aimed at bringing down the government. The 1926 general strike in Britain lasted only nine days and backed down before a far less authoritarian but still resolute government. In short, the strike would not replace the AK, but combined, they might replicate what the Polish workers achieved in the late 1980s. The Solidarity union federation, the sole surviving political opposition to the government, did manage to pressurize the hardline Warsaw regime into a power-sharing deal and eventually free-ish elections.

## Churches et al

Along with the unions, the churches were one of the few legal outlets for protest against apartheid. Nevertheless, the state continuously banned churchmen and their organizations, at one stage almost going as far as banning public prayer. During the 1984-86 period, two whole congregations, in Elsies River and Graaff Reinet, were detained. Pretoria particularly resented many of the churches' advocacy of the 'just war' concept and the doctrines of liberation theology that were often associated with it. With their purported biblical justifications of apartheid, it was the three main Dutch Reformed Church organizations that did most to discredit religion in the eyes of the blacks. In 1974 the South African Council of Churches (SACC), however, said the SADF was defending a 'fundamentally unjust society'. After the Soweto rebellion, many blacks tended to feel that any church that did not actively support their struggle was against hem. Some churches, especially the (apparently) conservative, three-million-strong Zionist Christian Church, remained aloof from the call to action, but many clerics responded with alacrity. In 1981 the Presbyterians called on their ministers to ignore the Mixed Marriages Act and to marry couples regardless of race. In 1982 Catholic bishops lambasted the SADF as 'an army of occupation' in Namibia; later that year 123 dissident Dutch Reformed ministers signed a document condemning apartheid. In 1983 the World Alliance of Reformed Churches, with local prompting, declared apartheid a heresy. In 1985 over 100 mainly black theologians and prominent Christians signed the Kairos Document that branded Pretoria as 'unreformable' and the 'enemy of the people of God'.

Pretoria retaliated, especially against the SACC, which represented twenty-two of the country's main churches. It banned, detained and harassed its leaders, including Beyers Naudé, a heroic Afrikaner, and Frank Chikane, who had close ties with the ANC. As Chikane put it in 1987, 'In 1982 I believed that protest could be non-violent but now the government has closed the space for non-violence.' Some less prominent churchmen died in detention; others were killed mysteriously outside prison but the most well-known clerics such as Archbishop Desmond Tutu, a Nobel Peace Prize winner, and Reverend Allan Boesak, a patron of the UDF, because of their international prominence, developed a degree of inviolability.

Individual churchmen had a dramatic effect on mobilizing blacks, particularly during the highly-charged atmosphere of mass funerals, as well, in some cases, urging moderation – for example, Tutu's condemnation of the necklace. Nonetheless, as in the case of union movement, the churches in South Africa were divided. Many conservative churchmen opposed liberation theology. The Zionist church was deliberately apolitical. Some of the fundamentalist 'born-again' faiths were ultra-conservative crusaders against 'communism'. In Latin America liberation theology was embedded in centralized Catholicism. It was not like that in South Africa. In short, Pretoria had its allies as well as its enemies in dog collars.

The more radical churches were, however, enmeshed in a wide network of other important anti-apartheid groups: civic associations, student bodies, educational organizations such as the National Education Crisis Committee, women's organizations and the Black Sash, to name but a few. In late 1989 the internal anti-apartheid groups, especially those who backed the ANC, regrouped themselves into the 'Mass Democratic Movement'. Nevertheless, by the end of the dramatic decade, state repression and more subtle divide-and-rule methods, as well as internal divisions helped to prevent the emergence of a unified mass social protest.

## Economic weapons

Politicians and academics have squabbled endlessly about the efficacy of sanctions, most notably in the case of South Africa. A historical survey of the hundred or so examples of sanctions imposed after 1914 would confirm the commonsensical conclusion that sometimes they work and sometimes they don't. The massive body of literature on the subject suggests that, apart from the purely punitive or symbolic considerations, sanctions have not been useful devices *on their own* to induce, persuade or compel a target state to comply. The theory of sanctions is straightforward: economic sanctions = economic deprivation = political change. The effectiveness of the first leg of the formula obviously depends on how comprehensive the sanctions are. The second element relates to the strength of the sanctioned economy and its abilities to evade and/or retaliate. The third, political results, depends largely upon psychological factors. Above all, to be effective, sanctions should have a clear political goal. The more specific that is, the more likely it is to be achieved.

Effective comprehensive sanctions were not imposed on South Africa, partly because sanctions became all things to all men (and women). They were seen as both a means to encourage revolution and a mechanism to induce a negotiated settlement. Sometimes they had little to do with change in South Africa and more to do with virtue-signalling in Western domestic politics.

There were good and bad arguments for sanctions against Pretoria. An important argument *against* sanctions was that economic progress would undermine apartheid. The liberal capitalist argument was essentially trade + economic growth = black mobility + more black political rights. But not all economists were prepared to predict the victory of the market over ideology. Neo-Marxist scholars insisted that capitalism and apartheid were fundamentally collaborative and that, *in extremis,* white capitalism would accept diminished profitability for the preservation of white supremacy. They pointed out, for example, that rapid economic growth in the 1960s coincided with the 'high apartheid' period. The debate, polarized by liberal and Marxist academics, centred on the questions of whether apartheid was an irrational historical aberration or a rational system of economic exploitation; and whether apartheid was an inflexible ideological belief system, like Nazism, or a cynical pragmatic means of domination that could adapt.[12] Supporters of

Boycotts were very effective

sanctions argued that the alternative was economic warfare, blockade, and direct military intervention. Sanctions, they said, could shorten the war, save lives and hasten negogiations. Moreover, Pretoria did not have a leg to stand on. The apartheid government had applied sanctions, very forcefully, against Rhodesia and Lesotho, for example. Crucially, the sanctioneers argued, they sent a message to whites that their racism had put them beyond the moral pale and it also sent a clear signal to the oppressed majority that the world had not forgotten them.

Opponents of sanctions insisted that whites were being driven into the proverbial laager, not to the conference table, and that blacks, not whites, were suffering from the economic weapons. And the blacks in the front-line states would suffer even more from comprehensive sanctions. Blacks in South Africa did not want sanctions that threatened their jobs, despite what the Tutus and Boesaks said.

Whether the majority of blacks supported sanctions was a moot point. The *Sanctions Handbook* published in 1987 said simply: 'In the South African context there are lies, damned lies and public opinion surveys on black attitudes to sanctions.'[13] Elite black opinion inside the republic, besides Buthelezi, appeared to favour sanctions, although it was illegal to publicly advocate such economic measures. The blacks-suffering-the-most argument was met by Tutu's regular rejoinder, 'When the ladder is falling, surely it's those at the top who will get hurt most, not those at the bottom.' Some union leaders expressed discreet concern about disinvestment. They wondered whether union solidarity would hold when four million were unemployed and had to face total sanctions. Nevertheless, the thrust of politically-conscious blacks inside the republic was, 'we are already suffering, so sanctions might help to shorten the misery.'

The don't-hurt-the-blacks argument looked shabbiest when it was paraded by foreign business people who had never shown the slightest interest in black welfare before. A better argument was that comprehensive sanctions would have shattered the feeble economies of the front-line states, as Pretoria passed on the hardships. But the black neighbours, or at least their authoritarian leaders, said they were prepared to make the sacrifices.

The arms embargo largely failed; instead it turned South Africa into a major producer and exporter of high-quality arms. The sports boycott did encourage rapid racial integration in most, if not all, areas of South African sport. But sport was not political power. A more powerful example was the refusal to roll over loans in 1985. One man in Chase Manhattan Bank set off a massive financial crisis. And this was triggered off by a conservative banker, not a hostile Soviet manoeuvre. As my friend and former tutor, Jack Spence, put it, 'It is difficult to see the directors of Chase Manhattan as the foot soldiers of Lenin.' The 1985 crash was a combination of hard-nosed foreign business concern at the level of profitability in South Africa, moral impulses generated by the anti-apartheid lobbies abroad, the resulting so-called 'hassle factor' in the boardrooms and finally long-term disinvestment, not as a protest against apartheid, but from fear of possible conditions under a future black-rule government.

Private actions by foreign companies, especially the banks, produced far more dramatic effects than official UN sanctions, partly because UN strictures were more easily evaded in a way that bank loans were not. A domestic variant existed: the interplay of private and public sanctions – consumer boycotts. The boycotts were sporadic and largely localized, but sometimes effective, especially in the Eastern Cape. The aims were to secure local political concessions (for example, the release of political organizers from detention) and to mobilize local communities. The state could ban organizations and meetings, it could stop funerals and arrest or shoot people but it could not force people to buy if they did not want to.

The often haphazard mix of international and domestic sanctions worked in some respects. It was partly a question of time. Sanctions against Rhodesia were said to have failed initially. In the short to medium term the Rhodesian economy went through an exuberant phase of growth generated partly by import substitution and swashbuckling sanctions-busting. But in the long term – the growth stage of a siege economy was said to be typically about eight to ten years – the economy ran right down. Sanctions supplemented the insurgency in forcing the Rhodesian government to the conference table. Sanctions, if not comprehensive, take time.

The Rhodesians, a tiny white tribe, fought almost to the end. The nuclear-armed Afrikaner superpower, it was assumed, would fight longer and harder than the Rhodesian *arrivistes*. It was not just Afrikaners who would have looked at conditions in the neighbouring black states and worried about the future. Many English, Greek, Portuguese and Jewish South Africans usually shared the same anxieties. Like their English-speaking compatriots, Afrikaners were also part of a cosy, spoilt, gadget-festooned suburbia whose economic pain threshold might have been lower than the rugged trekkers of the nineteenth century. In the end the efficacy of sanctions, like war, depended upon the nature of white resistance.

Also, profits were to be made as well from sanctions. Disinvestment allowed local capitalists to buy up companies at bargain rates. One man's sanctions were always another man's, or woman's, business opportunity. As with Rhodesia, often the most noisy and pious sanctioneers, especially in the Eastern Bloc and Africa, were the biggest sanctions cheats. Until Nelson Mandela was released sanctions were bound to stay. Economists talked about tightening them by, for example, running down the value of gold, a mainstay of the South African economy. White-oriented sanctions were suggested, such as banning all international flights or cutting mail. Anti-apartheid activists also returned to the possibilities of a naval blockade or 'quarantine' as John Kennedy called it.

Short of *force majeure*, such as foreign navies controlling South Africa's six major ports, sanctions were ultimately idealistic. They wanted Afrikaners to change their minds about racism. Most Afrikaners saw the issue as being asked to change their minds about their survival. Nevertheless, by late 1989, sanctions were beginning to make the whites choose between economic comforts and white domination. They used to have both. 'The ox-wagon was also a bandwagon,' as Conor Cruise O'Brien had put it.

*Waiting for the Barbarians*

In 1982 South Africa's leading novelist, J.M. Coetzee, published his *Waiting for the Barbarians.* His remarkable allegory described the evils inherent in all types of authoritarianism: the real enemy is fear. In Pretoria's case it was an overwhelming fear of the future. Black rule was inevitable but how and when would the 'permanent transition' become a settlement? The search for a negotiated peaceful deal created a veritable solutions industry in South Africa in the late 1980s. A whole new breed of white prophets arose; an anxious white population often turned their frequently unprofound placebos into bestsellers. Some of the technocratic prophets of boom suggested a 'high road' to the South African version of Japan and modified version of the Swiss cantonal system. Clutching at such straws may well have been what Antonio Gramsci, an earlier Marxist prophet, termed 'morbid symptoms of the interregnum'. Denis Beckett's more persuasive 1988 solutions book, *Fallacy of Heroes,* offered a more down-to-earth attempt to reverse the whites' tendency to think with their blood. Yet even his quasi-cantonal model, for all its blazing sincerity, was Utopian. At least these books attracted a wide audience. Many whites had previously avoided thinking about the future at all. As American Pulitzer Prize-winning writer Joseph Lelyveld observed, many white South Africans regarded revolutions in the same way that Californians regarded earthquakes – they tried not to think about it.

For all the intellectual attractions, the solutions industry was seen as a white sideshow to distract blacks from the real question of the transfer of power. The key to this was not any modification of apartheid. Frederik van Zyl Slabbert neatly summarized the necessary steps as 'unban, release, dismantle and negotiate'. The essential first step was the release of Mandela and the unbanning of the ANC. Pretoria worried that Mandela's release could cause as many problems as it might have solved. The government had called on the ANC to renounce violence before serious negotiations could take place. The armed struggle was the movement's main card. Why throw it away in advance? The game was on to find the right words. 'Suspend' violence maybe? The new phrase became 'a contribution to the creation of a climate which would promote peace'. Mandela's first official press release from prison, in July 1989, precisely endorsed those words. This statement followed Mandela's talk over tea at P.W. Botha's official residence, perhaps the most dramatic move ever made by any Afrikaner leader. Botha had in effect become Mandela's prisoner. This was Moses and the Pharaoh: the theme of the obsessive tyrant pleading with his prisoner to set him free had reverberated through the ages. And yet, to many Afrikaners, Mandela's release could have been a public symbol of white capitulation. The AWB, and maybe hard-line elements in the SADF and police, might have decided it was time to take up arms, against appeasers in Pretoria.

The ANC had achieved little militarily in thirty years of armed struggle. What precedents were there for a guerrilla army overthrowing a modern industrial state? The MK had lost nearly every contact with the SAP or army. Only a small proportion of the external ANC insurgents had managed to penetrate into the country. And its conventional allies, the Cubans, were departing. In purely military terms the SADF's counter-insurgency had been very successful. Pretoria was not about to be defeated militarily in the foreseeable future. Simply because the apartheid system was morally untenable did not mean that it was not militarily tenable. It was weak or indecisive, not cruel, governments that fell to such pressures. Pretoria had no external patron to pull the rug from under its feet as Vorster had done to the Rhodesian Front. South Africa was not a colony; no imperial capital could have summoned home the legions. Many securocrats did not feel defeated: at worst they considered a long holding operation. Perhaps a deal could still be done with Chief Buthelezi, leader of the most powerful African tribe? He would never have made it to the Finland Station. He would have ended up as a cross between Joshua Nkomo and Bishop Muzorewa, 'suffocated to death by white kisses'. This is a view from hindsight; at the time many intelligence officers wanted to continue backing the Zulu forces, and did so for years after Mandela was finally released. A Buthelezi-led holding operation, even if he been suicidal enough to have agreed, would have been a temporary no-win strategy.

Unsuccessful wars are often the antechambers of revolution; the SADF had not lost their fight against the total onslaught. Nor did the officer class feel stalemated, let alone defeated, as many Rhodesians did at the end of their long fight. Yet, as in Rhodesia, the end would come grudgingly, after seasons of bloodshed. The settlement came as result not of defeat but as the fruit of exhaustion.

Everyone was telling the whites to get off the tiger's back. No one was telling them how to survive once they had done so. A deal would take time even though everything was always expressed in 'the 'five-minutes-to-midnight heavy-breathing' politics. Pretoria's strategy had created innate dilemmas. Political stability was needed for reform, said the government, but its repression fuelled political instability. There was no escape. Reform raised up black hopes, then the jackboot crushed them, an almost deliberate formula for revolution.

Apartheid's phases had been stamped by Afrikanerdom's great men: Malan preached Afrikaner unity, Strydom the republican ideal; Vorster's rule was marked by pragmatism and tough security laws; and P.W. Botha's era was distinguished by the total strategy and militarism, tinged with reform. The beginning of F.W. de

Klerk's period suggested a new flexibility regarding negotiations with the ANC. President Botha had warned his people that they had to 'adapt or die'. As one of South Africa's most controversial playwrights, Pieter-Dirk Uys, put it, 'People have adapted a little … and died a lot. And we have swapped a laager for a bunker.' The just war against Hitler had led to that final bunker. Yet, despite the popular analogies, Afrikaner supremacists were not Nazis. There was room for pity as well as *Schadenfreude* over their largely self-induced predicament. That is a classic definition of a Greek tragedy. As the distinguished French philosopher Raymond Aron observed: 'When a party gives itself the right to use force against all its enemies in a country in which to start with it is in a minority, it condemns itself to perpetual violence.'

As we shall see, the Afrikaners did manage to break out of that vicious circle. Despite all the odds, the start of a settlement was around the corner in late 1989 as F.W. de Klerk struggled to bring peace. And yet ending apartheid was merely the first step in solving South Africa's *real* problems: overpopulation, unemployment, soil erosion, health (especially the AIDS pandemic), education, land redistribution and tribalism. The immediate *post-bellum* questions such as political restructuring, a new constitution, reconciliation and punishment, as well as rehabilitation of the war-wounded and an army of ex-prisoners would, by comparison, pale into insignificance. The hope was that South Africa could still become the engine for continental renaissance, the breadbasket for Africa, not another proverbial basket case.

## *Chapter 17*

# The End Game

One of Pretoria's persistent goals had been to split the ANC: to separate the so-called 'nationalists' from the more radical communists, to encourage a compliant 'internal' ANC as distinct from the hardline exile wing in Lusaka. Pretoria had always insisted that the imprisoned ANC leaders had to renounce the armed struggle. With a few exceptions, they had always refused. Mandela had never compromised on this crucial ANC position. Rejection of violence had to precede talks, said Pretoria. Nevertheless, the South African government leaders, including F.W. de Klerk, had been busy negotiating with the world's most famous political prisoner.

On 2 February 1990 President de Klerk finally dragged his National Party across the Rubicon. In a major speech, he announced, *inter alia,* the unbanning of the ANC, the PAC and the communist party, although the state of emergency was not lifted. It looked as though normal politics could begin in South Africa. On 11 February the black messiah was finally freed after twenty-seven years in prison. In his first speech, in Cape Town, Mandela, while conceding de Klerk's sincerity, warned: 'We have waited too long for our freedom; we can no longer wait. Now is the time for intensifying the struggle on all fronts. Our march to freedom cannot be stopped.'

The Mass Democratic Movement, the internal groups allied to the ANC, ecstatically welcomed their hero back into public life. The ANC in exile remained cautious, however. True, Mandela had been released but some political prisoners still languished in jail. And the state of emergency still gave the government vast and draconian powers, they complained. And yet most of the world's major leaders hailed de Klerk's historic steps. Margaret Thatcher, out of step with the European Community and the Commonwealth as usual, removed some of the minor 'voluntary' sanctions against Pretoria. Some activists argued that it was the right time for the quick kill: short, sharp, comprehensive sanctions could finish off the apartheid beast, while it was reeling on the ropes. Thatcher, however, argued that unless de Klerk was rewarded with some concessions for his boldness and courage he could fall victim to a purge from the reactionary right.

It was from this perspective that de Klerk and Mikhail Gorbachev were often compared. Both possessed the same combination of steel and charm. Like Mandela,

Nelson Mandela went from being the world's most famous prisoner to a worldwide secular saint. A later picture of the US Secretary of Defense, William Cohen, visiting Mandela's home near Umtata. (US DoD)

Gorbachev's and de Klerk's professional training had been in law. Both presidents were struggling to install the rule of law in their oppressive systems. Both knew that reform could collapse rather than modernize their autocracies. Even at the time, however, the Russian looked more fragile. The imminent collapse of the Soviet system was to deprive the ANC of its major ally. While the supporters of Mandela were shouting *amandla* (power) it was clear that real *amandla* was owned by the state. By 1990 the armed struggle had been relegated almost to the level of a mere nuisance. Some discontentment festered in the security forces, especially the police, but President de Klerk commanded a large and powerful military machine, which remained immune from defection, at least to the left. Gorbachev soon faced a palace coup and then the collapse of the whole grand Soviet edifice, but de Klerk was strong enough to handle the years of negotiations with the ANC and, crucially, other parties such as Inkatha.

The disappearance of the Soviet Union shocked even the most experienced Kremlinologists. The USSR had been a kind of alter ego, a demon that had nourished Pretoria's paranoia. It was no coincidence that the failed ideologies of Soviet communism and apartheid crumbled at the same time. America became

The collapse of the Berlin Wall and the end of the USSR changed the political dynamics in southern Africa

the only superpower but did not know what to do with that power, especially in Africa. The war against the Boers had been the main excuse for the dictators and secret police terrors in many of the front-line states: perhaps South Africa's democratization would be contagious. And yet nearly all the black-white colonial conflicts had turned into so-called 'black-on-black' civil wars. Would post-apartheid South Africa suffer the same fate as Angola or Mozambique? South Africa was the regional leviathan and the cornerstone to the economic and political salvation of southern and central Africa. Yet a vigorous black-ruled South Africa was everything the neighbouring states had desired, and dreaded. They wanted liberation but feared the republic's power.

## *The long haggle*

De Klerk and Mandela maintained an uneasy rapport, an odd-couple tango, for four years of constitutional horsetrading between the ANC and the still-ruling National Party. The international media were less interested now because of the virtual absence of large-scale formal violence to match, for example, the recent big, largely secret, battles in Angola. The local journalists were left with covering the continual killing, often tribal, between the Zulu Inkatha party and the PAC, ANC, and Black

Consciousness supporters. The so-called black-on-black violence of 1990-94 was no longer a simple morality tale of good versus evil. Some American journalists had analyzed the complexities of the region in superlative style, notably Joseph Lelyveld's *Move Your Shadow*. No one caught the country with so much brio, however, as Afrikaner journalist Rian Malan's *My Traitor's Heart.* Certainly, after Mandela's freedom, the conflict could no longer be refracted for American audiences through the prism of the civil rights movement as it had been. Some US journalists struggled to interpret the atrocities, for example, those committed by Winnie Mandela's personal followers in her 'football team', or the socialism of most, and the communism of many, in the ANC coalition by way of the simple analogy of the Mason-Dixon line. Many gave up. Local journalists could not. For example, Max du Preez and Jacques Pauw, of the *Vrye Weekblad,* took extraordinary risks in their exposure of the death squads inside the SAP. The most famous were the four young photographers who comprised the Bang Bang Club, Ken Oosterbroek, Kevin Carter, Greg Marinovich and João Silva. They risked their lives daily covering the inter-black fighting in the townships. Oosterbroek died, with camera in hand, after he was hit by a stray bullet. A few weeks after winning a Pulitzer Prize for his photograph of a starving child stalked by an expectant vulture in Sudan, Carter committed suicide. The two survivors, Marinovich and Silva, wrote their harrowing story in the *The Bang Bang Club*. Here is an excerpt on war correspondents' guilt:

> At times, we felt like vultures. We had indeed trodden on corpses, metaphorically and literally, in making a living; but we had not killed any of those people. We had never killed anyone; in fact, we had saved some lives. And perhaps our pictures had made a difference by allowing people to see elements of other people's struggles to survive that they would not otherwise have known about.[1]

The book was subtitled 'Snapshots from a hidden war'. Much fighting still went on – in secret. The main news story in South Africa was dubbed CODESA, the abbreviation for the Convention for Democratic South Africa, the formal negotiations started in 1991. Behind the political façade numerous mini-wars were raging. The covert Third Force elements, most notably the Civil Co-operation Bureau, were assassinating and torturing people. Other pro-apartheid groups were arming and training the Inkatha forces. There was much talk of confederal forces and not just the Zulus. Within formal SADF units and the SAP, Afrikaners were forming militant groups for a possible *Volkstaat*. The *Afrikaner VolksFront* was formed in May 1993 and was led by the charismatic ex-SADF chief, Constand Viljoen. Later this was associated in the Freedom Alliance with allies in Inkatha as well as Ciskei troops.

In his memoirs F.W. de Klerk claimed he did not know about the secret armies especially the Civil Co-operation Bureau and the SAP Vlakplaas units. And yet the

General Malan was sidelined by F.W. de Klerk

new president had been astute enough to keep the State Security Council going; disbanding it would have antagonized the militant right. Instead de Klerk moved senior SSC players such as Magnus Malan sideways. In September 1991 he made the proud general the Minister for Housing, Works, Water affairs and Forestry. Not much gunsmoke there. The president knew he had to defang the SSC long before the promised national elections in 1994. Dealing with the special forces was more touchy. The PAC and its armed wing, the Azanian People's Liberation Army (APLA), had not renounced the armed struggle. To the contrary, they promised, notably in their grandly named Operation GREAT STORM, to seize numerous white farms. In 1991 and 1992 the PAC launched over forty-one attacks, mainly from bases in the Transkei. The PAC attacks got so bad that the former MK chief of staff, Chris Hani, urged the PAC leadership 'to bite the bullet' and accept negotiations by suspending the struggle. Hani also said they should drop their slogan 'one settler, one bullet' because it was racist and encouraged the perception that it was correct and revolutionary to target whites. In October the Recce Commandos attacked and destroyed a number of PAC bases in the Transkei. The PAC eventually joined CODESA but Buthelezi was still getting a lot of white military backing and remained aloof from the electoral process. It was assumed he had the power to torpedo the election if he did not jump on board the train to democracy.

## *The first democratic election*

The years of political haggling over a new constitution drew to a close and the first one-person, one-vote election was set for May 1994. Ultra-conservatives in the white community, especially in the Neo-Nazi AWB, prepared for a last stand, or perhaps a retreat to some white-ruled redoubt in the Northern Cape. Some right-wingers, including AWB men, poured into the tottering homeland of Bophuthatswana to back the apartheid puppet, Lucas Mangope. The date was 17 March 1994, the day the awe factor for whites and white South Africa dissipated. Three armed Neo-Nazis, travelling through Mangope's dusty capital in a dilapidated green Mercedes, threw racial taunts at a group of blacks. A local black policeman fired at the car, fatally wounding the driver. The two whites with him stumbled out of the car, their hands in the air. But they still used derogatory terms about blacks to nearby journalists. Two minutes later both whites were killed, shot in the head by other black policemen. That picture was flashed around the world: a black man in uniform pointing a rifle at the head of a white man lying prostrate in the dirt. Such pictures had not been widely seen since the Congo massacres in the early 1960s and never in South Africa, still cocooned in the spluttering racism of apartheid's last days.

The old Africa hands among the resident press corps had expected the Afrikaner tribe to fight, as the Rhodesians had, especially when remembering the *bittereinders* who had campaigned to the last in the Boer War. The two lawyers, Mandela and de Klerk, however, managed to control their respective sides. Thousands of international correspondents flew in for the elections, expecting a bloodbath. The key question was would Buthelezi contest the election? I happened to be in the office of my good friend David Willers, editor of the *Natal Witness* in Pietermaritzburg, when the news came in that the mercurial Zulu leader would join in. David and I celebrated that it was likely to be peace rather than war. So the feared Zulu uprising in Natal and Johannesburg did not materialize. Nelson Mandela's ANC won the expected landslide. As a result the long-ruling National Party started to implode.[2] Many whites accepted black rule as inevitable, while others thought in cosmetic terms: they would allow the ANC into parliament in exchange for the resumption of international rugby tours. One cynical local journalist said to me in Johannesburg just after the election, 'South Africa was a first-world dictatorship, now it's a third-world democracy.' My own view was that, as in Zimbabwe, politics for whites would be like the weather – interesting but they couldn't do much about it.

### *The role of the media*

The apartheid philosophy was demonstrably evil but the question remained whether it had been *uniquely* evil. Some journalists argued that it was a special evil. Others found it tempting to take sides after witnessing a massacre or two. It was no wonder Pretoria accused foreign journalists of incitement. No media conspiracy existed, however; reporters tend to be too competitive, disorganized, busy or arguably inebriated to organize a successful conspiracy even if they ever wanted to. Most foreign correspondents did not crusade against Pretoria, despite the siren calls of the advocacy journalists and editors ensconced in the safe newsrooms at home. Still, the vast majority, even the crusty old Africa hands, with faces as lined as the terrain they traversed, were frequently appalled by Pretoria's inept manipulation of the media.

Most hacks, as journalist call themselves, felt that if they treated South Africa as a special case then they had to accept all the others such as the Khmer Rouge in Cambodia or Papa Doc in Haiti, for example. All notions of professional objectivity would have been blown out of the water. Those journalists who did take up cudgels for the ANC needed to understand that revolutions tend to devour their children. For example, were partisan foreign correspondents who crusaded for Mugabe prepared to stay in Zimbabwe and live under a dictatorship that destroyed an economy previously relatively vibrant in 1980 despite sanctions, war and no foreign aid? Mandela had become a secular saint, but what if he could in the future play a Kerensky to appalling and corrupt ANC leaders? Should journalists judge Africa by Western standards, or patronizingly make allowances? After all, human rights are, or should be, universal.

In terms of conventional war reporting – witnessing battles and campaigns – the fighting in southern Africa was generally poorly covered, especially apartheid's 'second front' in the neighbouring states. Here the terrain was difficult and reporting the wars often required feats of endurance, determination and basic military skills to survive. Above all, Pretoria went to great lengths to hide these wars from the public. While the fighting in Angola could involve thousands of combatants in a single battle, the guerrilla warfare and sabotage campaigns inside South Africa were badly orchestrated with few white casualties. Despite the clumsy propaganda of the government, which emphasized the Cold War threats, many whites just followed the herd. As in Rhodesia, people tended to believe what they wanted to believe, especially if it preserved the status quo.

In sixty years of post-colonial mayhem throughout the continent, apartheid was the most popular running African story in the West. This continued coverage could have been because the media often portrayed whites, nearly always fluent in English, in conflict with blacks, whose leaders had mastered English soundbites. Greater slaughter in neighbouring states, such as the mass butchery in Rwanda, did not inspire the same media interest, perhaps because it could not be easily portrayed in stark moral terms, good versus evil, justice versus apartheid, black versus white. One other hypothesis was that Johannesburg, compared with most other African cities, was a comfortable place to be based as a journalist, in lifestyle and access to modern communications and transportation (and good schools for the kids). All applied to me, by the way, except the kids. The front-line states in the struggle against apartheid, such as Zimbabwe or Zambia, did warn correspondents that they would have to move north to the Zimbabwean capital, Harare, or be banned from working in the front-line states. To no avail. When Zimbabwe banned Western journalists in 2008 none of its black neighbours dared whisper an official complaint because of misplaced regional, racial and anti-imperialist solidarity.

Did the many foreign reporters have any provable impact on the demise of apartheid – the much-touted (though bogus) CNN effect?[3] Despite the self-image of truculent indifference, most South African whites, especially in the government, were concerned about how the world viewed them. And, like most siege cultures, many whites were deeply religious, especially in the ruling

Afrikaner elites. The constant worldwide drumbeat of moral condemnation and sanctions did have an effect.

Though foreign correspondents colonized affluent white suburbs, the dangerous streets of the townships, where my colleagues George De'Ath or Ken Oosterboek were murdered, were testing environments. No single story or event comparable to, say, Vietnam's Tet Offensive doomed the regime. Rather, stories covered over a long period did cause political embarrassment for the Afrikaner rulers, including Steve Biko's murder, corruption in the government and the secret northern wars, especially when South African special force soldiers were captured. The often close cooperation between well-known foreign journalists and determined local correspondents, both black and white, sustained the pressure when Pretoria banned the cameras and kicked out foreign news reporters. A few correspondents betrayed their calling by extreme partisanship but the vast majority did not. Despite Pretoria's media management the story was relayed to the international public over the decades. This helped trigger the international political and economic pressures that eventually forced Pretoria to accept the inevitable. The ANC had hoped that the various fronts, from armed struggle to union power, would eventually bring down the apartheid superstructure; ironically, the incremental impact of the media coverage might have been just as effective at toppling the ramparts of white supremacy. Although the South African military was still by far the most powerful on the continent, the political war was lost.

F.W de Klerk and Nelson Mandela: reconciling black and white. Attending together an award ceremony in Philadelphia, Pennsylvania. (US Library of Congress)

### *The Rainbow Nation*

Mandela eschewed bitterness after decades of unjust incarceration and preached reconciliation for the new 'rainbow nation' of South Africa. Sanctions were ended and the exiles came home. Above all, the Truth and Reconciliation Commission displaced calls for Nuremberg-style trials. Victor's justice was avoided. After 1996 over a thousand public meetings were held where the many crimes of apartheid and atrocities by the insurgents were discussed, confessions were made, and sometimes amnesty as well as forgiveness were sought. F.W. de Klerk apologised while P.W. Botha called the whole thing a 'circus' and refused to attend.

Perhaps equally important was the formation of the SANDF, the South African National Defence Force. It was charged with providing the country with a balanced and modern force which was, above all, integrated. The former SADF was still the backbone but the amalgamation involved nine armies in all, including the former homelands as well as MK and APLA. France and the USA expected to play the role of honest broker but were irritated by the fact that Britain was asked to replicate its role in Zimbabwe. London sent a group of military trainers and senior civil servants to help reform the ministry of defence. This BMATT, British Military Advisory and Training Team, set up boards to assess the quality of the new forces; only a few very senior MK officers were excluded. Thousands of bogus guerrillas presented themselves for payment as well as training and sometimes the British trainers had to deploy their power of final veto. On one occasion a British lieutenant colonel, who had served with the SAS, had to stand between two large and armed groups of MK and APLA who were about to fight a pitched battle. Unarmed, he talked the leaders of both groups into reaching a peaceful deal. On one occasion, 6,000 MK soldiers went AWOL and demanded the resignations of the defence minister, the former MK leader, Joe Modise. The cadres felt that he had betrayed them. Other grievances followed about pay, conditions and the integration process. Many ex-MK men asked for Mandela to intercede. Eventually one of the toughest ex-MK men was made deputy minister of defence, Ronnie Kasrils. A white of Jewish background, Kasrils had been MK chief of intelligence and a prominent member of the SACP. He had undergone military training early in the 1960s in the USSR. He put his foot down with the SANDF and later he led the intelligence services.

The former SADF top brass still in service were relieved that Kasrils took charge but were concerned about their hiding the special forces in 45th Parachute Battalion rather than disbanding the Recces. One of Kasrils's first questions was 'Where are my Special Forces?' Two Recce units were restored though a third, based in Natal, perhaps because of its alleged connections with Inkatha death squads, was not restored. The old Recces were soon active in the Congo wars as well as training with British and French special forces.

Pretoria's neighbours were still wary of its power, both its military and economic clout. Early in the peace process, Washington had very quietly removed the six atomic weapons that had been assembled; South Africa became the first country to de-nuclearize. The modernized, albeit smaller and less efficient, armed forces of the new democratic republic did involve themselves in military action beyond its border, usually reluctantly and often with little success. Some of the old SADF professionals fought on but in such outfits as Executive Outcomes, which proved once more that privatized mercenary forces could be highly effective.

# PART V

# RAINBOW NATIONS?

# Chapter 18

# After the Fall

The collapse of the Cold War rivalry on the continent prompted many Africans to question their own one-party systems. The neighbours had all preached democracy for South Africa, so why could it not be practised elsewhere? Phrases such as the 'Second Liberation' and 'African Renaissance' peppered political discourse. In southern Africa, Mozambique found some peace and reconciliation partly based on the South African approach.

Sadly, after an encouraging turn of events in the south, Africa elsewhere was soon back to its cyclical crop of coups, famines and killing fields. As Mandela walked free, a long civil war in Liberia broke out. In the Horn of Africa, in Ethiopia, a famine of 'biblical proportions' broke out (to quote Michael Buerk's famous BBC documentary) and the civil war that had raged since 1974 died down in 1991, though Ethiopia and breakaway Eritrea would soon fight one of the most bloody wars over the most undesirable tract of desert. In the same region, the continent's longest war in Sudan, Africa's largest country, was to rumble on for a decade or two.[1] Then the state was divided. Africa's newest country, South Sudan, was already a failed state; soon it collapsed into Mad Max-style civil war. And as South Africa walked towards democracy, another Islamic insurgency had torn Algeria apart.

Nothing matched, however, the killing fields of Rwanda, where Hutu extremists killed perhaps 800,000 fellow Rwandans, mainly Tutsi, in 100 days. This extermination rate surpassed Hitler's. As with the holocaust of the Jews, much of the world chose to ignore Rwanda. It caught the UN and nearly all the veteran correspondents unprepared. Rwanda's genocide was not a tribal frenzy, nor anarchy, but the work of an organized and obedient society: men and women were convinced that mass annihilation was their *umganda*, their civic duty. The country's neighbours and the Western states chose not to recognize the atrocities. The US state department's spokeswoman was ordered not to use the term 'genocide', but deployed the slippery phrase 'acts of genocide' instead. The worst offender was the UN, which recalled all but a handful of peacekeepers who were operating in the country. Rwanda was soon framed as a refugee crisis which enabled, by default, many of the Hutu killers, the *Interahamwe,* to evade punishment. The refugee camps became humanitarian havens for the killers and more telegenic means for NGOs to portray a suffering Africa. Some of the Hutus responsible for the Rwandan massacres fled into Zaire, now the Democratic Republic of the Congo, after the Tutsi-led Patriotic Front took control of Rwanda. The new Rwandan government sent in its troops to kill Hutu militiamen hiding in the refugee camps in the Congo. This was partly the cause of the so-called 'first world war' in Africa.

Nine nations became embroiled in a long, complex ethnic and resource war in a vast land that has known little peace since the greedy and often cruel Belgian colonial administration quit in 1960. After five years and possibly five to six million deaths, a shaky ceasefire was signed. Although international television crews reported on the conditions in the refugee camps along the eastern borders of the Congo, the absence of roads and the presence of dense jungle and armed anarchy, as well the inevitable military secrecy in Africa, prevented any effective international coverage. This was a complex war and completely different from the Western portrayal of apartheid. Also, compassion fatigue about Africa had intruded, in a big way. After the US-led UN intervention in Somalia went disastrously wrong it discouraged Western involvement in complex emergencies. But it should not have excused the moral blindness about Rwanda, and tepid engagement in the even bigger calamity in the Congo.

### *Africa's First World War*

Robert Mugabe intensely disliked his role as Africa's prime liberator being usurped by the much greater man, Mandela. For historical reasons, democratic South Africa was always reluctant to throw its weight around in the region. And when it did, in Lesotho, in 1998, it proved a failure. Mugabe was determined to use his much smaller military and economic base to act as the regional peacemaker. Pretoria failed to prevent Mugabe's aggressive support for Laurent Kabila in the Congo and the recruitment of the other SADC nations, including Angola and Namibia, to enter the fray in the Congo. Time and time again Pretoria was to let Mugabe get away, literally, with murder.

Mugabe's open war in Mozambique had a clear logic, as did the covert previous campaign against apartheid. Zimbabwe's costly intervention in the Congo made little sense except as an extension of ZANU-PF cronyism. Just as the 'chefs', the party big-wigs, cleaned up at home, the Congo offered untold riches abroad to Mugabe's generals. The war killed hundreds of ordinary soldiers and further undermined the tottering economy, but a handful of new military millionaires laughed all the way to the bank. By African standards, Mugabe's army had performed well in Mozambique, but the ZNA was increasingly undermined, not least by the treatment of war veterans.

The War Veterans Association was led by Dr Chenjerai 'Hitler' Hunzvi. His wartime and medical credentials were extremely suspect, but as he became responsible for assessing the claims of the veterans, he was himself up to his neck in the scam (to the tune Z$45 million allegedly stolen by him). In parliament, Margaret Dongo, a brave independent member, albeit formerly a Mugabe stalwart, publicized the scandal. Led by the firebrand Hunzvi, over 50,000 veterans began to campaign for proper compensation, gratuities and pensions. Mugabe ignored them at first. The war veterans also demanded land, which helped re-ignite the simmering question of the white farmers who still owned much of the productive land (much of it bought with full government permission, *after* independence). Eventually Mugabe had to meet the veterans and promised to buy them off with money the state did not possess. The tens of thousands of veterans received a one-off payment of $2,500 and a continuous pension of $100 a month. In January 1998, in response to riots over price hikes in basic food stuffs, the army had to be called out onto the streets of the main towns to suppress the urban violence. This was the first time that the army had to act in the streets to prop up an increasingly unpopular government. At the same time, the Zimbabwe Congress of Trade Unions, led by Morgan Tsvangirai, began to flex its industrial muscle. The last thing the Zimbabwe economy needed was the expense of an unnecessary war in the Congo.

Mugabe was always more keen to strut on the world stage rather than address the technicalities of domestic economic governance, which appeared to bore him. With the end of the apartheid war and the traditional role of the front-line states, the Southern African Development Community (SADC) emerged as the main vehicle for regional diplomacy. In 1996 Mugabe had finagled his appointment as chairman of the defence arm of the Community (the Organ for Politics, Defence and Security Co-operation). This was his chosen mechanism to intervene in the Congo, portraying his personal ambitions as SADC diplomacy. From June 1997 Mugabe had also held the post of the chairman of the OAU, for a year. That was a useful network to intrigue with his allies in Luanda to work against what Mugabe feared would be the dominance of South Africa in the region, now that the psycho-political burden of apartheid was removed. On a personal level the relationship had been awkward. During the South African president's first state visit to Zimbabwe he spoke on the same platform as Mugabe; it was obvious that Mandela's bighearted speech carried a much deeper message than the shrill tirade of the Zimbabwean, even though both were couched in quasi-Marxist language. Later, in 1998, when both men were involved in mediating the latest Congo crisis, Mandela groaned to his assistant, 'Please don't tell me I have to speak to Comrade Robert again.'

The politics and wars of the Democratic Republic of Congo (formerly Zaire) almost defies succinct analysis. In brief, however, the end of the Cold War meant that President Mobutu's position in Zaire was far less important to his main patron, Washington. Simultaneously with the surge of African optimism after the election of Mandela, Rwanda suffered the most rapid genocide in modern history. When

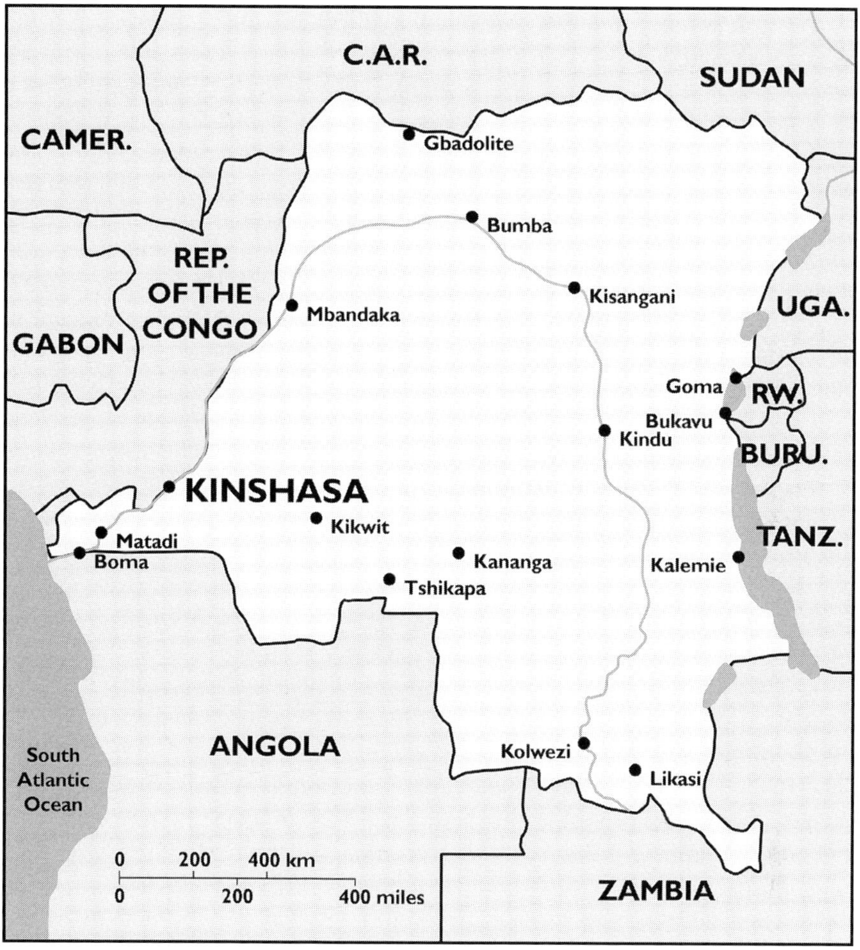


Africa's first world war

the relieving Tutsi-dominated troops marched into Rwanda many of the Hutu perpetrators of the massacres fled into the Congo. The new Rwandan government invaded next-door Zaire to flush out the militants (the *Interahamwe*) among the two million Hutu refugees and this helped boost the anti-Mobutu rebels; Laurent Kabila, an old adversary of Mobutu, was installed as president. Kabila's former rebel allies then sparked a new insurgency, but this time backed by Rwanda and Uganda. Kabila turned to Mugabe for help.

Mobutu had been detested by the southern African liberation movements because of his CIA connections in thwarting, particularly, the advance of the Marxist guerrillas in Angola and in Namibia. And, in 1998, Jonas Savimbi, the long-term ally of Pretoria, was still a significant military figure in Angola. When Kabila took over, South Africa's Thabo Mbeki was the first to fly to congratulate him on removing 'the man who stank' – Mobutu. Ideological payback was part of the pro-Kabila alliance.

Initially Mugabe was ambiguous about Kabila. His playboy background did not please the austere Zimbabwean. But Kabila claimed an affection for Maoism, and he had once spent time with Che Guevara, when the Cubans sent a small force to the Congo. Guevara himself despised Kabila because his revolutionary rhetoric was not matched by any action outside nightclubs and brothels. Cautiously, Moven Mahachi, the Zimbabwean defence minister, promised aid. Mugabe was keen to discourage South African entrepreneurs making further inroads into the Congo honeypot. A few weeks after Kabila's victory, the Zimbabwe Defence Industries won a small supply contract of half a million US dollars. Within six months ZDI had received orders for $140 million. And negotiations about new mining concessions were conducted in earnest. Most of the legal mining companies had shut up shop because the usual chaos in the Congo had been made even worse by the anarchy following Mobutu's fall. The new concessions needed professional military protection. Harare seemed to care little about the noisy European lawyers disputing the new Zimbabwean deals. This was a land grab almost as audacious as Cecil Rhodes's seizure of the Shona and Ndebele territories.

In August 1998 Mugabe decided to back Kabila fully, without consulting his party or cabinet, and persuaded his allies in the SADC, Angola and Namibia, to commit troops as well. The Zimbabwe Defence Forces (ZDF) component was relatively small in the beginning, about 3,000. As in Mozambique, however, 'mission creep' grew to feed operational demands. It eventually topped 10,000 troops plus air force and logistical support. The war would soon cost Harare around $1 million a day, although Mugabe always publicly asserted it was a 'self-financing war'. It was in one sense, except that the taxpayers paid for the war and senior generals and a few favoured Zimbabwean businessmen took all the profits.

Mugabe and Kabila had signed a formal contract on 4 September 1998. Zimbabwe would receive a 37.5 per cent interest in Gécamines, and 30 per cent of the company's profits were supposed to pay for Harare's war effort. The company, however, had over $1 billion in long-term debts. Like most of the DRC's companies it was not viable. Neither man made any money from that deal. Large areas of prime land in Katanga were also given to ZANU-PF interests, but no capital was available to develop the land there, or for that matter at home in Zimbabwe. Other state deals fell apart but some of the private military ventures did not. Nevertheless, Harare initially admitted that it was spending just $36 million a year on the Congo misadventure. Finally, Simba Makoni, the finance minister, was forced to confess that a more realistic figure was $200 million over two years. That was still a gross understatement. The World Bank put the figure at nearly $1 million per day and cut off a much-needed loan to Zimbabwe. The war costs shot up as Harare bought weapons from China ($72.3 million), MiGs from Libya and spare parts for BAe Hawks costing up to $10million. Defying Foreign Office advice, Tony Blair had insisted on allowing the British deal to go ahead. Opponents argued that the Hawks were using bombs with no guidance systems and it was inevitable that civilians would be killed. New Labour had come into power in 1997 with the promise of an ethical dimension to foreign policy. Arming Mugabe seemed to stretch the term 'ethical'.

The DRC had always been the richest of African states, with the poorest of inhabitants, because the mineral wealth was consistently looted, by the Belgian colonists and then kleptocratic domestic governments. Now the Zimbabwean lootocracy joined in. Senior officers and politicians set up a variety of companies that had officially bought mines from Kabila as part of the deal to give him military support. Western companies and lawyers helped launder much of the money made so that the proceeds ended up as clean cash in Swiss bank accounts. Richard Dowden, then head of Britain's Royal African Society, summed up the Congo malaise rather poetically: 'Anyone with a gun, a mobile phone and an airstrip can become a wealthy warlord. Ripped out of Africa, the loot then floats gently through the international free market system and comes to rest in the window of a jewellery shop, on the fingers of innocent lovers.'

Zimbabweans secured preferential trade deals not just for diamonds, cobalt and other minerals but for timber and other business concessions. Party securocrats, especially Emmerson Mnangagwa, were at the core of the vast protection racket. General Vitalis Zvinavashe, a top ZNA commander, set up a major logistics company to supply the war. Officers and men were encouraged to do their own deals in the country and the lower ranks were given special allowances by the army for serving in the Congo.

The details of the war were effectively kept secret by Mugabe, but often casualties could not be completely hidden, nor occasional rumours of mutinies against officers who were sacrificing their men purely to defend business profits. Zimbabwean journalists who tried to report on the ill effects of the war and particularly military disaffection with Mugabe, presumably from the officers who were not making enough money from the Congo, were arrested and tortured.

Although Zimbabwean and Angolan troops saved Kabila, they often suffered major reverses. For example, in what was termed the river wars, Rwandan-led forces had trapped over 3,000 largely Zimbabwean and Namibian troops at Ikela airport. Mugabe was said to be furious that so many of his troops were besieged. Pro-Kabila troops, with heavy Zimbabwean reinforcements, launched an assault to relieve the Ikela garrison; despite use of gunships and river-borne heavy artillery, they managed to secure only a short ceasefire to allow the Zimbabwean Air Force to airlift its troops out. On another occasion, 300 ZNA men had to seek refuge over the border in Zambia after being defeated in the DRC. So tough was the war at one stage that Harare brought back 75 per cent of its aviation from the DRC, partly because of the fear of their being permanently grounded because the Harare treasury was having major problems paying for spare parts for their planes. This might explain the alleged failure of a Zimbabwean flypast requested by Kabila for a celebration in Kinshasa. Six fighters left Harare, but only one managed to reach the DRC capital, because of malfunctions *en route* and at least one fatal crash.

On Tuesday 16 January 2001, around noon, President Kabila was sitting in his office at the presidential palace in Kinshasa, looking at some papers and chatting to an advisor. One of his bodyguards, Rashidi Kasereka, walked up to him as though he wanted to whisper something in his ear. Instead, he fired an automatic pistol at point-blank range straight into Kabila's head. He died almost immediately. Nevertheless, his dead body was flown to Harare under the pretext of seeking medical attention. When Kabila's son, Joseph, took over, Mugabe maintained his largesse, despite the accelerating military and political opposition in Zimbabwe. Officially, Harare's position was that it was waiting for a suitable UN peacekeeping force to replace the SADC forces. In August 2002, just after South Africa offered to contribute 1,500 troops to the UN force, Mugabe ordered his remaining infantry out.

When the UN published its second report on looting in the Congo in 2003, the Mugabe government refused to investigate some of the prominent Zimbabwean culprits indicted in the report. 'We did a good job in the DRC and we will not respond to malicious allegations by the British masquerading as the United Nations,' was the official response to UN accusations. Mugabe had long been almost paranoid not only about alleged British meddling in his country but also about South Africa taking over Zimbabwean business interests in both Mozambique and the DRC. At one stage, Mugabe thought that Pretoria might actually join the opposition forces to the SADC alliance in Congo. As it happened, South Africa did replace many of Zimbabwean interests in both countries, as Zimbabwe's economy, destabilized by the pointless Congo fiasco, made it impossible for it to function at home, let alone compete with the regional economic giant.

The Second Congo War, also known as Africa's World War, began in August 1998 and officially ended in July 2003, though large UN forces were still trying to keep an impossible peace as late as 2018. It was the largest war in modern African history, involving nine immediate state combatants, but many others from around Africa who stirred the pot, as well as an alphabet soup of twenty-five domestic militias. It killed an estimated 5.4 million people, mostly from disease and starvation. The war was also a financial disaster for the Zimbabwean treasury. Until the beginning of the new millennium, disaffected Zimbabweans wanted an end to bad policies – and opposition to the Congo war became a focus of discontent. After the Congo disaster, the aim was not reform of ZANU-PF and the removal of the more obvious gangsters, but rather the toppling of both Mugabe and his entire corrupted party.

*South Africa's failure to curb Mugabe*

Mandela was a great man but a poor president. He was too busy travelling the world, or later involved with his new third wife. Graca Machel, the widow of Samora. She was the only woman to have married two state presidents of two different republics. And she was the first African woman to become a British dame – perhaps the only dame who could strip an AK-47 in quick time. By standing down after one term, Mandela set an impressive example in Africa where few presidents have been keen to hand over power, at any time. Yet it meant that lesser men were bound to follow him. Thabo Mbeki was an intellectual with a poor feel for real politics. Late at night, alone in his study, smoking his trademark pipe, and sipping his favourite cognac, he must often have pondered – why did I take this job? It was a job for which he was ill-suited. And it showed, for example, in his catastrophic failure to accept the reality of the AIDS pandemic in his country, just as he failed to curb the dangerous antics of his neighbour, Robert Gabriel Mugabe.

The Zimbabwean president continued to administer his country as though he were running the politburo of a revolutionary army. After thirty-plus years in power he became increasingly mad, messianic and dictatorial. Initially, Mugabe was an austere man who did not indulge in pleasures of the flesh. In time, though, he turned a blind eye to the corruption in his own family, especially his avaricious second wife, Grace, as well as the greed of party leaders. They became like the pigs in *Animal Farm*, an elite above the law, in total control and living the lifestyle of the world's richest. The seizure of productive land caused famine. Much of the new lands, many given to party cronies, was not farmed. Soon the country became dependent on foreign food handouts. Attacks on foreign investors also ruined the economy while the war in the Congo emptied the coffers. Soon the

Mugabe ruined the Zimbabwean economy and created the second highest inflation in modern history

country endured the second highest inflation in modern history and its currency was replaced by the US dollar and the rand. Three million refugees fled, mainly to South Africa. It came to a crunch in 2008 when Mugabe lost the election but rigged the run-off with utter thuggery. President Thabo Mbeki held all the cards; in 1976 John Vorster had shown far more *cojones* when he forced Ian Smith to do a political deal with his black opponents. Mbeki never did that. South African pressure did, however, help create a government of national unity.[2]

Eventually Mugabe's dictatorial rule helped collapse the coalition government with the opposition, and Zimbabwe's economic tragedy deepened. South Africa's failure to democratize its neighbour led to a creeping Zimbabweanization of South Africa itself; not only obvious symptoms such as electricity cuts but also gross corruption under President Jacob Zuma.

### *'State capture'*

The South Africans had tied to mediate in various wars in its neighbours after the apartheid era. Initially, Pretoria had not managed to cut its old ally down to size. Jonas Savimbi was not killed until February 2002. His longterm opponent, José Eduardo dos Santos, had won his civil war but, despite all the oil wealth, the country's population remained desperately poor. Dos Santos agreed to step down in 2017 and his family empire was soon dismembered. Namibia chugged along while Botswana remained an exceptional example of sound political and economic management. In 2012 Afonso Dhlakama went back to Gorongosa to renew his struggle. State repression mounted in Zambia and Tanzania. The one positive change was the military toppling Mugabe in late 2017. The army commanders went to Mugabe's residence and told Grace Mugabe to shut up and 'stay in the kitchen where you belong'. The possibility that she would succeed Mugabe was too much for the military commanders. Mass street demonstrations in Harare welcomed the coup against Mugabe and especially Grace: 'Leadership is not sexually transmitted', said one prominent placard. The police had disappeared and the population appeared to welcome the new boss, Emmerson Mnangagwa. His nickname was 'Crocodile' for good reasons: he had supervised the massacres in Matabeleland in the early 1980s, as well heading the Central Intelligence Organisation. He had also ensured that rigged elections kept Mugabe in power, so Mnangagwa was no tree-hugging liberal. As the slogan ran in Harare: 'Same bus, different driver'. The tyrant had gone but the tyranny remained.

Zimbabwe's dictatorship had been tolerated by South Africa for a number of reasons. Mugabe's reputation as a liberation fighter held some sway at home and aboard. And yet the bottom line was that the victorious liberation parties were expected to stay in power. The trade union of crony parties in Zimbabwe, Angola, Namibia, Mozambique, and South Africa were all mutually dependent: if one was allowed to lose an election, a domino effect might topple some or all of

The people turn out in Harare to praise the army for toppling Mugabe

the rest. Not until some or all of the revolutionary parties were defeated in free elections would the region start to democratize. ZANU-PF had lost the first round of the 2008 election, and even in South Africa the ANC was losing friends and votes, partly because of the mass corruption of Jacob Zuma's presidency as well as the faltering economy. It all came to a head in 2018 with the escalating Gupta scandal, known as 'state capture', under which the billionaire Indian family had accumulated massive wealth and influence because of its close ties to the Zuma family. The ANC finally got rid of Zuma in early 2018: he fought hard to secure immunity, not least to avoid the first big corruption case; 783 cases relating to a huge arms deal. Cyril Ramaphosa, originally the choice of Mandela to succeed him, took over as the new state president while promising to clear out corruption and to start rebuilding the shattered economy and alleviate high unemployment.

*Post-bellum* South Africa had not endured civil war, nor kangaroo courts punishing the white supremacists who had lost their long fight with their neighbours, the Soviets and Cubans, as well as the internal majority. The crisis of expectations with the almost messianic ascendancy of Mandela was bound to cause disappointments. The so-called 'born-frees', the young generation born after apartheid, expected and demanded so much. Africa is still the world's youngest continent; south of the Sahara the median age is 18. It was lack of jobs for the young which helped fire up the Arab Spring in the north of the continent and it is youthful alienation that is telling the now stale revolutionary parties to ditch ideology and organize successful economies, new housing and decent schools and hospitals.

The days of the anti-colonial wars and fraternal assistance from the comrades in the USSR and China are long gone. True, China has largely replaced Western aid but Beijing can be as exploitative as its western predecessors. At the last count only sixteen of the fifty-four African countries were democratic. Between now and 2050 Africa's population will double to 2.5 billion and not all of them can try to cross the Mediterranean illegally. Bad governance is the main problem in Africa and at the current rate it will take nearly a hundred years for all African states to become democratic. African leaders have realized that they may need to hold elections sometimes, but many are not yet sure they should be free and fair. African states need:

President Jacob Zuma celebrating Armed Forces' Day in South Africa (SANDF)

- a free and fair press;
- an independent judiciary;
- an independent electoral commission;
- neutral and professional security forces;
- an independent central bank;

Since 1960 there have been 240 African heads of state and fewer than twenty can be said to have been good leaders. The vast majority were corrupt, incompetent and often cruel. Often they had to be removed by force.

The wars throughout Africa continued, whether to depose tyrants or fighting in African peacekeeping forces, notably in the Democratic Republic of the Congo. But elsewhere, too, for example in the Centtral African Republic, in March 2013, the South African National Defence Force lost fourteen soldiers during a thirteen-hour battle wth rebels in Bangui, the CAR capital. At home in South Africa, with mass unemployemnt, the politics of the belly raged on. Parties to the left of the declining ANC demanded the return of white-owned land, without compensation. This was Zimbabwe revisited. Just as Mugabe was in the habit of shadow boxing with long-dead white men in pith helmets, so too white exiles looked back in anger and sadness. In 2015, fifty years after UDI, I asked historian Sue Onslow what Rhodesia meant today. 'Rhodesia now exists only on the net,' she said. The scatterlings of Africa were now ruminating in Britain, Australia or New Zealand, communicating on Face Book and bemoaning the condition of 'the old country', lamenting that South Africa was rapidly following suit.

What Africa does not need is nostalgia, nor aid or charity. More NGO personnel, supervised by the proverbial 'Lords of Poverty', NGO fat-cat mandarins, now operate in Africa than colonial officials at the height of imperialism. If something is going wrong in an African country it is not usually that they do not have enough foreigners, they usually have too many. Africa needs trade: one other good reason for getting out of the EU's external trade tariffs. African leaders must stop blaming foreigners; Mugabe's party used to blame pin-prick sanctions or the weather for nearly all their woes. No foreign aid should be given to any dictatorships, except for immediate humanitarian relief in natural emergencies. Aid just funds the survival of dictatorships. African leaders must address the simple problem: two terms as head of state, maximum of eight to ten years, is more than enough. It is not a question of race. Tony Blair and Margaret Thatcher became messianic and even plain bonkers after ten years in power. The Westerners can't win but will be blamed if they do not intervene as in Rwanda or if they do as in Libya. On a personal note, I describe myself as a 'recovering interventionist'. We should stay out of foreign countries, especially Islamic ones, unless specially aiding disaster relief under UN auspices. The more the West intervenes the worse things become. Acceptance of that simple dictum should become the new total strategy for Africa.

*Appendix*

# The Structure of the South African Security System

NB: The independence of Namibia and the reforms of F.W. de Klerk brought major changes to the defence structures. The following information is a guide to the system that pertained during the most important wars covered in this book, namely the period of P.W. Botha's dominance until the end of the 1980s.

*Political control*

Until 1989 the complex security system comprised the SADF, the South African Police, Armscor, the three intelligence services, affiliated security services in the homelands and Namibia and, technically, the Prison Service. Security policy was generated by the State Security Council (SSC), in theory, for cabinet appraisal. The SSC consisted, usually, of senior ministers holding such portfolios as defence and foreign affairs, plus the chief the SADF and the head of police. It was chaired by the state president. Various senior civil servants and the head of Armscor, for example, were also invited to attend, as relevant. The SSC was the pinnacle of the National Security Management System (NSMS).

*The SADF structure*

The structure was headed in practice by the SSC. The chain of command was: president → SSC/cabinet → minister of defence → chief of the SADF → various councils/committees → the commanders of the four wings of the SADF (army, navy, air force and medical services). The main SADF planning organs were the Defence Command Council (DCC), the Defence Planning Committee (DPC) and the Defence Staff Council (DSC), all chaired by the chief of the SADF. The DCC managed overall strategy. The DPC was concerned with financial management and liaison with Armscor. The DSC co-ordinated the various branches of the SADF. Direct military command was exercised by the chief of the SADF via the chiefs of the four services though joint force commanders when a large combined operation was in progress. All the services had their main HQs in Pretoria, the 'military capital'.

## The National Security Management System:

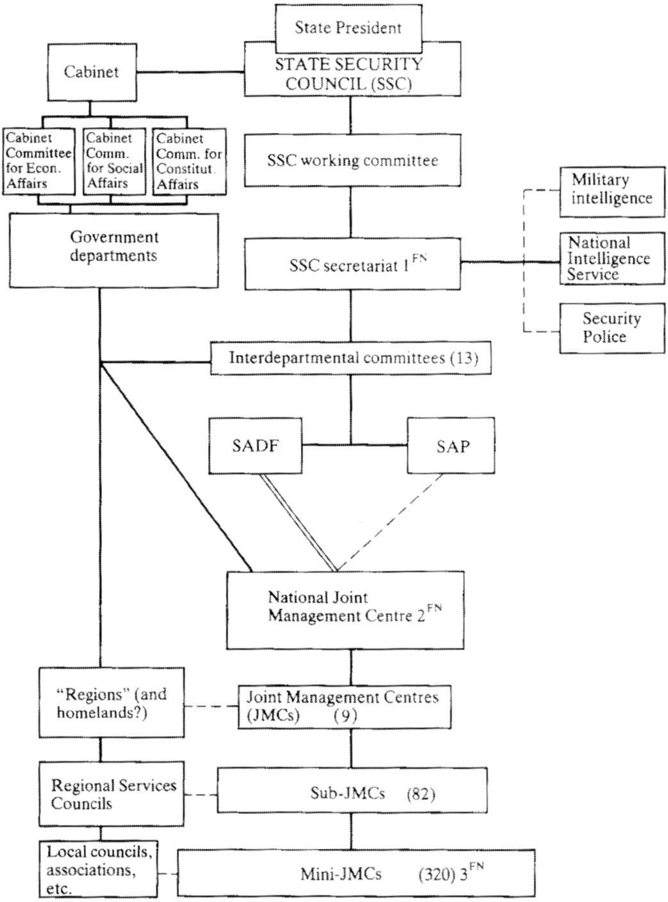


1. The secretariat has four main branches:
The National Intelligence Interpretation Branch;
The Strategic Communications Branch;
Strategy Branch;
Administration Branch.

The JMCs, sub-JMCs and mini-JMCs operated committees which roughly corresponded with the three main branches of the secretariat:
Joint Intelligence Committee;
Communications Committee;
Constitutional, Social and Economic Committee.
These committees were commonly referred to by their Afrikaans acronyms, respectively; GIK, KOMKOM, SEMKOM.

2. Like much of the system, some of its operational machinery was clouded in secrecy. The workings of the National Joint Management Centre were unclear.

3. The estimates of the number of mini-JMCs and sub-JMCs have varied.

The National Security Management System

The structure of the South African Defence Force:

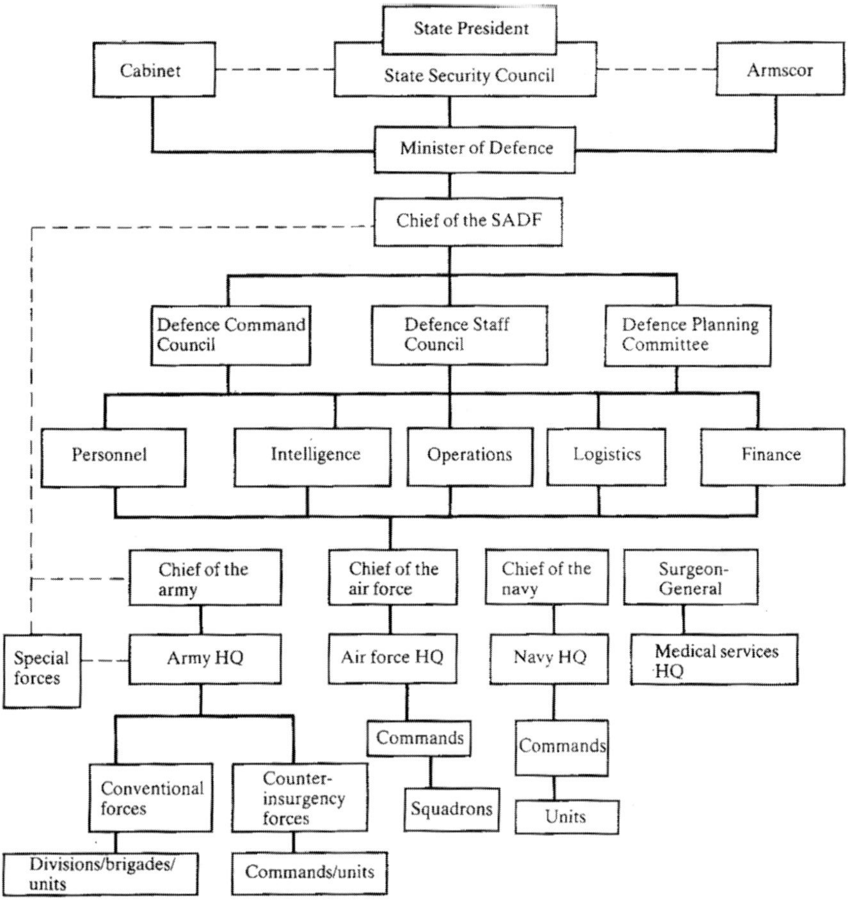


The Structure of the SADF

## *The branches of the SADF*

### The army

The army was by far the largest section of the SADF, employing over 80 per cent of total personnel. The army was divided into three main components: the conventional force, the territorial force and a large training element.

The conventional force comprised two mechanized divisions (each of which had one armoured and two mechanized brigades) and the parachute brigade. Permanent Force (PF) officers and some national servicemen formed the skeleton of the conventional force but the flesh was largely made up of citizen force (CF) reserve units. The army emphasized rapid deployment and combat mobility, since the conventional force was both the ground deterrent and large-scale offensive force as used in operations in Angola. After some difficulties experienced in Angola in the early 1980s, the parachute brigade was no longer intended for big airdrops but was deployed in smaller raiding or 'stopper' groups.

The territorial force was concerned with largely internal counter-insurgency. This force, comprising largely CF and commandos, was organized into ten regional commands, as well as Walvis Bay. The operations, using light infantry techniques, supported the police in case of serious guerrilla incursions. The territorial force also performed disaster relief and 'civic action' roles.

## Special forces

The SF operated as almost a distinct fifth wing of the SADF. The SF were directly responsible to the chief of the SADF. The elite forces were called Reconnaissance Commandos, or 'Recces'. This SAS-style force was founded in 1972 and consisted originally of five regiments, each with its own speciality. They were both PF and reservists. Other SF were 44 Parachute Brigade and 32nd (Buffalo) Battalion, in some ways South Africa's foreign legion. There were also specialist units in the SAP.

According to the International Institute for Strategic Studies (IISS) the total standing force in this period was 77,500. The PF complement was 19,000 (12,000 whites, 5,400 blacks and coloureds and about 2,000 women). The remainder was made up of about 58,500 national servicemen, CF and commandos (i.e. reservists).

### Equipment

Tanks: 250 Centurion/Olifant;
Armoured cars: 1,600 Elands (of various types with 90mm gun and 60mm mortar);
Infantry Combat vehicles: 1,500 including Ratel, Wolf etc;
APCs: 1,500 including Buffel, Hippo, Rhino etc;
Towed artillery: 175 x 25-pounder, 30 x 144mm. 75 x G-2, 40 x G-5;
Self-propelled artillery: 10 + G-6 155mm;
SAMs: 20 Cactus (Crotale), 54 Tigercat plus a big range of captured types such as SA-8/9/13/14; also Soviet AA guns;
Multiple rocket-launcher: 80 x Valkiri 127mm.

### Air Force

The SAAF was organized into two regions (Western and Southern) and four functional commands (Logistics, Air Space Control, Tactical Support and Training). Western Air Command, with its HQ formerly in Windhoek, was concerned with the war in Namibia. Southern Air Command had its HQ at the Silvermine complex near Cape Town. It was responsible for fisheries patrol, air-sea rescue and the helicopters that operated from naval vessels. Air Space

Command was tasked with early warning and air defence provided by Mirage F-1 and Mirage III aircraft, plus mobile SAM and AA systems. Tactical Support Command provided temporary air bases where the SAAF needed them. The SAAF size was 11,000 (4,000 conscripts and 400 women).

**Main SAAF equipment**

A total of 338 combat aircraft, including 116 operated by CF units), and 14 armed helicopters.

Bombers: 5 Canberra, 5 Buccaneer;

Fighter/ground attack: 29 Mirage IIIAZ, 80 Impala;

Fighters: 14 Mirages IIICZ, 19 Mirage IIICZ/EZ (being converted to Cheetah, perhaps 27 of the latter were in service);

Attack/training: 24 Impala;

Reconnaissance: 7 Mirage III;

Electronic warfare: 4 Boeing 707;

Reconnaissance/Maritime: 8 C-47, 20 Albatross P-16S;

Anti-submarine warfare: 8 Wasp HAS-1, 6 Alouette III;

Transport: 7 C-130B, 9 C-160Z, plus various VIP transports;

Helicopters: 14 Super-Frelons, 50 Pumas (some converted to Puma XTP1), 8- Alouette III;

Training: 130 Harvards, 29 Impala, etc.

Air to air missiles R-530, R-530 Magic, Sidewinder, Kukri V-3B

**Navy**

The Navy was the Cinderella of the SADF in terms of resources. It was organized into two sections: Naval Command with its HQ at Silvermine and its major base at Simonstown, and Naval Command East with Durban as its HQ. The main operational units were:

The Strike Craft flotilla based at Salisbury Island, Durban. The flotilla operated nine Israeli-designed, 430-ton, Minister-class strike craft, armed with Skerpioen ship-to-ship missiles, similar to the Israeli Gabriel. The missiles had a range of 26 nautical miles.

Submarine flotilla. The primary conventional maritime deterrent was based upon the three French Daphné-class boats.

Mine Warfare flotilla. Four locally built mine-countermeasures vessels and four Ton-class minesweepers.

Various inshore and support vessels. The South African Navy did have two frigates, modified Whitby-class. One, SAS *President Steyn*, had been stripped of its main components. The other, SAS *President Pretorius*, was in mothballs in 1989. A third frigate, SAS *Tafelberg,* had been sunk in an embarrassing accident with a replenishment ship in 1981.

SAN size: 6,500, including 900 marines, 1,500 conscripts and 300 women.

**Medical Service**
The 8,000-strong service was organized territorially in support of all the three fighting wings of the SADF.

## *Allied Forces*

**SWATF**
This force was established in August 1980. With 22,000 members, it was controlled by the SADF until late 1989. Thereafter it formed the nucleus of the independent Namibian armed forces.

**Homeland Armies**
The four so-called independent homelands each had their own security forces: Bophuthatswana – 3,100 men under arms; Ciskei – 1,000; Transkei 2,000; Venda – 1,500. Most had various light aircraft and armoured vehicles. There were also ethnically based army/police units in the non-independent homelands. The KwaZulu paramilitary police was probably the most powerful.

## *The South African Police*

The SAP was considered a paramilitary force, as was the South West African Police before it became the Namibian Police. *Koevoet* was a very active and effective COIN force in the SWA Police until it was disbanded in 1989. The SAP continued to support various specialist task forces in the republic.

**National**
The SAP incorporated the former SA Railways and Harbour Police;
Police Reserve (ex-members of the regular force, used as part-timers);
Reserve Police Force (part-time volunteers, mainly white but some Asians, coloured and blacks);
SAP *Wachtuis* (part-time volunteers, serving, for example, as radio operators).

**Regional/local**
Provincial Traffic Police
Municipal Traffic Police
Area Defence Units (voluntary part-time rural militias).

**African Areas**
'Independent' homeland police;
Non-independent homeland police (and paramilitary forces);

Township Municipal Law Enforcement Officers;
Township 'Kitskonstabels' ('Instant' police, trained for three weeks).

Beside the above, there were numerous private 'police' forces, ranging from the mine police, paid and controlled by the mining companies, to the hundreds of private security firms that guarded white residential and commercial areas. Private Security was one of the few growth areas. According to the *Star* (5 April 1989), the number had amounted to 200,000 private security officers, almost three times the size of the regular police. All wore uniforms of various types. Civilian vigilante groups ranged across the political spectrum. The best known type was the *Makgotla* run by traditional elders in Soweto. They were largely displaced on the left by the comrades and on the right by vigilantes such as *witdoeke* and the 'fathers', both said to be backed by the SAP.

*Civil Defence Network*

While not officially part of the SADF or SAP, a civil defence network operated nationally. In 1984 there were 646 civil defence units. Some were moribund and others quite active. Pretoria appeared to have had a very sophisticated system which could mobilize a large number of civilians down to individual street level.

*Intelligence Services*

South Africa had three intelligence services. One, the National Intelligence Service (NIS), was an independent body, while the Security Police was part of the SAP, and the directorate of military intelligence was an integral part of the SADF.

Until 1978 the most influential intelligence body was the Bureau for State Security (BOSS), founded in 1969, and led by the powerful General Hendrik van den Bergh. 'South Africa's very own Heinrich Himmler' was Helen Suzman's famous description; he was said to be the *eminence grise* behind John Vorster. Van den Bergh's empire collapsed in 1978 during the Muldergate scandal. BOSS, the security police (SP) and military intelligence had a very long and bitter history of inter-agency feuding. The rivalry was so intense that they spied on each other and obstructed each other's covert operations. The sharpest antagonism was between the military and BOSS. When P.W. Botha became premier he abolished BOSS and set up the Department of National Security (DONS) which was renamed the National Intelligence Service (NIS). NIS was headed by a young Free State political science professor, Lukas Niel Barnard. NIS fell into temporary disfavour, partly because of its involvement in the Seychelles fiasco in 1981. Military intelligence (especially its counter-intelligence section) was also criticized when the navy's Commodore Dieter Gerhardt, commander of the Simonstown base, and his wife, Ruth, were found guilty of spying for the Soviet Union in 1983. They were alleged, *inter alia*, to have passed on NATO secrets to Moscow, in itself not only an interesting comment on alleged Afrikaner solidarity but also on Pretoria's connections with Western intelligence.

By 1989 NIS was operating as a general think tank. It played an important role in preparing the agenda of the State Security Council and was heavily involved with the running of the SSC secretariat. NIS in general and Niel Barnard personally played a key role in the negotiations to end the SADF's role in Angola, paving the way for independence in Namibia.

The Security Police was concerned mainly with field intelligence. Throughout the 1960s and 1970s it kept a meticulous record of the activities of black nationalist groups throughout southern Africa. Its performance was very impressive from a security standpoint. After the 1984-86 domestic insurrection, it lost some ground because of the damage done to its extensive informer network. In the late 1980s it restored some of this network. The SAP monitored all internal dissidence across the political and racial spectrum.

The dominant service in the 1980s was military intelligence, partly because of P.W. Botha's close relationship with the military in general. In the 1970s the (then) much smaller SADF military intelligence directorate did not perform well, according to its counterparts in Rhodesia and elsewhere. Under Botha, however, its size, power and resources were expanded rapidly. It developed a 'strategic intelligence function' similar to the CIA's and it controlled the military aspects of the regional destabilization.

As in Western intelligence agencies inter-agency and intra-agency feuding over turf was a marked aspect of the republic's operations. Duplication and competition, however, were to some extent reduced by the centralization of command and control initiated b the SSC and the National Security Management System.

### *Secret forces*

Off the books, as it were, the army's special forces operated units which were responsible for assassinating ANC individuals and blowing up their homes and offices in the republic and abroad. Initially, the operations were under the generic code name of Operation BARNACLE, which covered a multitude of sins. Later the strike force was called by the Orwellian title of Civil Co-operation Bureau (CCB). Many of its crimes were articulated during the Truth and Reconciliation process after 1996. The police also ran a hit squad called after its base outside Pretoria, Vlaakplas. There were other secret units, most notably the arming and training of the anti-ANC forces among Inkatha. They were collectively known after 1990 as the 'Third Force'.

### *Manpower*

The core of the SADF was the regular professional element, the permanent force (PF). The PF and civilians employed by the SADF made up about 10 per cent of total strength. National servicemen comprised another 10 per cent, while the rest was composed of the citizen force, about 47 per cent, and the commandos.

The four basic periods of military commitment were:

1. All fit white male South Africans were liable for service from 18-55. National servicemen were conscripted initially for two years full-time. In 1990 it was reduced to one year, and then conscription was abolished.
2. Thereafter the whites were liable for 12 years in CF units. They were supposed to be called up for annual 'camps' (periods of further training or operational duty for up to three months, which should have amounted to 720 days in total). The alternative was for twenty years' part-time duty in a commando for those declared area-bound such as farmers. There were three main types of commando duty: rural, urban and industrial. Urban commandos assisted with crowd control, roadblocks, curfew enforcement etc. Industrial commandos protected 'key points', important commercial facilities. The most common form of commando duty, however, was rural COIN.
3. Then followed five years in the Active CF Reserve. Call-up in ths category was usually only during a national emergency.
4. Finally, controlled National Reserve for those who had completed the previous periods in a CF or commando unit; they were liable to twelve days call-up a year in an emergency until aged 55. Some volunteers served until 65.

Deferments from national service were allowed for a variety of reasons, including fulltime study. There were also very strict provisions for conscientious objection on formal religious but not political grounds. Opposition to the draft grew, particularly among young English-speaking South Africans. The reasons were various: political opposition to apartheid, the disruption to their careers and privileged, often middle-class English-speaking elite were often more discomfited by running around the bush with Afrikaner railway workers than by occupation duty in the bleak townships. Draft-dodging and emigration increased. National service also imposed major strains on the economy, because of the drain on the limited pool of white skilled manpower. Some companies provided 'make-up' pay to supplement employees who were called up. Perhaps one-fifth of companies paid full salaries. Although the government had provided guidelines to encourage companies to supplement national servicemen's pay, there was no legal obligation to do so.

The obvious alternative sources of personnel were white female and black, coloured and Asian volunteers. About 3,200 women were serving in uniform in the SADF. The Cape Corps for coloureds was revived in 1963. A compulsory scheme for coloured cadets was introduced but it met with great opposition and was abolished in 1979. A small number of Indians volunteered for service in the Navy. When coloureds and Indians were allowed to vote for the tricameral parliament in 1984, the government hinted that the vote entailed conscription obligations. The Indian and coloured parties in parliament opposed the draft. So only whites were ever conscripted. A volunteer black unit, 21st Battalion, based at Lentz near Johannesburg, was set up in 1974. It served as a training school for the various homeland forces.

The SADF tried to remove discrimination in pay and career prospects. The SWATF and SAP had black colonels. About 20,000 blacks, coloureds and Indians served in the SADF and allied homeland forces. In the former SWATF at least half were blacks. About half of the SAP (33,000) were black. That meant that about 64,000 blacks helped to defend the security system. Some suffered fatally from this collaboration; some black policemen appeared to have a brave sense of commitment to their communities and were concerned with crime, not politics. Mass unemployment perhaps helped swell the ranks.

As in Rhodesia, the SADF pushed up the age limit for white call-ups and turned to new immigrants. In 1984 it was made compulsory for immigrants between 15.5 and 25 to take up citizenship after five years' residence, thus making them liable for national service. This discouraged fresh immigration and caused a large number of expatriates, with sons, to quit South Africa. A small number of 'mercenaries', variously defined, served in the SADF. Most of them were Americans, British and Rhodesian professional soldiers as well as black and white Portuguese from Angola and Mozambique. A handful of Israelis, Europeans and South Americans were recuited, usually as SF, but the SADF was wary of absorbing foreigners because of the bad publicity surrounding the small number of mercenaries who deserted (especially from 32nd Battalion) and sold sensational stories to the press.

Not included are Armscor workers, SADF civilian employees, Prison Service personnel or allied guerrillas in UNITA and RENAMO.

# Endnotes

**Introduction**

1. *'Die Wallisers en die Afrikaners het baie gemeen – albei leef te na aan die Engelse en te ver van God.'* (*Beeld,* 9 December 1981.) Because 'Afrikaners' came early in the alphabet my quotation sometimes led books of Afrikaans quotations. See, for example, *Die Groot Afrikaanse Aanhalings-Boek* (Human and Rousseau, Cape Town, 1988.)

**Chapter 1: Pax Britannica**

1. James Morris, *Heaven's Command* (Penguin, Harmondsworth, 1986) p.422.
2. T. Davenport, *South Africa: A Modern History* (Macmillan, Johannesburg, 1987) pp.53 & 124. This quotation summarizes Davenport's views on the Great Trek and the later British expansion into the Eastern Cape.
3. Morris, op.cit., p.440.
4. Thomas Pakenham, *The Boer War* (Ball, Johannesburg, 1982) p.574.
5. The *Ossewabrandwag* (OB) (English: Ox-wagon Sentinel) was an anti-British and pro-German organization in South Africa during the Second World War, which opposed South African participation in the war. It was formed in Bloemfontein on 4 February 1939 by pro-German Afrikaners. Its military wing was called *Stormjaers* (assault troops). Thousands of OB supporters were interned during the war.

**Chapter 2: Winds of Change and War**

1. R. Cohen, *Endgame in South Africa*, (Currey/UNESCO, London, 1986) p.9.
2. For a pioneering discussion of this theme, see Paul Moorcraft, 'Towards the Garrison State,' in F. Clifford-Vaughan (ed), *International Pressures and Political Change in South Africa* (Oxford University Press, Cape Town, 1978).
3. Joseph Hanlon, *Beggar Your Neighbours* (Catholic Institute for International Relations, London, 1986) p.8.
4. For a summary of media representations of Africa, see Paul Moorcraft, *Dying for the Truth: The Concise History of Frontline War Reporting* (Pen and Sword, Barnsley, 2016) pp.129-51.
5. Christopher Othen, *Katanga 1960-63: Mercenaries, spies and the African nation that waged war on the world* (History Press, Stroud, 2015) p.42. This is a very racy

account of the war for Katangan secession, which was supported by some Western states and especially by the white-ruled governments in the south.

6. For one of the best narrative accounts of this period, see R.W. Johnson, *How Long Will South Africa Survive?* (Macmillan, Johannesburg, 1977) pp.58-9,214.
7. R. Levgold, 'The Soviet Threat to Southern Africa', *International Affairs Bulletin*, 8:1, Johannesburg, 1984, p.10.
8. At this time, I must confess I had a similar view of *some* of the SADF's military leaders. I wrote a book about it at the time: *Africa's Superpower* (Sygma/Collins, Johannesburg, 1981).
9. William Minter, 'Destructive Engagement: The United States and South Africa in the Reagan Era', in Phyllis Johnson and David Martin (eds) *Destructive Engagement* (Zimbabwe Publishing, Harare, 1986) p.294.

**Chapter 3: The Rise of Africa's Superpower**

1. Kenneth Grundy, *The Militarization of South African Politics* (Oxford University Press, Oxford, 1988) p.13.
2. The House of Assembly (known in Afrikaans as the *Volksraad*) was the lower house of South Africa from 1910 to 1981, the sole parliamentary chamber between 1981 and 1984, and the white representative house of the so-called 'Tri-cameral Parliament' from 1984 to 1994, when it was replaced by the current National Assembly. Throughout its history, it was exclusively constituted of white members who were elected to office predominantly by white citizens, though until 1960 and 1970, respectively, some black Africans and Coloureds in the Cape Province voted under a restricted form of suffrage.
3. For an informative account of this period, see diligent Afrikaner scholar Deon Geldenhuys's, *South Africa's Search for Security since the Second World War,* (South African Institute for International Affairs, Johannesburg, 1978) and Robert Jaster, *South Africa's Narrowing Strategic Options* (Adelphi Paper no. 159, International Institute for Strategic Studies, London, 1980) pp.9-21.
4. These Buccaneers were the centre of a major political controversy in Britain. By 1973 it was reported unofficially that six had crashed and the remaining planes were grounded for some time. South African pilots preferred the French Mirages and tended to regard the Buccaneer in the same light that their Luftwaffe counterparts regarded the unlucky US Starfighter.
5. André Beaufre, *Introduction to Strategy* (Faber and Faber, London, 1963) and *Strategy of Action* (Faber and Faber, London, 1967); John J. McCuen, *The Art of Counter-Revolutionary War* (Faber and Faber, London, 1968).
6. Philip Frankel, *Pretoria's Praetorians* (Cambridge University Press, Cambridge, 1984) pp.69 and 174.
7. Armscor was formed out of a merger of the Armaments Production Board (established in 1964) and the Armaments Development and Production Corporation (1968). For a general history of Armscor under apartheid, see

J. McWilliams, *Armscor: South Africa's Arms Merchants* (Brassey's, London, 1989).

8. For an early discussion about this issue, see Paul Moorcraft, 'The Military-Industrial Complex Under Siege', in Benjamin Franklin Cooling (ed) *War, Business and World Military-Industrial Complexes* (Kennikat, Port Washington, 1981).
9. Quoted in Anthony Sampson, *The Arms Bazaar* (Hodder and Stoughton, London, 1977) p.167.
10. See Glenn Cross, *Dirty War: Rhodesia and Chemical Biological warfare 1975-1980*, (Helion, Solihull, 2017). For a historical background on the Israeli connection, see Zdenek Červenka and Barbara Rogers, *The Nuclear Axis* (Friedmann, London, 1978). Also Al J. Venter, *How South Africa Built Six Atomic Bombs* (Ashanti, Johannesburg, 2008).

**Chapter 4: Angola (1961-1976)**

1. According to the official 1950 census, there were 30,089 *assimilados* in a total Angolan population of just over 4 million, less than 1 per cent. John Marcum's two-volume work provides an exhaustive background to the Angolan revolution, see select bibliography.
2. Gerald Bender, *Angola Under the Portuguese* (Heinemann, London, 1978) p.159.
3. Ian Beckett, 'The Portuguese Army: The Campaign in Mozambique, 1964-1974' in Ian Beckett and John Pimlott (eds) *Armed Forces and Modern Counter-Insurgency* (Croom Helm, London, 1985) p.136.
4. Douglas Porch, *The Portuguese Armed Forces and the Revolution* (Croom Helm, London, 1977) analyzes these events with great wit and lucidity.
5. John Stockwell, *In Search of Enemies* (Deutsch, London, 1978). Interestingly he discusses in detail South African-US collaboration, but he insisted that 'I saw no evidence that the United States formally encouraged them to join' (p.186).
6. Hilton Hamann, *Days of the Generals* (Zebra, Cape Town, 2001) p.38.
7. For a summary of this tension, see Paul Moorcraft, *Israel Since the Yom Kippur War* (Anglo-Israel Society, London, 1976).

**Chapter 5: Namibia (1966-1976)**

1. Peter Katjavivi, A *History of Resistance in Namibia* (Currey, London, 1988) p. 10; André du Pisani, *SWA/Namibia: The Politics of Continuity and Change* (Ball, Johannesburg, 1986) p. 36.
2. Quoted in Katjavivi, op. cit., p. 85.
3. Because I had recently lived and studied in Jerusalem (I lived in the Arab quarter) I spoke to some of the Israelis in Hebrew. Israeli instructors had been active in southern Angola in connection with UNITA (although the specific role of Israelis in Namibia was not clear). Whenever I met Israeli army personnel in Namibia they usually claimed to be journalists, or academics on study leave etc. Israeli instructors

were allegedly involved with the use of sophisticated devices for tracking human movement on the border.

4. John Ya Otto, *Battlefront Namibia* (Heinemann, London, 1982) p.42.
5. See, for example, *Brutal Force* (International Defence and Aid Fund, London, 1986) p.178. Cawthra's book was a classic anti-apartheid text on military issues.

**Chapter 6: Mozambique (1964-1975)**

1. Allen and Barbara Isaacman, *Mozambique: From Colonialism to Revolution* (Zimbabwe Publishing, Harare, 1983) p.98. The influential Portuguese secret policeman, Oscar Cardosa, suggested that one of his PIDE colleagues, Casimiro Monteiro, was the actual assassin.
2. Martin Meredith, *The First Dance of Freedom: Black Africa in the Postwar Era* (Abacus, London, 1984) p.251.
3. For a summary of the disintegration of the Portuguese army, see Barry Munslow, *Mozambique: The Revolution and its Origins* (Longman, London, 1983) pp.125-9. For a recent popular summary of the African wars in general, see Al J. Venter, *Portugal's Guerrilla Wars in Africa* (Helion, Solihull, 2015).
4. Joseph Hanlon, *Beggar Your Neighbours* (Catholic Institute for International Relations, London, 1986) p.38.
5. For a summary of military ties between Portugal, South Africa and Rhodesia, see Munslow, op. cit., pp.115-16.
6. The OAS (*Organisation Armée Secrète*) was the ultra right-wing group that refused to accept decolonization in Algeria. For a discussion of the OAS and the parallels between the end of white rule in northern and southern Africa, see Alistair Horne, *A Savage War of Peace: Algeria, 1945-1962* (Penguin, Harmondsworth, 1985).

**Chapter 7: Rhodesia (1965-1980)**

1. John Sprack, *Rhodesia: South Africa's Sixth Province* (International Defence and Aid Fund, London, 1974) p.26.
2. Robert Blake, *A History of Rhodesia* (Methuen, London, 1977) p.390.
3. Harry Oxley, Assistant Secretary, Rhodesian Ministry of Defence, and was for a while acting head civil servant of the Rhodesian MoD, interview with me in 1981. This theme was repeated in a number of other interviews with defence and intelligence officials.
4. See Harold Wilson, *A Personal Record: The Labour Government, 1964-1970* (Weidenfeld and Nicholson, London, 1971) p.164. Anthony Verrier (*The Road to Zimbabwe*, Cape, London, 1986) offers the idiosyncratic view that Britain placated Pretoria throughout the Rhodesian crisis because London relied on gold and uranium from South Africa.
5. Robert C. Good, *UDI: the International Politics of the Rhodesian Rebellion* (Faber, London, 1973) pp.293-4.

6. *Chimurenga* is a chiShona word which implies 'resistance'. It was also applied to uprisings against the settlers in the 1890s. Some historians have stressed the continuity of both wars. See, for example, Terence Ranger, *Revolt in Southern Rhodesia* (Heinemann, London, 1967). The concept of a 'third Chimurenga' was developed long after independence to suggest a continuation of the struggle against white farmers and black opposition.
7. Dudley Cowderoy and Roy Nesbit, *War in the Air* (Galago, Alberton, 1987) pp.47-8.
8. See Glenn Cross, *Dirty War: Rhodesia and Chemical Biological warfare 1975-1980* (Helion, Solihull, 2017).

   Dr Cross has certainly done his homework in *Dirty War*. He supports what I have said in my books that sometimes the small CBW campaign was killing more insurgents than conventional firepower. Perhaps the number killed was a few thousand but it did not change the course of the war.

   A handful of senior Rhodesians – Ken Flower, the head of the Central Intelligence Organization, and Chief Superintendent Michael 'Mac' McGuinness of the British South Africa Police – operated a very small programme in a number of rooms in two isolated Selous Scouts forts (and perhaps a lab in the University of Rhodesia, and a room in a house in the upmarket suburb of Borrowdale in the capital, Salisbury). Using basic laboratory skills, deploying agricultural and industrial chemicals, they poisoned batches of clothing, food, beverages and medicines for covert distribution to guerrillas. Pesticide containing parathion was used on clothing. Food and drinks were contaminated with a rat-killer containing thallium. Warfarin was put into bulk food such as the staple mealie meal. Cholera was used as an area denial weapon especially for water sources on the southern often drought-ridden routes used to enter the country. The Rhodesians experimented with anthrax, not least as an assassination tool.

   Rhodesia suffered one of the largest anthrax outbreaks in history, and it killed not only a large number of cattle but many humans too. Despite all the rumours and accusations by the guerrilla leaders, Dr Cross concludes that the anthrax epidemic was probably accidental, caused partly by the breakdown of the veterinary services at the end of the war. The book does not linger on the often lonely deaths of guerrillas who were left to die in the bush. Their colleagues would take their weapon, say goodbye and might give them some water. Nor does the book talk much of the experiments on captured guerrillas. What I found interesting was the second-order effects of the CBW campaign – many insurgents blamed witches and wizards. The literal witchhunts disrupted the guerrilla campaigns as much as the actual poisonings. Eventually many of the guerrillas worked out what was happening and elaborated methods of securing food supplies from more trusted stores and middle men.

   The small Rhodesian project was partly funded and resourced by South Africa, so it was natural that personnel and secrets migrated south at the end of the war in 1980. South Africa adopted it under its own 'Project Coast'. Both for moral and practical reasons, many South African army commanders were reluctant to use CBW, although the South African Police did experiment a little, not least in the dreaded *Koevoet* unit in South West Africa/Namibia. Accidents were reported there when local militiamen ate some of the contaminated food but there is little evidence of battlefield applications.

The Brits and Americans relieved the outgoing whites of their CBW programme as well as their handful of nukes. Nobody wanted the African National Congress leaders, even the secular saint, Nelson Mandela, getting their hands on WMD.

Rhodesia was a rare case of a government using CBW on its own rebel citizens. Syria is a more recent example. Both exhibit intelligence failures in the West. Or turning a blind eye. I had got wind of the CBW programme in the late 1970s, and Ken Flower wrote about it in 1987 in his very self-censored memoirs. The British knew something but the American agencies claimed not to have known anything until 1990. When the US was engulfed in its anthrax scare, they did look up the survivors of the Rhodesian programme. Ironically, some of them had suffered early grisly deaths – the results of CBW poisonings, their relatives believed.

For specialists, Dr Cross's book is very impressive. He is no stylist, however, and lack of hard documentary evidence does enforce necessary speculation and some unnecessary repetition. This is likely to be the last word on the subject. Few care now about the white supremacists' last stand in southern Africa, and yet the subject is very pertinent. It shows how a very basic and amateurish programme can inflict thousands of deaths in an asymmetric war. No wonder al-Qaeda and Daesh have been so fixated on the same type of evil endeavour.

9. Peter Stiff, *The Silent War* (Galago, Alberton, 2004) p.294.
10. For a remarkable first-hand account of fire-force operations, see Chris Cocks, *Fireforce* (Galago, Alberton, 1988). See also the detailed analysis in J.R.T. Wood, *Counter-Strike from the Sky: The Rhodesian All-Arms Fireforce* (30° South, Newlands, Johannesburg, 2009).
11. For an excellent account of the psychological war from both sides, see Julie Frederikse, *None But Ourselves: Masses vs the Media in the Making of Zimbabwe* (Ravan, Johannesburg, 1982).
12. Denis Beckett, 'The Tough Guys Lost – Despite the Lies', *Frontline,* February 1983. When I was a neighbour of Beckett in the arty suburb of Melville in Johannesburg (1981-87) I wrote regularly for this magazine, which Denis edited; he usually forgot to pay his contributors even after he had recruited top writers such as Rian Malan. Denis wrote and spoke in a fascinating mix of hip-hop English and Afrikaans.

**Chapter 8: Battle Lines Drawn**

1. Joseph Hanlon, *Apartheid's Second Front* (Penguin, Harmondsworth, 1986) p.2.
2. Quoted in R. Green and C. Thompson, 'Political Economies in Conflict: SADCC, South Africa and Sanctions' in Phyllis Johnson and David Martin (eds), *Destructive Engagement* (Zimbabwe Publishing, Harare, 1986) p.265.

3. Beggar My Neighbour is a card game suitable for small children that's also known as Beat Your Neighbour Out of Doors and Strip Jack Naked. It is a very simple game, requiring no strategy or planning at all. The objective of the game is to win all the cards from the other players. Some critics have said it's a sort of war game in that it encourages aggression in children. Hence the title of Hanlon's excellent book. See Joseph Hanlon, *Beggar Your Neighbours* (Catholic Institute for International Relations, London, 1986). Another seminal text is Johnson and Martin, op. cit. See also their *Apartheid Terrorism: The Destabilization Report* (Commonwealth Secretariat/Currey, London, 1989).
4. Author's interviews in 1984 with senior officials from ESCOM, the South African Electricity Supply Commission. What ESCOM planned and what FRELIMO would allow were two different matters, but the South African protection of the Cahora Bassa lines (replicating the defence of the dam during Portuguese colonial rule) was discussed in some detail with Maputo.
5. Hanlon, *Second Front*, op. cit., p.2. For an excellent summary of the history and debate about militarization in South Africa, see Kenneth Grundy, *The Militarization of South African Politics* (Oxford University Press, Oxford, 1988).
6. Vera Brittain, *Hidden Lives, Hidden Death* (Faber, London, 1988) p. 8. Brittain was quoting from UNICEF and SADCC estimates.
7. Many apartheid critics, especially in the West, blamed Geldenhuys. It was implied that the young political science professor supplied the deadly logic for destabilization. From my personal contacts I always assumed that Geldenhuys was a straightforward *verlig* academic, even though he was trusted by the reformers (sic) in military intelligence. Besides, there was a shortage of major strategic thinkers, academic or military, in South Africa, unlike Israel where the species proliferated. For an example of his work, see Deon Geldenhuys, *The Diplomacy of Isolation* (Macmillan, Johannesburg, 1984).
8. See Martin and Johnson (1986) op. cit. p.xxi.
9. Hanlon, *Beggar Your Neighbours* (1986) op. cit., p.50.

**Chapter 9: The big battles: Angola (1976-1989)**

1. Fred Bridgland, *Jonas Savimbi: A Key to Africa* (Macmillan, Johannesburg, 1986) p.192.
2. Ibid., pp.194-218.
3. John Marcum, 'Regional Security in Southern Africa – Angola,' *Survival*, January/February 1988, p.5.
4. Joseph Hanlon, *Beggar Your Neighbours* (Catholic Institute for International Relations, London, 1986) p.157.
5. Marcum, op. cit., p.6.
6. Willem Steenkamp, *Borderstrike: South Africa into Angola* (Butterworth, Durban, 1983) p.5.

7. Francis Toase, 'The South African Army: The Campaign in South West Africa/Namibia since 1966' in Ian Beckett and John Pimlott (eds) *Armed Forces and Modern Counter-Insurgency* (Croom Helm, London, 1985) p.214.
8. Helmut-Römer Heitman, *South African War Machine* (CNA, Johannesburg, 1985) p.152. Heitman, an SADF citizen force officer, was an author and journalist who was very well informed and generally reflected the official military viewpoint.
9. Marga Holness, 'Angola: the struggle continues,' in Phyllis Johnson and David Martin (eds), *Destructive Engagement* (Zimbabwe Publishing, Harare, 1986) p.100. Captain du Toit was released two and half years later in a prisoner swap. For a detailed account of the raid, see Peter Stiff, *The Silent War: South African Recce Operations, 1969-1994* (Galago, Alberton, 2004) pp.457-69.
10. According to Bridgland's autobiography of Savimbi, op. cit., p.470.
11. *Strategic Survey, 1986-1987* (IISS, London, 1987) p.189.
12. My interview in Jamba, 21 August 1986. See also Paul Moorcraft, 'A New Heart for the UNITA Army', *Jane's Defence Weekly*, 13 September 1986.
13. Greg Mills and David Williams, *Seven Battles that Shaped South Africa* (Tafelberg, Cape Town, 2006) p.181.

**Chapter 10: Namibia: from Afrikaner colony to independence (1976-89)**

1. Gavin Cawthra, *Brutal Force*, (International Defence and Aid Fund, London, 1986) p.182.
2. Figures quoted in *Strategic Survey, 1977* (IISS, London, 1978) p.39.
3. For details see Deon Geldenhuys, *The Diplomacy of Isolation* (Macmillan, Johannesburg, 1984) p.83.
4. Willem Steenkamp, *Borderstrike: South Africa into Angola* (Butterworth, Durban, 1983) p.62. Most military accounts by South African writers, especially serving officers, tended to be couched in the heroic mould or were bland because of official censorship. Steenkamp, the military correspondent for the liberal *Cape Times,* although he wrote from a SADF perspective, produced refreshingly frank accounts of the campaigns from the vantage-point of combat troops.
5. Helmut-Römer Heitman, *South African War Machine* (CNA, Johannesburg, 1985) p.144.
6. Andre du Pisani, *SWA/Namibia: The Politics of Continuity and Change* (Ball, Johannesburg, 1985) p.436.
7. Cawthra, op. cit., p.183.
8. Steenkamp, op. cit., p.185.
9. For an analysis of mine warfare and the range of South African anti-mine warfare equipment, see Peter Stiff, *Taming the Landmine* (Galago, Alberton, 1986) pp.86-125.
10. Cawthra, op. cit., p.179.
11. Heitman, op. cit., p.153.

12. David Pallister, Sarah Stewart and Ian Lepper, *South Africa Inc: The Oppenheimer Empire* (Simon and Schuster, London, 1987) pp.102-21.

**Chapter 11: Mozambique (1976-1992)**

1. Flower was in some ways privately proud of his creation. Despite his connection to RENAMO, which the Zimbabwe National Army fought for over a decade, Mugabe respected Flower and kept him on as CIO director for eighteen months and then as part-time consultant until 1986. Mugabe told Flower on a number of occasions that Machel also respected him. According to my final interview with Flower just before he died in 1987, the spymaster told me that just before Machel died in a plane crash the Mozambican president had asked Flower to visit Maputo as the president's personal guest, presumably to discuss RENAMO.
   The South African spy-journalist Gordon Winter claimed in his sensational (and inaccurate) book, *Inside BOSS,* that BOSS helped to create RENAMO. See Joseph Hanlon, *Mozambique: The Revolution Under Fire* (Zed, London, 1984) p.220. For an excellent account of the CIO's connections with RENAMO, see David Martin and Phyllis Johnson, 'Mozambique: To Nkomati and Beyond' in Phyllis Johnson and David Martin (eds) *Destructive Engagement* (Zimbabwe Publishing, Harare, 1986) pp.1-14.
2. There are various transliterations of the first RENAMO leader's name. This text follows the usage of RENAMO officials.
3. Quoted in Ken Flower, *Serving Secretly (*Murray, London, 1987) p.302. There is ambiguity here as in much of the rest of the heavily redacted final version. The document is dated April 1974. In the preceding paragraph Flower talks of the previous five years of RENAMO activity. There were apparently discussions about a Mozambican counterforce in the mid-1960s when Rhodesia's first pseudos were formed, later to become the Selous Scouts. In the early 1970s there were various discussions with the Portuguese. For practical purposes, 1976 may be taken as the date of RENAMO's birth.
4. Barbara Cole, *The Elite: the Story of the Rhodesian Special Air Service* (Three Knights, Amanzimtoti, 1984) p.245. See also Paul French, *To the edge: With the Rhodesian SAS and Selous Scouts*, (Helion, Solihull, 2012) pp.156-77.
5. Jack Wheeler, *RENAMO: The Mozambique National Resistance* (mimeo, report prepared for the Foreign Research Institute, California, June 1988) p.8.
6. DONS = Department of National Security and NIS = National Intelligence Service. During the Rhodesian war, Pretoria and Salisbury had a gentleman's agreement that they would not run agents in each other's territories without prior arrangement, nor should either ally poach agents. This understanding broke down after 1978. At the end of the war Pretoria recruited a large number of high-ranking agents in the police, army and intelligence services, for activation in the post-independence period. Flower felt that this was not on. Many were weeded out after Flower left the CIO, and they were imprisoned or fled to South Africa. For those who remained, see Chapter Twelve.

An example of South Africa leaking information/propaganda about Flower can be found in Aida Parker, 'How Lord C [Carrington] Sold Out Rhodesia,' *The Citizen*, 24 February 1982. Aida Parker, a charmingly eccentric if well-informed journalist, had a fixation that Flower was a British mole. She pursued her quarry as obsessively as Peter Wright dogged Roger Hollis in *Spycatcher.*

7. Martin and Johnson, op. cit., p.19. Also Joseph Hanlon, *Mozambique: Revolution under Fire* (Zed, London, 1984) p.227.
8. Hanlon, *Mozambique: Revolution under Fire,* op. cit., p.227.
9. The South African media loved to re-quote these anti-Russian stories. On 26 October 1986, for example, the *Sunday Star* quoted an occasion when Machel and the Soviet ambassador visited the Soviet pavilion at the Maputo industrial and agricultural fair. Machel was reported as taking a ride in a Russian limo which was on display. The smiling ambassador asked Machel how he liked the car. 'Very nice,' responded the Mozambican president, 'a very comfortable car indeed. But I am afraid I have the same tastes as you and I prefer a Mercedes-Benz.'
10. Quoted in Simon Jenkins, 'Destabilization in Southern Africa', *The Economist*, 16 July 1983, p.20.
11. Joseph Hanlon, *Apartheid's Second Front* (Penguin, Harmondsworth, 1986) p.109.
12. Alistair Sparks, 'The Beira Prospect', the *Star*, 3 December 1986.
13. Heribert Adam and Stanley Uys, 'From Destabilization to Neocolonial Control', *International Affairs Bulletin* (Johannesburg, 9:1, 1985) p.13.
14. Robert Grenier, 'Why do we let down the rebels with a real cause,' the *Sunday Telegraph,* 20 September 1987.
15. Cited in Stephen Emerson, *The Battle for Mozambique* (Helion, Solhull, 2014) p.198.

**Chapter 12: Zimbabwe (1980-1990)**

1. The six officers were all tortured, usually by electric shock treatment, and some were sexually abused, according to my interview with the white physician who examined them in prison. For full details see, Barbara Cole, *Sabotage and Torture* (Three Knights, Amanzimtoti, 1988).
2. Stephen Chan, *Mugabe: A life of power and violence* (I.B. Tauris, London, 2003). See also Paul Moorcraft, *Mugabe's War Machine* (Pen and Sword, Barnsley, 2011).

**Chapter 13: Fellow Frontliners**

1. For more details, see Peter Stiff, *The Silent War: The South African Recce Operations (1969-1994)* (Galago, Alberton, 2004) pp.410-26.
2. Robert Edgar, 'The Lesotho Coup of 1986', *South African Review 4* (Ravan, Johannesburg, 1987) p.380.
3. Susanne Daley, 'Tiny Neighbour Gives South African Army Rude Surprise', *New York Times,* 22 September 1998.

4. For a more personal account of my journalism in the three former protectorates, see Paul Moorcraft, *Inside the Danger Zones: Travels to Arresting Places* (Biteback, London, 2010) pp.57-62.
5. For details, see Peter Stiff, *The Silent War*, op. cit., pp.516-18.
6. Joseph Hanlon, *Beggar Your Neighbours* (Catholic Institute for International Relations, London, 1986) p.240.
7. According to my conversations with credible South African intelligence officers long after the assassination.
8. Mervyn Rees and Chris Day, *Muldergate: The story of the info scandal* (Macmillan, Johannesburg, 1989).
9. Author's interviews with some of the ex-Rhodesians who took part in the attempted coup. See also Mike Hoare, *The Seychelles affair* (Corgi, London, 1987).
10. 'Comores: Under New Management,' *Africa Confidential*, 22 January 1988.
11. Harvey Tyson, 'Were You in the War, Dad?' the *Star* (weekly edition) 17 November 1987.
12. Joseph Hanlon, *Apartheid's Second Front* (Penguin, Harmondworth, 1986) p.83.

**Chapter 14: Black Resistance**

1. Anthony Sampson, *Black and Gold* (Hodder and Stoughton, London, 1987) p.149.
2. Alf Stadler, *The Political Economy of Modern South Africa* (Croom Helm, London, 1987) p.159.
3. Mary Benson, *Nelson Mandela* (Penguin, Harmondsworth, 1986) p.108.
4. Tom Lodge, *Black Politics in South Africa since 1945* (Ravan, Johannesburg, 1983) p.241. In 1973 *Okhela*, a 'white consciousness' resistance group was set up in Paris. Its best known member was the Afrikaner poet, Breyten Breytenbach. Apparently Oliver Tambo encouraged this short-lived affiliate of the ANC as a possible counter-balance to the influence of the white-dominated SACP. After some quixotic adventures, which included the jailing of Breytenbach and the revelation that its chief spokesman had been a police informer, *Okhela* collapsed in 1979.
5. See Hugh Lewin, *Bandiet* (Heinemann, London, 1981) for a fascinating account of the life of a white political prisoner. Lewin described how the guards tried to humiliate Fischer by making him do the most menial jobs such as cleaning the latrines. Denis Goldberg was interviewed by Bram Fischer's great-nephew, Gavin, in the BBC Radio World Service programme, *Remembering Rivonia,* on 7 March 2018.
6. One of Fischer's two daughters, Ruth, was a personal friend. She told me in 1977 that a colonel in the security police, who was monitoring her father's final days outside prison, described the communist leader as a 'noble Afrikaner'.
7. Antjie Krog, *Country of my Skull* (Vintage, London, 1999) pp.269-70.
8. Stephen Davis, *Apartheid's Rebels* (Yale University Press, London, 1987) p.19. This is one of the best contemporary military histories; a more popular general history of the time was Heidi Holland, *The Struggle: A History of the African National Congress* (Grafton, London, 1989).

9. Gavin Cawthra, *Brutal Force* (International Aid and Defence Fund, London 1986) p.218.
10. Davis, op. cit, p.74.
11. Some of the best analyses of these disputes – often parodied – were in Denis Beckett's brilliantly eccentric *Frontline* magazine (some of it is now online). The February 1987 issue was about the civil wars in resistance politics. Nomavenda Mathiane contributed an article called 'Deadly Duel of the Wararas and the Zim-Zims'. 'Wararas' was the nickname for the Charterists, those who supported the Freedom Charter, such as the UDF and ANC. It implied people with no clear policy – the waars-waars, the 'what-wheres'. Zim-Zim stood for AZASM, the Azanian Students' Movement, founded in 1983 and affiliated to AZAPO. This wandered into the world of Monty Python and the *Life of Brian*'s debate about the variations on The People's Front of Judea.
12. For an account of my time with the gangs, see Paul Moorcraft, *Inside the Danger Zones* (Biteback, London, 2010) pp.51-4.

**Chapter 15: States of Emergency**

1. *Financial Mail,* 6 September 1985.
2. David Pallister, Sarah Stewart and Ian Lepper, *South Africa Inc.: The Oppenheimer Empire* (Simon and Schuster, London, 1987) p.185.
3. Quoted in Martin Meredith, *In the Name of Apartheid* (Hamish Hamilton, London, 1988) pp.205-6.
4. I am quoting from Suzman's speech in the Johannesburg City Hall, 5 August 1986. I sat in the audience by chance next to Harry Oppenheimer, one of the richest and most powerful businessmen in the world, let alone South Africa. I engaged him in casual conservation. He sat on his own without aides or, apparently, any bodyguards. It would have been unlikely in America, let alone in many other societies enduring a low-intensity war.
5. See Nicholas Haysom, *The Rise of Right-Wing Vigilantes in South Africa* (Centre for Applied Legal Studies, University of the Witwatersrand, 1986). See also his 'Vigilantes and the Militarization of South Africa' in Jacklyn Cock and Laurie Nathan (eds) *War and Society: The Militarization of South Africa* (Philip, Cape Town, 1989).
6. Rick Turner wrote a rather philosophical book called *Eye of the Needle*, about creating democracy in the republic. His first wife was Barbara Follet, the well-known Labour MP and 'Blair Babe', whose fourth husband was Welsh novelist Ken Follet whose first big hit, on a different subject, was also called *Eye of the Needle*. When, at a soirée in London, I pointed this out to Mrs Follet she did not think it an odd coincidence.
7. H. van Dyk, *Look at South Africa's Youth Politics* (SA Forum, 10:7, 1987).
8. Quoted in Peter Hawthorne and Bruce Nelan, 'Black Rage, White Fist,' *Time*, 5 August, 1985.
9. Howard Barrell, 'Conscripts to their Age: ANC Operational Strategy, 1976-86' (D. Phil. Thesis in politics, St Antony's College, University of Oxford, 1993) p.452.

10. The black danger, the red danger, the foreign danger were combined into one big danger.
11. Frederik van Zyl Slabbert, *The Last White Parliament* (Sidgwick and Jackson, London. 1985) p.147.

**Chapter 16: The Garrison State**

1. Alf Stadler, *The Policial Economy of Modern South Africa* (Croom Helm, London, 1987) p.83.
2. Quoted in Julie Frederikse, *South Africa: A Different Kind of War* (Ravan, Johannesburg, 1987) pp.8-10.
3. I would like to acknowledge the patient and expert assistance of at least one excellent regular officer in the SADF PR section, the then Colonel F. van Oudtshoorn, and the then Captain Leonard Knipe of the Cape Town SAP. In some ways a model policeman, Knipe assisted me when I made a TV documentary on the SAP and briefly advised me on a popular book on crime (later a major movie): Paul Moorcraft and Mike Cohen, *Stander: Bank Robber* (Galago, Alberton, 1984).
4. For a summary of war reporting in South Africa, see Paul Moorcraft, *Dying for the Truth: The Concise History of Frontline War Reporting* (Pen and Sword, Barnsley, 2016) pp.140-6.
5. Frederik van Zyl Slabbert, *The Last White Parliament* (Sidgwick and Jackson, London. 1985) p.105.
6. Denis Beckett, 'The Battle for Boksburg', *Frontline*, April 1989. I used to regularly write for the magazine in the 1980s. Equally regularly Denis would forget to pay me but it was hard not to like him, not least because he reminded me so much of madcap actor Gene Wilder.
7. Kenneth Grundy, *The Militarization of South African Politics* (Oxford University Press, Oxford, 1988) pp.68-9.
8. For some key texts on the praetorian debate, see Philip Frankel, *Pretoria*'s *Praetorians* (Cambridge University Press, Cambridge, 1984); Annette Seegers, 'The Military in South Africa', *South Africa International*, 16:4, April 1986; 'Security Tensions under the Emergency,' *Africa Confidential*, 17 June 1988; Paul Moorcraft, 'Day of the Generals', *Financial Mail,* 23 September 1988. For the debate about civil-military relations in Rhodesia, see Paul Moorcraft, 'The Fall of the Republic: The Collapse of White Power in Rhodesia' (D. Litt et Phil. Dissertation, University of South Africa, Pretoria, 1988).
9. Lewis Gann and Peter Duignan, *Why South Africa Will Survive* (Tafelberg, Cape Town, 1981) p.193.
10. K. Philips, 'The Private Sector and the Security Establishment' in Jaclyn Cock and Laurie Nathan (eds) *War and Society: The Militarisation of South Africa* (Philip, Cape Town, 1989) p.214.

11. David Pallister, Sarah Stewart and Ian Lepper, *South Africa Inc.: The Oppenheimer Empire* (Simon and Schuster, London, 1987) p.24. See also *The Economist,* 'The Oppenheimer Empire', I July 1989.
12. For a summary of the ideology versus pragmatic domination debate, see Paul Moorcraft, 'Towards the Garrison State,' in Frederick Clifford-Vaughan (ed) *International Pressures and Political Change in South Africa* (Oxford University Press, Cape Town, 1978). The seminal text was Heribert Adam, *Modernizing Racial Domination* (University of California Press, London, 1971).
13. Joseph Hanlon and R. Ormond, *The Sanctions Handbook* (Penguin, Harmondsworth, 1987) p.10.

**Chapter 17: The End Game**

1. Greg Marinovich and João Silva, *The Bang Bang Club: Snapshots from a Hidden War* (Arrow, London, 2001) p.261.
2. One of the best accounts of this period is Patti Waldmeir's *Anatomy of a Miracle* (Penguin, Harmondsworth, 1997).
3. For a full discussion of this, see Paul Moorcraft, *Dying for the Truth: The Concise History of Frontline War Reporting* (Pen and Sword, Barnsley, 2016).

**Chapter 18: After the Fall**

1. For full details, see Paul Moorcraft, *Omar al-Bashir and Africa's Longest War* (Pen and Sword, Barnsley, 2015).
2. For full details on the Mugabe regime, see Paul Moorcraft, *Mugabe's War Machine* (Pen and Sword, Barnsley, 2011). It was published in 2011 but I was one of the few who suggested the army would eventually topple the dictator.

# Select bibliography


Caute, David, *Under the Skin: The Death of White Rhodesia* (Allen Lane, London, 1983).

Chan, Stephen, *Southern Africa: Old Treacheries and New Deceits* (Yale University Press, London, 2011).

Chitiyo, Knox, *The Case for Security Sector Reform in Zimbabwe* (RUSI, September 2009).

Cilliers, J.K., *Counter-Insurgency in Rhodesia* (Croom Helm, Beckenham, Kent, 1985).

Cocks, Chris, *Fireforce: One Man's War in the Rhodesian Light Infantry* (Galago, Alberton, 1988).

Coltart, David, *The Struggle Continues* (Jacana, Auckland Park, Johannesburg, 2016).

Cross, Glenn, *Dirty War: Rhodesia and Chemical Biological Warfare 1975-1980*, (Helion, Solihull, 2017).

Dowden, Richard, *Africa: Altered States, Ordinary Miracles* (Portobello, London, 2008).

Fuller, Alexandra, *Don't Let's Go to the Dogs Tonight: An African Childhood* (New York: Random House, 2001*)*.

Gann, L. and T. Henriksen, *The Struggle for Zimbabwe (*Praeger, New York, 1981).

Godwin, Peter, *The Fear: The Last Days of Robert Mugabe* (Picador, London, 2010).

Godwin, Peter and Ian Hancock, *Rhodesians Never Die: The Impact of War and Political Change on White Rhodesia* (Oxford University Press, Oxford, 1993).

Grundy, Kenneth, *The Militarization of South African Politics* (Oxford University Press, Oxford, 1988).

Gumede, William, *Thabo Mbeki and the Battle for the Soul of the ANC* (Zed, London, 2007).

Hanlon, Joseph, *Beggar Your Neighbours* (Catholic Institute for International Relations, London, 1986).

_________, *Apartheid's Second Front* (Harmondsworth: Penguin, 1986).

Hamann, Hilton, *Days of the Generals* (Zebra, Cape Town, 2001).

Holland, Heidi, *Dinner with Mugabe* (Penguin, Johannesburg, 2008).

James, Lawrence, *Empires in the Sun: The Struggle for Mastery of Africa* (Weidenfeld & Nicolson, London, 2016).

Johnson, R.W., *How Long Will South Africa Survive?* (Macmillan, Johannesburg, 1977).

_______, *South Africa's Brave New World* (Penguin, London, 2010).

Kriger, Norma, *Guerrilla Veterans in Post-War Zimbabwe* (Cambridge University Press, Cambridge, 2003).

Marinovich, Greg and João Silva, *The Bang Bang Club* (Arrow, London, 2001).

Martin, David and Phyllis Johnson, Phyllis, *The Struggle for Zimbabwe* (Faber and Faber, London,1981).

Meredith, Martin, *The Past is Another Country: Rhodesia, 1890-1979* (André Deutsch, London, 1979).

_______, *Robert Mugabe: Power, Plunder and Tyranny in Zimbabwe* (Jonathan Ball, Johannesburg, 2002).

_______, *The First Dance of Freedom: Black Africa in the Postwar Era* (Abacus, London, 1984).

Moorcraft, Paul, *Mugabe's War Machine* (Pen and Sword, Barnsley, 2011).

_______, and Peter McLaughlin, *The War in Rhodesia: 50 Years on Since UDI* (Pen and Sword, Barnsley, 2015).

_______, *Dying for the Truth: The Concise History of Frontline War Reporting* (Pen and Sword, Barnsley, 2016).

Onslow, Sue *Cold War in Southern Africa* (Routledge, Abingdon, Oxford, 2009).

Pakenham, Thomas, *The Boer War* (Ball, Johannesburg, 1982).

Petter-Bowyer, Peter, *Winds of Destruction: The Autobiography of a Rhodesian Combat Pilot* (30° South, Newlands, Johannesburg, 2004).

Porch, Douglas, *The Portuguese Armed Forces and the Revolution* (Croom Helm, London, 1977).

Pringle, Ian, *Dingo Firestorm: The Greatest Battle of the Rhodesian Bush War* (Helion, Solihull, 2012).

Prunier, Gérard, *From Genocide to Continental War* (Hurst, London, 2009).

Ranger, Terence, *Peasant Consciousness and Guerrilla War in Zimbabwe* (Zimbabwe Publishing House, Harare, 1985).

Reid-Daly, Ron, as told to Peter Stiff, *Selous Scouts: Top Secret War* (Galago, Alberton, 1982).

Shubin, Vladimir, *The Hot Cold War: The USSR in Southern Africa* (Pluto, London, 2008).

Spence, J.E. and David Welsh, *Ending Apartheid* (Longman, London, 2011).

Stiff, Peter, *The Silent War: South African Recce Operations, 1969-1994* (Galago, Alberton, 2004).

Verrier, Anthony, *The Road to Zimbabwe* (Cape, London, 1986).

Wessels, Hannes, *A Handful of Hard Men: The SAS and the Battle for Rhodesia* (Casemate, Oxford, 2015).

Woods, Kevin, *The Kevin Woods Story: In the Shadow of Mugabe's Gallows* (30º South, Johannesburg, 2010).

# Index